Bravo/Miladinovic (Eds)

Concept and Implementation of CFC Legislation

Series on International Tax Law
Univ.-Prof. Dr. Dr. h.c. Michael Lang (Editor)
Volume 124

Concept and Implementation of CFC Legislation

edited by

Nathalie Bravo

Alexandra Miladinovic

Linde

Zitiervorschlag: *Author* in *Bravo/Miladinovic* (Eds), Concept and Implementation of CFC Legislation (2021) page

Bibliografische Information der Deutschen Nationalbibliothek
Die Deutsche Nationalbibliothek verzeichnet diese Publikation in der Deutschen Nationalbibliografie; detaillierte bibliografische Daten sind im Internet über http://dnb.d-nb.de abrufbar.

Hinweis: Aus Gründen der leichteren Lesbarkeit wird auf eine geschlechtsspezifische Differenzierung verzichtet. Entsprechende Begriffe gelten im Sinne der Gleichbehandlung für alle Geschlechter.

Das Werk ist urheberrechtlich geschützt. Alle Rechte, insbesondere die Rechte der Verbreitung, der Vervielfältigung, der Übersetzung, des Nachdrucks und der Wiedergabe auf fotomechanischem oder ähnlichem Wege, durch Fotokopie, Mikrofilm oder andere elektronische Verfahren sowie der Speicherung in Datenverarbeitungsanlagen, bleiben, auch bei nur auszugsweiser Verwertung, dem Verlag vorbehalten.

Es wird darauf verwiesen, dass alle Angaben in diesem Fachbuch trotz sorgfältiger Bearbeitung ohne Gewähr erfolgen und eine Haftung der Herausgeber, der Autoren oder des Verlages ausgeschlossen ist.

ISBN 978-3-7073-4405-9 (Print)
ISBN 978-3-7094-1158-2 (E-Book-PDF)
ISBN 978-3-7094-1159-9 (E-Book-ePub)

© Linde Verlag Ges.m.b.H., Wien 2021
1210 Wien, Scheydgasse 24, Tel.: 01/24 630
www.lindeverlag.at
Druck: Hans Jentzsch & Co GmbH
1210 Wien, Scheydgasse 31
Dieses Buch wurde in Österreich hergestellt.

Gedruckt nach der Richtlinie des Österreichischen Umweltzeichens „Druckerzeugnisse", Druckerei Hans Jentzsch & Co GmbH, UW-Nr. 790

Series Editor's Preface

The LL.M. program in International Tax Law at WU (Vienna University of Economics and Business) is available as either a one-year full-time or a two-year part-time program. Students not only attend a vast number of courses for which they prepare papers and case studies as well as sit numerous examinations but also write their master's theses. These theses are a prerequisite for the academic degree Master of Laws (LL.M.).

The program follows a scheme under which the master's theses of one particular program all examine various aspects of the same general topic. Previous general topics have included: Electronic Commerce and Taxation (1999/2000 full-time program), Partnerships in International Tax Law (2000/2001 full-time program), Transfer Pricing (1999/2001 part-time program), Exemption and Credit Methods in Tax Treaties (2001/2002 full-time program), Permanent Establishments in International Tax Law (2002/2003 full-time program), Non-Discrimination Provisions in Tax Treaties (2001/2003 part-time program), Triangular Cases (2003/2004 full-time program), Tax Treaty Policy and Development (2004/2005 full-time program), Source versus Residence in International Tax Law (2003/2005 part-time program), The Relevance of WTO Law for Tax Matters (2005/2006 full-time program), Conflicts of Qualification in Tax Treaty Law (2006/2007 full-time program), Taxation of Artistes and Sportsmen in International Tax Law (2005/2007 part-time program), Fundamental Issues and Practical Problems in Tax Treaty Interpretation (2007/2008 full-time program), Dual Residence in Tax Treaty Law and EC Law (2008/2009 full-time program), Taxation of Employment Income in International Tax Law (2007/2009 part-time program), The EU's External Dimension in Direct Tax Matters (2009/2010 full-time program), History of Tax Treaties (2010/2011 full-time program), Permanent Establishments in International and EU Tax Law (2009/2011 part-time program), International Group Financing and Taxes (2011/2012 full-time program), Limits to Tax Planning (2011/2013 part-time program), Exchange of Information for Tax Purposes (2012/2013 full-time program), Tax Policy Challenges in the 21st Century (2013/2014 full-time program), Global Trends in VAT/GST (2013/2015 part-time program), Non-Discrimination in European and Tax Treaty Law: Open Issues and Recent Challenges (2014/2015 full-time program), Preventing Treaty Abuse (2015/2016 full-time program), Limiting Base Erosion (2015/2017 part-time program), Taxation in a Global Digital Economy (2016/2017 full-time program), Arbitration in Tax Treaty Law (2017/2018 full-time program), Transfer Pricing and Value Creation (2017/2019 part-time program), Special Features of the UN Model Convention (2018/2019 full-time program), Hybrid Entities in Tax Treaty Law (2019/2020 full-time program) and Access to Treaty Benefits (2020/2021 full-time program).

Series Editor's Preface

The respective master's theses were published in edited volumes. The general topic for the 2019/2021 part-time program was Concept and Implementation of CFC Legislation. Daniel Blum and Yarif Brauner introduced the students to the subject matter at the beginning of the program. Nathalie Bravo and Alexandra Miladinovic held workshops in which the structure of the papers and the preliminary results were critically analysed. It was with great commitment that they supported the students who were preparing their theses. Their numerous suggestions helped to improve their quality and, as a consequence, the quality of the present volume. In my function as both the scientific director of the LL.M. program and the editor of this series, I would like to not only thank those two colleagues for their excellent engagement and efforts but to also express my gratitude to them.

Finally, I am also grateful to the students themselves. They pursued the program with great enthusiasm. This LL.M. program not only gave them the opportunity to interact with academics and scientifically qualified interns from all over the world and to acquire a wealth of knowledge, but they also learned how to effectively address and solve complex issues using a structured approach. The master's theses that are now available bear witness to this. I hope that the results of these papers will both influence scientific discussion and be of use to tax practitioners.

Michael Lang

Preface

This volume in the "Series on International Tax Law" includes the master's theses of the part-time students attending the 2019-2021 class of the postgraduate LL.M. programme in International Tax Law at WU (Vienna University of Economics and Business). The general topic for this year was "Concept and Implementation of CFC legislation". In the last couple of years, aggressive tax planning leading to tax base erosion has been in the focus of many academic and tax policy related debates. One focal point has been the taxable treatment of controlled foreign companies (CFC) established by resident taxpayers to shift income outside the country of residence and to achieve long-term deferral of taxation. In 1962, the first CFC rules were enacted in the United States in an attempt to effectively address the potential risks of profit shifting through CFCs. Since then, a number of jurisdictions have implemented similar rules. However, the rules have proven to be ineffective. As a result of the OECD/G-20 Base Erosion and Profit Shifting (BEPS) Project as part of Action Plan 3, recommendations were made regarding a more efficient design of domestic CFC rules. At the EU level, agreement with respect to the adoption of CFC rules was reached with Articles 7 and 8 of the anti-tax avoidance directive (ATAD) leading to a more uniform application of these types of rules among the EU Member States. Additionally, the United States has reformed its CFC rules and supplemented them with new and complex rules – the so-called Global Intangible Low Tax Income (GILTI) and the Base Erosion and Anti-Abuse Tax (BEAT). Considering the necessity of a comprehensive analysis of the treatment of CFCs in domestic law, EU law, and tax treaty law as well as general considerations regarding the interplay of the CFC rules with various other sets of rules and concepts, this volume intends to provide academic insights and an in-depth assessment of the specific aspects related to this topic. In particular, it analyses different approaches to successfully address base erosion and profit shifting through the use of CFC legislation and provides practical guidance for the effective implementation and application of CFC rules.

In the beginning, the reader is provided a general overview on CFC rules comprising the historical background and the policy considerations for implementing CFC legislation as well as different CFC approaches adopted in domestic legislations. Hence, this part focuses on the evolution and the development of CFC legislation and the various mechanisms that may be adopted in the application of the rules.

Subsequently, the second part is devoted to the criteria that is relevant for the effective designing of CFC rules with several chapters geared towards discussing the recommendations of the report on BEPS Action 3 and country specific CFC legislations. Thus, the reader is taken through the developments that have come about as a result of the BEPS Project, particularly concentrating on the definitions of foreign base company, control, CFC income, and the various exemptions and threshold requirements that may be adopted, among others, to reduce the administrative burden and compliance costs in the application of the rules. Furthermore, several chapters are dedicated to specific issues such as the computation of CFC income and the avoidance of double taxation of CFC income.

Moving ahead, the reader is presented with several chapters that discuss how CFCs are treated under EU law in the area of direct taxation. In particular, the reader is taken through chapters that deal with how CFCs are considered under Articles 7 and 8 of the ATAD. The chapters address the definition of CFCs, the two suggested approaches to the definition of taxable CFC income, the computation and attribution of CFC income as well as exceptions to the CFC rules under the ATAD. Furthermore, the reader is presented with an overview of how primary law could have an impact on the application of the ATAD provisions that form part of secondary law, especially in light of the jurisprudence of the Court of Justice of the European Union (CJEU) on this topic.

Last, the volume focuses on selected issues related to CFC rules. Inter alia, it discusses the interplay of CFC legislation and tax treaties, it addresses the relationship between CFC rules and general anti-abuse rules, it investigates possible implications of the proposed directive on the Common Consolidated Corporate Tax Base (CCCTB Directive) on CFC rules and it analyses alternative approaches to CFC legislation (such as the Global Anti-Base Erosion proposal of the OECD/G20 or GLOBE). Moreover, the volume comprises an analysis of the interrelationship between CFC rules and transfer pricing legislation as well as the balance between effective CFC rules and compliance burdens.

Without any doubt, the complexity of these topics provided the students with a challenge. Nevertheless, they have succeeded in creating an impressive academic compilation on this topic. It was our pleasure to support them in completing their research endeavours. We thank all of the students for their commitment and congratulate them on their successful graduation. In addition, we would like to express our sincere gratitude to the Linde Publishing House for the opportunity to publish this volume. Having Linde as a partner provides the professional cooperation needed to make a project such as this a success.

Vienna, June 2021

Nathalie Bravo
Alexandra Miladinovic

List of Authors

Olena Bokan

Olena Bokan was born in the Ukraine in 1980. She graduated with an MSc in Economics from Kyiv National University of T.Shevchenko (Ukraine) in 2003. In 2006, she obtained an MSc in Business and IT from the Aston University (UK). In her early career years, she worked as a financial controller in Ukrainian and international companies. In 2011, she established her own consultancy company in Kyiv in the area of international business and taxation. Since 2019 she is based in Prague and runs there a consulting company. She provides consulting services in the area of international taxation, investments, and various business matters to domestic and international clients.

Serena Bussotti

Serena Bussotti received a degree in economics and business law at Bocconi University in Milan, Italy. She has been working as a transfer pricing and international tax consultant since 2012 at an Italian tax firm mainly based in Milan, Pirola Pennuto Zei & Associati.

Fernanda Freitas Maciel

Fernanda Freitas Maciel was born in Pompéu, Minas Gerais, Brazil, in 1990. In 2015, she graduated in law at the Federal University of Ouro Preto, Brazil and, in 2019, she graduated in Accounting at the Pontifical Catholic University of Minas Gerais, Brazil. Currently, she is a transfer pricing consultant at Ernst & Young in Zurich, Switzerland.

Federico Giordano

Federico Giordano was born in Italy. In 2007, he graduated with honours from the University of Urbino with a degree in Business Administration. During his studies, he attended exchange study programmes in the United Kingdom and the United States. From 2007 to 2010, he worked in Milan at Big4 accounting firms, providing tax counsel in connection to both domestic and international tax matters, as well as M&A transactions and Real Estate practice, with a particular focus on REIFs and Trusts. In 2009, he obtained a Master's degree with full marks in tax law from Bocconi University in Milan. Since 2010, he has been working as an international tax advisor (salary partner from 2016) for both individuals and corporations at Marchionni & Partners; a regional tax and legal firm based in Italy and part of HLB International, a global network of independent advisory and accounting firms. In 2017, he was on secondment at Withum Smith+Brown, in New York. He is a statutory auditor for companies operating in manufacturing and other industries.

List of Authors

Lydia Gregorova

Lydia Gregorova graduated from the Faculty of Economics at Matej Bel University in Slovak Republic, and she received a degree in Public Economics and Administration. She has a finance and tax background, and she currently works as the Tax Country Lead Slovakia in Swiss Re in Bratislava.

Francesco Grieco

Francesco Grieco is a lawyer and certified public accountant who graduated from Bocconi University in Italy and had executive education at Harvard University in the United States. He has been working in China, Italy, and Luxembourg in the field of international taxation since 2013. Since then, he has worked within the network of BonelliErede, PricewaterhouseCoopers, and a company listed on the Dublin ISEQ and London stock exchanges, and taught transfer pricing and international taxation within graduate courses. Currently, he is working as a global international tax and transfer pricing specialist for a multinational company in Switzerland operating in the Oil & Gas industry.

Hannes Hilpold

Hannes Hilpold received a degree in business administration at the Leopold-Franzens-Universität Innsbruck in Austria. He has been working as a tax consultant and auditor in several international tax law firms in Milan (Italy) since 2006. Currently, he is tax advisor and partner at Bureau Plattner Milan (Italy).

Mike Kollar

Mike Kollar completed his degree in economics at the University of Economics in Bratislava Slovakia where he graduated with honors. He started in tax advisory, became a certified tax advisor in 2018, and is currently working in a senior role in the global tax department of ESET, one of the leading cybersecurity providers.

Jovdat Mammadov

Jovdat Mammadov was born in Baku, Azerbaijan. He holds the MBA academic title, jointly awarded by Wirtschaftsuniversität Wien and Technische Universität Wien. Previously, he received his master's degrees in law from Kutafin Moscow State Law University (MSAL) and in international relations from Diplomatic Academy of the Ministry for Foreign Affairs of Russia. From 2000 to 2011, he worked for the Organization for Security and Cooperation in Europe (OSCE) in various legal and managerial roles and, in 2012, he joined the United Nations (UNO) where he develops capacity-building programs and advises the organization on policy issues.

Niki Mitrakou

Niki Mitrakou graduated from the Faculty of Law and holds an LL.M in European Law from the National and Kapodistrian University of Athens. She is a qualified lawyer with work experience in law firms in Greece and Germany and has worked from 2018 to 2020 in the legal and compliance department of a leading US alternative investment firm, in Luxembourg. Currently, she is a tax advisor at PricewaterhouseCoopers in Athens.

Ludovica Ostorero

Ludovica Ostorero was born in Turin in 1983. In 2007, she completed her studies in Business and Accounting at Università degli Studi di Torino and graduated with honors. After a period of study in the United States, she started working in 2009 and, since 2012, she has been a certified public accountant and auditor. She currently works as a tax consultant in Turin, and she is a member of the Scuola di Alta Formazione of Turin.

Anca Pianoschi

Anca Pianoschi is a Romanian-American economist with extensive experience in banking, management, and taxation. She has a degree in International Economic Affairs from Babes-Bolyai University (BBU) Cluj-Napoca, Romania. Currently, she is running a consultancy boutique firm in Romania, offering mainly tax advice to domestic and foreign companies.

Kristína Reguliová

Kristína Reguliová received a degree in economics at the University of Economics in Bratislava in the Slovak Republic. Currently, she is a senior tax consultant at BMB Partners in Bratislava.

Peter Van Rompaey

Peter Van Rompaey received a Master's degree in Political and Social Sciences (KU Leuven, Belgium) and a Master's degree in Commercial and Financial Sciences – Tax law (EHSAL, Belgium). He is also a holder of the Vienna Transfer Pricing Certificate. In the past, he has worked for the Belgian tax authorities and a Big4 firm. As of 2000, he is a certified tax advisor. He is tax partner at RSM Belgium in Brussels, since 2007, dealing with national and international tax services for companies.

Rodrigo Saavedra Zepeda

Rodrigo Saavedra Zepeda earned his licentiate degree in law from Universidad Rafael Landívar and was admitted to practice in Guatemala in 2014. In 2017, he completed the LL.M. in International Law at the Graduate Institute of International and Development Studies (IHEID) in Geneva, Switzerland. Rodrigo has extensive experience advising both clients and governments on how to increase their competitiveness and impact through international trade. Currently, he works for the United Nations Conference on Trade and Development (UNCTAD), assisting developing countries in assessing their readiness to better engage in and benefit from e-commerce for development.

Iva Uljanić Škreblin

Iva Uljanić Škreblin received a degree in economics at the University of Zagreb, Faculty of Economics and Business, in the Republic of Croatia, in 2004. From 2004 until 2019, she worked at the Croatian Tax Administration as an income tax advisor and was also the first fiscal attaché of the Republic of Croatia since its full membership in the European Union. She represented the Republic of Croatia in working groups of the Council of the European Union for direct and indirect taxation. She is now working as a tax advisor at Primus savjetovanje in Zagreb.

Benjamin Florian Vlasich

Benjamin Florian Vlasich was born in 1986 in Austria. He has a degree in business law from the Vienna University of Economics and Business. In 2009, he started working for multiple tax advising companies. Then in 2015, he was publicly appointed as a tax advisor, in Austria. Since 2016, he has become a self-employed partner of an Austrian Tax Advising company, in Vienna.

Patrick Walchhofer

Patrick Walchhoferreceived a degree in Business and Economics at the Vienna University of Business and Economics. He has been working in various fields of national and international tax law since 2010. Currently, he is working at a tax advisory firm in Vienna, is finalizing his master thesis in the graduate program of Taxes in Accounting in Vienna, and started with his first exams to become a tax consultant.

Dawid Widzyk

Dawid Widzyk graduated from the University of Warsaw, Poland, in 2010, and obtained a master's degree in law. He also graduated from the Academy of Fine Arts in Warsaw in 2013 as a graphic designer. He worked as a tax lawyer and a legal attorney at international corporations and Polish boutique tax advisory firms, including the renowned Swiss and Polish law firm PATH. Dawid Widzyk is a partner in V4 Law Firm seated in Poland, Slovakia, Czech Republic, and Hungary.

Carmela Marina Zenzola

Carmela Marina Zenzola received a degree with honours in economics at the University of Bari in Italy. She attended a post-degree programme in multinational management and contracts at the University of Parma in Italy and a training programme on Chinese Economy at the Beijing University of Foreign Studies, in P.R. China, endorsed by the EU. She is a CPA and a certified auditor. After some years spent in the Far-East working for some MNEs, she has been working as a tax consultant in Milan focusing on international tax topics.

Table of Contents

Series Editor's Preface V
Preface VII
List of Authors IX
List of Abbreviations XV

CFC rules in general

Ludovica Ostorero
Historical background to CFC-rules and policy considerations 3

Iva Uljanić Škreblin
Different Approaches to the application of CFC rules 35

CFC criteria in general
(with particular focus on OECD BEPS Action 3 and country specific CFC-legislation)

Patrick Walchhofer
The concept of foreign base company and the application of CFC rules to transparent entities and PEs (switch over) 59

Kristina Reguliova
The role of the "control" concept under CFC rules 83

Peter Van Rompaey
The definition of CFC income 105

Fernanda Freitas Maciel
An analysis of CFC exemptions and threshold requirements 125

Federico Giordano
Computation of CFC Income 149

Serena Bussotti
Avoidance of double taxation of CFC income 173

CFC rules and EU law

Olena Bokan
CFC definition under the Anti-Tax Avoidance Directive (covered entities, control test, low taxation) 203

Carmela M. Zenzola
Taxable income under option 7(2)(a) of the Anti-Tax Avoidance Directive 231

Table of Contents

Jovdat Mammadov
Taxable income under Article 7(2)(b)
of the EU Anti-Tax Avoidance Directive 261

Anca Pianoschi
Computation and Attribution of CFC income under ATAD 295

Hannes Hilpold
Exceptions from the application of the CFC rules under article 7(3)
and (4) of the ATAD 327

Mike Kollar
CFC rules of the ATAD in light of the EU fundamental freedoms 355

CFC selected issues

Dawid Widzyk
CFC legislation and application of tax treaty law
(particular focus on Savings Clause of Article 1(3) OECD MC) 377

Rodrigo Saavedra Zepeda
The relationship between CFC rules and general anti-avoidance rules 399

Niki Mitrakou
Common Corporate (Consolidated) Tax Base and CFC-Rules 417

Benjamin Florian Vlasich
CFC Rules and Global Minimum Tax 435

Francesco Grieco
Interaction of CFC rules and transfer pricing rules 457

Lýdia Gregorová
Balance between effective CFC rules and compliance burdens 477

Series on International Tax Law 503

List of Abbreviations

Action 2	Base Erosion and Profit Shifting Project, Neutralizing the Effects of Hybrid Mismatch Arrangements, Action 2 – Final Report (2015)
Action 3	Base Erosion and Profit Shifting Action 3: Designing Effective Controlled Foreign Company Rules, Action 3 – 2015 Final Report
AEoI	Agreement on the Exchange of Information
AFIP	Administración Federal de Ingresos Públicos (Argentinian Federal Administration of Public Revenues)
AGI	Allowance for Growth and Investment
ALP	Arm's Length Principle
AOA	Authorized OECD Approach
Art.	Article
ATAD	Anti-Tax Avoidance Directive
ATAD I	Anti-Tax Avoidance Directive (Council Directive [EU] 2016/1164 of 12 July 2016 laying down rules against tax avoidance practices that directly affect the functioning of the internal market)
ATAD II	Anti-Tax Avoidance Directive II (Council Directive [EU] 2017/952 of 29 May 2017 amending Directive [EU] 2016/1164 regarding hybrid mismatches with third countries)
ATAP	Anti-Avoidance Tax Package
BEAT	Base Erosion and Anti-Abuse Tax
BEPS	Base Erosion and Profit Shifting
Bull. Intl. Taxn.	Bulletin for International Taxation – Journal IBFD
CbCR	Country-by-Country Reporting
CCTB	Common Corporate Tax Base
CCCTB	Common Consolidated Corporate Tax Base
CC(C)TB	Common Corporate (Consolidated) Tax Base
CEN	Capital Export Neutrality
CFC	Controlled Foreign Company/Controlled Foreign Corporation
CIN	Capital Import Neutrality
CIT	Corporate Income Tax
CITA	Corporate Income Tax Act
CJEU	Court of Justice of the European Union
Co.	Company
Commentaries	Commentaries on the Articles of the MC

List of Abbreviations

Corp.	Corporation
CSO	Cadbury Schweppes Overseas
DEMPE	Development, Enhancement, Maintenance, Protection, Exploitation
DIAN	Dirección de Impuestos y Aduanas Nacionales (Colombian National Tax and Customs Office)
DGI	Dirección General Impositiva (Uruguayan Tax Administration)
DTA	Double Tax Agreement
DTC	Double Tax Convention
DTT	Double Tax Treaty
e.g.	exempli gratia, for example
EC	European Commission
ECJ	European Court of Justice
ed.	editor
eds.	editors
EEA	European Economic Area
EEAA	European Economic Area Agreement
EFTA	European Free Trade Association
ETR	Effective Tax Rate
EU	European Union
EUR	Euro
FA	Formulary Apportionment
FBCI	Foreign Base Company Income
FBCSI	Foreign Base Company Sales Income
FBC Service Income	Foreign Base Company Services Income
FDII	Foreign Derived Intangible Income
FFA	Functional and Factual Analysis
FIF	Foreign Investment Fund
Forco	Foreign Company
FPHC	Foreign Personal Holding Company
FPHCI	Foreign Personal Holding Company Income
FTC	Foreign Tax Credits
G-20	Group of 20
G20 or G-20	Group of Twenty
GAAR	General Anti-Avoidance Rule
GILTI	Global Intangible Low Tax Income

List of Abbreviations

GLOBE	Global Anti Base Erosion
HMRC	Her Majesty's Revenue and Customs
i.e.	id est, that is
IBFD	International Bureau of Fiscal Documentation
IFA	International Fiscal Association
IFRS	International Financial Reporting Standards
IFSC	International Financial Services Centre
IIR	Income Inclusion Rule
IP	Intellectual property
IRC	Internal Revenue Code
IRS	Internal Revenue Service
ITA	Income Tax Act
LMU	Ludwig-Maximilians-Universität München
LOB	Limitations on Benefits Clause
LP or LPS	Limited Partnerships
MLI	Multilateral Convention to Implement Tax Treaty Related Measures to Prevent Base Erosion and Profit Shifting
MNC	Multinational Corporation
MNE	Multinational Enterprise
MNE Group	Multinational Enterprise Group
MS	Member State
MSs	Member States
MTC	Model Tax Convention
No.	Number
Nos.	Numbers
OECD	Organisation for Economic Co-operation and Development
OECD MC 2017	OECD Model Convention of 2017
OECD MC	OECD Model Tax Convention on Income and on Capital
OECD Model	OECD Model Tax Convention on Income and on Capital
Opco	Operational Company
para.	paragraph
paras.	paragraphs
PE	Permanent Establishment
PFIC	Passive Foreign Investment Company
PFIC rules	Passive Foreign Investment Company rules
POEM	Place of Effective Management

List of Abbreviations

PoW	OECD Programme of Work to Develop a Consensus Solution to the Tax Challenges Arising from the Digitalization of the Economy
pp.	pages
PPT	Principal Purpose Test
QEF	Qualifying Electing Fund
RUB	Russian rouble
SAAR	Specific Anti-Tax Avoidance Rules
Sec.	Section
SENIAT	Servicio Nacional Integrado de Administracion Aduanera y Tributaria (Venezuelan National Customs and Tax Administration)
SII	Servicio de Impuestos Internos (Chilean Internal Tax Services)
SoR	Switch over Rule
STTR	Subject to Tax Rule
SPF/KERT	Significant People Functions/Key Entrepreneurial Risk-Taking Functions
TCJA	Tax Cuts and Jobs Act
TEU	Treaty on European Union
TFDE	Task Force on Digital Economy
TFEU	Treaty on the Functioning of the European Union
TP	Transfer Pricing
TPR	Transfer Pricing Rules
UIT	Unidad Impositiva Tributaria (Peruvian Tax Unit)
UK	United Kingdom
UN	United Nations
UN Committee	United Nations Committee of Experts on International Cooperation in Tax Matters
UN Model	United Nations Model Double Taxation Convention between Developed and Developing Countries
UPE	Ultimate Parent Entity
US	United States of America
US Model	United States Model Income Tax Convention
US Treasury	US Department of the Treasury
US or USA	United States of America
USD	United States dollar
UTPR	Undertaxed Payments Rule

List of Abbreviations

VAT	Value Added Tax
WHT	Withholding tax
World Tax J.	World Tax Journal – Journal IBFD

CFC rules in general

Historical background to CFC-rules and policy considerations

Ludovica Ostorero

1. Introduction
2. The very beginning: CFC rules in the United States
3. The German CFC regime
4. CFC Implementation in Europe: current trends and proposals
5. A Nordic approach
6. Cadbury Schweppes: the repercussion on freedom of establishment
   6.1. Cadbury Schweppes case
   6.2. Columbus Containers and Olsen cases
7. Road to the BEPS Project: aims and challenges
8. Implementation of ATAD Directive
9. Outlooks and suggestions for the future of CFC legislation

1. Introduction

Controlled Foreign Companies (hereafter CFC) are common rules among EU Member States and OECD countries that have been adopted since the late 1960s in order to counteract the practice of corporations setting up companies in low tax jurisdictions.

The history of CFCs, although it can be considered quite short since its first introduction in the United States, has rapidly evolved in the past decade due to the implementation of BEPS[1] in 2015 and, more recently, with the introduction of the ATAD Directive[2] by the EU. The following chapter aims to briefly analyse the history of the CFC rules and the policy considerations behind the introduction of such rules.

While approaching the topic of controlled foreign companies and the reason why so many countries have, sooner or later, introduced CFC regulations is the definition and meaning behind the term 'deferral' that has been continuously used since 1913 in relation to tax matters. According to the Merriam-Webster vocabulary,[3] it is the act of delaying or deferring something; in tax, more specifically, deferral means the postponement of taxation to a later time.

According to international law and, more specifically, treaty law, income may be taxable under the laws of a country based on a link or '*nexus between that Country and the income or activities that generated the income*'[4] meaning that a country has the right to tax income generated within its territory (source taxation). On the other hand, a country '*may also impose tax on income because of a nexus between the country and the person earning the income*'[5] meaning that it has the right to tax income generated by its residents regardless of where the income is produced (residence taxation).[6]

Taxation of income at an international level is deemed to be based on simple principles:

- countries have a right to tax based on the source of income and on the basis of residence of the taxpayer;

---

1 OECD (2015), Designing Effective Controlled Foreign Company Rules, Action 3 – 2015 Final Report, OECD/G20 Base Erosion and Profit Shifting Project, OECD Publishing, Paris, https://doi.org/10.1787/9789264241152-en.
2 Council Directive (EU) 2016/1164 of 12 July 2016 laying down rules against tax avoidance practices that directly affect the functioning of the internal market, OJ L 193, 19.7.2016, p. 1–14.
3 Merriam-Webster vocabulary, online edition https://www.merriam-webster.com/thesaurus/deferral, check on print edition or other English vocabularies.
4 Brian J. Arnold, International Tax Primer, Wolters Kluwer, 3rd edition, 2016.
5 Ibid.
6 Based on the residence jurisdiction, persons are generally taxed on their worldwide income without reference to the source of such income. See also Brian J. Arnold, International Tax Primer, Wolters Kluwer, 3rd edition, 2016.

- the source state has the first right to tax; and
- the residence state has the right to tax the worldwide income while granting relief for income already subject to taxation in the source country.[7]

Based on the allocation rules laid down among countries in their respective double tax treaties, the approach chosen is that the residence state may have an unlimited right to tax while the source state may have a limited tax liability. This approach is the one chosen by the OECD in its model tax convention (OECD MTC) which has served as the basis for the majority of the existing double tax treaties among OECD members. The consequence of such an approach is that source state, based on the relevant allocation rule as provided in the tax treaty, may have the first right to tax.

According to Article 7[8] of the OECD MTC, each entity is therefore taxed in its state of residence. In order to avoid such taxation, companies resident in high tax jurisdictions have started to set up CFCs in low tax jurisdictions and move the passive income there and retain the profits generated. The subsidiaries would have eventually distributed the profits generated in such low taxed countries in the form of a dividend to the parent company. In such cases, taxes can be postponed or deferred until the income is either distributed as a dividend or the resident taxpayers sell the foreign subsidiary's shares.[9]

Given that, over the years, domestic corporations have formed foreign corporations with the aim of avoiding or deferring taxation, countries have started to introduce CFC legislation in their domestic tax law to both tackle tax avoidance schemes and protect their domestic tax revenues. With no CFC rules, taxpayers will be free to establish companies with no economic substance in low tax jurisdictions with the sole purpose of transferring profits.[10]

The policy objectives behind the introduction of CFC rules differ among the states that have enacted such legislation. However, fundamentally, CFC legislation is typically seen as an instrument to guard against the unjustifiable erosion of the domestic tax base by the export of investments to non-resident corporations.[11] Many states have implemented CFC legislation throughout the years, but not all regimes are the same. The different rules and the reason behind them have been partially explained by the fact that some states mainly follow a doctrine of

---

7   Arnold, evolution on CFC, December 2019.
8   Article 7, OECD Model Tax Convention on Income and on Capital, 2017.
9   Revuen Avi-Yonah and Oz Halabi, "US Subpart F legislative proposals: a comparative perspective" 2012, Law & Economics Working Papers 69. https://repository.law.umich.edu/law_econ_current/69.
10 Renata Fontana The Uncertain Future of CFC Regimes in the Member States of the European Union – Part 1, European Taxation, 2006 IBFD.
11 Peter K. Schmidt, Taxation of Controlled Foreign Companies in Context of the OECD/G20 Project on Base Erosion and Profit Shifting as well as the EU Proposal for the Anti-Tax Avoidance Directive – an Interim Nordic Assessment.

capital export neutrality whereas others follow a doctrine of capital import neutrality.[12]

Capital export neutrality (CEN) is achieved when countries tax their residents on their worldwide income, including income earned by their foreign subsidiaries, while capital import neutrality is achieved when *'taxpayers doing business in a country should be subject to the same tax burden irrespective of where they are resident'*.[13] Jurisdictions taxing on a worldwide basis are indeed following the CEN principle while countries that do not impose tax on foreign source income earned by foreign corporations controlled by residents are consistent with the capital import neutrality (CIN) principle. The balance between the aims of these two principles, between taxing foreign income and maintaining competitiveness without causing distortions in a world with no harmonized tax rates, has affected how states have designed their CFC rules. However, a clear and definitive adoption of those two principles has never been achieved, and countries usually adopt some variations.[14]

2. The very beginning: CFC rules in the United States

It has now become common knowledge, at least common among those approaching and studying CFCs rules, that the starting point is, indeed, the United States. They were the first country ever to introduce such legislation in the 1960s, and such legislation have paved the way and became the role model for CFC rules applied worldwide. The implementation of CFC regulations in the United States has been a long process that first started in the late 1930s, leading up to the introduction in 1962 of the first anti-deferral rule.[15] This was followed up by amendments over the past 50 years to the current reforms and proposals and also due to the introduction of OECD BEPS Project,[16] the Tax Cuts and Jobs Act (TCJA),[17] and the Global Intangible Low-Taxed Income (GILTI).[18]

From a historical point of view, before the implementation of the Revenue Act of 1913,[19] starting from the first revenue acts after the Civil War, there was no separation from a corporation and its owner and, generally, the principle of worldwide taxa-

---

12 Peter K. Schmidt, Taxation of Controlled Foreign Companies in Context of the OECD/G20 Project on Base Erosion and Profit Shifting as well as the EU Proposal for the Anti-Tax Avoidance Directive – an Intermin Nordic Assessment.
13 Brian J. Arnold, International Tax Primer, Worlters Kluwer, 3rd edition, 2016.
14 Ibid.
15 Revenue Act of 1962, Public Law 87-334, October 16, 1962, Section 12.
16 OECD (2013) Base Erosion Profit Shifting, OECD Publishing, https://doi.org/10.1787/23132612.
17 Tax Cut and Jobs Act TCJA, Public Law no. 115- 2017, 115th US Congress Public Law 97, 22/12/2017.
18 Global Intangible Low-Tax Income, GILTI, US Treasury Department n. 9866, section 951A.
19 Revenue Act 1913, An Act to reduce tariff duties and to provide revenue for the Government, 38 Stat.114 Public Law 63-16.

tion was not applied.[20] Thus, with the Revenue Act of 1913,[21] corporations have been formally treated as separate entities from their shareholders unless these corporations were '*created or organized, formed or fraudulently availed of for the purpose of preventing the imposition of the graduated surtax on individuals*'.[22] If so, shareholders of such corporations were required to include in their income the corporation's gains and profits whether or not they were distributed.[23]

Other revenue acts followed after the 1913 act and, in 1934, the Revenue Act[24] introduced one of the first anti-avoidance and postponement measures specifically to tackle the practice of US taxpayers forming a corporation '*and exchange for its stock his personal holding in stock, bonds or other income-producing property*'[25]; therefore, with such an exchange that was defined by congress as an 'incorporated pocketbook',[26] the income generated at the level of the corporation, unless later distributed, was not taxed at the level of the shareholders. In order to tackle this scheme, the Revenue Act of 1934 introduced an additional tax on undistributed profits of all corporations that fell under the definition of a 'personal holding company'.[27]

By 1937, tax avoidance schemes were put in place, one example being the scheme of 'foreign personal holding companies' established in tax havens to avoid taxation. On a request addressed to the congress by President Roosevelt,[28] a proposal was made to include the non-distributed income of such corporations into the gross income of their shareholders.

As stated by the joint committee[29] that proposed such a measure, the introduction of such legislation would definitely have not solved tax avoidance problems for the future.[30] Following the expansion of US investments in Europe and international markets after the end of World War II, by the 1950s, the increase of incorporation

---

20 The Deferral of Income Earned Though U.S. Controlled Foreign Corporations, A Policy Study, Office of Tax Policy, Department of the Treasury, December 2000.
21 Revenue Act 1913, An Act to reduce tariff duties and to provide revenue for the Government, 38 Stat.114 Public Law 63-16.
22 The Deferral of Income Earned Through U.S. Controlled Foreign Corporations, A Policy Study, Office of Tax Policy, Department of the Treasury, pg.105 – December 2000.
23 Ibid.
24 Revenue Act 1934, An Act to provide revenue, equalize taxation, and for other purposes, 73rd Congress, Session II, 24 May 1934.
25 The Deferral of Income Earned Though U.S. Controlled Foreign Corporations, A Policy Study, Office of Tax Policy, Department of the Treasury, pg.107, December 2000.
26 Also Prof. Avi Yonah, Back to the Future? The Potential Revival of Territoriality, Bulletin for International Taxation, October 2008.
27 The Deferral of Income Earned Though U.S. Controlled Foreign Corporations, A Policy Study, Office of Tax Policy, Department of the Treasury, pg.107, December 2000.
28 The Deferral of Income Earned Though U.S. Controlled Foreign Corporations, A Policy Study, Office of Tax Policy, Department of the Treasury, December 2000.
29 Ibid. with particular reference to the Joint committee intervention and letter of 1937, pg 7.
30 Ibid.

Historical background to CFC-rules and policy considerations

of foreign subsidiaries, deferral schemes, and tax advantages related to investments in either low-tax countries or tax havens rose again. As stressed by President Kennedy in his 1961 message to the congress the *'outflow of capital from the United States into investment companies created abroad whose principal justification lies in the tax benefits which their method of operation produces'*.[31] The Kennedy Administration then proposed a complete elimination of deferral by including the income of the foreign corporation at the level of the US shareholder. However, this proposal was not accepted by the congress due to concerns over CEN reasons.[32] At that time, congress assumed that most of active income earned outside the United States would have been taxed in countries with similar tax rates as those applicable by the United States so the CEN principle would not have been violated.[33] While one of the main concerns over the introduction of Subpart F was the relationship between capital export neutrality as proposed by the Kennedy Administration and capital import neutrality as supported by congress, many reasons were and still are the core policies to CFC legislation in the United States.

In 1962, although some concerns of President Kennedy were not included and therefore resulted in a *'political compromise'*,[34] CFC rules were finally introduced in the Internal Revenue Code[35] as Subpart F, requiring US shareholders to include in their gross income the pro-rata share of the passive income of the CFC and excluding the active income of the CFC.

As stated by the US Department of the Treasury,[36] the enactment of Subpart F rules was the result of five main reasons:

i. preventing tax haven abuse;
ii. taxing passive income in a timely manner regardless that such income was earned through a tax haven or not;
iii. promoting equity among US taxpayers through the concept of tax neutrality or efficiency;
iv. promoting economic efficiency; and
iv. competitiveness of US owned foreign corporations with the aim of stimulating investments abroad.

---

31 President Kennedy, H.R. Rep. No. 1447, 87th Cong., 2nd session 1962.
32 R.E. Krever, Chapter 1: Controlled Foreign Company Legislation: General Report in Controlled Foreign Company Legislation (G.W. Kofler et al. eds., IBFD 2020), Books IBFD.
33 Prof. Reuven S. Avi-Yonah, the U.S. Treasury's Subpart F report: plus ca change, plus c'est la meme chose?, IBFD 2001.
34 Yarif Brauner & C.A. Davis, Chapter 42: Controlled Foreign Company Legislation in the United States, in Controlled Foreign Company Legislation (G.W. Koflere et al. eds., IBFD 2020), Books IBFD.
35 Revenue Act 1962, An Act to amend the Revenue Act of 1954 to provide a credit for investment in certain depreciable property, to eliminate certain deficits and inequities and for other purposes, 87th Congress, May 11 and 12 1962.
36 The Deferral of Income Earned Though U.S. Controlled Foreign Corporations, A Policy Study, Office of Tax Policy, Department of the Treasury, chapter 2, December 2000.

Through the years, some authors have suggested the total repeal of Subpart F rules based on the assumption that the CEN should be followed rigorously, and the deferral mechanism was unnecessary and should be repealed. Others have suggested a more limited restructuring such as treating all European Union countries as one state for Subpart F purposes.[37]

Although some changes were made throughout the years, Subpart F and its scope remains intact. Both in 1976 and in 1986, the income categories of Subpart F were broadened,[38] and other anti-deferral rules have been enacted, most particularly, the Passive Foreign Investment Company (hereafter PFIC) regime in 1986.[39] The latter regime has been specifically designed to target portfolio investments made by US individuals in foreign corporations with the purpose of minimizing US tax liability.

As the years went by, different studies have shown[40] that the use of complex foreign corporation's structures was a common practice to keep US multinational profits abroad. Hence, with the enactment of the TCJA, new provisions were introduced such as the Foreign Derived Intangible Income (FDII), Base Erosion and Anti-Abuse Tax (BEAT), and the GILTI.

Before the introduction of the TCJA, it has been estimated that US multinationals held USD 2.6 trillion of foreign earnings outside the United States.[41] Some of the measures included in the TCJA, such as the ones mentioned above, directly aimed to reduce such a situation and encourage US MNEs to repatriate foreign investments while adding business tax incentives. One of the main consequence of TCJA is a shift from a worldwide taxation system to a partial territorial system.

The GILTI, though quite complex in calculation, can be defined as an 'estimate of the intangible income earned by a U.S. shareholder"[42] and provides that U.S. shareholders of *"any CFC must include its GILTI in gross income for a taxable year in a manner similar to inclusions of Subpart F income"*.[43] According the GILTI provision, US companies are subject to a minimum tax of 10.5% on income

---

37   Paul R. McDaniel, James R. Repetti, Diane M.Ring, Introduction to United States International Taxation, sixth edition, Wolters Kluwer Law&Business, 2014.
38   Yarif Brauner & C.A. Davis, Chapter 42: Controlled Foreign Company Legislation in the United States, in Controlled Foreign Company Legislation (G.W. Koflere et al. eds., IBFD 2020), Books IBFD.
39   Tax Reform Act of 1986, Public Law n.99-514, 99th U.S. Congress, October 22, 1986, Section 1235.
40   Sebastian Duenas, CFC Rules Around the World, Fiscal Fact, Tax Foundation, no.659, June 2019, with particular reference to pages 18–19.
41   Sebastian Duenas, CFC rules around the world, Tax Foundation, Fiscal Fact no.659, June 2019.
42   Yarif Brauner & C.A. Davis, Chapter 42: Controlled Foreign Company Legislation in the United States, in Controlled Foreign Company Legislation (G.W. Koflere et al. eds., IBFD 2020), Books IBFD.
43   Yarif Brauner & C.A. Davis, Chapter 42: Controlled Foreign Company Legislation in the United States, in Controlled Foreign Company Legislation (G.W. Koflere et al. eds., IBFD 2020), Books IBFD.

earned by CFC from a notional return of 10% on all intangible assets, like patents, trademarks and copyrights.[44]

The GILTI has been described by congress as 'the all-American adaptation of international anti-avoidance standards intended to dissuade MNEs from the pernicious practice of sheltering profits in low-taxed jurisdictions'.[45] The BEAT, on the other hand, targets the deduction of 'base-eroding payments made to foreign related parties'[46] such as interest, royalties, and service payments by adding back to US companies' taxable income such payments and taxing them at a rate of 10% (12.5% after 2025).

The GILTI is an expansion of the current CFC regimes in the United States but with a broader scope since it 'applies to all CFCs with GILTI, irrespective of the country in which the CFC is resident or the amount of foreign tax it pays'.[47] Therefore, it is an application that is, indeed, very different from the designated-jurisdiction approach used by most countries in their CFC rules.[48]

The TCJA has undoubtedly brought many benefits to US corporations that invested in the US market but, indeed, it raised many questions on whether it would be compatible at an international level. First of all, the tax on the GILTI imposed on CFC earnings could be seen as unfavourable in comparison to the CFC regimes applicable to most of the major trading partners of the United States[49] and, secondly, it will have major effects on the international fiscal policy, particularly at an European level.[50]

The approach taken by the United States is quite different from that taken by the OECD; following the introduction of Action 3 of OECD/G20 BEPS[51] that required the adoption or the extension of CFC rules, the OECD moved forward with the proposal included in the Inclusive Framework. In particular, the proposal included in Pillar Two regarding the Global Anti-Base Erosion (GloBE) consists of two rules: an income inclusion rule and a base eroding payments rule. The main outcome is the introduction of a minimum tax rate which should be

---

44 Brian J. Arnold, The Evolution of Controlled Foreign Corporation Rules and Beyond, Bulletin for International Taxation, December 2019.
45 C. Pérez Gautrin, US Tax Cuts and Jobs Act: Part 1 – Global Intangible Low-Taxed Income (GILTI), 73 Bulletin for International Taxation. 1 (2019), Journal Articles & Opinion Pieces IBFD.
46 Brian J. Arnold, The Evolution of Controlled Foreign Corporation Rules and Beyond, Bulletin for International Taxation, December 2019.
47 Ibid.
48 Ibid.
49 Hannelore Niesten, European Union/United States Unraveling the Recent Tax Reform: a Paradigm Shift in the International and EU landscape, European taxation, October 2018, Vol.58, n.10.
50 Ibid. The author also pointed out that, right after the TCJA was approved in 2017, the Finance Ministers of Germany, France, the United Kingdom, Italy, and Spain expressed their concerns about the GILTI arguing that it could discriminate against EU companies, increase the risk of double taxation, and distort international trade.
51 OECD, BEPS Action 3.

uniform throughout all countries and so applicable to all MNEs therefore aiming to target the same income as the CFC rules.

However, the chances to coordinate and harmonize a proposal on a minimum tax rate are indeed scarce; regardless of the lack of coordination and criticisms on the complexity of introducing a minimum tax rate, it is highly questionable whether the introduction of a minimum tax rate could entirely replace the current CFCs rules without any sort of implications and inequalities.

It is still an open issue if CFCs rules around the world, or at least the ones applicable by the trade leaders such as the United States and the EU, can be replaced in favour of other solutions or whether the countries should simply expand the application of their current CFCs rules to all income, active and passive, in order to tackle the threat of base erosion problem.

With the recent implementation of the GILTI, the United States has taken a step forward and taken another approach and direction compared to other OECD Member States. I do, however, wonder if such an approach would ultimately produce a positive effect and whether other countries shall follow the example set forth by the United States. The GILTI regime has been highly criticized for being too complex, and I suggest that it would eventually remain restricted to the United States if not repealed at all in the coming years in favour of a more coordinated approach.

3. The German CFC regime

CFC legislation was enacted in Germany in 1972, exactly eleven years after the implementation in the United States and, at that time, it was the only other country in the world and the first in Europe ever to introduce it. The rules, introduced as part of the Foreign Tax Act,[52] were based on US subpart F legislation and, although later revised in 1992 and 2003, only a few changes have been made to the rules while its overall system remained unchanged. (check again different opinions on this: see Rust in cfc legislation 2004)

Different from the policy reasons that led to the introduction of subpart F in the United States that were previously discussed, the policy considerations in Germany were not as clear.[53] Before the CFC rules were enacted, German companies were able to defer tax on profit of foreign companies until those profits were distributed and, therefore, one of the main reasons behind the introduction of CFC rules, and therefore to tackle deferral schemes, was to 'eliminate cross-border tax advantages and equate them with domestic situations'.[54]

---

52   Foreign Tax Act (FTA), September 8 1972.
53   J. Gerbracht, Chapter 17: Controlled Foreign Company Legislation in Germany, in Controlled Foreign Company Legislation (G.W: Kofler et al. eds., IBFD 2020), Books IBFD.
54   Ibid.

Historical background to CFC-rules and policy considerations

Another reason behind the introduction of CFC rules in Germany was to raise the foreign tax burden to the domestic level, as can be found in the parliamentary documents of 1971. *'Explicitly the legislator stated that there was no intention to penalize foreign activities hence the taxes suffered by a foreign subsidiary on passive income may be credited against corporate income taxes due in Germany'*.[55] However, given that domestic taxes on CFC income is subject to corporation and trade tax and there is no credit on trade tax, the overall result is a higher tax burden.

The structure of CFC legislation in Germany, also considering the changes that were made throughout the year, has basically remained static. According to German legislation, a CFC is a foreign corporation that shares capital or voting rights, is directly or indirectly majority owned by German resident shareholders, and generates passive income subjected to low taxation, i.e. income that is taxed at a tax rate below a threshold of 25%.[56]

German CFC rules have always targeted low-taxed passive business income and left out income from active business[57] (or, more specifically, all income that is not covered in the list of active income) and, until 2003, only some categories of passive income were targeted that were, in particular, ordinary passive income,[58] passive capital investment income, and passive capital investment income from intra-group financing activities.[59]

In 2003, the Tax Benefit Reduction Act eliminated the category of passive capital investment income from intra-group financing activities and changed the way resident German shareholders should include their passive income in their total income based on the proportional share of all CFC low-taxed passive income.[60]

Germany has enacted, through time, different types of CFC legislation, i.e. a simple and an extended version. According to the simple version, passive low taxed income is calculated at the level of the CFC and, if the criteria of passive income and low taxation are satisfied, then *'the low taxed passive income is deemed to be distributed to the shareholder in proportion to his holdings ... and the taxes paid by the foreign company can be deducted from the attributed income'*.[61] If the profits of a CFC are later distributed, the dividend is then tax exempted. This way, double

---

55 Stefan Weber and Martin Weiss, Legal Uncertainty in the Application of the German CFC Rules, Bulletin for International Taxation, June 2016.
56 Martin Weiss, recent development in the German tax treatment of CFCs, European taxation, 2015.
57 Guido Forster, Dirk Schmidtmann, CFC Legislation in Germany, Intertax, Vol.32, Issue 10, 2004; see also Weiss and Weber *at supra* note 49.
58 Ordinary passive income was taxed to German resident shareholders as if the income was distributed to them and is therefore defined as a deemed dividend; see also Guido Forster, Dirk Schmidtmann, CFC Legislation in Germany, Intertax, Vol.32, Issue 10, 2004.
59 Guido Forster, Dirk Schmidtmann, CFC Legislation in Germany, Intertax, Vol.32, Issue 10, 2004.
60 Guido Forster, Dirk Schmidtmann, CFC Legislation in Germany, Intertax, Vol.32, Issue 10, 2004.
61 A. Rust in M.Lang, H.J. Aigner, U. Scheuerle and M. Stefane, CFC Legislation, Tax Treaties and EC Law, Eucotax, Kluwer Law International, 2004.

taxation of the same profit is avoided.[62] Before 2003, the German CFC legislation treated 'the attributed income like real dividends'[63] and, consequently, tax treaty benefits were also extended to the 'fictitious dividends' or deemed dividend distributions producing the ultimate effect of lowering the incidence of German CFC rules.[64] With the introduction in 2003 of new regulation, the treaty protection and benefits that were first given to ordinary passive income were abolished, meaning that there was no more exemptions to such passive income. This was ultimately included in the overall German resident taxable income, and the relevance of CFC rules has undoubtedly increased.[65]

Pursuant to the extended version, the second type of CFC legislation enacted in Germany was to avoid the application of tax treaty protection on the fictitious dividends, so it was excluded for certain types of income such as capital investment income and the so called 'personal scope', i.e. the minimum interest a shareholder is bearing in a company was tightened and, in 2001, reduced to 1%.[66]

After the modifications that occurred in 2003, the difference between the two CFC models was drastically reduced with the only difference being the percentage of minimum holding: 50% under the simple CFC legislation and 1% under the extended type. Some authors have also argued that the changes made in 2003 have created a "shift in German tax law" by "*departing from the principle of capital import neutrality…to the principle of capital export neutrality*".[67]

German CFC rules were majorly affected after the ECJ decision in the *Cadbury Schweppes* case[68] since the German legislator introduced an escape clause in section 8 of the FTTA which provides an exemption of CFC rules if the CFC is based in the European Union or the European Economic Area and "the taxpayer can prove to the authorities that it pursues a real economic activity".[69]

More recently, the German legislator again updated the CFC rules by introducing a PE test providing that the income generated by the foreign PE could be considered as CFC income if it were generated by a corporation instead of a PE.[70] Such a rule

---

62   Ibid.
63   Ibid. See also Guido Forster, Dirk Schmidtmann, CFC Legislation in Germany, Intertax, Vol.32, Issue 10, 2004.
64   Guido Forster, Dirk Schmidtmann, CFC Legislation in Germany, Intertax, Vol.32, Issue 10, 2004.
65   Guido Forster, Dirk Schmidtmann, CFC Legislation in Germany, Intertax, Vol.32, Issue 10, 2004.
66   A. Rust in M. Lang, H.J. Aigner, U. Scheuerle and M. Stefane, CFC Legislation, Tax Treaties and EC Law, Eucotax, Kluwer Law International, 2004.
67   Guido Forster, Dirk Schmidtmann, CFC Legislation in Germany, Intertax, Vol.32, Issue 10, 2004.
68   UK, ECJ Case C-196/04 Cadbury Schweppes pls and Cadbury Schweppes Overseas Ltd v Commissioners of Inland Revenue, ECJ Case Law, IBFD. For further reference, please see also Mike Kollar's chapter in this book.
69   Martin Weiss, recent development in the German tax treatment of CFCs, European taxation, 2015.
70   Martin Weiss, recent development in the German tax treatment of CFCs, European taxation, 2015; this concept is also referenced as a substance carve-out, Jochen Gerbracht, Chapter 17: Controlled Foreign Company Legislation in Germany, in Controlled Foreign Company Legislation (G.W: Kofler et al. eds., IBFD 2020), Books IBFD.

can lead to a problematic situation: the switch from the exemption method to the credit method can be seen as a treaty override since most of Germany's tax treaties include the former method of relief instead of the latter.[71] However, as recent case law demonstrated, although a treaty override is a violation of international law, it is considered permissible in some cases and constitutional in Germany.[72]

German CFC rules have been more recently modified due to the implementation of the ATAD Directive,[73] although few changes were necessary since most of the directive requirements partly followed the already existing German CFC rules.[74]

After the publication of Deutsche Bank Report in 2018, German tax rules have been defined as particularly restrictive and outdated, putting non-German subsidiaries of German parent companies at a disadvantage.[75] As a response to this report, along with France, Germany is pushing toward the implementation of the OECD's Inclusive Framework Pillar 2 GLOBE Proposal that, although aiming mainly at taxation of the digital economy, also include rules involving CFCs.[76] Germany and France, in particular, are "converging at the OECD on the creation of a minimum tax"[77] therefore aiming to harmonize the international tax system and probably moving forward from the outdated CFC rules.

4. CFC Implementation in Europe: current trends and proposals

As mentioned in the previous chapter, Germany was the first European country to implement CFC legislation in 1972, but it was soon followed by other European jurisdictions. France introduced CFC legislation for the first time in 1980 mainly as a response to abusive practice related to its participation exemption regime. It is worth noting that France applies a strict territorial tax regime, meaning that only the profits generated in the country are subject to taxation in France.[78]

71　Martin Weiss, recent development in the German tax treatment of CFCs, European taxation, 2015.
72　Adrian Cloer and Tobias Hagemann, Constitutionality of Treaty Override, European taxation, 2016; see also reference to Federal Fiscal Court's order I R 66/09 and Decision of BVerfG 2 Bvl 1/12 December 15, 2015.
73　Council Directive EU 2016/1164 of 12 July 2016 Laying Down Rules against tax avoidance practices that directly affect the functioning of the internal market, OJ L 193.
74　The definition of a CFC included in the directive was already in line with Germany rules; some of the changes implemented regarded: the introduction of the substance escape provision of Art. 7.2 and the extension to EEA countries; and taxation of specific categories of income as required by Art. 7.1. However, Germany, differently than the ATAD, specifically provides for a list of active income that is not subject to CFC rules and passive income that is subject to CFC rules. For further reference, please see Germany – ATAD Implementation Tables, Tables IBFD. (2020).
75　Sebastian Dueñas, Comparing CFC Rules Around the World, Tax Notes International, 2019.
76　As stated in the previous chapter the rules introduced in Pillar 2 are an income inclusion rule and a base eroding payments rule.
77　Sebastian Dueñas, Comparing CFC Rules Around the World, Tax Notes International, 2019.
78　Sebastian Duenas, CFC around the world, Tax Foundation, Fiscal Fact, no.659, June 2019.

Under a pure territorial regime, French domestic corporations had the option of establishing subsidiaries in low-tax jurisdictions and, by the application of the participation exemption regime, dividends from foreign subsidiaries were subject to limited taxation[79] Therefore, the French CFC rules represent an exception to the principle of territoriality. The French CFC regime applies to resident companies that directly or indirectly hold a participation of more than 50% in a foreign subsidiary[80] in a country where the effective tax rate is at least 60% lower than the French tax rate.[81]

As like other European countries, France amended its own rules after the ECJ decision in the *Cadbury Schweppes* case[82] introducing a safe harbour provision. It states that CFC rules do not apply within the European Union unless the structure is purely artificial within the meaning and definition provided in the ECJ case mentioned previously, and its purpose is the avoidance of taxation.

France CFC legislation did not suffer any major modification to the Anti-Tax Avoidance Directive since the domestic legislation was already in line with the requirements of the directive. Although both Germany and France legislations were in line with the provision of the ATAD Directive, those countries released a joint statement in 2018, known as the Meseberg Declaration, supporting the European Commission's proposal for a directive establishing a Common Corporate Tax Base in order to 'foster tax harmonization in Europe'.[83] The declaration itself contained many common positions with regard to harmonization of the tax base and, with regards to CFC legislation, both countries agree on the introduction of an effective minimum tax on corporate profits provided by the ATAD Directive.

Such an initiative taken by Germany and France is also a response or, rightly put, a third option with regards to taxation of the digital economy and the Task Force on the Digital Economy set up by the OECD. While there is still no agreement on taxation of the digital economy, mainly two options had been identified.

The first option focused on the traditional internet companies criticizing the current system in which value creation is not taken into account in the allocation of taxing rights. European countries agreeing with this option are also in favour of the introduction or have already introduced a digital service tax (DTS), i.e. the United Kingdom, Spain, Italy, and France.

---

79   Currently, intercompany dividends related to a consolidated tax group will give rise to taxation of an add-back amount of 1% while, in the case of a tax-consolidated group, the amount is 5%.
80   French parent company holds 50% of the voting rights or 50% of financial rights or both.
81   P. Burg, France – Corporate Taxation sec. 10, Country Tax Guides IBFD.
82   UK, ECJ Case C-196/04 Cadbury Schweppes plc and Cadbury Schweppes Overseas Ltd v Commissioners of Inland Revenue, ECJ Case Law, IBFD. For further references please see also Mike Kollar's chapter in this book.
83   Klaus von Brocke, France and Germany Publish Common Position Paper on Common Corporate Tax Base, EC Tax Review, 2019/1.

Historical background to CFC-rules and policy considerations

The second option, mainly supported by the United States, mainly focuses on shifting taxation right to the market jurisdiction where the goods and services are consumed.[84]

The Germany and France proposal aims not to reallocate taxing rights among states but to enhance a way of strengthening the allocation rights in cases for which, when the tax burden of a foreign subsidiary is going to be too low, then a supplementary minimum tax shall be levied.[85] Such a proposal is, in a certain aspect, similar to the US' GILTI and BEAT regimes since both aim to tax foreign source profits (although the GILTI focuses on profits related to the use of tangible assets in foreign jurisdictions).

As stated in the previous chapter, the GILTI aims to tax foreign source profits that exceed a standard notional return on the use of tangible assets imposing a minimum tax. Given that the current US regime provides for a 80% foreign tax credit, the GILIT is basically similar to a minimum tax on foreign profits similar to the German-France proposal.

5. A Nordic approach

Nordic countries have also introduced CFC rules in their respective domestic legislation throughout the years. The first one was Sweden in 1989[86] as a result of the repeal of the Swedish Exchange Control Act. Although the reasons behind the introduction were not extensively explained, the objective was mainly to protect the tax base against tax planning involving companies in low-tax countries.[87]

Sweden was soon followed by Norway which introduced CFC legislation in 1992 as the result of the repeal of the regulations on currency control.[88] It is important to point out that Norway is not a Member State of the EU but is a European Free Trade Association (EFTA) State which signed the Agreement on the European Economic Area (EEA Agreement).[89]

Finland and Denmark introduced CFC legislation in 1994 and 1995, respectively, while Iceland was the last in 2009.

---

84   Johannes Becker, Joachim Englisch, The German proposal for an Effective Minimum Tax on MNEs Profits, Kluwer International tax blog, accessed December 2020.
85   Ibid.
86   Inkomstskattelag, Swedish Income Tax Act 1989.
87   Peter Koever Schimdt, taxation of CFC companies in context of OECD/G20 Project on Base Erosion and Profit Shifting as well as the EU Proposal for the Anti-Tax Avoidance Directive – an Interim Nordic Assessment, Nordic Tax journal, 2016.
88   Peter Koever Schimdt, taxation of CFC companies in context of OECD/G20 Project on Base Erosion and Profit Shifting as well as the EU Proposal for the Anti-Tax Avoidance Directive – an Interim Nordic Assessment, Nordic Tax journal, 2016.
89   Agreement on the European Economic Area – Final Act – Joint Declarations – Declarations by the Governments of the Member States of the Community and the EFTA States, OJ L 1, 3.1.1994, p. 3–522. The EEA Agreement was signed on January 1, 1994 between the EU Member States and three EEA EFTA State – Iceland, Liechtenstein and Norway – establishing a single internal market. Since Norway is not an EU Member State, the ATAD does not apply. However, the Norwegian CFC legislation is in line with both BEPS recommendations and ATAD provisions.

Although the policy reasons behind the introduction of CFC rules are quite similar among those countries, some differences can be traced in their respective rules and, in particular, changes made after the ECJ Cadbury Schweppes case, particularly the changes introduced in Denmark and Sweden. The Danish CFC legislation was amended in 2007 after the *Cadbury Schweppes* case,[90] but, differently from the majority of EU countries that tightened the rules, the Danish widened the scope of its application also to domestic subsidiaries and not only to foreign subsidiaries. According to the Danish legislature, this decision was based on the idea that there should not be different treatment among a domestic subsidiary resident in Denmark, a foreign subsidiary resident in the EU/EEA, or a foreign subsidiary resident outside the EEA.[91] The 2007 reform also aimed to shift from a transactional approach to an entity approach, meaning that the entire income of the subsidiary and not only the tainted one "*should be attributed to the parent company*" if the CFC rules are fulfilled.[92]

It still remains questionable if the Danish current CFC legislation is compatible and in line with the EU law and in particular with the provision enshrined in Article 49 of the TFEU. Although the National Tax Assessment Board has concluded that the legislation is in line with EU law, some authors' suggested that it still constitutes a restriction on the freedom of establishment producing a genuine tax advantage. It therefore treats the Danish parent company different whether the subsidiary is resident in Denmark or resident in a country with a level of taxation lower than the one in Denmark.[93]

Sweden CFC rules were also amended in light of Cadbury Schweppes and, in particular, following the ECJ judgement, the provision specified that CFC rules are not applicable if the foreign legal entity constitutes an actual establishment from which activities conducted for business reasons are carried out. The wording of the Swedish legislation does not follow the ECJ reference to "wholly artificial arrangements" made in the Cadbury Schweppes judgement and authors[94] have pointed out that such definition is "rather vague and...does not provide guidance on how to interpret it for tax purposes".[95]

---

90 UK, ECJ Case C-196/04 Cadbury Schweppes plc and Cadbury Schweppes Overseas Ltd v Commissioners of Inland Revenue, ECJ Case Law, IBFD
91 Peter Koever Schimdt, Are the Danish CFC rules in Conflict with the Freedom of Establishment? – An Analysis of the Danish CFC Regime for Companies in Light of ECJ Case Law, European Taxation, 2014.
92 Peter Koever Schimdt, Are the Danish CFC rules in Conflict with the Freedom of Establishment? – An Analysis of the Danish CFC Regime for Companies in Light of ECJ Case Law, European Taxation, 2014.+ same wording in CFC book also by same author.
93 Peter Koever Schimdt, Are the Danish CFC rules in Conflict with the Freedom of Establishment? – An Analysis of the Danish CFC Regime for Companies in Light of ECJ Case Law, European Taxation, 2014.
94 Jesper Barenfeld, Sweden's New CFC Regime after Cadbury Schweppes – Comments and Analysis, Bulletin for International Taxation, July 2008.
95 Jesper Barenfeld, Sweden's New CFC Regime after Cadbury Schweppes – Comments and Analysis, Bulletin for International Taxation, July 2008.

6. Cadbury Schweppes: the repercussion on freedom of establishment

6.1. Cadbury Schweppes case

Within the European Union, the cornerstone case that established a benchmark for all future cases and deeply impacted the CFC rules that was either later implemented or revised is the ECJ case Cadbury Schweppes.[96] The major issue that was brought to the ECJ for a preliminary ruling was whether the taxation of a resident company of a Member State on the profits of subsidiaries established in another Member State with a lower level of taxation constituted a restriction on the on the freedom of establishment as set out in Article 43 of the EC Treaty.[97]

In particular, in the case at hand, the resident company was established in the United Kingdom and the subsidiaries in Ireland, a country where the level of taxation on profits was lower than the one applicable in the United Kingdom.

In addition, the issue brought to the ECJ also concerned whether the possibility of restriction on the freedom of establishment was permissible when applied to wholly artificial arrangements whose purpose was to escape the domestic level of taxation on the State of the parent company.

The ECJ decided to examine the domestic legislation of the United Kingdom in light of the freedom of establishment and, in paragraph 42 of its judgment, stated that such freedom prohibits *"the Member State of origin from hindering the establishment in another Member State of one of its nationals or of a company incorporated under its legislation"*.[98] Following the reasoning of the ECJ, it was also stated that the application of the UK CFC legislation caused a *"tax disadvantage for the resident company to which the legislation on CFCs is applicable"*.[99] The result of the domestic CFC rules of the United Kingdom and the tax disadvantage as envisaged by the ECJ led to a situation in which the parent company was dissuaded to establish a subsidiary in a low-tax jurisdiction of another Member State, and this led to a restriction of the freedom of establishment of Article 43 of the EC Treaty.[100]

In its judgement, the ECJ went on by stating that

a national measure restricting freedom of establishment may be justified where it specifically related to wholly artificial arrangement aimed at circumventing the application of the legislation of the Member State concerned".[101] The ECJ continued

---

96 ECJ, 12 September 2006, Case C-196/04, Cadbury Schweppes plc, Cadbury Schweppes plc, Cadbury Schweppes Overseas Ltd v. Commissioners of Inland Revenue.
97 Art. 43 ECT Treaty now art.49 of TFEU.
98 ECJ C-196/04, para.42.
99 ECJ C-196/04, para.45.
100 Art. 43 ECT Treaty now art.49 of TFEU.
101 ECJ C-196/04, para.51.

emphasizing that *"the concept of establishment within the meaning of the Treaty provisions on freedom of establishment involves the actual pursuit of an economic activity through a fixed establishment in that State for an indefinite period...Consequently, it presupposes actual establishment of the company concerned in the host Member State and the pursuit of genuine economic activity there.*[102]

Given that the ECJ, in the following paragraphs of its judgement, stated that a restriction of the freedom of establishment is justifiable in order to prevent the creation of wholly artificial arrangements that do not reflect economic reality,[103] its final ruling permitted the application of UK CFC legislation in spite of the freedom of establishment in order to counter wholly artificial arrangements intended to escape the national tax normally payable.[104]

As it has been pointed out by some authors[105] the ECJ, in its ruling, has acknowledged that a company could benefit from a low-tax jurisdiction within the EU, however, demanding a physical presence and not just a "letter box" company. It is therefore justifiable that the allocation of activity throughout the territory of the EU could be "triggered by the low level of taxation, as long as the business is an active one".

With this in mind, it may be useful to analyze the dual nature of CFC rules: On the one hand, they are a measure of countering tax avoidance by eliminating cases of fraud or abuse; without CFC rules, a taxpayer could be *"free to establish companies without economic substance in low-tax jurisdictions for the sole purposes of transferring profits and reducing the overall tax burden"*.[106] Therefore, the common objective of CFC regimes is *"to counter tax-driven foreign investments and to protect the domestic tax base from erosion* [being] *a defensive measure against states that adopt harmful tax competition"*.[107]

On the other hand, given that the internal market is based on the principles of reciprocity, mutual recognition, and desirable tax competition, each Member State can *"develop a competitive and attractive economic infrastructure by levying low taxes, and the other Member States cannot counter this by applying more severe rules"*.[108] CFC rules, as the ones discussed in the Cadbury Schweppes case, could lead to internal market distortion and jeopardize its nature since it can be seen as a protectionist legislation the aim of which is to protect the internal market of the parent company Member State.[109]

---

102 ECJ C-196/04, para.54.
103 ECJ C-196/04, para.55.
104 ECJ C-196/04, para.75.
105 Meussen, Cadbury Schweppes the ECJ significantly limits the application of cfc rules, European Taxation, January 2007.
106 Renata Fontana, Uncertain future of cfc regime in the EU, part 1, 2006 IBFD.
107 Ibid.
108 Meussen, Cadbury Schweppes the ECJ significantly limits the application of cfc rules, European Taxation, January 2007.
109 See also on this point Schonfeld, Cadbury Schweppes: are the days of UK CFC Legislations Numbered?, IBFD, 2004.

Historical background to CFC-rules and policy considerations

It is now a well-established fact that CFC legislation follows the aims of the capital export neutrality principle while the internal market is commonly based on the capital import neutrality principle. The different tax systems in place within the territories of the EU that caused distortions and tax competition among Member States led some authors to think that the community should abandon the principle of the CIN in favour of adopting the principle of CEN.[110]

However, there is no a clear preference over those two principles, and Member States are free to apply them in their respective domestic legislation; bearing in mind that the UK tax system applied the CEN principle to all taxpayers, it might be questionable whether there could even be discrimination or restriction on the exercise of the freedoms of the EC treaty.

The exercise of fundamental freedoms may be affected by domestic legislation but, in order for the restriction to be justifiable, some requirements are necessary. Domestic legislation shall indeed be applied in a non-discriminatory manner, shall be justified by an imperative requirement in the general interest, be suitable for securing the attainment of the objective pursued, and shall not go beyond what is necessary to attain.[111]

It has been pointed out that CFC rules aiming to protect the internal market of the parent company Member state fall within the restriction category rather than satisfying the discrimination condition mentioned previously. Discrimination is used to define a situation in which a Member States imposes an obstacle on the exercise of the fundamental freedoms on the basis of barriers imposed to non-national or non-resident taxpayers. Restriction, on the contrary, clearly identifies a situation where a Member States hinders the access of its own nationals or residents to the market of another Member State.[112]

Some common restrictions apply to all CFC regimes, namely, unattractiveness of cross-border investments, a temporary economic double taxation in the case of a look-through approach; time mismatching of a fictitious dividend approach; and administrative costs that are, generally, more burdensome.[113] These common features can be justified by either Member States or their respective tax authorities by reasons of effective fiscal supervision, tax cohesion, protecting loss of tax revenues and, in general, combating tax avoidance mechanisms and abusive conducts. However, it appears difficult to really justify the use of such regulations throughout Member States for reasons other than protecting their respective tax base as a symbol of expressing their own tax sovereignty.

---

110 Jens Schonfeld, Cadbury Schweppes: are the days of UK CFC Legislations Numbered?, IBFD, 2004.
111 Renata Fontana, Uncertain future of cfc regime in the EU, part 2, 2006 IBFD.
112 Ibid.
113 Ibid.

Given that, at the time of the Cadbury Schweppes ruling and, as of today, there is still no harmonization in the corporate income tax field, its seems that the only way of reaching that would be a harmonized strategy leading to clear rules to counter low-tax jurisdictions and regimes. With the Cadbury Schweppes' ruling, the ECJ clearly limited the application of UK CFC legislation to wholly artificial arrangements and, as a response, Member States have started to amend their respective domestic legislations and adjusting them to the principles as ruled by the ECJ.

The United Kingdom itself introduced some changes in the Finance Bill of 2007 in order to expand the scope of the legislation to all subsidiaries, whether residents or not, and to exclude from its scope any income from commercial and industrial activities, limiting the application to only passive income.[114]Although some of those suggestions were not implemented, the United Kingdom enacted some changes in its CFC legislation in 2013 and later in 2019 as a response following the implementation of the ATAD Directive.[115]

6.2. Columbus Containers and Olsen cases

While surely the benchmark case on CFC legislation compatibility with EU fundamental freedom is still Cadbury Schweppes, the ECJ has dealt with other cases related to either compatibility of CFC legislation and possible breaches of EU Treaty fundamental freedoms. At the time Cadbury Schweppes was pending, another case was brought up for an ECJ ruling, i.e. *Columbus Container Service* case.[116]

Although discussed nearly at the same time *as Cadbury Schweppes*, the ECJ surprisingly did not choose to deal with the case in light of possible discrimination on the basis of freedom of establishment. The ECJ held that the German domestic provisions did not constitute a restriction on the freedom of establishment since

---

114 Guglielmo Maisto and Pasquale Pistone, A European Model for Member State's Legislation on the Taxation of Controlled Foreign Subsidiaries (CFCs) – part 1., European Taxation, October 2008.
115 Germany also proposed some changes similar to the ones proposed by the United Kingdom and, most in particular, amending the definition of passive income to harmonize it with the wording wholly artificial arrangement used by the ECJ. For further reference, please see Guglielmo Maisto and Pasquale Pistone, A European Model for Member State's Legislation on the Taxation of Controlled Foreign Subsidiaries (CFCs) – part 1.
116 ECJ case-298/2005, Columbus Container Services B.V.B.A: & Co. v. Finanzamnt Bielefeld-Innenstadt. The case at hand's main issue was whether the German domestic law providing for a switch-over clause, overriding the provision included in the Germany-Belgium tax treaty, was contrary to EC law. In particular, a German resident individual held 100% of a Belgium limited partnership that was treated as a company under Belgian law but transparent under German law. According to the Germany-Belgium tax treaty, the business profits of a Belgian partnership are attributed to a foreign PE of the Germans partners in Belgium and, in order to relieve double taxation, such profits are usually tax exempt. However, the German Foreign Tax Act provided for a switch-over clause to use the credit method instead of the exemption method for profits of a foreign PE that would fall under the general CFC rules if the foreign PE was a foreign company.

Historical background to CFC-rules and policy considerations

Columbus Container did not suffer any tax disadvantage in comparison with partnerships established in Germany. Surprisingly, the ECJ reasoning differs completely from the one in the Advocate General Mengozzi Opinion since the latter saw a breach of the freedom of establishment that could only be justified in the case of countering wholly artificial arrangements to circumvent national tax rules.[117]

It was clear that this case did not deal with specific CFC legislation since the ECJ was not concerned over any form of deemed income attributed to the partners, and it was established that the activities carried on by such a controlled partnership in the host Member State was actually a genuine activity. Therefore, the line of reasoning applied to *Cadbury Schweppes* based on an anti-abuse provision could not be applied in the *Columbus Container* case.[118]

The repercussion of the Cadbury Schweppes ruling went beyond the borders of the European Union and deeply influenced the decisions of the EFTA Court. Particularly affected was the ruling regarding the joined EFTA Court case E-3/13 and E-20/13 Olsen and Olsen[119] with regards to the interpretation of the rules on freedom of establishment and the free movement of capital in relation to domestic CFC legislation as implemented in Norway.

In particular, those cases concerned the interpretation of the rules on the freedom of establishment and the free movement of capital and, moreover, the interpretation of Articles 31[120] and 40 of the Agreement on the European Economic Area (EEA Agreement),[121] in relation to the Norwegian CFC rules that permit national taxation of capital placed in a low-tax country.

The Olsen cases concerned a trust established in Liechtenstein in order to hold the interests of the Norwegian Olsen family's certain companies. Due to domestic Liechtenstein tax rules, such a trust was exempt from ordinary wealth tax, income

---

117 Ad.General Mengozzi Opinion and Gerard T.K. Meussen, Columbus Container Services – A Victory for the Member STates' Fiscal Autonomy, European Taxation, 2008.
118 Gerard T.K. Meussen, Columbus Container Services – A Victory for the Member STates' Fiscal Autonomy, European Taxation, 2008.
119 Efta Court joined cases E-3/13 and E-20/13 Fred Olsen and Others and Petter Olsen and Others vs. The Norwegian State.
120 Article 31 of the EEA Agreement provides that there shall be no restrictions on the freedom of establishment of national of an EC Member State or an EFTA State in the territory of any other of these states. The provision also is applicable to the setting up of agencies, branches, or subsidiaries. The freedom of establishment shall also include the right to take up and pursue activities as self-employed persons and to set up and manage undertakings such as companies or firms formed in accordance with the respective domestic laws of either EC Member States or EFTA States under the same conditions granted for their own nationals.
121 Article 40 of the EEA Agreement states that, under the provisions of the agreement, there shall be no restrictions between contracting parties on the movement of capital belonging to persons resident in EC Member States or EFTA States and no discrimination based on the nationality or on the place of residence of the parties or on the place where such capital is invested.

tax, and capital gains in Liechtenstein upon the condition that it did not engage in economic activities there. Shares in a Dutch parent company were held through the trust. According to Norwegian CFC rules, trusts were considered as a form of independent undertaking or asset fund and, accordingly, the tax administration considered the participants of the trust to be liable for domestic CFC taxation on their share of the profits.

The issue referred to the court was mainly whether Articles 31 and 40 of the EEA Agreement, namely, freedom of establishment and free movement of capital, precluded Norwegian CFC rules that permitted taxation of capital placed in a trust established in a low-tax country and therefore whether such domestic regulations led to discrimination within the meaning of the EEA Agreement.

Although quite an extensive judgement, the EFTA court essentially repeated what the ECJ stated in Cadbury Schweppes. The restriction imposed by the Norwegian domestic CFC rules *"cannot be justified on the basis of anti-abuse consideration if the foreign entity is not fictitiously established in Liechtenstein and carries out a genuine economic activity"*.[122] The restrictions imposed by the Norwegian domestic law cannot be justified on the basis of a general anti-abuse scope; specifically in paragraph 166 of the judgement, the court states that "the need to prevent loss of tax revenue is not a matter of overriding general interest that would justify a restriction on a freedom guaranteed by the EEA Agreement. For the purposes of preventing tax avoidance, a national measure restricting the right of establishment or the free movement of capital may be justified where it specifically targets wholly artificial arrangements which do not reflect economic reality and the sole purpose of which is to avoid the tax normally payable on the profits generated by activities carried out on the national territory."[123]

Differently from the ECJ in *Cadbury Schweppes*, the EFTA Court went a little further in describing the concept of economic activity. In particular, the court stated that such a concept should not be interpreted narrowly and, specifically, in paragraph 96, the court stated that *"the concept of establishment under Articles 31 and 34 EEA has a specific EEA meaning and must not be interpreted narrowly. Thus, any person or entity, such as a trust, that pursues economic activities that are real and genuine must be regarded as taking advantage of its right of establishment under Articles 31 and 34 EEA."*[124]

By analyzing and comparing those cases, both courts tried to establish a certain degree of definition of economic genuine activity and economic substance that

---

[122] Daniel Smit, Substance Requirements for Entities Located in a Harmful Tax Jurisdiction under CFC rules and the EU Freedom of Establishment, Derivatives and Financial Instruments, November/December 2014, IBFD.
[123] EFTA E-3/13 and E-20/13 para. 166.
[124] EFTA E-3/13 and E-20/13 para. 96.

could be achieved by Member States or EEA States under their respective CFC regulations. However, in neither cases[125] was a clear definition given but rather some guidance that implies that an economic activity can be considered a genuine one whether there is an economic link and, therefore, "establishment means integration in the national economy and involves…the exercise of an economic activity and a physical location, both on a permanent basis or at least a durable one."[126]

What can be inferred by those cases discussed previously is whether CFC legislation implemented by states can be considered a restriction of freedom of establishment and, if so, whether there is a possible justification. From the court's judgements, it is clearly understandable that the

intention to benefit from a tax advantage is not itself sufficient to constitute an artificial arrangement and neither is the fact that the activities of the foreign entity could have been carried out by an entity established in the home state…What is decisive is the fact that the activity, from an objective perspective, has no other reasonable explanation but to secure a tax advantage. If this is the case, the arrangement is purely artificial".[127]

The establishment of a controlled foreign company in another Member State with a generally low-tax regime is not sufficient to deny the home state of the parent company the protection of freedom of establishment. In order to have protection, a CFC should have some minimum requirements such as economic genuine activity and substance and a physical presence. As previously stated, the mere fact that " *a CFC is established in a Member State where it benefits from general low- or no-tax regime does not justify the application of CFC rules."*[128]

The Cadbury judgment was delivered in 2006 and is still considered to be the benchmark case regarding CFCs. It has set a ripple effect in changing the domestic CFC regulations among Member States and EEA States as stated in the previous chapters.

The concept of minimum standards had a major influence in defying the backbone structure and ideas that are some of the cornerstone basis of two major developments that will be discussed further on, i.e. the BEPS Project and the ATAD Directive.

---

125 Daniel Smit, Substance Requirements for Entities Located in a Harmful Tax Jurisdiction under CFC rules and the EU Freedom of Establishment, Derivatives and Financial instruments, November/December 2014, IBFD
126 Ibid.
127 EFTA E-3/13 and E-20/13 para 175 and reference to Opinion of Advocate General Poiares Maduro in Case C-255/02 Halifax and Others [2006]ECR I-1609, points 70 and 71.
128 Opinion AG Cadbury Schweppes and Daniel Smit, Substance Requirements for Entities Located in a Harmful Tax Jurisdiction under CFC rules and the EU Freedom of Establishment, Derivatives and Financial Instruments, November/December 2014, IBFD

With particular reference to the connection between the Cadbury Schweppes case and BEPS and, in particular, the ATAD provisions, it can be sufficient to point out the exemptions and threshold requirements laid down in BEPS Action 3 and in Article 7, paragraph 7 of the directive. Such requirements, as anticipated with Cadbury Schweppes, currently serve as a test and benchmark for the rules set forth in the ATAD Directive.

Both provisions explicitly provide for a substance carve out mechanism to ensure the compatibility of the CFC rules with current EU law. Such a threshold and exemptions deal in particular with the possibility of excluding the application of CFC rules for those subsidiaries that can prove to be engaged in substantial activities, i.e. genuine activities, and not being set up only for the purposes of obtaining a tax advantage achieving, therefore, the idea of the "wholly artificial arrangement" idea discussed in the Cadbury Schweppes case.

7. Road to the BEPS Project: aims and challenges

Tax competition among states has led to a situation of international harmful tax competition due to exploitation of different tax regimes, aggressive tax planning, and tax treaty abuse, to name a few, that have been largely exploited by MNEs throughout the years. This situation, particularly in a prolonged austerity period, has caught the attention of international bodies and the political world in general.

The OECD made the first acknowledgement of the international tax environment in 1998 in its publication on harmful tax competition.[129] This report was indeed the first signal of "an important change of focus in international cooperation effort"[130] which also focused on three major problems that were identified at the time by the OECD Members, namely, tax evasion, tax avoidance and tax subsidies, and substantive tax competition.[131]

Given the continuing economic situation at the international level and the focus on international cooperation in order to counter aggressive tax planning schemes and tax avoidance measures, it comes as no surprise that the OECD started to work on the Base Erosion and Profit Shifting Project in 2013 by publishing its first report addressing such issues.[132] In the report, the OECD recognized six "key pressure areas", namely: i. International mismatches in entity and instrument

---

129 OECD (1998), *Harmful Tax Competition: An Emerging Global Issue*, OECD Publishing, Paris, https://doi.org/10.1787/9789264162945-en.
130 Ibid.
131 Hugh J. Ault, Some reflections on the OECD and the Sources of International Tax Principles, Tax Notes International, Vol.70, number 12, 2013 ; see also OECD (1998), *Harmful Tax Competition: An Emerging Global Issue*, OECD Publishing, Paris, https://doi.org/10.1787/9789264162945-en.
132 OECD (2013), *Addressing Base Erosion and Profit Shifting*, OECD Publishing, Paris, https://doi.org/10.1787/9789264192744-en.

Historical background to CFC-rules and policy considerations

characterization including hybrid mismatch arrangements and arbitrage; ii. Application of treaty concepts to profits derived from the delivery of digital goods and services; iii. The tax treatment of related party debt-financing, captive insurance, and other inter-group financial transactions; iv. Transfer pricing; v. The effectiveness of anti-avoidance measures; and vi. the availability of harmful preferential regimes.

Among the measure of effectiveness of anti-avoidance, major attention is given to CFC rules since they "*can prevent the shifting of profits by bringing the profits back into the domestic system of the residence country – or by taxing directly base eroding payment that the foreign party has received from a related party*".[133] Although the OECD acknowledged the importance of relying on CFC rules, such rules have been implemented, changed, weakened, and strengthened throughout the years since the first introduction in 1962 in the United States by those same OECD Member States that were complaining about base erosion and profit shifting. It is no surprise that states have changed their domestic tax legislation, CFC rules included, in order to attract foreign investors and therefore somehow encourage base erosion and tax avoidance in general.

The first report published in 2013 led to the development of the BEPS Project comprised of 15 actions published in 2015. In the statement released by the OECD introducing the final action stressed that the BEPS phenomenon is not a new one but rather a phenomenon that was cited by President Kennedy in his statement in 1961.[134] The "*increased media attention and the inherent challenge of dealing comprehensively with such a complex subject has encouraged the perception that the rules for the taxation of cross-border activities are regularly broken and that taxes are paid only by the naive. MNEs stand accused of dodging taxes all around the world and in particular in developing countries …*".[135]

BEPS Action 3 deals specifically with the issue of a controlled foreign company and stressed the policy consideration and the objectives that CFC rules commonly share. In particular, the OECD pointed out that all CFC rules share some general policy considerations,[136] namely:

1. CFC rules have a role as a deterrent measure and are designed to protect revenue by ensuring that profits stay within the tax base of the parent company rather than raising taxes on the income of the CFC. However, the final result may not be as such since, in some cases, those rules seem to grant a secondary taxing right to the residence jurisdiction.[137]

---

133 Hugh J. Ault, Some reflections on the OECD and the Sources of International Tax Principles, Tax Notes International, Vol.70, number 12, 2013.
134 See first chapter.
135 Pascal Saint Amans, Raffaele Russo, What the BEPS are talking about?, OECD Forum, 2013.
136 OECD BEPS Action 3, chapter 1, pag. 13.
137 OECD, BEPS Action 3. Pg. 13.

2. CFC rules interact with transfer pricing rules since the latter are intended to adjust the taxable profits of associated enterprises in order to eliminate distortions arising from transaction among related parties. The former are a way for a parent company to capture income that may not have been earned. However, CFC rules do not always act as a "backstop" since they might target the same income as transfer pricing rules.[138]
3. CFC rules may effectively prevent avoidance while reducing administrative and compliance burdens.

The OECD goes on by asserting that, although there are some common features, each jurisdiction may design CFC rules in order to achieve a variety of policy objectives depending on the jurisdictions' aim themselves. Although CFC rules are quite difference among states, the OECD points out two common differences that can affect the CFC rule:

1. Whether a jurisdiction has a worldwide or territorial tax system;
2. Whether a jurisdiction is a Member State of the European Union.[139]

Without going into many details over these two points, the OECD pointed out that, in designing CFC rules, jurisdictions should find a balance between taxing foreign income and the competitiveness concerns inherent in rules that tax the income of foreign subsidiaries. On a competitiveness level of CFC rules, the OECD identified two major problems. On one side, the different application, either broad, narrow or no application of a CFC may cause disadvantages among resident companies and foreign investors. On the other side, the application of CFC rules in the EU may cause the same competitiveness issues among Member States. On this latter issue, the OECD is aware that, if CFC rules should apply within the EU, such rules must be compatible with EU law.

The aim of the OECD is to set forth recommendations that can be implemented throughout the EU but leaving Member States the task to decide how their respective CFC rules should be compatible with EU law. In connection to this topic, the OECD recognized the ECJ ruling on Cadbury Schweppes as a milestone in defining CFC rules and, following the ECJ ruling, the OECD recommended that Member States should include a "substance analysis" in order to verify the carrying out of a genuine economic activity and the application of CFC rules to both domestic and cross-border subsidiaries.[140]

The recommendation in the final report states that control should be based on a 50% or more ownership test, either legal or economic, but countries can also apply a de facto control test; at the same time, countries wishing to achieve a policy

---

138 OECD, BEPS Action 3. Pg. 14.
139 OECD, BEPS Action 3. Pg. 15.
140 OECD, BEPS Action 3. Pg. 17.

Historical background to CFC-rules and policy considerations

goal can reduce the control threshold lower than 50%.[141] Another set of recommendations state that CFC rules should not apply depending on whether the CFC is taxed at a comparable tax rate than that applied by the residence country and even suggest to implement a listed-country approach.[142]

Although these are the aims and policy considerations as set out in Action 3, authors have pointed out that the "action… and the its preamble lack much content".[143] It is clear while reading Action 3 that the OECD sees CFC regulation as a domestic regime rather than regulations that should be coordinated among states in order to promote coordination rather than competition. Since CFC rules are implemented at a domestic level, different solutions are applied by different states and, as Prof. Brauner rightly pointed out, countries are in competition with each other. Therefore, a straightforward solution in order to coordinate tax policies is not taken into consideration and "*consequently, the policies of the source and residence countries are not reconciled; they either overlap, resulting in potential double taxation, or create gaps of coverage resulting in double non-taxation to the advantage of MNEs.*"[144]

Throughout the years, the OECD has legitimized CFC rules as not being in contradiction with EU law and the EC Treaty. so Action 3 is the first real effort done by the OECD itself, however, it lacks much substance in its application.

The OECD materials on CFC rules were criticized by many in the academic literature.[145] In general, BEPS is considered "an overwhelming project in its breadth; it seems to be about everything and nothing at the same time".[146] However, can BEPS be seen as a complete failure? Maybe we all have been too hasty in our judgement; the OECD has brought light to an international mistrust on tax competition and finally recognized and, more importantly, legitimized the idea that action should be taken.

It was, indeed, a first step, lacking much substance itself but with a core purpose that, if legislators would keep it in mind, might eventually pave the way to reforms in order to achieve coordination. Indeed, maybe, the final verdict came too soon.

---

141 OECD, BEPS Action 3, para.n.25 pg. 21.
142 OECD, BEPS Action 3, para.n.51 pg. 33.
143 Yariv Brauner,*What the BEPS*, 16 Fla. Tax Rev. 55 (2014), *available at* http://scholarship.law.ufl.edu/facultypub/642.
144 Ibid.
145 Arnold even suggests that the final report on Action 3 "was a total failure. Not only did it fail to require, or even recommend, that countries adopt CFC rules, but it also failed to provide any solid tax-design guidance for countries that might want to adopt CFC rules or improve their existing CFC rules. Why was Action 3 such a complete failure when other action items of the OECD/G20 BEPS Project resulted in minimum standards and firm recommendations that were taken up by several countries? My guess is that the failure of Action 3 reflects the schizophrenic attitude of developed countries to the OECD/G20 BEPS Project." In Brian J. Arnold, The Evolution of Controlled Foreign Corporations Rules and Beyond", Bulletin for International Taxation, 2019.
146 Yariv Brauner, *What the BEPS*, 16 Fla. Tax Rev. 55 (2014), *available at* http://scholarship.law.ufl.edu/facultypub/642.

8. Implementation of ATAD Directive

If the BEPS Project is the international response to address aggressive tax planning and competition, the Anti-Tax Avoidance Package is the EU answer to such a response. The package included four different documents, namely: a Communication on an External Strategy for Effective Taxation,[147] the amendment to the directive on mutual assistance,[148] a recommendation on tax treaties to add the genuine economic activity test to the principle purpose test (PPT)[149] and, most importantly, a proposal for an Anti-Tax Avoidance Directive (ATAD),[150] which is the most direct European response to the OECD BEPS Project.

The European Council speedily adopted the aforementioned package that was proposed in January 2016 on 12 July 2016. The aim of the ATAD Directive[151] is to give Member States a common minimum level of rules in order to tackle tax avoidance practices, a *de minimis* character, as stated in Article 3.[152] One of the key objectives of the directive is *"to improve the resilience of the internal market as a whole against cross-border tax avoidance practices"* and is therefore *"imperative to restore trust in the fairness of tax system and allow government to effectively exercise their tax sovereignty"*.[153]

This is different from BEPS for which *"actions are meant to reduce gaps and disparities, their openness and ambiguity is deceiving … the EC Anti Tax Avoidance Package is an acknowledgment that there is no single international standard, but rather coexisting national or regional interests on policies attracting investments, tax competition and tax protectionism."*[154]

The directive builds on the BEPS Project and concentrates on five anti-avoidance measures that states must introduce, specifically, an interest limitation rule,[155] exit taxation,[156] a general anti-abuse rule,[157] an anti-hybrid rule,[158] and CFC rules.[159]

---

147   COM (2016) 24 final, Communication from the Commission to the European Parliament and the Council.
148   COM (2016) 25 final. Proposal for a Council Directive amending Directive 2011/16/EU as regards mandatory automatic exchange of information in the field of taxation.
149   COM (2016) 271 final, Commission Recommendation of 28.1.2016.
150   COM (2016) 23 final. Proposal for a Council Directive laying down rules against tax avoidance practices that directly affect the functioning of the internal market.
151   Council Directive EU 2016/1164 of 12 July 2016 Laying Down Rules against tax avoidance practices that directly affect the functioning of the internal market, OJ L 193.
152   Ibid, Article 3.
153   Council Directive EU 2016/1164 of 12 July 2016 Laying Down Rules against tax avoidance practices that directly affect the functioning of the internal market, OJ L 193, Preamble.
154   Ana Paula Dourado, The EU Anti Tax Avoidance Package: Moving Ahead of BEPS?, Intertax, Vol.44, Issue 6 & 7, Kluwer Law International, 2016.
155   Council Directive EU 2016/1164 of 12 July 2016 Laying Down Rules against tax avoidance practices that directly affect the functioning of the internal market, OJ L 193, Article 4.
156   Ibid, Article 5.
157   Ibid, Article 6..
158   Ibid, Article 9.
159   Ibid, Articles 7 and 8.

Differently from the BEPS Project that has the form of soft law and only comprised non-binding recommendations, the ATAD is hard law, meaning that Member States must have either implemented or changed their respective domestic legislation by 1 January 2019.

The European Council and OECD recognized the political necessity and challenge behind implementation of CFC rules in the EU given that, during negotiation, not all Member States had CFC rules in their national legislation. Therefore, one of the main questions was whether the CFC rules of the ATAD could be "considered an effective CFC rule without giving rise to side effects".[160]

The directive sets forth some minimum requirements for CFC rules and definitions and tries to implement the BEPS recommendations. As stated in the preamble, paragraph 12, "in order to ensure that CFC rules are a proportionate response to BEPS concerns, it is critical that Member States that limit their CFC rule to income which has been artificially diverted to the subsidiary precisely target situations where most of the decision-making functions which generated diverted income at the level of the controlled subsidiary are carried out in the Member State of the taxpayer."[161]

The directive defines a CFC as "an entity established in Europe or elsewhere which is (1) controlled directly or indirectly by a parent company established in a Member State and (2) is subject to an 'actual' corporate tax rate that is lower than the one to which it would have been charged if it was established in the jurisdiction of the parent company."[162] Clearly the directive is consistent with BEPS Action 3, covering both legal and economic control and including permanent establishments of companies established in a Member State or in a third country.

What is controversial in this definition is the method used by the directive for establishing if the income of a controlled foreign company is sufficiently taxed. The directive clearly establishes the tax rate of the parent company's resident country as a benchmark, therefore, as it has been pointed out by the Confédération Fiscale Européenne (CFE) Fiscal Committee,[163] this may lead to a "race-to-the-bottom" issue.[164] Member States may be tempted to lower their corporate tax rate in order to attract investments from foreign countries. Although this seems consistent with BEPS recommendations regarding best practices, "it is not aligned with the

---

160 Gilles Van Hulle, Current challenges for EU Controlled Foreign Company Rules, Bulletin for International Taxation, December 2017.
161 Preamble to the Directive, para. 12.
162 Guglielmo Ginevra, The The EU Anti-Tax Avoidance Directive and the Base Erosion and Profit Shifting (BEPS) Action Plan: Necessity and Adequacy of the Measures at EU level, Intertax, Vol.45, Issue 2, Kluwer Law International, 2017.
163 Confédération Fiscal Européenne (CFE) Fiscal Committee Opinion Statement.
164 Ana Paula Dourado, The EU Anti Tax Avoidance Package: Moving Ahead of BEPS? Intertax, Vol.44, Issue 6 & 7, Kluwer Law International, 2016.

Directive general aim which is to guarantee uniform implementation by the Member States".[165]

Another critical point of the CFC rules included in the directive is the definition of CFC income as stated in Article 7. The directive gives Member States the possibility of applying two different methods as already stated by the OECD, namely, a "categorical approach", i.e. a list of income, or a "substantive approach" based on a substantive test including "the non-distributed income of the entity or permanent establishment arising from non-genuine arrangements which have been put in place for the essential purpose of obtaining a tax advantage."[166] The directive does not give a preferential method so Member States can either implement both or one of the two and, consequently, although in line with the recommendations of BEPS, this may lead to confusion rather than coordination among Member States.

With respect to this latter method, the directive gives a substance carve-out unequivocally intended to ensure the compatibility of CFC rules with the fundamental freedom of the treaty. The directive clearly considers the Cadbury Schweppes ECJ case[167] in designing such a rule requiring that a controlled foreign company should be "engaged in a substantive economic activity which ... cannot be defined as wholly artificial and it has to be supported by the relevant facts and circumstances".[168]

The directive's aim is clearly to uniform rules, CFCs among other, across the European Union but, given the nature of the directive itself, being a duty of each Member State to transpose it into their domestic legislation will give space to the tax policy background of each Member State to influence the implementation of CFC rules. The choice in defining the covered entities; the threshold control requirements; the definition of CFC income and low taxation; the use of black, grey, and white lists; the categorical or substantive approaches in establishing the taxable income; the computation and attribution of income rules; and the carve-out rules and relief methods may easily complicate the harmonization principle that the ATAD wishes to achieve. Recognizing that 28 Member States, at the time of the directive, now 27, have different tax systems in place and laying down only a minimum level of protection against tax avoidance and therefore leaving the

---

165 Guglielmo Ginevra, The The EU Anti-Tax Avoidance Directive and the Base Erosion and Profit Shifting (BEPS) Action Plan: Necessity and Adequacy of the Measures at EU level, Intertax, Vol.45, Issue 2, Kluwer Law International, 2017.
166 Council Directive EU 2016/1164 of 12 July 2016 Laying Down Rules against tax avoidance practices that directly affect the functioning of the internal market, OJ L 193, Article 7.2.(b).
167 ECJ, 12 September 2006, Case C-196/04, Cadbury Schweppes plc, Cadbury Schweppes plc, Cadbury Schweppes Overseas Ltd v. Commissioners of Inland Revenue.
168 Guglielmo Ginevra, The The EU Anti-Tax Avoidance Directive and the Base Erosion and Profit Shifting (BEPS) Action Plan: Necessity and Adequacy of the Measures at EU level, Intertax, Vol.45, Issue 2, Kluwer Law International, 2017.

details to be implemented by each Member States may not be enough to have coherent harmonization among states.

Different tax policies have coexisted for many years and will coexist for many year to come despite the effort to implement a common set of rules. It is clear that the reaction of Member States have been, not surprisingly, quite diverse: some Member States have adopted a strict set of CFC rules[169] while others a less strict set of rules.[170] Are those differences the results of each domestic corporate tax rules, are they to blame only to the gaps in the directive itself, or are they to blame to an imprecise transposition of directive rules into domestic legislations? As previously stated, CFCs are and always have been a set of rules protecting the domestic tax base of the parent company rather than a proper allocation of taxing rights among states. States tax income based on a worldwide or territorial principle, apply either the CIN or CEN principle, apply different definition of residence and source, and have different allocation of taxing rights rules.

9. Outlooks and suggestions for the future of CFC legislation

The purpose of this chapter was to give a brief overview of the history and policy considerations behind the implementation of CFC rules.

Starting from President Kennedy's speech in 1961, CFC rules have come a long way. The international tax panorama has been shaken to its core because of the financial crisis in 2008 with the recognition of international tax planning schemes implemented by MNEs. As a direct consequence, the OECD introduced BEPS in 2015, and the European Union soon followed with the implementation of the ATAD Directive.

However, a question still remains: Are all of these measures enough to really provoke a change in the long run? We are now currently living in an ever more digitalized world where the value creation and, therefore, profits are no longer anchored to a "material" business activity made of buildings, machineries, installations, and people working together in the same place. Would it still be possible to apply the current tax allocation rules between residence and source states in the future and, if not, what would be the new approach also related to CFC regulations?

---

169 Netherlands and Belgium: see Isabella de Groot and Barry Larking, Implementation of Controlled Foreign Company rules under the EU Anti-Tax Avoidance Directive, European Taxation, June 2019.
170 Ireland, Luxembourg and Malta: see again see Isabella de Groot and Barry Larking, Implementation of Controlled Foreign Company rules under the EU Anti-Tax Avoidance Directive, European Taxation, June 2019.

The current outlook is indeed full of possibilities and jurisdictions are now moving in different directions. One the one hand, the United States has expanded from their Sub-F provision into a new approach with the introduction of the GILTI in the TCJA.

Although it may be too soon to judge the full repercussion of this measure, it would be interesting to weigh in the current US administration direction under President Biden regarding whether it would repeal it or continue with it even though the approach of the current administration looks less protectionist compared to the previous one.

On the other hand, the OECD has also dealt with these issues with the introduction of the BEPS Action Plan in 2013 and its final reports in 2015.

On the other side of the Atlantic, the European Union, as a response to the OECD BEPS Project, has implemented the ATAD Directive. Although highly criticized, both measures tackle the problem arising from tax avoidance and introduced minimum standards and requirements to be followed.

Countries like Germany and France also released a joint proposal, included in the Meseberg Declaration, with regards, among other topics, to the taxation of the digital economy. Both countries declared their intention to foster tax harmonization within Europe and are deeply committed to a swift adoption of the CCTB Directive[171] In particular, one of the main features of the proposal is the harmonization of the corporate tax base with the introduction of general principles of profit and loss recognition.[172]

However, it can be questioned whether all of these measures taken together are efficient enough to really deal with the core problem. Considering all of these changes and proposals, a question comes to mind: Are we facing the demise of the CFC rules around the world? Jurisdictions have struggled in the past to protect their tax bases; the awareness of this issue was first brought to light almost a century ago in the United States. A lot has been done, but the problem still stands. Probably a new approach has to be taken into consideration, not unilaterally but with a common goal in mind.

This would require not only global cooperation but putting aside the protectionist point of view all together; however, a protectionist's thinking is once more surging throughout the international scenario, and Brexit is only the latest example. The risk of disruption of global cooperation is still very high, and the chances of a successful coordination may sometimes seem feeble.

---

171 Please see for further reference Niki Mitrakou's chapter in this book.
172 Klaus von Brocke, France and Germany Publish Common Position Paper on Common Corporate Tax Base, EC Tax Review, 2019/1.

As a final remark and from my personal point of view, the work of the OECD with BEPS is praiseworthy. I agree with the criticisms it faced but it indeed represented the awareness of a problem and the willingness to face it globally, or at least as globally as the reach of the OECD, for the first time.

It is probably too soon to really ponder the results of BEPS and the ATAD but, at the same time, it is probably also too soon to discharge the positive effects altogether.

Different Approaches to the application of CFC rules

Iva Uljanić Škreblin

1. Introduction
2. The application mechanisms with respect to CFC rules applied worldwide
    2.1. General information
    2.2. Deemed dividend approach
    2.3. Piercing-the-veil approach
    2.4. US PFIC rules
    2.5. Other approaches applied
    2.6. Spread of CFC rules worldwide
3. Analysis of the different application mechanisms of CFC rules
    3.1. General analysis
    3.2. Comparative analysis of different approaches from a theoretical perspective
    3.3. Empirical analysis based on different countries experiences
4. Challenges for the future application of CFC rules
5. Conclusion

1. Introduction

Controlled foreign corporation (CFC) rules usually are applied and introduced in domestic tax systems as anti-avoidance measures that may secure the national tax base by limiting the tax privilege. The privilege or benefit in terms of tax to be paid in the country in which the parent company is situated can be achieved by shifting the passive income to a CFC in a low tax country. In other words, the CFC rules in most of the cases are intended to be prophylactic instead of raising tax revenues.[1]

Thus, CFC rules are mostly relevant for multinational companies that are incorporated in a high tax country. The income of a foreign subsidiary generally is not subject to tax in the country of the shareholder because of the generally accepted separate-entity approach[2] even if the foreign corporation would be subject to full taxation on foreign income earned by the shareholder corporation directly. Thus, by setting-up a foreign corporation, a taxpayer (shareholder, parent company) can, absent special rules, defer taxation of foreign income until it is repatriated, for example, as a dividend.[3]

Furthermore, if the country in which the parent company is situated applies the exemption method, the overall tax burden at the group level can easily be lowered. However, even if the country of the parent company applies the credit method, the company can transfer its instruments that generate passive income to a subsidiary situated in a low tax country and decide not to distribute the profit at all. In this case, also at the level of the group, the tax burden can be lowered.[4] So, neither the reinvested nor the repatriated profits of such a subsidiary are usually taxed by the home country of the parent and the lower tax rate on the subsidiary's profit becomes final. Nowadays, when it is very easy to transfer financial assets and open companies worldwide, especially in countries that do not have corporation taxes or the taxes are very low, this kind of tax planning can be used by any company or even wealthy individuals.

In principle, based on the tax policy that is used regarding the taxation of foreign income of resident taxpayers, different approaches of CFC rules can be used to

---

1   Brian J. Arnold, "The Evolution of Controlled Foreign Corporation Rules and Beyond", *Bulletin for International Taxation* (2019, vol. 73, no. 12).
2   Nicholas Garfunkel, "Are all CFC-regimes the Same? The impact of the Attribution Method" *Tax Notes International* 59 (2010), pp. 53–74.
3   Office of Tax Policy, Department of the Treasury, "The Deferral of Income Earned Through US Controlled Foreign Corporations" (December 2000), https://www.treasury.gov/resource-center/tax-policy/Documents/Report-SubpartF-2000.pdf (accessed 15 February 2020).
4   Peter Koerver Schmidt, "Taxation of Controlled Foreign Companies in Context of the OECD/G20 Project on Base Erosion and Profit Shifting as well as the EU Proposal for the Anti-Tax Avoidance Directive – An Interim Nordic Assessment", *Nordic Tax Journal* (2016, Issue 2), pp. 87–112.

determine how the CFC's income will be treated in the country in which the parent company (or shareholder) is situated. Thus, when a country is taxing dividends received from foreign corporations, CFC rules may be intended to prevent the deferral of domestic tax on income earned by and accumulated in CFCs until that income is distributed. In this case, the *deemed dividend* approach seems to be the appropriate approach to be used since the CFC rules aim to prevent the postponement of the taxation of retained profits of a CFC. For this purpose, the profits are subject to tax even though no actual distribution has yet taken place.[5] When a country exempts dividends that are received by resident taxpayers from foreign corporations from taxation, the CFC rules may be intended to prevent the complete avoidance of domestic tax on income earned by and accumulated in CFCs as such income would be subject to tax in the residence country if earned directly. In this case, the *piercing-the-veil* approach seems to be more appropriate to use than the *deemed dividend* approach. However, also other tax policy objectives may be considered in designing CFC rules such as the trade-offs between the breadth of the rules and concerns about tax compliance and tax administration, the use of CFC rules as a backstop to transfer pricing rules, the relationship with foreign investment fund rules, and the extension of CFC rules to situations involving the use of CFCs to avoid foreign tax.[6]

In the following Chapters 2 and 3, the *deemed-dividend* and the *piercing-the-veil* approaches are described and analyzed further, as well as some alternative approaches that are used in several countries worldwide. Then, in Chapter 4, some challenges for the future application and possible worldwide harmonization of CFC rules are analysed. Last, Chapter 5 summarizes the findings of the thesis and ends with a conclusion.

2. The application mechanisms with respect to CFC rules applied worldwide

2.1. General information

The main, common elements of CFC rules determined in national tax legislations by tax jurisdictions that apply different CFC approaches are: (**1**) the determination of what is considered a controlled foreign company, (**2**) control over the CFC, (**3**) the determination of the resident taxpayer to which CFC rules apply, (**4**) the effective level of taxation to which the CFC is subject in its resident state,

---

[5] Martin Klokar, Mario Riedl, "Controlled Foreign Company Legislation in Austria" in: Michael Lang/Jeffrey Owens/Pasquale Pistone/Alexander Rust/Josef Schuch/Claus Staringer (eds.) Controlled Foreign Company Legislation (Amsterdam: IBFD, 2020) p. 70.

[6] Brian J. Arnold, "The Evolution of Controlled Foreign Corporation Rules and Beyond", *Bulletin for International Taxation* (2019, vol. 73, no. 12).

(5) the type of income of the CFC,[7] and (6) the determination of the income/profit attributable to the resident taxpayer.[8]

The most common approaches used in practice when implementing the CFC rules, classified according to the subject matter they tax, are the *piercing-the-veil* approach where the CFC is treated as a pass-through entity for the purposes of attributing CFC income and the *deemed dividend* approach where the fictious income (dividend) that the controlling company could receive from the CFC is taxable. In practice, there are also some hybrid approaches like the US PFIC rules, the approach that is applied based on the imputation criteria, the approach based on the calculation of a notional (deemed) profit to be attributed to the parent company, and others. These approaches will be described further in this chapter.

2.2. Deemed dividend approach

The *deemed dividend* approach in its very basic form consists of taxation of a "fictious dividend" that a resident company might have received based on the anticipation of the taxable event relating to the dividend distribution regardless of when and if such an event will actually occur. So, the country in which the parent company (i.e. the shareholder) is situated will actually tax a notional income of its resident taxpayer that has a controlled subsidiary (or qualified investment) abroad, and the tax treatment can build on existing dividend rules with which taxpayers and tax administrations are already familiar.[9]

The taxable event is still the perception of the dividend. It implies that the income is taxed when it is legally available for distribution and only the distributable portion of the CFC's income is imputed to the shareholder.[10] Furthermore, foreign taxes are normally deductible against imputed income (not against the domestic tax) since they actually reduce the dividend available for distribution, and fictitious distributions reduce the taxable basis of subsequent actual distributions. Also, the income is computed in accordance with the rules applicable to the CFC.[11]

The first state to introduce such a rule was the US with its "Foreign Personal Holding Company" (FPHC) in 1937 which taxed the US shareholder on a deemed div-

---

7   A lot of jurisdictions differentiate between the type of income that a CFC generates, i.e. is it passive (for example interest, dividends, royalties, rents, etc.) or active (generated from active business activity) since this element can also be an indication if the CFC is established for justified business reason or for tax avoidance.
8   Reuven S. Avi-Yonah, Nicola Sartori, Omri Marian, Global Perspectives on Income Taxation Law (New York: Oxford University Press, 2011), p. 160.
9   OECD, Designing Effective Controlled Foreign Company Rules, Action 3 – 2015 Final Report (2015), OECD/G20 Base Erosion and Profit Shifting Project, p. 63, http://dx.doi.org/10.1787/9789264241152-en (accessed 14 March 2020).
10 The portion subject to foreign taxes is not imputed, nor are losses (which cannot be distributed).
11 Daniele Canè, "Controlled Foreign Corporations as Fiscally Transparent Entities. The Application of CFC Rules in Tax Treaties", *World Tax Journal* (2017, vol. 9, no. 4).

idend of the FPHC income. In 1962, the US expanded its CFC rules by introducing the Subpart F rule that applied the same *deemed dividend* approach to passive income and even some type of active income earned through a controlled foreign corporation.[12] More details regarding the evolution of CFC rules in the US can be found in this book in the chapter „Historical background to CFC-rules and policy consideration" of Ludovica Ostorero.

The reason for adopting this approach was that, in those years, the treasury was of the opinion that, if the FPHC as a foreign person would be taxed directly in the US, this would represent a breach of the principles of international tax law. Namely, in the period between the 1930s and the 1960s, there was a rule widely accepted as a customary binding international law rule which prohibited taxing foreign corporations on foreign source income. Thus, the US, in order to avoid an outright breach of that rule, implemented the *deemed dividend* approach.[13] Even if this universal rule has changed afterwards, nowadays, there are still some countries that use the *deemed dividend* approach such as Indonesia, Germany (yet only for individuals but not for companies), Taiwan, Turkey, Uruguay, etc.

Moreover, the first alternative ("Model A") in the EU ATAD[14] that the EU Member States can choose to implement for their CFC rules includes an extended version of the *deemed dividend* approach. According to this approach, the controlling shareholders must include in their income their share of the CFC's dividends but also other types of passive income such as interest, royalties, gains from the disposal of shares, income from financial leasing, insurance, banking and financial activities, and income from sales and services purchased from and sold to associated enterprises if little or no value is added. Therefore, it is not a pure *deemed dividend* approach, and the EU Member States may choose to implement it also as a *piercing-the-veil* approach (i.e. *deemed income approach*), which is described further in the Section 2.3.[15]

In the literature, criticism was voiced with regard to the *deemed dividend* approach, for example, in the US mainly because of its complexity and tax planning

---

12 Reuven S. Avi-Yonah, Nicola Sartori, Omri Marian, Global Perspectives on Income Taxation Law (New York: Oxford University Press, 2011), p. 160.
13 Reuven S. Avi-Yonah, "The Deemed Dividend Problem", SSRN (2004), pp. 1–7 https://papers.ssrn.com/sol3/papers.cfm?abstract_id=572182 (accessed 5 March 2020).
14 Council Directive (EU) 2016/1164 of 12 July 2016 laying down rules against tax avoidance practices that directly affect the functioning of the internal market (OJ L 193, 19.7.2016).
15 The European Commission does not give guidance as to which approach the Member States should follow. However, in its explanatory statement, the Commission states that CFC rules have the effect of reattributing the income of a low-taxed controlled subsidiary to its parent company. The wording "reattributing" could indicate that the EU legislator tends towards a *piercing the veil* approach. However, on the other side, the provisions of Art. 7 and Art. 8 ATAD contain elements of *piercing the veil* and the *deemed dividend* approach. (Martin Klokar, Mario Riedl, "Controlled Foreign Company Legislation in Austria" in: Michael Lang/Jeffrey Owens/Pasquale Pistone/Alexander Rust/Josef Schuch/Claus Staringer (eds.) Controlled Foreign Company Legislation (Amsterdam: IBFD, 2020) p. 71).

opportunities.¹⁶ The problem is also that, if a CFC has losses, these typically are not considered in calculating shareholders' income. Furthermore, it may be questioned whether there is alignment of these rules with Article 10 of the OECD Model, especially in cases when the contracting states have agreed to exempt intercompany dividends from taxation. Thus, if the shareholders country applies the CFC rules based on the deemed dividend approach and taxes the deemed dividend, the question is if this is compatible with the treaty because there is no justified reason why the deemed dividend should be treated differently than the dividend actually paid.¹⁷ The same reasoning also applies for countries that have implemented the exemption method for foreign dividends received by resident taxpayers regardless of a bilateral treaty. Namely, the *deemed dividend* approach would not be suitable in this case since the taxation of deemed dividend would not be in line with the usual tax policy that is applied, there would be inconsistency in the domestic rules, and resident shareholders to which the dividend is not distributed would be discriminated against the shareholders to which the dividend is distributed.

2.3. Piercing-the-veil approach

After the *deemed dividend* approach, many countries started to adopt CFC rules where the shareholders of the CFC are taxed directly on the CFC's income on a pass-through basis, albeit this approach is, in economical terms, more equivalent to direct taxation of the CFC and not of the shareholders.¹⁸

The *piercing-the-veil* or *look-through* approach consists of disregarding a CFC's legal personality for tax purposes and the consequent taxation of the CFC's profits in the hands of the controlling shareholder. In this case, the treatment of the CFC is very similar to the treatment of partnerships that are considered to be transparent entities for tax purposes and are taxed at the level of the partners. Thus, in the *piercing-the-veil* approach, the CFC is treated as a kind of transparent entity. The taxable event is the realization of the income, not its perception. This kind of CFC rule attributes to the resident shareholder the activity generating the income and the income itself which is deemed to be the income of the resident shareholder and not of the CFC.¹⁹ This is close to the classical fiscal transparency pattern that is ordinarily applied to partnerships as stated above, and implies that imputed income

---

16   Reuven S. Avi-Yonah, "The Deemed Dividend Problem", SSRN (2004), pp. 1–7 https://papers.ssrn.com/sol3/papers.cfm?abstract_id=572182 (accessed 5 March 2020)
17   This question is analysed in W. Blum's article "Controlled Foreign Companies: Selected Policy Issues – or the Missing Elements of BEPS Action 3 and the Anti – Tax Avoidance Directive", *Intertax* (2018, vol. 46, issue 4), p. 309
18   Reuven S. Avi-Yonah, "The Deemed Dividend Problem", SSRN (2004) https://papers.ssrn.com/sol3/papers.cfm?abstract_id=572182 (accessed 5 March 2020)
19   Daniele Canè, "Controlled Foreign Corporations as Fiscally Transparent Entities. The Application of CFC Rules in Tax Treaties", *World Tax Journal* (2017, vol. 9, no. 4).

is taxed in the hands of the shareholder on realization and at the end of the entity's financial year. Moreover, the whole income of the CFC is imputed to the shareholder, including accumulated profits and profits subject to foreign tax but also losses are attributed to the shareholder. Furthermore, foreign taxes on the CFC's income are credited against the domestic liability of the shareholders and dividend distributions are disregarded for tax purposes.[20] In addition, when calculating the attributable income of the CFC according to the *piercing-the-veil* approach, the tax law of the shareholder's state of residence is decisive.[21]

Like in the case of the *deemed dividend* approach, the *piercing-the-veil* approach has also some difficulties in its implementation and was subject to criticism in the academic literature. For example, as *Dodge* opines, the pass-through system could be imposed only where shareholders could be presumed to have access to the accounting books of the CFC.[22] This implies that the CFC needs to be treated as a pass-through entity under foreign tax law or that shareholders have a significant stake in the corporation in order to obtain such information. Imposing a tax on the entire net income of the CFC would appear to be feasible under the usual business practice only when the percentage of control by shareholders is fairly high.[23]

However, countries like New Zealand have found a solution even for the situation when the shareholder does not have a substantial participation.[24] Namely, one of the major issues for attributing income from a foreign investment fund (FIF) is that the New Zealand investor usually has limited scope to obtain detailed information about its earnings to calculate its attributable income. Therefore, approximation can be applied in this case using different methods.[25]

As with the *deemed dividend* approach, there might again be a potential conflict with the tax treaty law. In particular, like *D. Canè* argues, Article 7 of the OECD Model (2014) bans the taxation of foreign enterprises that do not carry on a business in the territory of the contracting state insofar as the CFC qualifies as a taxable person (i.e. a company) in its residence state, i.e. in the other contracting state.[26]

---

20 Daniele Canè, "Controlled Foreign Corporations as Fiscally Transparent Entities. The Application of CFC Rules in Tax Treaties", *World Tax Journal* (2017, vol. 9, no. 4).
21 Martin Klokar, Mario Riedl, "Controlled Foreign Company Legislation in Austria" in: Michael Lang/Jeffrey Owens/Pasquale Pistone/Alexander Rust/Josef Schuch/Claus Staringer (eds.) Controlled Foreign Company Legislation (Amsterdam: IBFD, 2020) p. 71.
22 What would constitute a "significant stake" is a difficult issue.
23 Joseph M. Dodge, "A Combined Mark-to-Market and Pass-through Corporate-Shareholder Integration Proposal", Tax Law Review (Spring 1995, vol. 50, no.3), pp. 265–372.
24 Andrew M C Smith, Adrian J Sawyer, "Controlled Foreign Company Legislation in New Zealand" in: Michael Lang/Jeffrey Owens/Pasquale Pistone/Alexander Rust/Josef Schuch/Claus Staringer (eds.) Controlled Foreign Company Legislation (Amsterdam: IBFD, 2020) p. 472.
25 Taxpayers have five methods potentially available to determine the amount of FIF income to be attributed: (1) the attributable FIF method, (2) the comparable value method ("mark-to-market"), (3) the deemed rate of return method, (4) the fair dividend rate method, and (5) the cost method.
26 Daniele Canè, "Controlled Foreign Corporations as Fiscally Transparent Entities. The Application of CFC Rules in Tax Treaties", *World Tax Journal* (2017, vol. 9, no. 4).

Different Approaches to the application of CFC rules

However, if the CFC is treated fiscally in the same way as a transparent partnership, CFC legislation following the *piercing-the-veil* approach can be in line with tax treaty law if applied in accordance with the principles of the OECD Partnership Report. This view is supported also by A. *Rust*, who considers that, according to this type of CFC rule, shareholders are treated similarly to the partners of a partnership as they directly earn the income via the company.[27]

Furthermore, the problem with this approach can appear in situations where the resident country wants to tax only particular categories of income (e.g. passive income), known also as the *deemed income* approach.[28] For example, it could be more difficult to distinguish between items of income that should continue to benefit from the deferral and items that should be taxed at the time in which the income arises, i.e. to determine in each specific case if the actual income is the taxable one or not. As a consequence, taxpayers could have more incentives for tax planning (for example, to use the type of investment or arrangements that will result in less or zero taxation), non-disclosure of all of the information needed to determine the taxable items (transactions), recharacterized some transactions etc. Moreover, when the attributable income is determined as the net income (e.g., passive income less expenses) of the CFC company, expenses must be qualified as belonging to either active or passive income. Clearly, difficulties arise when the expenses cannot be simply attributed to active or passive income without further analysis.[29]

2.4. US PFIC rules

Except from the Subpart F rules, the US has also implemented another rule in order to tax certain foreign investments made by US shareholders, known as the *Passive Foreign Investment Company* regime or, in short, the PFIC regime. However, when a company that is considered a PFIC also qualifies as a CFC, the shareholder should be taxed under the Subpart F income rules, and the PFIC rules are not applicable. Oppositely, any CFC that is excluded from the ambit of the Subpart F rules because of the high foreign tax rule or the *de minimis* rule is still considered for the purposes of the PFIC rule according to the US Code.

The PFIC regime was enacted in 1986 to prevent avoidance (by dividing ownership of foreign entities among multiple shareholders) of the foreign personal holding company (FPCH) and controlled foreign corporation (CFC) rules.[30] A

---

27 Daniele Canè, "Controlled Foreign Corporations as Fiscally Transparent Entities. The Application of CFC Rules in Tax Treaties", World Tax Journal (2017, vol. 9, no. 4).
28 Reuven S. Avi-Yonah, "The Deemed Dividend Problem", SSRN (2004) https://papers.ssrn.com/sol3/papers.cfm?abstract_id=572182 (accessed 5 March 2020).
29 Reuven S. Avi-Yonah, "The Deemed Dividend Problem", SSRN (2004) https://papers.ssrn.com/sol3/papers.cfm?abstract_id=572182 (accessed 5 March 2020).
30 Tom Fuller, Roger M. Brown, Connie Angle, "PFIC Mark-to-Market Regulations Finalized", Intertax, Kluwer Law International (2004, vol. 32, issue 8/9), pp. 450–451.

foreign corporation is a PFIC if it satisfies either the passive income test or the passive asset test for the taxable year.[31] The shareholder of a PFIC share is taxed on the excess distributions received from PFICs and gains realized upon the sale of their PFIC shares.[32] These distributions and gains are allocated pro rata to each day in the investor's holding period and are subject to the highest tax rate of the respective taxable year and interest charges on taxes deemed to be owed in preceding tax years.[33] As a result of the highly punitive PFIC regime, a US taxpayer will end up deferring taxes but also accruing interest charges on the taxes that he did not pay in preceding tax years.

Alternatively to the above taxation rule, the **qualifying electing fund (QEF) rule**[34] and the **mark-to-market rule** (enacted in 1997 as a third alternative) may apply. The selection of either of these two rules should be made by the shareholder during the first tax year following the year in which the PFIC shares were acquired. The benefit of the decision to apply either of those rules is the avoidance of interest charges, but the taxpayers are taxed on the income attributed to them annually.[35]

US taxpayers that want to avoid the excess distribution regime but do not qualify for QEF treatment can make a mark-to-market election. To qualify for that treatment, the PFIC stock must be regularly traded on a qualified exchange, and a selection must be made beginning in the first tax year of the taxpayer's holding period for the PFIC stock. Under the mark-to-market treatment, the US taxpayer owning the PFIC shares must recognize as ordinary income annual increases in the market value of their PFIC shares. Annual losses in the value of PFIC shares are treated as ordinary losses only to the extent of previously recognized gains. Any gain on the sale or other disposition of marketable stock in a PFIC, shall be treated as ordinary income.[36]

---

31 According to US Code §?1297, the term "passive foreign investment company" means any foreign corporation if either of the following two requirements is met: (1) 75% or more of the gross income of such corporation for the taxable year is passive income (income from non-business operational activities, such as interest, rents, royalties, capital gains, currency gains, and dividends) – the passive income test or (2) the average percentage of assets held by such corporation during the taxable year that produce passive income or are held for the production of passive income is at least 50% – the passive asset test.
32 Excess distributions are actual distributions that are in excess of 125% of average distributions received in the preceding three years in which the PFIC shares were owned.
33 All capital gains from the sale of PFIC shares are treated as ordinary income for federal income tax purposes and thus are not taxed at preferential long-term capital gain rates, and capital losses upon disposition of PFIC shares cannot be recognized.
34 A timely QEF election is the preferred remedy for an owner of PFIC shares because US taxpayers are taxed only on the income attributed to them annually throughout the period in which the PFIC shares are owned.
35 Vadim Blikshteyn, Holtz Rubenstein Reminick LLP, "Passive Foreign Investment Companies", The Tax Adviser (October 2011), https://www.thetaxadviser.com/issues/2011/oct/clinic-story-04.html (accessed 13 May 2020).
36 Water's Edge Manual, Chapter 6 Passive Foreign Investment Companies, State of California, https://www.ftb.ca.gov/tax-pros/procedures/waters-edge-manual/chapter-6.pdf (accessed 28 January 2020).

Different Approaches to the application of CFC rules

To conclude, the PFIC approach is different than the two previously explained approaches in Sections 2.2 and 2.3, especially the mark-to-marked approach which actually taxes the capital gain (unrealized and realized) of the shares in the CFC on a yearly basis regardless of the income attributable and distributed to the shareholder. This seems a simpler alternative for the two other approaches discussed earlier, easier to apply, or a good supplement, especially when the fair market value can be determined based on the sales value on national exchanges (which is a publicly available information and does not require inside information of the foreign company nor a lot of documentation). Furthermore, the PFIC approach is also a good supplement to CFC rules which are, in most cases, limited by the control test and level of taxation in the country of the subsidiary for the following reason: in contrast to the CFC rules, the PFIC rules apply to any US shareholder (individual, corporation, partnership, trust) who owns any amount of stock, directly or indirectly, in any foreign corporation regardless of the extent of its passive earnings and regardless if the foreign corporation is set up in a low tax country or not.

2.5. Other approaches applied

Apart from the three approaches described in Sections 2.2, 2.3, and 2.4 of this chapter, in the literature, the following two approaches are also discussed: (1) the *diverted attribution pattern*, and (2) the *notional sum approach*.

The *diverted attribution pattern* recognizes the CFC as an opaque (i.e. non-transparent) company for tax purposes, however, its income is not computed at the CFC level like in the case of the *deemed dividend* approach but is rather attributed directly to its shareholders.[37] Thus, by using this approach, the results are very similar to the *piercing-the-veil* approach, but the main differences are that this approach still respects the legal personality of the CFC, and it normally does not provide for loss to be attributed to shareholders. Furthermore, this approach does not operate on the taxable event but on the imputation criteria. The CFC is still treated as a resident in the country where it is registered, but its income is diverted to another taxable person (the shareholder). The ordinary imputation criterion is thus derogated. For this reason, it can be concluded that this approach conflicts with tax treaty law, especially with Article 7 of the OECD Model, as is also argued by D. Canè.[38]

By applying the *notional sum* approach, resident shareholders are currently taxed on the increase in value that stems from the income earned by the CFC either as a notional sum corresponding to the portion of the CFC's profit calculated based

---

[37] Larissa Pimentel de Lima, "The relationship between Article 1(2) of the OECD Model Convention and domestic CFC rules in: Govind/Van West (eds.) Hybrid Entities in Tax Treaty Law (Vienna: Linde, 2020) p. 266.
[38] Daniele Canè, "Controlled Foreign Corporations as Fiscally Transparent Entities. The Application of CFC Rules in Tax Treaties", *World Tax Journal* (2017, vol. 9, no. 4).

on the rules determined by the shareholder's country or corresponding to the fair value[39] of their participation in the CFC.[40] One of the countries that applies this *notional sum* approach is the United Kingdom which taxes the profit of the CFC on an assumption that the CFC is a resident there, using the same rules as for the determination of the PE according to the OECD AOA approach, with the difference that this CFC deemed PE in United Kingdom does not generate any profit there.[41] Instead, what is attributable to the United Kingdom parent are profits generated outside the country from assets that are legally owned by the CFC and profits from risks contractually allocated to the CFC in situations where management of those assets and risks is exercised to a significant extent from the United Kingdom. For the determination of these deemed profits, a two-step analysis is used. Under the first step, the analysis requires the PE to be hypothesized as a separate enterprise with its own assets and risks. The second step is concerned with pricing the "dealings" between the deemed PE (i.e. the CFC) and other parts of the enterprise at an arm's length basis. Thus, attributable profits to the UK parent company do not represent the actual profits of the CFC on which UK corporation tax is chargeable; rather, they are calculated on a hypothetical basis. Furthermore, foreign taxes are not taken into consideration when computing the notional sum. However, this was not considered as a violation of the treaty agreement according to the UK Court of Appeal in its decision on the *Bricom Holdings Ltd v IRC* case (1997)[42] with the justification that what is apportioned to the taxpayer and subjected to tax is not the CFC's actual profits but a notional sum which is the product of an artificial calculation.

This approach implemented by the United Kingdom is the same as the one stipulated in EU ATAD, in Article 7(2)(b), known as the "Model B". Accordingly, the EU Member States can apply one of the two models to attribute CFC income to its resident shareholders: "Model A" (passive income and business income from transactions with related persons, as explained in Section 2.2) and "Model B" (non-genuine arrangements).[43] Thus, beside the *deemed income* approach ("Model

---

39   Also called "fair value" approach where the CFC is regarded as a legal entity with no fictitious dividend distribution. Instead, participation in the controlled entity is valued at fair value. Generated profits of the foreign company increase the value of participation. This increase in value is taxed at the shareholder's level. The PFIC mark-to-market rule is a type of "fair value" approach.
40   Daniele Canè, "Controlled Foreign Corporations as Fiscally Transparent Entities. The Application of CFC Rules in Tax Treaties", *World Tax Journal* (2017, vol. 9, no. 4).
41   HMRC internal manual, International Manual, Controlled Foreign Companies: The CFC Charge Gateway Chapter 4 – Profits attributable to UK activities: Introduction, https://www.gov.uk/hmrc-internal-manuals/international-manual/intm200100 (accessed 15 February 2021).
42   UK residents with foreign income or gains: corporation tax: Controlled foreign companies: Bricom Holdings Ltd v CIR, https://www.gov.uk/hmrc-internal-manuals/international-manual/intm167460 (accessed 12 February 2021).
43   Richard Krever, "General Report" in: Michael Lang/Jeffrey Owens/Pasquale Pistone/Alexander Rust/Josef Schuch/Claus Staringer (eds.) Controlled Foreign Company Legislation (Amsterdam: IBFD, 2020) p. 10.

A"), "Model B" is an alternative model (not a pure *deemed dividend* approach nor *piercing-the-veil* approach) according to which controlling shareholders must include in their income the CFC's income from "non-genuine arrangements" entered into for the essential purpose of obtaining a tax benefit (a transactional approach). For this purpose, an arrangement is determined as non-genuine to the extent that a CFC would not own the assets or bear the risks if it were not controlled by a company for which people functions related to those assets and risks are instrumental in generating the CFC's income. Therefore, the income to be included in the tax base of the taxpayer shall be limited to amounts generated through assets and risks that are linked to significant people functions carried out by the controlling company. The attribution of controlled foreign company income shall be calculated in accordance with the arm's length principle.

Thus, in this case, the attributable income is calculated as it was directly generated by the controlling company using the transfer pricing methodology, as is analysed in more detail in this book by Anca Pianoschi in chapter "Computation and Attribution of CFC income under ATAD", but the main or the essential purpose of this transaction must be obtaining a tax benefit. So, this is an additional requirement that must be fulfilled and not just the simple attribution of income generated by the CFC to its parent company which, in practice, is more difficult to implement. Some EU countries, like Poland, are of the same view and have argued that this approach provides for a case-by-case factual analysis that is likely to disproportionally increase administrative burdens relative to the projected additional tax yield and did not implement it.[44] Even the European Parliament recommended in its resolution to the Member States to implement the first alternative, recognized as the simpler and most efficient CFC rule.[45] However, beside the United Kingdom, there are countries that consider this approach better than "Model A" because it is more targeted on tax avoidance situations, so it has been implemented also by Belgium, Cyprus, Estonia, Hungary, Slovakia, and Latvia.[46]

2.6. Spread of CFC rules worldwide

The US was the first country to enact CFC rules, and it is probably the country with the most complex set of rules. The United States not only has CFC regimes provided for in its Subpart F and the PFIC rules, but also the Global Intangible Low-Taxed Income (GILTI) rules were enacted in 2017 in order to expand the

---

44 Adrian Wardzynski, "Controlled Foreign Company Legislation in Poland" in: Michael Lang/Jeffrey Owens/Pasquale Pistone/Alexander Rust/Josef Schuch/Claus Staringer (eds.) Controlled Foreign Company Legislation (Amsterdam: IBFD, 2020) p. 565.
45 European Parliament resolution of 26 March 2019 on financial crimes, tax evasion and tax avoidance (2018/2121(INI)), point 46.
46 Richard Krever, "General Report" in: Michael Lang/Jeffrey Owens/Pasquale Pistone/Alexander Rust/Josef Schuch/Claus Staringer (eds.) Controlled Foreign Company Legislation (Amsterdam: IBDF, 2020) p. 10.

breadth of the US CFC legislation. GILTI broadened the tax base for US multinational companies, not only making the US system more complex but also more aggressive against base erosion and profit shifting.[47]

After the United States, many countries introduced CFC rules, including pure territorial jurisdictions like Germany (1972), Canada (1975), Japan (1978), France (1980), United Kingdom (1984), New Zealand (1988), Australia (1990), Sweden (1990), Norway (1992), Denmark (1995), Finland (1995), Indonesia (1995), Portugal (1995), Spain (1995), Hungary (1997), Mexico (1997), South Africa (1997), South Korea (1997), Argentina (1999), Brazil (2000), Italy (2000), Estonia (2000), Lithuania (2002), Israel (2003), etc.[48]

The adoption of CFC rules increased gradually in the 21st century and then more rapidly after the global financial crisis in 2008 when the G20 countries put tax at the top of their agenda and the OECD started working on its base erosion and profit shifting (BEPS) project in order to found measures to fight tax evasion and avoidance. Eight years later, the adoption of the ATAD at the EU level gave the single most important impetus to a widespread adoption of a CFC regime.[49] However, even before the EU ATAD, the CFC rules were applied by numerous EU Member States. More than half of them (seven out of 12) used the *piercing-the-veil* approach (so they attributed to the controlling company the total income of the CFC), and the rest applied the *deemed dividend* approach by which just the passive income of the CFC was attributable to the controlling company.

For the purpose of this chapter, data from 45 countries has been analysed,[50] and the following result is determined: only four of the countries examined currently do not apply CFC rules (Andorra, North Macedonia, Taiwan,[51] and Ukraine), six of them introduced the CFC rules before 1990, 12 of them in the 1990s, 15 of them in the period from 2000 till 2018, and eight of them introduced CFC legislation in 2019 as result of the ATAD. The policy objectives behind the introduction of CFC rules in most of the countries analysed were: (1) to prevent deferral of passive income derived through low tax jurisdictions, (2) combat tax avoidance, (3) address tax evasion that was mainly related to tax arrangements involving tax ha-

---

47 Yariv Brauner, Christine A. Davis, "Controlled Foreign Company Legislation in the United States" in: Michael Lang/Jeffrey Owens/Pasquale Pistone/Alexander Rust/Josef Schuch/Claus Staringer (eds.) Controlled Foreign Company Legislation (Amsterdam: IBFD, 2020) p. 845–850.
48 Reuven S. Avi-Yonah, Nicola Sartori, Omri Marian, Global Perspectives on Income Taxation Law (New York: Oxford University Press, 2011), p. 160.
49 Richard Krever, "General Report" in: Michael Lang/Jeffrey Owens/Pasquale Pistone/Alexander Rust/Josef Schuch/Claus Staringer (eds.) Controlled Foreign Company Legislation (Amsterdam: IBFD, 2020) p. 4.
50 Countries analysed are: Andorra, Argentine, Australia, Austria, Belgium, Brazil, Bulgaria, Chile, China, Croatia, Cyprus, Czech Republic, Denmark, Estonia, Finland, France, Germany, Hungary, Indonesia, Israel, Italy, Japan, Latvia, Lithuania, Netherlands, New Zealand, North Macedonia, Norway, Pakistan, Peru, Poland, Portugal, Romania, Russia, Slovakia, South Africa, South Korea, Spain, Sweden, Taiwan, Turkey, Ukraine, the United Kingdom, Uruguay, and the United States.
51 Taiwan has adopted the legislation, but the rules are not yet applied.

vens, and (4) prevent multinational groups from shifting investment income to low-tax jurisdictions and repatriating it free of tax by means of the intragroup dividend exemption, etc. For eight of them, the objective was harmonization with the requirements of the ATAD and the recommendations of the OECD BEPS Action 3 Report. Regarding the approach applied, the majority applies the *piercing-the-veil* approach (21 of them) whereby nine of them[52] determine specific categories of attributable income (mostly passive income as specified in the "Model A" from the ATAD) and the rest (12 out of 21)[53] attributes the total income of the CFC to the resident shareholders, with some exceptions from the general rule.

Furthermore, six non-EU countries apply the *deemed dividend* approach (China, Indonesia, Israel, Taiwan, Turkey, Uruguay), six countries use a combination of the two approaches (Argentine, France, Germany, Spain, Pakistan and the United States), and seven of them have applied the alternative "Model B" from the ATAD (Belgium, Cyprus, Estonia, Hungary, Slovakia, Latvia, and the United Kingdom). Brazil does not have a specific CFC rule but a hybrid approach, i.e. it applies a worldwide income taxation whereby controlling companies are taxed on "adjustments in the investment value".[54]

3. Analysis of the different application mechanisms of CFC rules

3.1. General analysis

The differences among the CFC regimes in place, including the reason why some states have abstained from introducing CFC rules, can partly be explained by the fact that some states mainly support and want to achieve capital export neutrality whereas others support and want to achieve a capital import neutrality.[55] However, even states that normally apply the exemption method have enacted the CFC legislation. In these cases, the CFC rules thus prevent the outright exclusion from domestic taxation of certain foreign-source income.[56]

---

52 Australia, Austria, Bulgaria, Croatia, Czech Republic, Denmark, Lithuania, Peru and Romania.
53 Chile, Finland, Italy, Japan, Netherlands, New Zealand, Norway, Poland, Portugal, Russia, South Africa, Sweden.
54 Prof. Dr. Luís Eduardo Schoueri, Guilherme Galdino, "Controlled Foreign Company Legislation in Brazil", in: Michael Lang/Jeffrey Owens/Pasquale Pistone/Alexander Rust/Josef Schuch/Claus Staringer (eds.) Controlled Foreign Company Legislation (Amsterdam: IBFD, 2020), pp. 116–120.
55 The *capital export neutrality* relates to the theory that investors should pay the same taxes on income derived from domestic and foreign investments, so tax would be removed as a consideration behind the place of investment. The *capital import neutrality* relates to the theory that investors deriving income from foreign sources should pay the same taxes as local investors in the source destination to ensure they could compete on a level playing field with the local investors and, hence, the resident country of investors mainly apply the exemption method. (Richard Krever, "General Report" in: Michael Lang/Jeffrey Owens/Pasquale Pistone/Alexander Rust/Josef Schuch/Claus Staringer (eds.) Controlled Foreign Company Legislation (Amsterdam: IBFD, 2020) p. 3).
56 Daniel Sandler, "Tax Treaties and Controlled Foreign Company Legislation", *The Hague: Kluwer Law International* (1998).

In the case of EU, there is some criticism and doubts concerning the effectiveness of the CFC rules determined in the ATAD. Namely, albeit the obligation of Member States to implement in their domestic legislation CFC rules, the provisions in the directive are stipulated just as a minimum standard, so there are some doubts that the directive will achieve its goal. In addition to that, and not surprisingly, countries such as Belgium, Luxembourg, and the Netherlands that have traditionally acted as very popular jurisdictions in which multinationals may establish their CFCs have adopted the weakest form of CFC rules possible.[57] It is clear that these countries, and also several other EU Member States, adopted CFC rules only because it was a legal requirement set by the directive.[58] Some did so because they may lack the capacity to enforce the rules efficiently while the others, like the three mentioned above, did so because it is not in line with their general fiscal policy, strategy, and objectives; because they do not have a lot of cases of deferral of income to foreign subsidiaries (CFCs); or because are small, open economies (like Croatia) that strive to attract inbound foreign direct investments, etc.[59]

The right CFC approach to be used depends on the main purpose and main goal that the country wants to achieve. For example, one of the main goals of CFC rule can be to prevent taxpayers to shift their profits in low tax countries. If in this case the CFC rule is not address just to actual tax avoidance, negative externalities can occur, such as severe adverse consequences for bona fide taxpayers who are penalized by additional taxation, burdensome compliance requirements and possible interest on the amount expended on anticipated taxation. For these reasons, the *piercing-the-veil* approach and also "Model B" of the EU ATAD seems to be a better approach to tackle these problems. Additionally, to balance the situation, most CFC regimes distinguish between active and passive income thereby eliminating the benefit of deferral only in the case of passive income not related to active business activity in the country where the CFC is registered.

3.2. Comparative analysis of different approaches from a theoretical perspective

In relation to the effectiveness of the different approaches that are applied, it can be expected that the *deemed dividend* approach will result in higher state revenues compared to the *piercing-the-veil* approach. For example, in Uruguay prior to the *deemed dividend* approach, the *piercing-the-veil* approach was applied whereby

---

57 Brian J. Arnold, "The Evolution of Controlled Foreign Corporation Rules and Beyond", Bulletin for International Taxation (2019, vol. 73, no. 12).
58 Richard Krever, "General Report" in: Michael Lang/Jeffrey Owens/Pasquale Pistone/Alexander Rust/Josef Schuch/Claus Staringer (eds.) Controlled Foreign Company Legislation (Amsterdam: IBFD, 2020) p. 13.
59 Nevia Čičin Šain, Stjepan Gadžo, "Controlled Foreign Company Legislation in Croatia" in: Michael Lang/Jeffrey Owens/Pasquale Pistone/Alexander Rust/Josef Schuch/Claus Staringer (eds.) Controlled Foreign Company Legislation (Amsterdam: IBFD, 2020) pp. 185–186.

Different Approaches to the application of CFC rules

just certain types of CFC's passive income was attributable to the individual shareholder.[60] With the new approach, all passive income obtained by a CFC is being taxed in Uruguay as "dividends" when assigned to the resident individual. Thus, the income changes its nature. Currently, therefore, the type of passive income does not matter; as pointed out, when the entity obtains passive income, the income "mutates" to a dividend that is instantly assigned to the individual shareholder and taxed. That is why it is expected that this new approach may imply an increase in tax revenue for the Uruguayan Tax Authority. However, the effectiveness should not be measured only in the amount of tax revenues that are raised since this is not a primarily goal of almost all countries worldwide that have implemented CFC rules.

In relation to which of the approaches is better to tackle tax base erosion, i.e. avoidance in terms of shifting the profit to CFC countries, the OECD has concluded in its report[61] that both approaches seem equally appropriate in terms of dealing with BEPS. Therefore, the question of how to treat attributed income could be left for jurisdictions to decide in a manner that is coherent with domestic law.

The problem with the *piercing-the-veil* approach is that double taxation may result, for example, from multiple attributions of passive income to the direct controlling company and indirect controlling company within one or more countries;[62] the applicability of CFC rules and the switch-over clause to the same passive income; or from the applicability of CFC rules to the same passive income in several states, for example, in case of dual residents.[63] In case of the *deemed dividend* approach, however, there is also the possibility to have double taxation, especially for dual resident shareholders. The cross-border double taxation in these cases can be avoided through mutual agreement procedures when a treaty is applicable; by unilateral reliefs from double taxation using the credit method (which is better be-

---

60 Andrea Laura Riccardi Sacchi, "Controlled Foreign Company Legislation in Uruguay" in: Michael Lang/Jeffrey Owens/Pasquale Pistone/Alexander Rust/Josef Schuch/Claus Staringer (eds.) Controlled Foreign Company Legislation (Amsterdam: IBFD, 2020) pp. 864–865.
61 The OECD published the BEPS Action 3 Report entitled "Designing Effective Controlled Foreign Company Rules", outlining the issue in totality and making comprehensive recommendations. The report contains a set of building blocks that are designed to ensure that jurisdictions that choose to have CFC legislation must put in place the rules that effectively prevent taxpayers from shifting income to foreign subsidiaries with substantive outcomes of tax evasion or tax deferral.
62 For example, assume that company A resident in country A holds 100 percent of the shares in company B that is located in country B and that this company B holds 100 percent of the shares in a foreign entity C located in a low tax jurisdiction. If CFC rules are triggered due to the indirect control in country A and due to direct control in country B, income from the CFC – entity C – would be taxed both in country A and B. Conclusively, CFC rules do not avoid double CFC-taxation, and the possible double tax treaty between country A and B also does not address the double CFC taxation. For handling this situation, unilateral domestic rules for elimination of double taxation should be applied, for example, a tax credit in country A for the tax paid in country B.
63 Martin Klokar, Mario Riedl, "Controlled Foreign Company Legislation in Austria" in: Michael Lang/Jeffrey Owens/Pasquale Pistone/Alexander Rust/Josef Schuch/Claus Staringer (eds.) Controlled Foreign Company Legislation (Amsterdam: IBFD, 2020) p. 70.

cause it can even prevent double non-taxation); or by introducing domestic rules that will clearly determine which of the rules has priority over the other.

If the subject of comparison of the two main approaches would be the compliance and administrative costs, then the less expensive and less demanding approach would be the *deemed dividend* approach. The reason is because this approach does not require recalculation of profit based on the rule of the country of the controlling company. It is easier to obtain the information from the CFC especially in a situation when the taxpayer does not have a substantial control over the CFC. However, if specific requirements are determined (for example, that only the income generated from passive or non-genuine activities is attributable), the situation becomes more complex even for the *deemed dividend* approach.

In the taxpayers' view, the *piercing-the-veil* approach is a better solution when the CFC has losses because, in theory, this approach should take into consideration the losses when the taxable income is computed at the level of the controlling company. In the case of the *deemed dividend* approach, the losses of the CFC are not taken into account because the losses are not distributed to the shareholders. However, in practice, variations of these rules apply, and some countries that apply the *piercing-the-veil* approach do not allow for the attribution of losses to the controlling company.

Conclusively, there is no best approach for all situations, and each of the approach has its pro and contra sides. Thus, which approach a country should apply depends on different factors such as the national tax policy related to taxation of foreign income that is applied (capital import neutrality or capital export neutrality), capability of the tax administration, policy objectives behind the CFC rules, countries' economic development, profit deferral and tax avoidance occurrences and frequency, determination of the taxpayer to which the CFC rules will be applied (for individual the *deemed dividend* approach is more suitable), the level of control over the CFC that is required (if the level is very low, the *deemed dividend* approach would be better since the shareholders could not have a substantial interest in the CFC, and it would be more difficult to obtain the accounting books of the CFC and all of the relevant information), etc. Thus, before introducing CFC rules or amendments of the current CFC rules, a lot of factors must be considered in order to choose the most appropriate approach.

3.3. Empirical analysis based on different countries experiences

Whether unilateral action such as CFC rules in the country of the controlling company are efficient for achieving the policy objective determined for their introduction is essentially an empirical question. However, there are not many studies that have been published in this respect.

Different Approaches to the application of CFC rules

Among a few of the researchers, R. *Altshuler* and R. *Hubbard* (2003) analyzed the Tax Reform Act of 1986 that amended the US Subpart F provisions and made it more difficult to defer US taxes on overseas financial services income held in low-tax jurisdictions.[64] The paper finds that the change in legislation reduced the tax sensitivity of the international asset location decisions of US financial services firms, i.e., the attractiveness of low-tax countries, measured by the aggregated sum of financial assets received, was reduced by the tightening of the CFC rules. This means that the tightening of the anti-deferral provisions applicable to financial services companies has been successful in neutralizing the effect of host country income taxes (country where the CFC is registered) on investment location decisions.

On the other side, R. S. *Avi-Yonah* explained on the basis of three real examples why the United States should abolish the *deemed dividend* approach used in its "Subpart F" CFC rules.[65] The first example that he explained was Enron's *Apache* transaction. Enron has set up a Dutch company with common stock (owned by Enron's CFC) and preferred stocked (owned by an unrelated Dutch bank). With this structure, it has achieved avoiding the determination of Subpart F income because the *deemed dividend* rule depends on the existence of earnings and profits in the CFC. Namely, the Dutch company ownership instruments provided that no earnings distributions could be made on Enron's common stock as long as any preferred stock remained outstanding, Enron took the position that the common stock would not be entitled to any earnings and profits in such a hypothetical distribution and therefore that Enron had no Subpart F income from its CFC.

The second example was about the *Brown Group*, a US corporation which has Cayman CFC which set up a Cayman partnership (98% share).[66] The Cayman partnership was buying shoes in Brazil and reselling it to Brown Group in the United States. The key issue in this case was that, if this transaction was done directly by the Cayman CFC and not by the partnership (which is not treated as a CFC), then the income generated would trigger the CFC rule. However, the earning of the partnership was not taken into account as income of the Cayman CFC because Subpart F is the income of the US corporation, so the tax is imposed not on the partner (the CFC) but on its US shareholder parent. So even in this second example, the problem has arisen because of the *deemed dividend* rule that was applied. If Subpart F applied to tax the CFC directly, the existing regulation would have sufficed.

---

64 Rosanne Altshuler, Robert Hubbard, „The Effect of the Tax Reform Act of 1986 on the Location of Assets in Financial Services Firms", Journal of Public Economics (2003, v. 87), pp. 109–127.
65 Reuven S. Avi-Yonah, "The Deemed Dividend Problem", SSRN (2004) https://papers.ssrn.com/sol3/papers.cfm?abstract_id=572182 (accessed 5 March 2020).
66 Reuven S. Avi-Yonah, "The Deemed Dividend Problem", SSRN (2004) https://papers.ssrn.com/sol3/papers.cfm?abstract_id=572182 (accessed 5 March 2020).

The third example is the *Chain Deficit Rule*.⁶⁷ In order to allow US shareholders to take into account also losses of the CFC and any other member of the chain between the CFC and US shareholder, the US Code provides for a "chain deficit rule" that, in some situations (but not in others), enables the US shareholder to use deficits in the earnings and profits of other members of the chain to reduce Subpart F inclusions resulting from positive earnings and profits in one CFC member. However, this rule is very complex and very difficult to apply in practice since it depends on finding that the deficit arose from the same "qualified activity" as the earnings. Taxing the CFC directly on Subpart F income would avoid this complexity and eliminate the entire dependence on earnings and profits that results from the *deemed dividend* approach.

So, R. S. Avi-Yonah finally concludes that the *deemed dividend* approach in the United States should be abolished and replaced by direct taxation of CFCs when the tax may be collected from their US shareholders.⁶⁸ However, on the other side, there are also other authors that consider that the *piercing-the-veil* approach is very complex as well and that it should not be applicable in the United States.⁶⁹ The solution, in general, especially for a big country like the United States, might be to have more simpler CFC rules that cannot be easily avoided by taxpayers and to use a combination of the *deemed dividend* approach in case of minor participation in a foreign corporation and *piercing-the-veil* approach in case of substantial participation.

M. *Ruf* and A. J. *Weichenrieder,* in 2012 conducted an empirical study and concentrated on non-financial subsidiaries of German firms.⁷⁰ They used micro data for the period 1996 to 2006 to test whether the applicability of the German CFC rules reduced the amount of passive assets in the respective countries. The study concluded that the amount of passive assets was significantly affected and that the magnitude of the effect was economically relevant.⁷¹ This means that the applied CFC rules have achieved their goal and have minimized the deferral of passive assets of domestic companies to their controlled companies abroad.

However, in the case of small countries, a question may be posed regarding the justification of the introduction of CFC rules because of the inevitable increase in compliance costs and the added pressure on already limited capacities on tax au-

---

67   Reuven S. Avi-Yonah, "The Deemed Dividend Problem", SSRN (2004) https://papers.ssrn.com/sol3/papers.cfm?abstract_id=572182 (accessed 5 March 2020).
68   Reuven S. Avi-Yonah, "The Deemed Dividend Problem", SSRN (2004) https://papers.ssrn.com/sol3/papers.cfm?abstract_id=572182 (accessed 5 March 2020).
69   see Section 2.3 and the Dodge opinion.
70   Martin Ruf, Alfons J. Weichenrieder, "CFC Legislation, Passive Assets and the Impact of the ECJ's Cadbury-Schweppes Decision", CESifo Working paper no. 4461 (October 2013).
71   Martin Ruf, Alfons J. Weichenrieder, "CFC Legislation, Passive Assets and the Impact of the ECJ's Cadbury-Schweppes Decision", CESifo Working paper no. 4461 (October 2013).

thorities.[72] Namely, for these small countries, there is no analysis suggesting that the benefits of the CFC legislation will outweigh the costs for businesses and the tax administration.[73] Even in countries that have introduced CFC rules before the ATAD, like Finland, there is no comprehensive numeric data on the application of the CFC Act in terms of fiscal efficiency of the rule.[74] According to the Finland Tax Administration's data, it is not common that Finnish taxpayers would own CFCs. Thus, the primary purpose of the CFC legislation in Finland is not fiscal; its main purpose is to prevent arrangements that would fall under the CFC regime and, according to the Finland Tax Administration's data, the Finnish CFC Act has been successful at preventing such arrangements.[75]

Regarding the effectiveness of the current applied CFC rules, countries need to find a balance between the simplicity of the rules and their efficiency in counteracting tax avoidance, as is analysed further in this book in chapter "Balance between effective CFC rules and compliance burdens" of Lydia Gregorová. For example, Indonesia is one of the few countries that uses the *deemed dividend* approach and tends to have simpler rules. However, the tax authority has recognized that the current CFC rules are not sufficiently targeted to counter tax avoidance. Thus, it is expected that the applicable CFC regime will be amended in order to be more balanced thereby taking into consideration the BEPS Action Plan 3 recommendations to have CFC rules that are targeted to counter profit shifting opportunities and long-term deferral of taxation.

4. Challenges for the future application of CFC rules

In the Policy Note Addressing the Tax Challenges of the Digitalisation of the Economy[76] approved on 23 January 2019, the Inclusive Framework agreed to examine and develop different proposals grouped into two pillars.[77] *Pillar Two* is in-

---

72 Nevia Čičin Šain, Stjepan Gadžo, "Controlled Foreign Company Legislation in Croatia" in: Michael Lang/Jeffrey Owens/Pasquale Pistone/Alexander Rust/Josef Schuch/Claus Staringer (eds.) Controlled Foreign Company Legislation (Amsterdam: IBFD, 2020) p. 198.
73 Petra Kamínková, Jiří Kostohryz, "Controlled Foreign Company Legislation in Czech Republic" in: Michael Lang/Jeffrey Owens/Pasquale Pistone/Alexander Rust/Josef Schuch/Claus Staringer (eds.) Controlled Foreign Company Legislation (Amsterdam: IBFD, 2020) p. 233.
74 Kristiina Äimä, Henri Lyyski, "Controlled Foreign Company Legislation in Finland" in: Michael Lang/Jeffrey Owens/Pasquale Pistone/Alexander Rust/Josef Schuch/Claus Staringer (eds.) Controlled Foreign Company Legislation (Amsterdam: IBFD, 2020) p. 270.
75 Kristiina Äimä, Henri Lyyski, "Controlled Foreign Company Legislation in Finland" in: Michael Lang/Jeffrey Owens/Pasquale Pistone/Alexander Rust/Josef Schuch/Claus Staringer (eds.) Controlled Foreign Company Legislation (Amsterdam: IBFD, 2020) p. 270.
76 OECD, Program of Work to Develop a Consensus Solution to the Tax Challenges Arising from the Digitalisation of the Economy (2019), OECD/G20 Inclusive Framework on BEPS, OECD, Paris, www.oecd.org/tax/beps/programme-of-work-to-develop-aconsensus-solution-to-the-tax-challenges-arising-from-the-digitalisation-of-the-economy.htm (accessed 19 February 2020).
77 The Pillar Two proposals are based on the US GILTI and BEAT measures that were introduced as part of the 2017 US tax reform.

teresting because it focuses on the remaining BEPS issues and seeks to develop rules that would provide jurisdictions with a right to "tax back" when other jurisdictions have not exercised their primary taxing rights or the payment is otherwise subject to tax at an effective rate below a minimum rate. Within this context, the members of the Inclusive Framework have agreed to a program of work that contains, among others, the exploration of an inclusion rule that could supplement a jurisdiction's set of CFC rules. The income inclusion rule would ensure that the income of the MNE group is subject to tax at a minimum rate thereby reducing the incentive to allocate income for tax reasons to low taxed entities.

This proposal of a new minimum tax has similar fundamental design features of CFC rules. Thus, it is not surprising that there is some criticism regarding this *Pillar Two* proposal. So, for example, B. J. Arnold argues that the major difficulty with the *Pillar Two* proposal is its complexity and that the changes proposed to domestic law would involve complex legislation and would necessitate changes to tax treaties. The domestic legislation would require detailed rules similar to CFC rules which would result in enormous complexity and would require rules to ensure that the overlaps do not result in double taxation.[78] Furthermore, for some countries, like Argentina, for example, tax planning through the use of trusts is expanding, and structures that are more sophisticated will necessarily require changes in the CFC rules in the near future with respect to trust, i.e. there will be a need to introduce new specific CFC rules and maybe to determine a new approach just for them.[79]

At EU level, the future of CFC legislation is inextricably linked to the future of corporate income tax and the common consolidated corporate tax base (CCCTB) might solve the profit shifting issue and thus influence the abolition of CFC rules in the case of EU situations or the modification of the applied approaches.[80] Moreover, it can be expected that, as more and more jurisdictions legislate and enforce CFC rules, their effectiveness would come into question and appraisal.[81]

Finally, the CFC legislation has brought further complexity in the area of tax law, and structures that are more complex are being developed by taxpayers. Thus, whether the solution in the future will be to turn back to the approach from its first beginnings (when the *deemed dividend* approach was mostly applied) which will be supplemented with a more effective cooperation between tax administra-

---

[78] Brian J. Arnold, "The Evolution of Controlled Foreign Corporation Rules and Beyond", Bulletin for International Taxation (2019, vol. 73, no. 12).

[79] Axel A. Verstraeten, "Controlled Foreign Company Legislation in Argentina" in: Michael Lang/Jeffrey Owens/Pasquale Pistone/Alexander Rust/Josef Schuch/Claus Staringer (eds.) Controlled Foreign Company Legislation (Amsterdam: IBFD, 2020) p. 40.

[80] Petra Kamínková, Jiří Kostohryz, "Controlled Foreign Company Legislation in Czech Republic" in: Michael Lang/Jeffrey Owens/Pasquale Pistone/Alexander Rust/Josef Schuch/Claus Staringer (eds.) Controlled Foreign Company Legislation (Amsterdam: IBFD, 2020) p. 234.

[81] Muhammad Ashfaq Ahmed, "Controlled Foreign Company Legislation in Pakis-tan" in: Michael Lang/Jeffrey Owens/Pasquale Pistone/Alexander Rust/Josef Schuch/Claus Staringer (eds.) Controlled Foreign Company Legislation (Amsterdam: IBFD, 2020) p. 522.

tions (in terms of more possibilities of joint tax audits and more advanced automatic shares of information) is yet to be seen.

5. Conclusion

The policy objectives behind the introduction of the CFC rules differ among the states that have enacted such legislation. However, fundamentally, the CFC legislation is typically seen as an instrument to guard against the unjustifiable erosion of the domestic tax base by shifting investments to non-resident corporations in lower tax jurisdiction.

In their pure form, the difference between the *deemed dividend* approach and the *piercing-the-veil* approach is in the rules that will be applied for the calculation of attributable income to controlling shareholders. In the *piercing-the-veil* approach, the legal personality of the CFC is disregarded, so the attributable income is determined according to the computation rules in the country of the controlling company. Obviously, the latter approach is more complex and requires substantial participation of the shareholders to obtain the information required by the CFC to compute and determine the taxable income. The situation is even more complicated when just the passive income is attributable to the controlling company or when the CFC rule is applied only to non-genuine arrangements.

In the *deemed dividend* approach, by contrast, the legal personality of the CFC is not disregarded, so the attributable income is the pro-rata share of non-distributed profit determined according to the computation rules in the country of the CFC. Thus, the *deemed dividend* approach is less complex, requires less time, and brings less administrative burden. However, it is not suitable for countries that apply the exemption method for foreign dividends received by resident taxpayers. This could be one of the many reasons why most of the countries worldwide apply the *piercing-the-veil* approach instead of the *deemed dividend* approach.

In practice, national CFC rules contain elements of different approaches in order to be more robust, more focused on avoidance situations, and to more effectively achieve their main policy objective: to prevent the evasion or avoidance of taxes by shifting profits to corporations situated in low-tax countries while balancing between taxing foreign income and maintaining international competitiveness of domestic corporations and not impede, in particular, sound overseas business operations. Conclusively, which approach should be applied is a policy decision that each country needs to determine on their own based on the overall applied tax policy, goals that it wants to achieve, their tax administration's capability, profit deferral and tax avoidance occurrences, and other factors. Thus, the conclusion is that there is no unique fit for all solution, and it cannot be generally concluded that one approach is better than the other or that is the "best available" solution.

CFC criteria in general

(with particular focus on OECD BEPS Action 3 and country specific CFC-legislation)

The concept of foreign base company and the application of CFC rules to transparent entities and PEs (switch over)

Patrick Walchhofer

1. Introduction
2. Foreign Base Company as a CFC
   2.1. OECD BEPS Action 3 and its limitations
   2.2. Fiscally Transparent Entities and Permanent Establishments
   2.3. Anti-Tax Avoidance Directive Solution for transparent entities
3. Recognition of CFCs as fiscally transparent entities
   3.1. The structure of CFC rules versus the fiscal transparency pattern
4. No recognition of CFCs as fiscally transparent entities
5. Country specific CFC legislation
6. Austria
7. United States
8. Resumé

The concept of foreign base company and the application of CFC rules

1. Introduction

The principles of corporate taxation can be regarded as the separation principle and the transparency principle. In the former, the company and the shareholder are taxed separately, i.e. the profits of the company, on the one hand, and the income of the shareholder (dividends) on the other. Thus, taxation at the level of the company takes place irrespective of whether dividends are distributed. The transparency principle, unlike the separation principle, is not predominant in the taxation of corporations but in the taxation of sole proprietorships and partnerships. It considers them as non-income taxable entities which leads to the fact that profits and losses are only calculated at the level of the company but, at the same time, assumes that they would have accrued to the shareholders. As an exception to the foregoing, however, there are also countries that apply the transparency principle to corporations. This, therefore, raises the question that I address in my thesis of whether the CFC rules nevertheless apply to those countries that treat corporations as transparent or whether this is not feasible.

As it is discussable if transparent entities and permanent establishments are covered or should be seen as covered as well as to what extent by controlled foreign corporation rules (CFC rules), this master thesis focuses on the reasons for considering or not considering CFCs as fiscally transparent entities. It will give facts about Action 3[1] of the Base Erosion and Profit Shifting Project by the OECD (BEPS) with a focus on transparent entities and will point out limitations of the CFC rules. Furthermore, it will address solutions through the use of the tax avoidance of these entities, e.g. Anti Tax Avoidance Directive II (ATAD II). Finally, the thesis gives some information about the country specific CFC legislations from selected jurisdictions.

2. Foreign Base Company as a CFC

2.1. OECD BEPS Action 3 and its limitations

BEPS Action 3 contains recommendations on the design of the rules for controlled foreign companies (CFCs). These rules are intended to apply to companies in which a majority stake is held in a foreign company with the aim of preventing the shifting of income to a foreign subsidiary and the associated erosion of the tax base of the country of residence.[2] In this regard, a total of six points have been defined for possible implementation in national law for the countries. These are the definition of a CFC, CFC exemptions and threshold requirements, definition of

---

1 OECD Ctr. for Tax Policy and Admin., *Designing Effective Controlled Foreign Company Rules – Action 3: 2015 Final Report*, OECD/G20 Base Erosion and Profit Shifting Project (OECD 2015), International Organizations' Documentation IBFD [hereinafter: *Action 3*].
2 See footnote 1.

income, computation of income, attribution of income, and prevention and elimination of double taxation.[3]

In order that the income, after its calculation, can be attributed to the respective shareholder of a CFC, the following five process steps were created by the OECD:[4]

1. The attribution threshold should be tied to the minimum control threshold when possible, although countries can choose to use different attribution and control thresholds depending on the policy considerations underlying CFC rules. This means that all resident taxpayers who have the minimum level of control in a CFC in that jurisdiction are attributable to CFC income.
2. The amount of income to be attributed to each shareholder or controlling person should be calculated by reference to both their proportion of ownership and their actual period of ownership or influence (influence could for instance be based on ownership on the last day of the year if that accurately captures the level of influence).
3. Jurisdictions can determine when income should be included in taxpayers' returns and how it should be treated so that CFC rules operate in a way that is coherent with existing domestic law.
4. CFC rules should apply the tax rate of the parent jurisdiction to the income.[5]

The measures proposed by the OECD through the BEPS Project[6] to coordinate the application of tax treaties to transparent companies and CFCs treat CFCs and transparent entities separately in terms of their legislation. On the one hand, BEPS Action 2[7] (as amended by Action 6)[8] or its scope focuses relatively little on CFCs. On the other hand, countries' CFC regulations should cover transparent entities according to the recommendation of BEPS Action 3.[9]

A fiscally transparent entity is when the income legally earned by an entity is fiscally attributed to the underlying member/partner, aggregated to the overall income of the latter according to his personal circumstances and the relevant tax is

---

3 See footnote 1.
4 See footnote 1.
5 See footnote 1.
6 OECD Ctr. for Tax Policy and Admin., *Explanatory Statement – OECD/G20 Base Erosion and Profit Shifting Project* (OECD 2015) [hereinafter: *BEPS Project*]. For an overview of the topic and an assessment of the BEPS results, see, inter alia, M. Lang et al. (eds.), *Base Erosion and Profit Shifting (BEPS). The Proposals to Revise the OECD Model Convention* (Linde 2016).
7 OECD Ctr. for Tax Policy and Admin., *Neutralising the Effects of Hybrid Mismatch Arrangements – Action 2: 2015 Final Report*, OECD/G20 Base Erosion and Profit Shifting Project (OECD 2015), at 139, International Organizations' Documentation IBFD [hereinafter: *Action 2*]. An analysis can be found in A. Rust, *BEPS Action 2: 2014 Deliverable Neutralising the Effects of Hybrid Mismatch Arrangements and its compatibility with the non-discrimination provisions in tax treaties and the Treaty on the Functioning of the European Union*, British Tax Review 3, at 308–339 (2015).
8 OECD Ctr. for Tax Policy and Admin., *Preventing the Granting of Treaty Benefits in Inappropriate Circumstances – Action 6: 2015 Final Report*, OECD/G20 Base Erosion and Profit Shifting Project (OECD 2015), International Organizations' Documentation IBFD [hereinafter *Action 6*].
9 See footnote 1.

reduced by his personal deductions and allowances; most of all, the final tax must be determined as if the partner himself earned that income.[10]

> An entity is considered to be fiscally transparent with respect to the income to the extent the laws of that jurisdiction require the interest holder to separately take into account on a current basis the interest holder's share of the income, whether or not distributed to the interest holder, and the character and source of the income to the interest holder are determined as if the income was realized directly from the source that paid it to the entity.[11]

Transparent companies and CFC rules were basically very rarely subjected to an examination *in cumulo* just as, for example, the Partnership Report did not intend to address CFC rules. At the time, however, there was also little concern about their application in agreement situations, presumably in part because they were not yet as widespread. The long experience of US treaty practice and the Partnership Report almost certainly significantly influenced the work on the OECD's new rules regarding transparent entities. First, several amendments were made to the OECD Model Tax Convention in this regard and, subsequently, the Multilateral Agreement Implementing the BEPS Measures (MLI)[12] was adopted on 24 November 2016 (signed on 7 June 2017).

In order to avoid bilateral renegotiations of each individual agreement, the MLI supplements all tax treaties that are in force. This is how agreed changes are implemented in a synchronized manner (OECD, *Explanatory Statement,* at 3 et seq.). If two states have decided to ratify the MLI, it will be applied to the extent of the compatibility clauses and reservations of the signing parties (restrictions are possible through reservations according to Article 28) provided that it is preceded by a concluded tax treaty.[13]

Source taxation will be allowed for (i) passive income sourced in the same state where the CFC is incorporated (i.e. the home state of the CFC) and (ii) for passive income sourced in a country other than the home state of the CFC only (a) when the premises of the CFC constitute a permanent establishment and (b) to the extent that the item of income is attributable to that permanent establishment. In this case, the

---

10 OECD Ctr. for Tax Policy and Admin., *Neutralising the Effects of Hybrid Mismatch Arrangements – Action 2: 2015 Final Report*, OECD/G20 Base Erosion and Profit Shifting Project (OECD 2015), International Organizations' Documentation IBFD [hereinafter *Action 2*], at 141.

11 Website – International Revenue Service, Flow-Through-Entities.

12 OECD Multilateral Convention to Implement Tax Treaty Related Measures to Prevent BEPS (24 Nov. 2016), Treaties IBFD [hereinafter: Multilateral Instrument or MLI]; OECD, Explanatory Statement to the Multilateral Convention to Implement Tax Treaty Related Measures to Prevent BEPS (24 Nov. 2016), Models IBFD [hereinafter: Explanatory Statement].

13 On the relevance, scope, and limits of the compatibility clauses in regulating possible conflicts between the MLI and existing treaties, *see* N. Bravo, *The Multilateral Tax Instrument and Its Relationship with Tax Treaties*, 8 World Tax J. 3 (2016), Journals IBFD. For an analysis of legal and technical issues, *see* S. Austry et al., *The Proposed OECD Multilateral Instrument Amending Tax Treaties*, 70 Bull. Intl. Taxn. 12, at 683 et seq. (2016), Journals IBFD; and J. Hattingh, *The Multilateral Instrument from a Legal Perspective: What May Be the Challenges?*, 71 Bull. Intl. Taxn. 3/4 (2017), Journals IBFD.

residence state has to credit the foreign taxes to the shareholders (Article 11(1)(d) of the MLI). On the other hand, no credit obligation exists on the residence state (of the shareholders) for taxes that are levied by the state where the CFC is incorporated solely because this state considers the CFC to be a separate taxable entity. This occurs either when the premises of the CFC do not constitute a permanent establishment to which the specific item of income is connected. In these cases, taxation is levied by the state of the CFC not in accordance with – i.e. under the protection of – the treaty distributive rules but on the basis of that state's sovereign taxing power. Since treaties do not limit residence-based taxation by the state of incorporation of the CFC, the opt-out clause in Article 5(6) of the MLI allows the state of residence (of the shareholders) to refrain from its credit obligation.[14]

As far as CFC rules are concerned, Action 3 in the BEPS Project contains a set of recommendations entirely dedicated to them. The interplay between CFC rules and transparent entities is scrutinized in Actions 2 and 3. Action 2 specifically considers that the CFC rules could be an efficient defensive measure to prevent double non-taxation arising out of situations where a deductible payment is made to an entity that is transparent in its home state but opaque in the investors' state (deduction/non-inclusion outcome).[15]

The same CFC inclusion effect is also considered to neutralize branch mismatch structures as the public discussion draft of 22 August 2016 suggests.[16] This indicates that CFC rules are seen as a tool to include the (non-included) income stemming from a source that the taxpayer does not directly own, as BEPS Action 3 confirms.[17]

2.2. Fiscally Transparent Entities and Permanent Establishments

Article 1 (2) of the OECD Model already refers to the term of a "fiscally transparent entity":

> For the purposes of this Convention, income derived by or through an entity that is treated as wholly or partly fiscally transparent under the tax law of either Contracting State shall be considered to be income of a resident of a Contracting State but only to the extent that the income is treated, for purposes of taxation by that State, as the income of a resident of that State.[18]

---

14 See footnote 12.
15 *Action 2*, at 56 et seq., 64 et seq. and at 57, para. 150; *Action 3*, at 21, para. 24. On the coordination between CFC rules and anti-hybrid rules, *see* M.A. Kane, *The Role of Controlled Foreign Company Legislation in the OECD Base Erosion and Profit Shifting Project*, 68 Bull. Intl. Taxn. 6/7, at 324 (2014), Journals IBFD; G. Maisto, *Controlled Foreign Company Legislation, Corporate Residence and Anti-Hybrid Arrangement Rules*, 68 Bull. Intl. Taxn. 6/7, at 329 (2014), Journals IBFD.
16 OECD Ctr. for Tax Policy and Admin., Public Discussion Draft on Branch Mismatch Structures (BEPS Action 2), paras. 22-24 (OECD 2016).
17 *Action 3*, at 21–22 et seq., paras. 27–30.
18 Website – https://www.oecd.org/ctp/treaties/articles-model-tax-convention-2017.pdf.

With minimal changes, this term found its way into Article 3(1) of the MLI via BEPS Action 2 and replicates Article 1(2) of the OECD Model:

> For the purposes of a Covered Tax Agreement, income derived by or through an entity or arrangement that is treated as wholly or partly fiscally transparent under the tax law of either Contracting Jurisdiction shall be considered to be income of a resident of a Contracting Jurisdiction but only to the extent that the income is treated, for purposes of taxation by that Contracting Jurisdiction, as the income of a resident of that Contracting Jurisdiction.[19]

The purpose of this provision is to ensure that the source state grants treaty benefits in cases of different classification of the legal entity only if the condition is met that the income is considered by the other contracting state to be received by a resident of that state.[20] This provision was already contained in the old Article 4 (1) (d) of the *US Model (1996)* as well as in the subsequent Article 1 (6) of the US Model (2006) – of course, with slight differences.[21] With minor changes, it even found its way into many of the DTTs of the United States which is why the case law in this regard is of particular relevance for the interpretation of Article (3) (1) of the MLI.

Originally, the rule in the *US Model (1996)* was designed to address reverse hybrid situations that can result in double non-taxation. Reverse hybrid situations are those in which a US company is treated as taxable under the laws of the source state but is considered transparent in the United States. This is made possible, for example, by the US check-the-box system (see also section 5.3). The regulation in the *US models* of 2006 and 2016 as well as Article 3 (1) MLI go beyond reverse hybrid situations as they also explicitly address hybrid situations. These are cases in which US companies are considered non-transparent under US law but transparent under the law of the source state.[22]

---

19   See footnote 12.
20   *See* Rust, in *Klaus Vogel on Double Taxation Conventions* Vol. I, at 102, 121–122, marginal notes 5 and 50–53 (4th ed., A. Rust & E. Reimer eds., Wolters Kluwer Law & Business 2015); *United States Model Income Tax Convention Technical Explanation* para. 20 (15 Nov. 2006), Models IBFD [hereinafter: US Model Technical Explanation]; J. Kollmann, A. Roncarati & C. Staringer, *Treaty Entitlement for Fiscally Transparent Entities: Article 1(2) of the OECD Model Convention*, in Lang et al. (eds.), *supra* n. 1, at 1 et seq.
21   United States Model Income Tax Convention art. 4(1)(d)(1996), Models IBFD; United States Model Income Tax Convention art. 1(6) (15 Nov. 2006), Models IBFD [hereinafter: US Model (2006)].
22   The addition of the words "by or" in the first sentence of Art. 1(6) of the *US Model (2006)* – repeated in the *US Model (2016)* – refers to the perspective of the state that sees the entity as opaque and the income as "derived" by this entity (whereas the state that regards the entity as transparent – the United States in the case at hand – considers the same income as "derived through" the entity). These words were not present in the previous US Models. *See*, for further considerations, C. Kahlenberg, *Hybrid Entities: Problems Arising from the Attribution of Income Through Withholding Tax Relief – Can Specific Domestic Provisions be a Suitable Solution Concept?*, 44 Intertax 2, at 151 (2016); M. Seevers, *Taxation of Partnerships and Partners Engaged in International Transactions: Issues in Cross-Border Transactions in Germany and the US*, 2 Hous. Bus. & Tax L. J. 143, at 223 (2002).

On Feb. 17, 2016, the *United States Model Income Tax Convention,* Models IBFD, replaced the *US Model (2006).* The minor changes that were made in comparison to the previous versions of Article 1 (6) of the *US Model (2016)* are highlighted below:

> 6. For the purposes of this Convention, an item of income, profit or gain derived by or through an entity that is treated as wholly or partly fiscally transparent under the taxation laws of either Contracting State shall be considered to be derived by a resident of a Contracting State, but only to the extent that the item is treated for purposes of the taxation laws of such Contracting State as the income, profit or gain of a resident.[23]

Differences between Article 1(6) of the *US Model (2016)* and Article 1(2) of the *OECD Model* as implemented in Article 3(1) of the MLI, are minor as it is based on the *US Model.*[24]

Even after the long history of the US model (2006) and its Article 1 (6), it is still disputed whether the decision of the state of residence on the attribution of income has a binding effect on the decision of the source state. Furthermore, it is unclear whether a person receiving income is also the person liable to pay tax on that income.

It is clear that the Partnership Report has influenced the additions to the commentary of Article 1 of the OECD Model[25] with regard to the definition of a fiscally transparent entity because it is required that the final tax on the imputed income is calculated in accordance with the characteristics of the taxpayer, i.e. that person who is entitled to this income. It is not relevant how and at what level the tax base is calculated. The addition of paragraph 26.10 of the commentary to Article 1 of the OECD Model (2014) which states that "fiscally transparent" refers to those situations in which the income is taxed at the level of the shareholders (under the domestic law of a contracting state) was considered in the context of BEPS Action 2.

> This will normally be the case where the amount of tax payable on a share of the income of an entity or arrangement is determined separately in relation to the personal characteristics of the person who is entitled to that share so that the tax will depend on whether that person is taxable or not, on the other income that the person has, on the personal allowances to which the person is entitled and on the tax rate applicable to that person; also, the character and source, as well as the timing of the realization, of the income for tax purposes will not be affected by the fact that it has been earned through the entity or arrangement. The fact that the income is computed at the level of the entity or arrangement before the share is allocated to the person will not affect that result ...[26]

---

[23] Art. 1 (6) of the Model of the United States Model Income Tax Convention (2016).
[24] "For the purposes of *a Covered Tax Agreement,* income derived by or through an entity or arrangement that is treated as wholly or partly fiscally transparent under the tax law of either Contracting Jurisdiction shall be considered to be *income of* a resident of a Contracting Jurisdiction but only to the extent that the income is treated, for purposes of taxation by that Contracting Jurisdiction, as the income of a resident of that *Contracting Jurisdiction.*"
[25] Para. 26.10 of the additions to the *OECD Model: Commentary on Article 1* (2014). *See Action 2,* at 141.
[26] See footnote 23.

The fact that the OECD concept of a tax transparent entity does not require that the calculation of the tax base must be made according to those rules that apply to the taxpayer to whom the income is attributed through transparency represents a slight deviation from the pattern of pure tax transparency. If the rules of calculation of the tax base differ between the levels of the company and the partner, this position seems questionable. In the end, there is a difference in the treatment of the tax base (and taxes) of the partner who earns income through a transparent entity and the partner who earns the same income directly. The former partner is thus placed in a better position. According to the principle of homogeneity in the tax base calculation, the tax base should rather be calculated according to the partner's rules that apply to the same type of income in order to avoid such differences.

It seems that the concept of fiscal transparency is about fictitiously assuming that the taxpayer to whom the source of the income is directly attributed would have directly carried out the activity in question or would be the owner of the profitable property (*fictio iuris*).[27]

"*Under generally accepted principles, income attribution is in fact a consequence of the fiscal attribution of the relevant source income.*"[28] That the income retains the character that it has received defined by the source is thus a legitimate finding. From this perspective, the connection of the ownership of the interest in a transparent entity with the ownership of the assets and activities contained therein is given for legal purposes. The application of this concept can also be found in other legal paradigms. These include, for example, trusts, where the income is attributed to a taxable person other than the entity owning the profitable assets. In the latter, the term itself applies by analogy where not all of the principles of the Partnership Report apply to trusts.[29] A more complex situation in which the income is attributed to the partner but the underlying assets and activities to the transparent entity is also conceivable. However, this is not in line with the position of the OECD for which source and income constitute a whole pattern.

In principle, this particular concept of tax transparency could be adapted to certain CFC rules. In doing so, CFC rules replicate the essential elements of the tax transparency pattern: the separation between the legal right to the income and the relevant source as well as the potential tax subjectivity of the corporation.[30] Ultimately, whether CFC rules fall within the OECD's definition of fiscally transparent entities depends on the characteristics of the imputation mechanism.

---

27 *See* para. 2 of the *OECD Model: Commentary on Article 10* (2014).
28 D. Canè, *Controlled Foreign Corporations as Fiscally Transparent Entities. The Application of CFC Rules in Tax Treaties*, World Tax J. (2017), Journals IBFD, p. 533.
29 See R. Danon, Conflicts of Attribution of Income Involving Trusts under the OECD Model Convention: The Possible Impact of the OECD Partnership Report, 32 Intertax 5 (2004).
30 T. Tassani, Trasparenza [dir. trib.], Treccani.it – Diritto online (2015).

It is also, not least, that CFC rules could also apply to certain transparent entities and permanent establishments (PEs) if those entities earn income that raises BEPS concerns and those concerns are not addressed in another way.

2.3. Anti-Tax Avoidance Directive Solution for transparent entities

The Council Directive (EU) 2017/952 of 29 May 2017, Anti-Tax Avoidance Directive II (ATAD II),[31] is the newest legislation on hybrid mismatches with third countries. These amendments are intended to counteract the aggressive tax planning ostensibly used by multinational corporations.

One of the introductions by the ATAD II is the concept of reverse hybrid entity mismatch. Due to the different characterization of corporations by jurisdictions in terms of their taxation, it is possible that income is subject to double non-taxation. This is possible due to the fact that one state considers the corporation to be non-transparent while the other state considers it to be transparent.[32]

In the case of one or more related (directly or indirectly held) non-resident entities, the reverse hybrid concept applies if more than 50% of the voting rights, capital shares, or profit-sharing rights are held in such a hybrid entity and it is incorporated in a Member State. Based on the national laws of a Member State, hybrid companies may be considered fiscally transparent while, for the state in which it is not resident, it may be considered fiscally non-transparent. Under these circumstances, however, it makes sense to consider this hybrid entity as fiscally non-transparent in the Member State as it is thereby recognized as a taxable person (generating tax substrate instead of double non-taxation). However, for investment funds (and similar collective investment vehicles), the reverse hybrid rules do not take effect as they are subject to the Member State's investor protection rules due to its diversified portfolio of securities.[33, 34]

"Reverse hybrid" is defined by the OECD Report as follows: "... *any person [including any unincorporated body of persons] that is treated as transparent under the laws of the jurisdiction where it is established but as a separate entity [i.e. opaque] under the laws of the jurisdiction of the investor*".[35]

As of 1 January 2020, EU member states must apply the anti-hybrid measures of the ATAD II, although the implementation of countermeasures regarding reverse

---

31 Council Directive (EU) 2017/952 of 29 May 2017 amending Directive (EU) 2016/1164 as regards hybrid mismatches with third countries, OJ L 144, 7.6.2017, p. 1–11.
32 See footnote 24.
33 Deloitte, An overview for fund managers – The impact of ATAD II on real estate asset managers and the implications come 2020, REflexions magazine, issue 9, at 3.
34 Website – A brief guide on the new Anti-Tax Avoidance Directive (ATAD II).
35 OECD Report, at 56.

hybrid mismatches does not have to take place until 1 January 2022. Nevertheless, adoption of measures in this regard at an earlier date is feasible.[36]

3. Recognition of CFCs as fiscally transparent entities

First of all, we can distinguish two functionalities of CFC legislation: The piercing-the-veil approach, on the one hand, in which the controlled foreign corporation is regarded as a transparent entity. It therefore attributes the income when generated which is normally the shareholder's fiscal year in which the entity's financial year ends. The underlying rationale is that the shareholder is taxed on income that it would have earned directly without the interposition of the CFC. On the other hand, it is worked with the deemed-dividend approach in which a notional distribution of profits from the foreign company to its shareholders is assumed. So, it attributes the income as soon as distributions become possible since it subjects to tax a fictitious distribution.[37]

CFCs should be considered as transparent units for different reasons, both theoretical and practical. The theoretical one concerns DTTs in particular. It refers to the imbalance created by the CFC rules (meaning the DTA law and the uneven distribution of taxation right) and is akin to that created by the approach of fiscal transparency. It has been mentioned by *Lang*[38] that, as much as one has to acknowledge that the contracting state taxes the partnership while the other taxes the shareholders according to their national laws, one has to acknowledge that the former state taxes the CFC while the latter taxes the income of the shareholders of the CFC which is attributed to them under the CFC laws. Irrespective of the national legislation, treaties are not taking an allocation decision; they just accept the allocated amount as determined by national law.[39] Since the rules of distribution, regardless of the laws of the two countries, do not necessarily require the income to be allocated to the same beneficiary, the treaties will still be applicable even if the income is allocated to different beneficiaries.[40] The absence of global tax coordination therefore leads to circumstances where both contracting states levy taxes on the identical income in the possession of differing persons. However, only the common issues already encountered with respect to partnerships are raised by the CFC rules.

---

36 Deloitte, Anti-Tax Avoidance Directive – Implementation of measures to counter hybrid mismatch arrangements, at 4–6.
37 See footnote 24.
38 M. Lang, *CFC Regulations and Double Taxation Treaties*, 57 Bull. Intl. Taxn. 2, at 54–55 (2003), Journals IBFD.
39 *See*, inter alia, J. Wheeler, *The Missi Keystone of Income Tax Treaties* at 23 (IBFD 2012), Online Books IBFD. It should not be surprising that a lack of global tax coordination creates situations where both the contracting states tax the same income.
40 Danon, *supra* n. 41; id., *Qualification of Taxable Entities and Treaty Protection*, 68 Bull. Intl. Taxn. 4/5 (2014), Journals IBFD; Lang, *supra* n. 44; H. Ault, *Issues Related to the Identification and Characteristics of the Taxpayer*, 56 Bull. Intl. Taxn. 6, at 263 (2002), Journals IBFD. This assumption emerges also from the *Partnership Report, supra* n. 17.

To reach the common target of combating tax avoidance, the need to ensure the coordination of both domestic and non-domestic tax laws was evident after the BEPS Project. This provides the systematic justification. A clearly welcomed outcome is the fact that the application of the partnership approach to CFCs can promote the coherent application of CFC rules in treaty scenarios.[41]

The structure of the CFC rules constitutes another argument in favour of considering CFCs as fiscally transparent entities. Consequently, an analysis of the core elements of each type of CFC rule has to be carried out. CFC legislation that follows the piercing-the-veil approach can be consistent with tax treaty law if applied in accordance with the principles of the Partnership Report because it essentially replicates the features of the partnership approach, *Rust* explained. Moreover, he argues that shareholders are treated similarly to partners in a partnership as they generate income directly through the company. For treaty purposes, he subsequently explains why certain CFC rules can shape fiscally transparent entities.[42]

3.1. The structure of CFC rules versus the fiscal transparency pattern

Elements indirectly and directly affecting the final tax calculation are the basic features of a tax transparency approach with the former group referring to the attribution, qualification, and calculation of taxable income. A partial or complete attribution of income based on a ratio is pursued within the framework of the tax transparency principle of the OECD approach which is why even a merely partial attribution of income (e.g. implementation of a "deemed dividend" approach) through the CFC regulations can fulfill the requirements in principle. In the following, it will be explained in more detail that, although within the CFC rules, in principle, no consolidation of the tax bases – namely, that of the company and that of the (controlling) shareholder – is permitted, both the tax transparency approach and the CFC rules allow the inclusion of these bases. In addition, the imputation under the fiscal transparency approach should neither affect the taxation date nor the source and nature of the income.

Since chargeable income is viewed as if it were domestic business income, the CFC rules based on the piercing-the-veil approach respect these requirements. Minimal variations from normally being considered and calculated as operating income under the rules applicable to the shareholder may be provided, but this does not change the substance.[43] Normally, imputed income attributed to the shareholder on a pro rata basis would be calculated separately but, for OECD purposes, there is no difference at which level it is calculated.

---

41 *OECD CFC Legislation*, supra n. 14.
42 Rust, in Lang et al. (eds.), *supra* n. 24, at 494–496.
43 Whereas, for individuals, the tax rate may vary. Hence, for them, the CFC is not completely transparent since imputed income would normally be subject to progressive rates.

The direct impact on the final tax is found in the second group where the correspondence of the final tax with the personal characteristics of the taxable entity is required in the definition of tax transparent entity in Article 3 (1) of the MLI. Since a tax incurred in a foreign country affects the final tax under both the piercing-the-veil and the transparency approaches, these taxes are credited against the taxes incurred in the domestic country. In this case, it is fictitiously assumed that the shareholder would have realized income directly and that this would also be taxed accordingly. This is not the case under the deemed dividend CFC regime where the deduction of foreign taxes from attributed income is generally prohibited.

Additional rules for the avoidance of double taxation do not appear to be material for the classification of a CFC as fiscally transparent and are not explicitly addressed by the OECD:

Dividends distributed by the CFC may either not be recognized by the shareholder or may be deducted from the actual distributions up to the amount of the previously imputed income; dividends exceeding the imputed income are generally tax-exempt or fully taxable – depending on the level of taxation of the CFC in its home country.[44]

A so-called switchover rule is applied in Italy, for example, if a foreign company is subject to a nominal tax rate of less than 50% of the Italian standard tax rate and dividends distributed by the CFC are fully taxable. However, an indirect tax credit is granted in those cases where an effective business activity is carried out by the CFC. If the dividends along the repatriation chain are subject to effective taxation of more than 50% of the Italian nominal or effective tax rate, the switchover rule does not apply. For purposes of the participation exemption rule, the same requirement of effective taxation applies. This requirement must be met from the first year of ownership of an interest in the CFC in order to qualify for the capital gains exemption and, if not met, will result in fully taxable gains. However, provided that the CFC actually conducts business, there is the indirect tax credit of the taxes borne by the CFC. In essence, economic double taxation is imposed only when the CFC earns active income.[45]

The relief from economic double taxation on the sale of the shareholding in the CFC may likewise be provided by an increase in the tax base of the shareholding by a reduction in the sale price and by a deduction from the tax paid on the sale. Since losses can be offset against the partner's liability, the second element affecting the tax calculation is that of loss pass-through. Income and losses should thus pass through in equal measure in the case of pure fiscal transparency and be

---

44 D. Canè, *Controlled Foreign Corporations as Fiscally Transparent Entities. The Application of CFC Rules in Tax Treaties,* World Tax J. (2017), Journals IBFD, p. 536.
45 *See* Silvani, *supra* n. 29, at sec. 7.2.1.3.

added to the shareholder's total income. Trusts,[46] however, are an example of the fact that, in practice, there are cases in the context of tax transparency where no losses are allowed through, but only income since losses are not taken into account by the OECD. Undoubtedly, this is what the OECD intended to address and, consequently, should be included in the definition of a fiscally transparent entity.[47] Furthermore, treaties address income rather than losses, so Canè does not consider loss pass-through as crucial to characterize a CFC as fiscally transparent.[48] Besides, the separate calculation of the final taxation of a taxable person is possible on the basis of his personal allowances and deductions according to the OECD. *"Separate taxation of imputed income – namely, whether it is aggregated to the shareholder's overall income or taxed in a separate basket – undoubtedly represents a distinctive characteristic of many CFC rules, which does not normally feature a fiscally transparent entity."*[49]

In fact, by consolidating imputed income with the shareholder's income from other sources and offsetting it against losses and personal deductions would, in fact, result in such a pure transparency pattern directly affecting the tax to be paid. From CFC rules such as those in Germany[50] that have implemented a deemed dividend approach and allow imputed income to be added to the total income of the shareholder (other CFC rules provide for separate taxation and are based on a piercing-the-veil approach[51]), it is apparent in practice that hardly any rules allow for loss pass-through. Politically, there is a trend toward making separate taxation a necessary formality for the defensive function of CFC rules.[52] Finally, a defensive function of CFC rules would become obsolete if a surrogate fiscal consolidation effect with the low-taxed subsidiary takes place due to the fact that foreign losses are allowed to reduce domestic taxable income.

---

46 Under Italian law, for instance, income accrued by a trust shall be imputed to the beneficiary – in proportion to their interest and regardless of actual distribution – to the extent that they are identified in the relevant trust deeds and are entitled to (i.e. have the enforceable right to) receive a share of these profits. From a theoretical standpoint, this cannot be regarded as a pure fiscal transparency since the trust is not a potential taxable person but rather a form of diverted attribution of income to persons that do not legally own the relevant source. For an overview of trust taxation in Italy, *see* G. Maisto, *Taxation of Trusts in Italy*, in *Taxation of Trusts in Civil Law Jurisdictions: 2nd Symposium of International Tax Law* at 153- 186 (J.L. Chenaux et al. eds. Schulthess 2010).
47 *See* Rust & Reimer (eds.), *supra* n. 34, at 122, m.no. 53; M. Scherleitner, *Thoughts on the Potential Effects of the OECD/G20 BEPS Action Plan on Collective Investment Vehicles – Part I*, 70 Bull. Intl. Taxn. 10, at 604 (2016), Journals IBFD; Sanghavi, *supra* n. 10, at 358.
48 D. Canè, *Controlled Foreign Corporations as Fiscally Transparent Entities. The Application of CFC Rules in Tax Treaties*, World Tax J. (2017), Journals IBFD, p. 537.
49 See footnote 40.
50 Lampert, Bittermann & Harms, *supra* n. 18, at 21 and 27; Perdelwitz, *supra* n. 26).
51 Art. 167(6) of the Italian Income Tax Code.
52 Which *Action 3* recommends and Art. 8(1) of the ATAD also implements. *Action 3*, at paras. 99 and 102- 108; Assonime, *supra* n. 18, at 6 and 16. Accordingly, most CFC rules – such as Art. 209 B of the *Code general des impôts* before the 2006 amendments – provide for separate taxation of the imputed income thus radically impeding a CFC's pass-through losses; and when aggregate taxation is admitted, pass-through losses are explicitly excluded. The only CFC rules allowing aggregate taxation and pass-through losses were the Canadian ones (*OECD CFC Legislation, supra* n. 14, at 77).

For shareholders of a corporation, separate taxation under the CFC rules essentially replicates the tax system to which the income would also be subject if it had been earned directly. This income, which is imputed to the shareholder, is considered business income as in Italy and in many other countries, for example, and is calculated in the same way and is subject to the tax rate that applies to corporate shares. Accordingly, separate taxation does not necessarily result in a different tax regime than that applicable to the shareholder. The shareholder is subject to personal tax on the income fictitiously assumed for him even in periods in which he has not reported any income. Likewise, he may be subject to personal tax if the CFC has suffered losses during this period. However, since this is in line with the basic ideas of the CFC rules, separate taxation is, in principle, not to be regarded as a decisive counter-argument.[53]

Finally, the OECD requires that the final tax on imputed income must be subject to the shareholder's personal allowances in order for a corporation to qualify as fiscally transparent. Since subjective allowances should theoretically hinder the operation of CFC rules, this requirement appears to be met because certain non-profit organizations, for example, that, by their nature, are exempt from income tax, will also be exempt for this imputed income.[54]

The fact that a piercing-the-veil CFC generally does not allow personal imputations and deductions by shareholders to offset separately computed tax on imputed income represents the only difference from the OECD's fiscal transparency approach. This characterizes the imputed income tax more as a real tax that is nevertheless consistent with the underlying rationale of the CFC legislation and the policy option.[55]

4. No recognition of CFCs as fiscally transparent entities

There are several political and legal reasons why CFCs should not be considered fiscally transparent entities.

That states suffer negative budgetary consequences as a result if the tax substrate is partially or entirely reduced by the shifting of taxing rights can be cited as a policy reason. When classifying a CFC as transparent, it is assumed that the income is received directly by the shareholder through the premises of the intermediary CFC (this also applies to permanent establishments). As a result, if there is an applicable treaty (that provides for the exemption of business income from a permanent establishment in that country) between the country of residence and the

---

53   See footnote 44.
54   See footnote 44.
55   See footnote 44.

source country, the income of the shareholder must be exempted by its country of residence.[56] Apart from the exemption method, any tax levied on the CFC would have to be credited by the residence state in terms of the imputation method.[57]

Other reasons are based on the assumption that a piercing-the-veil approach cannot be reconciled with international tax rules. The prohibition of taxation of foreign entrepreneurs who do not carry on business in the home country that arises from the primary distribution rule of Article 7(1) of the OECD Model is the basis of the objections to the compatibility of a CFC regime with tax treaties. Belgium's comments on Article 1 of the OECD Model can be particularly emphasized at this stage:[58]

> ... where a Contracting State taxes one of its residents on income derived by a foreign entity by using a fiction attributing to that resident, in proportion to his participation in the capital of the foreign entity, the income derived by that entity ...that State increases the tax base of its resident by including in it income which has not been derived by that resident but by a foreign entity which is not taxable in that State in accordance with the Convention. That Contracting State thus disregards the legal personality of the foreign entity and therefore acts contrary to the Convention.[59]

However, it has also been argued that neither the attribution of passive and low-taxed income of a CFC instead of its total profit nor taxation based on the residence of the controlling shareholder is prevented by Article 7 (1) of the OECD Model. This corresponds exactly to the way some CFC rules work. The French CFC rules were adapted in 2006 to include a deemed dividend approach, and they now overcome the business profit characterization.[60] France now refrains from violating tax treaty law and considers foreign income as deemed dividends.[61]

The question of who is understood by the term "enterprise" in the sense of Article 7 (1) of the OECD Model seems fundamental: While the CFC state will consider the CFC as an enterprise, the state of the shareholder may consider this shareholder as an enterprise. For this reason, by assuming that a "piercing-the-veil" CFC rule refers to the profits of the CFC and that these are also taxed as those of the CFC, there is a contradiction between Article 7 (1) of the OECD Model and this CFC

---

56   Rust, in Lang et al. (eds.), supra n. 24, at 494–495. See also Action 3, at 69, para. 137.
57   Rust, in Lang et al. (eds.), *supra* n. 24, at 496.
58   R. Fontana, The Uncertain Future of CFC Regimes in the Member States of the European Union – Part 1, 46 Eur. Taxn. 7, at 263 (2006), Journals IBFD; L.E. Schoueri & M.C. Barbosa, Brazil: CFC Rules and Tax Treaties in Brazil: A Case for Article 7, in Tax Treaty Case Law around the Globe 2015 at 79–82 (M. Lang et al. eds., Linde/IBFD 2016).
59   See footnote 54.
60   Details in J. Benamran, *France – Corporate Taxation* sec. 10.4., Country Analyses IBFD (accessed 9 Feb. 2017).
61   D. Gutmann, *Droit fiscal des affaires* at 496 (Montchrestien 2010); N. Gaoua & A. Ribeiro, *French CFC Legislation: An Illustration of Recovery from a "Tax Treaty Override" Situation*, 53 Eur. Taxn. 9, at 451 (2013), Journals IBFD. Interestingly, the French CFC rule, enacted in 1980, was the first CFC rule adopted in a country where residents are not subject to corporation tax on foreign-sourced income (territoriality principle).

rule. The result of the interpretation of the words "profits of a company" by the French Conseil d'Etat in 2002 in the Schneider case[62] was that France had no possibility to tax these profits. This arose from the fact that the taxed profits (according to Article 209 B of the Code général des impôts) were, from the French point of view, profits of a company resident in Switzerland which fall under Article 7 (1) of the treaty.

It is also claimed that the piercing-the-veil approach would invalidate Article 5 (7)[63] with its anti-single-entity clause that respects the separate legal identity of a sub-subsidiary and Article 10 (5)[64] which prohibits extraterritorial taxation. However, the taxation rights of the controlling shareholder's country of residence are not affected as Article 10 (5) only concerns the withholding taxation of the CFC. Moreover, the original purpose of this paragraph was not to prevent the application of the CFC rules but to counteract the extraterritorial taxation of dividends as imposed by the United States, among others.[65]

CFC rules are fundamentally different from a pure transparency rule, according to another reason why they should not be treated as a fiscally transparent entity. That "*CFC rules based on the notional sum approach and the diverted imputation approach*"[66] differ significantly from the tax transparency rule, according to the case law, is because it considers the resident shareholder as the person to whom income earned domestically is attributed but not as the one who receives the income earned abroad. Accordingly, it is not Article 7 of the OECD Model Tax Convention that should be applied but Article 21.

The UK CFC regime, based on the notional amount approach, did not violate Article 11 of the Income and Capital Tax Treaty between the Netherlands and the United Kingdom (2008),[67] according to the UK Court of Appeal in Bricom Holdings Limited v. IRC.[68] This was based on the fact that a notional amount was assumed to be income that was taxed in the case of a person deemed to be resident in the United Kingdom. The notional amount attributed to the resident share-

---

62   FR: *Conseil d'Etat*, 28 June 2002, no. 232.276, *Société Schneider Electric*, 4 International Tax Law Reports 4, at 1077 (2002).
63   Reimer, in Rust & Reimer (eds.), *supra* n. 34, at 397-398, mm.nno. 394-396.
64   Haslehner, in Rust & Reimer (eds.), *supra* n. 34, at 760, m.no. 143.
65   Para. 23 of the *OECD Model Convention on Income and on Capital: Commentary on Article 1* (15 July 2005), Models IBFD.
66   D. Canè, *Controlled Foreign Corporations as Fiscally Transparent Entities. The Application of CFC Rules in Tax Treaties*, World Tax J. (2017), Journals IBFD, p. 540.
67   *Convention between the Government of the United Kingdom of Great Britain and Northern Ireland and the Government of the Kingdom of the Netherlands for the Avoidance of Double Taxation and the Prevention of Fiscal Evasion with Respect to Taxes on Income and on Capital Gains*, art. 12 (26 Sept. 2008), Treaties IBFD [hereinafter: *Neth.-UK Income and Capital Tax Treaty*].
68   See D. Sandler, *Tax treaties and controlled foreign company legislation – A world premier in the United Kingdom*, British Tax Review 5, at 544-553 (1996); id., *Tax treaties and controlled foreign company legislation*, British Tax Review 1, at 52-61 (1998).

holder for transparency reasons did not correspond to the income of the CFC in this case, according to the court's finding.

In 2014, a similar result was reached in the Vale case by the Brazilian Superior Court of Justice that affected a diverted attribution rule for CFC.[69] What is particular about this is that it created a difference between CFC rules that follow the piercing the veil pattern and those written under the diverted attribution approach. At the same time as changing the application of the rule to align it with a purely fictitious totals approach, the scope of application was massively narrowed in its entirety which was ultimately owed to Law 12, 973/2014 after a series of rulings. "Profits earned by foreign controlled companies" are no longer "added to the profits of the parents" under Brazilian law.[70] Rather, an "adjustment to the investment account equivalent to the profits earned by the directly or indirectly controlled foreign companies" must now be made by the resident taxpayer in its financial statements.[71]

Even the OECD confirms with references of the OECD commentary to Article 7 and Article 10 of the CFC rules that there are clear distinctions between CFC rules due to the notional sum approach and the piercing-the-veil approach.[72] Paragraph 10.1 of the OECD Commentary on Article 7 of the OECD Model Tax Convention (2003), which remains unchanged to this day, states that the CFC rules are aimed at taxing the profits of residents and are not restricted by treaties. Additions to Article 1 (3) of the OECD Model Tax Convention, which were implemented in Article 11 (1) of the MLI based on the recommendation of Action 6 of the BEPS Project, reaffirm the view that provisions of a treaty do not affect a state's right to tax its own residents. This is precisely the case when the partnership approach or certain CFC rules are applied by a state. The commentary on Article 10 further confirms the structural differences between CFC rules (such as under the "deemed dividend" approach versus the ones following the "piercing the veil" approach) as fictitious dividends can be subsumed under Article 10 (1) of the OECD Model.[73]

---

69 Superior Court of Justice, Appeal No. 1.325.709/RJ of April 24, 2014, 17 International Tax Law Reports 4, at 643 (2015).
70 Unofficial translation taken from Schoueri & Barbosa, *supra* n. 20, at 85. *See*, for details, P. Violin, *The Brazilian CFC Regime: Recent Developments*, 68 Bull. Intl. Taxn. 4/5 (2014), Journals IBFD; id., *The Brazilian CFC Regime: Update on Recent Developments*, 68 Bull. Intl. Taxn. 9 (2014), Journals IBFD.
71 See footnote 59.
72 *See Action 6*, at 85, para. 59, addition 26.8 to the *OECD Model: Commentary on Article 1* (2014); *Action 3*, at 13, paras. 6-7; para. 14 of the *OECD Model: Commentary on Article 7* and para. 37 of the *OECD Model: Commentary on Article 10*. *See also* EU Council Resolution C 156/1, *supra* n. 21.
73 Provided that the fictitious dividend is not specifically exempted under a different norm. Many treaties concluded by Germany indeed provided for the exemption of intercompany dividends. K. Vogel, On Double Taxation Conventions at 622, mm.nno. 97 et seq. (3rd ed., Kluwer Law International 1996).

5. Country specific CFC legislation

CFC regimes differ across countries. A large number of them are targeting passive income although active income is also targeted frequently. Low taxation is a common requirement as well. Though CFC rules would appear, based on their name, only to apply to corporate entities, many countries include trusts, partnerships, and PEs in limited circumstances to ensure that companies in the parent jurisdiction cannot circumvent CFC rules just by changing the legal form of their subsidiaries.

6. Austria

Austrian legislators introduced key aspects of the ATAD within the framework of the Annual Tax Act 2018 (Jahressteuergesetz 2018).[74] What is more, Austria introduced the first CFC regulations with the adoption of Articles 7 and 8 of the ATAD. Low-taxed passive income generated through a controlled company is attributed to the controlling entity according to Section 10a of the CITA. As a matter of fact, it is often debated that Austria finally introduced a CFC regime because Austria did not adopt one for quite a long time. This is obvious when having a look at the years of implementations of CFC rules in other European countries such as Germany (1972), France (1980), Spain (1995), or Italy (2000). In Austria, the CFC legislation requires that a CFC obtains passive income in a low-taxed country as defined in Section 10a paragraph 2 CITA. Austria has decided in favour of the "categorical approach" when implementing the ATAD.[75] It implies that only specific passive income of a company abroad is subject to CFC taxation. Non-distributed passive income of the CFC is attributed to the controlling company in accordance with Section 10a paragraph 1. no 1 CITA. However, the CFC legislation in Austria is applicable only if the three criteria set out in Section 10a paragraph 4 CITA are met simultaneously:[76, 77]

- no. 1: Passive income amounts to more than one third of the total income of the foreign corporation (de minimis limit).[78]
- no. 2: The foreign corporation is controlled by the domestic corporation (controlling event).[79]

---

74   AT: Jahressteuergesetz 2018, BGBl I 2018/62 (JStG 2018). The provision was only slightly amended by the Tax Reform Act 2020 (AT: Steuerreformgesetz 2020, BGBl I 2019/103 [StRefG 2020]).
75   See footnote 74.
76   See Materials on Annual Tax Act 2018, Explanatory Notes to Government Proposal No. 36 26th Legislative Period, 22 et seq; see also in detail M. Schilcher & P. Knesl, in *KStG*31 (B. Renner/E. Strimitzer/M. Vock eds, LexisNexis 2018), § 10a, para. 124 et seq.
77   See also G. Kofler/R. Krever E./M. Lang/J. Owens/P. Pistone/A. Rust/… C. Staringer (2020). *Controlled foreign company legislation*, IBFD.
78   Art. 7 para. 3 first sentence ATAD.
79   Art. 7 para. 1 lit. a ATAD.

- no. 3: The foreign corporation does not exercise any significant economic activity (proof of substance).[80]

The provisions of CITA Section 10a paragraph 6 broadens the scope of coverage of the CFC legislation to cover dual residency of No. 1 and non-resident permanent establishments of No. 2. However, Section 10a paragraph 7 CITA is not affected by this paragraph.[81] A consequence of the fact that the scope is extended to cover national companies based in Austria and whose place of effective management is located in a foreign country is that, because of the "tie-breaker rule", national companies with dual residency are not liable to worldwide taxation when a double taxation agreement is applicable. Consequently, they are similar to CFCs (Section 10a paragraph 6 no. 1 CITA).[82] According to Section 10a paragraph 6 no. 2 CITA, even if the double taxation agreement foresees the exemption method, the CFC rules are applicable to non-resident permanent establishments.[83] Marchgraber/Zöchling[84] found that, as a consequence of the situation that companies that are subjected to unlimited tax liability can have no further reliance on the exemption method, there is a treaty override.[85]

According to the Austrian addition tax, foreign corporations can be considered as controlled intermediate companies.[86] This refers to "foreign legal entities without owners that are comparable to a domestic corporation on the basis of a comparison of types and whose registered office is abroad".[87]

Due to the neutrality of the legal form, foreign permanent establishments are also included.[88] With regard to permanent establishments, Section 10a (6) 2 KStG

---

80 Art. 7 para. 2 penultimate sentence ATAD. See in more detail Section 6.2, The Austrian Substance Test and EU Law.
81 See M. Schilcher & P. Knesl, in *KStG*31 (B. Renner/E. Strimitzer/M. Vock eds, LexisNexis 2018), § 10a, para. 264.
82 See Materials on Annual Tax Act 2018, Explanatory Notes to Government Proposal No. 36 26th Legislative Period, 26; M. Schilcher & P. Knesl, in *KStG*31 (B. Renner/E. Strimitzer/M. Vock eds, LexisNexis 2018), § 10a, para. 268 et seq.
83 See G. Mayr/E. Titz, *Umsetzung der Anti-BEPS-RL: Hinzurechnungsbesteuerung ergänzt Methodenwechsel nach § 10 Abs 4 KStG*, RdW 2018, 317, 326.
84 See C. Marchgraber/H. Zöchling, *§ 10a KStG: Passiveinkünfte bei niedrig besteuerten Auslandsaktivitäten*, ÖStZ 2018, 388, 393.
85 See also G. Kofler/R. Krever E./M. Lang/J. Owens/P. Pistone/A. Rust/… C. Staringer (2020). *Controlled foreign company legislation*, IBFD.
86 A comparison of types is required (cf. Schilcher/Knesl, Die Körperschaftsteuer, § 10a KStG, marginal no. 17); on the concept of a foreign corporation, see also ibid, no. 139; see also V. Oberrader, *Hinzurechnungsbesteuerung nach § 10a KStG – Eine Darstellung der neuen Gesetzesstelle mit Schwerpunkt auf dem Substanztest (2019)*, Johannes Kepler Universität Linz.
87 KStR 2013, Entwurf Wartungserlass 2019, no. 1248ad; see also V. Oberrader, *Hinzurechnungsbesteuerung nach § 10a KStG – Eine Darstellung der neuen Gesetzesstelle mit Schwerpunkt auf dem Substanztest (2019)*, Johannes Kepler Universität Linz.
88 See Sec. 10a (1) in conjunction with Sec. 6 (2) KStG; See also Schilcher/Knesl, Die Körperschaftsteuer, Sec. 10a KStG, no. 272; Schlager, SWI 2018,363; On the problem of hybrid foreign companies, see in detail Kollruss, SWI 2019, 248ff; see also V. Oberrader, *Hinzurechnungsbesteuerung nach § 10a KStG – Eine Darstellung der neuen Gesetzesstelle mit Schwerpunkt auf dem Substanztest (2019)*, Johannes Kepler Universität Linz.

adds "even if the double taxation agreement provides for an exemption". This standardizes a so-called "treaty override".[89] As a result, the additional taxation is applicable to foreign permanent establishments irrespective of a DTA.[90] By including permanent establishments, controlled foreign partnerships can also be subject to the additional taxation.[91]

The Austrian legislator additionally stipulates that dual-resident corporations with their place of management abroad (domiciled in Austria, therefore, a domestic corporation) can be the object of addition taxation.[92] The place of management under treaty law is decisive.[93] The initiative proposal for the Tax Reform Act 2020[94] provides, as an editorial change, that only those (dual-resident) domestic companies are covered "that are domiciled abroad under a double taxation treaty"

The reverse case of a dual-resident corporation (place of management in Austria, registered office abroad) is already covered by the term "foreign corporation".[95] However, such corporations are, in any case, subject to unlimited tax liability in

---

[89] See also Schlager, SWI 2018,363; Marchgraber/Zöchling, ÖStZ 2018,393; According to Mayr/Titz, this will be relevant especially for financing branches in Switzerland (cf. Mayr/Titz, RdW 2018,326); see also V. Oberrader, *Hinzurechnungsbesteuerung nach § 10a KStG - Eine Darstellung der neuen Gesetzesstelle mit Schwerpunkt auf dem Substanztest (2019)*, Johannes Kepler Universität Linz.

[90] See Schlager, SWI 2018,363; This does not entail a treaty violation (cf. KStR 2013, draft maintenance decree 2019, margin no. 1248ex); see also V. Oberrader, *Hinzurechnungsbesteuerung nach § 10a KStG - Eine Darstellung der neuen Gesetzesstelle mit Schwerpunkt auf dem Substanztest (2019)*, Johannes Kepler Universität Linz.

[91] See Schilcher/Knesl, Die Körperschaftsteuer, § 10a KStG, no.141; IdS also Fellinger, Jahrbuch Bilanzsteuerrecht 2018, 163mVa Kirchmayr in BEPS (2017),121 f; In other publications, a controlled company is also referred to as a control object (see Schilcher/Knesl, Die Körperschaftsteuer, § 10a KStG, no. 21 mwN); see also V. Oberrader, *Hinzurechnungsbesteuerung nach § 10a KStG - Eine Darstellung der neuen Gesetzesstelle mit Schwerpunkt auf dem Substanztest (2019)*, Johannes Kepler Universität Linz.

[92] See Section 10a (6) 1 KStG; ErlRV 190 BlgNR XXVI. GP, 23; See also Pedritz-Klar/Petritz, taxlex 2018, 205; see also V. Oberrader, *Hinzurechnungsbesteuerung nach § 10a KStG - Eine Darstellung der neuen Gesetzesstelle mit Schwerpunkt auf dem Substanztest (2019)*, Johannes Kepler Universität Linz.

[93] See Schilcher/Knesl, Die Körperschaftsteuer, § 10a KStG, marginal note 270; also the initiative motion for the Tax Reform Act 2020 -StRefG 2020, 984/A XXVI GP, 46; see also V. Oberrader, *Hinzurechnungsbesteuerung nach § 10a KStG - Eine Darstellung der neuen Gesetzesstelle mit Schwerpunkt auf dem Substanztest (2019)*, Johannes Kepler Universität Linz.

[94] Initiativantrag zum Steuerreformgesetz 2020 - StRefG 2020, 984/A XXVI. GP,Eingebracht am 3. July 2019, 7; The initiative motion followed (with the same content regarding Section 10a KStG) the draft assessment of the Tax Reform Act 2019/2020, 147/ME; The editorial amendment is intended to clarify that these provisions are applied mutatis mutandis only if a domestic corporation is deemed to be resident abroad under the applicable double taxation treaty (Initiativantrag zum Steuerreformgesetz 2020 -StRefG 2020, 984/A XXVI. GP,46); see also V. Oberrader, *Hinzurechnungsbesteuerung nach § 10a KStG - Eine Darstellung der neuen Gesetzesstelle mit Schwerpunkt auf dem Substanztest (2019)*, Johannes Kepler Universität Linz.

[95] See KStR 2013, draft maintenance decree 2019, margin no. 1248ad; See also Schilcher/Knesl, Die Körperschaftsteuer, § 10a KStG, margin no. 19; This interpretation regarding domestic and foreign companies coincides with the prevailing opinion on § 10 KStG (cf. ibid mVa Strimitzer/Vock, Die Körperschaftsteuer, § 10 KStG, margin no. 74 mwN); see also V. Oberrader, *Hinzurechnungsbesteuerung nach § 10a KStG - Eine Darstellung der neuen Gesetzesstelle mit Schwerpunkt auf dem Substanztest (2019)*, Johannes Kepler Universität Linz.

Austria, and the right of taxation is usually not restricted by a DTA. However, income that is to be exempted by Austria may have to be recorded in Austria through the addition taxation.[96]

Section 10a (8) KStG provides for a special exception for foreign finance companies. As proposed by the ATAD as an exemption option, these can be exempted from the addition provided that no more than one third of the liability income is generated within the group.[97] Group-internal financing companies are therefore not exempted.[98]

7. United States

The conceptual application of CFCs in the United States treats a foreign corporation as a CFC for US tax purposes if it is owned by at least one US person. In the most common cases, a CFC will result in taxable income under Foreign Base Company Incomes.[99] In cases where residents, green card holders, or citizens of the United States own more than 50% of the company, a company with such income is considered to be owned by "U.S. persons." For purposes of IRC § 951, "U.S. persons" also include those persons classified as trusts, certain estates, and domestic partnerships and corporations.[100]

This category of Foreign Base Company Incomes can be broken down into the subcategories of Foreign Personal Holding Company Income, Foreign Base Company Sales Income, Foreign Base Company Service Income, and Foreign Base Company Oil-Related Income. Taxable income then consists of the sum of these.[101]

> "For purposes of determining who is a US shareholder and CFC status, stock owned directly, indirectly, and constructively is taken into account (IRC § 957)."[102] This is considered a measure to prevent shares from being given away to family members or contributed to offshore structures and trusts, which is why these are also referred to as "look-through" rules.[103]

---

96 See Schilcher/Knesl, Die Körperschaftsteuer, § 10a KStG, no. 20;According to the tie-breaker rule of the OECD-MA, which is usually included, the place of management is decisive for persons other than natural persons if this and the company's registered office are different (see OECD Model Tax Convention, Article 4 (3)); see also V. Oberrader, *Hinzurechnungsbesteuerung nach § 10a KStG – Eine Darstellung der neuen Gesetzesstelle mit Schwerpunkt auf dem Substanztest (2019)*, Johannes Kepler Universität Linz.
97 See also Raab, SWK 2018, 847 f; Mayr/Titz, RdW 2018, 326 f; see also V. Oberrader, *Hinzurechnungsbesteuerung nach § 10a KStG – Eine Darstellung der neuen Gesetzesstelle mit Schwerpunkt auf dem Substanztest (2019)*, Johannes Kepler Universität Linz.
98 See ErlRV 190 BlgNR 26. GP 27; See also Raab, SWK 2018, 848; see also V. Oberrader, *Hinzurechnungsbesteuerung nach § 10a KStG – Eine Darstellung der neuen Gesetzesstelle mit Schwerpunkt auf dem Substanztest (2019)*, Johannes Kepler Universität Linz.
99 See also footnote 76.
100 See also footnote 76.
101 See also footnote 76.
102 See also footnote 76.
103 See also footnote 76.

The concept of foreign base company and the application of CFC rules

> "Being a CFC means that your foreign company needs to consider Subpart F of the US tax code. As a result, certain types of income of this corporation may be taxable as earned in the United States. Conversely, most income that is not Subpart F income can be retained tax deferred in the corporation."[104]

While the Subpart-F rules were fundamentally created to capture passive or mobile income, they also aggregate certain incomes

> that are intended to implement other policy goals. These rules include certain income in the category of Subpart F income that violates US international boycott rules; income derived from countries with which the US does not conduct diplomatic relations; and income paid in the form of illegal bribes and kickbacks.[105]

> For United States federal income tax purposes, US corporations and foreign entities of the type that can be publicly traded must be treated as corporations. For many other business entities, however, there is an option to elect to be treated either as a corporation or as other than a corporation."[106] "A business with a single owner does not file a separate tax return, but rather reports its net income on Schedule C of the owner's individual tax return. Generally, all net income from sole proprietorships is also subject to payroll taxes under the Self-Employed Contributions Act (SECA). Partnerships file an entity-level tax return (Form 1065), but profits are allocated to owners who report their share of net income on Schedule E of their individual tax returns. Under "check the box" regulations instituted by the US Department of the Treasury in 1997, limited-liability companies can elect to be taxed as partnerships. General partners are subject to SECA tax on all their net income, while limited partners are only subject to SECA tax on "guaranteed payments" that represent compensation for labor services.[107]

8. Resumé

Firstly, it has been shown that, in some cases, CFCs can be treated as transparent entities. Indeed, CFC rules produce effects and involve problems comparable to the partnership approach that are relatively unexplored for states that have historically considered foreign partnerships as opaque for fiscal purposes.

Secondly, the legal framework of tax treaties has been tested to assess whether it supports such an interconnected application of CFC rules. It has been found that the new provisions for transparent entities, only recently implemented in the Multilateral Convention, can be consistently applied even in CFC situations.

The additions to Articles 1(2)-(3) and 23(1) of the OECD Model, as transposed in Articles 3, 5(6)-(7) and 11(1)(d) of the MLI, allow a balanced application of treaties to CFCs whereby distributive rules are not applied unilaterally, and income allocation conflicts can be solved without resorting to the attribution rule of the source state.

---

104 See also footnote 76.
105 See Sections 952(a)(3)–(5).
106 Website – https://ieglobal.vistra.com/knowledge/country-compliance-alerts/2011/9/ united-states-check-box-entity-selection-context-foreign.
107 Website – https://www.taxpolicycenter.org/briefing-book/what-are-pass-through-businesses.

It seems that the dividing line between fiscally transparent entities and CFCs lies in the technical details of the concerned CFC legislation. From this perspective, the piercing-the-veil approach seems to meet the OECD concept of fiscal transparency in the taxable event (i.e. the generation of income); in the way the CFC's income is imputed to the shareholder and determined; in the timing of the attribution; as well as in the way economic double taxation is relieved. Even the very end result is the same: current taxation of foreign-sourced undistributed profits in the hand of a resident taxable person.[108]

Separate taxation of imputed income impedes loss pass-through and the ability to compensate between the liability on imputed income and the personal deductions of the shareholder. However, separate taxation conforms to the rationale of CFC rules and is also a common effect of schedular tax systems that do not always allow compensation between income and losses from different sources of income (at least for individual shareholders). Therefore, it should not be seen as a decisive difference between CFCs and fiscally transparent entities.

This thesis advocates that the normative and interpretative materials concerning transparent entities and CFCs can support a coordinated application of CFC legislation at the tax treaty level in order to tackle base erosion and profit shifting. Such coordination is possible by applying the principles set out for partnerships to CFC rules that adopt a fiscal transparency approach.

Attribution of income under these CFC rules obtains the same result, in fact, as under the transparency approach, i.e. the inclusion in the parent jurisdiction of an item of income derived by a non-resident entity (or arrangement). Application, by analogy, of the same rules therefore appears legitimate[109] and useful for solving the problems that (hybrid) transparent entities normally pose at treaty level.

To conclude, it is the need to coordinate tax legislation to counteract BEPS that mostly suggests extending the rules for transparent entities to CFCs based on the piercing-the-veil approach.

---

108 See, inter alia, Arnold, supra n. 12; E.R. Larkins, International Commerce through a Foreign Subsidiary: Navigating the Anti-Haven Tax Shoals of the Internal Revenue Code, 9 Intl. Tax & Bus. Law 64, at 67 (1991- 1992).
109 The idea that OECD Model Tax Convention on Income and on Capital (26 July 2014), Models IBFD [hereinafter OECD Model], art. 1(2) may also cover CFCs seems accepted; see D. Sanghavi, BEPS Hybrid Entities Proposal a Slippery Slope, Especially for Developing Countries, 85 Tax Notes Intl. 4, at 358 (2017).

The role of the "control" concept under CFC rules

Kristina Reguliova

1. **Introduction**
2. **The control concept under CFC**
    2.1. Type of control
        2.1.1. Figure 1: Example of the legal control test
        2.1.2. Figure 2: Example of the economic control test
    2.2. The level of control
        2.2.1. Figure 3: Concentrated ownership requirement (acting-in-concert concept, related parties)
        2.2.2. Figure 4: Acting-in-concert concept (unrelated parties)
    2.3. The exemptions
    2.4. Future replacement of the CFC by CCCTB
3. **Different control threshold between CFC legislation for corporate entities and individuals**
    3.1. CFC rules for individuals in Slovak Republic
4. **Conclusion**

1. Introduction

The digital era developed conjointly with international business and globalization. This progress has opened the space for base erosion and profit shifting. The uprising extent of BEPS, thanks to a digital economy and globalization, caused the political importance worldwide that persists or is even more critical for countries nowadays.

Many countries realized that it might be easier to tackle the profit shifting and base erosion in international business more effectively through international cooperation. The key factor for the cooperation was the awareness that national-based prevention is insufficient due to the obsolete domestic and international rules for international taxation established in an economic environment characterized by a lower degree of economic integration across borders.[1]

The joint work in this matter on the OECD level was initiated in 2013 in the report "Addressing Base Erosion and Profit Shifting" which analyzed the BEPS related background and ended up in the BEPS final reports consisting of 15 actions.[2]

The controlled foreign corporation (CFC) regulation is included in Action 3 of the BEPS Project and enables a country to tax income or profit from a foreign entity controlled by a domestic taxpayer according to the domestic law. Action 3 introduced a recommendation on setting the CFC rules in domestic regulation to become an effective measure; hence, it falls under the CFC domestic measures.[3] Regardless, each country could adjust the recommendations by implementing them to the domestic tax system and country's special issue targeting. Even if the country adjusts the CFC rules to its tax system, it must consider that CFC rules can be effective only if they comply with other countries' tax systems.[4] Therefore, the OECD recommendation was drafted. Some countries applied the CFC rules

---

1 OECD Addressing Base Erosion and Profit Shifting (2013), OECD Publishing. Executive Summary.
2 The 15 Actions of the BEPS project are divided into:
Minimum standards (Actions 5, 6, 13, 14).
Reinforced international standards (Actions 6, 7, 8–10, 13).
Domestic Measures (Actions 2, 3, 4, 12).
Analytical reports (Actions 1, 11, 15).
3 The CFC recommendations are based on six building blocks:
   1. Rules for defining a CFC (including the definition of control).
   2. CFC exemption and threshold requirements.
   3. Definition of CFC income.
   4. Rules for computing income.
   5. Rules for attributing income.
   6. Rules to prevent or eliminate double taxation.
If all countries adopted the CFC rules complying these six building blocks, the application should ensure a reliable international framework (i.e. standardization among countries) and prevent the conflicting interactions of different tax regimes.
4 OECD (2015), Designing Effective Controlled Foreign Company Rules, Action 3 – 2015 Final Report, OECD/G20 Base Erosion and Profit Shifting Project, OECD Publishing, Paris. P. 3-4, http://dx.doi.org/10.1787/9789264241152-en.

before the OECD initiative. In that case, the review and adjustment of "old" CFC rules are necessary. The first CFC rules were enacted in 1962.[5] For being a soft law instrument, the OECD work is not legally binding. It intends to give a positive example for the other countries participating in the project. In the wake of the BEPS Project, the European Union introduced the so-called anti-avoidance tax package (ATAP) which also included CFC legislation as part of the ATAD initiative.[6] The CFC within the ATAD needed to be implemented into the national legal systems of the Member States. Hence, the CFC rules applied by the EU Member States must comply with EU law at any time. To read more about the ATAD, see the part CFC definition under the Anti-Tax Avoidance Directive of this publication.

This master thesis analyzes only one of the key building blocks of the CFC legislation, the control concept, and its application. At the beginning, the standard implementation sources are reviewed, such as OECD recommendations of the "primary implementation manual for CFC legislation", including the ECJ resolution as the element that influenced the legislation implemented among the EU countries. It will then examine the CFC legislation that applies also for individuals and was introduced in the Slovak Republic recently, focusing primarily on different approaches to natural persons in comparison to corporate entities. The CFC approach to natural persons raised some general issues such as the questionable necessity of setting the CFC rules for natural persons and the lower control threshold for the qualifying control compared to corporate entities.

2. The control concept under CFC

The control and its exercise are an essential concept commonly used in different tax legislations for different purposes. The conjoined factor for setting the control level criterion is to find the responsible "someone" for the companies' activity. The responsibility is expressed by the level of control in percentage. The necessary level of control varies among the different types of tax legislation. Some tax jurisdictions set a secondary condition for granting the benefit besides the appropriate control level, such as the time duration of the control. The time duration should ensure the authenticity of the control.[7]

---

[5] It was in the United States, and the CFC was any foreign corporation in which more than 50% of the voting stock was directly owned by one or more US corporations for any day of the taxable year of the foreign corporation. Sebastian Duenas, CFC Rules Around the World (Tax Foundation, 2019), Fiscal Fact No. 659, June 2019, p. 3.

[6] The ATAD initiative was implemented in the Council Directive (EU) 2016/1164, laying down rules against tax avoidance practices that directly affect the internal market's functioning (ATAD I). The Council Directive (EU) 2017/952 amended ATAD I regarding hybrid mismatches with third countries (ATAD II), and both mirror the measures introduced in the OECD Action plan applied in EU legislation. The ATAD constitutes only minimum standards, and states can incorporate more protective rules to protect the domestic tax base.

[7] Benefit should not be granted to an artificial change of ownership to gain the benefit.

For example, the control concept is used by the Parent-Subsidiary Directive[8] and transfer pricing legislation. The Parent-Subsidiary Directive stipulates that dividends are tax-exempt if the parent company holds at least 10% of the company's capital for at least a two-year period. The aim of the directive is to remove tax obstacles in the area of profit distribution impacting group companies within the European Union only (primary to abolishing the withholding tax and preventing double taxation of profit). The minimal percentage of shares developed during the time from 25% to 10%. There was no intention to set the general control threshold for other legislation. This percentage could represent the minimum threshold only.[9] The transfer pricing rules set by the OECD Transfer Pricing Guidelines for MNE and Tax Administrations[10] defined the associated enterprises according to Article 9, "Associated enterprises" of the Model Tax Convention on Income and on Capital (OECD MC).[11] The definition is set for both corporate entities and natural persons and is defined by direct or indirect participation in management, control, or capital. There is diversity in interpretation of Article 9 of the OECD MC. Some countries understand the definition as legal and economic control, and some have a broader understanding of de-facto control. Anyhow, each country sets the qualifying percentage for direct and indirect participation.[12] For instance, a threshold is set as follows: in the Czech Republic, at least 25% (voting rights, registered capital, a person otherwise associated[13]), the Slovak Republic at least 25% (close person with economic, personal, or other ties), Indonesia at least 25% (equity, same controlling party, family relationship), Brazil at least 10% of capital, Germany at least 25% (share, exercise of controlling influence, holding of substantial participation), Italy more than 50% (in the capital, voting rights, profits). Resulting from these few examples, the percentage of the level of control and type of control by defining related parties vary in the transfer pricing legislation.

The OECD Final Report on Action 3 on CFC rules, representing the manual for their application, comprise recommendations on the design of the control con-

---

8 *Council Directive 2011/96/EU of 30 November 2011 on the standard system of taxation applicable in the case of parent companies and subsidiaries of different Member States.*
9 Joao Santos Pinto, The Role of the Concept of Control under CFC Legislation within the European Union vis-á-vies Third Countries, European Taxation (2013), p. 95.
10 OECD (2017), OECD Transfer Pricing Guidelines for Multinational Enterprises and Tax Administrations 2017, OECD Publishing, Paris.
11 OECD (2017), Model Tax Convention on Income and Capital: Condensed Version 2017, OECD Publishing.
12 Lang Michael, Cottani Giammarco, Petruzzi Raffaele, Storck Alfred, Fundamentals of Transfer Pricing, A Practical Guide, (Vienna 2019: Wolters Kluwer), p.14-15.
13 The definition of "persons otherwise associated" means a person participating in the management or control of another person, the identical person, or close persons participating in the management or control of other persons (excluding members of the supervisory boards) with a close relationship, controlling and controlled, by the same controlling person that created a legal relationship predominantly to reduce a tax base or increase a tax loss.

cept.¹⁴ The CFC under Action 3 of the BEPS Project is defined as a subsidiary in which residents (including corporate entities, individuals, or others such as a trust, PE, or partnership) of other countries hold participation (a participation means holding of shares, voting rights, having right to profit), at a minimum, of more than 50% of control (separately, aggregately, directly, indirectly). According to the OEDC's conclusion, the required minimum control reflects the countries' view that resident shareholders should only be taxed on income earned by a foreign company if they appear to have had some input in how, when, and where that income was earned."¹⁵ Most of the countries use the minimum control threshold of more than 50% by legal entities while, on the contrary, for individuals, the threshold is below 50% of control (mostly "more than 25%"). It shows a different approach to the legal entities compared to individuals.

According to the BEPS recommendation, the CFC rules' application should be triggered if four steps are identified. Firstly, the transaction is between related parties. Secondly, the relationship is between controlling and controlled companies (mainly between the parent company and its subsidiary).¹⁶ Thirdly, the controlling party can exercise control or has sufficient influence and, lastly, the exercised percentage of the control share needs to meet the threshold under local CFC legislation.¹⁷

A resident shareholder's ability to exercise sufficient influence over a foreign company should indicate the level of control, and a sufficient level of control gives the resident shareholder opportunity to shift profits. Simultaneously, the level of control could set the limitation of the CFC's rules' scope (under a certain level of control, the shareholder does not fall into the scope of the CFC) and thereby reduce the compliance and cost burden of shareholders, for instance, minority shareholders. The minority shareholders are excluded by setting the qualifying control level threshold at more than 50% because minority shareholders do not have sufficient influence over the company. Countries could make CFC rules stricter compared to the OECD recommendation by using a lower percentage of the control threshold and thereby include the minority shareholders into the scope of the CFC. Only a few countries used this advantage and lowered the qualifying percentage below 50% for legal entities (such as Finland, Portugal, Poland).

As is obvious from the four steps identifying a CFC above, the role of the control concept is an essential element of the CFC legislation concept. If there is no con-

---

14 OECD (2015), *Designing Effective Controlled Foreign Company Rules, Action 3 – 2015 Final Report, OECD/G20 Base Erosion and Profit Shifting Project, OECD Publishing, Paris.* P. 9–10, http://dx.doi.org/10.1787/9789264241152-en.
15 OECD (2015), Public Discussion Draft BEPS ACTION 3: STRENGTHENING CFC RULES, p. 27.
16 In general, direct taxation falls in the exclusive competence of Member States.
17 OECD (2015), *Designing Effective Controlled Foreign Company Rules, Action 3 – 2015 Final Report, OECD/G20 Base Erosion and Profit Shifting Project, OECD Publishing, Paris.* P. 21, http://dx.doi.org/10.1787/9789264241152-en.

trol, there is no CFC. Therefore, it is necessary to understand what control means. According to the Glossary of Tax Terms of the OECD, the general definition of control for tax purposes is as follows:

> The capacity of one person to ensure that another person acts in accordance with the first person's wishes, or the exercise of that capacity. The exercise of control by one person over another could enable individuals and corporations to avoid or reduce their tax liability. A company is usually regarded as controlling another company if it holds more than 50% of the latter company's voting shares. However, the definitions vary according to country and situation.

The OECD recommendations determined the control for CFC purposes by two factors: a) the type of control and b) the level of control. Types of control are divided into general groups: specifically legal control, economic control, de facto control, and control based on consolidation. Countries can choose if local legislation incorporates all four types or only some of them. It is carried out at each country's discretion, but the practice shows that almost all countries incorporated at least the legal, economic, and de facto control test.

2.1. Type of control

In its recommendations, the OECD recognizes four types of control: economic, legal, de-facto, and control based on consolidation.[18]

The legal control test examines the legal view of the domestic law on exercised control. It is focused on holding of shares and voting rights. However, the legal control could be only formal, and the control might be exercised by someone else.

2.1.1. Figure 1: Example of the legal control test

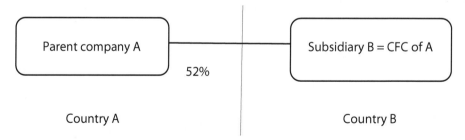

Figure 1 above illustrates the legal control of the parent company A residing in a country A over the subsidiary B residing in a country B. Other parent companies

---

18 OECD (2015), *Designing Effective Controlled Foreign Company Rules, Action 3 – 2015 Final Report*, OECD/G20 Base Erosion and Profit Shifting Project, OECD Publishing, Paris. P. 23–25, http://dx.doi.org/10.1787/9789264241152-en.

are holding the remaining shares of 48% in subsidiary B. Under the condition that country A follows the rule "more than 50% of the shares create the CFC", only parent company A controls the CFC in country B under the legal control test.

By contrast, the economic control test focuses more on economic facts rather than on legal documents. This test follows the entitlement on the company's value as a right on profit, capital, or assets. The legal information about holding-percentage of shares in the company or voting rights is not essential when examining the economic test.

2.1.2. Figure 2: Example of the economic control test

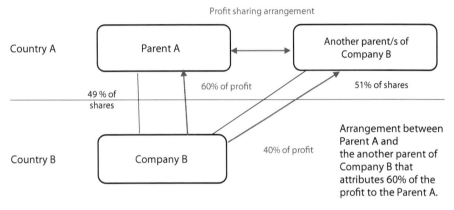

Note: The grey text follows the economic control test.

Despite parent A not meeting the CFC legal control's threshold of more than 50% in Example 2 above, there is an arrangement between parent A and another parent/s of company B according to which 60% of company B's profit is attributed to parent A. Based on the economic control test, parent A has the CFC in state B. In this example, the legal and economic tests collide; for both tests, the control threshold is met thus legal control of another parent of company B (in the case of a company with two parents) is at the level of 51% and, at the same time, the economic control of parent A is at the level of 60% of the profit. Such a situation steams the problem of income attribution (51% and 60% are more than 100% of participation). This disproportion in control qualification may lead to over-attribution of an income and will have to be prevented by incorporating domestic law attribution rules. In the case of parent companies located in different jurisdictions, the double taxation issue can arise as well because the same amount of income (overattributed part of the income) might be taxed in two different parent jurisdictions if both jurisdiction incorporated CFC rules that collide.

The de-facto test complements the economic and legal control tests and represents the anti-avoidance measure (substance over form) which cross-checks the legal and economic facts and circumstances and recognizes the substance. The analysis under the de-facto control test should verify who exercises or influences the control over the company by examining the concrete circumstances and facts on a case-by-case basis. Thereby, the de-facto control test should confirm or exclude the existence of control or controlling influence even if the economic and legal control tests would not be recognized or match the qualifying control threshold for the CFC. This kind of test brings an uncertainty for taxpayers and tax authorities from the practical application point of view.[19]

The last of the four types of control tests is based on IFRS consolidation.[20] The IFRS consolidates the accounting data of a group of companies worldwide based on shares and voting rights. The company's statements include information about interests in other entities. The group's consolidated statements start at the level of a parent company and contain the data of all subsidiaries of the parent company classified for consolidation. If a company needs to apply the IFRS and is part of the consolidated statements of the group, there must be some level of legal or economic control. A group can change the IFRS scope as desired by adjusting the legal or economic control.[21] In this respect, it should be borne in mind that consolidation is mandatory only for publicly traded companies but optionally useful for other companies.[22]

The OECD recommends applying at least a two-level control test as a minimum standard by incorporating the legal and economic control tests. These two tests are mechanical and easy to follow for the tax authority and the taxpayers. Therefore, they bring the least administrative burden, but they are also easy to circumvent. Thus, the OECD suggests the incorporation of the three-level control test as a best practice.[23] The best practice three-level control test complements the minimum standard by the de-facto test. The de-facto control test is advisable as it creates an anti-avoidance component of the minimum standard test. It is based on a

---

19 Brian J. Arnold, The Evolution of Controlled Foreign Corporation Rules and Beyond, (IBFD, Bulletin for International Taxation, 12/2019), p. 6.
20 *OECD (2015), Designing Effective Controlled Foreign Company Rules, Action 3 – 2015 Final Report, OECD/G20 Base Erosion and Profit Shifting Project, OECD Publishing, Paris. P. 24–25,* http://dx.doi.org/10.1787/9789264241152-en.
21 *The IFRS annual report is subject of an independent audit which should ensure conformity to reality. However, the history showed that, sometimes, the audit is not independent, e.g. the well-known Enron scandal in 2001 allowed by the advisory company Arthur Andersen which ended the existence of this advisory company (audit and accountancy) and changed the big five group of advisory companies into the actual big four group.*
22 Regulation (EC) No 1606/2002 of the European Parliament and of the Council of 19 July 2002 on the application of international accounting standards, Official Journal of the European Communities, Article 4.
23 According to the Cambridge Dictionary, best practice means a working method or set of working methods that are officially accepted as being the best to use in a particular business or industry.

complex case-by-case analysis; therefore, it is administratively and provably challenging for the tax authority as well as for the taxpayers.

In connection to the control test, a question arises of how the control test should be applied in time. The controlling entity could change during the monitoring period often, and it is desirable since the controlling entity decides whether to change. This might lead to opportunities for tax planning. The OECD Report determined the relevant point in time only indirectly. The OECD dealt with this question in Action 3 by describing rules for the attribution of income, and the question was the subject of the discussion in the Public Discussion draft to BEPS Action 3 by the question of how much CFC income should be attributed to the shareholder.[24] The issue was the fairness of attribution of the whole CFC income at the end of the year to the "end year" shareholder if the ownership lasted only a portion of the year. The final recommendation of the OECD is the calculation based on the duration of ownership/influence during the year calculated at the end of the year.[25] Such an approach shows that the control is examined during the year, and the tax authority, according to the approach of OECD, should not rely on the controlling ownership at the end of the year. However, it is up to each country whether it will follow the OECD recommendation or sets a different rule for the ownership examination time point.

2.2. The level of control

When the type of control is determined, the next step is to identify if and who can exercise the control or influence. This should be represented by the qualifying threshold of control for being a CFC. The controlling influence is represented by the execution of the entity's strategic decisions rather than the day-to-day decisions about the CFC's activities.[26] In this respect, the recommendation of the OECD and the EU's ATAD sets the threshold at the level of more than 50% of the control.[27, 28] In general, only the control at a level of more than 50% allows the shareholder to exercise absolute control over a company, e.g., the shareholder could alone decide how much and when the profit of the CFC is distributed. The

---

24 OECD (2015), Public Discussion Draft BEPS ACTION 3: STRENGTHENING CFC RULES, p. 55-60.
25 OECD (2015), Designing Effective Controlled Foreign Company Rules, Action 3 – 2015 Final Report, OECD/G20 Base Erosion and Profit Shifting Project, OECD Publishing, Paris. P. 61–62, http://dx.doi.org/10.1787/9789264241152-en.
26 OECD (2015), Designing Effective Controlled Foreign Company Rules, Action 3 – 2015 Final Report, OECD/G20 Base Erosion and Profit Shifting Project, OECD Publishing, Paris. P. 24, http://dx.doi.org/10.1787/9789264241152-en.
27 OECD (2015), Designing Effective Controlled Foreign Company Rules, Action 3 – 2015 Final Report, OECD/G20 Base Erosion and Profit Shifting Project, OECD Publishing, Paris. P. 25, http://dx.doi.org/10.1787/9789264241152-en.
28 Council Directive (EU) 2016/1164 of 12 July2016 laying down rules against tax avoidance practices that directly affect the functioning of the internal market, OJ L 193 (19 July 2016) p. 11 (Article 7 Controlled foreign company rule).

shareholder might try to circumvent the threshold of 50% by fragmentation of ownership to more than one company in different jurisdictions. To prevent such fragmentation circumvention, the direct and indirect shares are an object of verification according to local legislation. However, countries could differ in applying the control test to the direct and/or indirect ownership.

A shareholder with a level of control lower than 50% represents a minority shareholder who cannot exercise the control without the alliance with another shareholder. Despite the OECD's recommendation, countries might set a lower percentage than recommended by the OECD or EU as a stricter rule to achieve the CFC threshold, so-called gold-plating (country goes over the minimum standard). As a result of the lower percentage, a minority shareholder could qualify as a CFC. In fact, under certain conditions a lower percentage of control also enables the company to control. Control exercised by minority shareholders is demonstrated on the figures below.

In the Final Report, the OECD indicates three ways to verify the level of control of non-majority shareholders.[29] The first way uses the acting-in-concert concept, which targets minority shareholders that are related parties situated in different jurisdictions. It prompts the parent company to split the subsidiary shares into two or more related companies placed in different jurisdictions. Thereby, the threshold in one of the other jurisdictions is not met. If the jurisdictions apply "acting-in-concert with a related party", it would aggregate the interest of related parties to meet the control threshold.

---

29 OECD (2015), *Designing Effective Controlled Foreign Company Rules, Action 3 – 2015 Final Report*, OECD/G20 Base Erosion and Profit Shifting Project, OECD Publishing, Paris. P. 9–10, http://dx.doi.org/10.1787/9789264241152-en.

2.2.1. Figure 3: Concentrated ownership requirement (acting-in-concert concept, related parties)

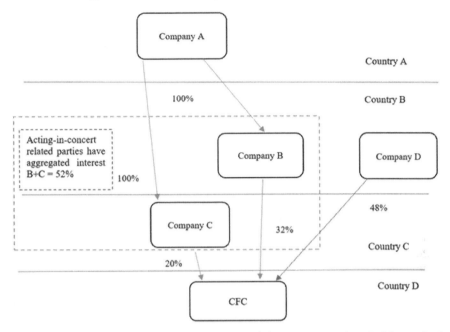

Figure 3 above demonstrates the structure of the minority shareholders which might create a situation in practice that enables related minority shareholders to exercise control. No shareholder has a CFC's controlling share in country D, i.e., there is no more than 50% interest in the CFC in country D. Thus, there is no company with a controlling share of its CFC in country D. However, it shows that company A owns 100% of companies B and C. Country B applies the related party or resident acting-in-concert rule. Hence, company B in country B will undergo the acting-in-concert test. Companies B and C are owned by the same shareholder. The CFC controlling threshold is deemed to be met. This rule is established to circumvent situations when interest is artificially split into separate companies located in different jurisdictions to avoid reaching the CFC controlling threshold. In country B, the CFC's income of 32% will be attributed to company B. Basically, the acting-in-concert test is a process of searching for controlling interest by aggregating interests of related parties. The income is attributed at 32% real interest in the CFC in order to avoid double taxation of the CFC's income in case country C applied the acting-in-concert criterion as well (avoidance of an over-attribution of income).

The second way to prove the control exercised by minority shareholders is similar to the first one, but it examines the control of unrelated parties acting conjointly to exert influence. Even if none of the shareholders has a controlling share of the CFC, by acting-in-concert (i.e. coordinating their actions, the controlling interest or influence might be exercised. In such a situation, the acting-in-concert test may apply. The interest of all the shareholders who coordinate their actions will be aggregated, and their control limited considering the jurisdiction legislation. This test's negative aspect is the demand for proof and analyses, especially if these unrelated parties are residents in different jurisdictions. The acting-in-concert by unrelated parties is demonstrated in Figure 4 below. To prove acting-in-concert with an unrelated party, we need a fact–based analysis.

2.2.2. Figure 4: Acting-in-concert concept (unrelated parties)

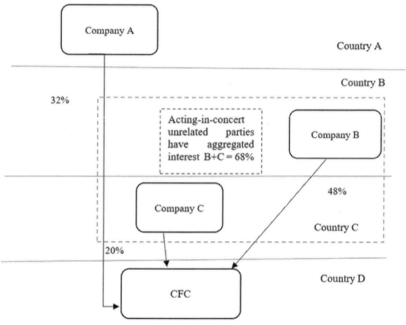

The last, third way, is searching for the concentration of ownership. The shares of the related and unrelated parties in the subsidiary aggregate together unless a defined threshold is met. The concentration covers only shareholders residing in the same jurisdiction. In some countries, this provision applies only to residents with ownership from a certain threshold, e.g., the shares of residents are aggregate if the shareholder holds at least 1% or more of shares. In China, the limited threshold for CFC rules includes the situation in which the individual Chinese resident holds directly or indirectly more than 10% and, jointly, the residents have more than 50% of control over the CFC.[30]

---

30   Michael Lang and col., *Controlled Foreign Company Legislation*, (IBFD, 2020), p. 157–159.

For the application of the CFC legislation within the EU, it is important to keep in mind that, besides the control test, the secondary, no less critical test must be met: the activity in the state of subsidiary location is not real economic activity created solely to benefit from the lower tax rate or special tax regime.[31] Nevertheless, another way around it, the CFC legislation could not apply if the control test is passed even if the subsidiary fulfils the genuine economic activity criterion (the subsidiary has the substance). It creates the interaction between the control concept and the genuine economic activity test.[32] When we are in a third country situation, the genuine economic activity test does not play a role. The ECJ case law introduced this genuine economic activity test. The case law is relevant for the EU Member States because it provides the uniform interpretation of European law, and ECJ concerns the compatibility of the national legislation of the concrete country with EU law.[33]

The CFC legislation's breakthrough was the decision of the ECJ in the Cadbury Schweppes case in 2006 (C-196/04) examining the compliance of the United Kingdom's CFC regulation with EU law. The result was that CFC legislation as such harms the freedom of establishment. The reasoning of the ECJ's decision was based on the primary motive that CFC legislation was introduced to be a counteraction of tax avoidance; therefore, the country legislation must, in order to be justified, target the concrete situation not only the general terms such as the level and type of control and the low tax rate in the subsidiary jurisdiction. Besides examining the control concept, this decision introduced a further criterion for successful justification, i.e. the necessity of the examination of the real economic activity test on the subsidiary side but only if the CFC situation is placed in the EU area. The domestic legislation of the EU Member State has to comply with EU law and target only wholly artificial arrangements. After the Cadbury Schweppes judgment, many Member States changed their national legislation (such as Sweden, Spain, France, and Germany).[34]

2.3. The exemptions

The practical application of the CFC rules comprising the control test and level of control test is mainly complex, demanding analyses and research, and countries may even establish their own hybrid rules that combine different options of the OECD's CFC recommendations. The answer to why CFCs differ among coun-

---

31 Council Directive (EU) 2016/1164 of 12 July2016 laying down rules against tax avoidance practices that directly affect the functioning of the internal market, OJ L 193 (19 July 2016) p. 12 (Article 7 Controlled foreign company rule, para 2 a)).
32 Sebastian Duenas, CFC Rules Around the World, Fiscal Fact, No. 659, Jun 2019, p. 15.
33 FREEDOM OF ESTABLISHMENT, GUIDE TO THE CASE LAW Of the European Court of Justice on Articles 49 et seq. TFEU, European Commission, Ref. Ares (2017) 1839123-06/04/2017, p. 2.
34 Anders Köhlmark, New CFC Legislation in Sweden, International Bureau of Fiscal Documentation (2004), p. 225 – 232 and Sebastian Duenas, CFC Rules Around the World, Fiscal Fact, No. 659, Jun 2019.

tries is that each country defines the domestic CFC policy to target the relevant companies and individuals specifically for the domestic situation. The domestic policy sets the local CFC criterion based on evaluating the existing risks of losing revenues by profit shifting and base erosion and, at the same time, the country wants to keep the attractivity for foreign investors. It is an alchemy to balance both goals. Based on the resulting risk, the exemptions and threshold requirements are established. In fact, exemptions and threshold requirements define transactions out of the scope of local CFC legislation.

The OECD exemption recommendations result from conclusions agreed by countries participating in the Final Report.[35] In this respect, the final report mentioned three types of exemptions and threshold requirements.[36] The first type of exemption is the "De minimis threshold" covering companies with a low or insignificant risk of profit shifting and base erosion for the country. The limited threshold amount defines the exemption as a fixed amount or a certain percentage of attributable income. According to the minimal threshold, the country is interested in the potential CFC income if the amount or/and percentage of income is met; otherwise, the income falls out of the domestic CFC scope. In case the country decides to apply the fixed amount threshold combined with the percentage limitation, the exemption may be defined as an exemption of an attributable income representing less than 5% of the gross income of the CFC but maximum EUR 100,000 in total. To read more about this topic, see the part CFC threshold requirements and exemptions of this publication.

Combined exemption de minimis test fixed amount plus %	EUR	EUR
gross income of a CFC	1 500 000	2 500 000
attributable income to the shareholder	60 000	150 000
5% from the gross income	75 000	125 000
exemption max. EUR 100,000	100 000	100 000
exemption applicable	yes	no

---

35   OECD (2015), Designing Effective Controlled Foreign Company Rules, Action 3 – 2015 Final Report, OECD/G20 Base Erosion and Profit Shifting Project, OECD Publishing, Paris. P. 9–10, http://dx.doi.org/10.1787/9789264241152-en.
36   Final report OECD page 33.
   1. A set de minimis amount below which the CFC rules would not apply.
   2. An anti-avoidance requirement that would focus CFC rules on situations with a tax avoidance motive or purpose.
   3. A tax rate exemption where CFC rules would only apply to CFCs residents in countries with a lower tax rate than the parent company.

Thus, if the de minimis threshold is set to the small investments abroad, they are thereby excluded from the CFC scope. The de minimis threshold is used, for example, by Australia, Canada, China, Germany, Spain, the United States, and Chile. On the contrary, Belgium does not apply this rule. The de minimis threshold is a mechanical test that is quite simple and easy to apply by a country and therefore causes a smaller administrative burden.[37]

The second test recommended by the OECD is to add additional requirements in the form of an anti-avoidance measure based on motive or purpose testing to strengthen the mechanical test representing the de minimis test. Anti-avoidance requirements are based on an individual case-by-case analysis. Whenever a mechanical test is passed, the anti-avoidance measure may help avoid applying for the exemption if anti-avoidance criteria are met.[38] Countries mostly add a principal purpose test or an anti-fragmentation rule to the mechanical test. In case the anti-avoidance measures are in question, the burden to prove the existence of avoidance is carried over to the country. On the contrary, if a shareholder wants to use a mechanical exemption, the burden of proof is on the shareholder (must prove his right for applying for exemption from CFC legislation). Some countries introduced CFC legislation instead of covering taxpayers' circumventing transactions by anti-avoidance measures to prevent the carry-over of the burden of proof from the taxpayer to the country (no CFC). For instance, while considering the introduction of CFC rules for individuals, Slovakia could have covered the individuals by general anti-avoidance rules rather than introducing the CFC for individuals. To prevent the carry-over of the burden of proof from the taxpayer to the country, the CFC rules for individuals were established (such a position is more favourable for the country). Once the anti-avoidance measures are invoked, it often ends with a long-lasting dispute between the tax authority and the taxpayer with questionable success. Therefore, countries try to target the use of CFCs precisely and clearly to be easy to prove.

The third type of exemption is based on the tax rate above a certain level (i.e. tax rate benchmark). The CFC rules target entities that benefit from a low foreign tax rate. The parent country's tax rate benchmark is compared to the CFC's jurisdiction's nominal or effective tax rate. If the tax rate in the CFC location is lower than the tax rate benchmark due to this fact, the income of the CFC is not exempt

---

37 Michael Lang and col., *Controlled Foreign Company Legislation*, (IBFD, 2020).
38 According to the HMRC internal manual published 9 April 2016 and updated on 17 July 2020, the United Kingdom applies the motive test:
 A controlled foreign company satisfies the motive test for an accounting period if it meets both of the following conditions:
  - *when a transaction (or transactions) reflected in the company's profits in the accounting period has or have achieved a reduction in United Kingdom tax, either the reduction was minimal, it was not the main purpose, or one of the main purposes of the transaction(s) to achieve that reduction; and*
  - *it was not the main reason or one of the main reasons for the company's existence in that period to achieve a reduction in UK tax by a diversion of profits from the United Kingdom.*

according to the parent jurisdiction. This exemption encourages tax planning in countries with a medium tax rate. The easiest way to distinguish countries that fall into the category of a high-tax or low-tax jurisdiction is to compile a list of low-tax jurisdictions (i.e. black list) and a high- and medium-tax jurisdictions (i.e. white list). Such lists should be understood as statements of how the parent jurisdiction examines the foreign jurisdictions and should bring legal certainty for the taxpayer. Regardless, the use of the black and/or white list should be joined with an additional condition of a specific type of income or activities.

2.4. Future replacement of the CFC by CCCTB

The European Commission introduced the idea of a Common Consolidated Corporate Tax Base (CCCTB) in the Proposal for a Council directive on a CCCTB.[39] Under the proposal, the CCCTB would be mandatory for the groups of companies of substantial size set based on the total consolidated revenue as evidenced in the consolidated financial statements.[40] The directive is aimed at companies established under the laws of a EU Member State that have one or more subsidiaries. To read more about the CCCTB, see part CFC rules and CCCTB of this publication.

The concept of the CCCTB should replace the CFC legislation on relations between group members of the European Union under the condition that EU countries agree on the concept in the future. The CFC legislation will still be valid in a situation between an EU country and a third country. To apply the consolidated group tax base, the control concept is defined which sets the control test identifying the subsidiary and, therefore, the group of companies could be taxed together. The parent company has a qualifying subsidiary in the case of a direct share if:

i) The extent of control > 50% of voting rights (i.e. legal view of control) and
ii) The extent of ownership > 75% of equity or rights to profits > 75% (entitlement to profit) (i.e. combination of economic view of control).

By examining the indirect control (indirect share) of a subsidiary, the calculation is adjusted by ascertaining the indirect share. If the qualified subsidiary fulfils the percentage, it is automatically assumed that the indirect subsidiary satisfied the criterion (by 100%). In order to calculate the criterion, the control is estimated by multiplying the subsidiary's direct and indirect interest at each tier. There is no possibility to adjust the percentage to the needs of the country. Compared to the OECD CFC recommendation and the ATAD, these criteria for control recogni-

---

39 European Commission, Proposal for a COUNCIL DIRECTIVE on a Common Consolidated Corporate Tax Base (CCCTB), Strasbourg, 25.10.2016, COM(2016) 683 final, 2016/0336 (CNS).
40 The threshold is set on the level of consolidated group revenue exceeding EUR 750 000 000 (verified for the last financial year).

tion are stricter as subsidiaries are included in the consolidated tax base if the legal control is more than 50% and economic control is more than 75% at the same time. The OECD recommendation is more than 50% for each type of control, and qualifying is the achievement of one or another type of control. The CCCTB favours that the taxpayer to qualify for the threshold because the taxpayer (parent company) wants to consolidate the tax base (losses and profits are offset in the consolidated tax base). In the case of the CFC rules, taxpayers tried to prevent or circumvent to qualify for the CFC rules because the unrealized profits from a CFC are taxed at the parent company level.[41]

To summarize the second chapter, the mechanical tests (such as legal or economic control, tax rate exemption, or de minimis threshold) are easy to apply by countries and create a smaller administrative burden, but these tests are also easy to circumvent by taxpayers. By contrast, the de facto control test or additional anti-avoidance measures are proof demanding tests on the countries side and therefore bring an administrative burden. The burden of proof of the taxpayer's anti-avoidance behaviour is carried over to the country, mostly resulting in disputes or law suits running for years. Contrary, if the taxpayer wants to benefit from tax legislation, the burden of proof is on the taxpayer's side to submit the proof if the right is put into question. To achieve the best results from CFC legislation, usually mechanical and anti-avoidance tests are combined. Thus, if the mechanical test is passed, the anti-avoidance test takes its place. The CFC rules based on the anti-avoidance measures should be applied after the complex assessments of relevant circumstances. To find the balance between the CFC's rules' effectiveness (control test, exemption, administrative burden) and to remain attractive for the foreign investors is alchemy. The CFC legislation application differs if the subsidiary and the parent company are placed in the EU or if there is a third country included. In the EU situation, there is an interaction between the control concept and the genuine economic activity test, and the CFC legislation applies only if, in the situation at hand, a wholly artificial structure is identified.

According to the document "Communication on Business Taxation for the 21st century"[42] published by the European Commission in May 2021 the future of the CFC rules might differ from the outline described in this Chapter.

---

41 European Commission, Proposal for a COUNCIL DIRECTIVE on a Common Consolidated Corporate Tax Base (CCCTB), Strasbourg, 25.10.2016, COM(2016) 683 final, 2016/0336 (CNS), p. 22–23 and European Commission, Commission Staff Working Document Impact Assessment Accompanying the document Proposal for a Council Directive on a Common Corporate Tax Base and a Common Consolidated Corporate Tax Base (CCCTB), Strasbourg, 25.10.2016, SWD (2016) 341 final, p. 95.

42 European Commission, Communication from the Commission to the European Parliament and the Council, Bussiness Taxation for the 21st Century, COM(2021) 251 final, Brussels, 18.5.2021. communication_on_business_taxation_for_the_21st_century.pdf (europa.eu)

3. Different control threshold between CFC legislation for corporate entities and individuals

Countries worldwide apply CFC rules mainly to corporate entities, but some countries also introduced the CFC rules for individuals (e.g., Germany, Slovakia, Israel, Italy). This chapter will describe different approaches to the control concept related to corporate entities and individuals. Then, the different approaches will be demonstrated on the country example.

The OECD's Action 3: 2015 Final Report recommends the classifying threshold for exercising control at the level of more than 50% whereby as covered residents are included corporate entities, individuals, or others, exercising control.[43] Thus, the OECD does not differ between individuals and corporate entities by establishing the CFC recommendations. The ATAD initiative of the EU does not force EU Member States to introduce CFC rules for individuals. Thus, if the concrete country introduced the CFC for individuals in addition to the CFC rules for corporate entities, this decision might result from the economic reasons of a concrete country, e.g. no parent companies are located in the country, and the business in the country is done by oligarchs. For such a country, the CFC rules for individuals make more sense than the CFC for corporate entities.[44]

By applying CFC rules for corporate entities, countries followed the OECD and the ATAD recommendations and incorporated the standard threshold of control at a level of more than 25% or 50%. A lower threshold was incorporated only exceptionally (e.g., Russian Federation, Sweden). Although the opposite situation appears if we talk about the CFC rules for individuals. For individuals, the control's qualifying threshold starts at the level of more than 10% and is mostly below 50%. Countries established rules that are more rigid more rigid rules and an easier to achieve qualifying threshold of control for individuals than for corporate entities. The CFC rules for individuals can negatively influence minority investors. The rules can deter them because they could be taxed on the CFC income even if they cannot influence the CFC activity and did not receive dividends. This low threshold results in a compliance burden and uncertainty for the sharehold-

---

43 OECD (2015), *Designing Effective Controlled Foreign Company Rules, Action 3 – 2015 Final Report*, OECD/G20 Base Erosion and Profit Shifting Project, OECD Publishing, Paris. P. 21, http://dx.doi.org/10.1787/9789264241152-en.

44 Some European countries believe that the anti-abuse measures cover individuals, and it is unnecessary to implement special CFC rules on top of them. In light of this idea and the ATAD, Hungary does not apply CFC legislation for the natural persons any longer, but a GAAR might track the CFC revenues. The difference between the CFC legislation (applicable inside of the EU or EEA) and a GAAR is that the CFC needs to be self-reported. It obligates the taxpayer to self-report the CFC and to compute the tax base according to the rules set by the domestic law whereby, with a GAAR, it is up to the responsible tax authority to identify the CFC and the artificial structure (it is necessary to prove the artificial structure) and tax it accordingly. From my perspective, it is easier for the tax authority to implement and use the CFC legislation.

ers. It is questionable if the shareholder can exercise any control over the subsidiary at such a low level. Such a low level of control applied by the EU Member State may implicate not just the freedom of establishment but the free movement of capital as well. The main distinguishing criterion between freedom of establishment and free movement of capital is the ability to exercise control. The harm of the free movement of capital only arises when the threshold is reduced below the "significant influence" level.[45] If the shareholder can exercise control, the freedom of establishment is at stake, and if the shareholder cannot exercise the control, the free movement of capital is at stake. To distinguish between the ability of a shareholder to exercise control and therefore have a significant influence (according to the ECJ, the "significant influence" is called "exert a definite influence" on the company) and the acquisition of shares solely with the intention of financial investment without obtaining a significant influence is clarified in ECJ case C-35/11 (13.11.2012).[46] When the shareholder holds a lower percentage of interest in the company than 50%, the free movement of capital is harmed. The ECJ clarified in another case, C-135/17 (26.2.2019),[47] when the restriction on the free movement of capital is justified by overriding reasons in the public interest only. In this case, countries participating justified it because of safeguarding the balanced allocation of the power to impose taxes between Member states and third countries, preventing tax evasion and avoidance.[48] The court went back to the Cadbury Schweppes case and referred to the matter of wholly artificial arrangements. The ECJ concludes that the CFC rules' application in cases in which the shareholder holds shares at least 1% of its shares is justified if it might result from an artificial scheme. To read more about ECJ case law, see the part CFC rules of the Anti-Tax Avoidance Directive in light of the EU fundamental freedoms of this publication.

3.1. CFC rules for individuals in Slovak Republic

According to the ATAD, the Slovak Republic introduced CFC legislation in 2018.[49] Even if the first draft wording of the legislation concerning the effectiveness of CFC rules included regulating both individuals and corporate entities, the law's effective wording touched only the corporations. The CFC rules for the corporate entities are effective since 1 January 2019.

A CFC is a company or a subject with its seat abroad if a tax resident of the Slovak Republic owns alone or together with the related subject (using the same terms as

---

45 OECD (2015), Designing Effective Controlled Foreign Company Rules, Action 3 – 2015 Final Report, OECD/G20 Base Erosion and Profit Shifting Project, OECD Publishing, Paris. P. 30, http://dx.doi.org/10.1787/9789264241152-en.
46 C-35/11 (13.11.2012) in the Test Claimants in the FII Group Litigation v Commissioners of Inland Revenue.
47 C-135/17 (26.02.2019) in the X GmbH v Finanzamt Stuttgart – Körperschaften.
48 Point 71 of the ECJ case C-135/17 (26.2.2019).
49 The rules for the controlled foreign companies are part of the Act No. 595/2003 on Income.

for transfer pricing) directly or indirectly more than 50% in the registered capital, voting rights, or right on a share in profits of this company or subject. At the same time, the tax due that is paid by the CFC abroad is lower than the difference between the corporate income tax of the CFC that is computed according to the relevant section of the Slovak ITA and the tax paid by the CFC abroad, i.e., the difference between the tax due abroad and the tax computed under the Slovak ITA is more than 50%. The same rule would be set for a permanent establishment abroad of the Slovak resident. The CFC legislation for corporate entities uses the transactional approach. The controlling company's taxable income will include revenues of the CFC that are raised by one or more partially or wholly artificial arrangements set to achieve a tax advantage.[50]

The Slovak Republic is a small country where subsidiaries prevail over the parent companies; thus, it is unlikely that an MNE parent company could be set up in Slovakia. For the timing of this legislation to be useful, it must cover natural persons as well due to the prevailing oligarchs' business structures. The CFC legislation for individuals should capture structures where oligarchs cover their business by holding companies situated in low tax jurisdictions. The newly introduced concept goes over the minimum standard proposed by OECD and the EU, i.e., gold-plating. After introducing the CFC legislation for individuals, it showed up that it hits a broader scale of individuals. The main concerns evoked the qualifying control threshold set at the level of more than 10% in CFC (direct or indirect share in capital, voting rights or profit, or exerting real control).[51] The exemption was designed to excuse the minority investor with income no more than EUR 100,000 or if the effective taxation is more than 10%. All affected individuals tried to change the control level to the general level of more than 50%, e.g. some investors investing in start-ups abroad were afraid of the effect of the 10% control on start-ups that normally generate losses in the first years of their activities. In the end, the compromise that was achieved was an additional condition that the CFC will apply only in the case of an artificial structure (no real business, no substance) and postponing of the effectiveness of the legislation for one year.

The response of the Slovakian individuals who will be affected by the CFC rules for individuals in 2022 is the consideration of changing their residency to the country where the CFC rules do not apply to individuals.[52] They declivitous some of the neighbouring countries of Slovakia (i.e. Czech republic, Hungary, Poland). The country must be the Member State of the EU. As a result of the new CFC leg-

---

50   The explanation of the term "artificial" is based on the transfer pricing principle, and artificial arrangement covers the arrangement that the CFC would not perform if it would not be controlled by the resident company that performs the significant functions bounded with the CFC assets.
51   JUDr. Ing. Miriam Galandová, Ph.D., LL.M., FCIArb., Nové CFC pravidlá pre fyzické osoby, Bulletin Slovenskej komory daňových poradcov (1/2021), p. 6–12.
52   Information is based on personal communication with the four richest residents in Slovakia who will be affected by the CFC rules for individuals.

islation, the individuals scrutinized their existing structures of conducting business, and they realised that it does not work any longer along with the CFC for individuals. They are afraid that the pure holding structures would not fulfil the real activity exemption provided by the Slovakia legislation. With the 10% qualifying controlling threshold for the CFC for individuals (low threshold), the state chooses the strategy "all or nothing" which can lead to losing of the richest residents of Slovakia by changing their residency and their future investments at the same time. These affected individuals are doing business, making investments, and creating jobs in Slovakia.

4. Conclusion

This master thesis concludes that the CFC legislation analysis' general result is the diversity of the CFC rule application, including the diversity of the control concept. The prevailing type of control test is legal control supplemented by economic control (both are mechanical tests), and the level of control is mostly set at the level of more than 50%. Thanks to this level, the ability to exercise control or influence is more than expected. Countries apply the CFC regulation for the corporate entities, and few countries also included natural persons.

The most significant difference in the percentage for setting the control level is between the corporate entities and the natural persons. The threshold for natural persons is much lower, beginning at the level of 10%. Such a low level of qualifying control can jeopardize the free movement of capital, deter investment abroad, and bring a compliance burden for individuals. Any qualifying level of control set below 50% raises the question of whether the shareholder can exercise control over the subsidiary and, even if so, they can only exercise limited control over the subsidiary.

The ECJ justified the application of the low threshold for qualifying control for having a CFC by overriding reasons in the public interest only and under the possible artificial scheme because, in other situations, for example, a portfolio investment, the minority investor cannot exercise the control or influence the decisions of the CFC. The CFC legislation's breakthrough was the decision of the ECJ in the case of Cadbury Schweppes in 2006, examining the fulfilment of the CFC regulation within EU law. The result was that a CFC, as such, harms the freedom of establishment (when the control threshold is more than 50%), which is important and forced upon the EU countries to incorporate the real economic activity rule along with the control demands. Since the control is in the CFC, and the CFC generates profit due to the local management's decisions, the profit could not be attributed to the shareholder before it is distributed based on the level of ownership. The CFC can reinvest profit into the CFC and not distribute it to the shareholder (as the permanent status).

Lastly, the CFC legislation might be substituted by a GAAR. Understandably, countries choose the CFC because the activity is carried over to the shareholder. Thanks to the set rules defined by the CFC legislation, such as the definition of a CFC, the level of control, type of control, exemptions, and the process of computation of the tax base is tax self-reported, computed and paid "willingly" by the taxpayer (shareholder). In contrast, the GAAR expects the action on the side of the responsible tax authority to this mechanism. I believe it is favourable from the country's perspective to incorporate the CFC rules for corporate entities and individuals along with the GAAR. However, by setting the thresholds of control, exemptions, tax rate, and doing the control test, the CFC legislation aims to avoid base erosion and profit shifting. Setting any qualifying control level or type of control should not go beyond the aim of the primary purpose of the legislation and bring a bigger compliance burden, uncertainty for the taxpayer, and determent of investments for the country.

Regarding the Slovak CFC legislation for individuals' certain issues, such as what it might bring or take from Slovakia, have been brought up. On one hand, the legislation undoubtedly hits the nail on the head because the affected individuals tested their holding structures and realised that it does not work with CFC for individuals any longer. On the other hand, the state chose the "all or nothing" strategy which can cause losing some of the richest Slovak residents and the future investments at the same time. The legislation is being discussed for the second time before it enters into force on 1 January 2022. Whether the income for the national budget has increased or lost investments should be evident by the end of 2023.

The definition of CFC income

Peter Van Rompaey

1. **General introduction**
2. **OECD BEPS Approach**
   2.1. General introduction
   2.2. Defining the CFC income
   2.3. Categorical analysis
      2.3.1. Legal classification
      2.3.2. Relatedness of parties
      2.3.3. Source of income
      2.3.4. Policy considerations
   2.4. Substance analysis
   2.5. Excess profit analysis
   2.6. Application of the income on a transactional or an entity basis
      2.6.1. Entity approach
      2.6.2. Transactional approach
3. **Practice Implementation into Domestic Law**
   3.1. CFC legislation in Belgium
      3.1.1. General description of the CFC rules
      3.1.2. Definition CFC income
   3.2. CFC legislation in China
      3.2.1. General description of the CFC rules
      3.2.2. Definition CFC income
   3.3. CFC legislation in US
      3.3.1. General description of the CFC rules
      3.3.2. Definition CFC income
4. **Comparison Different Approaches: Practical Case**
   4.1. Facts of the case
   4.2. CFC treatment in Belgium
   4.3. CFC treatment in China
   4.4. CFC treatment in US
   4.5. Comparison of the different approaches
5. **Conclusion**

The definition of CFC income

1. General introduction

Controlled Foreign Company or CFC (hereafter CFC) rules are relatively new in the history of taxes. In 1962, the United States of America (US) was the first country to enact CFC rules. The main purpose was to gather information about US companies overseas and to track foreign tax credits.[1] The Tax Cuts and Jobs Act of 2017 implemented new rules that further curbed deferral and effectively expanded the scope of US worldwide taxation.[2] Essentially, CFC rules aim to prevent individuals and corporations of stashing funds in CFCs to avoid domestic taxation.[3]

CFC rules also aim to end possible tax abuse schemes. MNEs (Multinational Enterprise) are shifting profits from high tax jurisdictions to low tax jurisdictions. For example, CFC in low tax jurisdictions generate revenues from transactions with group companies outside the home State of the CFC. The CFC income in principle requires little or no substance in the State of residence. As long as the CFC does not distribute profits to the shareholders, a tax deferral can be realized. However, avoiding such deferral can be reached by CFC legislation and undistributed profits become taxable.[4] CFC rules draw the line between deferral and no deferral for countries with a tax system on a worldwide basis.[5] For countries with a territorial tax system, it will be the difference between inclusion or exemption.[6] If a foreign company can be considered as a CFC, the income will be included in the taxable profit of the shareholder. If the conditions for a CFC taxation are not met, the foreign income will be exempt for the shareholder. These two different trajectories will encourage countries to take different conflicting CFC legislation approaches.[7]

Policy considerations will be important in order to understand the choices States make for their CFC legislation.[8] Tax systems, which are based upon a worldwide tax system, will normally use a broad application of CFC rules. A broad application remains, in this case, being consistent with the overall tax system of the Parent jurisdiction with priority given to the taxation of foreign income. States with a territorial system of taxation will normally apply CFC rules in a narrower manner.

---

1 Sebastian Duenas, 'CFC Rules Around the World', *Fiscal Fact Tax Foundation* (2019) No. 659, p. 3.
2 Yariv Brauner/Christine A. Davis, 'Controlled Foreign Company Legislation in the United States' in Georg Kofler, Michael Lang, Jeffrey Owens, Pasquale Pistone, Alexander Rust, Josef Schuch, Karoline Spies, Claus Staringer (eds.) *Controlled Foreign Company Legislation* (Amsterdam: IBFD, 2020) p. 625.
3 Brian J. Arnold, 'OECD/International – The Evolution of Controlled Foreign Corporation Rules and Beyond', *Bulletin for International Taxation* (2019) No. 12, p. 11.
4 Luc De Broe, 'De invoering van CFC-wetgeving in het WIB 1992, Een praktische benadering van een overbodige bepaling opgelegd door Europa', *Algemeen Fiscaal Tijdschrift* (2019) No. 4, p. 7.
5 In a pure worldwide tax system, residents are taxable on their worldwide income regardless of where the income is derived.
6 In a pure territorial tax system, the country taxes only income derived within its borders, irrespective of the residence of the taxpayer.
7 M.A. Kane, 'The Role of Controlled Foreign Company Legislation in the OECD Base Erosion and Profit Shifting Project', *Bulletin for International Taxation* (2014), No 6/7, p. 326.
8 R.G. Bader, *CFC legislation in the European Union and the alternative CSC concept* (Tilburg University, 2012) p. 213.

These States will in principle tax income that is clearly diverted from the Parent State, with giving priority to competitiveness.[9, 10]

The result is that countries will base their CFC rules on different income definitions. Certain countries will use a stricter definition of income categories, other countries a more comprehensive definition. The result is the implementation of extremely complex CFC legislation, whereby a general answer to a CFC question is not possible: different domestic systems must be analysed before a position can be taken.

This Master's thesis analyses the definition of CFC income. We will describe the different definitions of the CFC concepts. This Master's thesis aims to answer the research question: how have different countries implemented different methods into their domestic system to determine the CFC income? We will analyze whether the use of these different methods will lead to different results in taxation; that is, have a lower or higher taxation rate.

In Section 2, we will analyze the Organisation for Economic Co-operation and Development (OECD) approach in the Base Erosion and Profit Shifting (BEPS) Action Plan 3. In Section 3, we will describe the implementation of CFC rules into domestic law of the following countries: Belgium, China and US. These countries were chosen based upon the criteria of different approaches (passive/active income – transactional or entity based) and different regions (European Union and non- European Union). Section 4 includes a practical case to clarify the different approaches. The purpose is to demonstrate how the choice for a specific approach can lead to a different outcome. Finally, we will summarize our conclusions in Section 5.

2. OECD BEPS Approach

2.1. General introduction

The OECD dedicated a separate Action Plan to the CFC rules as the organization believes that CFC rules can avoid profit shifting opportunities and long-term deferral of taxation. The OECD failed in imposing one global standard, which could be implemented for this Action Plan.[11] Contrary to such a standardized approach, the OECD offered recommendations in the form of the following building blocks:

---

9   M. Lang, *Introduction to the Law of Double Taxation Conventions* (Vienna: Linde, 2013) p. 27–30; OECD (2015), *Designing Effective CFC Rules, Action 3 – 2015 Final Report*, OECD/G20 Base Erosion and Profit Shifting Project, OECD Publishing, No. 13, p. 15.
10 OECD (2015), *Designing Effective CFC Rules, Action 3 – 2015 Final Report*, No. 14–15, p. 15–16.
11 Brian J. Arnold, *Bulletin for International Taxation (2019)* p. 13; Peter Koerver Schmidt, 'Taxation of Controlled Foreign Companies in Context of the OECD/G20 Project on Base Erosion and Profit Shifting as well as the EU Proposal for the Anti-Tax Avoidance Directive – An Interim Nordic Assessment', *Nordic Tax* (2016) nr. 005, p. 10.

definition of a CFC, CFC exemptions and thresholds, definition of income, computation of income, attribution of income and prevention and elimination of double taxation.

2.2. Defining the CFC income

For a foreign company, which is considered as a CFC, the question arises which income must be included in possible corrections of the taxable basis in the resident State of the shareholder. The income that will be attributed to the shareholder is the CFC income.

The OECD states that CFC rules must include a definition, which makes it possible to attribute BEPS concerned income to the shareholders in the Parent country. Based upon the concern to have some flexibility for the countries to choose their own definition, which will depend on the degree of BEPS risk in that country, the OECD does not impose a mandatory system, instead it allows some degree of freedom.[12] Hence, Arnold concludes that Action Plan 3 was a 'total failure'. In his view, the report failed in requiring that countries adopt CFC rules and also in providing a 'solid tax-design guidance for countries that might want to adopt CFC rules or improve their existing CFC rules'.[13] Moreover, Schmidt concludes that the OECD recommendation appears 'weak and unfocused'.[14] This strong language shows the high expectations about the final outcome of the BEPS project; however, these expectations were not met.

Countries are encouraged to implement CFC rules. The fact that countries can chose different definitions of the CFC income, it is inevitable that it will lead to complex situations. These situations will be

analysed in the next Section. We conclude from this observation that a unique definition of CFC income would have avoided these conflicts.

The non-exhaustive OECD list for defining the CFC income includes the following approaches: the categorical analysis, the substance analysis, the excess profits analysis, the transactional and entity approaches. Hereafter we will describe the different suggested approaches in more detail.

2.3. Categorical analysis

The categorical analysis uses different categories of income.

The different categories can be based upon the legal classification of the income, the relatedness of the involved parties or the source of income.[15]

---

12   OECD (2015), *Designing Effective CFC Rules, Action 3 – 2015 Final Report*, No. 72–73, p. 43.
13   Brian J. Arnold, *Bulletin for International Taxation* (2019) p. 13.
14   Peter Koerver Schmidt, *Nordic Tax* (2016) No. 005, p. 10.
15   OECD (2015), *Designing Effective CFC Rules, Action 3 – 2015 Final Report*, No. 76, p. 44.

2.3.1. Legal classification

Income, in many countries, is categorized based upon its legal classification. Categories that do frequently occur in practice within a CFC context are the following: dividends, interest, insurance income, royalties, IP income and sales and services income. These categories consisting mainly of passive income are in principle geographically mobile and thus BEPS concerned.[16] The underlying principle of the categorical approach is that income from business activities undertaken in a CFC State or active income will raise less BEPS concerns.[17] Examples of countries with a CFC system based upon a legal classification are the following: US (under Subpart F), Russia, Denmark, Spain, Netherlands.

2.3.2. Relatedness of parties

A categorical analysis could also be based upon the relatedness of the involved parties. Certain existing CFC systems focus more on the fact that the income was earned within a group context. The justification for such a model is that group transactions and its pricing are more easily shifted. The relatedness of companies is used as an indication that income is possibly shifted to a CFC.[18]

2.3.3. Source of income

A third system is based upon the source of income. If business activities are effectively undertaken in a certain (CFC) country, the income from these activities raises less BEPS concerns. If the income is realized in another country, profit shifting could be an issue because operational profits could be shifted to the CFC country. For that reason, certain CFC systems use categories of income which are based upon the place where the income was earned. Income is treated as CFC income under these rules if the income is based upon sales or service transactions delivered to a party located in the Parent jurisdiction.[19] An example of a country with a CFC system based upon the source of income is: Belgium.

2.3.4. Policy considerations

A country that is implementing CFC rules can choose from a broad or limited category of income definition. The choice of the country will be based upon the balance in which the country wants to reach between the preservation of the domestic tax base and fostering competitiveness of home country firms in their foreign activities.[20]

---

16   OECD (2015), *Designing Effective CFC Rules, Action 3 – 2015 Final Report*, No. 78, p. 44.
17   Cane D., 'Controlled Foreign Corporations as Fiscally Transparent Entities. The Application of CFC Rules in Tax Treaties', *World Tax Journal* (2017) p. 530.
18   OECD (2015), *Designing Effective CFC Rules, Action 3 – 2015 Final Report*, No. 79, p. 46.
19   OECD (2015), *Designing Effective CFC Rules, Action 3 – 2015 Final Report*, No. 80, p. 46.
20   M.A. Kane, *Bulletin for International Taxation* (2014); Cui Xiaojing/Zhang Han, 'China (People's Rep.) – Chinese Controlled Foreign Company Rules in the Post-BEPS Era: New Developments', *Asia-Pacific Tax bulletin* (2018) No 2.

The definition of CFC income

The categorical approach reflects many existing CFC rules and is therefore familiar.[21, 22] The categorical analysis is also the basis for Model A in the European Union (EU) Anti-Tax Avoidance Directive (ATAD), which explains why several EU Member States have chosen this model.[23]

The choice of countries will have an impact on the competitiveness: two main issues arise.[24] First, countries with more broadly defined categories will have a competitive disadvantage, because companies will be taxed under the CFC rules on a larger number of income categories. Thus, foreign subsidiaries will have a heavier tax burden than subsidiaries of countries with less broad categories. Further, local companies established in the low tax jurisdiction will have a lower taxation. For example, a Belgian company with a CFC in Bermuda is (under conditions) subject to tax on the CFC's attributable income. On the other hand, a local Bermuda company can enjoy a tax rate of 0%. As a result the Bermuda CFC of a Belgian company bears a heavier tax burden than a local Bermuda company.[25]

Second, MNEs in countries with broadly defined categories or with higher tax rates will have a competitive disadvantage compared to MNEs that are established in countries with more limited defined categories, with lower tax rates or without a CFC legislation. These MNEs will be confronted with higher actual tax rates, even if the CFCs are based in the same country. For example, if CFC rules are strictly applied, multinationals in France pay on the CFC attributable income a tax rate of 31%, while other companies in countries without a CFC legislation with less stringent CFC rules will have a lower tax burden. Both examples show that the competitiveness of a country can be impacted by the CFC legislation.[26]

It is clear that the choice of the different methods in the categorical analysis will be based upon internal policy considerations.

2.4. Substance analysis

A second method is the substance analysis. This method looks at the involvement of the CFC and the activities for the determination of the CFC income. Substance, including people, premises, assets and risks are the basis for the CFC income: is the CFC able to earn the income itself?[27] In the past, most EU countries used a substance analysis in combination with a categorical analysis.[28] After the imple-

---

21   OECD (2015), *Designing Effective CFC Rules, Action 3 – 2015 Final Report*, nr. 76, p. 44.
22   Examples of countries that used the categorical approach before the approval of the BEPS Action plan: Germany, Spain.
23   Currently 14 EU Member States have opted for Model A. See further under section 3.1.
24   Brian J. Arnold, *Bulletin for International Taxation* (2019) p. 10.
25   Cui Xiaojing/Zhang Han, *Asia-Pacific Tax bulletin* (2018) No 2, par. 3.2.
26   Cui Xiaojing/Zhang Han, *Asia-Pacific Tax bulletin* (2018) No 2, par. 3.2.
27   OECD (2015), *Designing Effective CFC Rules, Action 3 – 2015 Final Report*, No. 81, p. 47.
28   Sebastian Duenas, *Fiscal Fact Tax Foundation* (2019) p. 12.

mentation of the EU ATAD Directive, both systems exist in the EU in a separate way, as the ATAD Model A is in line with the categorical approach, and Model B is a form of substance analysis.[29]

A substance analysis is possible as a threshold test or a proportionate analysis. A threshold test can be considered as an all-or-nothing test: a certain size of activity by the CFC is sufficient for excluding the income for the CFC rules. If the CFC is below the activity threshold, the total income will be considered as CFC income. The proportionate analysis will determine the CFC income in a proportional way: the part, which is related to the business activity of the CFC will be excluded from the CFC treatment. The remaining part will be considered as CFC income. The advantage of the proportionate analysis is that CFC income is only based upon the income that is not resulting from genuine economic activities.[30]

The advantage is that CFC rules will be more accurate. The CFC rules will only be applied if the CFC did not develop a substantial activity as described in the different options in the previous paragraph. Under the other methods, it is possible that CFC income will be taxed under the CFC rules, even if the CFC developed substantial activities.[31] Many existing CFC rules apply the substance analysis as a carve out rule in combination with a categorical approach.[32] An example can be found in the Nordic CFC regimes[33] and the CFC rules in Spain.[34]

2.5. Excess profit analysis

The third method is the excess profit analysis. This method is similar to the framework for Global Intangible Low-Tax Income (GILTI) in the US.[35] CFC income is based upon the excess of the normal return. This means that a normal return for the activities will be attributed to the CFC and will not be taxed under the CFC rules. The income above this normal return will fall under the application of the CFC rules.[36] A normal return could be calculated based upon a rate of return with respect to an equity investment and the amount of eligible equity.[37]

The most important advantage of the excess profit analysis approach is that it involves a simpler, more mechanical approach than the substance analysis. It re-

---

29 Council Directive (EU) 2016/1164 of 12 July 2016 laying down rules against tax avoidance practices that directly affect the functioning of the internal market, 19.7.2016, OJ L 193/1.
30 OECD (2015), *Designing Effective CFC Rules, Action 3 – 2015 Final Report*, No. 82, p. 47.
31 OECD (2015), *Designing Effective CFC Rules, Action 3 – 2015 Final Report*, No. 83, p. 47.
32 OECD (2015), *Public Discussion Draft BEPS Action 3: Strengthening CFC Rules*, OECD/G20 Base Erosion and Profit Shifting Project, OECD Publishing, par. 81.
33 Peter Koerver Schmidt, *Nordic Tax* (2016) p. 12.
34 Sebastian Duenas, *Fiscal Fact Tax Foundation* (2019) p. 27.
35 Sebastian Duenas, *Fiscal Fact Tax Foundation* (2019) p. 12.
36 OECD (2015), *Designing Effective CFC Rules, Action 3 – 2015 Final Report*, No. 87, p. 49.
37 OECD (2015), *Designing Effective CFC Rules, Action 3 – 2015 Final Report*, No. 89, p. 49.

The definition of CFC income

sponds to the remarks, of certain economists, that profit shifting out of high-tax countries is often related to excessive intellectual property (IP) returns.[38] The method will tax IP income on the level of the parent, also in case a minimal level of activity is realized in the CFC State. The most important disadvantage is that it can also lead to over-inclusion or under-inclusion as the normal return may not approximate the return of the assets and activities of the CFC.[39]

2.6. Application of the income on a transactional or an entity basis

The different types of analysis, as described under the previous Sections 2.3. to 2.5, can be applied on a transactional basis or on an entity basis.[40]

2.6.1. Entity approach

The entity approach qualifies the entity as a CFC if a certain minimum level of CFC income has been reached. Once this minimum level has been reached, the entire income will be considered as CFC income, even if a part of the income is not BEPS related. The advantage is that less administrative burden and compliance costs, and a higher degree of certainty can be expected.[41] Once the criteria are met, the taxpayer knows whether the income is subject to CFC taxation, therefore, no additional administration is required.

The most important disadvantage is that the outcome is not totally in line with the factual situation. CFC income will not be included if it concerns only a smaller part of the total income. On the contrary, non-CFC income will be included if the concerned thresholds are reached. Such a situation is defined by the OECD as over-inclusive or under-inclusive.[42] The fact that local CFC rules must determine, under the entity approach, the minimum level of CFC income before the CFC rules will be applicable, it is in our opinion also a weak element and will lead to legal uncertainty and eventually double taxation.

The "all-or-nothing" approach leads to a potential important impact on the limited increase or decrease in the development of passive activities: a small increase of passive activities can lead to taxation of the total income; a small decrease of passive activities will lead to an exemption.[43]

---

38 OECD (2015), *Public Discussion Draft, BEPS Action 3, Strengthening CFC Rules*, No. 125, p. 52.
39 OECD (2015), *Public Discussion Draft, BEPS Action 3, Strengthening CFC Rules*, No. 125, p. 52.
40 OECD (2015), *Designing Effective CFC Rules, Action 3 – 2015 Final Report*, No. 95, p. 50.
41 OECD (2015), *Designing Effective CFC Rules, Action 3 – 2015 Final Report*, No. 95–96, p. 51.
42 OECD (2015), *Designing Effective CFC Rules, Action 3 – 2015 Final Report*, No. 95–96, p. 51.
43 R.G. Bader, *CFC legislation in the European Union and the alternative CSC concept*, p. 299.

2.6.2. Transactional approach

The CFC income under the transactional approach is based upon individual streams of income. Each individual stream of income must be analysed before a conclusion of CFC taxation can be reached. Such analysis would not be necessary under the entity approach once the minimum thresholds are reached. As the analysis under the transactional approach is based upon individual transactions, the outcome of it will be more accurate. Minimum thresholds could be used to avoid additional compliance costs for companies with a limited passive income.[44]

According to the OECD, the transactional approach would be more in line with the policy purposes of the BEPS project. The main reason is that the transactional approach requires consideration of each stream of income. For this reason, the method would be better targeted to specific types of income more effectively than the entity approach.[45]

The transactional method focuses on the amount of passive income derived through the CFC. This approach uses a mere horizontal separation of income based upon the type of income. The transactional approach would lead to the taxation of the total amount of tainted income, which also includes components connected to an "active" activity carried out by the CFC; for example, received interest in the context of produced economic output. Bader states that such a horizontal approach is not sufficient, as active income could also be taxed.[46]

The transactional approach also results in a lower risk of double taxation because passive profit; that is, profit that does not arise from operational activities, under this option can only lead to taxation if there is a connection with key functions situated in a Parent country.[47]

3. Practice Implementation into Domestic Law

3.1. CFC legislation in Belgium

3.1.1. General description of the CFC rules

The first country in our analysis is Belgium, an OECD and EU Member State. It was also chosen as an example of a country with strict CFC rules against active companies.

---

44 OECD (2015), *Designing Effective CFC Rules, Action 3 – 2015 Final Report*, No. 95–97, p. 51.
45 OECD (2015), *Designing Effective CFC Rules, Action 3, 2015 Final Report*, No. 97, p. 51.
46 R.G. Bader, *CFC legislation in the European Union and the alternative CSC concept*, p. 224.
47 Pieter Deré/Gilles Van Hulle, 'Herschudt de Belgische CFC-regel de kaarten?', *Fiscale Actualiteit* (2018) No. 18/25-02, p. 1.

Belgium introduced new CFC rules only after the obligation as foreseen by the ATAD Directive.[48] A CFC is under article 7 (1) of the ATAD Directive, an entity that meets the following conditions as implemented by Belgium:[49] (1) in case an entity holds a (in)direct participation of more than 50% of the voting rights, or owns (in)directly more than 50% of capital or is entitled to receive more than 50% of the profits; and (2) the actual corporate tax paid on its profits is lower than the difference between the corporate tax that would have been charged under the applicable corporate tax system in Belgium and the actual corporate tax paid.

Belgian legislation foresees that the full amount of the CFC income is included in the tax base of the Parent company if the aforementioned conditions are met.

3.1.2. Definition CFC income

Belgium has chosen the ATAD Model B to target undistributed profits of a foreign company that arise from non-genuine structures that are set up for the essential purpose of obtaining a tax benefit. A "non-genuine" construction is established, just in case assets are identified that are owned by the CFC, while the Parent company is responsible for the strategic decisions.[50]

Article 7 ATAD Directive offers two different building blocks on which an internal CFC provision can be constructed. Under Model A, certain predefined categories of undistributed passive income such as dividends, interest, royalties and income from financial activities of the CFC are attributed to the Parent company. Model A can be compared with the OECD Categorical Analysis.[51] Under Model B, as implemented by Belgium, undistributed income of the CFC from non-genuine arrangements that have been put in place for the essential purpose of obtaining a tax advantage is attributed to the Parent company. Model B can be compared with a combination of the OECD Methods of the Substance Analysis[52] and the Transactional Approach.[53, 54] In addition, there is also a non-genuine construction if risks are identified for the CFC that are congenital to the CFC, but for which strategic decisions are made by the Belgian Parent company.

---

48 Applicable as from 1 January 2019 – assessment year 2020; art. 185/2 Belgian Income Tax Code 1992.
49 Article 7, Council Directive (EU) 2016/1164 of 12 July 2016 laying down rules against tax avoidance practices that directly affect the functioning of the internal market, 19.7.2016, OJ L 193/1, p. 11; Belgian Parliament, Proposal to reform the corporate income tax, 20 December 2017, DOC 54, 2864/001, p. 48.
50 Belgian Parliament, Proposal to reform the corporate income tax, 20 December 2017, DOC 54, 2864/001, p. 48.
51 Section 2.3.
52 Section 2.4.
53 Section 2.6.2.
54 Belgian Parliament, Proposal to reform the corporate income tax, 20 December 2017, DOC 54, 2864/001, p. 47.

3.2. CFC legislation in China
3.2.1. General description of the CFC rules

The second country in our analysis is China. China was chosen as it is not an OECD member, being an important economic player and as an example of CFC rules related to passive income.

The CFC regime was introduced in China in 2008. The CFC rules were created to prevent Chinese multinationals from leaving profits in low-tax jurisdictions, through arrangements, without business substance.[55]

For determining the CFC rules in China, three conditions must be met. The first condition is that Chinese resident shareholders must control the CFC company whereby the minimum thresholds are included in Chinese tax law. According to the second condition, the CFC must be established in a low tax country. Low-tax countries are countries with an effective tax rate below 50% of the Chinese tax rate of 25% (= 12,50%). The third condition is that the fact that the CFC profit is not distributed or is only distributed in a reduced way, it is not motivated by reasonable business reasons.[56]

Certain exceptions exist in different situations.[57]

3.2.2. Definition CFC income

CFC income refers to profits in low-tax countries which are not distributed whereby no reasonable business needs exist for this action. China uses a substantive approach supplemented by a transactional approach. If the foreign company is considered to be CFC, all the income will be taxed in China based upon the first approach. In supplementary order, also the transactional method is used. The transactional method gives companies the chance to exempt profits from CFC taxation if the company can prove that the positive profits contribute to regular business activities.[58]

3.3. CFC legislation in US
3.3.1. General description of the CFC rules

The third country in our analysis is the US, an OECD member as an example of CFC rules related to active income. It is undoubtedly the country with the most

---

[55] Sebastien Duenas/Daniel Blum, 'How Controlled Foreign Rules Look Around the World: China', *Tax Foundation* (2020).
[56] Li Na, 'Controlled Foreign Company legislation in China' in Georg Kofler, Michael Lang, Jeffrey Owens, Pasquale Pistone, Alexander Rust, Josef Schuch, Karoline Spies, Claus Staringer (eds.), *Controlled Foreign Company Legislation*, (Amsterdam: IBFD, 2020) p. 110.
[57] Li Na, in Georg Kofler, Michael Lang, Jeffrey Owens, Pasquale Pistone, Alexander Rust, Josef Schuch, Karoline Spies, Claus Staringer (eds.), *Controlled Foreign Company Legislation*, p. 111.
[58] Li Na, in Georg Kofler, Michael Lang, Jeffrey Owens, Pasquale Pistone, Alexander Rust, Josef Schuch, Karoline Spies, Claus Staringer (eds.), *Controlled Foreign Company Legislation*, p. 111.

The definition of CFC income

complex set of rules. The assessable income was initially passive income but the amount of foreign income subject to US tax has expanded with the adoption of GILTI, which can also include active income.[59]

In principle, the US does not tax foreign companies when it does not receive income from the US or does not engage in activities within the US. The US does tax all income from US worldwide legal persons. In order to reduce double taxation, companies can apply a tax credit for income from foreign participations. This income remains untaxed until income is distributed to the US shareholder. Subpart F works by treating US shareholders of a CFC as if they receive their proportional share of certain categories of income from the CFC.

3.3.2. Definition CFC income

The US uses a categorical analysis to define CFC income based upon a legal distinction. Subpart F is characterized by many exceptions within the categories of income.[60] Different categories of Subpart F Income exist.[61] The most significant category is Foreign Base Company Income (FBCI)[62] consisting of Foreign Personal Holding Company Income (FPHCI), Foreign Base Company Sales Income (FBCSI) and Foreign Base Company Services Income (FBC Service Income).

FPHCI consists of different items such as dividends, interest and royalties, although, certain items are excluded. These exceptions mainly refer to assets that are, in an important way, used in an active business such as dividends or interest payments from companies with a substantial part of their assets used in an active trade or business.[63]

FBCSI is income derived from the sale or purchase of personal property with a related person where the property which is purchased (or sold) is manufactured outside the country of incorporation and the property is sold for use (or purchased for use) outside such foreign country.[64]

---

59 Yariv Brauner/Christine A. Davis, in Georg Kofler, Michael Lang, Jeffrey Owens, Pasquale Pistone, Alexander Rust, Josef Schuch, Karoline Spies, Claus Staringer (eds.), *Controlled Foreign Company Legislation*, p. 625; IRS, 'Examining Process (part 4): International Program Audit Guidelines (chapter 61), Controlled Foreign Corporations (section 7), Controlled Foreign Corporations (No. 4.61.7)' (18 October 2019)
https://www.irs.gov/irm/part4/irm_04-061-007 (accessed 25 July 2020) (in the following footnotes, this document will be referred to as 'Manual IRS').
60 IRS, 2014, "Subpart F Overview", LB&I International Practice Service Concept Unit, pp. 7–10 https://www.irs.gov/pub/int_practice_units/DPLCUV_2_01.PDF (accessed 25 July 2020); Manual IRS, No. 4.61.7.5.2.
61 Manual IRS, No. 4.61.7.6.2.
62 As defined in IRC 954; Yariv Brauner/Christine A. Davis, 'Controlled Foreign Company Legislation in the United States' in Georg Kofler, Michael Lang, Jeffrey Owens, Pasquale Pistone, Alexander Rust, Josef Schuch, Karoline Spies, Claus Staringer (eds.), *Controlled Foreign Company Legislation*, p. 628.
63 Manual IRS, No. 4.61.7.14.
64 Manual IRS, No. 4.61.7.15.

FBC Service Income is income derived in connection with the performance of technical, managerial, engineering, architectural, scientific, skilled, industrial, commercial or "like services" for or on behalf of any related person outside the country under the laws of which the CFC is created or organized.[65]

Brauner indicates that the US Subpart F system is primarily transaction based, but they also include a jurisdictional component.[66] Before the US tax reform in 2017, the regime taxed the passive income.[67] Other rules were recently added to the Subpart F rules to avoid deferral of US taxes such as the Passive Foreign Investment Company (PFIC) and the Global Intangible Low-Taxed Income or GILTI.[68]

4. Comparison Different Approaches: Practical Case
4.1. Facts of the case

The facts in this case are based upon the example from the Belgian explanatory memorandum regarding the law implementing the CFC rules and on examples from the OECD Transfer Pricing Guidelines.[69] We completed the case with hypothetical financial information.

Operational Company (Opco)A[70] is a resident company of the analyzed jurisdiction. It is part of an international group and it holds all shares of Forco B,[71] a company based in country X, which is a central IP company and a service provider for certain group services. Opco A develops all Research and Development (R&D) activities. When R&D activities result in an invention, Opco A transfers all rights of the invention to Foreign Company (Forco) B. Each time an invention is transferred, Forco B pays a fee of EUR 100 to Opco A.

Forco B employs three IP lawyers who manage the patents. Forco B itself does not develop R&D activities. Forco B prepares the patent applications and registers it in its name. Forco B is responsible for the management of the patents, the renewal of them, and so on. If a patent is obtained, Forco B grants a license to Opco A, with the right to sublicense in a non-exclusive way. Opco A pays royalties for this

---

65 Manual IRS, No. 4.61.7.20.
66 An item of passive income between entities in the same jurisdiction can be excluded from Subpart F income if certain conditions are met.
67 Yariv Brauner/Christine A. Davis in Georg Kofler, Michael Lang, Jeffrey Owens, Pasquale Pistone, Alexander Rust, Josef Schuch, Karoline Spies, Claus Staringer (eds.), *Controlled Foreign Company Legislation*, p. 626.
68 Section 1297-1298 IRS.
69 Luc De Broe, *Algemeen Fiscaal Tijdschrift* (2019) pag. 9; Belgian Parliament, Proposal to reform the corporate income tax, 20 December 2017, DOC 54, 2864/001, p. 48; Belgian Parliament, Proposal to reform the corporate income tax, 20 December 2017, DOC 54, 3147/001, 19; OECD (2017), *OECD Transfer Pricing Guidelines for Multinational Enterprises and Tax Administrations 2017*, OECD Publishing, Annex to Chapter VI, Examples 1–3.
70 Operational Company A.
71 Foreign Company B.

The definition of CFC income

license. The charged amount is considered by the tax authorities as an arm's length price. The license agreement stipulates that Opco A is responsible for the improvement of the patent.

Opco A uses the patent protected technology to produce digital sports watches: smartwatches, activity trackers, and so on. The sale thereof is successful and brings Opco A EUR 100 million (annual turnover).

All decisions regarding possible licenses of the patent by Forco B are determined by the Opco A's board of directors. All negotiations of license agreements are made by directors of Opco A in the name and on behalf of Forco B with assistance from Forco B's legal team. One of these lawyers is also a director of Forco B and has the authority to sign. In case of violations of the Forco B patents or when Forco B itself is accused of infringement of someone else's patent, all decisions regarding the defense strategy are taken through the board of Opco A after advice by Forco B's legal team and by the lawyers appointed by Forco B in consultation with Opco A.

The substantial royalties received by Forco B are taxed up to 20% against the standard rate of 20% (effective tax rate = 4%). In a second alternative scenario the taxes for Forco B amounts to 20% on 100% of the profits (effective tax rate = 20%).

Forco B also delivers administrative services and employs enough people for these functions. Forco B has an invoice margin of 10% on the concerned costs. The margin can be considered as an arm's length margin. Opco A is invoiced EUR 1.200.000. This income is hypothetically taxed under the same previous mentioned tax rate.

The results of Opco A can be summarized as follows:

OPCO A

COSTS		INCOME	
Operational costs	85.000.500	Turnover sales products	100.000.000
Service fee Forco B	1.200.000		
Royalties ad 10%	10.000.000	Turnover transfer R&D rights	500
Total costs	96.200.500	Total income	100.000.500
Profit	3.800.000		
Taxes ad 25%	950.000		
Profit after taxes	2.850.000		

The results of Forco B can be summarized as follows:

FORCO B (STATE X)

COSTS		INCOME	
Legal costs	300.000	Turnover (royalties)	10.000.000
Other costs related to services	2.000.000	Service fee	2.200.000
Turnover transfer R&D rights	500		
Total costs	2.300.500	Total income	12.200.000
Profit	9.899.500		
Taxes ad 20% (on 20%)	395.980		
Profit after taxes	9.503.520		
Effective tax rate	4,00%		

The question arises as to what the consequences are for the application of the CFC rules in the different described countries.

4.2. CFC treatment in Belgium

Opco A is a Belgian resident company.

Based on the transactional approach, profits of a CFC from non-genuine structures, which are set up for obtaining a tax benefit, will be taxed in Belgium. A non-genuine construction exists just in case assets are identified, which are owned by the CFC, while the (Belgian) Parent company is responsible for the strategic decisions.

Although Forco B is the legal owner of the patents, its contribution to the Development, Enhancement, Maintenance, Protection, Exploitation (DEMPE)[72] functions are limited to file and maintenance of the patent (Maintenance) and to provide legal assistance with the licensing process and with the IP protection procedures (Protection).

Opco A is responsible for the following functions: development of the invention (Development), improvement of the IP (Enhancement), production by means of license on the patent (Exploitation), strategic decisions regarding the exploitation of the patent and active negotiation of licenses (Exploitation), and decisions on protection procedures (Protection). The majority of the DEMPE functions are thus not performed by Forco B, but by Opco A.

---

[72] Development, Enhancement, Maintenance, Protection, Exploitation; the ATAD Directive refers to the significant people's functions which is a concept of the OECD Transfer Pricing Guidelines. After the OECD BEPS Action Plan 8, the key functions must be determined based upon the DEMPE test; cf. OECD Guidelines, 2017, § 6.32 and following and Annex to Chapter VI.

Also, the most important risk in connection with the patent is for Opco A, as the company uses the patent for its production. The OECD Transfer Pricing Guidelines, therefore, conclude that as Opco A is not reimbursed by Forco B for these key functions that play an essential role in profit realization of Forco B, and the activities performed by Forco B are activities more of an administrative support nature or routine and do not involve risks, a significant portion of the royalties can be attributed to Opco A. Forco B is only entitled to an arm's length fee for its management and legal functions and also for the administrative services.[73]

Assuming hypothetically that the standard functions of Forco B would be remunerated under the normal transfer pricing rules based upon a cost-plus method (e.g. 10%), the most important part of the royalty profits would be taxed in Belgium under the CFC rules based upon the transactional approach as the DEMPE functions are performed by Opco A. The additional income for Opco A would be, in that case, EUR 9.669.450.[74]

In the alternative scenario, the effective taxes for Forco B equal 20% (instead of 4%). therefore, no CFC rules must be applied in Belgium, as the actual corporate tax paid is more than 50% of the Belgian tax rate.

4.3. CFC treatment in China

Opco A is a Chinese resident company.

CFC income in China refers to profits in low-tax countries, which are not distributed whereby no reasonable business needs exist for this action. We can assume, in this case, that no sound business reasons are available for justifying the fact that no profits were distributed, considering the realized tax savings. If no proper justification is available for this conduct, no exceptions can be applied and Forco B can be considered as a CFC. The result is that all the income of Forco B will be taxed in China. An additional profit of EUR 9.899.500 can be attributed to Opco A and will be taxed in China. The exception as foreseen in Chinese tax law cannot be applied as the most important part of the income for Forco B is not related to active business operations.

In supplementary order, the Chinese tax authorities could also use the transactional method. As described under the previous Section, it cannot be ignored the fact that Forco B is effectively granting administrative services within the group. Forco B should be remunerated for these services with a limited profit. Also, under the transactional approach, it is clear that the most important part of the CFC profit will be taxed in China, but the impact will be minor. Based upon the facts of this case, the additional profit for Opco A under the CFC rules is EUR 9.669.450.

---

73 OECD Transfer Pricing Guidelines (2017), § 6.32 and following and Annex to Chapter VI.
74 Cost-plus result for Forco B is EUR 230.050; difference with profit before CFC (EUR 9.899.500) is EUR 9.669.450.

In the alternative scenario, the effective taxes for Forco B equal 20%; further, no CFC rules must be applied in China as the minimum tax rate condition is fulfilled.

4.4. CFC treatment in US

Opco A is a US resident company.

Under the Subpart F rules, the US uses a categorical analysis to define the CFC income. The royalties as described in our practical case do fall under a Subpart F category; that is, FPHCI. As more than 70% of the gross income of Forco B is FPHCI, the total royalty income of Forco B will be considered as FPHCI and will be taxed in the US. No exceptions can be applied. If Subpart F taxation would not be applicable, a GILTI-inclusion (and thus taxation) could be applicable.

In the alternative scenario, the effective taxes for Forco B equal 20%. Therefore, CFC rules must also be applied as US tax laws do not foresee a minimum taxation condition. However, the global impact of taxation in the US will be limited, as a tax credit for the higher taxes ad 20% paid by the CFC is normally foreseen.

4.5. Comparison of the different approaches

The results of the different approaches can be summarized as follows:

Summary impact CFC taxation	Additional profit	
	Taxation ad 4%	Taxation ad 20%
Belgium		
Under Transactional approach	9.669.450	0
China		
Under Substantive law	9.899.500	0
Under Transaction law	9.669.450	0
US		
Under Subpart F	9.899.500	9.899.500

The different approaches indicate that the results of the application under the transactional approach leads to a lower taxation than under the categorical approach and the substantive approach.

Belgium and China (under the transaction law) apply the transactional approach. In this approach only the transactions, which are not justified by functions and assets of the CFC, will be taxed in Belgium and China. Transactions, which can be justified by the operational activities of the CFC, with own assets and persons, will not be included in the CFC taxation under the transactional approach. In our case, the difference with the other approaches in CFC profit that would be taxed in these countries is EUR 230.050. Depending on the circumstances of the case, the differences can be much higher or more limited.

China (under the substantive law) and the US are including the total profit of CFC in their taxation. The approaches in these countries are not totally the same; however, they have a common characteristic of not being based on transactions. As the most important part of the CFC income is passive income, which is not justified by operational business transactions, the total amount of the CFC profit will be taxed. The final outcome of this approach is that the profit of the CFC that will be taxed in the Parent country can be much higher (in our case EUR 230.050).

5. Conclusion

The definition of CFC income is important. Once a foreign company is considered as a CFC, it is necessary to have a clear system that indicates which part of the income of the CFC will be taxed in the Parent country. An effective system will lead to avoiding profit shifting or to avoiding deferral. In this Master's thesis, we analysed the fact that such an effective and clear system currently does not exist. Different systems are in place. Depending on the policy objectives of a country, a broad CFC system has been implemented, a rather broad system or a more limited system, which is more linked to the existing transfer pricing rules. The outcome, therefore, is that CFC legislation has become a complex set of rules, which can lead to double taxation.

The OECD did not succeed in bringing together the different policy objectives in one CFC standard. The failure of this ambition is shown by the approved BEPS Action Plan 3, which includes only a 'menu' of possible models to determine the CFC income. The different models are based upon a categorical analysis (legal classification, relatedness of parties, source of income), substance analysis or the excess profit analysis. The different models can be applied on an entity basis or on a transactional approach.

The income related blocks in the BEPS approach will finally determine whether effective taxation in the residence State of the Parent company is possible. The advantage of the OECD approach in giving recommendations is that each country has the possibility to take final decisions about CFC rules, based upon its own tax and economic policy strategy. The disadvantage is, however, that countries are following different approaches, which can lead to the fact that CFC income is not taxed, or CFC income is double taxed. The fact that no common approach has been imposed, will lead to different implementations and different domestic CFC systems. Such an approach could lead to extreme tax planning and uncertainty for the taxpayer.[75]

---

75   Cui Xiaojing/Zhang Han, *Asia-Pacific Tax bulletin* (2018) No 2.

The final result of the lack of consensus between governments is that a complex set of rules will determine whether CFC taxation will be realized. The use of the different models will lead to different outcomes. Based upon the domestic provisions of 3 countries, we analysed these differences.

First, an important observation is the fact that the transactional approach will lead to a lower CFC taxation, just in case the CFC is also involved in operational activities, which are executed with their own assets and employees. The CFC analysis under the transactional approach will accept such activities, if they are remunerated in an appropriate manner, as described in the examples of Belgium and China (transaction law). Under the categorical approach and the substantive approach, the operational activities will not be excluded from CFC taxation, if this concerns only minor activities, which are below the different thresholds. Therefore, the final outcome is that the global CFC profit will be included whereas this is not the case under the transactional approach. We described this situation for China (substantive law) and the US.

Second, an observation is that the fact that a minimum tax rate condition is applicable can lead to a different outcome. If no minimum tax rate condition is included in domestic law, as foreseen in the US, a large application of the CFC rules is foreseen. Even if no tax havens are in scope, CFC legislation must be applied, which leads to an additional administrative burden.

Third, an observation is that the definition of the income categories under the categorical approach is important. Even if the foreign company is considered to be a CFC and the foreign tax rate is rather low, CFC taxation will not be realized if the concerned income is not included in the list of tainted income. In our analysis, we have seen that certain countries are using rather broad lists of tainted income; for example, the US and other countries have a more limited list. The result of these differences is that similar situations of a CFC in two different countries will lead to a different CFC taxation.

The OECD and the EU missed an important chance to introduce a clear and effective set of CFC rules. The result of this lack of consensus is that currently complex CFC rules exist and consequently will lead certain countries to CFC taxation, while in other countries CFC rules will not be applied. Differences exist because countries are using different methods and approaches, different income categories and different minimum CFC tax rates. The result of this situation is that the foundations have been laid for double taxation, the application of complex rules, and the beginning of several discussions to be expected in the future before courts.

As the transactional approach does not have an important added value to the existing transfer pricing rules, we are in favour of one CFC standard, which is based upon the entity approach. The EU approach in its Model A, including the exception whereby foreign companies would not be considered as a CFC if less than one-third of the income is passive income, is in our opinion a standard that could work as an effective approach. It gives the advantage of having a model that is clear for all countries, tax authorities and MNEs, which need to apply it in practice. The use of such a common method will lead to a less administrative burden and costs, as for most companies, it will be rather straightforward to decide whether or not it is a CFC. An additional analysis would be necessary only in a limited number of cases for companies with passive income around the one-third threshold.

On the one hand, where a fair distribution of taxes is intended, extra attention is necessary for efficiency, feasibility and clarity. The implementation of one CFC model would increase the efficiency and the clarity, which we are currently missing in the amalgam of existing CFC systems. Although a first important step has been set to put the CFC legislation on the political agenda for many countries, a second step is absolutely necessary to blend the existing systems to one CFC standard. However, as we know from the evolution of tax laws, the famous Dutch author Willem Elsschot wrote already in 1910 (in a non-tax context): "Between dream and deed, laws and practical objections stand in the way."[76]

---

[76] Willem Elsschot (1882–1960), Het Huwelijk.

An analysis of CFC exemptions and threshold requirements

Fernanda Freitas Maciel

1. Introduction
2. CFC exemptions and threshold requirements under the OECD/G20 BEPS Action 3
   2.1. CFC exemptions and threshold requirements in general
   2.2. De minimis threshold
   2.3. Anti-avoidance requirement
   2.4. Tax rate exemption
   2.5. Observations on the CFC exemptions and threshold requirements
3. Analysis of CFC exemptions and threshold requirements in Latin American countries
   3.1. The adoption of CFC exemptions and threshold requirements
   3.2. The specific cases of Brazil and Colombia
   3.3. Observations on the CFC Regimes adopted in Latin America
4. Conclusion

An analysis of CFC exemptions and threshold requirements

1. Introduction

The Action 3 final report of the OECD/G20 Base Erosion and Profit Shifting (BEPS) Project aims to strengthen the controlled foreign company (CFC) rules by identifying the main challenges related to CFCs and establishing the technical and practical framework to address these challenges. In this regard, the OECD provides recommendations organized as building blocks through which it analyzes the key aspects that should be considered by countries in order to develop and implement effective CFC rules.[1] According to the OECD, CFC rules should be developed in a way that they target taxpayers that represent a high risk to using CFCs for profit shifting purposes and, at the same time, they should reduce the administrative and compliance burden as much as possible.[2] Therefore, CFC exemptions and threshold requirements comprise one of the building blocks analyzed by the OECD that aims at alleviating those burdens and facilitate the application of CFC rules in practice. In Chapter 3 of the Action 3 final report, the OECD particularly addresses some exemptions and threshold requirements that could be implemented by countries to limit the scope of CFC rules, i.e., *de minimis* thresholds, the anti-avoidance requirement and the tax rate exemption.[3]

In this context, there are two primary aims of the present chapter. The first one is to analyze the CFC exemptions and threshold requirements adopted by Latin American countries, and the second one is to ascertain whether the OECD recommendations under the BEPS Action 3 Final Report, in particular with respect to the CFC exemptions and threshold requirements, have been implemented in those countries. In doing so, the author first performs an examination of the CFC exemptions and threshold requirements under OECD/G20 BEPS Action 3. Afterwards, an analysis is conducted of the exemptions and threshold requirements adopted by the Latin American countries. This is followed by a brief analysis of Brazil and Colombia, considered by the author as specific cases due to the fact that they have not included any exemptions or threshold requirements in their CFC regimes.

It is worth noting that the present analysis was limited to the countries that, at the time of the research, have already implemented CFC rules or rules that have been considered as similar or even comparable to the conventional CFC rules, namely Argentina, Brazil, Chile, Colombia, Mexico, Peru, Uruguay, and Venezuela.

---

1   OECD (2015), Explanatory Statement, OECD/G20 Base Erosion and Profit Shifting Project, OECD, p. 13–14. Available at www.oecd.org/tax/beps-explanatory-statement-2015.pdf.
2   OECD (2015), Designing Effective Controlled Foreign Company Rules, Action 3 – 2015 Final Report, p. 33. Nevertheless, OECD states that even those taxpayers considered as low risk for profit shifting may be required to submit compliance reports in order to ensure the effectiveness of the CFC rules.
3   OECD (2015), Designing Effective Controlled Foreign Company Rules, Action 3 – 2015 Final Report, OECD/G20 Base Erosion and Profit Shifting Project, OECD Publishing, Paris, p. 33. Available at http://dx.doi.org/10.1787/9789264241152-en.

Among those jurisdictions, the only OECD member countries are Mexico (since May 1994), Chile (since May 2010), and Colombia (since April 2020).[4] Argentina, Brazil, Peru, and Uruguay, although not member countries of the OECD, are members of the OECD/G20 Inclusive Framework on BEPS.[5] Venezuela is the only analyzed country that is neither a member of the OECD nor of the Inclusive Framework on BEPS.

2. CFC exemptions and threshold requirements under the OECD/G20 BEPS Action 3

2.1. CFC exemptions and threshold requirements in general

CFC exemptions and threshold requirements aim to limit the scope of the CFC rules thereby excluding those taxpayers, transactions, and/or incomes classified as low-risk of profit shifting and, therefore, targeting those that would represent a higher-risk. In this regard, the exemptions and threshold requirements would ensure the effectiveness of the CFC rules insofar as they establish a precise framework where those rules would be applicable.[6]

Generally, the objective of the exemptions and threshold requirements will depend on whether the CFC rules are based on either the so-called entity approach or the so-called transactional approach or on a combination of both.[7] Under the entity approach, also known as the jurisdictional approach,[8] CFCs that carry on certain business activities or whose income that would be considered as attributable to the shareholders under the CFC regime (e.g. passive income, such as interests and intellectual property income) is below a certain amount or percentage, will be exempt from the CFC rules. The entity approach, therefore, exempts all income derived by those CFCs that fall below certain thresholds and/or meet some activities requirements.[9] As it is explained by Brian J. Arnold (2019), *"this all-or-nothing result is the essential characteristic of the entity approach"*.[10] On the other

---

4   List of OECD Member countries. Available at: https://www.oecd.org/about/document/list-oecd-member-countries.htm (accessed 24 May 2020).
5   Members of the OECD/G20 Inclusive Framework on BEPS. Available at: https://www.oecd.org/tax/beps/inclusive-framework-on-beps-composition.pdf (accessed 24 May 24, 2020).
6   OECD (2015), Designing Effective Controlled Foreign Company Rules, Action 3 – 2015 Final Report, p. 33.
7   OECD (2015), Designing Effective Controlled Foreign Company Rules, Action 3 – 2015 Final Report, pp. 50–51. See also Brian J. Arnold, *International Tax Primer*, 4th Edition, (Alphen aan den Rijn: Wolters Kluwer, 2019) pp. 133–134.
8   Peter Koerver Schmidt, 'Chapter 14: Controlled Foreign Company Legislation in Denmark' in: Georg Kofler/Richard Krever/Michael Lang/Jeffrey Owens/Pasquale Pistone/Alexander Rust/Josef Schuch (eds.) *Controlled Foreign Company Legislation* (IBFD, 2020), p.1 https://research.ibfd.org/#/doc?url=/document/cfcl_p02_c14 (accessed 14 February 2021).
9   OECD (2015), Designing Effective Controlled Foreign Company Rules, Action 3 – 2015 Final Report, pp. 50–51.
10 Brian J. Arnold, *International Tax Primer*, 4th Edition, (Alphen aan den Rijn: Wolters Kluwer, 2019) p. 131.

hand, the transactional approach requires the analysis of each transaction in which the CFC is involved and whether or not this transaction results in income that should be attributable to the shareholders under the CFC rules. The transactional approach is considered to be more precise if compared to the entity approach, although it also would increase the compliance and administrative burden, being considered, therefore, more costly.[11] Countries can also use a combination of both entity and transactional approaches in order to implement the exemptions and threshold requirements in their CFC regimes, this being the case, for instance, in Australia, New Zealand, and the United States (US) that, as explained by Brian J. Arnold (2019), *"use a transactional approach but provide an exemption for CFCs whose tainted income is less than a specified percentage of its total income"*.[12]

2.2. De minimis threshold

Under the BEPS Action 3 Final Report, the *de minimis* threshold was one of the three types of CFC exemptions and threshold requirements considered by the countries involved in the project and analyzed by the OECD.[13] The *de minimis* threshold can be defined as a cap, and all CFCs or the CFC incomes that fall below that cap are disregarded for the purposes of the CFC rules. As it is explained by the OECD in the BEPS Action 3 Final Report, countries usually *"provide an entity-based exemption where the entity's attributable income is less than either a certain percentage of the CFC's income or a fixed amount of the CFC's income or where the taxable profits are less than a fixed amount"*.[14]

The *de minimis* threshold has been widely implemented in the CFC regimes around the world. A well-known example are the *de minimis* thresholds adopted in the CFC rules in the United States according to which the total CFC income will be disregarded if the sum of the CFC's gross foreign base company income (FBCI) and gross insurance income is less than the lesser of 5% of its gross income or USD 1 million in a taxable year.[15] In addition to this, there is also a *"full inclusion rule"* in the US CFC regime for which all of its gross income will be re-

---

11 OECD (2015), Designing Effective Controlled Foreign Company Rules, Action 3 – 2015 Final Report, p. 51. See also Brian J. Arnold, *International Tax Primer*, 4th Edition, (Alphen aan den Rijn: Wolters Kluwer, 2019) pp. 131–132.
12 Brian J. Arnold, *International Tax Primer*, 4th Edition, (Alphen aan den Rijn: Wolters Kluwer, 2019) p. 132.
13 OECD (2015), Designing Effective Controlled Foreign Company Rules, Action 3 – 2015 Final Report, p. 33.
14 OECD (2015), Designing Effective Controlled Foreign Company Rules, Action 3 – 2015 Final Report, pp. 33–34.
15 Foreign base company income (FBCI) is defined as the sum of the foreign personal holding company income (e.g. dividends, interest, and royalties), foreign base company sales income and foreign base services income. Insurance income is defined as any income that (i) derives from the issuing (or re-

garded as FBCI if the gross FBCI of a CFC exceeds 70% of its gross income in a taxable year.[16] Another example is the *de minimis* threshold adopted by the CFC legislation in the Republic of Korea according to which the CFC will be exempted from the Korean CFC rules if its income actually earned, defined as the "*net income per book before deducting the corporate tax*", is below 200 million Korean Won (approximately EUR 150,000) per year.[17] Similarly, the Russian CFC regime exempts the CFC from the CFC regime if its profits are below RUB 10 million (approximately EUR 128,000) as of 2017.[18]

In the European Union, Council Directive (EU) 2016/1164, so-called as the Anti-Tax Avoidance Directive (ATAD),[19] also provides for two possible ways of establishing a *de minimis* threshold in the CFC rules applicable to non-distributed incomes derived from "*non-genuine arrangements which have been put in place for the essential purpose of obtaining a tax advantage*".[20] In Article 7(4) of the ATAD, an entity or a permanent establishment may be exempted from the mentioned CFC rules if (i) the accounting profits are no greater than EUR 750,000 and its passive income (defined as "*non-trading income*") is no greater than EUR 75,000; or if (ii) the accounting profits are up to 10% of its operating costs in a taxable period.[21]

---

insuring) of insurance or annuity contracts and (ii) would be taxed under Subchapter L of Chapter 1, so-called Insurance Companies, if they were derived from an insurance company located in the United States. See Sections 952(a), 953(a) and 954(a) of the Internal Revenue Code of the US.
See also Yariv Brauner/Christine A. Davis, 'Chapter 42: Controlled Foreign Company Legislation in the US' in: Georg Kofler/Richard Krever/Michael Lang/Jeffrey Owens/Pasquale Pistone/Alexander Rust/Josef Schuch (eds.) *Controlled Foreign Company Legislation* (IBFD, 2020), pp.1–5 https://research.ibfd.org/#/doc?url=/document/cfcl_p02_c42 (accessed 14 February 2021). See also Section 1.954-1(b)(1)(i) of the Internal Revenue Code of the US.

16 Yariv Brauner/Christine A. Davis in: Georg Kofler/Richard Krever/Michael Lang/Jeffrey Owens/Pasquale Pistone/Alexander Rust/Josef Schuch (eds.) *Controlled Foreign Company Legislation* (IBFD, 2020), p.5 https://research.ibfd.org/#/doc?url=/document/cfcl_p02_c42 (accessed 14 February 2021). See also and Section 1.954-1(b)(1)(ii) of the Internal Revenue Code of the US.
17 Ji-Hyun Yoon/Ji-Heon Jin, 'Chapter 35: Controlled Foreign Company Legislation in the Republic of Korea' in: Georg Kofler/Richard Krever/Michael Lang/Jeffrey Owens/Pasquale Pistone/Alexander Rust/Josef Schuch (eds.) *Controlled Foreign Company Legislation* (IBFD, 2020), pp.1–3 https://research.ibfd.org/#/doc?url=/document/cfcl_p02_c35 (accessed 14 February 2021).
18 Nikolai Milogolov/Kermen Tsagan-Mandzhieva, 'Chapter 32: Controlled Foreign Company Legislation in Russia' in: Georg Kofler/Richard Krever/Michael Lang/Jeffrey Owens/Pasquale Pistone/Alexander Rust/Josef Schuch (eds.) *Controlled Foreign Company Legislation* (IBFD, 2020), p.4 https://research.ibfd.org/#/doc?url=/document/cfcl_p02_c32 (accessed 14 February 2021). Currency converted in Oanda currency converter tool https://www1.oanda.com/currency/converter/ (accessed 23 May 2020).
19 Council Directive (EU) 2016/1164 of 12 July 2016 laying down rules against tax avoidance practices that directly affect the functioning of the internal market, OJ L 193 (19 July 2016).
20 Council Directive (EU) 2016/1164 of 12 July 2016 laying down rules against tax avoidance practices that directly affect the functioning of the internal market, OJ L 193 (19 July 2016), p. 1 (p. 12, Article 7(2)(b)).
21 Council Directive (EU) 2016/1164 of 12 July 2016 laying down rules against tax avoidance practices that directly affect the functioning of the internal market, OJ L 193 (19 July 2016), p. 1 (p. 12, Article 7(4)). See also Hannes Hilpold, 'Exceptions from the application of the CFC rules under article 7(3) and (4) of the ATAD' in: Nathalie Bravo/Alexandra Miladinovic (eds.) *Concept and Implementation of CFC Legisla-*

Despite being widely adopted, in the BEPS Action 3 Final Report, the OECD raises a concern related to the fact that the *de minimis* thresholds may not be the most precise way to limit the scope of the CFC rules if not implemented in combination with additional safeguards, so-called anti-fragmentation rules or similar anti-abuse provisions. Anti-fragmentation rules are those that target taxpayers aiming to avoid the application of *de minimis* thresholds through the fragmentation of the income between multiple CFCs thus ensuring that each one falls below the threshold. One example of anti-fragmentation rules is a provision that establishes that the income earned by all related CFCs must be computed together in order to ascertain whether it can be regarded as attributable income under the CFC regime, i.e., for the purposes of the *de minimis* threshold verification.[22] However, when the CFC rules provide for *de minimis* thresholds combined with safeguards, the chance to avoid its application could be reduced.[23]

Nevertheless, the need to implement safeguards to ensure the effectiveness of *de minimis* thresholds would also vary from one country to another, e.g. whether *de minimis* thresholds are high enough that fragmentation would be considered viable from the business perspective and, therefore, the *de minimis* threshold would need to be safeguarded. For instance, the implementation of safeguards in Russia was considered to be ineffective given the low *de minimis* threshold adopted there (i.e., RUB 10 million, approximately EUR 128,000) with the fragmentation being considered a more expensive alternative.[24] On the other hand, Germany decided to implement a safeguard rule under its CFC regime. The German *de minimis* threshold provides that CFC income will be exempted from the attribution to the German shareholders if the passive income does not represent more than 10% of the total gross income. Additionally, as a safeguard rule, there is an "*absolute ex-*

---

tion, Series on International Tax Law, Volume 124 (Vienna: Linde, 2021). See also Rodrigo Saavedra Zepeda, 'The relationship between CFC rules and general anti-avoidance rules' in: Nathalie Bravo/Alexandra Miladinovic (eds.) *Concept and Implementation of CFC Legislation*, Series on International Tax Law, Volume 124 (Vienna: Linde, 2021). See also Niki Mitrakou, 'Common Corporate (Consolidated) Tax Base and CFC-Rules' in: Nathalie Bravo/Alexandra Miladinovic (eds.) *Concept and Implementation of CFC Legislation*, Series on International Tax Law, Volume 124 (Vienna: Linde, 2021).

22 The US CFC regime provides for an anti-fragmentation rule, so-called "anti-abuse rule" in Section 1.954-1(b)(4)(i) of the Internal Revenue Code, which states the following: "*For purposes of applying the de minimis test of paragraph (b)(1)(i) of this section, the income of two or more controlled foreign corporations shall be aggregated and treated as the income of a single corporation if a principal purpose for separately organizing, acquiring, or maintaining such multiple corporations is to prevent income from being treated as foreign base company income or insurance income under the de minimis test. A purpose may be a principal purpose even though it is outweighed by other purposes (taken together or separately).*"

23 OECD (2015), Designing Effective Controlled Foreign Company Rules, Action 3 – 2015 Final Report, pp. 34–36.

24 Nikolai Milogolov/Kermen Tsagan-Mandzhieva in: Georg Kofler/Richard Krever/Michael Lang/Jeffrey Owens/Pasquale Pistone/Alexander Rust/Josef Schuch (eds.) *Controlled Foreign Company Legislation* (IBFD, 2020), p.4 https://research.ibfd.org/#/doc?url=/document/cfcl_p02_c32 (accessed 14 February 2021).

emption limit", according to which the CFC income will be only exempted if it does not exceed EUR 80,000 for both the CFC and the German taxpayer.[25]

2.3. Anti-avoidance requirement

The second type of the CFC exemptions and threshold requirements mentioned by the OECD under the BEPS Action 3 Final Report is the anti-avoidance requirement. This also known as "*a motive exemption*"[26] and would only target transactions and structures in which the CFCs are used with the purpose of tax avoidance and, therefore, only those would fall under the scope of the CFC rules. Although not being analyzed further in the Action 3 Final Report, it has not been excluded by the OECD as one possible way to address base erosion and profit shifting under the CFC rules.[27]

The ATAD provides for an anti-avoidance rule with regard to the application of the CFC rules in the European Union. As it is stated in Article 7(2)(b) of the ATAD, one of the options provided for Member States for the taxation of CFCs' income is called "*Model B*".[28] A Member State shall determine the inclusion in the taxpayers' taxable base of the non-distributed incomes of entities or permanent establishments regarded as CFCs provided that those incomes were derived from arrangements (so-called "*non-genuine arrangements*") laid down for the essential purpose of tax avoidance.[29] As an example, Latvia was one of the Member States that has implemented Model B of the ATAD under its corporate income tax law.[30]

---

25 Jochen Gerbracht, 'Chapter 17: Controlled Foreign Company Legislation in Germany' in: Georg Kofler/Richard Krever/Michael Lang/Jeffrey Owens/Pasquale Pistone/Alexander Rust/Josef Schuch (eds.) *Controlled Foreign Company Legislation* (IBFD, 2020), p.4 https://research.ibfd.org/#/doc?url=/document/cfcl_p02_c17 (accessed 14 February 2021). See also Martin Weiss, 'Recent Developments in the German Tax Treatment of CFCs', *European Taxation* (2015), p. 439 (p. 441).
26 Brian J. Arnold, *International Tax Primer*, 4th Edition, (Alphen aan den Rijn: Wolters Kluwer, 2019) p. 134.
27 OECD (2015), Designing Effective Controlled Foreign Company Rules, Action 3 – 2015 Final Report, p. 36.
28 Isabella de Groot/Barry Larking, 'Implementation of Controlled Foreign Company Rules under the EU Anti-Tax Avoidance Directive (2016/1164)', *European Taxation* (2019), p. 261 (p. 265).
29 Council Directive (EU) 2016/1164 of 12 July 2016 laying down rules against tax avoidance practices that directly affect the functioning of the internal market, OJ L 193 (19 July 2016), p. 1 (p. 12, Article 7(2)(b)).
30 Karlis Ketners, 'Chapter 22: Controlled Foreign Company Legislation in Latvia' in: Georg Kofler/Richard Krever/Michael Lang/Jeffrey Owens/Pasquale Pistone/Alexander Rust/Josef Schuch (eds.) *Controlled Foreign Company Legislation* (IBFD, 2020), p.3 https://research.ibfd.org/#/doc?url=/document/cfcl_p02_c22 (accessed 14 February 2021). See also Hannes Hilpold, 'Exceptions from the application of the CFC rules under article 7(3) and (4) of the ATAD' in: Nathalie Bravo/Alexandra Miladinovic (eds.) *Concept and Implementation of CFC Legislation*, Series on International Tax Law, Volume 124 (Vienna: Linde, 2021). See also Rodrigo Saavedra Zepeda, 'The relationship between CFC rules and general anti-avoidance rules' in: Nathalie Bravo/Alexandra Miladinovic (eds.) *Concept and Implementation of CFC Legislation*, Series on International Tax Law, Volume 124 (Vienna: Linde, 2021). See also Niki Mitrakou, 'Common Corporate (Consolidated) Tax Base and CFC-Rules' in: Nathalie Bravo/Alexandra Miladinovic (eds.) *Concept and Implementation of CFC Legislation*, Series on International Tax Law, Volume 124 (Vienna: Linde, 2021).

2.4. Tax rate exemption

The third and last type of the CFC exemptions and threshold requirements analyzed by the OECD under the BEPS Action 3 Final Report was a tax rate exemption that is also the OECD's recommendation for this building block.[31] The tax rate exemption could be defined as a benchmark established for the tax rates which can be a fixed amount or a percentage of the tax rate to which the parent company is subject, and all the CFCs subject to a tax rate above this benchmark would be exempted from the CFC rules.[32] This type of exemption has also been widely adopted by countries. According to the OECD, there are two main reasons why countries have decided to adopt it. Firstly, it could ensure that the CFC rules would only target companies that are considered as high risk of profit shifting and benefitting from the low tax rate of the CFC's jurisdiction. Secondly, it would reduce the compliance and administrative burden.[33]

There are different approaches that countries could choose for implementing the tax rate exemption and ascertaining whether the CFC's tax rate should be considered as low and, therefore, the CFC rules being applicable. One of the approaches is an exemption based on a case-by-case analysis in which the determination of the CFC's tax rate will be defined, e.g., statutory tax rate or effective tax rate, and compared to a given benchmark. Another approach is through the publication of a list of countries in which all of the CFCs will be considered to pay a low tax rate and will fall under the scope of the CFC rules, the so-called *"blacklist"*. A similar list, the so-called *"whitelist"*, can also be used to determine all of the countries in which the CFCs are considered to pay a tax rate above the given benchmark and should therefore be exempted from the CFC rules. In this case, all CFCs located in jurisdictions other than those included in the list will either be automatically subject to the CFC rules or they will be subject to a case-by-case analysis.[34] As an illustration, the Russian CFC regime provides for both a benchmark for the comparison of the CFC's tax rate with the tax rate to which the parent company is subject and also for lists to define from which countries the CFCs may be exempted.[35]

---

[31] OECD (2015), Designing Effective Controlled Foreign Company Rules, Action 3 – 2015 Final Report, p. 33.
[32] OECD (2015), Designing Effective Controlled Foreign Company Rules, Action 3 – 2015 Final Report, p. 37.
[33] OECD (2015), Designing Effective Controlled Foreign Company Rules, Action 3 – 2015 Final Report, p. 36.
[34] OECD (2015), Designing Effective Controlled Foreign Company Rules, Action 3 – 2015 Final Report, pp. 36–37.
[35] Precisely, this is explained by Nikolai Milogolov and Kermen Tsagan-Mandzhieva (2020) as follows: *"First, one of the necessary (but not sufficient) conditions for a CFC to be tax-exempt in Russia is that the CFC's effective tax rate is at least 75% of the weighted average tax rate (the effective and weighted average tax rates are calculated in accordance with the tax code). Second, a CFC should not be a tax resident in a jurisdiction "blacklisted" by the MinFin and the Federal Tax Service. However, compared to worldwide practice, this "blacklist" is formed depending on whether a country effectively exchanges tax information with Russia. Third, a CFC is also tax-exempt in Russia if the CFC is incorporated and a tax resident in an EAEU Member State (Kazakhstan, Belarus, Armenia, Kirghizia) – thus these countries represent a "whitelist"."* Nikolai

2.5. Observations on the CFC exemptions and threshold requirements

The Action 3 final report of the BEPS Project has the key objective to strengthen the CFC rules in the most effective way possible. That is, the design and implementation of CFC rules must clearly focus on the situations and taxpayers that represent a high risk of profit shifting. At the same time, it should be easily applicable by both taxpayers and tax administrations, i.e. establish a low administrative and compliance burden.

With regard to the effectiveness of the CFC exemptions and threshold requirements analyzed above, the anti-avoidance requirement could be considered as the least effective. From the perspective of the tax administration, the anti-avoidance requirement could increase the administrative burden as a detailed case-by-case analysis would need to be undertaken in order to ascertain whether the specific case has the purpose of tax avoidance. From the perspective of the taxpayers, the anti-avoidance requirement could increase the legal uncertainty as the situations and/or transactions that are within the scope of the CFC rules may not be clearly defined.

On the other hand, the *de minimis* threshold could establish a more precise framework in which the CFC rules apply because it is either a percentage or a fixed amount. From both perspectives of the tax administrations and the taxpayers, the *de minimis* threshold might mean a lower administrative and compliance burden as well as a higher legal certainty. Nevertheless, the *de minimis* threshold rule might add some complexity to the CFC regime given the necessity to combine it with anti-fragmentation or anti-abuse rules depending on the threshold amount as well as the risk for the rule to be avoided through fragmentation.

As a conclusion, the tax rate exemption might be considered the most effective among those CFC exemptions and threshold requirements that are analyzed, either if implemented as a benchmark for the tax rates or through the publication of lists that clearly identify the countries that are automatically within or without the scope of the CFC regime or both. The tax rate exemption would be easier to be applied by the tax administration and allows focusing the resources on those situations that represent the higher risk of profit shifting. In addition, it would represent a high legal certainty for the taxpayers as the framework in which the CFC rules should be applicable are clearly defined and a low compliance burden as it would not require much effort and many resources for the taxpayers to be compliant.

Milogolov/Kermen Tsagan-Mandzhieva in: Georg Kofler/Richard Krever/Michael Lang/Jeffrey Owens/Pasquale Pistone/Alexander Rust/Josef Schuch (eds.) *Controlled Foreign Company Legislation* (IBFD, 2020), p.3 https://research.ibfd.org/#/doc?url=/document/cfcl_p02_c32 (accessed 14 February 2021).

3. Analysis of CFC exemptions and threshold requirements in Latin American countries

3.1. The adoption of CFC exemptions and threshold requirements

In Latin America, almost all of the countries that have implemented CFC rules in their legislations have decided to adopt a combination of exemptions and threshold requirements to limit the scope of the CFC regime. The only exceptions are Brazil and Colombia which have not implemented any CFC exemption nor threshold requirements and will be briefly analyzed in a separate subchapter.

Argentina is one of the Latin American countries that has implemented a tax rate exemption combined with threshold requirements, including a *de minimis* threshold, under its CFC regime. The Argentinian CFC regime is provided for in the Article 133 of the income tax law (*Ley de Impuesto a las Ganancias*)[36] regulated by the Regulatory Decree 1170/2018 and was amended in 2017 through Law 27,430,[37] so-called the Tax Reform Law. One of the aims of the tax reform was to set up a CFC regime that is more consistent with the OECD recommendations under BEPS Action 3. Although not being a member country of the OECD, Argentina is a member of the OECD/G20 Inclusive Framework on BEPS and has been striving to strengthen its relationship with the OECD and to position itself in a better place on the international stage.[38]

The new Argentinian CFC regime is applicable to three categories of foreign entities, i.e., (i) trusts, private interest foundations, and other similar structures provided that they are controlled by a resident in Argentina;[39] (ii) foreign entities that are not regarded as taxable entities in the jurisdiction in which they are incorporated, domiciled, or located;[40] and (iii) foreign entities that do not fall under the scope of the two categories described previously provided some requirements are concurrently met.[41] Among those requirements are the tax rate exemption and the threshold requirements.

The threshold requirements adopted under the Argentinian CFC regime provide that foreign entities will be only regarded as a CFC if (i) they do not have enough substance (e.g. sufficient personnel) to carry out their activities, (ii) when their passive income (e.g. dividends, interests, royalties, etc.) represents more than 50%

---

36 Decree 649, published in the Official Gazette on 06 August 1997.
37 Regulatory Decree 1170, published in the Official Gazette on 26 December 2018; Ley (Law) 27,430, published in the Official Gazette on 29 December 2017.
38 Florencia Fernández Sabella, 'Argentina's New Controlled Foreign Company Rules Following the OECD/G20 Base Erosion and Profit Shifting Project', *Bulletin for International Taxation* (2019), p. 442 (p. 442). See also https://www.oecd.org/latin-america/countries/argentina/ (accessed 25 July 2020).
39 Article 133(d) of the Income Tax Law (Decree 649/1997).
40 Article 133(e) of the Income Tax Law (Decree 649/1997).
41 Article 133(f) of the Income Tax Law (Decree 649/1997). See also Florencia Fernández Sabella, 'Argentina's New Controlled Foreign Company Rules Following the OECD/G20 Base Erosion and Profit Shifting Project', *Bulletin for International Taxation* (2019), p. 442 (p. 442).

of the total income in a given fiscal period (i.e. a *de minimis* threshold),[42] or (iii) when their income results, directly or indirectly, in deductible expenses for tax purposes for their related parties resident in Argentina.[43] The foreign entities will be deemed to have sufficient substance and will therefore not fall within the scope of the CFC regime if they have valid commercial reasons and are consistent with the activities that they carry out in terms of infrastructure, assets, and qualified personnel. In addition, the foreign entities will also be considered to have enough substance if, despite not having sufficient material and human resources, their Argentine shareholder certifies that the required substance is effectively provided by another foreign third party as long as any of the following requirements is met: (i) this third party is related to the foreign entity in which the Argentine shareholder participates; or (ii) this third party is incorporated, domiciled, or located in the same jurisdiction of the foreign entity provided that it is neither a non-cooperative jurisdiction nor a tax haven.[44] It is worth noting that non-cooperative jurisdictions are those that do not have an exchange of information agreement or have an agreement but do not comply with it nor a double tax treaty with an exchange of information clause in place with Argentina. Tax havens are defined as those jurisdictions in which the income tax rate is less than 60% of the Argentinian income tax rate currently established at 25%.[45]

The Argentinian CFC regime also provides for a tax rate exemption that establishes a percentage of the Argentinian income tax rate as a benchmark and all of the CFCs that are subject to tax rates below this benchmark will fall under the scope of the CFC rules provided all other requirements are met. In this regard, if the tax effectively paid by the CFC in the jurisdiction in which it is incorporated, domiciled or located, is less than 75% of the tax that would have been paid under the Argentinian Income Tax Law, the CFC will fall under the scope of the CFC regime. This requirement is considered to be automatically met without admitting evidence to the contrary if the foreign entity is incorporated, domiciled, or located in a non-cooperative jurisdiction or in a tax haven.[46] Differently from the other

---

42 The passive incomes under scope are listed in the Article 165(VI).6 of the Regulatory Decree 1170/2018.
43 Article 133(f)(3) of the Income Tax Law (Decree 649/1997).
44 Article 165(VI).5 of the Regulatory Decree 1170/2018. See also Axel A. Verstraeten, 'Chapter 3: Controlled Foreign Company Legislation in Argentina' in: Georg Kofler/Richard Krever/Michael Lang/Jeffrey Owens/Pasquale Pistone/Alexander Rust/Josef Schuch (eds.) *Controlled Foreign Company Legislation* (IBFD, 2020), p.3 https://research.ibfd.org/#/doc?url=/document/cfcl_p02_c03 (accessed 14 February 2021).
45 Articles 15 and 69(a) of the Income Tax Law (Decree 649/1997). See also Axel A. Verstraeten in: Georg Kofler/Richard Krever/Michael Lang/Jeffrey Owens/Pasquale Pistone/Alexander Rust/Josef Schuch (eds.) *Controlled Foreign Company Legislation* (IBFD, 2020), p.4 https://research.ibfd.org/#/doc?url=/document/cfcl_p02_c03 (accessed 14 February 2021).
46 Article 133(f)(4) of the Income Tax Law (Decree 649/1997). See also Axel A. Verstraeten in: Georg Kofler/Richard Krever/Michael Lang/Jeffrey Owens/Pasquale Pistone/Alexander Rust/Josef Schuch (eds.) *Controlled Foreign Company Legislation* (IBFD, 2020), p.3 https://research.ibfd.org/#/doc?url=/document/cfcl_p02_c03 (accessed 14 February 2021).

An analysis of CFC exemptions and threshold requirements

CFC regimes implemented in Latin America that, in some cases, have adopted only different types of the *"black list"*, the Argentinian Federal Administration of Public Revenues (*Administración Federal de Ingresos Públicos*, AFIP) publishes two lists in order to identify those jurisdictions considered as cooperative and those considered as non-cooperative. The list with the cooperative jurisdictions encompasses 126 countries and territories, e.g., the OECD member countries, and the non-cooperative list consists of 95 countries and territories, e.g., Bolivia, Cape Verde, and Montenegro.[47]

Chile has also implemented a combination of tax rate exemptions and threshold requirements in its CFC regime. Chile has been a member country of the OECD since 7 May 2010 and, as such, has been implementing the measures recommended by the OECD under the BEPS Project in order to tackle tax avoidance, base erosion, and profit shifting.[48] The CFC regime can be considered as one of the measures adopted by Chile in this regard. It is provided for in Article 41(G) of the Chilean Income Tax Law (*Decreto Ley* 824), first implemented through Law 20,780 (Tax Reform Law of 2014) and later amended by Law 20,899 (Tax Reform Law of 2016)[49] which aimed to address the OECD recommendations under the BEPS Project in the Chilean CFC regime.[50]

In contrast to the Argentinian CFC regime, the Chilean CFC regime provides for a higher *de minimis* threshold that is also regarded as a *"contamination rule"* according to which, if the passive income represents more than 80% of the total income of the CFC, the total of the income derived by the CFC will be regarded as passive income and will fall under the scope of the CFC rules.[51] However, this rule will not be applicable if at least one of the following conditions is met: (i) when the passive in-

---

[47] The full list with the cooperative jurisdictions can be found in https://www.afip.gob.ar/jurisdicciones Cooperantes/cooperantes/periodos.asp (accessed 25 July 2020). The full list with the non-cooperative jurisdictions can be found in https://www.afip.gob.ar/jurisdiccionesCooperantes/no-cooperantes/periodos.asp (accessed 25 July 2020).

[48] List of OECD Member countries. Available at: https://www.oecd.org/about/document/list-oecd-member-countries.htm (accessed 01 August 2020).

[49] Decree Law 824, published in the Official Gazette on 31 December 1974; Law 20,780, published in the Official Gazette on 29 September 2014; Law 20,899, published in the Official Gazette on 08 February 2016.

[50] As it is precisely explained by Andrés Bustos B. and Felipe Yañez V. (2020): "As like most of the OECD countries, the main policy behind Chilean CFC rules is to prevent abuse of deferral of residence-country tax on the income not directly related to the exercise of commercial or industrial activities (passive income) of certain foreign controlled companies and, at the same time, not to interfere with the ability of residents to carry on legitimate foreign business activities." Andrés Bustos Baraona/Felipe Yáñez, 'Chapter 9: Controlled Foreign Company Legislation in Chile' in: Georg Kofler/Richard Krever/Michael Lang/Jeffrey Owens/Pasquale Pistone/Alexander Rust/Josef Schuch (eds.) *Controlled Foreign Company Legislation* (IBFD, 2020), pp.2–4 https://research.ibfd.org/#/doc?url=/document/cfcl_p02_c09 (accessed 14 February 2021).

[51] Cristián Gárate / Felipe Yáñez, 'Chapter 8: Chile', in: Michael Lang/Jeffrey Owens/Pasquale Pistone/Alexander Rust/Josef Schuch/Claus Staringer (eds.) *Implementing Key BEPS Actions: Where Do We Stand?* (IBFD, 2019), https://research.ibfd.org/#/doc?url=/document/ikb_p02_c08 (accessed 22 February 2021).

come of the CFC does not exceed 10% of its total income; (ii) when the value of the assets capable of producing passive income does not exceed 20% of the total assets value of the CFC; or (iii) when the effective tax rate to which the passive income of the CFC is subject in the jurisdiction in which it is domiciled, established, or constituted is at least 30%. This tax rate exemption approach differs from the approach followed by the Argentinian CFC regime which provides for a benchmark (i.e. 75%) of the Argentinian tax rate instead. Additionally, in contrast to the Argentinian CFC regime, the passive income of the CFC will be disregarded for Chilean CFC regime purposes when it does not exceed 2,400 *Unidades de Fomento* (an inflation-indexed unit of account), currently equivalent to approximately EUR 77,085.[52]

The Chilean CFC regime also provides for a requirement related to CFCs constituted, domiciled, or resident in a territory or jurisdictions that are considered to have preferential tax regimes. All of the income derived through CFCs constituted, domiciled, or resident in such territories or jurisdictions will be deemed as passive income and will fall under the scope of the CFC rules. The Chilean taxpayer may refute this presumption by proving that the income of the CFC does not qualify as passive income as it is defined under the Income Tax Law. The territory or jurisdiction will be considered to have preferential tax regimes if they meet at least two of the following requirements: (i) the effective tax rate to which the foreign source incomes are subject is less than 50% of the additional income tax rate applicable in Chile (currently established at 35%);[53] (ii) there is no exchange of information agreement in place with Chile or there is an agreement but it is not yet in force; (iii) they lack transfer pricing rules that follow the OECD standards; (iv) they do not meet the OECD standards in terms of exchange of information and fiscal transparency; (v) they have preferential tax regimes in place that do not meet the international standards according to the OECD; and (vi) they only tax the income generated, produced, or sourced in their own territories. The OECD member countries will not be subject to this rule.[54] It is worth mentioning that the Chilean Internal Tax Services (*Servicio de Impuestos Internos,* SII) has published a list with the countries considered to have preferential tax regimes through Exempt Resolution No. 124/2017,[55] later updated through Exempt Reso-

---

52 Article 41(G)(C) of the Income Tax Law (Decree Law 824/1974). See also Andrés Bustos Baraona/Felipe Yáñez in: Georg Kofler/Richard Krever/Michael Lang/Jeffrey Owens/Pasquale Pistone/Alexander Rust/Josef Schuch (eds.) *Controlled Foreign Company Legislation* (IBFD, 2020), p.3 https://research.ibfd.org/#/doc?url=/document/cfcl_p02_c09 (accessed 14 February 2021). See also Circular Letter No. 40 of 08 July 2016, available at http://www.sii.cl/normativa_legislacion/circulares/2016/circu40.pdf (accessed 01 August 2020).
According to the Central Bank of Chile, 1 Unit of Account amounts to 28,666.51 Chilean Pesos and 1 Euro amounts to 892.52 Chilean Pesos. Available at: https://www.bcentral.cl/en/home (accessed 01 August 2020).
53 Article 58 of the Income Tax Law (Decree Law 824/1974).
54 Article 41(H) of the Income Tax Law (Decree Law 824/1974).
55 Exempt Resolution No. 124, published in the Official Gazette on 19 December 2017. Available at: http://www.sii.cl/normativa_legislacion/resoluciones/2017/reso124.pdf (accessed 13 August 2020).

An analysis of CFC exemptions and threshold requirements

lution No. 55/2018.[56] The latest version of the list is the longest among those Latin American CFC regimes that were analyzed and encompasses 147 jurisdictions, e.g. the United Arab Emirates, Costa Rica, Cuba, and Thailand. The list is considered by the Chilean Internal Tax Services as having a preliminary character and is thus being used as a guidance to the application of the CFC rules.[57]

Mexico also provides for a tax rate exemption combined with threshold requirements to limit the scope of its CFC regime, although its CFC regime might be considered less complex than the Chilean and Argentinian CFC regimes.[58] Mexico has been a member country of the OECD since 18 May 1994 and its CFC regime was implemented in 1997 in Title VI, Chapter I of the Income Tax Law (*Ley del Impuesto sobre la Renta*).[59] The latest amendment in the Mexican CFC regime was made through the so-called Tax Reform of 2020 as some amendments would be in force as of fiscal year 2020. It aimed to broaden the scope of the CFC rules, especially with regards to the concept of control. Additionally, it also changed the name of the CFC regime from Preferential Tax Regimes (*De Los Regímenes Fiscales Preferentes*)[60] to Controlled Foreign Entities Subject to Preferential Tax Regimes (*De Las Entidades Extranjeras Controladas Sujetas A Regímenes Fiscales Preferentes*), among other amendments.[61]

Under the Mexican CFC regime, the tax residents in Mexico and also the foreign residents that have a Permanent Establishment in Mexico are obligated to pay the income tax in Mexico on the incomes derived abroad through foreign entities subject to preferential tax regimes. According to the income tax law, the incomes of the foreign entities will be considered as subject to preferential tax regimes when they are not subject to any taxation or to a tax rate lower than 75% of the income tax rate that would have been paid in Mexico.[62] This is currently established at 30% which is a higher benchmark if compared to the 50% established in the Chilean CFC regime.[63] Nevertheless, the CFC regime in Mexico also provides for

---

56 Exempt Resolution No. 55, published in the Official Gazette on 05 July 2018. Available at: http://www.sii.cl/normativa_legislacion/resoluciones/2018/reso55.pdf (accessed 13 August 2020).
57 Francisco Ossandón Cerda, 'Normas CFC en Chile: Análisis Particular Del Requisito De Control De Entidades Extranjeras Del Artículo 41 G de la LIR', *Revista de Estudios Tributarios* (2019), p. 11 (pp. 23–24).
58 During the research, the author of the present chapter found one scholar that has the opinion that the Mexican CFC regime does not provide for a *de minimis* threshold. See David Domínguez, 'Chapter 23: Mexico', in: Michael Lang/Jeffrey Owens/Pasquale Pistone/Alexander Rust/Josef Schuch/Claus Staringer (eds.) *Implementing Key BEPS Actions: Where Do We Stand?* (IBFD, 2019), https://research.ibfd.org/#/doc?url=/document/ikb_p02_c23 (accessed 22 February 2021).
59 Law that amends the income tax law and other regulations, published in the Official Gazette on 29 December 1997. Available at: https://sidof.segob.gob.mx/notas/4905187 (accessed 07 August 2020).
60 Decree that issues the income tax law, published in the Official Gazette on 11 December 2013. Available at https://sidof.segob.gob.mx/notas/5325373 (accessed 07 August 2020).
61 Decree that amended the income tax law, published in the Official Gazette on 09 December 2019. Available at: https://sidof.segob.gob.mx/notas/5581292 (accessed 07 August 2020).
62 Article 176 of the Mexican Income Tax Law.
63 Article 9 of the Mexican Income Tax Law.

a *de minimis* threshold. According to it, the incomes derived through foreign entities that carry out business activities will not fall within the scope of the CFC rules if the passive income represents less than 20% of the total income. This is in opposition to the 50% *de minimis* threshold adopted under the Argentinian CFC regime and the 10% *de minimis* threshold adopted by the Chilean CFC regime, although Chile also provides for the 80% *de minimis* threshold or "contamination rule", as explained above. The *de minimis* threshold will not be applicable when more than 50% of the foreign entity income is sourced in Mexico or have represented a deduction in Mexico directly or indirectly.[64]

In Peru, the scope of the CFC regime is also limited through a tax rate exemption and threshold requirements. Peru is not a member country of the OECD, but it is considered as *"one of the most active Partner countries"* by the organization, and it is also a member of the OECD/G20 Inclusive Framework on BEPS.[65] The Peruvian CFC regime is called the International Fiscal Transparency Regime (*Régimen de Transparencia Fiscal Internacional*), and it is provided for in Chapter XIV of the Income Tax Law (*Ley del Impuesto a la Renta*).[66] It was enacted through Legislative Decree No. 1120/2012[67], and the latest amendment was made through Legislative Decree No. 1381/2018[68] which aimed to include the non-cooperative jurisdictions in the scope of the CFC regime and to include the concept of a preferential tax regime in the income tax law. According to the statement of reasons of Legislative Decree No. 1381/2018, the amendments would be necessary because the previous national legislation would not be in accordance with the best international practices, e.g. those established by the OECD in the BEPS Project, to combat international tax avoidance.[69]

In the Peruvian CFC regime, the foreign entities will be considered as a CFC and fall under the scope of the CFC rules in the following cases: (i) when they are established, resident or domiciled in non-cooperative jurisdictions or in tax havens or (ii) when they are not subject to any taxation or are subject to a tax rate lower than 75% of the tax rate they would have been subject in Peru that is currently established at 29.5%.[70] The Peruvian CFC regime also establishes the conditions in which the passive income of the foreign entity will not be attributable for the CFC regime purposes. Among those conditions, there is a tax rate exemption estab-

---

64 Article 176 of the Mexican Income Tax Law.
65 Available at: https://www.oecd.org/latin-america/countries/peru/ (accessed 09 August 2020).
66 Supreme Decree No. 179-2004-EF, published in the Official Gazette on 08 December 2004).
67 Legislative Decree No. 1120, published in the Official Gazette on 18 July 2012. Available at: https://www.gob.pe/institucion/mef/normas-legales/226832-1120 (accessed 09 August 2020).
68 Legislative Decree No. 1381, published in the Official Gazette on 24 August 2020. Available at: http://www.leyes.congreso.gob.pe/Documentos/2016_2021/Decretos/Legislativos/2018/01381.pdf (accessed 09 August 2020).
69 Statement of reasons of the Legislative Decree No. 1381/2018, available at: http://spij.minjus.gob.pe/Graficos/Peru/2018/Agosto/24/EXP-DL-1381.pdf (accessed 09 August 2020).
70 Article 55 of the Supreme Decree No. 179-2004-EF (Income Tax Law).

lishing that the passive income will be exempt from the CFC regime if they are subject to a tax rate higher than 75% of the Peruvian tax rate. In addition to the mentioned tax rate exemption, there are also two *de minimis* thresholds among those conditions. The first *de minimis* threshold exempts the passive income if its total amount is lower than 5 Peruvian Tax Unit (*Unidad Impositiva Tributaria*, UIT). This amount is equivalent to approximately EUR 5,132[71] which is a much lower amount if compared to the similar *de minimis* threshold established by the Chilean CFC regime (approximately EUR 77,085). This calculation excludes the passive income sourced in Peru and also those that fall under the scope of the tax rate exemption. Similar to the Mexican CFC regime, the second *de minimis* threshold establishes that, when the passive income represents 20% or less of the total income of the CFC, it will not be attributable for the CFC regime purposes.[72] Additionally, following the same approach as the Mexican CFC regime, the Peruvian CFC regime provides for a "*contamination rule*" according to which, when the total passive income is higher than 80%, the total income of the CFC will be regarded as passive income for the CFC rules purposes.

Moreover, there is a legal presumption establishing that all the income derived through CFCs located in non-cooperative jurisdictions or in tax havens will be regarded as passive income.[73] Following the same "*blacklist*" approach as the Chilean CFC regime, the non-cooperative jurisdictions or tax havens are those included in a list provided in Appendix I of the Regulatory Decree of the Income Tax Law (*Reglamento de la Ley del Impuesto a la Renta*) which currently includes 44 jurisdictions, e.g. Anguilla, Antigua and Barbuda, Bermuda, Cayman Islands, among others, although this list is much shorter if compared to the Chilean list of 147 jurisdictions.[74] The Regulatory Decree also establishes the requirements for a country to be included in the mentioned Appendix, which includes, for instance, the absence of an exchange of information agreement with Peru or a double tax convention that does not include an exchange of information clause or having an income tax rate of 0% or less than 60% of the Peruvian income tax rate. The Regulatory Decree also establishes the conditions that a jurisdiction or territory can be excluded from the mentioned list,

---

71 According to the government of Peru, 1 Peruvian Tax Unit amounts to 4,300 Nuevo Soles https://www.gob.pe/435-valor-de-la-uit (accessed 09 August 2020). In addition, 1 Euro amounts to 4,189 Nuevo Soles https://www.bcrp.gob.pe/index.php (accessed 09 August 2020).
72 Article 115 of the Supreme Decree No. 179-2004-EF (Income Tax Law).
73 Article 114 of the Supreme Decree No. 179-2004-EF (Income Tax Law).
74 Supreme Decree No. 122-94-EF, as amended by the Supreme Decree No. 086-2020-EF, published in the Official Gazette on 21 April 2020. See also Manuel Augusto Carrión Camayo, 'Chapter 28: Controlled Foreign Company Legislation in Peru' in: Georg Kofler/Richard Krever/Michael Lang/Jeffrey Owens/Pasquale Pistone/Alexander Rust/Josef Schuch (eds.) *Controlled Foreign Company Legislation* (IBFD, 2020), p.2 https://research.ibfd.org/#/doc?url=/document/cfcl_p02_c28 (accessed 14 February 2021).

e.g., being a member country of the OECD or having an exchange of information agreement in force with Peru, among others.[75]

Uruguay may also be mentioned among the Latin American countries that have implemented specific thresholds to limit the scope of its CFC regime which may be considered as a special CFC regime because, in contrast to all of the other CFC regimes implemented in Latin America, it is only applicable to natural persons. Uruguay is not an OECD member country, but it is a member of the OECD/G20 Inclusive Framework on BEPS. In Uruguay, the CFC regime was enacted in 2010 through Law 18.718[76] which included the regime in the Uruguayan Tax Code.[77] The regime was later amended through Law 19.484 in 2017 that aimed "*to comply with the international standards on tax transparency, anti-money laundering and counter-terrorist financing*" thereby including a few regimes in the Uruguayan legislation.[78]

According to the Uruguayan CFC regime, the individual taxpayers that are shareholders in foreign entities will fall within the scope of the regime only in situations in which the foreign entities are located in low or no taxation jurisdictions or that benefit from a low or no taxation special regime.[79] The definition of a low or no taxation jurisdiction is provided in Decree No. 40/017[80] according to which the countries, jurisdictions, or special regimes will be regarded as such when they meet the following conditions: (i) when they subject the income sourced in Uruguay to an effective tax rate lower than 12% as opposed to the benchmark approach followed by Argentina, Chile, Mexico, and Peru; and (ii) when there is no exchange of information agreement or a double tax convention with an exchange of information clause in force with Uruguay or, being in force, it is not fully applicable to all of the taxes covered by the agreement or the convention. The Uruguayan CFC regime also provides for an effective compliance requirement according to which those countries or jurisdictions that do not effectively comply with the exchange of information will also be considered as low or no taxation.[81]

---

75 Article 86 of the Regulatory Decree of the Income Tax Law (Supreme Decree No. 122-94-EF). See also Manuel Augusto Carrión Camayo, in: Georg Kofler/Richard Krever/Michael Lang/Jeffrey Owens/Pasquale Pistone/Alexander Rust/Josef Schuch (eds.) *Controlled Foreign Company Legislation* (IBFD, 2020), p.2 https://research.ibfd.org/#/doc?url=/document/cfcl_p02_c28 (accessed 14 February 2021).
76 Law 18.718, published in the Official Gazette on 24 December 2010.
77 *Texto Ordenado* enacted through the Decree 338 in 28 August 1996 and amendments.
78 Andrea Laura Riccardi Sacchi, 'Chapter 43: Controlled Foreign Company Legislation in Uruguay' in: Georg Kofler/Richard Krever/Michael Lang/Jeffrey Owens/Pasquale Pistone/Alexander Rust/Josef Schuch (eds.) *Controlled Foreign Company Legislation* (IBFD, 2020), p.2 https://research.ibfd.org/#/doc?url=/document/cfcl_p02_c43 (accessed 14 February 2021).
79 Article 7 bis of the Decree 338/1996 (*Texto Ordenado 1996*).
80 Decree No. 40, published in the Official Gazette on 13 February 2017.
81 Article 1 of the Decree 40/017. See also Andrea Laura Riccardi Sacchi in: Georg Kofler/Richard Krever/Michael Lang/Jeffrey Owens/Pasquale Pistone/Alexander Rust/Josef Schuch (eds.) *Controlled Foreign Company Legislation* (IBFD, 2020), p.2 https://research.ibfd.org/#/doc?url=/document/cfcl_p02_c43 (accessed 14 February 2021).

Similar to Chile and Peru, the Uruguayan Tax Administration (*Dirección General Impositiva,* DGI) also follows the *"blacklist"* approach and publishes a list with the countries, jurisdictions, and special regimes considered as low or no taxation. The latest version of the list was published through Resolution No. 2440/020[82] that has been in force since 1 January 2021 that consists of 39 countries, jurisdictions, and special regimes and is the shorter list among the Latin American CFC regimes that follow the *"blacklist"* approach.[83]

Venezuela is also among the Latin American countries that have adopted specific exemptions and threshold requirements to limit the scope of its CFC regime, so-called the International Fiscal Transparency Regime (*Del Régimen de Transparencia Fiscal Internacional*). According to the Venezuela Fiscal Transparency regime, those taxpayers resident in Venezuela that have made investments directly or indirectly through an intermediary person, in branches, legal entities, investment funds, and joint ventures, among others, located in low tax jurisdictions will fall under the scope of the regime.[84] The definition of a low tax jurisdiction was published by the Venezuelan National Customs and Tax Administration (*Servicio Nacional Integrado de Administracion Aduanera y Tributaria,* SENIAT) through the Administrative Ruling SNAT/2004/0232.[85] Similar to the fixed amount approach followed by the Uruguayan CFC regime, those jurisdictions in which the total income, the total assets, or any part of them are not subject to any taxation or are subject to a tax rate equal or lower than 20% will be considered as low tax jurisdictions, which is a higher rate if compared to the 12% established by Uruguay.[86] In the same way as Chile, Peru, and Uruguay, Venezuela also follows the *"blacklist"* approach, and its list with the regarded low tax jurisdictions consists of 83 countries and territories.[87] Furthermore, the countries or territories with which Venezuela has a double tax convention with an exchange of information clause will not be

---

82 Resolution DGI No. 2440, published in the Official Gazette on 28 December 2020.
83 The full list comprises the following countries: Angola, Antigua and Barbuda, Ascension Island, Brunei, Commonwealth of Dominica, Guam, Co-operative Republic of Guyana, Republic of Honduras, North Keeling Island, Christmas Island, Saint Helena, Norfolk Island, Pitcairn Islands, Pacific Islands, Republic of Fiji, Republic of Maldives, Falkland Islands, Republic of Palau, Solomon Islands, US Virgin Islands, Jamaica, Hashemite Kingdom of Jordan, Republic of Kiribati, Federal Territory of Labuan, Republic of Liberia, Niue, Collectivity of French Polynesia, Commonwealth of Puerto Rico, Kingdom of Tonga, Republic of Yemen, Sint Maarten, Overseas Collectivity of Saint Pierre and Miquelon, Sultanate of Oman, Svalbard, Kingdom of Eswatini, Tokelau Islands, Tristan da Cunha, Tuvalu and Republic of Djibouti. See also Andrea Laura Riccardi Sacchi in: Georg Kofler/Richard Krever/Michael Lang/Jeffrey Owens/Pasquale Pistone/Alexander Rust/Josef Schuch (eds.) *Controlled Foreign Company Legislation* (IBFD, 2020), p.3 https://research.ibfd.org/#/doc?url=/document/cfcl_p02_c43 (accessed 14 February 2021).
84 Article 100 of the Income Tax Law (*Ley de Impuesto sobre la Renta*), published in the Official Gazette No. 38.628 on 16 February 2007.
85 Administrative Ruling (*Providencia Administrativa*) SNAT/2004/0232, published in the Official Gazette No. 37.924 on 26 April 2004.
86 Article 1 of the Administrative Ruling SNAT/2004/0232.
87 Article 2 of the Administrative Ruling SNAT/2004/0232.

classified as low tax jurisdictions regardless of their tax rate or whether they are part of the list provided in the ruling.[88] Notwithstanding the latter provision and similar to the Uruguayan effective compliance requirement, those countries or territories that do not provide the information requested by Venezuela based on the exchange of information clause will be regarded as low tax jurisdictions.[89]

Moreover, the Venezuelan regime also provides for two *de minimis* thresholds. The first one establishes that those incomes derived from business activities carry out in low tax jurisdictions will fall out of the scope of the regime when more than 50% of the total assets of the investments consists of fixed assets used to carry out the mentioned activities and are located in such jurisdictions. The second *de minimis* threshold provides that the latter provision will not be applicable, i.e. those investment incomes derived from business activities will fall within the scope of the regime when more than 20% of the total income obtained by the taxpayer's investments in low tax jurisdictions is derived from the transfer of use or temporary use or benefit of assets, dividends, interests, capital gain from the sale of movable, or immovable property or royalties.[90]

3.2. The specific cases of Brazil and Colombia

Brazil can be classified as a specific case because its CFC regime does not provide for any exemption or threshold requirements. Brazil is not an OECD member country, although it has been considered by the OECD as the *"most engaged Key Partner"* over the past two decades.[91] Brazil is also a member of the OECD/G20 Inclusive Framework on BEPS. The Brazilian CFC regime was enacted in the Brazilian legislation through Law No. 12,973/2014[92] and was later regulated through Normative Instruction No. 1,520/2014.[93] With regards to the Brazilian CFC regime and its comparison with the OECD recommendations under the BEPS Action 3 Final Report, the precise explanation provided by Prof. Sergio André Rocha (2017) is worth mentioning:[94]

> This is probably the Report's [BEPS Action 3 final report] *building block* [CFC Exemptions and Threshold Requirements] *that most clearly opposes Brazil's international tax policy regarding CFCs. The reason for such contradiction is that this topic highlights the OECD's concern with using CFC rules to prevent base erosion and profit shifting. However, from a Brazilian standpoint, CFC rules are a standard taxing instrument that is not exclusively focused on avoiding BEPS.*

---

88 Article 3 of the Administrative Ruling SNAT/2004/0232.
89 Article 4 of the Administrative Ruling SNAT/2004/0232.
90 Article 101 of the Income Tax Law.
91 Available at https://www.oecd.org/brazil/ (accessed 13 August 2020).
92 Law 12,973, published in the Official Gazette on 13 May 2014.
93 Normative Instruction 1,520, published in the Official Gazette on 08 December 2014.
94 Sergio André Rocha, *Brazil's International Tax Policy* (Rio de Janeiro: Lumen Juris, 2017) pp. 226–227 https://ssrn.com/abstract=3048899 (accessed 13 August 2020).

An analysis of CFC exemptions and threshold requirements

The OECD's recommendation in this second block – basically focused on providing exemptions and limits to CFC rules – is completely out-of-line with Brazil's policy, since it demonstrates OECD's concern to balance CFC rules' effectiveness and the overall level of administrative burden for the companies.

Considering the fact that the Brazilian CFC regime does not aim to combat tax avoidance, many Brazilian scholars do not consider the Brazilian regime as a "true CFC regime".[95] Nevertheless, in the present study, the author adopted a broader' concept of CFC legislation and, therefore, included Brazil among those Latin American countries that have implemented a CFC regime.

Similar to Brazil, Colombia can also be considered as a specific case because it has decided to not limit the scope of its CFC regime with exemptions and threshold requirements. On 28 April 2020, Colombia became the 37th member country of the OECD, and it is also member of the OECD/G20 Inclusive Framework on BEPS.[96] The Colombian CFC regime was enacted in 2016 through Law 1819 (Tax Reform Law of 2016)[97] which included the CFC regime in Decree 624/1989 (National Tax Statute).[98] In official ruling No. 0386-10/04/2018 that aimed to provide clarifications and guidance on the interpretation of the Colombian CFC rules, the National Tax and Customs Office (Dirección de Impuestos y Aduanas Nacionales, DIAN) stated that the Colombian CFC regime arose from BEPS

---

95 Sergio André Rocha, *Brazil's International Tax Policy*, p. 111, FN 296. It is worth highlighting the opinion of Prof. Luís Eduardo Schoueri and Guilherme Galdino (2020): *"Whether or not Brazil has CFC legislation depends on what should deemed to be the main features of such legislation. Accordingly, if a CFC is considered as a SAAR, i.e., aiming at specific situations whereby resident companies would be able to choose low tax jurisdictions, than it would immediately be concluded that there is no need for such in Brazil. Accordingly, already in the adoption of worldwide taxation in Brazil, a full transparency regime was adopted. [...] On the other hand, should a broader concept be adopted for CFC legislation that would not consider only abusive situations (SAAR), then Brazil has CFC rules. However, as the authors adopt the strict concept of CFC legislation, the unrestricted Brazilian regime is hereinafter referred to as the "worldwide income taxation" legislation ("WWIT legislation")."* Luís Eduardo Schoueri/Guilherme Galdino, 'Chapter 7: Controlled Foreign Company Legislation in Brazil' in: Georg Kofler/Richard Krever/Michael Lang/Jeffrey Owens/Pasquale Pistone/Alexander Rust/Josef Schuch (eds.) *Controlled Foreign Company Legislation* (IBFD, 2020), p.1 https://research.ibfd.org/#/doc?url=/document/cfcl_p02_c07 (accessed 14 February 2021).
96 Available at https://www.oecd.org/colombia/colombia-accession-to-the-oecd.htm (accessed 02 August 2020).
97 Law1819, published in the Official Gazette on 29 December 2016.
98 Decree 624, published in the Official Gazette on 30 March 1989. The Colombian CFC regime was later amended by Law 1943, published in the Official Gazette on 28 December 2018, which amended Article 885 of Decree 624/1989 and established two presumptions that could be considered as de minimis thresholds. The first presumption stated that, when the passive income of the CFC represented 80% or more of its total income, all of the income would be deemed as passive income and, as a consequence, would fall under the scope of the CFC regime. On the contrary, the second presumption stated that, when the active income of the CFC was at least 80% of its total income, all of the income would be deemed as active income and would fall out of scope of the Colombian CFC regime. However, Law 1943/2018 was declared unconstitutional by the Constitutional Court of Colombia through Sentence No. C-481 of 2019. Available at: http://www.suin-juriscol.gov.co/viewDocument.asp?id=30038453#ver_30205295 (accessed 22 February 2021).

Action 3. It also indicated that its key characteristics are the international fiscal transparency and the anti-deferral of the income tax on passive income.[99]

Although the implementation of the CFC regime in Colombia is a consequence of BEPS Action 3, the regime has some deviations from the OECD recommendations in the Action 3 Final Report, including those related to the CFC exemptions and threshold requirements.[100] In this regard, as precisely explained by Héctor Andrés Falla Cubillos (2020), the Colombian CFC regime "did not contemplate exceptions for its application, particularly in those cases where the CFCs are not subject to effective tax rates significantly low compared to the Colombian tax rate".[101]

3.3. Observations on the CFC Regimes adopted in Latin America

The present chapter aimed to analyze the CFC exemptions and threshold requirements adopted by the Latin American countries that have already implemented the CFC regime under their legislations, i.e. Argentina, Brazil, Chile, Colombia, Mexico, Peru, Uruguay, and Venezuela. Moreover, it aimed to ascertain whether the OECD recommendations under the BEPS Action 3 Final Report, in particular with respect to the CFC exemptions and threshold requirements, have been embraced in Latin America.

The Latin American countries analysed in the present chapter had already implemented CFC rules in their legislation before the publication of the BEPS Action 3 Final Report with the exception of Colombia whose CFC regime was enacted in 2016. Nevertheless, the analysis leads to the conclusion that the BEPS Project, especially Action 3, has been the grounds for several legislative changes that aimed to amend or to implement the CFC regime in the Latin American countries. This is the case of Argentina, Chile, Colombia, and Mexico which made it explicit that the modifications, or the implementation as is the case of Colombia, of their CFC regimes occurred because of the OECD recommendations under BEPS Action 3. Peru and Uruguay, although not specifically mentioning BEPS Action 3, have also amended their CFC legislation to comply with the OECD recommendations and the best international practices as well as to combat international tax avoidance. Brazil and Venezuela are the only countries that have not amended their

---

99 *Concepto General Unificado* (Ruling) 0386, published in the Official Gazette on 10 April 2018. Available at: https://cijuf.org.co/normatividad/concepto-general-unificado/2018/concepto-general-00386.html (accessed 02 August 2020).
100 Natalia Quiñones, 'Chapter 10: Colombia', in: Michael Lang/Jeffrey Owens/Pasquale Pistone/Alexander Rust/Josef Schuch/Claus Staringer (eds.) *Implementing Key BEPS Actions: Where Do We Stand?* (IBFD, 2019), https://research.ibfd.org/#/doc?url=/document/ikb_p02_c10 (accessed 22 February 2021).
101 Héctor Andrés Falla Cubillos, 'Reflexiones sobre el Régimen de entidades controladas del exterior en Colombia', *Revista Instituto Colombiano de Derecho Tributario* (2020), p. 19 (p. 42).

An analysis of CFC exemptions and threshold requirements

CFC regimes to be consistent with the BEPS Project. Nevertheless, the Venezuelan CFC regime could be considered more consistent with the OECD recommendation under BEPS Action 3 with regards to the exemptions and threshold requirements if compared to the Brazilian regime.

The analysis of the CFC exemptions and threshold requirements adopted by Latin American countries has shown that almost all of them, with the exception of Brazil and Colombia, have implemented a combination of exemptions and threshold requirements to limit the scope of their CFC rules, thereby trying to focus their CFC rules to combat the tax avoidance, base erosion, and profit shifting. Among those countries, Chile, Peru, Uruguay, and Venezuela have also implemented lists with the non-cooperative jurisdictions while Argentina has implemented a combination of two lists. One provides for the non-cooperative jurisdictions and the other for the cooperative jurisdictions. The combination of a tax rate exemption with the publication of lists is also recommended by the OECD under the BEPS Action 3 Final Report because it would facilitate the application of the CFC regime by the tax authorities, and they would also allow the taxpayers to know the risk in advance of falling under the scope of the CFC regime.[102]

In conclusion, the CFC regimes of the Latin American countries analyzed in the present chapter could be considered largely consistent with the OECD recommendations under the BEPS Action 3 Final Report, specifically with regards to the building block in scope in the present analysis, namely, the CFC exemptions and threshold requirements. The Latin American CFC regimes could still be improved. This is the case, for instance, of the Mexican CFC regime, in particular its *de minimis* threshold. It does not focus on avoiding BEPS situations as it does not exempt those CFCs from the CFC regime that, although their passive income represents more than 20% of the total income, carry out valid economic activities,[103] among others, that have already been precisely pointed out by some scholars.[104] Nevertheless, the implemented exemptions and threshold requirements, combined in many cases with the publication of lists, have established what could be considered as a good framework for the application of the CFC rules. It could also allow targeting the situations representing a higher-risk of tax avoidance, base

---

102 OECD (2015), Designing Effective Controlled Foreign Company Rules, Action 3 – 2015 Final Report, p. 36.
103 David Domínguez, 'Chapter 23: Mexico', in: Michael Lang/Jeffrey Owens/Pasquale Pistone/Alexander Rust/Josef Schuch/Claus Staringer (eds.) Implementing Key BEPS Actions: Where Do We Stand? (IBFD, 2019), https://research.ibfd.org/#/doc?url=/document/ikb_p02_c23 (accessed 22 February 2021).
104 See Luis Maria Méndez/Mirna Solange Screpante, 'Chapter 2: Argentina', in: Michael Lang/Jeffrey Owens/Pasquale Pistone/Alexander Rust/Josef Schuch/Claus Staringer (eds.) *Implementing Key BEPS Actions: Where Do We Stand?* (IBFD, 2019), https://research.ibfd.org/#/doc?url=/document/ikb_p02_c02 (accessed 22 February 2021). See also Cristián Gárate/Felipe Yáñez, in: Michael Lang/Jeffrey Owens/Pasquale Pistone/Alexander Rust/Josef Schuch/Claus Staringer (eds.) *Implementing Key BEPS Actions: Where Do We Stand?* (IBFD, 2019), https://research.ibfd.org/#/doc?url=/document/ikb_p02_c08 (accessed 22 February 2021).

erosion, and profit shifting. It is worth noting that the Brazilian and the Colombian regimes would not be compliant with the OECD recommendations under this building block insofar as they have a rather broad scope and do not provide for any exemptions or threshold requirements.

4. Conclusion

The BEPS Action 3 Final Report aims to identify the main challenges related to CFCs and to provide the technical guidance on how to address these challenges, in particular in relation to the development and implementation of effective CFC rules. One of the key challenges is the limitation of the scope of the CFC rules which should target the taxpayers and structures that represent a high risk of profit shifting and, at the same time, alleviate the compliance and administrative burden. In Chapter 3 of the Action 3 Final Report, the OECD analyzes some exemptions and threshold requirements that could be adopted to limit the scope of CFC rules, i.e., *de minimis* thresholds, the anti-avoidance requirement, and the tax rate exemption.

The present chapter analyzed different countries' CFC regimes in order to ascertain whether the CFC exemptions and threshold requirements have been implemented as a way of limiting the scope of the CFC rules. The vast majority of the countries analyzed have adopted at least one type of exemption or threshold requirement in their CFC regimes as they seem to be practical and to make the application of the CFC rules more feasible for both taxpayers and the tax administration.

Computation of CFC Income

Federico Giordano

1. Introduction
2. The computation rules under the Final Report on BEPS Action 3
   2.1. General rules on the computation of the CFC taxable income
   2.2. Computation of the CFC taxable income under the law of the parent jurisdiction
   2.3. Computation of the CFC taxable income under the law of the CFC jurisdiction
   2.4. Option for the taxpayer to choose either jurisdiction's computational rules
   2.5. Computation of the CFC taxable income under Common Standard as the International Financial Reporting Standards (IFRS)
   2.6. The tax treatment of subsidiary losses under CFC rules
3. The implementation of the CFC rules in the EU Anti-Tax Avoidance Directive (ATAD)
   3.1. General rules on the calculation of the CFC taxable base under Articles 7 and 8 of ATAD
4. Comparing the applicability of the CFC computation rules around the World
   4.1. The Italian CFC rules
   4.2. The German CFC rules
   4.3. The Dutch CFC rules
   4.4. The U.S. CFC rules
5. Conclusion

Computation of CFC Income

1. Introduction

The Organisation for Economic Co-operation and Development (OECD) Final Report on Base Erosion and Profit Shifting (BEPS) Action 3 (named 'Designing Effective Controlled Foreign Company Rules') provides recommendations on this matter based on six building blocks: 1. Definition of a Controlled Foreign Company (CFC), 2. CFC exemptions and threshold requirements, 3. Definition of income, 4. Computation of income, 5. Attribution of income, 6. Prevention and elimination of double taxation[1]. The OECD report aims to provide guidelines for legislators to identify effective CFC rules to avoid profit shifting to foreign entities.

The intent of this thesis is to analyse the recommendations the OECD has made in the Report on Action 3 for computing CFC income, taking into account both the policy goals of the action under discussion and the experiences acquired by some countries that have been applying CFC rules in recent years[2].

In order to understand the recommendations for computing CFC income outlined within BEPS Action 3 it is to be taken into account the main purpose of BEPS that was to close loopholes in international tax laws that allow multinational companies to shift profit to low or no-tax jurisdiction and then acquire competitive advantage compared with other companies.

This thesis is divided in five main Chapters. After the Introduction Chapter, the second Chapter presents an overview of the computation rules under the Final Report on BEPS Action 3. In order to provide a comprehensive framework, the third Chapter, briefly describes general rules on the calculation of the CFC taxable base under Council Directive no. 2016/1164/EU[3] (ATAD) that, despite BEPS Action 3, has established *inter alia* a minimum standard with reference to CFCs.

With the aim to provide some examples to better understand the current scenario, Chapter four describes the CFC rules that are in place in some European jurisdictions and in the United States (U.S.), which was the first jurisdiction to adopt CFC rules in 1962[4]. Chapter 5 sums up and concludes this thesis.

---

1 OECD (2015), 'Designing Effective Controlled Foreign Company Rules', Action 3 – 2015 Final Report, OECD/G20 Base Erosion and Profit Shifting (BEPS) Project, OECD Publishing, Paris, Executive summary, p. 9–10.
2 Eva Palatická, 'Implementation of a CFC Rule: Rules to Compute and Attribute Income' in Limiting Base Erosion, Controlled Foreign Company Rules and the EU, Michael Lang (Ed.), Erik Pinetz and Erich Schaffer (Eds.), Series on International Tax Law, Linde, 2017, p. 1/14.
3 Council Directive (EU) 2016/1164 of 12 July 2016 laying down rules against tax avoidance practices that directly affect the functioning of the internal market (ATAD).
4 Brian J. Arnold, ''International Tax Primer', Kluwer Law International, IV edition, January 15, 2019, par. 7.3.1.

2. The computation rules under the Final Report on BEPS Action 3

In the context of this constituent element of the CFC, the final report identifies the method of calculating the income of a CFC. In this regard, it provides recommendations on: (i) which country rules should apply, and (ii) the assessment of whether specific rules need to be applied for calculating CFC income. These guidelines are not mandatory; acceding countries have the option of adopting them if they agree with their national policy objectives[5]. It is to be noted that there is a considerable variation in the CFC rules of countries with respect to the computation rules.

In practice, most Multinational Enterprises (MNEs) have trouble calculating CFC income, especially when local requirements and rules for CFC reporting, accounting, and tax information vary from those in the parent company's jurisdiction. This frequently requires them to duplicate accounting and tax reporting, as well as keeping data on file for an extended period of time about applicable carry forwards and tax adjustments with reference to the CFC[6]. In order to better understand the recommendations *ratio* it is important to note that one of the causes of the BEPS issue is the use of low-tax affiliated non-resident taxpayers to route income from a resident business *via* the low-tax non-resident affiliate. To address this problem, several countries have implemented CFC regulations[7].

As stated in the BEPS Action Plan, BEPS issues are primarily posed by situations in which taxable income is arbitrarily separated from the activities that produce it. These circumstances jeopardize the legitimacy of the entire tax system and can exacerbate the difficulty in meeting revenue targets[8]. Furthermore, when taxpayers plan to shift taxable income away from the jurisdiction where income-generating activities are conducted, other taxpayers may end up bearing a larger share of the burden[9] "as corporations operating only in domestic markets or refraining from BEPS activities may face a competitive disadvantage relative to enterprises MNEs that are able to avoid or reduce tax by shifting their profits across borders"[10].

---

5 Cui Xiaojing, Zhang Han, 'Chinese Controlled Foreign Company Rules in the Post-BEPS Era: New Developments', Asia-Pacific Tax Bulletin, Volume 24, No. 2 (2018), IBFD.
6 Comments received on Public Discussion Draft BEPS Action 3: Strengthening CFC Rules, 5 May 2015, part 1, p. 251.
7 Action Plan on Base Erosion and Profit Shifting, OECD, No. 60839 2013, p. 16.
8 OECD/G20, Addressing the Tax Challenges of the Digital Economy – Action 1: Final Report (OECD/G20 2015), International Organizations' Documentation IBFD, n. 5, p. 78.
9 Ibid.
10 Ibid.

2.1. General rules on the computation of the CFC taxable income

The Final Report on BEPS Action 3 provides four options for the computation of CFC related income before arriving at a recommendation, namely, (i) computation under the law of the parent jurisdiction; (ii) computation under the law of the CFC jurisdiction; (iii) option for the taxpayer to choose either jurisdiction's computational rules; that is, (i) or (ii); and (iv) computation by using a common standard such as the International Financial Reporting Standard (IFRS) or any internationally accepted accounting standard.

2.2. Computation of the CFC taxable income under the law of the parent jurisdiction

According to the recommendations, the law-based calculation of the parent jurisdiction (the jurisdiction applying the CFC rules) is probably the most appropriate option for calculating the CFC income to be attributed to shareholders. This is because this choice is consistent with the previously mentioned BEPS concerns and allows for the reduction of tax administration costs[11]. In fact, applying this option significantly reduces any benefit from shifting taxable income away from the jurisdiction in which activities producing income are effectively conducted and, generally, permit to tax income where value is created[12].

However, such a policy would require MNE subsidiaries to recalculate their profits annually under the laws of the parent jurisdiction, which may result in significant compliance costs for the MNE. Furthermore, it may result in circumstances where differences in the tax base calculation in the parent and subsidiary jurisdictions cause an otherwise high-taxed subsidiary to be regarded as having a low effective rate of tax[13]. For example, structural differences in the calculation of the taxable base (including timing differences and criteria for the recognition of income and expenses) could affect the calculation of the effective tax rate in different jurisdictions.

As an example of the computation of the CFC taxable income under the law of the parent jurisdiction, Article 167 of the Italian Tax Code (*Testo Unico sulle Imposte sui redditi*, TUIR[14]), on par. 7, states that incomes from CFCs are determined according to the Italian provisions applicable to a persons resident that

---

11 Ibid.
12 The Davis Tax Committee, "Second and Final Report on Base Erosion and Profit Shifting", September 2016, p. 195.
13 OECD Secretary-General Report to G20 Finance Ministers and Central Bank Governors, Japan, June 2019, p. 49.
14 Presidential Decree of 22 December 1986, No 917; official publication: Gazzetta Ufficiale (G.U.), General Series No. 302, Ordinary Supplement No 126; publication date: 31 December 1986.

holds business income, except Article 86, par. 4 TUIR; that is, capital gains and are taxed separately at the corporate tax rate; that is, 24% as per 2021. Therefore, the Italian lawmaker would choose the first option, recommended by the OECD, since the relevant provisions to be applied belong to the parent company's jurisdiction. This choice is logically consistent with BEPS Action 3 and has the ability to reduce costs for the tax authorities[15]. Italy included in its CFC rules not only passive income but also all income that is earned by a foreign-related company[16].

A further example is that of Spain, where Article 91(8) of the Spanish personal income tax (*Impuesto de Renta sobre las Personas Fisicas*, IRPF[17]) and Article 100(9) of the Corporate Taxation Act (*Ley del Impuesto sobre Sociedades*, LIS[18]), provide that the amount of positive income to be attributed to the parent company is computed according to the principles and criteria established in the LIS and in other provisions relating to the determination of corporate tax base[19]. It is to be noted that the rules in Spain, despite the rules in force at the Italian level, only apply tax to CFCs on passive income. However, it seems that the CFC legislation in both Italy and Spain is aligned with the standards recommended by the OECD. The Italian rules will be analysed in more detail in Chapter 4.

Likewise in France, for example, the profits of the foreign entity are added to the tax base of the parent company and taxed according to French tax law. Furthermore, the losses of the parent company can offset the profits of the CFC, but the losses of a CFC cannot be used to offset the income of the parent company (in some cases the losses can be carried over and used in subsequent fiscal years)[20]. It is to be noted that the French CFC legislation does not apply to companies within the European Union (EU) unless the foreign structure is considered an artificial scheme.

Examples can be found in developing countries as well. Colombia[21], for example, has OECD-oriented CFC rules in which the foreign entity's taxable income is calculated by applying Colombian tax rules[22].

---

15 As per BEPS Action 3 (p. 57), some "jurisdictions could achieve a broadly similar outcome by starting with the income calculated according to the rules of the CFC jurisdiction and then adjusting the income in line with the rules of the parent jurisdiction".
16 For more details on the Italian CFC rules, see Chapter 4, par. 4.1.
17 Law of 28 November 2006 No 35, official publication: Boletín Oficial del Estado (B.O.E) No 285/2014; publication date: 29 November 2006.
18 Ibid.
19 Peter Wenzel, "Making Germany's CFC Rules Effective Again: A Comparative Analysis to Spain's and UK's CFC Rules to Find the Best ATAD Compliant Approaches Provided in the OECD/G20's Report on Designing Effective CFC Rules", Universidad Católica de Murcia, Programa de Doctorado en Ciencias Sociales, February 2019.
20 Sebastian Dueñas, 'How Controlled Foreign Corporation Rules Look Around the World: France', January 21, 2020, Tax Foundation.
21 Colombia has become the OECD's 37th Member country.
22 Tim Sanders (Ed.), 'The inward investment and international taxation review', The Law Reviews, Tenth Edition, February 2020, p. 89.

Computation of CFC Income

An example is provided below to illustrate the computation of the CFC taxable income under the law of the parent jurisdiction.

Country X	€	Country Y	€
Subsidiary P&L		Computation of the CFC taxable income in the Parent jurisdiction	
Revenues from sales	1000	Subsidiary taxable income	150
Royalties on license	200	Tax adjustment 1	32
General expenses	600	Tax adjustment 2	−100
Rent	150		
Salaries	100		
Entertainment	100		
Telephone	40		
Depreciation	60		
Profit = Taxable base	150	Taxable base	282

Some assumptions have to be made in order to simplify the computation process:

- under Country X (CFC jurisdiction) tax rules all of the expenses necessary to run a business are tax-deductible, including office rent, salaries, telephone costs, entertainment expenses and depreciations;
- under Country Y (parent jurisdiction) tax rules telephone cost are tax deductible in the limit of 20% (adjustment 1) and entertainment expenses are not deductible (adjustment 2).

Country Y includes in its CFC rules not only passive income but also all income that is earned by the freeing entity.

2.3. Computation of the CFC taxable income under the law of the CFC jurisdiction

A second option is to use the rules of the CFC jurisdiction to assess income. However, the report itself highlights how this practice would not be consistent with the objectives of Action 3, since the use of the rules of the CFC jurisdiction could allow a reduction in the assigned income at the parent company level. Moreover, due to its greater complexity it could also increase the administration costs for the tax administration, which would be forced to apply unfamiliar rules[23].

---

23 OECD (2015), 'Designing Effective Controlled Foreign Company Rules', Action 3 – 2015 Final Report, OECD/G20 Base Erosion and Profit Shifting (BEPS) Project, OECD Publishing, Paris, p. 57.

For example, the Argentine CFC rules are not perfectly in line with the above-mentioned OECD recommendation. As stated in sections 133.d, 133.e, 133.f and 133, last paragraph, of the Income Tax Law (*Ley de Impuesto a las Ganancias*, LIAG[24]), Argentine law identifies which CFC income should be considered in a given tax year through the application of the rules of the CFC resident jurisdiction[25].

It is obvious that allowing taxpayers the use of the CFC jurisdiction's rules to calculate the taxable income would create room for manipulation of the tax base.

In fact, BEPS activities would distort competition, as companies that only operate in domestic markets or refrain from engaging in BEPS activities can find themselves at a competitive disadvantage compared to MNEs that can escape or minimize tax by moving income across borders[26]. For example, the CFC jurisdiction could consider some expenses to be deductible that are not deductible in the parent jurisdiction. This may allow manipulation of the taxable base by MNEs that could determine a reduction in the overall effective tax rate by shifting profit in more favourable tax jurisdictions.

Considering the example presented in Section 2.2 above, in which case the CFC taxable income is computed under the law of the CFC jurisdiction, the parent company would tax the amount of euro 150; that is, the CFC taxable base; hence, taking advantage of the entire tax deduction of telephone costs and entertainment expenses.

2.4. Option for the taxpayer to choose either jurisdiction's computational rules

Allowing taxpayers to choose either jurisdiction's rules for calculating income is another option, but this would open up possibilities for tax planning[27] and arbitrage, resulting in significant revenue losses for many States. The practice of 'cherry picking' would allow MNEs an unfair advantage that, again, would distort competition. Based on this analysis, this option appears to be less applied since no example of countries applying it has been identified.

---

24 As codified by Decree No. 649/97 (B. O. 6.8.97), Exhibit EC II-2, as last amended.
25 Florencia Fernández Sabella, 'Argentina's New Controlled Foreign Company Rules Following the OECD/G20 Base Erosion and Profit Shifting Project', Bulletin for International Taxation September 2019, IBFD, p. 444.
26 OECD/G20, Addressing the Tax Challenges of the Digital Economy – Action 1: Final Report (OECD/G20 2015), International Organizations' Documentation IBFD, n. 5, p. 78.
27 Ibid. note 23.

2.5. Computation of the CFC taxable income under Common Standard as the International Financial Reporting Standards (IFRS)

A final option under the OECD Final Report on BEPS Action 3 would be to compute income using a common standard, for example, the International Financial Reporting Standards (IFRS). According to the explanatory section of the OECD final report, the benefit of this further approach is that it could potentially lead to international consistency, since all CFCs and parent jurisdictions will be required to use identical rules for calculating CFC income, regardless of the CFC's or parent's residence. However, given that most countries do not use these criteria to calculate taxable income, this approach could result in an increase in administrative and compliance costs, if taxpayers are required to recalculate the CFC's income using standards not applied by the parent jurisdiction or the CFC jurisdiction[28].

Studies comparing the standard process of adjusting financial accounting data to tax requirements, using a common IFRS tax base, show that this option results in a higher tax burden than the first one i.e. 'computation of the CFC taxable income under the law of the parent jurisdiction')[29]. That said, if companies around the world are given the ability to calculate CFC taxable income in accordance with a common standard, such as IFRS, there will be no harmful tax behaviour by MNEs. In fact, applying a common accounting standard to all subsidiaries will ensure that differences in accounting standards between subsidiaries do not cause distortions[30]. On the contrary, the use of different accounting standards at the subsidiary level would, for example, create the possibility of distortions arising from intercompany transactions.

Despite the growing trend towards the application of IFRS around the world, its implementation as a common standard for calculating the tax base, in many countries, would affect constitutional restrictions on the states' taxing powers and create a greater administrative burden for both taxpayers and for tax offices. Moreover, governments are hesitant to implement such a common concept be-

---

28 Ibid, p. 58.
29 Eva Palatická, 'Implementation of a CFC Rule: Rules to Compute and Attribute Income' in Limiting Base Erosion, Controlled Foreign Company Rules and the EU, Michael Lang (Ed.), Erik Pinetz and Erich Schaffer (Eds.), Series on International Tax Law, Linde, 2017, p. 3/14. See also: Simona Jirásková and Jan Molín, 'IFRS Adoption for Accounting and Tax Purposes: An issue based on the Czech Republic as Compared with Other European Countries', 16th Annual Conference on Finance and Accounting, ACFA Prague 2015, 29th May 2015. See also: Christoph Spengel, 'International Accounting Standards, Tax Accounting and Effective Levels of Company Tax Burdens in the EU', European Taxation, July/August 2003, p. 253–266.
30 Public consultation document Global Anti-Base Erosion Proposal ("GloBE") – Pillar Two, 8 November 2019 – 2 December 2019, p. 10.

cause it would require alignment with other provisions[31]. Consequently, for the reasons mentioned above, it will remain an elusive goal. Therefore, it is possible to agree with the OECD's arguments in the explanatory section of the report, where the fourth alternative (i.e. 'computation of the CFC taxable income under Common Standard as the IFRS') is in a disadvantageous position in comparison to the first alternative ('computation of the CFC taxable income under the law of the parent jurisdiction')[32].

It is important to note that the OECD issued a Consultation Document on 8 November, 2019 , Pillar Two[33], which suggests that generally accepted accounting principles should be used to determine whether an enterprise's foreign-source income is subject to tax at a rate lower than the minimum rate. For this purpose, acceptable accounting standards could be the IFRS or some other acceptable standard used by the ultimate parent of a multinational group. However, the final amount would be subject to adjustment in order to eliminate the permanent and temporal differences between accounting profits and taxable income[34].

It can be argued that Pillar Two is intended to supplement the OECD/G20 BEPS Project and provide a "comprehensive solution" to the issue of profit shifting to low-taxed jurisdictions, and thus serves as a natural complement to the BEPS measures already in place[35]. Nevertheless, this last option would be more complex compared with the first one and therefore, less easy to apply. In fact, computing the tax base using a common standard presents some challenges for tax administrations. More specifically, since the auditors may be unfamiliar with the accounting standards used by each of the international jurisdictions, it may be difficult for the parent company's tax administration to audit the income of controlled companies that use a different accounting standard from the one used in the parent jurisdiction[36].

2.6. The tax treatment of subsidiary losses under CFC rules

The OECD Report also recommends that a CFC's income be measured using the parent jurisdiction's laws, and that the offset of CFC losses be limited to profits of the same CFC or those in the same jurisdiction[37].

---

31 Eva Palatická, 'Implementation of a CFC Rule: Rules to Compute and Attribute Income' in Limiting Base Erosion, Controlled Foreign Company Rules and the EU, Michael Lang (Ed.), Erik Pinetz and Erich Schaffer (Eds.), Series on International Tax Law, Linde, 2017.
32 Ibid, p. 3/14.
33 OECD, Public Consultation Document: Global Anti-Base Erosion Proposal ("GloBE") – Pillar Two, 8 Nov. 2019, available at www.oecd.org.
34 Brian J. Arnold, 'The Evolution of Controlled Foreign Corporation Rules and Beyond', Bulletin for International Taxation, December 2019, IBFD, p. 644.
35 Aldo Castoldi and Piero Bonarelli, 'Pillar One: le misure dell'OCSE per governare le sfide dell'economia digitale', Fiscalità & Commercio Internazionale n. 12/2020, Wolters Kluwer Italia, p. 7.
36 OECD, Public Consultation Document: Global Anti-Base Erosion Proposal ("GloBE") – Pillar Two, 8 Nov. 2019, p. 10.
37 Ibid, p. 58.

Computation of CFC Income

Over the last years, before arriving at this second recommendation, discussions have been undertaken on various treatments of loss limitation in respect to designing effective CFC legislation. The most crucial issue to be resolved seemed to be the question "whether CFC losses should only be offset against CFC profits or whether they can also be used against profits in the parent company"[38]. It should be noted that enabling loss relief can take several forms, and countries' approaches can vary in this regard depending on whether the situation is purely domestic or cross-border[39].

Many existing CFC regulations only provide for an offsetting between the CFC's losses and the profits of that CFC or another CFC in the same jurisdiction, which is the recommended solution, since it prohibits the CFC losses from being offset against the parent company's profits. Allowing CFC losses to be offset against the profits of parent companies or CFCs in other jurisdictions may promote loss manipulation in the subsidiary jurisdiction[40].

In the absence of such a limit in the legal system, taxable profits in the hands of the parent company would be distorted because the latter could pay taxes on less wealth than the one was actually made[41].

Example

Parent is a resident in Country A and Sub B is a wholly owned subsidiary in country B that is a CFC. Country A has CFC rules. In year 1, Parent earns 1000 and Sub B earns 500 of CFC income. Parent has 200 in losses and Sub B has 1000 in losses. This is illustrated in the below Figure.

Figure 5.1   Loss limitation

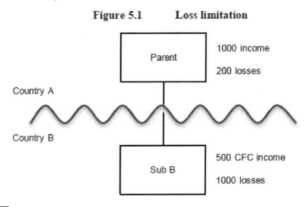

---

38   OECD (2015), 'Designing Effective Controlled Foreign Company Rules', Action 3 – 2015 Final Report, OECD/G20 Base Erosion and Profit Shifting (BEPS) Project, OECD Publishing, Paris, Explanation part, Sec. 103.
39   Eva Palatická, 'Implementation of a CFC Rule: Rules to Compute and Attribute Income' in Limiting Base Erosion, Controlled Foreign Company Rules and the EU, Michael Lang (Ed.), Erik Pinetz and Erich Schaffer (Eds.), Series on International Tax Law, Linde, 2017.
40   OECD (2015), 'Designing Effective Controlled Foreign Company Rules', Action 3 – 2015 Final Report, OECD/G20 Base Erosion and Profit Shifting (BEPS) Project, OECD Publishing, Paris, p. 58..
41   On this matter, Action 3, p. 58 et *seq*. provides some examples that demonstrate the dynamics that arise when the loss limitation rule is applied / not applied at the parent level.

If Country A's CFC rules do not limit the losses of Sub B to the income of Sub B, then Parent will only be taxed on 300 because the full 1200 of losses will be offset against the full 1500 of income. If, however, Country A's CFC rules do limit the losses of Sub B to the income of Sub B, then Parent will be taxed on 800 (1000 – 200), and no income will be attributed to Parent from Sub B because all of Sub B's attributable income will be offset by the losses, and the remaining 500 could potentially, depending on Country A's CFC rules, be carried forward to be used against Sub B's future income. This limit will prevent use of CFCs to reduce the taxable income in the parent jurisdiction[42].

Furthermore, European countries must note that all acts relating to the fiscal powers exercised by EU national courts must be consistent with EU law[43].

As noted accordingly in the OECD Report on Action 3, "Member states of the European Union should determine whether a restriction of CFC losses would be consistent with the fundamental freedoms of the European Union."[44] When a CFC is identified and many past losses have been accrued in order to offset future profits, and the parent company has not been able to prove that this was not done on purpose, this would raise the suspicion of abuse. In this case, it is better to avoid compensating for losses both at the CFC and at the parent level[45]. As the OECD Report correctly states and recommends in terms of loss importation "[m]any countries have domestic law provisions designed to prevent tax avoidance that deal with these situations and these could equally be applied to the CFC's computation of income."[46] In terms of CFC loss relief, it can be argued that applying parent company jurisdiction loss offset rules is appropriate insofar as losses within a CFC can be used to offset profits in other entities within the CFC jurisdiction[47].

3. The implementation of the CFC rules in the EU Anti-Tax Avoidance Directive (ATAD)

This Chapter briefly describes general rules on the calculation of the CFC taxable base under Council Directive no. 2016/1164/EU[48] (ATAD). In order to present a comprehensive framework, it is important to provide general information on the ATAD, in fact, despite BEPS Action 3 it has established *inter alia* a minimum stand-

---

42 Ibid.
43 Ibid.
44 OECD/G20 Base Erosion and Profit Shifting Project, Designing Effective Controlled Foreign Company Rules, Action 3: Final Report, 2015, Chapter 5 – Rules for Computing Income, Notes 3.
45 Eva Palatická, 'Implementation of a CFC Rule: Rules to Compute and Attribute Income' in Limiting Base Erosion, Controlled Foreign Company Rules and the EU, Michael Lang (Ed.), Erik Pinetz and Erich Schaffer (Eds.), Series on International Tax Law, Linde, 2017.
46 Ibid, Sec. 108.
47 Comments received on Public Discussion Draft BEPS Action 3: Strengthening CFC Rules, 5 May 2015, part 1, p. 251.
48 Council Directive (EU) 2016/1164 of 12 July 2016 laying down rules against tax avoidance practices that directly affect the functioning of the internal market (ATAD).

ard with reference to CFCs[49]. This topic is dealt in detail in Chapter 13, "Computation and Attribution of CFC income under ATAD" by Anca Pianoschi, and therefore it will only be briefly mentioned in connection with the subject of this piece of work. In general, it is important to note that some of the OECD BEPS guidelines were incorporated by the EU Council into the ATAD, which is now mandatory for member states. Before the OECD released the BEPS project guidelines, countries such as Italy, France, Germany, and the United Kingdom had already adopted similar laws. However, because of the ATAD, they had to make changes to their laws[50].

To better understand the transition within the EU and, more widely, at the global level, it appears appropriate to examine general rules on the calculation of the CFC taxable base under ATAD. The Directive's aim is to prevent companies from shifting profits to countries where taxes are minimal or non-existent in order to minimize overall tax burdens. The aim is to reallocate the profits of a subsidiary company that is subject to minimal or no taxes to the parent company. It should be noted, however, that member states can consider exempting from this tax framework those entities with low profits or profit margins, as these factors are associated with a lower risk of tax avoidance.

3.1. General rules on the calculation of the CFC taxable base under Articles 7 and 8 of ATAD

The ATAD obliges EU Member States to introduce measures, including CFC rules, that would ensure "effective taxation and transparency"[51], restore "fairness and a level playing field"[52] and set a "common minimum level of protection"[53] of the EU against BEPS due to MNEs exploiting discrepancies and mismatches between different countries' tax systems.

Thus, EU Member States should take on board the recommendations provided in Article 7: 'Controlled foreign company rule' and Article 8: 'Computation of controlled foreign company income' of the final ATAD in setting appropriate CFC measures, which according to Article 11 of the Directive should have been included into the national tax systems by 31 December 2018[54].

---

49 To address the most popular form of aggressive tax planning, all Member States must implement five legally binding anti-abuse measures: an exit tax, rules on controlled foreign companies, a general anti-abuse rule (GAAR), limitations on interest deductions, and rules to avoid double non-taxation of certain incomes.
50 Sebastian Dueñas, 'CFC Rules Around the World', Fiscal Fact No. 659, Jun. 2019, Tax Foundation., p. 11
51 Communication from the Commission to the European Parliament and the Council ('Chapeau Communication'), Anti-Tax Avoidance Package: Next steps towards delivering effective taxation and greater transparency in the EU, SWD (2016) 6 final, January 28, 2016.
52 Ibid.
53 Ibid.
54 Julia De Jong, 'Controlled Foreign Company Rules and the EU' in Limiting Base Erosion, Controlled Foreign Company Rules and the EU, Michael Lang (Ed.), Erik Pinetz and Erich Schaffer (Eds.), Series on International Tax Law, Linde, 2017, p. 294.

The limits provided by the application of Article 7 of the Directive concern specify:

- the percentage of the parent company's holding in the subsidiary;
- the tax rate applicable in the country of the subsidiary;
- the categories of income involved;
- the method of calculating the tax base[55].

When an entity or permanent establishment is qualified as a CFC, the profit is included in the parent company's tax base. The ATAD offers EU Member States the option of choosing between two approaches for calculating CFC profits. The first approach (the 'categorical approach') produces a list of income that can be attributed to the parent company's tax base, such as royalties, interest, and dividends[56] (cd. 'passive income'). In order to comply with the fundamental freedoms, this approach shall not apply where the controlled foreign company carries on a substantive commercial activity supported by staff, equipment, assets and premises, as shown by relevant facts and circumstances[57].

The second approach ('substantive approach') states that the non-distributed profit of the entity or permanent establishment resulting from a non-genuine arrangement placed, for the essential purpose of gaining a tax advantage, shall be included in the tax base by the EU Member State of the parent company[58].

A map indicating the type of foreign-sourced income subject to CFC rules over Europe has been published on Tax Foundation website[59].

---

55 According to Article 7 § 1 of ATAD "[t]he Member State of a taxpayer shall treat an entity, or a permanent establishment of which the profits are not subject to tax or are exempt from tax in that Member State, as a controlled foreign company where the following conditions are met:
   (a) in the case of an entity, the taxpayer by itself, or together with its associated enterprises holds a direct or indirect participation of more than 50 percent of the voting rights, or owns directly or indirectly more than 50 percent of capital or is entitled to receive more than 50 percent of the profits of that entity; and
   (b) the actual corporate tax paid on its profits by the entity or permanent establishment is lower than the difference between the corporate tax that would have been charged on the entity or permanent establishment under the applicable corporate tax system in the Member State of the taxpayer and the actual corporate tax paid on its profits by the entity or permanent establishment.
   For the purposes of point (b) of the first subparagraph, the permanent establishment of a controlled foreign company that is not subject to tax or is exempt from tax in the jurisdiction of the controlled foreign company shall not be taken into account. Furthermore the corporate tax that would have been charged in the Member State of the taxpayer means as computed according to the rules of the Member State of the taxpayer. (…)"
56 ATAD, Article 7 § 2 (a).
57 Ibid.
58 Ibid, Article 7 § 2 (b).
59 A. Kristina Zvinys, 'CFC Rules in Europe', August 20, 2020, https://taxfoundation.org/controlled-foreign-corporation-rules-cfc-rules-in-europe-2020/.

Computation of CFC Income

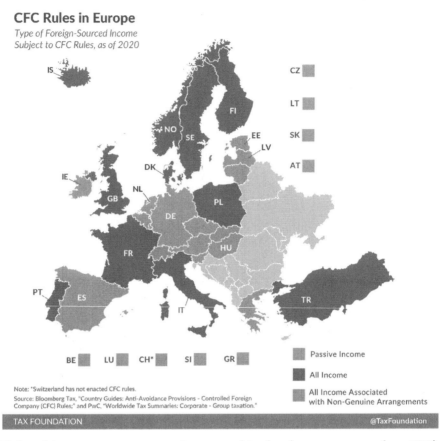

Eight of the twenty-seven countries covered in the above map tax only a CFC's passive income: Austria, the Czech Republic, Germany, Greece, Lithuania, the Netherlands, Slovenia, and Spain.

Denmark, Finland, France, Iceland, Italy, Norway, Poland, Portugal, Sweden, Turkey, and the United Kingdom tax both active and passive income earned by a CFC.

Belgium, Estonia, Hungary, Ireland, Latvia, Luxembourg, and Slovakia tax all profits associated with non-genuine arrangements.

Based on the map, the only country that has yet to implement CFC regulations is Switzerland.

Most countries' CFC regulations have a number of exemptions. Many EU member states do not apply CFC regulations to subsidiaries operating within EU borders[60].

---

60   Ibid.

With respect to the 'categorical approach', "the income to be included in the tax base of the taxpayer shall be calculated in accordance with the rules of the corporate tax law of the Member State where the taxpayer is resident for tax purposes or situated"[61]. Losses incurred by the entity do not have to be included in the tax base, although they can be carried forward and used in subsequent tax periods.

The 'alternative method' allows the taxpayer to include the entity's non-distributed profits resulting from non-genuine agreements put in place for the sole purpose of receiving a tax advantage[62].

As a result, as indicate in ATAD (Article 8 § 2): "the income to be included in the tax base of the taxpayer shall be limited to amounts generated through assets and risks which are linked to significant people functions carried out by the controlling company".

In each of the preceding cases, the CFC rule includes guidelines to eliminate double taxes in two situations:

- in the case of dividend payments from the CFC;
- in the case of the sale of the stake in the CFC.

Finally, the Member State of which the taxpayer is a tax resident must allow a deduction from the tax liability of the tax paid by the entity or permanent establishment.

4. Comparing the applicability of the CFC computation rules around the World

Our aim in this Chapter is to describe the CFC rules in place in some European jurisdictions and in the United States.

4.1. The Italian CFC rules

Having entered into force in 2002[63], the Italian CFC rules have been the subject, in the last decade, of important regulatory interventions that have changed requirements and scope, considerably. The measure has been revised many times over the years, most recently in 2006, when it was expanded to include related (but not controlled) companies, and in 2010, when it was expanded to include countries not on the 'black list' of privileged tax regimes. The definition of a privileged tax regime was further changed in 2015[64].

---

61 Ibid, Article 8 § 1.
62 Ibid, Article 7 § 2 (b). In this regard, "an arrangement or a series thereof shall be regarded as non-genuine to the extent that the entity or permanent establishment would not own the assets or would not have undertaken the risks which generate all, or part of, its income if it were not controlled by a company where the significant people functions, which are relevant to those assets and risks, are carried out and are instrumental in generating the controlled company's income", see ATAD, Article 7 § 2 (b).
63 Law 342 of 2000, implemented by Ministerial Decree No. 429 of November 21, 2001, published in the Official Gazette, No. 288, of December 12, 2001
64 G. Rolle, 'New ATAD-based CFC Regime in Italy', Bloomberg Tax, January 10, 2020.

Legislative Decree No. 142 of November 29, 2018, implementing Council Directive (EU) 2016/1164 of 12 July 2016, known as the Anti-Tax Avoidance Directive (ATAD), setting out new rules against tax avoidance, was the most recent revision. As stated in Recital No. 2 of the ATAD, the Directive was intended at "implementing the OECD BEPS conclusions at the EU level". More specifically, the changes introduced to article 167 of the Income Tax Code (ITC) by Legislative Decree no. 142/2018 incorporate articles 7 and 8 of the ATAD, as well as some of the recommendations of the OECD BEPS 2015 Final Report on Action 3[65] ("Designing Effective Controlled Company Rules")[66]. Indeed, it can be argued that, since ATAD comply with BEPS Action 3, Italian CFC legislation should comply with BEPS[67]. The tax framework governing CFCs pursuant to Article 167 of the ITC, as rewritten by Article 4 of Legislative Decree No. 142/2018, envisages, even in the absence of actual distribution, the direct allocation of the income produced by enterprises, companies, or entities with a privileged tax regime to resident taxpayers, who hold controlling interests in such enterprises, companies or entities.

The CFC rules apply if the resident taxpayer has control of the foreign company or entity with a privileged tax regime as identified under Article 167 § 4 of the ITC. Pursuant to Article 167 § 4 of the ITC, as amended by Article 4 of Italian Legislative Decree No. 142/2018, the CFC rules apply if the following conditions are both met:

- Non-resident controlled taxpayers are subject to actual taxation lower than half of what they would have been subject to if resident in Italy;
- More than one third[68] of the income they make falls into one or more of the categories of income qualified as 'passive income'[69].

---

65 The Final Report of Action 3 provides detailed recommendations for the design of CFC rules that countries should consider if they want to introduce a new CFC regime or amend an existing one.
The Action 3 Final Report provides detailed suggestions for the design of CFC rules that countries should consider if they want to introduce a new regime or amend an existing one.
66 Ibid.
67 Ibid.
68 This rule complies with Article 7 § 3 of ATAD.
69 The following are considered to be passive income:
- Interest and other financial asset income;
- Royalties and other intellectual property income;
- Dividends and other income derived from the selling of equity investments;
- Income from financial leasing;
- Income from insurance, banking, and other financial activities;
- Income deriving from transactions for the purchase and sale of goods with little or no added economic value, carried out with parties that directly or indirectly control the controlled non-resident taxpayer, are controlled by it, or are controlled by the same party that controls the non-resident entities;
- Income deriving from the provision of services, with little or no added economic value, carried out in favour of parties who, directly or indirectly, control the non-resident controlled taxpayer, are controlled by it, or are controlled by the same subject that controls the non-resident entity; for the purpose of identifying services with little or no added economic value, the indications contained on Ministerial Decree of May 14, 2018, should be taken into account.

The CFC rule does not apply when the foreign controlled entity engages in "substantial economic activity, supported by personnel, equipment, assets and premises" according to § 5 of Article 167 of the ITC. The exemption clause is similar to that of Article 7 2 (a) of the ATAD and meets the requirements defined by the European Union's Court of Justice (CJEU) in its decision in the Cadbury Schweppes case[70].

In general terms, in order to verify the first condition, it is necessary to compare the actual foreign taxation (equal to the ratio between the foreign tax and the pre-tax profit resulting from the financial statements filed in the foreign State) and the 'virtual' taxation that the subsidiary would have been subject to in Italy on the same income (equal to the ratio between the tax that would result by redetermining foreign income by Italian regulations and the same pre-tax profit). Essentially, to verify the level of actual taxation, it is necessary to make a comparison between the 'effective foreign tax rate' and the 'virtual domestic tax rate'. The latter calculated by determining the income resulting from the financial statements filed abroad based on Italian corporate tax provisions[71].

If the CFC rules apply, the income of the CFC are deemed to be the income of the Italian resident taxpayer. This income, to be determined under the Italian tax rules governing the calculation of business income and attributed proportionally to the Italian shareholders, are taxed separately at the tax rate for Italian-resident corporations (for 2021 is 24 percent) with no possibility to utilize tax losses, other than those of the CFC. In line with BEPS Action 3, any loss generated by the CFC may be carried forward to the subsequent fiscal years in order to offset any future income of the same CFC[72].

Note that in order to avoid double taxation on income, profits that have already been taxed at the controlling entity level under the CFC rules are exempt under Article 167 § 10 of the ITC. Furthermore, tax paid by the foreign company in its home country can be deducted from the Italian tax liability[73]. Both laws have remained unchanged since they were already in compliance with the requirements of Article 8 of the ATAD[74].

As previously analysed in Section 3.1, ATAD proposes two alternative approaches to tax CFCs:

1) The 'categorical approach' (Article 7§ 2 (a)); and
2) The 'substantive approach' (Article 7 § 2(b)).

---

70 Ibid.
71 It is useful to highlight that the Agenzia delle Entrate (Italian Revenue Agency), on the occasion of "Telefisco 2019" (annual conference dedicated to tax news organized by Il Sole 24 Ore.) confirmed that, for the purposes of calculating the 'virtual domestic tax rate', it is necessary to make exclusive reference to the IRES (corporate tax) and not to the IRAP (regional tax on productive activities), see Diego Avolio, 'CFC: nel calcolo del tax rate conta solo l'IRES' ['CFC: only the IRES counts in tax rate calculation'], IPSOA Quotidiano, Wolters Kluwer, February 2, 2019,
72 Georg Kofler et al, 'Controlled Foreign Company Legislation', November 2020, IBFD, p. 264.
73 Article 167 § 9 of the ITC.
74 Ibid.

On one hand, under the 'categorical approach', only the CFC's passive income is taxed in the parent's hands unless the CFC engages in a substantive economic activity supported by personnel, equipment, assets and premises. However, according to Article 7 § 3 of the ATAD a EU Member State may choose not to treat an entity or permanent establishment as a tax transparent CFC, if one third or less of the foreign entity's income qualifies as 'passive income'[75]. On the other hand, under the 'substantive approach', if the CFC qualifies as a non-genuine agreement, the controlling entity must include all of the CFC's non-distributed profits in its tax base.

Since all of the CFC's income is taxed in the hands of the controlling entity, it is clear that the Italian CFC rules adopt the 'substantive approach'. However, one of the conditions of the Italian CFC rules; that is, more than one third of the income qualifies as 'passive income', comes from the so called 'safe harbour rule' under the 'categorical approach'[76]. It can, therefore, be concluded that the Italian CFC rule results in a mix of the two approaches.

4.2. The German CFC rules

Germany has in place a CFC regime, since 1972, the year in which the Foreign Transaction Tax Act (FTTA; *Außensteuergesetz* (AStG)) was introduced. Following the German legislation, a CFC occurs at the end of fiscal year, when voting rights are in the hand of the majority of German residents[77]. It is vital to determine the *delta* between the tax rate applied to CFC and the virtual tax to be paid in Germany.

In order to calculate if a foreign subsidiary paid in proportion less taxes, the effective rate is to be determined and calculated as the effective rate ratio between tax paid for passive CFC income and tax base hypothetical paid for a residence.

In order to measure the ratio, the CFC is regarded as a German company; the rule is applied if the foreign tax liability is less than 25 percent of the virtual domestic taxes. Then, according to German CFC rules, any level of taxation below 25 percent is considered to be low taxation[78].

The German CFC rules apply to passive income derived by a CFC from sources not listed in a list of active income. The calculation of passive income depends on the application of the German provisions on the determination of taxable income (section 10 § 3 of the FTTA). Note that only operating expenditures that economically relate to the passive income can be deducted in calculating the income[79]. Once the

---

75 A. Silvestri, P. Ronca, 'Italy amends CFC rules in corporate tax reform', August 22, 2019, International Tax Review.
76 Ibid.
77 Under the German CFC regime, the control threshold for CFC purposes is 50 percent.
78 Sebastian Dueñas, 'How Controlled Foreign Corporation Rules Look Around the World: Germany', February 18, 2020, Tax Foundation.
79 Georg Kofler et al, 'Controlled Foreign Company Legislation', November 2020, IBFD, p. 219.

CFC passive income has been determined, the amount is added to the German shareholder's taxable income and taxed accordingly on the basis of their participation in the foreign entity. Such passive income qualifies as a 'deemed dividend' to be attributed to the German parent company irrespective of any effective distribution[80]. This deemed dividend is not subject to any participation exemption.

In order to avoid double taxation, non-refundable taxes paid by the CFC may be attributed to the German entity. Furthermore, in line with BEPS Action 3, CFC's losses cannot be attributed to the German entity, but they can be carried forward to cover any CFC's income in a subsequent fiscal year[81]. It should also to be emphasised that it is not possible to compensate losses between different CFCs[82].

In a 2018 report, Deutsche Bank[83] explains that Germany's CFC rules are particularly stringent. According to the report, the German CFC rules are outdated, and that their original purpose was to ensure that a portion of foreign income was adequately taxed in Germany. Moreover, the report states that German tax law penalises non-German subsidiaries of German parent companies in other countries. The lower tax rate, according to the report, appears to be too high, with a 25 percent threshold triggering enforcement of the rules[84].

In sum, the German tax law would need to be tweaked in order to apply the standards that the EU requires as a minimal, based on the ATAD[85].

4.3. The Dutch CFC rules

Before it became mandatory, the Netherlands did not have a CFC regime. In fact, it was not until January 2019 that the Dutch tax system adopted CFC rules[86]. The CFC rules are intended to target corporate taxpayers that have a direct or indirect interest in a subsidiary of more than 50 percent or who dispose of a permanent establishment in either a low-taxed jurisdiction; that is, a statutory corporate income tax rate of less than 9 percent or a non-cooperative jurisdiction that is expressly specified by the Dutch Ministry of Finance[87]. Under certain conditions, part of the income of the CFC is included in the taxable base of the parent company[88].

---

80 Ibid.
81 Ibid. note 77.
82 Ibid. note 78.
83 Deutsche Bank Research, 'German corporate taxes', September 14, 2018.
84 Ibid.
85 Ibid.
86 Sebastian Dueñas, 'How Controlled Foreign Corporation Rules Look Around the World: Netherlands', July 8, 2019, Tax Foundation.
87 On December 28, 2018, the Netherlands released in the Government Gazette a list of 21 low-tax jurisdictions to assist in the introduction of new measures to combat tax avoidance.
These jurisdictions either have no corporation tax or have a corporation tax rate that is lower than 9%.
88 PwC, 'Worldwide Tax Summaries – Netherlands', July 6, 2020, https://taxsummaries.pwc.com/netherlands/corporate/group-taxation.

Computation of CFC Income

The CFC rules of the Netherlands apply to the calculation of passive income, including but not limited to dividend, interest and royalty income, income from financial leasing, income from insurance, banking and other financial activities.

Under the Dutch law, if passive income does not exceed 30 percent of the overall income, this income it is not taken into account and it is not attributed to the shareholder. The rules allow companies to deduct the costs that contribute to the formation of the passive income[89]. Then, if a foreign entity is qualified as a CFC, the CFC's undistributed income, that is, passive income minus related costs, shall be (i) calculated according to the Dutch provisions, (ii) included in the Dutch taxable base and, finally, (iii) subject to Dutch corporate income tax[90]. As a result, the Dutch tax law needs to be applied when calculating CFC income, such as the participation exemption regime, interest deduction limitation rules and transfer pricing adjustments. Furthermore, in order to avoid double taxation, the corporate tax actually paid by the foreign entity or permanent establishment may be deducted from the parent company's income taxes due in the Netherlands[91].

Back in the days, the Dutch tax system was regarded as complex and susceptible to tax evasion[92] and this attracted investors. However, as major tax systems, given the introduction of CFC rules, the Dutch jurisdiction, as other jurisdictions do, now protects its tax revenue from erosion and profit shifting. It is evident that the Netherlands is experiencing a series of adjustments that would create a system complying with international standards recommended by the OECD and taken on board by the European Union Council[93].

4.4. The U.S. CFC rules

In the United States (U.S.), CFC rules were first implemented in 1960 and have undergone several amendments since then. The U.S. standard for control aims to establish whether a foreign company is a CFC. Under § 957 (a) if a U.S. company controls more than 50 per cent of the votes or value of a foreign entity, it qualifies as a CFC. This threshold can be reached by considering direct, indirect and constructive ownership assessments[94].

---

89 Sebastian Dueñas, 'How Controlled Foreign Corporation Rules Look Around the World: Netherlands', July 8, 2019, Tax Foundation.
90 EY, 'Netherlands enacts new CFC legislation: Impacton multinational enterprises', January 29, 2019, https://www.ey.com/en_gl/tax-alerts/netherlands-enacts-new-cfc-legislation---impact-on-multinational-enterprises.
91 Georg Kofler et al, 'Controlled Foreign Company Legislation', November 2020, IBFD, p. 325.
92 A. Lejour, 'The political economy of tax reforms', CPB Netherlands Bureau for Economic Policy Analysis, 2016/08, p. 9.
93 Ibid. note 88.
94 Sebastian Dueñas, 'How Controlled Foreign Corporation Rules Look Around the World: United States of America', June 24, 2019, Tax Foundation.

The Internal Revenue Code provides the following definition of a U.S. shareholder[95]: "a (...) person[96] (...) who owns (...) 10 percent or more of the total combined voting power of all classes of stock entitled to vote of such foreign corporation, or 10 percent or more of the total value of shares of all classes of stock of such foreign corporation". Once a company has been classified as a CFC, it must determine what foreign income should be taxed in the U.S.

U.S. shareholders of a CFC include amounts of the CFC's E&P (earnings and profits) in their domestic taxable income when the CFC distribute a dividend or recognises certain categories of income, known as subpart F income.

Usually, income that falls into one of the categories defined in Subpart F of the Internal Revenue Code is adjusted to comply to U.S. income tax provisions and then taxed under the tax law of the United States[97]. In particular, income from a CFC that is determined under Subpart F must be added to the taxable income of the U.S. shareholder in the year the income is earned by the CFC. As a result, the CFC income will be taxed at the U.S. income tax rate in the hands of the shareholder. CFC 's E&P is calculated at the level of each foreign entity and then attributed to the U.S. shareholder for taxation[98].

> Under § 952 "the term "subpart F income" means, in the case of any controlled foreign corporation, the sum of–
> (1) insurance income (as defined under section 953),
> (2) the foreign base company income (as determined under section 954),
> (3) an amount equal to the product of–
>   (A) the income of such corporation other than income which–
>   (i) is attributable to earnings and profits of the foreign corporation included in the gross income of a United States person under section 951 (other than by reason of this paragraph), or
>   (ii) is described in subsection (b), multiplied by
>   (B) the international boycott factor (as determined under section 999),
> (4) the sum of the amounts of any illegal bribes, kickbacks, or other payments (within the meaning of section 162(c)) paid by or on behalf of the corporation during the taxable year of the corporation directly or indirectly to an official, employee, or agent in fact of a government, and
> (5) the income of such corporation derived from any foreign country during any period during which section 901(j) applies to such foreign country."

It is to be noted that Subpart F qualification can, in some cases, apply to all the income of a foreign entity. Foreign subsidiaries that generate Subpart F income that accounts for more than 70 percent of the entity's gross income, qualify as 'full in-

---

95 See § 951.
96 A U.S. person is defined as a U.S. citizen or resident or a domestic entity. See § 957(c) and 7701(a)(30).
97 Sebastian Dueñas, 'How Controlled Foreign Corporation Rules Look Around the World: United States of America', June 24, 2019, Tax Foundation.
98 Ibid.

clusion' entities[99]. This means that all their income is considered Subpart F income[100]. If a CFC has no E&P in a certain tax year, the Subpart F income may be deferred for U.S. tax purposes. In such a case, the deferred Subpart F income would be attributed to the U.S. shareholder's taxable income, in the year in which the CFC generates E&P[101].

With regard to loss relief, Subpart F income from one CFC generally may not be offset by Subpart F loss of another CFC. Furthermore, qualified deficit, that is, a loss measured under applicable tax law, in E&P may only offset Subpart F income in the same category[102]. In particular, under the qualified deficit rule of § 952(c)(1)(B), a prior-year E&P deficit may be used to limit a qualified shareholder's current year Subpart F income in the same CFC if such deficit "is attributable to the same qualified activity as the activity giving rise to the income being offset".

In order to avoid double taxation, in the case where a U.S. shareholder is a domestic corporation, they may be eligible for a foreign tax credit in the U.S. for foreign taxes paid by the CFC on Subpart F income. Furthermore, CFCs' E&P that have been included in the income of the U.S. shareholder as Subpart F income are not taxed again when they are actually distributed to such shareholder[103].

For the intent of this thesis, GILTI[104] ('global intangible low-taxed income') and PFIC[105] ('passive foreign investment companies') regimes are not the object of this study.

Despite the U.S. being the first country to adopt the CFC rules and based on the author's analysis, it appears to be the country with the most complex set of rules[106] aimed at avoiding tax deferral schemes. In addition, it can be concluded that the U.S. adopts the 'transactional approach'[107] under which only certain types of income of a CFC are attributed to the U.S. shareholder.

5. Conclusion

In the view of the author, in can be concluded that the Final Report on Action 3 of the OECD/G20 BEPS project, in some respects, failed. In fact, it did not require

---

99   See § 954(b)(3)(B).
100 PwC, Viewpoint, '11.10.2 US subpart F income', April 30, 2019.
101 Ibid.
102 See § 952(c)(1)(B)(ii).
103 PwC, 'Doing Business in the United States', 2020, https://www.pwc.com/gx/en/tax/newsletters/tax-controversy-dispute-resolution/assets/pwc-doing-business-in-the-united-states.pdf.
104 Starting from 2017, a U.S. shareholder is required to include in income the 'global intangible low-taxed income' (GILTI) of its CFCs.
105 Income from 'passive foreign investment companies' (PFICs) is also subject to special regulations aimed at eliminating the benefit of deferral.
106 Ibid. note 97.
107 Brian J. Arnold, 'International Tax Primer', Kluwer Law International, IV edition, January 15, 2019, par. 7.3.2.3.

that countries implement CFC rules. It also provided no safe tax planning guidance for countries that had been interested in adopting CFC rules or improving their existing CFC rules. Although the EU asked its Member States to adopt CFC rules, contrary to the OECD/G20 BEPS Project's inability to make a firm recommendation for countries to adopt CFC rules, the rules' minimum requirements are not stringent, and they may even be ineffective[108].

With regards to the computation approach, after having analysed the applicability of the CFC rules, in some countries, it is to be noted that most of such countries require the income of the CFC that is subject to the CFC country's tax to be computed in accordance with the parent jurisdiction's computational rules as recommended by BEPS Action 3. It should also be noted that this option was chosen because it was consistent with BEPS' concerns and because it reduced tax administration costs.

While the majority of EU countries have adopted most of ATAD requirements, some countries are still in different stages of enforcing the rules[109], especially extra-EU countries that are not required to meet the ATAD standard in respect of CFC rules. It could be argued that harmonising CFC rules is still a long way off and much has to change in order to reduce tax competition between countries.

Since there is no harmonization around the world, it is also noteworthy that MNEs can still use a number of law-tax jurisdictions to acquire the most convenient tax rate for their profits and then obtain ad advantage in the conduct of business. It is also important to note that not all countries have the same capacity and resources for implementing rules. Furthermore, one important issue for countries that are not capital exporters is whether CFC rules are necessary or are implicitly a prerequisite to join international organisations such as the OECD[110]. It is often appropriate for capital exporting countries to have CFC rules in order to strengthen their tax structures while promoting multinational corporations' ability to invest globally. This is not the case in some developing countries, for example, India, where CFC rules have not been enforced and no current attempts to amend or introduce international tax rules have been made. It is possible that the reason for this is that not all countries have sufficient resources to handle tax reforms that would add to the system's complexity.

Since CFC rules are among the most complicated tax provisions, they necessitate a high level of technical competence backed by a substantial financial commitment, which is a difficult challenge for many countries, especially emerging coun-

---

[108] Brian J. Arnold, 'The Evolution of Controlled Foreign Corporation Rules and Beyond', Bulletin for International Taxation, December 2019, IBFD, pp. 639–640.
[109] Sebastian Dueñas, 'Tax Avoidance Rules Increase the Compliance Burden in EU Member Countries', March 28, 2019.
[110] Sebastian Dueñas, 'CFC Rules Around the World', Fiscal Fact No. 659, Jun. 2019, Tax Foundation.

tries. This may be one of the reasons why some countries[111] are still in the earliest stages of their CFC rules and most of the countries analyzed by the OECD[112] have no CFC rules in place.

However, due to tax competition, it is foreseeable to conclude that in the next few years more and more countries will adopt CFC rules to avoid profits shifting to low-taxed countries. Furthermore, the computation under the law of the parent jurisdiction is to be generally preferred, both because it complies with the recommendation made in BEPS' project and limits room for the manipulation of a tax base.

---

111 E.g. Austria (2019), Belgium (2017), Bulgaria (2019), Czech Republic (2019), Colombia (2017), Croatia (2019), Luxemburg (2019), Malta (2019), Poland (2015), Romania (2018), Slovenia (2019), Slovak Republic (2019).
112 The OECD collected data on progress related to the implementation of Action 3 and in particular, whether a jurisdiction has CFC rules in place. For detailed data: https://qdd.oecd.org/subject.aspx?Subject=CFC.

Avoidance of double taxation of CFC income

Serena Bussotti

1. Introduction
2. The purpose of the CFC rule from a tax policy perspective: a comparison between CIN and CEN countries' approach
   2.1. The purpose of CFC regime: a general overview
3. The OECD recommendations to prevent or eliminate double taxation under the CFC regime and the ATAD Directive
   3.1. The BEPS Project and the OECD recommendations in Action 3
   3.2. Foreign tax credit: item, timing, and country issues
   3.3. Foreign tax credit: the interaction with anti-abuse provisions
   3.4. Foreign tax credit: the interaction with the CFC regimes of multiple countries
   3.5. Foreign tax credit: the non-deductible passive income
   3.6. Issues related to the foreign tax exemption
   3.7. Some further considerations
4. The measures to avoid double taxation implemented by countries and their consistency with the BEPS Action 3 main policy considerations
   4.1. Measures to avoid double taxation for CFCs in Germany
   4.2. Measures to avoid double taxation for CFCs in France
   4.3. Measures to avoid double taxation for CFCs in Spain
   4.4. Measures to avoid double taxation for CFCs in Sweden
   4.5. Measures to avoid double taxation for CFCs in Indonesia
   4.6. Measures to avoid double taxation for CFCs in Brazil
5. Conclusions

1. Introduction

From its introduction until to date, one of the main issues concerning the controlled foreign company (hereafter briefly also CFC) provision was its consistency to the tax policy goals pursued by countries[1].

Starting from a general overview on the tax policy goals that are pursued through CFC legislation for both capital import neutrality (CIN) and capital export neutrality (CEN) countries, this thesis will focus on one of the policy considerations outlined by the OECD in BEPS Action 3 – the avoidance of double taxation of CFC income. Specifically, the thesis explains if – and why – the effective avoidance of double taxation is important and consistent with both the CFC policy goals and the tax policy systems implemented by countries. Additionally, to what extent the countries should deal with all the more complex situations that, following the CFC application, cause double taxation.

The analysis is carried out by identifying the main situations in which double taxation could arise taking into consideration both those already included in BEPS Project Action 3 and what the interested parties have raised during the preliminary public consultation of the Action 3 document.

The study is then supported by the examination of what Germany, Spain, Sweden, France, Indonesia, and Brazil have implemented at the domestic level to avoid double taxation following CFC application as representative for both CEN and CIN countries.

2. The purpose of the CFC rule from a tax policy perspective: a comparison between CIN and CEN countries' approach

2.1. The purpose of CFC regime: a general overview

Many states have introduced CFC regimes[2] in the last 40 years as anti-tax avoidance instruments; indeed, many countries allow the exemption from the application of the regime in case taxpayers succeed in demonstrating the *genuine* nature of the economic activity carried out by the foreign controlled company[3].

---

1 *Indirect credit versus exemption: double taxation relief for intercompany distribu-tions*, Georg Kofler, Bulletin for international taxation, February 2012.
2 Germany, France, Italy, Spain, the United Kingdom, Poland, and most of the European countries (except Austria that has only recently introduced the CFC provisions).
3 The genuine nature is intended as a real economic activity that is performed with adequate means and structure. Essentially, the concept was received in ATAD Directive (Council Directive (EU) 2016/1164 of 12 July 2016) as defined in the Cadbury Schweppes ruling (Case C-196/04).

The reasons for the introduction of the CFC regimes needs to be identified in the origin of these provisions starting from their first introduction in the United States, the pioneer of the CFC[4]. The policy study published in 2000 by the Office of Tax Policy – US Department of the Treasury with the title *"The Deferral of Income Earned Through U.S. Controlled Foreign Corporations"* exposes the main policy reasons that drove the preliminary introduction of CFC legislation during the Kennedy administration in the 1960s. The document at issue underlined the consistency of the CFC provisions with the US tax policy goals that are aligned with the *capital export neutrality* (hereafter also CEN) principle.

Before identifying the general tax policy goals typical for CEN countries, it is sufficient to point out here that the main goal for the United States to introduce the CFC provision in the 1960s was basically to prevent the tax deferral on the profits realized by controlled foreign entities with US shareholders[5] (i.e. avoid the timing deferral of income taxation). The US CFC legislation has been significantly amended during the years[6] with the intent to be more effective and to put in place measures even more consistent with the economic trends and the CEN tax policy goals. Consequently, the anti-deferral purpose declared by United States for the CFC's first introduction was joined by the anti-avoidance goal (i.e. avoid the shifting of income in tax havens)[7].

After the United States, many other countries introduced CFC provisions[8] at a domestic level that are properly designed to be consistent with their own tax systems.

IN 2015, the BEPS[9] Project pushed the countries[10] to reconsider its own CFC legislation to be more effective and consistent with both anti-avoidance and anti-deferral purposes and, at the same time, to reduce as much as possible (or better avoid) the double taxation resulting from CFC application overall in certain situations[11].

---

4 Office of Tax Policy – US Department of the Treasury, *the Deferral of Income Earned Through U.S. Controlled Foreign Corporations*, 2000.
5 Office of Tax Policy – US Department of the Treasury, *The Deferral of Income Earned Through U.S. Controlled Foreign Corporations*, 2000.
6 For example, the GILTI and the BEAT regimes were introduced after the last tax reform (also referred as TCJA). Please refer to Christine Davis, *Is the Tax Cuts and Jobs Act GILTI of ANTI – Simplification?*, Virginia Tax review, volume 38, No 315, 2019.
7 *A Small Fish in a Big Pond: The International Tax Options of Belgium*, Frans Vanistendael, Bulletin for International Taxation, June 2017
8 See footnote n. 4.
9 OECD/G20 *Base Erosion and Profit Shifting Project*, OECD Publishing, Paris, 2015. The document on CFC is the Action 3. Refer to footnote n. 8.
10 OECD (2015), *Designing Effective Controlled Foreign Company Rules, Action 3* – 2015 Final Report, OECD/G20 Base Erosion and Profit Shifting Project, OECD Publishing, Paris. http://dx.doi.org/10.1787/9789264241152-en, Paragraph 20.
11 *Indirect credit versus exemption: double taxation relief for intercompany distributions*, Georg Kofler, Bulletin for international taxation, February 2012.

Before analysing the reactions to the BEPS Project on CFC tax policy considerations – by focusing on the avoidance of double taxation – it is important to identify the peculiarities of both the territorial and worldwide tax systems. As already said above and observed for the United States, the CFC rules and their implementation depends on the tax policy perspective assumed by countries. In this respect, it needs to distinguish between:

- CIN countries[12]: Capital import neutrality countries aim to obtain a fair domestic tax system for inbound investments – independently from the investor's residence – usually by exempting the income generated by the foreign business activities from domestic taxation. CIN countries are substantially in line with the territorial tax system that exempts foreign source income from domestic taxation;
- CEN countries[13]: Capital export neutrality countries aim to obtain a fair domestic tax system for both inbound and outbound investments, usually by crediting from foreign taxes paid on the income generated by the foreign business activities. CEN countries are substantially in line with the worldwide tax system for which all of the income (both domestic and foreign source) attributed to residence taxpayers is taxed in the same manner at a domestic level, and a credit is granted for the foreign taxes paid on foreign source income.

Beside the above listed main tax policies (CEN and CIN), there are further approaches[14] that differ one from the other basically for the purpose and the way to achieve it[15].

However, irrespective of the specific tax policy implemented by the country, it is possible to identify a common goal for the CFC provisions: the protection of the shareholder's tax base[16].

Indeed:

- in the case that the CFC provisions are designed as anti-deferral measures, the residence state's position (of the shareholder) is substantially the same for territorial and worldwide tax systems[17] (and so for CIN and CEN tax policies). In

---

12 *Indirect credit versus exemption: double taxation relief for intercompany distributions,* Georg Kofler, Bulletin for international taxation, February 2012.
13 *Indirect credit versus exemption: double taxation relief for intercompany distributions,* Georg Kofler, Bulletin for international taxation, February 2012.
14 Reference is made to National Neutrality – NN – Capital Ownership Neutrality – CON – and National Ownership Neutrality – NON.
15 *Indirect credit versus exemption: double taxation relief for intercompany distributions,* Georg Kofler, Bulletin for international taxation, February 2012 and Controlled foreign companies: selected policy issues – or the missing elements of BEPS Action 3 and the anti-tax avoidance directive", Daniel W. Blum, Inter-tax, volume 46, issue 4.
16 *The evolution of controlled foreign corporation rules and beyond,* Brian J. Arnold, Bulletin for international taxation, december 2019
17 *Controlled foreign companies: selected policy issues – or the missing elements of BEPS Action 3 and the anti-tax avoidance directive,* Daniel W. Blum, Inter-tax, volume 46, issue 4, page 302.

both of the cases, the shareholder's state is interested in protecting the corporate tax base of its domestic company from deferral and in ensuring the taxation of the income at the shareholder level[18].

- on the other hand, if the CFC rules are implemented as anti-avoidance measures, the goal is again to prevent the deduction of base-eroding payments at the shareholder's level[19] but also taking into account the tax position of the foreign controlled entity. This approach therefore includes the necessity to define (i) what is a base-eroding payment and (ii) how much the level of taxation on that diverted income in the foreign country is relevant[20]. This further element of evaluation (i.e. the tax position of the controlled foreign company) assumes more importance for CIN countries in respect of CEN ones. Indeed, to be consistent with the CIN principle, the level of taxation in the CFC country can never be the main element to evaluate for the CFC application. Otherwise, the tax policy of CIN countries (and so territorial tax systems) is undermined[21] as the CFC would imply a deviation from the foreign source income exemption whenever the controlled entity is located in a low-tax rate country (and the location of a controlled company in a low-tax jurisdiction cannot be considered *per se* as abusive and an avoidance transaction)[22]. This is the reason why, in case of genuine business activities carried out by the company located in the CFC country, the relevant low level of taxation should not cause the CFC rules application (i.e. no CFC income to be picked up at the controlling shareholder level for tax purposes)[23]. This is aligned with the solution applied by the European Commission[24], and it is consistent with the CIN principle as it is focused on the substance of the economic activity. Substantially, the derogation from the said neutrality principle is justifiable when the passive income (namely, royalties, interest expenses, and dividends) of the foreign controlled entity indicate a non-genuine business activity at the CFC country level.[25]

---

18 *Controlled foreign companies: selected policy issues – or the missing elements of BEPS Action 3 and the anti-tax avoidance directive*, Daniel W. Blum, Inter-tax, volume 46, issue 4, page 302.
19 *Controlled foreign companies: selected policy issues – or the missing elements of BEPS Action 3 and the anti-tax avoidance directive*, Daniel W. Blum, Inter-tax, volume 46, issue 4, page 302.
20 *Controlled foreign companies: selected policy issues – or the missing elements of BEPS Action 3 and the anti-tax avoidance directive*, Daniel W. Blum, Inter-tax, volume 46, issue 4, page 303.
21 *Controlled foreign companies: selected policy issues – or the missing elements of BEPS Action 3 and the anti-tax avoidance directive*, Daniel W. Blum, Inter-tax, volume 46, issue 4, page 304 and *Diritto tributario Europeo*, Pasquale Pistone, G. Giappichelli Editore, 2019, para-graph 1.4.1.3.4.
22 *Diritto tributario Europeo*, Pasquale Pistone, G. Giappichelli Editore, 2019, paragraph 1.4.1.3.4.
23 *Controlled foreign companies: selected policy issues – or the missing elements of BEPS Action 3 and the anti-tax avoidance directive*, Daniel W. Blum, Inter-tax, volume 46, issue 4, page 304.
24 Council Directive (EU) 2016/1164 of 12 July 2016 laying down rules against tax avoidance practices that directly affect the functioning of the internal market, the so called ATAD, Article 7.
25 *Controlled foreign companies: selected policy issues – or the missing elements of BEPS Action 3 and the anti-tax avoidance directive*, Daniel W. Blum, Inter-tax, volume 46, issue 4, page 305.

In conclusion, the purpose of a CFC regime shall be evaluated in a comprehensive manner and mainly together with (i) the tax policy system implemented by the country and (ii) the specific CFC domestic provisions (i.e. what triggers the application of the CFC rules? Under which circumstances do the CFC provisions come into play?).

In any case, the effective avoidance of double taxation on CFC income affects the achievement purpose of the tax policy as explained above (by undermining the tax neutrality). Indeed, the OECD considered the avoidance of double taxation as one of the fundamental policy considerations of the BEPS Project[26]. This is so that each country is free to implement the CFC regime according to its own tax policy system. However, double taxation should always be avoided[27] as, otherwise, each tax system is compromised.

3. The OECD recommendations to prevent or eliminate double taxation under the CFC regime and the ATAD Directive

3.1. The BEPS Project and the OECD recommendations in Action 3

As already mentioned before, in 2015, the so called BEPS[28] Project was concluded and, in October 2015, the report *Designing Effective Controlled Foreign Company Rules* (hereafter also BEPS Project Action 3) was published. The document basically includes recommendations to prevent profit shifting of income into foreign subsidiaries located in low-taxed jurisdictions.

Chapter 1 of the document at issue deals with the importance of including CFC rules into each domestic tax system as more than one tax policy's objectives can be reached through the implementation of these provisions[29]. Indeed, each country is called to design and implement its own CFC provisions to be as effective as possible and in line with the objectives pursued through its domestic tax policy. According to the BEPS Project, all of the CFC rules implemented by countries should be based on one or more of the following policy considerations.[30]

(i) The function of a CFC as a deterrent measure[31]

---

26 OECD (2015), *Designing Effective Controlled Foreign Company Rules, Action 3* – 2015 Final Report.
27 *Controlled foreign companies: selected policy issues – or the missing elements of BEPS Action 3 and the anti-tax avoidance directive*, Daniel W. Blum, Inter-tax, volume 46, issue 4, page 302.
28 Base Erosion and Profit Shifting (BEPS).
29 OECD (2015), *Designing Effective Controlled Foreign Company Rules, Action 3* – 2015 Final Report, Chapter 1.
30 OECD (2015), *Designing Effective Controlled Foreign Company Rules, Action 3* – 2015 Final Report, Chapter 1.
31 OECD (2015), *Designing Effective Controlled Foreign Company Rules, Action 3* – 2015 Final Report, Chapter 1, paragraph 7.

As a deterrent measure, CFC legislation allows preventing taxpayers to allocate excessive profits to the controlled foreign companies, making the opportunity of shifting profits to low-tax jurisdictions less attractive (because of the unfavourable taxation on CFC income)[32].

(ii) The interaction of CFC rules with transfer pricing provisions[33]:

The interactions of the CFC rules with the other tax provisions, especially with transfer pricing rules, allow preventing base erosion and profit shifting practices in line with the BEPS Project when the other tax provisions (i.e. transfer pricing rules) fail[34].

(iii) The balance between the effectiveness of the CFC provisions in pursuing the goals and the interest of not increasing the administrative burdens and compliance costs:[35]

In this respect, it is necessary to avoid that the CFC provisions increase the administrative tax burdens on both taxpayers and tax administrations[36] and, at the same time, guaranteeing that the prescribed policy goal is pursued. Speaking in general terms, it means that it is necessary to find the right balance between a standard provision and an overly tailor-made one[37]. Indeed the risk of designing a standard CFC rule is that its main function is reduced because it also deals with situations in which deferral or avoidance phenomena are not actually detected (resulting in a distortion and discouraging investment)[38]. On the other side, a tailor-made provision with a sophisticated application could result in excessive compliance costs and administrative tax burdens for both taxpayers and tax administrations that need to comply with the CFC rules[39]. For all of these reasons, the provision of specific exemption from the CFC rules in the case that certain requirements are met is useful to identify the said balance.

(iv) The balance between the effectiveness of both the CFC provisions and the rules to avoid double taxation[40].

---

32 OECD (2015), *Designing Effective Controlled Foreign Company Rules, Action 3* – 2015 Final Report, Chapter 1, paragraph 7.
33 OECD (2015), *Designing Effective Controlled Foreign Company Rules, Action 3* – 2015 Final Report, Chapter 1, paragraphs 8 and 9.
34 OECD (2015), *Designing Effective Controlled Foreign Company Rules, Action 3* – 2015 Final Report, Chapter 1, paragraphs 8 and 9.
35 OECD (2015), *Designing Effective Controlled Foreign Company Rules, Action 3* – 2015 Final Report, Chapter 1, paragraph 10.
36 OECD (2015), *Designing Effective Controlled Foreign Company Rules, Action 3* – 2015 Final Report, Chapter 1, paragraph 10.
37 OECD (2015), *Designing Effective Controlled Foreign Company Rules, Action 3* – 2015 Final Report, Chapter 1, paragraph 10.
38 OECD (2015), *Designing Effective Controlled Foreign Company Rules, Action 3* – 2015 Final Report, Chapter 1, paragraph 10.
39 OECD (2015), *Designing Effective Controlled Foreign Company Rules, Action 3* – 2015 Final Report, Chapter 1, paragraph 10.
40 OECD (2015), *Designing Effective Controlled Foreign Company Rules, Action 3* – 2015 Final Report, Chapter 1, paragraph 11.

Avoidance of double taxation of CFC income

As far as the prevention or elimination of double taxation for CFCs is concerned, the OECD sets out recommendations in Chapter 7 of the said document under examination[41]. Indeed, one of the main policy considerations raised by the BEPS Project is to ensure that the CFC rules do not lead to double taxation[42]. In this respect, it needs to point out that countries with a worldwide taxation system usually grant a credit for taxes paid abroad on foreign sourced income[43] while countries with a territorial system (even partial) apply for tax exemption of certain foreign income.[44] However, as considered in the following paragraphs, the said measures (i.e. credit and exemption method) if not properly integrated in the domestic tax system are ineffective in many situations, and the result is that double taxation is not completely avoided.

After the above listed policy considerations, Chapter 7 of Action 3 focuses on the fourth one, and it outlines recommendations to avoid the double taxation raised in specific situations of CFC rules application, as described below.

Firstly, BEPS Project Action 3 document identifies that double taxation may arise when the attributed CFC income is subject to corporate tax in the CFC jurisdiction[45] and, at the same time, to CFC taxation in the shareholder company's or controlling company's country[46]. This is the most common situation that many countries[47] used to face when introducing CFC legislation. In the case at issue, the double taxation is then avoided by granting (from the shareholder or controlling company's jurisdiction) a foreign tax credit for the taxes actually paid in the residence country of the CFC company by the same CFC company[48]. Basically, it talks about the so called *indirect credit method*[49] that prescribes offsetting the foreign taxes paid by the CFC company with the shareholder's taxes due to the attributed CFC income by considering that income as economically owned by the

---

41 OECD (2015), *Designing Effective Controlled Foreign Company Rules, Action 3* – 2015 Final Report, Chapter 1, paragraph 11.
42 OECD (2015), *Designing Effective Controlled Foreign Company Rules, Action 3* – 2015 Final Report, Chapter 7, paragraph 121.
43 OECD (2015), Designing Effective Controlled Foreign Company Rules, Action 3 – 2015 Final Report, Chapter 1 and Indirect credit versus exemption: double taxation relief for intercompany distributions, Georg Kofler, Bulletin for international taxation, February 2012.
44 OECD (2015), Designing Effective Controlled Foreign Company Rules, Action 3 – 2015 Final Report, Chapter 1 and Indirect credit versus exemption: double taxation relief for intercompany distributions, Georg Kofler, Bulletin for international taxation, February 2012.
45 OECD (2015), *Designing Effective Controlled Foreign Company Rules, Action 3* – 2015 Final Report, Chapter 7, paragraph 122.
46 OECD (2015), *Designing Effective Controlled Foreign Company Rules, Action 3* – 2015 Final Report, Chapter 7, paragraph 124.
47 For example in Italy, Spain, Germany, the United Kingdom, the United States, etc.
48 OECD (2015), *Designing Effective Controlled Foreign Company Rules, Action 3* – 2015 Final Report, Chapter 7, paragraph 124.
49 *Indirect credit versus exemption method: double taxation relief for intercompany distributions*, Georg Kofler, Bulletin for international taxation, February 2012.

shareholder. Substantially, the shareholder is called to make and advance payment on the income for which taxation should be otherwise deferred[50].

It is understood that the tax credit granted for the foreign taxes paid is for taxes paid by another taxpayer resident in the CFC country[51]. Certainly, it is the most effective method to eliminate double taxation if the exemption method cannot be used due to its inconsistency with CFC rules[52]. Indeed, the exemption method undermines the CFC purpose since it does not allow subjecting the foreign income allocated to the CFC company to tax[53].

On the other hand, the deduction method is much less effective[54] since it operates only at the tax base level (i.e. by deducting the CFC taxes from the relevant tax base in the shareholder's country) and not on the taxes to be paid. The following example can help to understand the said weakness of the deduction method in eliminating the double taxation in respect of the most effective indirect credit method.

	DEDUCTION METHOD	INDIRECT CREDIT METHOD
CFC income attributed to the shareholder	1.000	1.000
Foreign taxes paid by CFC on its income	50 (i.e. tax rate 5% * 1.000)	50 (i.e. tax rate 5%)
Shareholder's country tax rate	20%	20%
Total tax burden on shareholder for CFC rule application	20% * (1.000–50) = 190 Through the deduction method, the foreign taxes paid reduced the taxable income of CFC (i.e. 1.000–50). Therefore, 950 of CFC income is double taxed.	20% * (1.000) = 200–50 = 150 Through the indirect credit method, the foreign taxes paid are credited against the domestic taxes due on CFC income (i.e. 200–50).

---

50 *Indirect credit versus exemption method: double taxation relief for intercompany distributions*, Georg Kofler, Bulletin for international taxation, February 2012.
51 OECD (2015), *Designing Effective Controlled Foreign Company Rules, Action 3 – 2015 Final Report*, Chapter 7, paragraph 125.
52 OECD (2015), *Designing Effective Controlled Foreign Company Rules, Action 3 – 2015 Final Report*, Chapter 7, paragraph 125.
53 OECD (2015), *Designing Effective Controlled Foreign Company Rules, Action 3 – 2015 Final Report*, Chapter 7, paragraph 125.
54 OECD (2015), *Designing Effective Controlled Foreign Company Rules, Action 3 – 2015 Final Report*, Chapter 7, paragraph 125.

Avoidance of double taxation of CFC income

	DEDUCTION METHOD	INDIRECT CREDIT METHOD
Effective tax rate/burden	(190+50)/1.000 = 24%	(150+50)/1.000 = 20%
Conclusion	The higher tax burden of 4% following the deduction method in respect of the tax rate of the shareholder's country (i.e. 20%) – or the effective tax burden of the indirect credit method – is because a part of income (i.e. 950) is double taxed anyway through the deduction method.	

From the table above, it is evident that the deduction method is much less effective that the credit method in eliminating the double taxation. Again, this ineffectiveness undermines the tax policy system implemented by countries: in case of double taxation, the tax neutrality of both CIN and CEN countries is not met, and the investment choices are influenced by the fact that some investments involving CFCs could cause double taxation, making the resident shareholder less competitive on the international market[55]

Moreover, according to the BEPS Project Action 3, the indirect credit method is able to effectively eliminate double taxation provided that (i) it is based on the foreign taxes actually paid (and not credited or qualified taxes for reimbursement), and (ii) it is limited to the amount of domestic taxes due on the foreign income[56].

As far as foreign taxes to be credited are concerned, the suggestion included in BEPS Project Action 3 is to consider all of the taxes borne by the CFC company and referred to as income; in this sense, also withholding taxes should be included[57].

Secondly, double taxation could arise in the case that more than one country applies CFC rules so that the same income (of a CFC's jurisdiction) is taxed in more than one country due to the simultaneous application of several CFC legislations[58]. If that should be the case, the document recommends again that a tax credit for the taxes actually paid by the CFC company is granted provided that, for those foreign taxes, no further tax reliefs have been recognized[59].

---

55 *The evolution of controlled foreign corporation rules and beyond*, Brian J. Arnold, Bulletin for international taxation, december 2019.
56 OECD (2015), Designing Effective Controlled Foreign Company Rules, Action 3 – 2015 Final Report, Chapter 7, paragraph 125.
57 OECD (2015), Designing Effective Controlled Foreign Company Rules, Action 3 – 2015 Final Report, Chapter 7, paragraph 125.
58 OECD (2015), Designing Effective Controlled Foreign Company Rules, Action 3 – 2015 Final Report, Chapter 7, paragraphs 126–130.
59 OECD (2015), Designing Effective Controlled Foreign Company Rules, Action 3 – 2015 Final Report, Chapter 7, paragraphs 126–130.

It is worth pointing out that the case under examination occurs only if more than one country considers the same subsidiary as a CFC and if they simultaneously taxed the same foreign CFC income disregarding that also other group shareholders are doing the same.

The BEPS suggestion to avoid an uncoordinated and simultaneous application of different domestic CFC rules is to define a hierarchy among the domestic CFC rules that are potentially applicable to the case[60]. The said suggestion substantially deals with the definition of a set of rules in order to identify which domestic CFC rule has priority over the others and, as a consequence, which country has to grant the tax credit in order to avoid double taxation[61]. As a matter of consistency with the CFC function, the prioritized CFC rules should be those of the controlling shareholder that is closer to the CFC company in the ownership structure[62].

The third situation for which BEPS Action 3 identifies in order to ensure that double taxation is avoided is when dividends are distributed by a CFC company or in case its shares are sold[63]. It is necessary to exempt that income from taxation in order to avoid that they are double taxed because both dividends and eventual capital gains have already been taxed in the previous years because of CFC rules' application[64]. Indeed, BEPS Project Action 3 suggests exempting the foreign dividends distributed by the CFC in the case that they derive from CFC income that is already taxed at the shareholder's level[65]. This exemption should be granted through a specific provision when the requirement for applying the so called "participation exemption" regimes are not met[66]. The participation exemption regimes exempt dividends received from a controlled company from taxation provided that certain requirements are met. For example, in order to apply the participation exemption in Italy, it is necessary that the dividends do not come from a controlled company that is located in a CFC country[67]. Otherwise, the dividends exemption does not apply. Therefore, in order to avoid the double taxation in the

---

60   OECD (2015), Designing Effective Controlled Foreign Company Rules, Action 3 – 2015 Final Report, Chapter 7, paragraphs 126–130.
61   OECD (2015), Designing Effective Controlled Foreign Company Rules, Action 3 – 2015 Final Report, Chapter 7, paragraphs 126–130.
62   OECD (2015), Designing Effective Controlled Foreign Company Rules, Action 3 – 2015 Final Report, Chapter 7, paragraphs 126–130.
63   OECD (2015), Designing Effective Controlled Foreign Company Rules, Action 3 – 2015 Final Report, Chapter 7, paragraphs 131–134.
64   OECD (2015), Designing Effective Controlled Foreign Company Rules, Action 3 – 2015 Final Report, Chapter 7, paragraphs 131–134.
65   OECD (2015), Designing Effective Controlled Foreign Company Rules, Action 3 – 2015 Final Report, Chapter 7, paragraphs 131–134.
66   OECD (2015), Designing Effective Controlled Foreign Company Rules, Action 3 – 2015 Final Report, Chapter 7, paragraph 131.
67   Italian Income Tax Code, Presidential Decree 917/1986, articles 47 and 89 (3).

Avoidance of double taxation of CFC income

case of CFC dividends, Italy introduced a specific provision[68] that prescribes the exemption of dividends in the case that the income of the controlled company was subject to a CFC regime in the previous fiscal years (reference is made to the income from which the dividends are deemed to originate)[69].

It is obvious that, for the avoidance of double taxation purposes, only the income previously subject to the CFC rules is entitled to benefit of the exemption for the dividends that are subsequently distributed[70]. Therefore, the percentage of income subject to CFC rules needs to be identified and the exemption granted to dividends paid out on a proportional basis. In this respect, it is in line with the BEPS Action 3 policy consideration to assume that the dividends distributed belong first to the income subject to CFC rules (and therefore already taxed at the sharcholder level)[71].

Another issue that the Action 3 document suggests considering is the withholding taxes that is applied – if any – by the CFC country when the dividends are paid out. In this case, indeed, it is appropriate to guarantee a foreign tax credit on the withholding taxes applied by the source state[72].

The same considerations expressed above can also be extended in case of sales of CFC shares[73]. Considering that each country has its own approach to tax capital gains, the subsequent relief of double taxation shall be defined accordingly in order to be in line with the specific country tax policy[74].

3.2. Foreign tax credit: item, timing, and country issues

The measure proposed by BEPS Action 3 to avoid double taxation for the first two situations listed above (i.e. tax credit) can, however, be both insufficient and inconsistent for the main reasons that will be explained below. It is worth remembering that, when BEPS Project Action 3 was drafted and published for public consultation purposes, most of the interest parties[75] were called to express their opinions on the measures included in the document, criticizing the limits set out to the tax credit method for relieving the double taxation in certain CFC cases.

---

68 Italian Income Tax Code, Presidential Decree 917/1986, article 47-bis.
69 Italian Income Tax Code, Presidential Decree 917/1986, article 47-bis.
70 OECD (2015), Designing Effective Controlled Foreign Company Rules, Action 3 – 2015 Final Report, paragraph 132.
71 OECD (2015), Designing Effective Controlled Foreign Company Rules, Action 3 – 2015 Final Report, Chapter 7, paragraph 132.
72 OECD (2015), Designing Effective Controlled Foreign Company Rules, Action 3 – 2015 Final Report, Chapter 7, paragraph 133.
73 OECD (2015), Designing Effective Controlled Foreign Company Rules, Action 3 – 2015 Final Report, Chapter 7, paragraph 134.
74 OECD (2015), Designing Effective Controlled Foreign Company Rules, Action 3 – 2015 Final Report, Chapter 7, paragraph 134.
75 Comments Received On Public Discussion Draft BEPS Action 3: Strengthening CFC Rules 5 May 2015 Part 1 And 2.

This is mainly because the interested parties observed that the avoidance of double taxation is wholly reached through the tax credit system only if no limitation to item, country, or fiscal year[76] exists.

The reference shall be made, for example, to the cases in which the tax credit is recognized only for certain foreign taxes (for example, for income taxes and not for trade taxes[77]). As a matter of fact, double taxation on income for foreign taxes not being creditable is not avoided.

Further concerns arise in the case that the CFC country tax rate is higher than that of the parent/controlling jurisdiction; therefore, the relevant recognition of the tax credit is misleading if both the carrying forward and the reimbursement request of the tax credit in excess are denied. Indeed, in all of the said cases, economic double taxation is not avoided, and the BEPS Action 3 policy objective is far from being reached.

This is true if the total income at a shareholder level is negative so that no foreign taxes can be actually credited; at the same time, the carried forward loss is reduced due to the positive CFC income[78]

In this regard, the so-called "deduction method" could be useful in situations when the excess tax credit cannot be carried forward, and it helps in mitigating the double taxation phenomena by deducting the foreign taxes (qualified as deductible costs for determining the shareholder's tax base)[79]. This is an alternative (less generous) mechanism than the foreign tax credit method, and it allows reducing the double taxation phenomena[80]. Under the deduction method, the foreign taxes paid (on CFC income) are considered as costs and then deducted from the shareholder's taxable income. Therefore, even if it is far from wholly eliminating double taxation, it can be considered a good compromise anyway in respect to a full tax credit method that implies higher administrative tax burdens for both taxpayers and tax administrations. Indeed, in the case that the tax burdens to comply with the law are excessive, the tax credit is granted years and years after

---

76   Comments Received On Public Discussion Draft BEPS Action 3: Strengthening CFC Rules 5 May 2015 Part 1 And 2, by BASF SE, by Federation of German Industries (BDI) and by International Chamber of Commerce.
77   Comments Received On Public Discussion Draft BEPS Action 3: Strengthening CFC Rules 5 May 2015 Part 1 And 2, by BIAC. In Germany, for example, the foreign tax credit on CFC cannot be credited against the trade taxes applied on business income. Please refer to *"The provision of the EU ATA Directive regarding CFC rules"*, Till Moser and Sven Hentschel, Intertax volume 45 issue 10, 2017.
78   In Switzerland, for example, the shareholders' companies shall offset the CFC income attributed with their losses, missing the opportunity of the foreign tax credit. Please refer to Comments Received On Public Discussion Draft BEPS Action 3: Strengthening CFC Rules 5 May 2015 Part 1 And 2 by Swiss Holdings.
79   Comments Received On Public Discussion Draft BEPS Action 3: Strengthening CFC Rules 5 May 2015 Part 1 And 2 by Beiten Burkhardt.
80   Comments Received On Public Discussion Draft BEPS Action 3: Strengthening CFC Rules 5 May 2015 Part 1 And 2 by Mouvement des Enterprises de France (MEDEF) and by Beiten Burkhardt.

the request; the consequence is that, in the meantime, double taxation occurred, compromising the tax neutrality of the tax policy systems. In this scenario, the deduction method mentioned before assumes relevance as an, alternative and it can also be considered as consistent with the CFC function.

As far as the timing issues are concerned (i.e. fiscal year limitation), it is worth noting that there are no specific and coordinated rules among countries able to regulate the statute of limitations for assessment purposes[81]. Again, no common indications exists on when specific items of income and expense should be included in the tax base[82] For example, reference is made to situations in which adjustments (to the tax base of the CFC company) occurs following tax audits. Of course, they make the application of the tax credit quite more complex due to taxes that the taxpayer of the CFC country can be asked to pay also several years after the end of the accounting period[83]. This issue usually occurs in a case of transfer pricing adjustments[84] made by the local tax authorities. The only remedy to avoid the double taxation on CFC income after those tax adjustments is to allow the shareholder to credit the additional taxes that are borne on CFC income after the tax authority assessments or to make the shareholder eligible for the tax reimbursement. These remedies seem complex since they imply the scrutiny and evaluation of further elements, making the double taxation the *lowest price to pay* in respect of the increased compliance costs[85].

Moreover, in order to properly identify the actual taxes paid by the CFC, tax refunds and rebates should be taken into account in order to determine the fair tax credit to be granted on the CFC income. However, also in this case, it seems far from being easily implemented since it significantly increases the administrative burden on taxpayers and tax administrations as it would require a procedure to trace taxes back to the relevant tax periods and income[86].

3.3. Foreign tax credit: the interaction with anti-abuse provisions

The interaction between CFC rules and transfer pricing is something discussed in the BEPS Action 3 Report as already pointed out above when dealing with the tax

---

81   Comments Received On Public Discussion Draft BEPS Action 3: Strengthening CFC Rules 5 May 2015 Part 1 And 2 by Mouvement des Enterprises de France (MEDEF) and by KPMG.
82   Comments Received On Public Discussion Draft BEPS Action 3: Strengthening CFC Rules 5 May 2015 Part 1 And 2 by Mouvement des Enterprises de France (MEDEF) and by KPMG.
83   Comments Received On Public Discussion Draft BEPS Action 3: Strengthening CFC Rules 5 May 2015 Part 1 And 2 by National Foreign Trade Council, Inc.
84   As well as tax adjustments following the application of the anti-avoidance rules.
85   Comments Received On Public Discussion Draft BEPS Action 3: Strengthening CFC Rules 5 May 2015 Part 1 And 2 by Japan Foreign Trade Council, Inc. and by SwissHoldings.
86   Comments Received On Public Discussion Draft BEPS Action 3: Strengthening CFC Rules 5 May 2015 Part 1 And 2 by Valente Associati GEB Partners.

policy considerations set out by the OECD. However, the Action 3 document that was published does not give any practical solutions in this respect as it solely suggests to properly manage the situations in which the interaction gives rise to double taxation and to implement effective measures to avoid it[87]. As far as a domestic tax provision is concerned (i.e. transfer pricing rules and general or specific anti-abuse provisions), it could be useful to define a "rule" in order to identify which provision takes priority over the others[88] and which are the remedies to eliminate any double or multiple taxation that has occurred.

In this sense, any limitation in time for granting the relief (as already discussed above), should be avoided, so that any transfer pricing adjustment – occurred after the closing of the fiscal period – does not generate a double taxation on CFC income.

3.4. Foreign tax credit: the interaction with the CFC regimes of multiple countries

The same income can also be subject to more than one CFC rule by multiple states[89]. The only solution proposed by BEPS Action 3 is to define a hierarchy among the domestic CFC rules that would be applicable in order to identify which country has the right to apply its domestic CFC rules first[90]. The hierarchy rule mentioned in the OCED document is based on the preliminary calculation by each country involved of:

(i) the effective tax rates borne by the controlled company submitted to the test (referred to the low taxation test) that triggers the CFC rules[91];
(ii) the taxes actually paid on the CFC income by the CFC in order to define the tax credit to wholly avoid the double taxation[92].

Once the previous calculations are performed, it is possible to identify how many countries are going to apply their domestic CFC rules and tax the CFC income at the domestic level. At this stage, the hierarchy rule comes into play, and it uniquely defines which country has the priority to tax the CFC income. In general terms, the 'hierarchy rule' could work by giving priority to the closer shareholder

---

87 Comments Received On Public Discussion Draft BEPS Action 3: Strengthening CFC Rules 5 May 2015 Part 1 And 2. Almost all the commentators have the same view.
88 For example, the thin capitalization rule that limits the deduction of interest expenses to a certain percentage (30% according to the European Directive) of the EBITDA.
89 OECD (2015), Designing Effective Controlled Foreign Company Rules, Action 3 – 2015 Final Report, Chapter 7, paragraphs 126–130.
90 OECD (2015), Designing Effective Controlled Foreign Company Rules, Action 3 – 2015 Final Report, Chapter 7, paragraphs 126–130.
91 Comments Received On Public Discussion Draft BEPS Action 3: Strengthening CFC Rules 5 May 2015 Part 1 And 2 by Japan Foreign Trade Council, Inc.
92 Comments Received On Public Discussion Draft BEPS Action 3: Strengthening CFC Rules 5 May 2015 Part 1 And 2 by Japan Foreign Trade Council, Inc.

Avoidance of double taxation of CFC income

(i.e. located in the intermediate country closer to the CFC in terms of direct control). If it should be the case, the CFC policy goal (as a deterrent measure protecting the shareholders' tax base) is met if both the following tax credits are recognized:

- the first shareholder (i.e. the closer one) that applies the CFC rules recognizes the foreign taxes paid by the foreign entity;
- the ultimate shareholder that applies the CFC provision grants a tax credit (in addition to the tax credit grant for the taxes paid in the CFC state) for the taxes already paid in the intermediate jurisdiction (by the before mentioned closer shareholder).

It is evident that the application of this rule implies a significant administrative burden on both the taxpayer and the tax administrations and makes the CFC policy goal (i.e. avoidance of double taxation) difficult to reach[93]. Indeed, in order to definitively avoid double taxation and grant the appropriate tax relief, a coordinated system among the countries applying the simultaneous CFC rules is necessary. However, if – and to what extent – each country is obligated to coordinate with the other countries involved when it applies its own CFC rules (in terms of income subject to double taxation and taxes creditable) is not clarified in BEPS Action 3.

It is worth underlining that the proposed "hierarchy rule" could primarily be used to define which states have the right to apply the CFC rule, thus inhibiting all of the others from the relevant application[94]. The said application of the "hierarchy rule" would prevent any further double taxation issue since it would avoid the simultaneous application of more than one CFC provision, and it would be the most effective manner to reach the policy goal of a CFC regime without adding further elements of complexity.

It is necessary to underline that the risk of double (or even multiple) taxation increases in the case that the CFC rules address also foreign-to-foreign stripping (i.e. in case the base erosion phenomenon goes beyond the direct controlled company that plays as an intermediate company for another foreign company that is indirectly controlled by the same shareholder). In the case of hierarchy rule application, this latter works as a deterrent measure not only by protecting the shareholder's tax base but also by preventing the said foreign-to-foreign stripping phenomena.

Instead, if no hierarchy rule is prescribed among the countries involved, it is very difficult to identify the company – and so the country – that has the priority from

---

93 Comments Received On Public Discussion Draft BEPS Action 3: Strengthening CFC Rules 5 May 2015 Part 1 And 2 by Japan Foreign Trade Council, Inc and by PricewaterhouseCoopers LLP.
94 Comments Received On Public Discussion Draft BEPS Action 3: Strengthening CFC Rules 5 May 2015 Part 1 by Swissholding.

a taxing right perspective[95] Consequently, the same double taxation phenomena described above for the simultaneous application of more than one CFC regime occurred. So, also in this case, an hierarchy rule should be defined in order to decide which domestic CFC rule applies first and, as a consequence, which country is entitled to first include all of the CFC income (of the direct and the indirect subsidiary)[96].

However, as already observed, the limit in applying such a rule is always the same: it implies a significant administrative burden on both taxpayer and tax administrations to demonstrate the taxes paid in more than one jurisdiction and on the same income.

3.5. Foreign tax credit: the non-deductible passive income

The tax credit recognized on the CFC income succeeds in eliminating double taxation to the extent that the passive income is considered as deductible in the shareholder jurisdiction (acting as payor) and subject to no or low taxation in the CFC jurisdiction[97] (acting as recipient). Otherwise, if the deduction of the passive income paid by the shareholder to the CFC company is denied[98], the tax credit is insufficient, and the double taxation (following the non-deductible expenses for the payor) remains.

Indeed, the denied deduction of passive income in the hands of the shareholder and the simultaneous application of CFC provisions leads to multiple taxation of the same income[99]. A first time, double taxation arises following the non-deductibility of the passive income expenses paid by the shareholder: the same income is taxed in the hands of the shareholder (as a non-deductible tax payment) and in the hands of the CFC[100].

Subsequently, another double taxation phenomenon arises when the CFC provisions apply, and the same CFC passive income (paid by the shareholder to the CFC company) is attributed and taxed at the shareholder level[101].

---

95 Comments Received On Public Discussion Draft BEPS Action 3: Strengthening CFC Rules 5 May 2015 Part 1 by Astrazeneca.
96 Comments Received On Public Discussion Draft BEPS Action 3: Strengthening CFC Rules 5 May 2015 Part 1 And 2 by Astrazeneca.
97 Comments Received On Public Discussion Draft BEPS Action 3: Strengthening CFC Rules 5 May 2015 Part 1 And 2 by BAS and by KPMG.
98 For example, due to the domestic thin cap rules that limit the deduction of certain passive income such as interest and royalties.
99 Comments Received On Public Discussion Draft BEPS Action 3: Strengthening CFC Rules 5 May 2015 Part 1 And 2 by BASF and by KPMG.
100 Comments Received On Public Discussion Draft BEPS Action 3: Strengthening CFC Rules 5 May 2015 Part 1 And 2 by BASF and by KPMG.
101 Comments Received On Public Discussion Draft BEPS Action 3: Strengthening CFC Rules 5 May 2015 Part 1 And 2 by BASF and by KPMG.

Avoidance of double taxation of CFC income

An example can help to clarify the phenomenon:

- the royalty is paid by the shareholder located in **country A** (hereafter also source country) whose tax law does not allow the deduction of the royalty payment to another entity resident in a foreign jurisdiction (hereafter also CFC country);
- the effective tax rate born by the company of the CFC country is considered too low by the source country and the activity performed by the controlled company is not considered as genuine business; therefore, the CFC rules apply in the source country at the parent company level;
- as a consequence of the CFC application, the royalty income is included by the source country in the shareholder's taxable base;
- the royalty income is taxed twice: once by the source country according to its domestic CFC rules and a second time because of the application of the source country's tax rule which denies the royalty deduction.

It should therefore be necessary to introduce a general escape clause in addition to clear rules to define tax relief that enables taxpayers to avoid double or multiple taxation in the cases described above[102].

The same occurs in the case of a company (other than the shareholder's and, hereafter, for sake of simplicity, **company A**) that pays an amount (i.e. passive income) to the CFC company and a withholding tax on this payment is applied[103]. When CFC rules apply at the shareholder level, the taxes to be credited should also include the withholding taxes paid in the source jurisdiction by company A if it is applied on the same passive income taxed at the shareholder's level under its domestic CFC rules[104]. Otherwise, double taxation is unavoidable.

3.6. Issues related to the foreign tax exemption

The measure proposed by BEPS Action 3 to avoid double taxation for the third situation (i.e. tax exemption for dividends paid out and capital gain realized after the CFC shares sale) can result in inefficiency in many cases. The comments of the interested parties in this respect for the public consultation purposes of BEPS Action 3 also emphasize the weakness of this measure[105].

---

102   Comments Received On Public Discussion Draft BEPS Action 3: Strengthening CFC Rules 5 May 2015 Part 1 And 2 by BASF and by KPMG.
103   Comments Received On Public Discussion Draft BEPS Action 3: Strengthening CFC Rules 5 May 2015 Part 1 And 2 by International Alliance For Principled Taxation.
104   Comments Received On Public Discussion Draft BEPS Action 3: Strengthening CFC Rules 5 May 2015 Part 1 And 2 by BASF and by KPMG.
105   Comments Received On Public Discussion Draft BEPS Action 3: Strengthening CFC Rules 5 May 2015 Part 1 And 2 by Swissholdings, by United States Council for International Business and by Mouvement des Enterprises de France (MEDEF).

First of all it shall be observed that the implementation of the exemption method requires the application of an efficient and coordinated method to determine if the dividends have been already taxed (directly or indirectly) as income under CFC provisions[106]. Indeed, in the case that more than two jurisdictions are involved, the dividends' distribution could generate the payment of additional taxes in each country (i.e. withholding taxes paid in the source state or other corporate tax on CFC income not recognized by the shareholder jurisdiction for the tax exemption of distributed dividends)[107].

Moreover, even in the case that the participation exemption regimes apply for the paid out dividends, many countries[108] do not provide for a total exemption. Indeed, the quota of dividends exempted from taxation is around 95%; as a consequence, the residual 5% of dividends is actually double taxed and no further tax reliefs are granted.

All of these issues are not taken into account in BEPS Action 3.

3.7. Some further considerations

Due to the lack of consensus of interested parties on alternative solutions that are more efficient[109], the limited tax credit and the participation exemption remain the two main recommendations included in the final version of BEPS Action 3[110] to avoid double taxation without specific measures addressed to the complex situations that could occur as described above.

The major concern expressed by the interested parties intervened in the public discussion[111] of Action 3 is that the proposed approaches appear to be unable to guarantee the pursuing of the CFC policy goals because the double taxation could not be avoided in many cases. It goes without saying that the effective pursue of the avoidance of double taxation as OECD policy consideration depends both on the coordination of countries for the measures adopted to relieve double taxation

---

106 Comments Received On Public Discussion Draft BEPS Action 3: Strengthening CFC Rules 5 May 2015 Part 1 And 2 by Swissholdings, by United States Council for International Business and by Mouvement des Enterprises de France (MEDEF).
107 Comments Received On Public Discussion Draft BEPS Action 3: Strengthening CFC Rules 5 May 2015 Part 1 And 2 by Swissholdings, by United States Council for International Business and by Mouvement des Enterprises de France (MEDEF).
108 For examples, Spain does not allow the 100% exemption of dividends paid out even already taxed under CFC rules by Swissholdings, by United States Council for International Business and by Mouvement des Enterprises de France (MEDEF).
109 Comments Received On Public Discussion Draft BEPS Action 3: Strengthening CFC Rules 5 May 2015 Part 1 And 2 by Swissholdings, by United States Council for International Business and by Mouvement des Enterprises de France (MEDEF).
110 OECD (2015), Designing Effective Controlled Foreign Company Rules, Action 3 – 2015 Final Report, Chapter 7.
111 Comments Received On Public Discussion Draft BEPS Action 3: Strengthening CFC Rules 5 May 2015 Part 1 And 2. The large majority of the commentators have this view.

and for the collection of evidence to obtain the tax reliefs. Moreover, the recommendations of the OECD document are quite general so that the countries have a lot of flexibility to implement them locally, making the risk of double taxation increasing more and more[112].

However, if the tax policy goal of double taxation avoidance is not reached through the CFC, the provision leads to distortions since the tax neutrality of the tax systems for both CEN and CIN countries is undermined. Indeed, it is undisputable that, if a CFC application carries on to double taxation (for example, under the cases examined in the previous paragraphs):

- for CEN countries, the domestic shareholders investing abroad in CFC countries are penalized in respect of domestic investments since they suffer double taxation if the credit method does not work properly. Consequently, the domestic and foreign investments are not taxed in the same manner anymore as the tax burden on the first one is significant higher due to double taxation (failing the prerequisite of CEN);
- for CIN countries, the foreign investments that are usually exempted are not only taxed at the domestic tax rate in the case of a CFC but they are also double taxed.

It is therefore evident that the proper functioning of the tax credit method – and the exemption, in some cases – is something on which countries shall focus for pursuing different tax policy goals. All that being stated, it is interesting to understand to what extent countries are (and should be) doing everything possible to avoid double taxation and which costs they are available to suffer.

Before answering the previous questions and concluding, the following paragraph carries out an overview on what has been implemented domestically[3] by some countries chosen by the author in order to understand how countries reacted to BEPS Action 3. The choice of the countries was driven by, on one hand, their peculiarities in CFC provisions and, on the other hand, by their key role in Europe (i.e. Germany) and as developing countries (i.e. Brazil).

4. The measures to avoid double taxation implemented by countries and their consistency with the BEPS Action 3 main policy considerations

As already discussed above, BEPS Action 3 includes recommendations to avoid double taxation following the application of CFC provisions; however, it does not always deal with all of the situations from which double or multiple taxation could arise because CFC provisions apply. Once BEPS Action 3 was published,

---

112 Comments Received On Public Discussion Draft BEPS Action 3: Strengthening CFC Rules 5 May 2015 Part 1 And 2, by AFME/Finance for Europe, by BBA/ The voice of banking, by BIAC.

some OECD Countries[113] started a tax reform in order to align their domestic regulations with the recommendations included in the BEPS Project referring to CFCs. Notwithstanding, the CFC provision system now in force for each country is still far from being fully compliant with the main BEPS policy considerations and the more complex situations described above (from which the double taxation arises) are not regulated.

4.1. Measures to avoid double taxation for CFCs in Germany

German tax law[114] prescribes that, following the application of domestic CFC rules, a foreign tax credit is granted to the shareholder in order to avoid that the income that is attributed is taxed both in the shareholder's country and in the CFC jurisdiction.

In addition, the distribution of dividends by a CFC company and capital gains realized on the sales of CFC shares are tax exempt.

In particular, the German tax law prescribes:

- the opportunity to offset the foreign tax credit with the corporate and income tax but totally excluding the local trade tax[115];
- the recognition of foreign taxes to be credited to those actually paid by the CFC company[116];
- the recognition of foreign taxes to be credited if not eligible for the refund[117];
- the tax exemption on dividends (at 95%) paid out by the CFC company (for which income has been previously subject to tax in the parent jurisdiction) to seven years from the CFC rules application[118];
- the tax exemption on capital gains realized on the sale of shares of a CFC controlled company (for which income has previously been subject to tax in the parent jurisdiction) to seven years from the CFC rules application[119].

Moreover, in the case that:

- more than one CFC rule applies on a simultaneous and on the same income,

---

113 For example, Austria introduced a CFC regime for the first time after the BEPS Project. Please see Austria – ATAD Implementation Table, IBFD, last review 8 January 2020.
114 Foreign Transactions Tax Act (Außensteuergesetz), sections 7–20.
115 The provision of the EU ATA Directive regarding CFC rules, Till Moser and Sven Hentschel, Intertax volume 45 issue 10, 2017.
116 Foreign Transactions Tax Act (Außensteuergesetz), sections 12, section 34 of the Income Tax Act and section 26 of the Corporate Income Tax Act.
117 Foreign Transactions Tax Act (Außensteuergesetz), sections 12, section 34 of the Income Tax Act and section 26 of the Corporate Income Tax Act.
118 Income Tax Act, section 3.
119 Income Tax Act section 3.

- the foreign tax credit is in excess against the domestic German tax of the relevant fiscal year,

the German tax law prescribes the possibility for the German shareholder to opt for the deduction method[120].

4.2. Measures to avoid double taxation for CFCs in France

French tax law[121] prescribes that, following the application of domestic CFC rules, a foreign tax credit is granted to the shareholder in order to avoid that the income attributed is taxed both in the shareholder's country and in the CFC jurisdiction. Specifically, according to French tax law:

- the offset of the foreign tax credit on a CFC with domestic taxes on the same income is limited to corporate and income taxes[122], including withholding taxes[123];
- the recognition of foreign taxes to be credited is limited to those actually paid by the CFC company[124];
- the recognition of foreign taxes to be credited is limited to those that cannot qualify for a refund[125];
- he tax exemption on dividends (at 99%) does not apply if the dividends are paid out by a CFC company located in a non-cooperative country[126] (otherwise, the exemption applies)[127];
- the offset of long-term capital gains realized on the sale of shares of a CFC controlled company with similar long-term capital losses[128] is allowed.

Moreover, a special provision is prescribed in the case of permanent establishments that qualify for French CFC rules application with regard to the French shareholder. Indeed, the French CFC rules can also be extended to the branches. The main reason for this extension can be identified in the fact that, consistent with the policy goals of its territorial tax system, France tends to exempt from taxing the income attributed to foreign branches of its resident mother companies[129].

---

120 Foreign Transactions Tax Act (Außensteuergesetz), sections 7–20.
121 Article 209B of the tax code (CGI).
122 The provision of the EU ATA Directive regarding CFC rules, Till Moser and Sven Hentschel, Intertax volume 45 issue 10, 2017.
123 Article 209B of the tax code (CGI).
124 Article 209B of the tax code (CGI).
125 Article 209B of the tax code (CGI).
126 It means that countries that do not deal with transparency, BEPS implementation, and fair tax competition requirements as requested by the EU. Reference to https://ec.europa.eu/commission/presscorner/detail/en/MEMO_19_1629.
127 'CFC rules around the world', Sebastian Duenas, Tax foundation, n. 659, June 2019.
128 Article 209B of the tax code (CGI).
129 Please see, for example, the convention for the avoidance of double taxation of income and capital and for the prevention of fiscal evasion and fraud between the government of the French Republic and the government of the Italian Republic concluded on 5 October 1989.

Consequently, in the case that the branch is located in a source country where it is subject to low-taxation (without performing a real business activity and receiving active income), there are no policy reasons to exclude the permanent establishment from the CFC application. Otherwise, the anti-avoidance phenomenon fight with CFC rules for companies is circumvented through the incorporation of branches[130].

In order to allow this specific *treaty override*, many tax treaties against double taxation concluded between France and other countries expressly includes a clause that allows France to apply CFC legislation to attribute the taxing right on the branch business profits to the French shareholder[131] (by derogating from the exemption mechanism).

Otherwise, if no specific clauses for French CFC provisions are included in the tax treaty, the French CFC rules cannot apply[132], even if the business profits of the foreign branches are exempted from taxation in France.

It is evident that, in France, there are no specific remedies prescribed to deal with the peculiar situations set out in the BEPS Action 3 document nor is the deduction method (as is prescribed in Germany) contemplated. The French situation is further complicated by the extension of the domestic CFC regime to foreign branches that are usually exempted from taxation in France: something that domestic French legislation had not been used to facing.

4.3. Measures to avoid double taxation for CFCs in Spain

The double taxation due to the application of Spanish CFC rules is avoided[133] by granting a foreign tax credit to the resident shareholder for both CFC income and dividends paid out. Also, the permanent establishments of Spanish companies that are located in CFC countries are subject to the Spanish CFC rules; the exemption of business income of the foreign branch of a Spanish mother company under tax treaty provisions – if any – is waived for the application of CFC rules[134]. The provision is substantially the same as that already explained for France.

---

130 A fully similar provision is prescribed in countries like Italy that implemented a partial territorial tax system and usually tax the business profits of foreign branches in Italy by recognizing a tax credit. As a consequence, the Italian CFC regime is not generally extended to the branches unless the taxpayer opts to apply for the branch exemption regime (i.e. the business profits of the foreign permanent establishments are not subject to tax in Italy). The same happens for Spain.
131 Article 209B of the tax code (CGI).
132 Article 209B of the tax code (CGI).
133 Spanish corporate income tax, '*CFC rules around the world*', Sebastian Duenas, Tax foundation, n. 659, June 2019 and *Controlled Foreign Company Legislation*, Michael Lang, Jeffrey Owens, Pasquale Pistone, Alexander Rust, Josef Schuch, Claus Staringer, IBFD, 2020, Chapter 36.
134 Spanish corporate income tax, *CFC rules around the world*, Sebastian Duenas, Tax foundation, n. 659, June 2019 and *Controlled Foreign Company Legislation*, Michael Lang, Jeffrey Owens, Pasquale Pistone, Alexander Rust, Josef Schuch, Claus Staringer, IBFD, 2020, Chapter 36.

Moreover, Spanish law prescribes that:

- the foreign tax credit can be offset with the corporate and income tax[135] to which the CFC income is subject in Spain, withholding taxes included;
- the recognition of foreign taxes to be credited is limited to those actually paid by the CFC company and each of its controlled entities[136] that distribute profits to the CFC[137];
- the tax exemption on dividends (at 95%) paid out by the CFC company (whose income has been previously subject to tax in the parent jurisdiction)[138];
- the tax exemption on capital gains realized on the sale of shares of a CFC controlled company (whose income has been previously subject to tax in the parent jurisdiction)[139].

4.4. Measures to avoid double taxation for CFCs in Sweden

Sweden[140] prescribes that, following the application of domestic CFC rules, a foreign tax credit is granted to the shareholder in order to avoid that the income attributed is taxed both in Sweden (parent company country) and in the CFC jurisdiction. Specifically, Sweden law prescribes that:

- the foreign tax credit can be offset with the corporate and income taxes[141] to which the CFC income is subject in Sweden; also, municipal tax can be offset[142];
- the recognition of foreign taxes to be credited, and it limits them to those actually paid by the CFC company[143];
- the excess of a foreign tax credit can be carried forward in the next five years[144];
- in the case that the foreign taxes paid by the CFC can be deducted as expenses for the parent company taxable base purposes, and those taxes can also be creditable; the effective foreign tax credit is reduced by the amount of Swedish tax that is saved due to the foreign tax deduction[145];

---

135 Implementing key BEPS Action: Where do we stand?, IBFD, January 2019, part 2, chapter 31.
136 The minimum percentage of participation of the CFC company in the subsidiary shall be 5%. If it should be the case, the taxes paid by the controlled company of the CFC can be credited if the relevant profits have been paid out to the CFC and then attributed to the parent company according to the CFC rules.
137 Implementing key BEPS Action: Where do we stand?, IBFD, January 2019, part 2, chapter 31.
138 Implementing key BEPS Action: Where do we stand?, IBFD, January 2019, part 2, chapter 31.
139 Implementing key BEPS Action: Where do we stand?, IBFD, January 2019, part 2, chapter 31.
140 Chapter 39a of the ITA Swedish Income Tax Act.
141 The provision of the EU ATAD Directive regarding CFC rules, Till Moser and Sven Hentschel, Intertax volume 45 issue 10, 2017.
142 Chapter 39a of the ITA Swedish Income Tax Act (No. 1229 of 1999).
143 Chapter 39a of the ITA Swedish Income Tax Act (No. 1229 of 1999).
144 Chapter 39a of the ITA Swedish Income Tax Act (No. 1229 of 1999).
145 Chapter 39a of the ITA Swedish Income Tax Act (No. 1229 of 1999).

- the tax exemption on dividends (at 100%) paid out by the CFC company (whose income has been previously subject to tax in the parent jurisdiction) without any relief for eventual withholding taxes paid by the source state;
- the tax exemption on capital gains realized on the sale of shares of a CFC controlled company (whose income has been previously subject to tax in the parent jurisdiction).

Moreover, Sweden prescribed an "innovative" provision that is significantly effective at reducing the double taxation phenomena: the excess tax credit (resulting from the taxed paid at the CFC level) can be carried forward by the Sweden shareholder. Since Sweden has a partial territorial tax system, it can be argued that the said provision is fully in line with its tax policy perspective[146]. Indeed, in the case that the territorial tax system deviates from the tax exemption of foreign source income – as it is the case with the CFC rules application – it should at least give the opportunity to carry forward the unused tax credit to be used to offset the CFC taxable income attributed to the shareholder in future years[147]. Otherwise, the result is the foreign investments being subject to a higher effective tax rate in respect of that applied to (i) domestic investments and (ii) foreign investments in no CFC case.

4.5. Measures to avoid double taxation for CFCs in Indonesia

According to the Indonesian law, double taxation due to the CFC rules application is not avoided by recognizing a foreign tax credit for the CFC taxes that are paid as prescribed for all of the above listed countries. Indeed, the Indonesian CFC rules were amended in FY 2017 with the introduction of the so called "deemed dividend approach"[148]. According to the said rule, the income of the CFC is attributed to the shareholder as a fictitious dividend (i.e. deemed CFC dividend)[149], so that it is considered as the attribution of the CFC profit after tax. The double taxation on the subsequent actual dividend distribution by the CFC to the shareholder is avoided by offsetting the deemed dividends and the actual ones[150]. However, this offsetting is available for the dividend distributed within the five years after the deemed dividend attribution to the Indonesian shareholder[151]. Always with reference to the actual dividend distribution (and not for the deemed dividends), Indonesian law recognizes a foreign tax credit limited to the withholding taxes paid on the inbound CFC dividends[152].

---

146 Implementing key BEPS Action: Where do we stand?, IBFD, January 2019, part 2, chapter 32.
147 Implementing key BEPS Action: Where do we stand?, IBFD, January 2019, part 2, chapter 32.
148 Regulation No. PMK-107/PMK.03/2017 issued by the Indonesian Ministry of Finance.
149 Regulation No. PMK-107/PMK.03/2017 issued by the Indonesian Ministry of Finance, article 3.
150 Regulation No. PMK-107/PMK.03/2017 issued by the Indonesian Ministry of Finance.
151 Regulation No. PMK-107/PMK.03/2017 issued by the Indonesian Ministry of Finance, article 6.
152 Please refer to the Indonesian income tax law, Article 24 and to Regulation No. PMK-107/PMK.03/2017 issued by the Indonesian Ministry of Finance that sets out specific limitations for the amount of the foreign tax creditable.

Moreover, Indonesian law prescribes that:

- the foreign tax credit suffers a per country limitation if dividends are distributed by different countries[153];
- the recognition of foreign withholding to be credited is limited to those of the direct CFC (and not extended to those paid on the dividends distributed from an indirect CFC to a CFC directly owned by the shareholder)[154].

It is evident how the Indonesian CFC rules are quite far from the BEPS Action 3 reccomendations by ignoring the double taxation phenomena due to most of the situatons outlined in the OECD document. Indeed, through the before mentioned provisions (i.e. by offsetting the deemed dividend with the actual distributed dividends and by recognizing as creditable only the withholding taxes on distributed dividends), double taxation is only mitigated. Indeed, the CFC taxes paid on the deemed dividends are never considered as creditable and no specific rules are in force to avoid double taxation in the case of CFC shares alienation.

4.6. Measures to avoid double taxation for CFCs in Brazil

The Brazilian law No. 12,973/2014 prescribed a foreign tax credit to avoid double taxation on CFC income attributed to the Brazilian shareholder. That foreign tax credit is limited to the taxes actually paid by the CFC company and to the taxes payable in Brazil on the CFC income attributed to the Brazilian shareholder[155].

Similar to the previously described Indonesian system, the withholding taxes paid on dividends distributed by the CFC company are creditable but only referred to the dividends distributed by the direct CFC (and not extended to the withholding taxes paid on the dividends distributed from an indirect CFC to a CFC directly owned by the shareholder)[156].

Moreover, Article 87 of law No. 12,973/2014 introduced a beneficial regime for specific industries (i.e. beverage, food, and construction) that is in force until 2022. This favourable rule prescribes a presumed tax credit up to 9% (i.e. independent of the taxes paid in the CFC country and creditable) to be deducted from the shareholder's taxes that are due after the CFC income attribution[157]. This results in increasing the foreign taxes to be deducted at the Brazilian shareholder

---

153 KPMG, „Amended Controlled Foreign Company rules", Tax News Flash, August 2017. The provisions commented by KPMG are always in force since they refer to Regulation No. PMK-107/PMK.03/2017 issued by the Indonesian Ministry of Finance.
154 KPMG, „Amended Controlled Foreign Company rules", Tax News Flash, August 2017. The provisions commented by KPMG are always in force since they refer to Regulation No. PMK-107/PMK.03/2017 issued by the Indonesian Ministry of Finance.
155 Please refer to the law No. 12,973/2014.
156 Please refer to the law No. 12,973/2014, article 87.
157 Please refer to the law No. 12,973/2014, article 87.

level and to favour the said industries for both inbound and outbound investments (aligned with the essence of a CEN tax policy that is proper in Brazil[158]).

The Brazilian CFC rules are not fully aligned with BEPS Action 3 recommendations as not only are the more complex situations not covered but also all of the cases that deal with very common situations such as CFC shares disposal. However, the favourable regime (i.e. the presumed additional tax credit of 9%) is something that helps in realigning the CFC rules with the policy goals of Brazil as a CEN country, pushing for fair market competitiveness by reducing the distortion that double taxation causes.

5. Conclusions

It is evident how the answer of the countries to eliminate double taxation following the CFC rules application is not able to deal with all of the possible situations identified in the previous paragraphs. It is also obvious that the effort of each country in making the tax credit method – and the exemption, in some cases – work is something that differs according to the tax policy system that is implemented and to the CFC policy goals.

For countries that implemented a territorial tax system (such as Germany, France, Sweden, and Spain), the most important thing is to ensure that the double taxation on foreign income is avoided as much as possible as its CIN tax policy is highly undermined by a CFC application and by consequent double taxation. It is indeed evident that the provisions on double taxation avoidance of the CIN countries examined above are more structured in respect of those of Brazil and Indonesia (as CEN countries) as they try to cover as many situations as possible. This is also the main reason why they used to restrict the cases to which the domestic CFC rules apply as much as possible (i.e. for example, only in the case of no genuine business activities), by reducing the situation in which the 'exemption' for foreign income is waived. As described in the first part of this thesis, the main goal of CFC legislation for CIN and CEN countries is to primarily avoid the erosion of the domestic shareholder's tax base. This caused the evaluation of further elements for CFC application in CIN countries (apart from low taxation) including the existence of base eroding payments and genuine business activity as the international competitiveness shall be protected[159]. Additionally, these elements actually help to restrict the cases in which the CFC rules apply by addressing the provisions solely to the situation in which the tax avoidance exists.

---

158 „Controlled Foreign Company Legislation", Michael Lang, Jeffrey Owens, Pasquale Pistone, Alexander Rust, Josef Schuch, Claus Staringer, IBFD, 2020, Chapter 7.
159 *The evolution of controlled foreign corporation rules and beyond*, Brian J. Arnold, Bulletin for international taxation, december 2019.

Avoidance of double taxation of CFC income

On the other hand, for CEN countries such as Brazil and Indonesia, the taxation – at domestic level – of foreign investments is already consistent with their tax policy. Indeed, differently from CIN countries, the main policy goal pursued with the CFC application by CEN countries is to reduce the deferral taxation of foreign income that, in the case of distribution, would have been taxed anyway at a domestic level (even without CFC rules). At the same time, they are even much less worried about the possible distortion that occurs if double taxation remains (since they could apply domestic remedies) even if it has a negative effect undermining the competitiveness of CEN countries in investing abroad. A clear example is Brazil that is a CEN country, and its domestic provision to avoid double taxation in CFC cases is focused on implementing a fair domestic tax system for both inbound and outbound investments, guarantying the same tax treatments and incentives. This is the reason why to guarantee the tax neutrality for certain industries, a presumed tax credit in case of CFC application has been introduced to prevent the double taxation phenomena that could affect industries that Brazil wants to protect.

Therefore, the policy ambition of BEPS Project Action 3 to avoid double taxation due to domestic CFC rules application is still far to be reached since it presumes that countries with different tax policy systems and goals coordinate with each other and find a compromise in many divergent situations.

One could object that, if double taxation remains and it is tolerable by countries, the goals of CFC rules (both as anti-avoidance measures and as anti-deferral) are more important than the tax neutrality on which the tax systems are based. It is also true that it needs to take into account a further obstacle to a coordinated approach among countries to avoid double taxation: the high administrative burden (for both tax authorities and taxpayers) that such a coordination implies.

The result is that, to date, most of the cases of double taxation due to CFC rules identified in this thesis still remain without protection, and this unavoidably affects the competitiveness of multinational companies on the market that shall incur further tax costs due to double taxation. As underlined by some authors[160], all of these issues would maybe have been avoided if the BEPS Project Action 3 was focused more on preventing double non-taxation through the CFC provisions instead of avoiding double taxation due to a CFC application.

---

160 *The evolution of controlled foreign corporation rules and beyond*, Brian J. Arnold, Bulletin for international taxation, December 2019.

CFC rules and EU law

CFC definition under the Anti-Tax Avoidance Directive (covered entities, control test, low taxation)

Olena Bokan

1. Introduction
2. Defining CFC rules within the ATAD Framework
   2.1. CFC rules in the ATAD
   2.2. Entities in the scope of the ATAD
   2.3. Control tests applied to CFC
   2.4. Notion of low taxation
   2.5. Observations and Conclusive Remarks on the CFC definition in the ATAD
3. Implementation of the CFC rules in EU Member State
   3.1. General remarks and overview
   3.2. CFC rules and the definition of "entities" implemented by the EU Member States
   3.3. Provisions of the control test in the EU Member States
   3.4. Implementation of the definition of the "low taxation"
   3.5. Analysis of several issues and challenges related to the implementation of the CFC definitions
4. Conclusions

1. Introduction

Fair taxation and control over tax avoidance at the international level had become a high priority for many governments in the late 2000s.[1] After the initiation of the BEPS Project by which the OECD aimed to tackle tax base erosion and profit shifting practices, the OECD had prepared and issued, among others, its final report on BEPS Action 3 designing effective controlled foreign company rules (hereinafter, BEPS Action 3 Report). The major aim of the BEPS Action 3 Report was to provide the countries with the comprehensive recommendations of how to tackle profit shifting through controlled foreign companies (hereinafter: CFC).[2]

Following the presentation of the OECD BEPS final report, the EU Member States' representatives predicted that many EU countries would rush to implement the proposed rules into their tax systems,[3] each of them already having their own tax system. The lack of a common tax system in the EU could lead to an ineffective implementation of the proposed initiative. Therefore, the European Commission proposed a common framework with a minimum standard to ensure the implementation of the BEPS recommendations across all the 28 EU Member States.[4] The European Council approved the initiative and following the necessary procedures and, on 12 of July 2016, adopted Council Directive (EU) 2016/1164 on rules against tax avoidance practices that affect the internal market of EU, which is known as the so-called anti-tax avoidance directive (hereinafter: ATAD).

This paper covers specifics of ATAD Article 7 "Controlled foreign company rule" in relation to the definitions of entities, the control test, and the notion of "low taxation". Section two will provide a legal overview of the definitions and criteria outlined in Article 7. First, a definition of the entities will be covered in Chapter 2.2. Second, Chapter 2.3 will elaborate on the control test to define the CFC. Finally, the notion of "low taxation" will be presented in Chapter 2.4. Furthermore, subsequent chapters of section 3 will provide an overview on the way the definitions mentioned above were implemented by the EU Member States. This does not intend to provide a comprehensive overview but rather to demonstrate a distinction in the implementation approach between the EU Member States. Finally, an analysis of some challenges and issues that arose over the course of the implementation of the ATAD will be presented in Chapter 3.5. The paper concludes with observations on whether the ATAD CFC rules provide the consistent and common rules to ensure fair taxation and protection of the internal market.

---

1 Council Directive (EU) 2016/1164 of 12 July 2016 laying down rules against tax avoidance practices that directly affect the functioning of the internal market, Official Journal of the European Union, (2016), L 193, hereinafter: ATAD.
2 OECD (2015), *Designing Effective Controlled Foreign Company Rules – Action 3: Final Report*, OECD/G20 Base Erosion and Profit Shifting Project, (OECD 5 Oct. 2015) (Paris: OECD).
3 Caroline Docclo, 'The European Union's Ambition to Harmonize Rules to Counter the Abuse of Member States' Disparate Tax Legislations', *Bulletin for International Taxation* (2017), p.367.
4 At the time of implementation, Great Britain was the member of the EU.

2. Defining CFC rules within the ATAD Framework
2.1. CFC rules in the ATAD

The ATAD was developed as a minimum standard for the EU Member States in order to ensure a minimum level of protection of their tax systems. As such, by adopting the ATAD, the European Council provided each EU Member State with the required tax avoidance rules and, simultaneously, with flexibility for how to implement these rules. The ATAD incorporated six anti-BEPS measures for which three of them were based on OECD BEPS recommendations: 1) the interest limitation rules; 2) the CFC rules, and 3) measures against hybrid mismatches.[5] In the following, the focus will be put on the CFC rules adopted in the ATAD.

CFC rules are laid down in the Articles 7 and 8 of the ATAD, and their aim is to ensure the effective taxation of a parent company and to prevent the profits being transferred outside of the Member State to the subsidiary with substantially lower taxation. To this end, the profits of the subsidiary should be attributed to the parent company and taxed at the profit tax rate of the latter. In order to eliminate double taxation matters in such cases, when the profit of the subsidiary is taxed twice, i.e. at the subsidiary's level and at the level of the parent company, the parent jurisdiction shall provide a deduction for the taxes already paid by the subsidiary.

The ATAD defines a CFC as a foreign entity based in a low-tax jurisdiction that is controlled by a parent company that is situated in a country with higher rates of profit taxation. Each of the components of the CFC definition will be analysed in detail. First, Chapter 2.2 addresses the definition of the entities covered by the ATAD. Then, Chapter 2.3 will elaborate on defining the level of control of the parent company under the rules of the ATAD. Finally, Chapter 2.4. will concentrate on the notion of low taxation as one of the criteria established by the ATAD.

2.2. Entities in the scope of the ATAD

According to the ATAD, the CFC rules apply to all taxpayers subject to corporate income tax (hereinafter: CIT) in the EU Member States that have a subsidiary or a permanent establishment (PE) in low-tax jurisdictions. Particularly, Article 7 of the ATAD stipulates that EU Member States in which the parent company is based should consider the foreign entity, or a PE, as a CFC, when *"the profits are not subject to tax or are exempt from tax in that Member State"*[6] and meeting other predefined conditions that are considered below.

---

5   The other three are based on the proposed Common Consolidated Corporate Tax Base Directive (hereinafter: CCCTB): 4) exit taxation rule, 5) GAAR rule, and 6) the switch-over clause.
6   ATAD, Article 7 (1).

To point out, the EU law defines the parent company as a resident of the Member State for tax purposes according to the laws of the EU Member State that is subject to CIT without the possibility to be exempt or to substitute such tax.[7] Furthermore, the parent company should have a minimum shareholding or voting rights of at least 10% in the capital of the company based in the other state.[8] To highlight, the percentage of the shareholding in the CFCs differs according to the tax law of each EU Member State with the ATAD recommended minimum standard of more than 50%, which will be covered in more detail in subchapter 2.3 below. Consequently, a subsidiary is the company for which the capital includes the shareholding of the parent company or grants the voting rights to the parent company.[9]

Moreover, EU law provides the list of the parent companies that includes various forms of corporate entities existing in EU Member States such as limited liability companies, public limited companies, associations, and all other forms of entities that are subject to corporate income tax.[10] Notably, the ATAD rules did not specify the legal form of the entities at the parent level and only stipulates that the rules should be limited only to corporate taxpayers. Therefore, this leaves the definition of the entities covered by the ATAD quite broad. The reason behind that can be that the major aim of the European Council was to provide the EU Member States with a minimum requirement, but one that would be flexible enough to be adjusted to a specific tax system. In turn, it can be arguable whether such an approach provides benefit to the law of EU Member States as many states that did not have any CFC rules prior to the implementation of the ATAD merely adopted the same wording of the ATAD into their national tax law.[11] Therefore, this left the taxpayers with uncertainty and the necessity for additional clarification.

It is important to mention that the OECD proposed that the definition of entities covered by CFC rules should not be limited only to cover corporations but to cover any corporate body or entity in order to prevent the possibility to avoid the rules in any case, such as through transparent entities. Nevertheless, transparent entities are not covered by the ATAD rules due to the fact that the profit of such entities is or should already be taxed at the level of the partners or shareholders in one of the EU Member States. This matter can be problematic and was already addressed by the OECD in 2015 in its final report. In this report, the OECD had pointed out that, in the case that the profit of the transparent entities, such as

---

7   Council Directive (EU) 2011/96/EU of 30 November 2011 on a common system of taxation applicable in the case of parent companies and subsidiaries of different Member States, Official Journal of the European Union, (2011), L345/8, Article 2(a), hereinafter: Parent-Subsidiary Directive.
8   Parent-Subsidiary Directive, Article 3 (1)(a).
9   Parent-Subsidiary Directive , Article 3 (1)(b).
10 Parent-Subsidiary Directive, Annex I.
11 Czech Republic, Malta, Ireland, and other countries that did not have CFC rules before 2019 transposed the wording of the ATAD into their national law, giving no clarifications to the covered entities.

partnerships, is not taxed in the EU Member State, this state should apply the CFC rules to such transparent entity in order to ensure taxation.[12] The report also provides that the EU Member State may consider such transparent entity as a CFC in order to apply the rules and to tax income of such transparent entity before it might be shifted to the other transparent entity,[13] preventing tax avoidance at each level of complex structures. Nevertheless, the European Council considered that inclusion of the transparent entities would enlarge the list of taxes beyond the CIT covered by the ATAD and would cause a lengthy negotiation to find the common ground within the EU. Therefore, it had limited the application only to those entities that are considered as taxpayers for the purposes of the CIT.

The language of the ATAD provisions states that any taxpayer subject to CIT is covered under the CFC rules thus PEs subject to the CIT of the parent company of one EU Member States situated on the territory of the other EU Member State are also subject to CFC rules. To clarify, the PE is defined as:

> ... fixed place of business situated in a Member State through which the business of a company of another Member State is wholly or partly carried on in so far as the profits of that place of business are subject to tax in the Member State...by virtue of national law.[14]

Moreover, the ATAD stipulates that the CFC rules should address situations not only in the EU but also in third countries. Therefore, if the PE of the entity that is a resident of a third state is subject to the CIT in the EU Member State where it is based, such PE is also covered by the provisions of the ATAD[15] and should comply with the CFC rules.[16] The fact that ATAD provisions extend its effect not only to the residents of the EU but also to the residents of third states shows that the European Council was aiming to ensure fair taxation of all taxpayers, including PEs of non-resident entities.

According to the ATAD, the CFC rules adopted by the EU Member States that address the entities and PEs not only within the EU but also in the third countries, should comply with the EU fundamental freedoms and target the CFCs that do "*not carry on a substantial economic activity*"[17]. This requirement was developed in the European Court of Justice (hereinafter: ECJ) jurisprudence with regards to

---

12 For more on transparent entities in: *The concept of foreign base company and the application of CFC rules to transparent entities and PEs* (switch-over) by Patrick Walchhofer.
13 OECD (2015), *Designing Effective Controlled Foreign Company Rules – Action 3: Final Report*, OECD/G20 Base Erosion and Profit Shifting Project, (OECD 5 Oct. 2015) (Paris: OECD), p. 22, para. 27
14 Parent-Subsidiary Directive, Article 2(b).
15 Caroline Docclo, *Bulletin for International Taxation* (2017), p.369
16 ATAD, Article 1.
17 ATAD, preamble, section 12, paragraph 2.

the freedom of establishment, most notably in the decision on the Cadbury Schweppes case.[18, 19, 20]

Furthermore, the ATAD covers entities or PEs that generate their profits from the artificial operations that are developed to obtain a tax advantage. For this purpose, the ATAD specifies such operations as "non-genuine" when entities do not possess the assets needed, do not assume the relevant risks, and do not employ the staff to execute the respective functions.[21] At the same time, the ATAD introduces a substance carve-out provision that provides that CFC rules should not apply to the entities with "*substantive economic activity supported by staff, equipment, assets and premises...*" which can be proven by the factual analysis.[22]

Finally, the ATAD states that, in order to eliminate high administrative and compliance costs, the EU Member States may not apply CFC rules towards entities with low margin or minimum profit due to the low risk of shifting the profit from such companies to CFCs.[23]

2.3. Control tests applied to CFC

The fact that the foreign entity is controlled by the parent company distinguishes whether such foreign entity qualifies as a CFC. To this end, Article 7(1) of the ATAD defines specific conditions, namely, legal and economic levels of control. From the legal point of view, the taxpayer itself or together with its associated parties based in the EU Member State should directly or indirectly hold at least 50% of the voting rights and have a major power to appoint the managing body in the foreign company, i.e. to exercise its control over the foreign company.[24] To clarify, the ATAD defines associated enterprises as (a) an entity in which the taxpayer directly or indirectly holds or (b) an individual or entity that directly or indirectly holds in the taxpayer a participation in terms of voting rights or capital ownership of 25 percent or more or is entitled to receive 25 percent or more of the profits of that entity or of the taxpayer.[25] The economic control, on the other hand, requires that the shareholder owns more than 50% of the capital of the entity or should be entitled to more than 50% of the profits of that foreign entity.

---

18 UK: ECJ, 12 September 2006, Case C-196/04, *Cadbury Schweppes v. Commissioners of Inland Revenue*, (2006)
19 OECD (2015), Designing Effective Controlled Foreign Company Rules – Action 3: Final Report (2015), p.17, para 20
20 For more on ATAD and EU fundamental freedoms in: *CFC rules of the Anti-Tax Avoidance Directive in light of the EU fundamental freedoms* by Mike Kollar.
21 ATAD, Article 7 (2)(b).
22 ATAD, Article 7 (2)(a).
23 ATAD, preamble, section 12, paragraph 1.
24 For more on control concept in : *The role of the "control" concept under CFC rules* by Kristina Reguliova.
25 ATAD, Article 2 (4).

ATAD, Article 7 (1)(a). specifies the following:

1. The Member State of a taxpayer shall treat an entity, or a permanent establishment of which the profits are not subject to tax or are exempt from tax in that Member State, as controlled foreign company where the following conditions are met:
   (a) in the case of an entity, the taxpayer by itself, or together with its associated enterprises holds a direct or indirect participations of more than 50 percent of the voting rights, or owns directly or indirectly more than 50 percent of capital or is entitled to receive more than 50 percent of the profits of that entity; ...

Therefore, in order to protect the internal market against corporate structures avoiding taxation, the ATAD covers not only majority shareholdings of respective levels of control exercised by the parent companies but also defines direct and indirect ownership of the CFC through the associated enterprises. Consequently, control over the CFC should be assessed at the level of the parent company through the evaluation of its share of ownership in its intermediate holding company that holds the shares in such CFC. However, there may be the case that, while calculating the level of control in the low-taxed entity through the intermediate holding company, the parent company executes less than 50% of the control threshold. Then, the CFC rules are still to be applied if the parent and its intermediary holding company each have more than 50% of the shareholdings at each level of the ownership structure.[26]

Thus, defining the level of control through indirect participation prevents the parent companies from arranging the structure of ownership of the CFC entity through several minor shareholders by splitting the level of ownership among them below the threshold of 50%. Nevertheless, the European Council and the OECD emphasize that, while direct and indirect levels of control render CFC rules more effective, such approach may cause double taxation which should be eliminated by the EU Member States. For that reason, the ATAD provides a few provisions regarding the prevention of double taxation such as, in the case of the dividends distributed from the CFC to the parent company, the taxpayer should exclude from the taxable base the part of profit that was previously included in the taxable base of the taxpayer and taxed.[27] Next, the double taxation should be avoided in the case that an alienation of the shareholdings or proceeds to be taxed in the parent company jurisdiction were already included in the taxable base of the parent company.[28] Finally, the taxpayers should be granted a deduction of the tax paid by the CFC in its jurisdiction.[29]

---

26 OECD (2015), *Designing Effective Controlled Foreign Company Rules – Action 3: Final Report*, OECD/G20 Base Erosion and Profit Shifting Project, (OECD 5 Oct. 2015) (Paris: OECD), p.29, para 47.
27 ATAD, Article 8(5).
28 ATAD, Article 8(6).
29 ATAD, Article 8(7).

Although the ATAD provides a minimum standard and allows the Member States to implement lower thresholds of control into their national CFC rules, the ATAD also recommends that, in order to comply with the ECJ case law, the Member States should be careful with the application of the lower participation threshold as this might be considered as an infringement of the fundamental freedoms.[30] So, in order to comply with free movement of capital, a Member State should not reduce the shareholding threshold of 50% in the foreign entity if the CFC rules of a Member State spread beyond the territory of the EU. This is due to the fact that, unlike the freedom of establishment, the right of the free movement of capital can be invoked beyond the territory of the EU[31] therefore hindering the effectiveness of the application of the Member State' CFC rules. Nevertheless, should an EU Member State decide to reduce the threshold lower than 50%, it should exclude entities based in the third countries that are not engaged in non-genuine operations from the law.[32] Therefore, the ATAD recommends that an EU Member State should focus on the entities lacking economic substance.[33]

Both the legal and economic types of control are relatively easy to access and therefore might not cause much administrative burden to the tax authorities. However, as corporate law enables companies to exercise flexible terms of shareholder participations, various corporate structures may cause a misleading understanding of who precisely exercises the control over the CFC entity. Therefore, an additional assessment should be conducted to identify the CFC controlling body. Although the ATAD does not go beyond the above specified types of control and provides for a minimum standard, some EU Member States could consider implementing additional tests. Such additional tests were likewise proposed by the OECD report. In particular, the EU Member States may apply, in addition to the tests under the minimum standard, the *de facto* analysis, or define control on the basis of consolidation[34] The *de facto* analysis enables the tax authorities to evaluate who has a significant level of control of the CFC through the execution of the important decisions such as entering into agreements or daily operational activity. It mainly serves as a supplement to the economic and legal control analyses due to the difficulty of collection of the relevant proof and high administrative costs. In addition, such analysis is always a matter of a subjective approach which lacks efficiency in comparison to the objective technical legal and economic anal-

---

30 ATAD, preamble, section 12, para. 2.
31 Caroline Docclo, *Bulletin for International Taxation* (2017), p.375.
32 In the case UK: ECJ, 12 September 2006, C-196/04 Cadbury Schweppes plc, Cadbury Scheweppes Overseas Ltd v. Commisioners of Inland Revenue, the ECJ concluded that CFC legislation should not be applied to the subsidiaries based in the low tax countries if such subsidiaries can prove their real economic activity.
33 ATAD, preamble, section 12, para. 2.
34 OECD (2015), *Designing Effective Controlled Foreign Company Rules – Action 3: Final Report*, OECD/G20 Base Erosion and Profit Shifting Project, (OECD 5 Oct. 2015) (Paris: OECD), p.23, para 35.

yses.[35] According to the OECD, the test of control based on consolidation considers whether the accounts of the subsidiary are consolidated into the financial accounts of the parent company.[36] As such, this test is in line with the abovementioned tests consisting of a legal analysis and de facto analysis. According to the International Financial Reporting Standards (hereinafter: IFRS), the accounts of the subsidiary should be consolidated in case the parent has a substantial influence right due to its share of voting rights in such entity.[37] Taking into account the substantial administrative costs of execution and a subjective effect, the additional control tests mentioned above might not serve as a reliable mechanism for application by the tax authorities. Therefore, the OECD recommends that countries should focus on legal and economic tests and develop specific national tax law provisions to ensure that the rules are applied effectively[38].

2.4. Notion of low taxation

An equally important criterion in defining CFC rules is the provision regarding low tax entities or entities based in low tax jurisdictions. For many years, it was attractive for various businesses to set up structures that included subsidiaries in low tax jurisdictions. Therefore, in order to prevent profit shifting from the parent company based in the high tax country, the OECD advised in its report to implement the threshold of the CIT that the jurisdiction below that will be considered as low-taxed.

Accordingly, Article 7 (1)(b) of the ATAD included a second provision of the CFC rules regarding the tax on profit paid by the foreign entity in the low-tax jurisdiction. As such, if the CIT paid by the foreign entity or a PE is lower than the difference between the CIT payable in the parent company and the CIT paid in the foreign company,[39] the profit of such entity should be taxed at the level of the parent company. To specify, Article 7(1)(b) of the ATAD provides that the entity should be considered as controlled by the EU parent company if:

> ... (b) the actual corporate tax paid on its profits by the entity or permanent establishment is lower than the difference between the corporate tax that would have been charged on the entity or permanent establishment under the applicable corporate tax system in the Member State of the taxpayer and the actual corporate tax paid on its profits by the entity or permanent establishment.

---

35 OECD (2015), *Designing Effective Controlled Foreign Company Rules – Action 3: Final Report*, OECD/G20 Base Erosion and Profit Shifting Project, (OECD 5 Oct. 2015) (Paris: OECD), p.24, para 35.
36 OECD (2015), Designing Effective Controlled Foreign Company Rules – Action 3: Final Report, OECD/G20 Base Erosion and Profit Shifting Project, (OECD 5 Oct. 2015) (Paris: OECD), p.24, para 35.
37 OECD (2015), Designing Effective Controlled Foreign Company Rules – Action 3: Final Report, OECD/G20 Base Erosion and Profit Shifting Project, (OECD 5 Oct. 2015) (Paris: OECD), p.25, para 35.
38 OECD (2015), Designing Effective Controlled Foreign Company Rules – Action 3: Final Report, OECD/G20 Base Erosion and Profit Shifting Project, (OECD 5 Oct. 2015) (Paris: OECD), p.25, para 36.
39 ATAD, Article 7 (1)(b).

One of the important features in defining the CFC threshold concerning the requirement of low taxation is the calculation of the relevant tax rate. In this respect, it would be advisable or more accurate to take into the calculation the effective rate of the tax paid by the entity in the foreign country rather than the statutory tax rate. Although the ATAD does not provide any recommendations on the type of tax rate paid by the CFC, the OECD pointed out in its report that, while the statutory tax rate is less administratively burdensome, the effective tax rate provides a more accurate comparison of the tax paid by the entity in the low-tax jurisdiction.[40]

Considering various propositions of the EU Member States regarding the tax threshold, the European Council considered a tax of less than 50% of the CIT that would have been paid in the relevant Member State as the most appropriate.[41] As a matter of fact, during the negotiations, the EU Member States were considering a wide range of the tax threshold varying between 33% and 75% of the CIT in the parent jurisdiction.[42] Moreover, the European Council points out that the proposed recommendations are the minimum standards, and the EU Member States may apply a higher threshold of the national income tax in order to protect the national market and ensure effective taxation.[43] It points out that the EU Member State *"could... use a sufficiently high tax rate fractional threshold"* if it is relevant to the national tax system.

Furthermore, Article 7 (1,b) stipulates that PEs of the CFC for which profits are exempt from the tax in the jurisdiction of the CFC should not be taken into account for the purposes of the CFC rules at the parent level in the EU Member State.[44] The same refers to the income of the CFC derived through a PE based in the other country and taxed at the high rate. In this case, the tax authorities of the parent company will not provide tax relief to the CFC.[45] As stated above, the ATAD provides that PEs are subject to CFC rules in the case that their profits are not taxed at the level of the parent company. However, if a PE was denied a tax exemption under the national tax law, the CFC rules should not be applied as such PE is already treated as a CFC.[46]

2.5. Observations and Conclusive Remarks on the CFC definition in the ATAD

It is vital to point out that the major aim of the CFC rules within the ATAD was to develop the common rules for all EU Member States to tackle the profit of the EU

---

40 OECD (2015), *Designing Effective Controlled Foreign Company Rules – Action 3: Final Report*, OECD/G20 Base Erosion and Profit Shifting Project, (OECD 5 Oct. 2015) (Paris: OECD), p.37.
41 Caroline Docclo, *Bulletin for International Taxation* (2017), p.375.
42 Caroline Docclo, *Bulletin for International Taxation* (2017), p.375.
43 ATAD, preamble, para.12.
44 ATAD, Article 7 (1)(b).
45 Caroline Docclo, *Bulletin for International Taxation* (2017), p.375.
46 ATAD, preamble, section 12, paragraph 1.

parent company that were diverted to the low-taxed foreign entity. These rules were adopted as a minimum standard and provided a certain degree of flexibility to the EU Member States to adopt them. Consequently, the definitions of the covered entities were developed without a certain degree of clarity but limited to those who are payers of the CIT. This fact, in turn, provided that the European Council, while developing the ATAD, did not include transparent entities in order to not extend the taxes covered beyond the CIT. However, as already mentioned above, not covering transparent entities might potentially give a possibility to avoid profit taxation through the complex structures thereby undermining the aim of the law.

Although, the definition of the control clearly covers legal and economic levels of control over the foreign subsidiary, the control test in the case of indirect ownership may clearly create double taxation. Therefore, it will not only jeopardize the current business structures of the international companies but also increase the administrative burden of taxpayers to eliminate excessive taxation. This can be exemplified if some of the EU Member States would not consider granting a credit of the tax paid in the CFC jurisdiction. Naturally, the EU law should be adopted in a way to prevent any double taxation, nevertheless, the taxpayer may face a risk of being trapped in such period and taxed twice. Furthermore, while defining the actual level of control, EU Member States should design their rules, on the one hand, in accordance with the minimum standard of the ATAD but, on the other hand, to follow EU primary law such as rights guaranteed by the fundamental freedoms. Therefore, some of the EU Member States may trigger the infringement process due to the complications arising from following the ATAD and fundamental freedoms.

Furthermore, in defining the criteria of the low tax rate, the European Council does not provide any details with regards to the type of the applied tax rate: effective or statutory. The OECD, in turn, provides that effective tax rates would rather effectively reflect the tax burden of the foreign entity. Therefore, this matter is left for the consideration of each EU Member State that may provide substantial deviation of the common CFC approach within the EU.

Overall, the European Council had equipped every EU Member State with the basic set of ani-avoidance rules that were agreed on the EU level. Nevertheless, these rules should be read together with the OECD BEPS Final Report in order to clearly understand the specific meaning of the rules designed by the ATAD. Although the ATAD had followed the developments of the OECD, it had left some of the reflect issues open that were mentioned above. In the opinion of the author, the ATAD will need to be amended to provide more clarity in the open issues that will presumably be raised over the course of the application of the CFC rules by the taxpayers and tax authorities.

3. Implementation of the CFC rules in EU Member State
3.1. General remarks and overview

As a result of the long-lasting work presented by the OECD in its Action 3 report and subsequent adoption of the ATAD in 2016, the majority of the EU Member States had successfully implemented the proposed tax-avoidance measures into their national tax law by 1 January 2019. Such measures were developed specifically to protect the internal market, ensure fair taxation, and stop tax avoidance practices within the EU.

The specific approach of the implementation of the CFC rules, and the ATAD in general, within the Member States can be considered through three different groups. The first group is comprised of the Member States that already had CFC rules in line with the ATAD provisions and did not implement the ATAD specifically. These are: Germany, Greece, Portugal, France, and the United Kingdom[47]. The second group includes the states that already had the CFC rules in place and adjusted their rules according to the prerequisites of the ATAD such as: Denmark, Lithuania, Spain, Sweden, Finland, Hungary, Romania, Poland, and Italy. Furthermore, the third group comprises those countries that did not have incorporated CFC rules prior to the ATAD and had implemented the ATAD CFC rules, namely. Austria, Belgium, Bulgaria, Croatia, the Czech Republic, Estonia, Ireland, Latvia, Luxembourg, the Netherlands, Slovenia, the Slovak Republic, Cyprus, and Malta.[48] It is worth mentioning that some of the Member States had implemented their CFC legislation much earlier than the specified deadline, and some are still amending their existing tax law. For example, Romania and Poland implemented their CFC rules by 1 January 2018 whereas, Germany, having already CFC law, is expecting to adopt the new bill with the amendments in 2021.[49]

According to the ATAD, the Member States were allowed to transpose CFC provisions fully into their national legislation or to use them as a minimum standard, implementing the rules that could be broader or stricter. For example, the EU Member States were free to adopt the higher threshold of the tax rate paid in the CFC jurisdiction. While the ATAD provides the threshold of not less than 50% of the tax rate of the parent company, the EU Member State may increase it up to 75%, as was proposed by some during the negotiation process.[50] As a result, the EU Member States were able to adjust the CFC rules considering their own tax systems, ensuring effective taxation in each of them, and assessing the impact on

---

47　Overall, the UK CFC law was in accordance with the ATAD, however, some amendments were implemented before 1 January 2019.
48　Oana Popa, 'An Overview of ATAD Implementation in EU Member States', *European Taxation* (2/3 2019), p.120 (59).
49　Petra Eckl, Felix Schill, 'Reform of the German Controlled Foreign Company Rules', *European Taxation* p. 247 (6, 2020)
50　Caroline Docclo, *Bulletin for International Taxation* (2017), p.375.

the investment climate, providing the needed level of protection of their internal economy.

Furthermore, the implementation of the CFC rules had required from some of the EU Member State to look for the balance between protection against tax avoidance and the country competitiveness for the taxpayers[51]. This can be exemplified by Malta and the Netherlands which had to implement the CFC rules and the ATAD fully into their national legislation.

At the same time, those countries that had already had CFC rules in action before the adoption of that ATAD had gained a chance to amend them in accordance with the ATAD or specify unclear provisions. For example, in Germany, scholars and professional practitioners have, for years, requested from the legislator to specify the definition of the low-taxed income or tax rate used under the CFC rules.[52] Thus, the adoption of the ATAD had finally provided the country with such an opportunity. The draft bill containing amendments to the German CFC rules was published at the end of 2019 in relation to the ATAD.[53]

While adopting CFC rules, the EU Member States had a possibility to choose between two models. "Model A" provides for rules that target foreign entities with passive income and income from transactions with associated parties whereas "Model B" tackles companies engaged in non-genuine transactions. Most of the countries had adopted "Model A" with the combinations of the rules, including those of "Model B".[54]

In essence, the ATAD had been developed as a vital legal vehicle in order to ensure the implementation of the unified rules against aggressive tax planning and tax avoidance within the EU. To highlight, these measures were implemented also by countries that previously positioned themselves as open economies and had substantial tax advantages in comparison to the other EU Member States such as: the Netherlands, Malta, and Cyprus[55]. Therefore, although it had deprived such Member States their tax attractiveness and potential investments, the initially settled goal of protection and fair taxation had been achieved due to the ATAD.

This chapter will analyse more closely the different means of implementation of the various definitions provided in the ATAD in the national legislation of the EU Member States. First, Chapter 3.2 will describe the approach used by the EU

---

51   Isabella de Groot/Barry Larking, 'Implementation of Controlled Foreign Company Rules under the EU Anti-Tax Avoidance Directive (2016/1164)', *European Taxation*, (2019), p.262 (6, 59).
52   Petra Eckl/Felix Schill, *European Taxation* p. 247 (6, 2020).
53   Petra Eckl/Felix Schill, *European Taxation* p. 247 (6, 2020).
54   Richard Krever, 'Chapter 1: Controlled Foreign Company Legislation' in: Michael Lang/Jeffrey Owens/Pasquale Pistone/Alexander Rust/Josef Schuch/Claus Staringer (eds.) *Controlled Foreign Company Legislation*, (Amsterdam: IBFD, 2020), para. 1.1, p.2.
55   Gillen Van Hulle, 'Current Challenges for EU Controlled Foreign Company Rules', *Bulletin for International Taxation* (12, 2017), p.720.

Member States in defining "entities" under the ATAD. Then, Chapter 3.3 will expand on provisions of the control test adopted by the EU Member States. Furthermore, Chapter 3.4 will describe the implementation of the provisions of the low taxation of the foreign entities under the ATAD. Finally, Chapter 3.5 will touch upon several issues related to the implementation of the CFC rules.

3.2. CFC rules and the definition of "entities" implemented by the EU Member States

In many EU Member States, the definition of the CFC rules was adopted by all Member States in accordance with the wording of the ATAD. As such, the CFC rules apply in the case that the taxpayer controls more than 50% of the shares in the foreign entity that generates passive income and is located in the low-taxed jurisdiction or taxed at the substantially lower rate in comparison to the tax rate of the taxpayer. For example, such wording of the ATAD provisions were fully transposed into the national law of the Czech Republic[56], Malta[57] and Croatia[58].

Most of the EU Member States consider a taxpayer to be a resident for the tax purposes in the EU Member State, including PEs of the foreign enterprises deriving the income from the territory of the EU Member State. This applies, for example, in Germany, the Netherlands, Austria, Finland, Luxemburg, Ireland, and others.[59] Additionally, some of those EU Member States extended their definitions of the taxpayers according to their national tax policies. For example, Germany extended the definition of the taxpayer to include not only companies but also individuals and related parties.[60] Ireland considers a taxpayer, for the purposes of the CFC, an Irish resident company, branch, or agency that controls a non-resident foreign company.[61] In Austria, the CFC rules apply – along with broad meaning of entity – also to private foundations.[62] In contrast, Hungary does not include individuals in its CFC rules whereas Slovakia had presented the draft law of CFC rules concerning the individuals but had not adopted the draft at the time of the writing of this paper.[63, 64]

---

56 Dr.Tigran Mkrtchyan, Czech Republic – Corporate Taxation, section 10, subsection 10.4, *Country Tax Guides IBFD*.
57 Conrad Cassar Torregiani, Malta – Corporate Taxation, section 10, subsection 10.4, *Country Tax Guides IBFD*.
58 Paul Suchar/Bojan Đukić/Lada Rajković, Croatia Corporate Taxation, section 10, subsection 10.4, *Country Tax Guides IBFD*.
59 Isabella de Groot/Barry Larking, *European Taxation*, (2019), p.262 -263 (6, 59).
60 Petra Eckl/Felix Schill, *European Taxation* p. 248 (6, 2020).
61 Stephen Ruane, Ireland – Corporate Taxation section 10, subsection 10.4, *Country Tax Guides IBFD*.
62 Yvonne Schuchter/Alexander Kras, Austria – Corporate Taxation section 10, subsection 10.4, *Country Tax Guides IBFD* (accessed 3 Aug. 2020).
63 Richard Krever in: Michael Lang/Jeffrey Owens/Pasquale Pistone/Alexander Rust/Josef Schuch/Claus Staringer (eds.) *Controlled Foreign Company Legislation*, (Amsterdam: IBFD, 2020), Vol.17, para. 1.3, p.4.
64 For more on control concept in: *The role of the "control" concept under CFC rules* by Kristina Reguliova.

With regard to PEs, overall, the countries are taxing PEs of the foreign entity based in the EU Member State or the PE of the taxpayer located in the foreign country based on the principle of the worldwide taxation – unless those PEs that are based in the other country are tax exempt according to bilateral tax treaties. In particular, Hungary had excluded the PEs based in non-EEA[65] countries and protected under its bilateral tax agreements from the CFC rules in order to eliminate the contradiction between the CFC rules and bilateral tax agreements. Similarly, Belgium does not tax PEs of the CFC if they are tax exempt under the provisions of the bilateral tax treaties between the jurisdiction of the CFC and the jurisdiction of the PE.[66] However, it is worth mentioning that Belgium had included transparent entities into the definition of entities covered by the ATAD.[67]

In addition to the CFC entities that satisfy the criteria defined by the ATAD, some countries had developed additional laws to cover roll-up funds[68] which normally do not fall under the definition of the CFC. The major objective is to prevent avoidance of the taxation through funds placed abroad that include a number of shareholders with their shareholdings below the defined threshold thus allowing tax deferral for a certain time period. To mention a few, this law was introduced in Austria, Belgium, Poland, and the United Kingdom.[69] Nevertheless, offshore discretionary funds, which provide the possibility not to allocate the income of the fund to the beneficiary until the decision of the trustee, are left without specific CFC rules.[70]

Finally, the majority of the Member States had extended their CFC rules to the residents of third countries and members of EEA Agreement following the recommendation of the ATAD to implement the control threshold of minimum 50% and the substance escape provision to comply with EU case law. For instance, Ireland excluded companies from its CFC rules that fulfil the test of essential purpose (when the main purpose of its activity is not a tax advantage) and the

---

65 Non-EEA countries – countries, which are not in the European Economic Area, such as Switzerland and the UK.
66 Gilles Van Hulle/ Jean-Philippe Van West, 'Chapter 6: Controlled Foreign Company Legislation in Belgium' in: Michael Lang/Jeffrey Owens/Pasquale Pistone/Alexander Rust/Josef Schuch/Claus Staringer (eds.) *Controlled Foreign Company Legislation*, (Amsterdam: IBFD, 2020), Vol.17, para. 6.1.3, p.2.
67 Gilles Van Hulle/ Jean-Philippe Van West in: Michael Lang/Jeffrey Owens/Pasquale Pistone/Alexander Rust/Josef Schuch/Claus Staringer (eds.) *Controlled Foreign Company Legislation*, (Amsterdam: IBFD, 2020), Vol.17, para. 6.1.1, p.1.
68 Roll-up funds constitute an offshore investment fund with the rolled-up coupons that assign the interest gained in the invested securities back into the fund rather than to be paid in cash. Therefore, it was used to avoid income tax.
69 Richard Krever in: Michael Lang/Jeffrey Owens/Pasquale Pistone/Alexander Rust/Josef Schuch/Claus Staringer (eds.) *Controlled Foreign Company Legislation*, (Amsterdam: IBFD, 2020), Vol.17, para. 1.6, p.5.
70 Richard Krever in: Michael Lang/Jeffrey Owens/Pasquale Pistone/Alexander Rust/Josef Schuch/Claus Staringer (eds.) *Controlled Foreign Company Legislation*, (Amsterdam: IBFD, 2020), Vol.17, para. 1.7, p.5.

test for non-genuine activities (when the company has to prove the availability of assets, risks deployment, and functions provided by relevant staff).[71] Similarly, in Germany, foreign entities are exempt from CFC rules if they are situated in EEA Member States, perform genuine economic activities, and the EU Directive on Mutual Assistance is applicable between the states.[72] Notably, the Netherlands provides a tax exemption to a foreign CFC in the case that it has office space and the employment costs burden is not less than EUR 100 000.[73]

3.3. Provisions of the control test in the EU Member States

The majority of the EU Member States had defined control over a foreign entity in accordance to the provisions of the ATAD. As such, a shareholding of 50% that a taxpayer holds directly or indirectly in a foreign entity enables the application of the CFC rules. Following the provisions by the ATAD, particular EU Member States applied stricter requirements to the control test. For example, Finland and Sweden consider the entity controlled by its taxpayers at the threshold of 25%.[74] Moreover, Ireland had adopted CFC rules based on the existing "close company rules" for which "close company" is a company controlled by five or more participants who can also be directors and hold not only voting rights and a share in the company capital but also have a right to acquire capital and distribute the assets at the time of company liquidation.[75] Therefore, CFC Irish rules are considered to be of a wide coverage of any type of control, including the right of the Irish tax resident to appoint the board of directors of the CFC, which exceeds the minimum ATAD provisions.[76] Furthermore, German corporate legislation additionally includes CFC rules on invested capital. In such a case, the shareholding threshold of 1% that is in the possession of one German resident is enough to apply the CFC rules.[77]

In addition, indirect control of the taxpayer over the foreign entity through the associated parties was defined by some EU Member States[78] at the level of 25% and more of voting rights or capital and profit of the subsidiary which, in turn, holds not less than 25% of CFC. This can be shown by means of an example. An

---

71　Stephen Ruane, Ireland – Corporate Taxation section 10, subsection 10.4, Country Tax Guides IBFD (accessed on 02 August 2020).
72　Andreas Perdelwitz, Germany – Corporate Taxation sec. 10, subsection 10.4, Country Tax Guides IBFD (accessed 2 August 2020).
73　Hendrik-Jan van Duijn & Kim Sinnige, Netherlands – Corporate Taxation sec. 10., subsection 10.4, Country Tax Guides IBFD (accessed 3 August 2020).
74　Isabella de Groot, Barry Larking, *European Taxation*, (2019), p.263.
75　Stephen Ruane, Ireland – Corporate Taxation section 10, subsection 10.5, Country Tax Guides IBFD (accessed on 11.02.2021).
76　Stephen Ruane, Ireland – Corporate Taxation section 10, subsection 10.4, Country Tax Guides IBFD (accessed on 11.02.2021).
77　Petra Eckl/Felix Schill, *European Taxation* p. 248 (6, 2020).
78　Finland, Austria, Luxemburg.

Austrian holding company (AT1) holds 25% of an Austrian company (AT2) which, in turn, owns 50% of the shares in a Hungarian company. According to this approach, it is considered that a Hungarian company is indirectly controlled by AT1 though the economic shareholding of AT1 in a Hungarian company constitutes only 12,5% (25% x 50%). The above example demonstrates that legal ownership of at least 25% of shareholding at each level of ownership is suffice to constitute the indirect control of the holding company over the CFC.

Furthermore, some states implemented the control test differently through the associated parties. For example, Belgium did not include in the law to add the shareholding of the associated party to the shareholding of the taxpayer in the calculation of the level of control.[79] In other words, the Belgian CFC rules apply if there is at least a 50% shareholding of the capital or profit held by the Belgian parent, directly or indirectly, in the CFC. Moreover, the Netherlands and Luxemburg consider the interest held by the taxpayer in the CFC based on the shareholding of the associated party. As such, in the case that an associated company of the Dutch taxpayer has 70% of the shares in the foreign company but the Dutch taxpayer holds only 40% in an associated company, the actual interest of the Dutch taxpayer in the CFC will be considered as 70%. In other words, the *de facto* analysis is not relevant in the Netherlands.[80]

Equally important, the majority of the EU Member States considered control over the foreign company not only as a percentage of the shares but also as a type of shareholding and included the following types of participations in their law: shares, shares with voting rights, participations in the capital, or rights in dividends[81]. The major goal was to eliminate manipulation within the terminology of the corporate law of different countries and, as a consequence, to prevent the avoidance of the control test.[82]

Similarly, most of the countries have gone further and added a *de facto* analysis to test the control over the foreign entities. As such, Denmark provides that it is not necessarily needed to have more than 50% of shares but to exercise "deciding influence". Though, should the Danish parent company hold more than 50% shareholding in the foreign entity but prove that it does not exercise deciding influence, the CFC rules will not be applied.[83] By contrast, Poland defines de facto con-

---

79   Isabella de Groot, Barry Larking, *European Taxation*, (2019), p.263.
80   Isabella de Groot, Barry Larking, *European Taxation*, (2019), p.264.
81   Richard Krever in: Michael Lang/Jeffrey Owens/Pasquale Pistone/Alexander Rust/Josef Schuch/ Claus Staringer (eds.) *Controlled Foreign Company Legislation*, (Amsterdam: IBFD, 2020), Vol.17, para. 1.2, p.3.
82   OECD (2015), *Designing Effective Controlled Foreign Company Rules – Action 3: Final Report*, OECD/ G20 Base Erosion and Profit Shifting Project, (OECD 5 Oct. 2015) (Paris: OECD), p.24, para 35.
83   Peter Koerver Schmidt, 'Chapter 14: Controlled Foreign Company Legislation in Denmark' in: Michael Lang/Jeffrey Owens/Pasquale Pistone/Alexander Rust/Josef Schuch/Claus Staringer (eds.) *Controlled Foreign Company Legislation*, (Amsterdam: IBFD, 2020), Vol.17, para. 14.1 p.2.

trol in the case of *"legal, economic and factual control"*.[84] To point out, Belgium had introduced the test of control based on the place of the decision making related to the CFC. As a result, the Belgian CFC legislation applies not only in cases of non-genuine transactions but also in cases when CFC may have assets, offices, and employees if all of the decision-making processes are actually in the hands of the Belgian parent.[85]

Moreover, to reduce the administrative burden of control in instances of many shareholders but with relatively small proportions of shares, some EU Member States apply the control test to the fewer number of the shareholders, such as five or less, which will, in total, constitute a level of control of 50% and more in the foreign entity.[86]

Finally, the period during which the taxpayer holds a share is not defined in the ATAD and should therefore be established by the national law of each Member State. Therefore, such criterion varies from country to country. In Germany, for example, such a period is defined as a fiscal year of the company.[87] By contrast, Ireland had implemented that the control test should be done throughout the existence of the CFC, reflecting the changes in the ownership.[88] As such, in the case that the owner of the interest in the CFC changes within a year, it should be reflected in the financial records of Irish taxpayer accordingly. Nevertheless, mostly all Member States define CFC control based on the data of share or interest holders at the end of the fiscal year of the CFC.[89]

3.4. Implementation of the definition of the "low taxation"

Overall, the EU Member States were following the ATAD provisions while adopting their "low taxation" criteria. In particular, they had adopted a comparable taxation approach together with the assessment of the CFC transactions and activity. As a rule, the taxation rules comparable with those of the EU Member States are perceived to be relatively safe in terms of tax avoidance for the EU Member States and provide none or very low possibility for the tax deferral. As provided in the

---

[84] Richard Krever in: Michael Lang/Jeffrey Owens/Pasquale Pistone/Alexander Rust/Josef Schuch/Claus Staringer (eds.) *Controlled Foreign Company Legislation*, (Amsterdam: IBFD, 2020), Vol.17, para. 1.2, p.3.
[85] Gilles Van Hulle/ Jean-Philippe Van West, 'Chapter 6: Controlled Foreign Company Legislation in Belgium' in: Michael Lang/Jeffrey Owens/Pasquale Pistone/Alexander Rust/Josef Schuch/Claus Staringer (eds.) *Controlled Foreign Company Legislation*, (Amsterdam: IBFD, 2020), Vol.17, para. 6.1.4, p.2.
[86] Stephen Ruane, Ireland – Corporate Taxation section 10, subsection 10.5, Country Tax Guides IBFD (accessed on 11.02.2021).
[87] Andreas Perdelwitz, Germany – Corporate Taxation section 10, subsection 10.4, *Country Tax Guides IBFD* accessed on 03 August 2020).
[88] Isabella de Groot, Barry Larking, *European Taxation*, (2019), p.264.
[89] Petra Eckl, Felix Schill, *European Taxation* p. 248 (6, 2020).

ATAD, the EU Member States had full authority to establish their rates of "low taxation" whereas some had implemented a list of the countries towards which the CFC rules applied automatically.

According to the ATAD, CFC rules are applied in the case that the profit tax executed in the CFC jurisdiction is lower than the difference between the CIT charged in the country of the parent and the actual CIT paid by the entity in the foreign country. At the same time, the ATAD provides a minimum standard for the rules, therefore, the countries were allowed to define their own "low tax" definitions. Some Member States entirely transposed the wording of the ATAD with regards to this matter into their CFC rules. For example, this approach was followed by the Czech Republic and Malta. In contrast, others had defined specific tax rates such as, in Austria, the tax rate is set to the effective 12,5% rate; in Sweden, it equals 55% of the local CIT rate; in Finland, it comprised 3/5 of the domestic CIT; and the Netherlands considers the entity as a CFC if the statutory rate is equal to 9%.[90] At the same time, in Germany, the low tax rate is set at 25% and based on the effective tax rate. In the case that the tax rate in a CFC jurisdiction is higher than 25% but then the entity was provided with the tax relief that minimizes the tax rate, Germany will treat the entity based on the effective rate.[91] Furthermore, some EU Member States had addressed the income of the CFCs that is not taxed until the distribution, such as in Estonia. In these cases, Austria, for example, compares the Austrian CIT rate and the nominal CIT rate of the foreign state.[92, 93]

Considering the fact that the ATAD does not provide the instructions to which extent the profit of the CFC should be attributed to the parent company, this rule differs in various EU Member States. For instance, Ireland defines that CFC rules are applied to any undistributed profits for the accounting period less any relevant distributions such as dividends to EEA or EU residents subject to income tax.[94] The Dutch CFC rules apply to all passive income of the foreign entity less any related costs during the accounting period, provided there were no interim distributions to the parent or intermediary company.[95] In Austria, the CFC rules

---

90 Isabella de Groot, Barry Larking, *European Taxation*, (2019), p.264.
91 Petra Eckl, Felix Schill, *European Taxation* p. 254 (6, 2020).
92 Martin Klokar/Mario Riedl 'Chapter 5: Controlled Foreign Company Legislation in Austria' in: Michael Lang/Jeffrey Owens/Pasquale Pistone/Alexander Rust/Josef Schuch/Claus Staringer (eds.) *Controlled Foreign Company Legislation*, (Amsterdam: IBFD, 2020), Vol.17, para. 5.2.3, p.4.
93 However, in the case of Estonia, the so called, 'distribution tax' 20% (or 14%) would not trigger CFC rules in Austria, as such rate is higher than 12,5%.
94 Stephen Ruane, Ireland – Corporate Taxation section 10, subsection 10.4, *Country Tax Guides IBFD* (accessed on 03 August 2020)
95 Hendrik-Jan van Duijn, Kim Sinnige, Netherlands – Corporate Taxation sec. 10, subsection 10.4, *Country Tax Guides IBFD* (accessed 3 August 2020).

state that, in the case that the passive income of the foreign entity comprises more than one third of the total income, it is added to the taxable base of the parent company but to the extent of the shareholding of the latter.[96]

Furthermore, the Member States had to set their own rules related to the calculation of the tax base of the CFCs. According to the recommendations of Article 7 (1) of the ATAD, the computation of the CIT of the foreign entity should be calculated according to the accounting rules of the parent company. As a result, the tax base of the CFC should be recalculated in accordance with the accounting rules of the taxpayer. Nevertheless, Austria had addressed the situations of the difference in the assessment of the CFC profits (for example, due to differences in depreciation rules or the attribution of losses from previous years) which may lead to a lower than 12,5% effective tax rate. In such cases, Austrian CFC rules will not be applied to the foreign entity.[97]

Following the recommendation of the ATAD, some Member States implemented black lists with the countries that are automatically considered a CFC under national tax law. For instance, Poland has its own list of countries engaged in "harmful tax competition" such as, for example, Andorra, the British Virgin Islands, Hong Kong, the Marshall Islands, Monaco, the Netherlands, etc.[98] Similarly, the Netherlands had defined a list of non-cooperative countries where: 1) the statutory income tax is less than 9% and 2) these countries are in the EU list of non-cooperative countries, among them, e.g. Belize, British Virgin Islands, Guernsey, Isle of Man, Jersey, etc.[99]

Finally, most of the EU Member States had adopted the provisions of the ATAD with regards to the deduction of the foreign CIT paid in the CFC jurisdiction[100]. Nevertheless, the foreign tax deduction will be granted only to the extent of the actual tax burden of the CFC entity. For example, Germany provides a tax credit limited to the amount of tax paid less any refunds provided either to the CFC itself or to the intermediary company that has a share in such entity.[101]

---

96 Yvonne Schuchter, Alexander Kras, Austria – Corporate Taxation section 10, subsection 10.4, *Country Tax Guides IBFD* (accessed 3 August 2020).
97 Martin Klokar/Mario Riedl in: Michael Lang/Jeffrey Owens/Pasquale Pistone/Alexander Rust/Josef Schuch/Claus Staringer (eds.) *Controlled Foreign Company Legislation*, (Amsterdam: IBFD, 2020), Vol.17, para. 5.2.3, p.4.
98 Magdalena Olejnicka, Poland – Corporate Taxation sec. 10, subsection 10.4, *Country Tax Guides IBFD* (accessed 3 August 2020).
99 Hendrik-Jan van Duijn & Kim Sinnige, Netherlands – Corporate Taxation sec. 10., subsection 10.4, Country Tax Guides IBFD (accessed 3 August 2020).
100 ATAD, Article 8 (7).
101 Andreas Perdelwitz, Germany – Corporate Taxation section 10, subsection 10.4, *Country Tax Guides IBFD* accessed on 03 August 2020).

3.5. Analysis of several issues and challenges related to the implementation of the CFC definitions

According to research, the major challenge of the ATAD implementation process was to harmonize disparate tax regimes and ensure common tax avoidance practices among the EU Member States. Although every state had transposed CFC rules into their national legislation based on the ATAD provisions, the law was adopted with deviations depending on the peculiarities of each state's tax policy; some of them will be considered below.

As stated previously, the ATAD allowed the Member States some flexibility in implementing their own rules according to their tax policies but following the provisions of the ATAD as a minimum standard, ensuring that the national tax law will be in line with the directive. Although all Member States had implemented, and some amended, their CFC rules according to the provisions of the directive, the differences in the interpretation or peculiarities of the national tax system draw a number of challenges faced by the states.

To begin with, there is no uniformity in the definition of the covered entities transposed by the EU Member States into their national tax law. Therefore, some EU Member States included only legal entities subject to the CIT such as Malta, the Czech Republic, the Netherlands. Whereas, the others, such as Belgium, covered not only CIT tax payers but also transparent entities. Some of the EU Member States went further and included roll-up funds in their CFC rules, among them: Austria, Poland, and the United Kingdom. However, majority of the EU Member States still did not address the discretionary funds in their law.[102] The EU Member States justify their position regarding the matter by other existing anti-avoidance rules. Nevertheless, the discretionary funds provide tax deferral for the income of the funds until its attribution to the beneficiary or tax avoidance in the case of the investment loss.[103] This still leaves the legal opportunity to avoid taxation.

Furthermore, Germany has its CFC rules applied not only to the legal entities but also to individuals.[104] This example was planned to be followed by the Slovak Republic, but the new law is still not adopted. Therefore, as can be seen, various interpretation of the entities increase difficulty in harmonization of the rules within the internal market for all participants, not only to taxpayers but also to tax authorities. Moreover, leaving the some of the legal entities not covered still provides the possibility of gaps in tax laws of some countries.

---

102 Richard Krever in: Michael Lang/Jeffrey Owens/Pasquale Pistone/Alexander Rust/Josef Schuch/Claus Staringer (eds.) *Controlled Foreign Company Legislation*, (Amsterdam: IBFD, 2020), Vol.17, para. 1.6, p.5.
103 Richard Krever in: Michael Lang/Jeffrey Owens/Pasquale Pistone/Alexander Rust/Josef Schuch/Claus Staringer (eds.) *Controlled Foreign Company Legislation*, (Amsterdam: IBFD, 2020), Vol.17, para. 1.7, p.5.
104 Petra Eckl/Felix Schill, *European Taxation* p. 248 (6, 2020).

With regards to the definition of control, the rules within the EU also deviate substantially. Despite the fact that almost all of the EU Member States implemented the rules based on the 50% threshold of shareholding in the foreign entity, Sweden and Finland consider the control already at 25% of the shareholding. Moreover, some EU Member States had supplemented them with criterion of the de facto test which will be a decisive factor of the test. For example, in Denmark, the law states that, in the case that the taxpayer exercises "deciding influence", the CFC rules should be applied. On the contrary, if the Danish taxpayer holds more than 50% of the shares but does not exercise such influence, there will be an escape from the CFC rules.[105] This approach may trigger the ineffectiveness of the CFC rules. What is more, the broad definitions of control via various expressions, such as "deciding influence" or "legal, economic or factual" control, bring the risk of subjective evaluation from the side of the taxpayer and the tax administration. Inevitably, they cause substantial administrative burden and are time consuming and costly for both parties.

Furthermore, one of the challenges related to the rules of the control faced by countries that already had their CFC law in force is that such laws may contradict with the ATAD's main objective to protect the internal market from tax avoidance. For example, additional CFC rules on income from the invested capital in Germany where a shareholding of 1% for one German resident is sufficient to apply the CFC rules is not required by the ATAD. Many scholars and practitioners in Germany claim that having such rules violates the ATAD or can be impractical and, therefore, need to be replaced only with the ATAD. They claim that, since the ATAD does not provide special treatment of the passive income from invested capital, in order to continue such a special regime, it should be justified by the legislator from the perspective of protection of the internal market.[106]

Furthermore, an analysis of the implementation of the "low taxation" criteria reveals that not only some of the EU Member States approached the law according to their national interest but also that some of them had faced unaddressed legal issues. While defining the rate that indicates low taxation, the ATAD minimum standard of protection does not take into consideration the EU Member States with federal and municipal taxation of income. To demonstrate, the newly developed draft bill in Germany provides that not only federal income tax should be accounted for the purpose of calculating the tax paid by a CFC but also municipal trade tax. The reason behind is that the federal income tax rate in Germany is 15% and, increased by the solidarity surcharge of 5,5%, it constitutes approximately 15,82%. Following the formula provided by the ATAD, the threshold of low taxa-

---

105 Richard Krever in: Michael Lang/Jeffrey Owens/Pasquale Pistone/Alexander Rust/Josef Schuch/Claus Staringer (eds.) *Controlled Foreign Company Legislation*, (Amsterdam: IBFD, 2020), Vol.17, para. 1.2, p.3.
106 Petra Eckl, Felix Schill, *European Taxation* p. 250 (6, 2020).

tion should be around 7,9% which would address only offshore jurisdictions, leaving the EU countries with no attention, thus enabling the gap in German tax law. Nevertheless, should the German legislator adopt the new bill, it may contradict the provisions of the ATAD in which it states that only CIT at the country level should be taken into account which equates to 15,82%. Considering the above, the directive lacks specific clarifications for the EU Member States that have the two-tier system of income taxation that is executed by different levels of governance.[107]

In addition to the above, the municipal trade tax, which is applied to corporate income in Germany, does not apply to the foreign entities in case such entities do not have their PEs in the country. Therefore, such entities are subject to limited tax liability and always treated as CFCs as their corporate tax equates to 15,82%, which is substantially lower than the established 25%. Therefore, under the German CFC rules, in this case, even entities from countries commonly perceived as reliable, such as France, deem to be a CFCs.[108]

As mentioned previously, some Member States did not set the specific tax rate that is considered to be the threshold for low taxation. Instead, they implemented the provisions of the ATAD approach for which the calculation of the CFC tax is done according to the accounting standards of the parent company. Some scholars claim, though, that this approach would cause substantial compliance costs, uncertainty, and potential disputes for the taxpayer. Therefore, the provision of the CFC tax rate or specific rules to avoid uncertainty, such as countries in the black list,[109] would enable the taxpayers to eliminate unnecessary costs and amend or develop business structures to be compliant with the new tax rules.

Moreover, according to the directive, the CFC tax should be computed according to the rules of a Member State. As had been described previously, the EU Member States provide exemptions for CFC income based on the substance escape provision. However, due to the lack of uniformity in the implementation and the approach, at the point of computation of the taxable base of parent company, the EU Member States implement computation rules differently which may cause some issues. To demonstrate, in the Netherlands, exempted CFC income is not included in the taxable base of the Dutch parent whereas, in Austria, exempted income is included in the taxable base of the Austrian taxpayer.[110] Both instances provide protection of the internal market but may lead to the more favourable tax treatment of one EU Member State in comparison to the other.

---

107 Petra Eckl, Felix Schill, *European Taxation* p. 254 (6, 2020).
108 Petra Eckl, Felix Schill, *European Taxation* p. 253 (6, 2020).
109 Gilles Van Hulle/ Jean-Philippe Van West, 'Chapter 6: Controlled Foreign Company Legislation in Belgium' in: Michael Lang/Jeffrey Owens/Pasquale Pistone/Alexander Rust/Josef Schuch/Claus Staringer (eds.) *Controlled Foreign Company Legislation*, (Amsterdam: IBFD, 2020), Vol.17, para. 6.1.3, p.2.
110 Isabella de Groot, Barry Larking, *European Taxation*, (6, 2019), p.270.

On the positive side, the European Council clearly understood peculiarities of the political constraints of the EU Member States and provided a few options of how to implement CFC rules. In fact, the directive's provisions provided a two-option approach for identifying CFCs. The first approach targets CFCs with undistributed passive income according to Article 7(2)(b) with exemptions covered by the substance escape clause. The other exemption, introduced due to the EU Member States' negotiations, provides that in the case that passive income is less than one third of overall income of the CFC, such entity cannot be treated as a CFC. The second option relates to the CFCs engaged in the non-genuine arrangements with a major aim of "obtaining a tax advantage".[111] Non-genuine arrangements were defined not only as the lack of assets and control over the risks but also lack of "significant people functions"[112] needed to generate the income.

As a result of the non-genuine arrangements' definition, the ATAD defines the control over the foreign entity based on where the significant management decisions had been executed, so-called place of effective management (hereinafter: POEM) which solves the problem of dual residency of the parent company. As such, in the case that two Member States would treat the same entity as their resident, which will inevitably lead to the taxation and CFC rules obligations in both countries, the ATAD provides that the residency of a state is defined by the POEM.[113] To point out, until now, there is no available public information with regards to the practical resolution of any disputes related to the dual residence issue due to the ATAD provisions.

Additional issues arising over the course of the ATAD implementation related to double taxation may arise at the level of the intermediary company and the parent. Such is the case of an intermediary company that is based in one EU Member State and a parent based in the other EU Member State, and they hold a share in the CFC. They both will be subject to the CFC rules in their respective states, causing the matter of double taxation. In this respect, the ATAD does not provide recommendations regarding the tax credit of the tax paid by the intermediary company at the level of parent company but only generally refers to the tax credit paid by the foreign entity in its residence state.[114] As a result, double taxation may arise on the basis of the missing provisions in the directive concerning the credit of the tax paid by the intermediary company.[115]

Likewise, the matter of double taxation arises even due to the misinterpretation of the directive's provisions by some Member States and the implementation of the rules with their own perception. To demonstrate, the ATAD provides relief from

---

111 ATAD, Article 7 (1)(b).
112 ATAD, Article 7 (1)(b).
113 Gillen Van Hulle, *Bulletin for International Taxation* (12, 2017), p.721.
114 ATAD, Article 8 (7).
115 Gillen Van Hulle, *Bulletin for International Taxation* (12, 2017), p.721.

double taxation for the tax paid by the CFC. Nevertheless, Belgium, for example, did not implement such a provision in its CFC rules, stipulating that such a legislator's position is established to discourage Belgian taxpayers from using CFCs.[116] However, Malta and the Czech Republic implemented all provisions related to the matter. Nevertheless, the EU Commission letter of formal notice already addressed the case of Belgian CFC rules to bring its rules in accordance with the directive provisions and eliminate the double taxation of the tax paid by the CFC.[117]

Definitely, the latest research demonstrates that, although CFC legislation contributed substantially to the tax avoidance and fair taxation among the Member States, some of them were opposed to implementing it due to their positioning as tax friendly countries,[118] as can be seen in the Netherlands, Malta, and Cyprus, to name a few. The others, though, had implemented CFC regime, lacking expertise and training among the tax officers of how to handle the CFC rules and evaluate control over the rules.[119] Consequently, these possible drawbacks may trigger the ineffectiveness of the CFC rules within the EU. Therefore, in order to prevent any negative outcomes, the implementation process should be additionally addressed in order to ensure positive results for all Member States.

4. Conclusions

While CFC rules have been implemented by the EU Member States for more than two years, the countries' reports demonstrate that a substantial number of challenges still need to be overcome. Some of them were caused by the possibility of the EU Member States to implement their own rules though following the minimum requirements of the ATAD whereas others were caused due to the misinterpretation issues.

As a matter of fact, although the introduction of the CFC rules have been discussed for years, there are still some unaddressed issues in the field of entity definitions that will be in place until their resolution. For example, transparent entities were included in the CFC rules of Belgium but not in the majority of the EU Member States. Moreover, Germany had individuals covered by their CFC rules whereas the other countries followed the provisions of the ATAD and covered only legal entities. To point out, the fact that discretionary funds are not included

---

116 Isabella de Groot, Barry Larking, *European Taxation*, (6, 2019), p.271.
117 European Commission, 'July Infringement Package: key decisions', published on 2 July 2020 (Brussels) https://ec.europa.eu/commission/presscorner/detail/en/inf_20_1212 (accessed on 20 February 2021).
118 Richard Krever in: Michael Lang/Jeffrey Owens/Pasquale Pistone/Alexander Rust/Josef Schuch/Claus Staringer (eds.) *Controlled Foreign Company Legislation*, (Amsterdam: IBFD, 2020), Vol.17, para. 1.9, p.6.
119 Richard Krever in: Michael Lang/Jeffrey Owens/Pasquale Pistone/Alexander Rust/Josef Schuch/Claus Staringer (eds.) *Controlled Foreign Company Legislation*, (Amsterdam: IBFD, 2020), Vol.17, para. 1.9, p.6.

in the current CFC provisions but that the roll-up funds are addressed by some Member States proves the nonconformity within the EU.

Furthermore, enabling the EU Member States to implement their own CFC rules more broadly brought to light vaguely defined definitions of control like "deciding influence" as in Denmark, for example. Therefore, this affords the opportunity to not only the risk of subjective evaluation but also to possible substantial administrative burden and costs for the taxpayer. Subsequently, it would be more effective to eliminate broad definitions in the future and instead provide clear definitions for various situations that the particular country wants to address.

As a matter of fact, while developing the ATAD, the European Council focussed on the minimum standards and provided Member States with the flexibility to implement the CFC rules into their national legislation. Nevertheless, the lack of clear instructions caused misinterpretations and, sometimes, no implementation of the ATAD provisions to the EU Member States. The example of Belgian legislator not transposing the relief from double taxation of the tax paid by the CFC demonstrates that the Member State either should additionally clarify the provisions, or it may face the potential infringement procedure initiated by the commission. Nevertheless, uncertainty and changes in the law may cause substantial costs for the taxpayers when adjusting their business structures according to the new law amendments.

To emphasize, for those countries that already had CFC rules before the ATAD implementation, the need to adjust the existing CFC rules with the ATAD provisions is vital. The legislator of countries, such as Germany, should consider the primary goal of the ATAD and existing rules to eliminate any contradictions or unnecessary provisions, considering the provisions of ATAD to ease the burden for tax administrations and taxpayers.

Furthermore, in order to harmonize the different taxation systems of the EU Member States, it is important to address pivotal issues at the level of the European Commission. As demonstrated by the example of Germany, leaving the issues of federal and municipal taxes as well as shareholding of 1% into investment capital to the consideration of the state causes high disputes and uncertainty among scholars and practitioners, on the one side, and legislators on the other.[120] Similarly, additional clarification should be provided by the European Council in order to address the issue of implementation of the computation rules with regards to the exempted CFC income in order to eliminate different implementation practices by the EU Member States.

Consequently, the deviations in the CFC rules of the various EU Member States demonstrate that, although all EU Member States have their CFC rules now in

---

120 Petra Eckl, Felix Schill, *European Taxation* p. 254 (6, 2020).

force, the application still lacks conformity and unification. In the author's opinion, such issues need to be addressed at the level of the EU and should not be left at the consideration of each EU Member State. Nevertheless, notwithstanding the differences of the implementation processes and challenges faced by the EU Member States, the CFC rules and other provisions of the ATAD enabled 27 different countries to implement the common framework against tax avoidance practices. Therefore, CFC rules implemented through the ATAD are a valuable instrument of internal EU market protection. Surely, to overcome all of the challenges described in this chapter, and there are probably more to come in the near future, the joint assistance and cooperation between the Member States will be vital in order to ensure the success of the implementation and functioning of the EU common legal provisions.

Taxable income under option 7(2)(a) of the Anti-Tax Avoidance Directive

Carmela M. Zenzola

1. **Introduction**
   1.1. Topic
   1.2. Specific purpose and scope
   1.3. Approach and research method
   1.4. Outline of the thesis
2. **CFC taxable income under ATAD**
   2.1. The definition of taxable income
   2.2. Taxable income and CFC rationale
      2.2.1. Anti-deferral rationale
      2.2.2. Anti-abuse rationale
      2.2.3. Anti-tax avoidance rationale
3. **The boundaries to the concept of income**
   3.1. Two flexible options
   3.2. The background to the categorical approach
   3.3. Pros and cons of the categorical approach
4. **The categorical approach: a legal classification**
   4.1. Article 8(2)(a) in the "presidency compromise"
   4.2. Article 7(2)(a): the final version
   4.3. Dividends
   4.4. Income from the disposal of shares
   4.5. Interest or any other income generated by financial assets
   4.6. Income from insurance, banking, and other financial activities
   4.7. Income from financial leasing
   4.8. Royalties or any other income generated from an intellectual property
   4.9. Income from invoicing companies that earn sales and services income from goods and services purchased from "and" sold to associated enterprises "and" add no or little economic value
   4.10. Deductions and treatment of losses
   4.11. Conclusions
5. **The EU Primary Law and the "substance carve-out" rule**
   5.1. Pursuing compliance with the fundamental freedoms
   5.2. Third Countries
   5.3. The Burden of proof
6. **Final considerations**

1. Introduction

1.1. Topic

The objective of this thesis is to define the concept of taxable income for the purposes of the CFC regime. The ATAD Directive devises, among others, a specific methodology aiming to identify the taxable income of a CFC (entity or PE). This methodology is based on the classification of predefined types of income and is therefore called the "categorical approach". The purpose of the thesis is also to explore whether the specific classification of income contemplated by the categorical approach is consistent with the aims of the directive. Each individual class of income may, in fact, be defined and taxed differently in each Member State, thus giving rise to tax planning phenomena. Consequently, the classification of CFC taxable income is a very critical issue for taxpayers, tax authorities, and tax advisors.

1.2. Specific purpose and scope

This thesis attempts to provide an answer to the following research questions:

(i) What is the purpose of Article 7(2)(a)?
(ii) Is the categorical approach efficient to reach ATAD goals?
(iii) Is it coherent with the effect of reattributing the income of a low-taxed CFC to its parent company that becomes taxable in the state where it is resident for tax purposes?
(iv) Is the list of income items exhaustive, or are there items that could be included or excluded?
(v) Could there be other approaches coherent with the ATAD?
The answers to the above questions appear complex despite the fact that the categorical approach may seem relatively simple. However, the effectiveness of the categorical approach depends on how this methodology has been implemented by domestic laws in compliance with the main principles of the European law.

1.3. Approach and research method

The approach of this thesis is primarily that of a legal study. However, being a master thesis, it also has a practical and operational slant. It also aims to assess how the categorical approach has been implemented in some significant Member States, such as Germany, Spain, Austria, Denmark, Finland, and the Netherlands. In addition, it intends to analyze the categorical approach in light of the tax policy goals of these selected Member States. These countries have provided particularly significant examples of the implementation of the categorical approach. Anyway, this thesis does not adopt a pure comparative method, and reference to the above-mentioned countries is made as practical exemplifications. A substantial part of this thesis is based upon literature research.

1.4. Outline of the thesis

The following chapters try to address the issues above. Chapter 1 will set out the theoretical rationale for the introduction of a specific taxation aimed at affecting the income of CFCs. Chapter 2 will analyze the legal genesis and the international background of the categorical approach. Chapter 3 delves into the income classification of the categorical approach and focuses on each single class of income. Chapter 4 will explore the relationship with the primary law of the European Union and its implications.

2. CFC taxable income under ATAD
2.1. The definition of taxable income

According to Preamble number 12 of the ATAD[1], the main objective of the CFC regime consists in *"re-attributing the income of a low-taxed controlled subsidiary to its parent company"*. In order to efficiently achieve this aim, it is essential to define what is meant by "income" for CFC purposes, how to delimit this concept so as not to be so broad as to entail a risk of double taxation that undermines economic competition, and whether there are possible justifications for such constraints.

The ATAD definition of taxable income for CFC purposes stands as an attempt to combine BEPS recommendations on one hand, the legacy of the ECJ settled case law and the EU primary legislation on the other hand. In addition, political priorities of the Member States also play an important role. In order to meet various requirements, the ATAD provides for three different methodologies to address the definition of income[2]. As briefly represented in Preamble number 12 of the directive, CFC rules may target:

1. an "entire" low-taxed entity's – or permanent establishment's – income (entity approach);
2. "specific" categories of passive income (categorical approach);
3. income that has "artificially" been diverted to the entity (or to the permanent establishment).

---

[1] Council Directive (EU) 2016/1164 of 12 July *2016 laying down rules against tax avoidance practices that directly affect the functioning of the internal market,* OJ L 193 (19 July 2016) also known as the ATAD Directive, Preamble n. 12.

[2] From a general point of view, the concept of income does not exist in itself as an economic concept. In theory, it is to be determined as a fiction through the application of legal assumptions that ideally try to build the taxable base as close as possible to economic operations and business transactions. D. W. Blum, Controlled Foreign Companies: Selected Policy Issues – or the Missing Elements of BEPS Action 3 and the Anti-Tax Avoidance Directive, *Intertax,* (2018), vol. 46, issue 4, p. 298, par. 3. J. Prebble, Ectopia, the Root Cause of the Ineliminable Fictions of Income Tax Law, (2006), Working Paper presented to a conference of the Western Regional Council of the Institute of Chartered Accountants of India, Mumbai, 30 November 2006.

These are not alternative methodologies as one or more of them may coexist. Thus, Member States can implement a variety of CFC structures according to the rationale at which they aim.

2.2. Taxable income and CFC rationale

The three methodologies that the ATAD uses to determine income as stated in Preamble number 12 underlie the three rationales of the CFC regime as highlighted by the relevant doctrine on ATAD[3].

2.2.1. Anti-deferral rationale

The option of including the entire low-taxed entity's (or PE's) income in the taxpayer's tax base is consistent with the anti-deferral rationale. The system of full inclusion of CFC income (also called the entity approach) has been adopted in those countries where the anti-deferral motive is prioritized[4]. As an anti-deferral measure, a CFC regime favours capital export neutrality (CEN) by placing foreign investments on the same level of taxation as those existing in the parent company's jurisdiction. However, capital import neutrality (CIN) which considers the tax treatment of investments from the point of view of the controlled entity's jurisdiction may be undermined since CFC income could be taxed in both jurisdictions.

The "entity approach" (full income inclusion) was adopted to determine CFC income under the first proposal of Article 8 ATAD.

The tax base of a taxpayer shall include the non-distributed income of an entity when the following **conditions** are met:[5]

(a) the taxpayer by itself or together with its associated enterprises as defined under the applicable corporate tax system holds a direct or indirect participation of more than 50 percent of the voting rights, owns more than 50 percent of capital, or is entitled to receive more than 50 percent of the profits of that entity;
(b) under the general regime in the country of the entity, profits are subject to an effective corporate tax rate lower than 40 percent of the effective tax rate that would have been charged under the applicable corporate tax system in the Member State of the taxpayer;

---

3   D. W. Blum, Controlled Foreign Companies: Selected Policy Issues – or the Missing Elements of BEPS Action 3 and the Anti- Tax Avoidance Directive, *Intertax*, (2018), vol. 46, issue 4. B. J. Arnold, The Evolution of Controlled Foreign Corporation Rules and Beyond, *Bulletin for International Taxation* (2019).
4   Among those countries, Finland, Estonia, Italy, France, Bulgaria, the United Kingdom (except for capital gains). See also, R. Fontana, The Uncertain Future of CFC Regimes in the Member States of the European Union – Part 1, *IBFD Bulletin*, June 2006. R. Russo, *Fundamentals of International Tax Planning* (Amsterdam: IBFD, 2003) pag. 65.
5   European Commission, Proposal for a Council Directive laying down rules against tax avoidance practices that directly affect the functioning of the internal market, Brussels, 28.1.2016, COM(2016) 26 final, 2016/0011 (CNS), art. 8.

(c) more than 50 percent of the income accruing to the entity falls within any of the following categories:
   (i) interest or any other income generated by financial assets;
   (ii) royalties or any other income generated from intellectual property or tradable permits;
   (iii) dividends and income from the disposal of shares;
   (iv) income from financial leasing;
   (v) income from immovable property, unless the Member State of the taxpayer would not have been entitled to tax the income under an agreement concluded with a third country;
   (vi) income from insurance, banking and other financial activities;
   (vii) income from services rendered to the taxpayer or its associated enterprises;

The rule provided for a subjective requisite and an objective requisite that triggered the CFC regime[6]. The approach based on specific income categories represented the third step of the objective requisite. So, if those requisites were met, the entity approach applied, and the entire non-distributed income of the entity (or PE) was subject to taxation in the hands of the controlling company. According to this approach, also called "piercing the corporate veil"[7], the taxpayer and the subsidiary are deemed to be one sole entity from a tax point of view, and the income earned by the CFC is taxed directly in the hands of the shareholders. However, this structure was not considered efficient to pursue the objectives foreseen in ATAD Preamble number 12 and was subsequently set aside.

2.2.2. Anti-abuse rationale

From a CIN perspective, in order to not undermine the tax competitiveness of investments abroad, in some cases, tax jurisdictions of parent companies may permit tax deferral. Many countries have reached a compromise solution between pursuing CEN without undermining tax competition on investments abroad (CIN protection)[8]. In this perspective, CFC rules as anti-deferral rules are adopted as long as they are limited to specific categories of passive income[9] while active income is taxed by the parent jurisdiction only in the case of distribution. Hence, tax deferral is allowed only for active income so as to not impair the CIN in the foreign countries of which the subsidiaries are resident, and passive income is taxed under the CFC regime[10].

2.2.3. Anti-tax avoidance rationale

The ATAD enriches the CFC rationale with a third perspective: the *"fight against tax avoidance and aggressive tax planning, both at the global and EU levels"*[11]. So,

---

6   Italy, Brazil and Sweden apply CFC rules according to the entity approach. Until 2010, the New Zealand CFC rules also taxed all of the income of CFCs.
7   The relationship between the ATAD and the BEPS Project is analyzed in the chapter of Jovdat Mammadov.
8   See the cases of the Netherlands which implemented a combination of approaches, and Bulgaria, Finland and France which deviated from both models.
9   C. Turley, D. Chamberlain, M. Petriccione, *A New Dawn for the International Tax System* (Amsterdam: IBFD, 2017), Part. 2, Ch. 8, par. 8.1. See also par. 8.1.1. for the concept of „*good deferral*".
10 This compromise solution has its source in the US CFC rules set in 1962. L. Burns, Rethinking the Design of Australia's CFC Rules in the Global Economy, *IBFD Bulletin*, July 2005, p. 262.
11 General Secretariat of the European Council, Conclusions, 18 December 2014, EUCO 237/14, par. I.3.

CFC income definition is also supposed to be consistent against tax avoidance that is generally achieved through the creation of "artificial" economic activities in the jurisdiction of the entity or the permanent establishment[12] within the Union and in third countries as specified in Preamble number 12.

3. The boundaries to the concept of income
3.1. Two flexible options

In accordance with the objectives outlined above, the concept of income[13] is designed as a flexible one so as to address the priorities of each individual Member State. Moreover, income should be an easy-to-determine concept in order to limit *"administrative burden and compliance costs"*[14] while maintaining business competitiveness. To this end, the EU legislator has designed Article 7(a) ATAD on CFC income according to two approaches:

1. The categorical approach – Article 7(2)(a);
2. The transactional approach – Article 7(2)(b);

The categorical approach consists of allocating the entity's (or PE's) income to the taxpayer provided that income falls into certain categories set out in a given list and regardless of any actual distribution. It is based on the assumption that certain types of income, named "passive income", lend themselves as an instrument for tax base stripping, especially parent stripping or foreign base stripping and time deferral of taxation. Passive income is produced without an intense rooting of capital, assets, risks, or functions in the foreign jurisdiction. In other words, it has no or low "tax nexus"[15] with the foreign jurisdiction. For those reasons, passive income can be easily displaced from one jurisdiction to another without significant economic barriers or economic side-effects. Passive income stems from functions, assets or risks for which legal ownership can be legally shifted from one jurisdiction to another. Thus, they can be legally relocated for taxation purposes. Passive income is not the antithesis of active income as they may be interconnected and, in any case, passive income comes from economical activities. Moreover, many CFC rules may also target active income for mere tax deferral purposes.

---

12 European Commission, Proposal for a Council Directive laying down rules against tax avoidance practices that directly affect the functioning of the internal market, Brussels, 28.1.2016, COM(2016) 26 final, 2016/011 (CNS), Explanatory Memorandum. In the first proposal for a council directive, dated 24 January 2016, a CFC regime aimed at tackling the profit shifting mainly related to infra-group schemes where mobile passive income, especially deriving from the ownership of intangible assets, is shifted to low-tax subsidiaries.
13 D. W. Blum, Controlled Foreign Companies: Selected Policy Issues – or the Missing Elements of BEPS Action 3 and the Anti- Tax Avoidance Directive, *Intertax*, (2018), vol. 46, issue 4, 298, par. 5.
14 ATAD Directive, Preamble n. 12.
15 For a definition of tax nexus, see also OECD/G20 Base Erosion and Profit Shifting Project Action 5: Agreement on Modified Nexus Approach for IP Regimes or European Commission Report of the Commission Expert Group on Taxation of the Digital Economy. pp.41–49.

According to the transactional approach, the simplest units of the tax base analysis are the single transactions or arrangements between the parent company and the controlled entity or permanent establishment. If certain characteristics or requisites arise[16], those items trigger CFC income[17].

Table 1

Approaches[18]	TAX BASIS	
	Transactional	Entity
Categorical – legal classification	Model A* Article 7(2)(a) ATAD	Italy[19], Finland[20], Ireland, Poland
Substance-based	*Model B*** *Article 7(2)(b) ATAD*	*Outlined in the BEPS report, Action 3*
Excess profit return	*Outlined in the BEPS report, Action 3*	*Outlined in the BEPS report, Action 3*

* Although it is not possible to draw a clear separation between Model A and Model B, as these models have been implemented in mingled ways in some cases, according to a *Deloitte study*, „EU Anti-tax Avoidance Directive, Implementation of controlled foreign companies rules", February 2020, fourteen countries adhered to Model A: Italy, Portugal, Spain, Greece, Croatia, Slovenia, Austria, Romania, Poland, Czech Republic, Germany, Denmark, Lithuania, and Sweden. Sweden, however, does not extend CFC regime to foreign permanent establishments' income. According to a *PWC analysis*, „Overview of the implementation of the Anti-Tax Avoidance Directive into Member States' domestic tax laws", December 2019, the same countries adhered to Model A, but Germany has not opted for either Model A nor for Model B.

** According to a *Deloitte* and a *PWC* study (see note above), ten countries have adhered to Model B: Ireland, UK, Belgium, Slovakia, Hungary, Latvia, Estonia, Malta, Cyprus, Luxembourg. Hungary switched from model A to model B since 01/01/2019[21].

---

16 J. De Jong in E. Pinetz, E. Schafferley, Limiting Base Erosion: Schriftenreihe IStR Vol. 104 (Vienna: Linde, 2017), pag. 298.
17 The transactional approach in Art. 7(2)(b) ATAD will be analyzed in the chapter of Jovdat Mammadov.
18 See also I. M. de Groot & B. Larking, Implementation of Controlled Foreign Company Rules under the EU Anti-Tax Avoidance Directive (2016/1164), 59 *Eur. Taxn.* 6 (2019), *Journal Articles & Opinion Pieces IBFD*, par. 5.1.2 and following.
19 The implementation of the ATAD Directive by Italy envisages an entity approach for which the entire CFC income is taxed in the hands of the parent company by applying a „look through" taxing technique.
20 K. Äimä & H. Lyyski, Chapter 15: Controlled Foreign Company Legislation in Finland in: G.W. Kofler et al. (eds.), *Controlled Foreign Company Legislation* (Amsterdam:IBFD, 2020).
21 B. Kolozs & A. Köszegi, Chapter 18: Controlled Foreign Company Legislation in Hungary in: G.W. Kofler et al. (eds.), *Controlled Foreign Company Legislation* (Amsterdam:IBFD, 2020).

3.2. The background to the categorical approach

The idea of using the categorical approach as the fish-net to catch "passive income" within CFC rules goes back many years. The United States was the first country to attempt to elaborate on "passive income". In 1962, it introduced the CFC rules in their Internal Revenue Code, Subpart F. A previous tax rule, dated 1937, aiming at taxing foreign personal holding companies where individuals could avoid US tax by getting passive income through controlled foreign companies inspired CFC rules. However, provisions have never specified any definition of passive income. They have only provided a classification for it since the United States considered that the mere listing of income categories was a very effective *"tool for ensuring current taxation in the US of certain types of highly mobile income, including passive income earned by foreign corporations with majority US ownership"*[22] and to counter tax deferral[23]. As an example, on the subject of sheltering income with non-cash losses from businesses in which the taxpayers do not participate[24] (IRC, Sec. 469(c), 1986 and subsequent), the tax code provides three types of gross income:

1. active activity gross income;
2. passive activity gross income;
3. portfolio activity gross income.

According to the given definition, "Income is passive activity gross income if generated by activities that involve the conduct of a trade or business in which the taxpayer does not materially participate or by rental activities". Income from intangible assets, such as patents, copyrights, and literary compositions, is excluded from passive income if the taxpayer has spent significant personal efforts in the creation of those assets. Moreover,

> *I.R.C. defines portfolio activity gross income as*
> (1) income from any activity that generates interest, dividends, annuities, or royalties and
> (2) gain or loss from the disposition of:
>   (a) investment property that is not used in a passive activity and
>   (b) the sale of assets that produce investment income.[25]

On the subject of CFC taxable income, Subpart F[26] rules include the following categories:

---

[22] C. Turley, D. Chamberlain, M. Petriccione, *A New Dawn for the International Tax System* (Amsterdam: IBFD, 2017), Part. 2, Ch. 8, par. 8.1.2. Y. Brauner, M. Herzfeld, United States, IFA Cahiers 2013 – Volume 98A, *The taxation of foreign passive income for groups of companies*, p. 783 and on.
[23] P. A. Glicklich, U.S. Taxation of E-Commerce under Subpart F – Missing Pieces Leave Uncertainty, *IBFD Bulletin*, Sept./Oct. 2001. J. Rogers, E.P. Lemanowicz, *United States*, IFA Cahiers, 2001.
[24] H. D. Sprohge, Passive Activity Losses in Light of the New Section 469 Temporary Regulations, Idea Exchange@UAkron, (1988) Akron, *Tax Journal Akron Law Journals*, pag. 131.
[25] US I.R.C. CFR § 469 (e)(1)(A)(i)(I)-(III); CFR § 1.469-2T (c)(3)(i)(A)(i)-(ii).
[26] US I.R.C. CFR § 954.

- Foreign base company income – FBCI (§ 954(a)) which is the sum of:
  - Foreign personal holding company income – FPHCI (§ 954(c));
  - Foreign base company sales income among CFCs[27] (§ 954(d));
  - Foreign base company services income among CFCs (§ 954(e));
  - Foreign base company oil related income (§ 954(g));
  - Special rule for income derived in the active conduct of banking, financing, or similar business;
- Insurance income (§ 953);
- Others.

The item FPHCI includes eight categories: (a) dividends, interest, rents, royalties and annuities, (b) gains from certain property transactions (e.g. investment assets, stock and partnership interests), (c) gains from commodities transactions, (d) foreign currency gains, (e) income equivalent to interest, (f) income from notional principal contracts, (g) payments in lieu of dividends, and (h) income from certain personal service contracts[28]. Capital gains should not be considered passive income if they are derived from the disposal of assets producing active income.

The OECD did not fundamentally criticize the outcome of the categorical approach as applied in the United States as a tool to reattribute income of a low-taxed controlled subsidiary to its parent company and it has even supported it in some respects[29]. Thus, the US experience served as a litmus test for other experiences in other countries and, in some respects, also for the BEPS Project and, consequently, for the elaboration of the categorical approach in the ATAD Directive.

3.3. Pros and cons of the categorical approach

ATAD lawmakers revealed a bias in favour of the categorical approach for the following considerations. Firstly, it represents a fair compromise between the safeguarding of CEN (capital export neutrality) and CIN (capital import neutrality). Secondly, it directly targets those types of income that international doctrine and established ECJ jurisprudence would consider as "passive" income[30]. Thirdly, it allows for a relatively simple and cost-effective implementation. The great advantage of the categorical approach based on a legal classification and the reason why it has been chosen in many jurisdictions, although applied in different ways, is the simplicity in its assessment and application. However, the categorical approach has the disadvantage that it targets some items of income irrespective of the fact that they can derive from sources that have genuinely produced that income from a substantive or active economic activity performed in the other state. Thence, the risk of double taxation arises although the relief methods might be applied.

---

27 Intended as related parties.
28 US I.R.C. CFR § 954(c)(1)(A)-(H).
29 Y. Brauner, M. Herzfeld, United States, IFA Cahiers 2013 – Volume 98A, *The taxation of foreign passive income for groups of companies*, p. 784.
30 CJEU, 3 October 2013, C-282/12, Itelcar; CJEU, 13 March 2014, C-375/12, Bouanich; CJEU, 23 April 2008, C-201/05, CFC GLO.

4. The categorical approach: a legal classification

Article 7(2)(a) adopted the categorical approach as one of the two best methods to reattribute the undistributed CFC income. Article 7(2)(a) mirrors BEPS Action 3[31] which outlined certain items as "passive income" in accordance with international practice[32]. The BEPS recommendations propose a classification based on the legal definition of income as further elaborated by the ATAD. While BEPS only provides a "recommendation" for which items should be included in the list for the categorical approach, the ATAD provides a list of income items that constitute a "minimum standard"[33] from which member countries may deviate and set provisions that are more rigorous in order to achieve the objectives of the directive. Anyway, in both cases, the list of income items is *not exhaustive* and is left open so that member countries can select or remove items as long as they are characterized by the following *hallmarks*:

(i) income is a geographically mobile income, or
(ii) it is earned due to interaction with related parties;
(iii) it is passive income by its nature[34].

In other words, "CFC rules generally include income that has been separated from the underlying value creation to obtain a reduction in tax"[35].

4.1. Article 8(2)(a) in the "presidency compromise"

The intermediate elaboration of the ATAD, named the "presidency compromise", revised the previous framework for Article 8(2)(a) on CFC income. The entity approach was abandoned in favour of the categorical approach which is elevated as one of the two preferred methodologies aiming at *"re-attributing the income of a low-taxed controlled subsidiary to its parent company"*[36]. Article 8(2)(a)

---

[31] OECD/G20 Base Erosion and Profit Shifting Project, Designing Effective Controlled Foreign Company Rules, Action 3, Paris 2015 Final Report, chapt. 1 and 4. On the relationship between BEPS and ATAD Directive, please see also European Commission – Fact Sheet, The Anti-Tax Avoidance Package – Questions and Answers, Brussels, 28 January 2016; European Commission, Communication from the Commission to the European Parliament and the Council, Anti-Tax Avoidance Package: Next steps towards delivering effective taxation and greater tax transparency in the EU, {SWD(2016) 6 final}, Brussels, 28.1.2016 COM(2016) 23 final, par. 3.

[32] C. HJI Panayi, 'The ATAD's CFC Rule and its Impact on the Existing Regimes of EU Member States' in: Pistone and Weber (eds.), *The Implementation of Anti-BEPS Rules in the EU: A comprehensive Study*, (Amsterdam:IBFD, 2018), chap. 16.1.

[33] Art. 3 ATAD Directive, „Minimum level of protection". R. Danon, 'Some Observations on the Carve-Out Clause of Article 7(2)(a) of the ATAD with Regard to Third Countries' in: Pistone and Weber (eds.), *The Implementation of Anti-BEPS Rules in the EU: A comprehensive Study*, (Amsterdam:IBFD, 2018), chap. 17.1.

[34] M. Dahlberb, B. Wiman, General report, par. 2.3.3 in IFA Cahiers 2013 – Volume 98A, *The taxation of foreign passive income for groups of companies*.

[35] BEPS, Action 3, p. 43.

[36] Council of the European Union, Brussels, 24 May 2016, OR.en, 9431/16, FISC 83, ECOFIN 498, „Presidency Compromise", Preamble n. (12). The other option is the transactional method in Art. 8(2)(b).

featured the list of income categories as follows which was thereby confirmed in the last final version as Article 7(2)(a) ATAD.

> *Where an entity or permanent establishment is treated as a controlled foreign company under paragraph 1, the Member State of the taxpayer shall include in the tax base:*
> (a) the non-distributed income of the entity or the income of the permanent establishment which is derived from the following categories:
> - interest or any other income generated by financial assets;
> - royalties or any other income generated from intellectual property;
> - dividends and income from the disposal of shares;
> - income from financial leasing;
> - income from insurance, banking and other financial activities;
> - income from invoicing companies that earn sales and services income from goods and services purchased from and sold to associated enterprises, and add no or little economic value;

The list of categories does not consider income from immovable property and real estate anymore which had appeared in the previous version. In the initial ATAD proposal, non-distributed income from immovable property was included as a CFC tax base unless the Member State of the parent company would not be entitled to tax the income on the basis of a tax treaty[37]. Income from immovable property may have specific characteristics such as the absence of active economic activities involving the participation of the tax-payer that make it suitable for inclusion in the list of passive CFC income. However, the real estate income may not raise concerns of tax avoidance and profit stripping from a low-taxed controlled subsidiary to its parent company due to the immovability of the tax base[38]. Moreover, it was argued that the management of real estate is *per se* an active and genuine business. That is why immovable property and real estate income was removed from the CFC income list under the categorical approach. However, Spain has taken a different approach. Article 100.3 a) Spanish corporate income tax (CIT) provides that income derived from the "*entitlement to rustic and urban real estate or real rights that fall upon them*" is included in CFC income as the first category of tainted income unless real-estate income derives from a business activity (unless it is assigned to a business activity). Since Article 7(2)(a) is a "minimum standard" allowing the Member States to further its requirements, Spanish CFC domestic law will not cause compatibility problems with ATAD rules[39]. According to the German approach based on an explicit list of active income so that passive income is determined by exclusion from active income, rental income from

---

[37] The initial Atad proposal dated 28 January 2016 included income from immovable property in the list of categories of non-distributed income. The proposal was as follows: (…) *(v) income from immovable property, unless the Member State of the taxpayer would not have been entitled to tax the income under an agreement concluded with a third country.*
[38] European Commission, Taxation Trends in the European Union, Data for the EU Member States, Iceland and Norway, 2019, ed., DG Taxation and Customs Union, pag. 46.
[39] G.W. Kofler et al. (eds.), *Controlled Foreign Company Legislation*, (Amsterdam:IBFD, 2020), chapt. 36.

movable and immovable property is considered passive income unless it is earned in the context of an activity carried out on a commercial basis under section 8(1) number 6 AStG[40].

4.2. Article 7(2)(a): the final version

In the final version of Article 7(2)(a), the ATAD adopted the enumerative technique so that this provision includes a list of categories of income that are allegedly considered as passive income and, as such, targeted to be considered within the scope of the CFC rules. Based on this approach, passive income can be divided into four main areas according to the specific nature of the enumerated items (see Table 2). The four areas are the following:

1. Income from shares;
2. Financial income;
3. Income generated from intellectual property;
4. Sales and services income.

If we compare the BEPS version to the ATAD legal income classification, the following table comes out. Article 7(2)(a) expands the formal wording and adds additional items such as income from the disposal of shares, income generated from financial assets, income from banking and other financial activities, income from financial leasing for which inclusion was already suggested by the BEPS Project[41], and income from invoicing companies.

Table 2: Legal classification

	Passive income (areas)		BEPS – Action 3	ATAD Art. 7(2)(a)
1	Income from shares	1	Dividends	(i) Dividends and income from the disposal of shares
2	Financial income	2	Interest	(ii) Interest or any other income generated by financial assets
		3	Insurance income	(iii) Income from insurance, banking and other financial activities
		4	–	(iv) Income from financial leasing
3	Income generated from an intellectual property	5	Royalties and IP income	(v) Royalties or any other income generated from an intellectual property

---

40 P. Eckl & F. Schill, Reform of the German Controlled Foreign Company Rules, 60 *Eur. Taxn.* 6 (2020), *Journal Articles & Papers IBFD*, par. 3.3.5.
41 BEPS, Action 3 added that jurisdictions could also include further categories of income, such as rents and leasing fees, note 4, p. 52.

	Passive income (areas)		BEPS – Action 3	ATAD Art. 7(2)(a)
4	Sales and services income	6	Sales and services income	(vi) Income from invoicing companies that earn sales and services income from goods and services purchased from and sold to associated enterprises, and add no or little economic value

4.3. Dividends

According to the ATAD itemization, dividends are considered passive or tainted income and therefore included *per se* in CFC income. "*Dividend in its economic sense is the return on an equity investment in a corporate entity*[42]. The directive does not offer a definition of dividends, the scope of which remains very general and thus very flexible[43]. It requires the inclusion of dividends irrespective of whether they are portfolio or non-portfolio dividends[44] nor does it consider any other kind of characterization. Non-portfolio dividends and PE profits usually benefit from tax exemptions in the parent company's residence state and thence can raise concerns about double non-taxation or very long deferral from domestic taxation which ultimately turns into avoidance of domestic tax on income[45]. On the other hand, the directive does not transpose certain concrete situations that do not give rise to any concerns according to the BEPS Project and would therefore be worthy of exclusion from a CFC scope. The cases are the following ones:

1. dividends paid out of the active income of a subsidiary;
2. dividends exempted from taxation (as happens in many jurisdictions) if those dividends would have been exempted from taxation in the parent jurisdiction had they been earned by the parent company directly;
4. dividends paid out of an active trade or business of dealing in securities and thus linked to the CFC's trade or business.

As it is rather easy to shift equity, dividends could be consequently shifted as purely "passive" income (i.e. income that does not arise from any underlying activity). The assumption that dividends are passive income has been interpreted differently among the EU countries. Germany has adopted a unique legislative tech-

---

[42] M. Helminen, *The International Tax Law Concept of Dividend*, Series on International Taxation, vol. 36, (Wolters Kluwer, 2017), „*Dividend distribution is a transaction in which corporate profits are distributed to the owners of the corporate entity without the corporate entity's expectation of receiving anything in return*".
[43] For one of the definitions of dividends, see the Commentary on the OECD Model Tax Convention par. 24 to Article 10(3). S. E. Bärsch, The Definitions of Dividends and Interest Contained in the OECD Model, Actual Tax Treaties, and the German Model, (2014), 42, *Intertax*, Issue 6, pp. 433–444.
[44] A dividend paid to a company when that company has a voting interest sufficient to exercise an influence in the company (usually amounting to at least 10% of the voting power) paying the dividend.
[45] B. J. Arnold, The Evolution of Controlled Foreign Corporation Rules and Beyond, *Bulletin for International Taxation* (2019) par. 3.1 (p. 631–648).

nique consisting of deriving passive income from a negative assumption that passive income is any type of income that is not explicitly stated to be active income. Section 8(1) AStG contains the catalogue of active income and also selective exceptions[46]. Germany considers dividends as active income provided that some requisites occur: the subsidiary is not located in a low-tax country (tax rate of less than 25 per cent), dividend derives from designated positive activities, and it is not a hybrid payment. In detail, Germany has adopted a "reverse" entity approach by treating all income of the subsidiary company as harmless for CFC purposes, provided that income derives from specified activities listed in section 8(1) AStG as "active" income. On the other hand, if income derives from activities that are not included in the active catalogue, then it triggers CFC legislation. Besides, in some countries, dividend income from fourth- or lower-tier companies[47] automatically qualifies as passive income even if the dividends originated from companies that are engaged in active trade or business[48]. The inclusion of dividends among targeted passive income for CFC treatment has at least two undesirable consequences especially when it comes to holding companies that regularly make dividend distributions. Assume that a group consists of a parent company in one state and a holding company in another state that, in turn, controls operating companies. Firstly, the same holding company would be subject to CFC rules for the years in which it distributes dividends to the parent company and not for the other years. So, a holding can be treated as a CFC in one year but not in another year with a consequent increase in administrative burdens. Moreover, those dividends would be subject to the CFC regime irrespective of whether they result from genuine economic activities but would be taxed in the hands of the parent company in "mass" terms. *"This will result in classification and tracking issues (i.e., contaminated and non-contaminated income need to be distinguished)"*[49]. Secondly, in the case of multiple tiers' companies for which a dividend is distributed by the third-tier and then by the second-tier company, there is a sound risk that dividend is taxed twice as a case of double taxation, which is a negative effect that should be eliminated. A solution to this issue could be the implementation of a *"switch-over"* clause[50] or the exclusion from taxation of distributions by lower-tier subsidiaries so that only the ultimate recipient (the parent company) can be taxed on dividends.

---

46 The German Foreign Transaction Tax Act (FTTA), § 8. S. Weber & M. Weiss, Legal Uncertainty in the Application of the German CFC Rules, 70 *Bulletin for International Taxation* 6 (2016), Journal Articles & Opinion Pieces IBFD.
47 P. Eckl, The tax regime for controlled foreign corporations, *Eur. Taxn.* 1 (2003), IBFD, par. 3.2.
48 Steuersenkungsgesetz (Tax Reduction Act, StSenkG), 23 October 2000, Federal Law Gazette 2000I, p. 1433.
49 CFE Fiscal Committee, Opinion Statement FC 3/2016 on the European Commission's proposal for an Anti-Tax Avoidance Directive, Brussels, 28 January 2016, par 3.4.
50 Although the introduction of "switch-over" clauses should not, in itself, present general profiles of incompatibility with EU law (see ECJ, case law C-298-05 dated 6 December 2007, Columbus Container Services BVBA & Co. vs Finanzamt Bielefeld-Innenstadt), in view of the fact that the OECD BEPS Project does not provide for the general introduction of switch-over clauses in the countries participating in the project, the general introduction of such a clause could penalize the activities of European companies and constitute an interference with the tax policy of the Member States.

4.4. Income from the disposal of shares

Capital gains deriving from the disposal of shares for which dividends are qualified as passive income usually will remain qualified as passive income. However, capital gains arising from the sale or disposal of shares in companies that primarily conduct an active business may be considered as active income. An issue to be addressed is the relationship between the CFC regime and the capital gains exemption regime. In many countries such as Germany, Sweden, Austria, Spain, and Romania, income from the disposal of active shares is exempt according to domestic taxation[51]. Therefore, in the implementation of a CFC rule, some countries such as Austria have added the remark: *"to the extent that these (income) would be taxable for the participating corporation"*[52]. In other words, the CFC regime applies if the capital gain income is taxed in the state of the parent company. If, on the other hand, the jurisdiction of the parent company considers such income as exempt, then there is no reason to subject it to the CFC regime, otherwise it would be taxed under the CFC regime even though it is entitled to exemption. In some other jurisdictions, if the seller is a credit institution or financial service institution that does not qualify for the domestic participation exemption, then the income from the disposal of shares is considered passive income and subjected to CFC rules[53]. In these circumstances, double taxation can arise. On the other hand, as a tool to avoid double non-taxation, a CFC regime also covers income from the capital gain of the disposal of shares provided that the capital gain is taxed in the jurisdiction of the parent company that acknowledges the tax credit, if any, for the tax paid in the CFC country. In the United Kingdom, there is a general exclusion for all types of capital gains whereas an increasing number of countries, such as Denmark, exempt capital gains arising from the disposition of an IP.

4.5. Interest or any other income generated by financial assets

Most of the countries that have adopted the categorical approach of Model A[54] (Italy, Portugal, Spain, Greece, Croatia, Slovenia, Austria, Romania, Poland, Czech Republic, Germany, Denmark, Lithuania, and Sweden) have included financial income as an item of the passive income list. Interest and financing income is assumed to be passive income as the parent company can easily shift it to the low-taxed CFC by providing it the necessary financial resources in order for the CFC to grant back loans or other financing services (like letters of patronage,

---

51   C. Turley, D. Chamberlain, M. Petriccione, *A New Dawn for the International Tax System* (Amsterdam: IBFD, 2017), Part. 2, chapt. 8, table 8.5. G.W. Kofler et al. (eds.), *Controlled Foreign Company Legislation* (Amsterdam:IBFD, 2020).
52   Sec. 10a par. 2 n. 3 CITA.
53   P. Eckl & F. Schill, Reform of the German Controlled Foreign Company Rules, 60 *Eur. Taxn.* 6 (2020), Journal Articles & Papers IBFD, par. 3.3.8.
54   See supra table 1.

guarantees, etc.) worthy of remuneration[55]. In general, interest and financial income is treated as passive income if financial services do not represent genuine financial activities in the CFC jurisdiction. However, the approach is different for banking and insurance activities performed by financial institutions. In general, these activities are genuine economic activities, bound up with local regulations being location-based activities. Therefore, they generally enjoy the non-application clause provided for in Article 7(2)(a) which contains an exclusion from CFC regime for substantially economic activities[56]. According to the Spanish implementation, income from lending, financial, and insurance activities between related parties is included in the CFC regime if it generates a deductible cost for the resident parent company[57]. Additionally, income from derivative instruments is included in CFC income except from those derivatives covering risk deriving from an economic activity. According to German CFC rules, the rising and lending of funds is active income if the taxpayers *"prove that the CFC raises the capital exclusively on foreign capital markets and not from the taxpayer or an associated person"*[58]. In order to protect intra-group treasury activities or group finance centres, the CFC rules may provide for interest exclusions. As an example, the Spanish regulations provide that the positive income derived from the transfer of capital to third parties shall be understood as coming from the carrying out of credit and financial activities. This is valid unless the transferor and the transferee belong to a group of companies irrespective of residence and the obligation to draw up consolidated annual accounts as long as the revenue of the transferee derives at least by 85% from the exercise of economic activities[59]. This behaviour would possibly lead to the overleveraging of the parent and overcapitalization of the CFC without an economic justification in both jurisdictions. It was noted that the categorical approach on interest could also be combined with a *"look-through rule"* that would consider interest to be active finance income if deductible by the payor against its active business income[60]. Accordingly, this rule would treat in-

---

55 Interest and financing income is more likely to raise this concern when it has been earned from related parties. BEPS Action 5 suggests that the *relatedness of parties* can be used as an indicator that the income in question can raise profit shifting concerns. Action 5 envisages a sort of test, a "related party test" or "related party rule", to check if the financial income remunerates genuine financing flows from the parent to the CFC to finance active business instead of shifting profit from the parent company to the CFC. BEPS Action 3, Paris 2015 Final Report, chapt. 4, p. 46 and p. 53, note 4. See also D. W. Blum, Controlled Foreign Companies: Selected Policy Issues – or the Missing Elements of BEPS Action 3 and the Anti-Tax Avoidance Directive, *Intertax*, (2018), vol. 46, issue 4, pp. 306, par. 4.2.
56 C. Turley, D. Chamberlain, M. Petriccione, *A New Dawn for the International Tax System* (Amsterdam: IBFD, 2017), Part. 2, chapt. 8, table 8.3.
57 Spain art. 100.4 g CIT.
58 P. Eckl & F. Schill, Reform of the German Controlled Foreign Company Rules, 60 *Eur. Taxn.* 6 (2020), Journal Articles & Papers IBFD, par. 3.3.6.
59 Spain CIT, Art. 100 (3)(b), L. 27/2014. G.W. Kofler et al. (eds.), *Controlled Foreign Company Legislation* (Amsterdam:IBFD, 2020), chapt. 36, par. 2.3.1.
60 A. Ting, The Politics of BEPS – Apple's International Tax Structure and the US Attitude towards BEPS, 69 *Bull. Intl. Taxn.* 6/7 (2015), Journal Articles & Opinion Pieces IBFD, para. 3.

terest paid out of active earnings as active in order to exclude that interest from CFC rules. However, it was also noted that such a rule could raise foreign-to-foreign base stripping issues.

4.6. Income from insurance, banking, and other financial activities

The analysis of this item involves distinguishing between entities engaged in financial activities in a structured manner or regulated entities (such as banks, financial institutions, etc.) and other entities or non-regulated entities. In general, taxable income from financial, insurance, mortgage, or banking activities is included in passive income. If such income is exempt, then it should not be included in the CFC income. Income from insurance, banking, and other financial activities is considered *per se* as CFC income on the assumption that the income arising from the insurance of risks can be shifted away from jurisdictions in which those risks are located and into a low-tax jurisdiction. In cases of organized financial services, such as banks or insurance companies, income may not raise the same concerns because of the regulatory environment settings in terms of risks, capital, and remuneration. According to the Danish CFC approach, subsidiaries that qualify as regulated entities in terms of financial institutions under Article 2(5) ATAD are excluded from the CFC regime if no more than one third of the CFC income stems from operations with group related parties or associated persons. Additionally, CFC rules apply if the value of the subsidiary's financial assets exceeds 10% of the value of the subsidiary's total assets (asset test). In other words, they qualify for an exemption from CFC regime if they collect financial income in the context of a structured activity that has commercial substance as demonstrated by exceeding certain parameters. Interestingly, the list of Danish passive income also includes taxable gains and deductible losses on CO_2 quotas and CO_2 credits as well as taxable gains and deductible losses on debt claims, debt, and financial contracts[61]. According to some thinking, if derivative contracts (forward contracts, etc.) serve as hedging instruments for active transactions, they should not be included in passive income.

As to regulated entities (such as banks) that are subject to capitalization regulations and other requirements, rules designed to attribute CFC income should recognize that any rules on overcapitalization should take account of such requirements and should not attribute CFC income just because an entity is required to maintain a certain level of capital for non-tax purposes (such as for credit, market, and operational risks).

---

61   A. Riis, *Amendments Danish CFC tax rules – are we there yet?*, 25 november 2019, Aritax Law publishing. P. Koerver Schmidt & J. Bundgaard, 'Denmark', chapt. 14 in: M. Lang et al. (eds.), *Implementing Key BEPS Actions: Where Do We Stand?* (Amsterdam:IBFD, 2019), Books IBFD. G.W. Kofler et al. (eds.), *Controlled Foreign Company Legislation* (Amsterdam:IBFD, 2020), Books IBFD, chapt. 14, par. 1.

4.7. Income from financial leasing

Many operating lessees take "ownership" of the asset via finance leases (rather than outright purchase). Contracts of finance leases can be legally placed in low-tax countries so that, under the dislocated finance leases, the operating lessor will record income that will be regarded as lease rentals receipts. On the other hand, the parent company might transfer assets to the CFC via loan agreements at low rental fees. To avoid disruptions in the leasing industry and to ensure that the lessor is both the legal and also the economical owner of the assets under financial leasing, income from financial leasing is regarded as CFC passive income[62]. Countries such as Austria, Croatia, and Denmark have included financial leasing and subleasing (Spain) including gains and losses from the sale of assets used in connection with financial leasing in the list of passive income[63].

4.8. Royalties or any other income generated from an intellectual property

Income from royalties or any other income generated from intellectual property[64] is considered *per se* as CFC income on the assumption that IP assets are highly mobile. The income from these assets can easily be shifted from the location where the value of the assets was created to low-tax jurisdictions. According to BEPS Action 3, IP income raises several CFC concerns because the IP income is particularly easy to manipulate. An IP can be exploited, and related income can be distributed in many different forms, all of which may have different formalistic classifications under the CFC rules of different countries. For instance, income from the IP could be embedded in income from sales and therefore be treated as active sales income under the CFC rules. Moreover, IP assets are often hard-to-value assets[65] because of the difficulty in finding comparable assets, and their cost base may not be accurate for measuring the income they can generate. In addition, in the case of an IP that is embedded in other goods or services, it is often difficult to separate the income directly earned from the underlying IP asset from the income that is earned from associated services or products. CFC rules that use a categorical analysis based on legal classification often attempt to address the concerns raised by IP income by separating royalties and treating them as attributable using OECD trans-

---

62   IFA Cahiers 1990 – Vol. 75a. *Taxation of cross border leasing.*
63   G.W. Kofler et al. (eds.), *Controlled Foreign Company Legislation* (Amsterdam:IBFD, 2020), Books IBFD.
64   For one of the definitions of royalties, see Article 12 and related Commentary on the OECD Model Tax Convention.
65   Public Discussion Draft on BEPS Action Item 8: Hard-to-Value Intangibles (OECD, 4 June 2015): Hard-to-value intangibles include "*intangibles or rights in intangibles for which, at the time of their transfer in a transaction between associated enterprises, (i) no sufficiently reliable comparables exist; and (ii) there is a lack of reliable projections of future cash flows or income expected to be derived from the five transferred intangible, or the assumptions used in valuing the intangible are highly uncertain.*"

fer pricing guidelines (2017). BEPS Action 3[66] makes reference to income generated from some sort of intellectual property (IP) as underlying the income from digital goods and services. As shown in Pillar 1 and Pillar 2, income from digital goods escapes the classification under income from intellectual property and is to be detected using completely different tools[67]. A very broad definition of income from IP can be seen in the list provided by Denmark which indicates *"payments of any kind received as compensation for the use of or the right to use intangible assets as well as gains and losses connected to the transfer of intangible assets"* as passive income for ATAD purposes. This is a very broad definition covering any income derived from the exploitation of an IP at the subsidiary level. Some jurisdictions provide for the exclusion of royalties from passive income if intangibles have been developed at the entity (or PE) level. Spain does not include royalties in passive income as does the United States which considers royalties as active income depending on the organizational setup related to the local exploitation of the IP. According to the German approach, royalties are considered as active income if the IP is developed at the subsidiary level. In this case, they are excluded from the CFC provisions pursuant to section 8(1)(6) AStG.

4.9. Income from invoicing companies that earn sales and services income from goods and services purchased from "and" sold to associated enterprises "and" add no or little economic value

This item is one of the most intricate and controversial legal definitions both because of its wording and its complex content. The international tax debate[68] has often focused on the need to avoid that, through the transfer of sideline activities, income from sales and services attributable to the parent company's jurisdiction is shifted to a CFC's low-tax jurisdiction. Article 7(2)(a) picks the *"income from invoicing companies that earn sales and services income from goods and services purchased from and sold to"* other entities if the following two requisites occur:

---

66   BEPS, Action 3, page 52, note 6.
67   OECD, Pillar 1 and Pillar 2. B. J. Arnold, The Evolution of Controlled Foreign Corporation Rules and Beyond, 73 *Bull. Intl. Taxn.* 12 (2019), Journal Articles & Opinion Pieces IBFD: according to this author, CFC rules would be preferable to the Inclusive Framework proposal on the OECD/ G20 Base Erosion and Profit Shifting Project (Pillar Two) for a uniform minimum tax on all CFC income. See also P. Pistone et al., The OECD Public Consultation Document "Global Anti-Base Erosion (GloBE) Proposal – Pillar Two": An Assessment, 74 *Bull. Intl. Taxn.* 2 (2020), Journal Articles & Opinion Pieces, IBFD, par. 2–3.
68   According to the BEPS Project (see Chapt. 4, par. 4.2.1.1), income from sales and services does raise concerns in at least two contexts: *(i)* invoicing companies that earn sales and services income for goods and services that they have purchased from related parties and to which they have added little or no value; and (ii) IP income that was shifted into the CFC and to which the CFC has added little to no value.

Taxable income under option 7(2)(a) of the Anti-Tax Avoidance Directive

1. Proceeds derive from operations with *"associated enterprises"* as defined in ATAD Article 2(4)[69];
2. Proceeds derive from operations that *"(...) add little or no economic value"*.

The text of the article states that companies that purchase from "and" sell to their associated companies fall under the scope of the provision whereas companies that purchase from "third parties" and sell to group affiliates, or the opposite, should not generate a passive income. In other words, CFC income applies if the transactions have both a "cross-border" element (buying from abroad or selling abroad) in a transaction of goods or services "and" both legs of the transaction with a related party (so called "invoicing companies")[70]. As illustrated below, in case 1, the proceeds fall under the scope of CFC income; in case 2, proceeds cannot be considered as CFC income.

Table 3

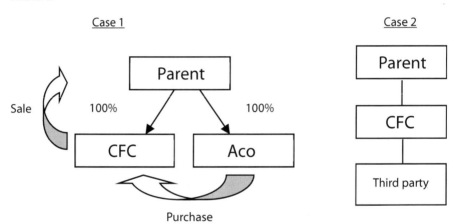

Moreover, the provision refers to invoicing companies that *"add no or little economic value"*. The question arises as to how to identify the extent of the "value added in a transaction". The EU promoted a Joint Transfer Pricing Forum (JTPF)[71] to analyse intercompany services that are routinary in nature, i.e. do not generate added value for the parties involved. The EU Forum stated that the concept of "added value" is to be interpreted in relation to the nature of the services rendered,

---

69　ATAD Art. 7(2)(a): *'Associated enterprise' means: (a) an entity in which the taxpayer holds directly or indirectly a participation in terms of voting rights or capital ownership of 25 percent or more or is entitled to receive 25 percent or more of the profits of that entity; (b) an individual or entity which holds directly or indirectly a participation in terms of voting rights or capital ownership in a taxpayer of 25 percent or more or is entitled to receive 25 percent or more of the profits of the taxpayer; If an individual or entity holds directly or indirectly a participation of 25 percent or more in a taxpayer and one or more entities, all the entities concerned, including the taxpayer, shall also be regarded as associated enterprises".*

70　C. Turley, D. Chamberlain, M. Petriccione, *A New Dawn for the International Tax System* (Amsterdam: IBFD, 2017), table 8.7.

the provider, and the beneficiary. The purpose of the EUJTPF analysis was to verify the criterion for determining the compensation agreed upon for the services included in the service agreement, the advantage obtained by the company receiving the service, the fairness of the compensation, and the effectiveness of the services[72]. However, the EUJTPF list of services is very extensive and far-reaching. Rather, for the purposes of Article 7(2)(a), one can resort to the OECD Transfer Pricing Guidelines (TP Guidelines) (2017) which identifies low (or no) value-adding trading activities under the application of the *arm's length principle*[73]. In detail, TP Guidelines[74] contain the definition for what the international best practice defines as "low value-adding services", namely:

- Auxiliary services;
- Services that are not part of the multinational entity's core business;
- Services that need no intangible asset and do not contribute to their creation; and
- Services that do not involve an assumption or control of significant risk by or give rise to significant risks for the service provider.

The above list has the advantage of being concise, practice-oriented, and straightforward to apply. Although the application of the criteria above might be useful to the purpose, real cases still imply subjective evaluations. Some authors have described some particular cases which I find particularly interesting as they well represent the difficulties for the implementation of this income category[75]. If we think of the operations performed by the service providers, distributors, contract, and toll manufacturers, then *"it could be disputable whether a service or activity can be deemed "auxiliary", "non-core" or "non-risk bearing". In other words, services or activities may or may not be deemed low value-adding depending on the specific context and circumstances"*[76]. Let us consider the example in Table 3: the parent company controls a Hong Kong trading company (HKCFC) that:

---

71 EUJTPF, JTPF Report: Guidelines on Low Value Adding Intra-Group Services, DOC: JTPF/020/REV3/2009EN, Brussels, February 2010. Annex I of the paper provides a list of intra-group services commonly considered low-value-adding services. The services mentioned are the following: information technology, human resources; marketing services; legal services; accounting and administration services; technical services; quality control; and other services.

72 According to the JTPF, a *mark-up* (i.e. the difference between the cost of an asset or service and its selling price) is applied to these types of services which is generally within a range of 3–10% but usually close to 5%. The identification of such values does not allow to exclude *a priori* the application of higher percentages if these are justified by the case.

73 In the preamble of the very first proposal, item (10), for a council directive laying down rules against tax avoidance practices that directly affect the functioning of the internal market, European Commission, Brussels, 28.1.2016, the *arm's length principle* was cited as a reference principle in assessing the income attributed to the parent company, COM(2016) 26 final, 2016/011 (CNS).

74 OECD, Transfer Pricing Guidelines, Special Considerations for Intra-Group Services, D. Low value-adding intra-group services, (2017), chap. VII, par. 7.45, 7.47 et seq.

75 A. Silvestri, P. Ronca, Italy amends CFC rules in corporate tax reform, *International Tax Review*, 22 agosto 2019.

76 D. Avolio, CFC e proventi a basso valore aggiunto in attesa di chiarimenti, *Il Fisco*, 8/2020.

a) purchases raw materials from a group affiliate (other than ParentCo);
b) performs a "standard" quality check on the raw materials; and
c) sells the raw materials back to ParentCo.

Under these facts, it could be reasonably concluded that HKCFC performs a low value-adding activity falling within the scope of the CFC. On the other hand, the conclusion may be different if:

i) ParentCo's final customers demand the highest standards of quality;
ii) HKCo is requested by ParentCo to perform a very accurate quality check on the raw materials according to the "best practice"; and
iii) HKCo's personnel need special expertise, skills, and training to perform the above quality check.

In the latter case, since HKCo's services add a high value, it follows that the income does not fall within the scope of CFC income. In any case, when the CFC effectively adds no or little economic value, it should achieve little remuneration based on transfer pricing principles and, therefore, the income to be taxed in the hands of the parent entity, according to the CFC rules, should not be significant. Furthermore, ATAD Article 7(2)(a)(*vi*) says that passive income is an "earned" one, meaning that income should be not only invoiced but also cashed-in before being taxed in the hands of the parent company. Anyway, this aspect has not yet been clarified. Spain preferred not to introduce this type of tainted income because it was considered unnecessary in light of the general design of CFCs. Germany considers trading activities as generally active unless the business activities take place between related parties. However, income remains active if evidence is provided that the business is commercially organized with appropriate documentation. Portugal has adopted a restrictive implementation that considers trading income as tainted income even if it arises from transactions with unrelated parties[77].

4.10. Deductions and treatment of losses

Article 7(2)(a) ATAD does not specify how to deduct the respective direct and indirect costs from each item of passive income to determine the taxable income. Some countries such as Denmark and the Netherlands have chosen to explicitly state that deductible expenses are an integral part of passive income items and, as such, should be deducted according to local rules[78]. Thus, costs relating to passive income should be deducted from passive income. In the case of losses deriving from one or more of the categories defined as CFC passive income (passive ex-

---

[77] P. Eckl & F. Schill, Reform of the German Controlled Foreign Company Rules, 60 *Eur. Taxn.* 6 (2020), Journal Articles & Papers IBFD. G.W. Kofler et al. (eds.), *Controlled Foreign Company Legislation* (Amsterdam:IBFD, 2020), Books IBFD.

[78] Danish CIT, sec. 32 SEL 1960. G.W. Kofler et al. (eds.), *Controlled Foreign Company Legislation* (Amsterdam:IBFD, 2020), Books IBFD, 'Netherlands', chapt. 24, par. 2.2.3.

penses higher than passive revenues), Article 8 ATAD does not clearly state whether those losses should offset future CFC taxable income deriving exactly from the same categories or if those losses could be used to offset taxable income whatever category to which the income belongs. In general, if the CFC generates losses, there is no attribution to the shareholder. Vertical loss compensation with other income of the taxpayer is therefore not possible. Instead, the loss is carried forward and can offset future CFC income. If a CFC generates negative passive income in one area and positive passive income in another, these shall be offset in accordance with general principles. Alternatively, losses should be stored and tracked until the same kind of passive income arises, possibly within a certain time frame[79].

4.11. Conclusions

After analysing the types of income envisaged by the categorical approach under Article 7(2)(a) (so called Model A), it can be said that the directive has essentially achieved its aim of providing a flexible guidance list for re-attributing the income allocated in low-tax entities (and PE) to the parent company. Model A is a "minimum standard" as individual Member States may deviate from the provision and may introduce requirements that are more rigorous and more restrictive *"to safeguard a higher level of protection of national corporate tax bases"*, pursuant to Article 3 ATAD. Member States adhering to Model A have implemented this methodology with substantial uniformity, albeit adopting variations in tune with their own tax competition policy.

5. The EU Primary Law and the "substance carve-out" rule

5.1. Pursuing compliance with the fundamental freedoms

The categorical approach lends itself to reflections of whether a *priori* taxation based on legal categories entails a restriction to the fundamental freedoms protecting the EU internal market: the freedom of establishment (Article 49 TFEU), and the free movement of capital (Article 63 TFEU)[80]. The question is whether a formulaic listing of given income items triggering taxation in the hands of a taxpayer is compliant with the aims of the EU market functioning notwithstanding

---

79   For a general comment on CFC losses, see G. Maisto, P. Pistone, A European Model for Member States' Legislation on the Taxation of Controlled Foreign Subsidiaries (CFCs) – Part 1, *European Taxation* (Amsterdam:2008), para. 3.5. The treatment of losses in art. 8 ATAD will be analyzed in the chapter of Anca Pianoschi.

80   Treaty on the Functioning of the European Union (Consolidated version 2012), OJ C 326 (2012). The Treaty itself does not define what "capital" is, so it is common practice to interpret this legal term based on Directive 88/361, Appendix.

Taxable income under option 7(2)(a) of the Anti-Tax Avoidance Directive

the limitations developed by the ECJ[81] on measures preventing tax abuse. Reservations on this model as a challenge to the EU fundamental freedoms have been reported since the first proposal for a directive against tax avoidance[82]. Consequently, a disapplication clause (also named exemption clause) was added. It was engineered as a "substance carve-out". In Article 8(2) of the first proposal for a council directive, dated 28 January 2016[83], the disapplication clause reads as follows:

> Member States shall not apply paragraph 1 where an entity is tax resident in a Member State or in a third country that is party to the EEA Agreement or in respect of a permanent establishment of a third country entity which is situated in a Member State, unless the establishment of the entity is wholly artificial or to the extent that the entity engages, in the course of its activity, in non-genuine arrangements which have been put in place for the essential purpose of obtaining a tax advantage.

In this respect, the CFC regime would have applied if the entity had been a wholly artificial one or an entity engaged in non-genuine arrangements that had the essential purpose of obtaining a tax advantage. Several concerns arose around this version because of its complexity. A later draft version, the so called "presidency compromise", dated 24 May 2016[84], reported the further concept of the *"valid commercial reasons"* which replaced the approach based on wholly artificial entities. This concept was also mentioned in Preamble number 13 which stated that: *"(...) To comply with the fundamental freedoms, the income categories should be combined with a substance carve-out aimed to limit, within the Union, the impact of the rules to cases where the CFC has not been established for valid commercial reasons"*. Additionally, Article 8(2)(a), the penultimate paragraph of the presidency compromise stated that: the categorical approach *shall not apply where the taxpayer can establish that the controlled foreign company has been set up for valid commercial reasons and carries on an economic activity supported by commensurate staff, equipment, assets and premises which justify the income attributed to it"*. Several delegations brought up a few concerns to delimit the scope of intra-EU/EEA CFC, which should have been limited to wholly artificial enti-

---

81 CJEU, 12 September 2006, C-196/0412, Cadbury Schweppes and Cadbury Schweppes Overseas. CJEU, 23 April 2008, C-201/05, The Test Claimants in the CFC and Dividend Group Litigation v Commissioners of Inland Revenue. CJEU, 7 September 2017, C-6/16, Eqiom SAS, formerly Holcim France SAS, Enka SA v. Ministre des Finances et des comptes publics.
82 European Commission, Proposal for a Council Directive laying down rules against tax avoidance practices that directly affect the functioning of the internal market, Brussels, 28.1.2016, COM(2016) 26 final, 2016/011 (CNS), Preamble 10.
83 European Commission, Proposal for a Council Directive laying down rules against tax avoidance practices that directly affect the functioning of the internal market, Brussels, 28.1.2016, COM(2016) 26 final, 2016/0011 (CNS).
84 Council of the European Union, Proposal for a Council Directive laying down rules against tax avoidance practices that directly affect the functioning of the internal market, Brussels, 24 May 2016, OR.en, 9431/16, FISC 83, ECOFIN 498.

ties as the ECJ had extensively represented the (subjective and objective) requirements needed to enforce the CFC regime to wholly artificial entities in its case law[85]. Moreover, the verb *"commensurate"* and the wording *"which justify the income attributed to it"* were removed since they do not appear in the ECJ case law, and it would not be easy to apply them. Finally, the motive test (*"valid commercial reasons"*) was removed since it was based on subjective considerations of the economic reasons underlying the incorporation of a CFC. On the contrary, objective factors were introduced both to emphasize that the test was of a *"substantive"* nature[86] and to reach a political compromise between the nexus principle of the economic activity and the wholly artificial entity's principle[87]. In the final version[88], Article 7(2)(a) ATAD states that the categorical approach *"shall not apply where the controlled foreign company carries on a substantive economic activity supported by staff, equipment, assets and premises, as evidenced by relevant facts and circumstances"*[89]. The so-called "substance carve-out" acts as a "non-application clause" of the CFC categorical approach. Preamble number 12 of the directive explains it as follows *"To comply with the fundamental freedoms, the income categories should be combined with a substance carve-out aimed to limit, within the Union, the impact of the rules to cases where the CFC does not carry on a substantive economic activity."*[90] It is worth noting that the angle of the "substantive economic activity" underlying this exception is purely objective. The taxpayer must prove some objective requirements related to the existence of a real and actual economic activity supported by staff, equipment, assets, and premises and evidenced by relevant facts and circumstances. The "substance carve-out" of Article 7(2)(a) appears to leave aside the notion of "wholly artificial arrangements" already addressed by the ECJ in Cadbury Schweppes' case law which still represents a cornerstone in the application of anti-abuse provisions. However, although the two formulations appear to differ significantly, it is considered that, for the purposes of proving the new exemp-

---

85 CJEU, 12 September 2006, C-196/04, Cadbury Schweppes and Cadbury Schweppes Overseas, para. 65–70.
86 Council of the European Union, Brussels, 13 June 2016 (OR.en), Political agreement, 10067/16, FISC 101 ECOFIN 587.
87 A. Rigaut, Anti-Tax Avoidance Directive (2016/1164): New EU Policy Horizons, 56 *Eur. Taxn.* 11 (2016), Journal Articles & Opinion Pieces, IBFD.
88 See the general approach by the General Secretariat of the Council. The Member States reached political agreement on a final compromise text for the ATAD with no objections raised during the "silence procedure" that ended on 20 June 2016. W. Haslehner, G. Kofler, A. Rust, EU Tax Law and Policy in the 21st Century, Kluwer Law International, Eucotax European Taxation, (2016), Zuidpoolsingel, par. 14.02, note 83: the final version of the Netherlands Presidency compromise text (hereinafter 'the Final Netherlands Compromise Text') that contained the compromise reached in ECOFIN on 17 June 2016 was subject to the silence procedure, 10426/16, FISC 104 ECOFIN 628, and was formally adopted in ECOFIN of 12 July 2016, available at https://data.consilium.europa.eu/doc/document/ST-10426-2016-INIT/en/pdf.
89 ATAD Council Directive (EU) 2016/1164 of 12 July 2016, art. 7(2)(a) paragraph 2.
90 ATAD Council Directive (EU) 20146/1164 of 12 July 2016, Preamble 12.

tion, reference can still be made to the elaboration of both expressions of community derivation (see Court of Justice and, in particular, judgment C-196/04, Cadbury-Schweppes)[91]. It must, however, be considered that the new expression "substantive economic activity" would appear to be broader than the previous wording. It would enable the disapplication of the CFC rules even where the activity of the foreign entity does not consist in the industrial or commercial activity, but it only consists in collecting income such as dividends, royalties or interest (e.g. in the case of holding companies). In these cases, a lean structure would be consistent with its activity[92]. The objective test at issue seems to be more restrictive than that of the artificial entity since the parent company not only has to prove the absence of artificial economic activity (negative evidence) but also has to provide positive evidence that the entity conducts a substantial economic activity to which staff, equipment, assets, and premises are devoted whereby all are substantiated by facts and circumstances. So, uncertainties arise with respect to companies with a minimal structure such as holding and finance companies but which nevertheless conduct substantial business activity. According to part of the doctrine, for an intra-EU CFC, the substantive economic test can still be interpreted in light of the case law concerning "wholly artificial arrangements"[93]. In order to avoid uncertainties, the Netherlands has introduced a specific model in which the substance carve-out is conceived as a safe harbor provision[94] in which, if certain requirements related to corporate governance and the labour force are met, substantive economic activity is deemed to exist. Differently, Denmark has decided not to implement the substance carve-out as it is considered that the provision of a non-application clause may undermine the objectives of the CFC regime as outlined in the directive[95].

---

[91] M. Klokar & M. Riedl, Chapt. 5: 'Controlled Foreign Company Legislation in Austria' in: G.W. Kofler et al. (eds.), *Controlled Foreign Company Legislation*, (Amsterdam: IBFD, 2020), para. 6.

[92] S. Geringer, Criteria for the Application of Anti-Abuse Provisions to Holding Companies under CJEU Case Law: Their Significance in Interpreting and Applying ATAD Provisions, 60 *Eur. Taxn.* 10 (2020), Journal Articles & Opinion Pieces IBFD, par. 2.3.

[93] R. J. Danon, 'Some Observations on the Carve-Out Clause of Article 7(2)(a) of the ATAD with Regard to Third Countries' in: Pistone and Weber (eds.), *The Implementation of Anti-BEPS Rules in the EU: A comprehensive Study*, (Amsterdam:IBFD 2018), chap. 17.3.1. R.J. Danon, Chapter 10: EU Fiscal Protectionism versus Free Movement of Capital: The Case of the ATAD CFC Categorical Model in European Tax Integration: Law, Policy and Politics (P. Pistone ed., IBFD 2018), Books IBFD. C. Turley, D. Chamberlain, M. Petriccione, *A New Dawn for the International Tax System* (Amsterdam: IBFD, 2017), Part. 2, Ch. 8, par. 8.1.3.

[94] R.P.C. Adema, J.N. Bouwman & I.J.J. Burgers, Chapter 24, par. 2.2.4.: 'Controlled Foreign Company Legislation in the Netherlands' in: G.W. Kofler et al. (eds.), *Controlled Foreign Company Legislation*, (Amsterdam: IBFD, 2020).

[95] P. Koerver Schmidt, Chapter 14: 'Controlled Foreign Company Legislation in Denmark' in: G.W. Kofler et al. (eds.), *Controlled Foreign Company Legislation*, (Amsterdam: IBFD, 2020). P. Koerver Schmidt, Are the Danish CFC Rules in Conflict with the Freedom of Establishment? – An Analysis of the Danish CFC Regime for Companies in Light of ECJ Case Law, 54 *Eur. Taxn.* 1 (2014), Journal Articles & Opinion Pieces IBFD.

5.2. Third Countries

Pursuant to Article 7(2)(a), last paragraph, if the CFC is a resident of a third country that is not a party to the EEA[96] agreement, a Member State may refrain from applying the "substance carve-out" exemption. In other words, if a Member State does not grant the substance carve-out exception to the CFCs that are resident of an extra-EEA country, taxpayers may not disapply the CFC regime even though they can give evidence that the CFC exercises a substantive economic activity. In this regard, a parent company whose CFC is located in a third counties would not be enabled to invoke the disapplication clause even in the evidence of an active business thereof. Consequently, the income of the entity (or PE) would be taxed in the hands of the parent company under the categorical approach. In this context, the question arises as to whether the different treatment between intra EU/EEA and third countries' CFC disapplication clause entails an unjustified restriction of the fundamental freedoms protected by EU primary law. The question presupposes a characterization issue and, precisely, whether such a restriction is framed within the free movement of capital under Article 63 TFEU or as a restriction of the freedom of establishment under Article 49 TFEU in which its scope of protection is covered within the European Union and does not extend to third countries. In this second perspective, a difference in treatment between intra-EU/EEA and extra-EEA application of CFC rules could be compatible with EU primary law. Moreover, as CFC ownership rules require the control of at least 50% of the shares or profit of the entity, thus assuming the possibility of exercising a significant influence on the CFC so as to determine its activities, a restriction of the freedom of establishment would be involved. In the first perspective, a difference in the application of the substance carve-out between intra-EU/EEA and extra-EEA CFCs also entails an unjustified restriction to the free movement of capital in light of which different treatment between intra-EU and extra-EU CFCs would be unjustified and against the fundamental freedoms of the European Union. However, these restrictions to fundamental freedoms could find justifcation in the context of the effectiveness of fiscal supervision of extra-EEA CFCs which are commonly marked by a lack of exchange of information, and the need to avoid profit stripping and tax abuse[97]. The Netherlands extended the substance carve-out to third countries mainly to reduce the administrative burden on

---

96 The European Economic Area, abbreviated as EEA, consists of the Member States of the European Union (EU) and three countries of the European Free Trade Association (EFTA) (Iceland, Liechtenstein, and Norway; excluding Switzerland).
97 R. J. Danon, 'Some Observations on the Carve-Out Clause of Article 7(2)(a) of the ATAD with Regard to Third Countries' in: Pistone and Weber (eds.), *The Implementation of Anti-BEPS Rules in the EU: A comprehensive Study*, (Amsterdam:IBFD, 2018), chap. 17.5.2.3. C. HJI Panayi, 'The ATAD's CFC Rule and its Impact on the Existing Regimes of EU Member States' in: Pistone and Weber (eds.), *The Implementation of Anti-BEPS Rules in the EU: A comprehensive Study*, (Amsterdam:IBFD, 2018), chap. 16.3.

taxpayers and streamlining business operations but, above all, to consolidate the attractiveness as a tax residence of companies acting as group holding companies. Finland has also extended the substance carve-out to third countries but under two types of requirements: the first one is the presence of an agreement on the exchange of information; the second one is the conduct of specific production activities such as industrial and comparable production or service activities, shipping activities, sales, and marketing activities related to such activities[98]. Finally, Finland does not apply the substance carve-out to jurisdictions considered as non-cooperative and therefore included in the EU's black list[99]. These procedures also serve the purpose of allowing those third countries to be removed from blacklists created for the purposes of the non-application clause of the substance carve-out. With a technique opposite to that envisaged by Finland, Austrian legislation provides a list of non-substantive activities whose exercise by the CFC prevents it from benefiting of the substance carve-out. These activities include those of holding companies and conduit companies[100]. As an alternative, the Netherlands states that, if the foreign entity carries out substantive activity that could be demonstrated, this could lead to an exclusion of the CFC status even in low-tax jurisdictions.

5.3. The Burden of proof

The effective application of the "substance carve-out" requires streamlining the burden of proof, otherwise, any possible restriction on fundamental freedoms would risk not being proportional to the aims of the directive. In the first draft[101], the burden of proof was placed on the tax authorities in consideration of the anti-abuse nature of the CFC rule. The presidency compromise[102] provided a reversal

---

[98] K. Äimä & H. Lyyski, Chapter 15: Controlled Foreign Company Legislation in Finland in: G.W. Kofler et al. (eds.), *Controlled Foreign Company Legislation* (Amsterdam:IBFD, 2020). A. Tokola, The Implementation of the Controlled Foreign Company Rules in the EU Anti-Tax Avoidance Directive in Finland, Luxembourg and the Netherlands – The Effects on the Holding Company Structures of Finnish Groups, 72 *Bull. Intl. Taxn.* 3 (2018), Journal Articles & Opinion Pieces IBFD.

[99] Council conclusions on the revised EU list of non-cooperative jurisdictions for tax purposes (2021/C 66/10), Official Journal of the European Union 26.2.2021.

[100] In some cases, the ECJ's interpretation has considered the activities of holding companies engaged in mere asset management as not necessarily wholly artificial and
not reflecting economic reality. See Deister Holding AG and Juhler Holding A/S (C-504/16 and C-613/16), paras. 64–73 and 79. S. Geringer, Criteria for the Application of Anti-Abuse Provisions to Holding Companies under ECJ Case Law: Their Significance in Interpreting and Applying ATAD Provisions, 60 *Eur. Taxn.* 10 (2020), Journal Articles & Opinion Pieces IBFD, par. 2.3.

[101] European Commission, Proposal for a Council Directive laying down rules against tax avoidance practices that directly affect the functioning of the internal market, Brussels, 28.1.2016, COM(2016) 26 final, 2016/0011 (CNS).

[102] Council of the European Union, Proposal for a Council Directive laying down rules against tax avoidance practices that directly affect the functioning of the internal market – Presidency compromise, Brussels, 24 May 2016, FISC 83, ECOFIN 498, 9431/16 and Preamble n. 13.

of the burden of proof on the taxpayer who was required to give evidence of the valid commercial reasons that justify the set-up of the CFC carrying on economic activity supported by consistent and appropriate staff, equipment, assets, and premises. Moreover, the adoption of white[103]-, grey-, or black-lists of third countries was introduced so as to graduate the burden of proof according to the location of the CFC within the EU/EEA or in third countries. The reversed *onus* on the taxpayer was assessed as legally sound[104]. Furthermore, this approach was consistent with the recommendations of the BEPS report which appears to propose a reversed burden of proof to demonstrate a sufficient level of substance, and that the CFC under analysis be not wholly artificial[105]. The burden of proof was ultimately revised by the council whose major aim was to promote the effective cooperation between taxpayers and financial authorities in the awareness that only transparency in the exchange of information could ultimately enable the pursuit of the objectives targeted by the categorical approach, namely, the anti-deferral, anti-abuse, and anti-tax avoidance goals. The wording of the final provision does not explicitly specify who bears the burden of proof of the existence of the "substantive economic activity". As pointed out in Preamble number 12 "*It is important that tax administrations and taxpayers cooperate to gather the relevant facts and circumstances to determine whether the carve-out rule is to apply*". It can be inferred that the council aimed at promoting cooperation between the taxpayer and the tax authorities to collect evidence about facts and circumstances to determine whether the CFC carries a substantive economic activity. Only through the effective collaboration between the parties it can it be possible to gather grounded evidence about staff, equipment, assets, and premises of the CFC[106]. So, the final developments of the rule espose the *onus* lying on both the taxpayer and the tax authorities. Notwithstanding the content of Preamble number 12, Austria and the Netherlands have designed the burden of proof to be on the taxpayer[107].

---

[103] Sweden adopted a system of a so-called basic whitelist and secondary whitelist in order to exclude certain jurisdictions from being characterized as low-tax countries regardless of the actual tax rates that are normally applied. I.M. de Groot & B. Larking, Implementation of Controlled Foreign Company Rules under the EU Anti-Tax Avoidance Directive (2016/1164), 59 *Eur. Taxn.* 6 (2019), Journal Articles & Opinion Pieces IBFD, par. 4.4.2.3

[104] General Secretariat of the Council, General approach, Proposal for a Council Directive laying down rules against tax avoidance practices that directly affect the functioning of the internal market, Brussels, 24 May 2016, OR.en, 9432/16, FISC 84, ECOFIN 499, par. III – Key Open Issues, point 20.

[105] BEPS, Action 3 Final report, par. 1.2.2, point 22, p. 17.

[106] W. Haslehner, G. Kofler, A. Rust, EU Tax Law and Policy in the 21st Century, Kluwer Law International, Eucotax European Taxation, (2016), Zuidpoolsingel, par. 14.02, p. 327.

[107] R.P.C. Adema, J.N. Bouwman & I.J.J. Burgers, Chapter 24: 'Controlled Foreign Company Legislation in the Netherlands' in Controlled Foreign Company Legislation (G.W. Kofler et al. eds., IBFD 2020), para. 2.2.4.

6. Final considerations

Exhaustive treatment of all of the implications related to the implementation of the categorical approach proposed by the ATAD directive is not easily reacheable due to the multifaceted way Member States have implemented it. Nevertheless, it can be inferred that Model A combined with the option of Model B constitutes an efficient and reasoned attempt to achieve the objectives of the directive, namely, the effect of reattributing the income of a low-taxed controlled subsidiary to its parent company. However, a list of passive income based on a characterization on legal grounds still may entail some administrative burdens and possible risks of double taxation for which implications have not yet been thoroughly addressed.

Taxable income under Article 7(2)(b) of the EU Anti-Tax Avoidance Directive

Jovdat Mammadov

1. The OECD BEPS and the EU ATAD
2. The Relevance of CJEU Case Law to Model B (Transactional Approach)
3. The CFC Income Definition under Model B (Transactional Approach)
4. The Relevance of the EU Fundamental Freedoms to Model B (Transactional Approach)
5. The CFC Profits Attributable to Activities in EU Member State
6. Conclusion

1. The OECD BEPS and the EU ATAD

In response to challenges presented by the OECD 2013 Report on addressing BEPS, the OECD 2013 BEPS Action Plan recognized several sources of BEPS concerns. This culminated into the "OECD 2015 BEPS Final report on Action 3 – Designing Effective CFC Rules" which provided recommendations in the form of six building blocks of effective CFC rules. Thus, CFC rules aim to prevent artificial profit shifting and long-term deferral of taxation. The ATAD builds upon the OECD BEPS Project by closing existing loopholes in EU rules and forms part of a larger anti-tax avoidance package. The ATAD aims to provide a minimum level of protection for the EU internal market, strengthen protection against aggressive tax planning, and ensure a harmonized and coordinated approach in the EU to implementation of certain measures against BEPS. The ATAD came into force on 1 January 2019 and set out minimum standards across a range of anti-avoidance measures that include detailed rules in relation to CFCs within the EU.

Since CFC rules were successfully pioneered in 1962 in United States, many jurisdictions have followed in their footsteps on CFC regimes. However, due to certain design features, many of existing CFC rules were often not able to tackle BEPS risks effectively. Prior to the ATAD, some of the EU Member States already had experience with CFC regimes.

The ATAD is a result of compromise between fundamentally different views from EU Member States. Thus, it provides them with certain flexibility to implement CFC rules which allows them to choose between two approaches: (1) a standard rule – CFC income (categorical approach) under Article 7(2)(a) – called "Model A"; and (2) an alternative rule – CFC income (transactional approach) under Article 7(2)(b) – called "Model B". EU Member States also have the option to exclude certain CFCs. In other words, they can choose either Model A (categorical approach) or Model B (transactional approach) to determine CFC income.[1] Thus, the ATAD introduced a general rule to the tax base of EU Member States for assessing the tax liabilities of their taxpayers.

The standard CFC rule (Model A) is based on the provisions of paragraphs 1, 2(a), and 3 of Article 7 of the ATAD. Thus, Model A (categorical approach) under Article 7(2)(a) of ATAD is focused on "specific types of income [profit]" (called "passive income categories") that are considered to raise BEPS concerns. For further information on Model A (categorical approach) under Article 7(2)(a) of the ATAD, the reader is referred to existing overviews.[2]

The alternative CFC rule (Model B) is based on the provisions of paragraphs 1, 2(b), and 4 of Article 7 of the ATAD. Thus, Model B (transactional approach) under

---

1   EC Decision, 2019/1352 of 2 April 2019 on the UK's State aid, recital 43.
2   Carmela Zenzola, Taxable income under option 7(2)(a) of the ATAD.

Article 7(2)(b) of the ATAD is focused on "the level of activity [operation] in the CFC tested by reference to SPF/KERT [functions] performed within the [company]"[3] and requires attributing undistributed income (chargeable profits) of a CFC to a controlling company "from non-genuine arrangements which have been put in place for the essential purpose of obtaining a tax advantage". In other words, the controlling company must include that undistributed income (chargeable profits) of its CFC that is derived from SPF/KERT functions caried out in the controlling EU Member States into its taxable base that is liable for a CFC charge (tax). However, the Model B (transactional approach) is not subject to a "substance carve-out clause [substance escape clause]" because it is in compliance with the EU fundamental freedoms, and thus "it does not restrict the freedom of establishment".[4]

At present, nine EU Member States, among them Belgium (2017), Cyprus (2019), Estonia (2000), Hungary (1997), Ireland (2019), Latvia (2019 for companies), Luxembourg (2019), Malta (2019), Slovakia (2019), and the former EU Member State – the United Kingdom (1984) opted for Model B (transactional approach) under Article 7(2)(b) ATAD, while one country, the Netherlands (2007), chose the combination of two models (Model A and Model B).[5] However, seven out of nine EU Member States that opted for Model B (transactional approach), among them Belgium, Cyprus, Ireland, Latvia (for companies), Luxembourg, Malta, and Slovakia, did not have a CFC regime until the ATAD made it mandatory beginning 1 January 2019. Interestingly, Switzerland – a country surrounded by EU Member States for which economic and trade agreements with the EU are governed through acceptance of certain aspects of EU legislation – does not have a CFC regime to date.[6]

Next, EU Member States may choose, under Article 7(4) CFC rule/SAAR of ATAD (called "safeguards clause"), to apply two de minimis exemptions for Model B (transactional approach) under Article 7(2)(b) ATAD. These exemptions protect taxpayers from a CFC charge (tax) in situations when the CFC has (1) "low accounting profits" (called "profit escape") and (2) "a low profit margin" (called "costs escape"). At present, five EU Member States, among them Cyprus, Hungary, Ireland, Luxembourg (except for non-trading income of no more than EUR 75000), Malta, and the former EU Member State – the United Kingdom that opted for Model B (transactional approach) apply both profit escape and costs escape exemptions. Further, two EU Member States, namely, Estonia and Latvia, only apply a profit escape exemption with accounting profits of no more than EUR 750000. However, three EU Member States, namely, Belgium, the Netherlands, and Slovakia, do not apply any exemptions.[7]

---

3   Francisco Alvarez, The ATAD CFC – All Roads Lead to Cadbury Schweppes, Kluwer ITB, 2020.
4   EC Decision, 2019/1352 of 2 April 2019 on the UK's State aid, recital 172.
5   PwC, Overview of the implementation of the ATAD into EU MSs' domestic tax laws, PwC NL TKC, 2020.
6   https://qdd.oecd.org/data/CFC/ALL.
7   PwC, Overview of the implementation of the ATAD into EU MSs' domestic tax laws, PwC NL TKC, 2020.

This study relies on CFC rules from Ireland which adopted a CFC regime in 2019 and the United Kingdom which adopted CFC regime in 1984 for assimilation of complex information on CFC regimes and interpretation of taxable income under Article 7(2)(b) ATAD. Though CFC legislation varies across EU Member States, CFC regimes from Ireland and the United Kingdom are highly representative and important for the design of this study because both countries adopted the alternative CFC rule (Model B) under Article 7(2)(b) ATAD. For this reason, the CFC regime of Ireland illustrates a typical example of EU Member States that opted for Model B (transactional approach) to maintain their competitive corporate tax system with a view of pursuing economic strategies of attracting foreign investment. The United Kingdom's CFC regime is equally important for this study because the United Kingdom has longstanding experience in the application of CFC rules as it was the third European country, after Germany (1972) and France (1980), that introduced a CFC regime into its legislation in 1984.[8] Furthermore, the United Kingdom was an EU Member State that insisted on flexibility in relation to CFC rules that would allow EU Member States to design their own rules consistent with the OECD anti-BEPS recommendations, a result of which was the inclusion of Model B (transactional approach) in the ATAD.[9] Despite the United Kingdom's exit from the EU as of 31 January 2020, its CFC rules remain a highly relevant source of information and could thus be studied by those EU Member States that do not have or have little experience with Model B (transactional approach). This study is not intended to produce a comparative analysis of CFC regimes of all of the EU Member States that opted for Model B (transactional approach) which would go beyond the scope and the purpose of it, and thus the reader is referred to existing overviews.[10]

Instead, this study undertakes a review of CFC rules in relation to taxable income under Model B (transactional approach) of Article 7(2)(b) ATAD as a contribution to discussion on their interpretation and application under the ATAD, albeit some EU Member States may have their peculiarities. Since the ATAD CFC rules apply EU-wide, this study, insofar as is possible, interprets these rules not by reference to a particular national CFC regime but rather by reference to general principles of CFC rules common to most EU Member States that opted for Model B (transactional approach). In doing so, this study reviews relevant CJEU case law in order to understand the way that the CJEU-defined two-pronged test (an objective and a subjective test) helps to determine abuse of law under the GAAR and the CFC rule/SAAR (Model B) of the ATAD. Further, this study offers important insights into Model B (transactional approach). It goes on to analyse in detail the definition of taxable income under Model B (transactional approach) and ex-

---

8   Sebastian Dueñas, CFC Rules Around the World, Tax Foundation, 2019.
9   Anzhela Cédelle, The EU ATAD: A UK Perspective, British Tax Review, 2016.
10 Georg Kofler et al., Controlled Foreign Company Legislation, IBFD, 2020.

plains differences between (1) a non-genuine (artificial) arrangements test and (2) the essential purposes test under Article 7(2)(b) in conjunction with Article 6 of the ATAD. In particular, it addresses the issue on whether Model B (transactional approach) is in compliance with the Cadbury Schweppes criteria. Furthermore, it describes and analyses five basic steps through the application of the SPF/KERT test under the AOA to help to understand and determine a CFC's undistributed income (chargeable profits) arising from non-genuine arrangements that are attributable to activities in a related EU Member State. It concludes that Model B (transactional approach) of Article 7(2)(b) ATAD constitutes a proportionate response to BEPS risks.

2. The Relevance of CJEU Case Law to Model B (Transactional Approach)

CJEU case law plays an important role in the application of the ATAD and helps to interpret the key concepts, especially the concept of "wholly artificial arrangement", with regard to abuse of law (as recognized in literature by many commentators)[11] because both the CFC rule/SAAR and the GAAR in the ATAD contain an objective and a subjective test similar to the PPT/OECD. Further, the review of CJEU case law helps to understand the way to apply its two-pronged test (an objective and a subjective test) in order to analyse the structure of Model B (transactional approach) under Article 7(2)(b) ATAD and determine conditions that constitute abuse of law under the CFC rule/SAAR and the GAAR of the ATAD.

In this regard, when defining the elements of abuse in EU law, the CJEU ruled, for the first time, in Emsland-Stärke, that the abuse of rights consists of the two-pronged test:

> (1) "a combination of objective circumstances in which, despite formal observance of the conditions laid down by the Community [EU] rules, the purpose of those rules has not been achieved", and (2) "a subjective element consisting in the intention to obtain an advantage from the Community [EU] rules by creating artificially the conditions laid down for obtaining it".[12]

The CJEU applied its two-pronged test in tax matters for the first time in the Halifax case in which it ruled that two mutually depending elements are required to constitute an abusive practice:

> (1) "notwithstanding formal application of the conditions laid down by the relevant provisions of the [EU law] and the national legislation transposing it, [the transactions must] result in the accrual of a tax advantage the grant of which would be contrary to

---

11   Błażej Kuźniacki, The CJEU case-law relevant to the GAAR under the ATAD, University of Bologna Law Review, 2019.
12   CJEU, 14 December 2000, C-110/99, Emsland-Stärke, para 52, 53.

the purpose of those provisions" (objective test), and (2) "it must also be apparent from a number of objective factors that the essential aim of the transactions concerned is to obtain a tax advantage" (subjective test).[13]

Since then, the CJEU remains consistent in its views on how to determine the concept of abuse in EU law. This is evident from the recent CJEU ruling on the Danish Beneficial Ownership cases in which the CJEU, by examining the issue concerning the constituent elements of the concept of abuse in EU law, reaffirmed its previous views that proof of an abusive practice (abuse of rights) requires performing the two-pronged test (an objective and a subjective test). For this reason, the CJEU explained that "[e]xamination of a set of facts is therefore needed to establish whether the constituent elements of an abusive practice are present, and in particular whether economic operators have carried out purely formal or artificial transactions devoid of any economic and commercial justification, with the essential aim of benefiting from an improper advantage".[14]

Thus, the CJEU-defined two-pronged test is the standard for determining abuse of law in the area of EU taxation. In view of the review of CJEU case law, some commentators suggest that the CJEU confirmed "a general legal prohibition of abuse [of law], yet it has not prescribed a normative standard for assessment in the form of lying down specific criteria as to when abuse of rights is to be presumed". However, the CJEU, through its case law, developed certain criteria that the same commentator categorizes into two relevant case groups. In the first category of cases, especially regarding Article 49 (right of establishment) and Article 63 (free movement of capital) of the TFEU, the CJEU "departs from a narrow understanding of abuse [of law as referred to] the Cadbury Schweppes criteria". This category of cases defines that an infringement on the EU fundamental freedoms by "a national tax burdening measure is justified when": (1) "there is a wholly artificial design"; (2) "the fundamental freedom is formally applicable, but its original objective is frustrated"; and, (3) "the tax subject strives exclusively for a tax advantage". The CJEU, in the second category of cases, "follows instead a broad understanding of abuse [of law as referred to] the Halifax criteria". This category of cases defines that "a tax advantage can be refused by [EU MS] when": (1) "the scope of the EU secondary law is formally opened"; but (2) "the tax advantage granted is incompatible with ratio legis [the policy reason and underlying purpose] of [that EU] secondary law"; and (3) "essentially [not exclusively] a tax advantage is intended". In this context, this commentator takes the position that the design of Article 6 (GAAR) in the ATAD is based on the broad Halifax criteria.[15]

---

13 CJEU, 21 February 2006, C-255/02, Halifax plc et al., para 74, 75.
14 CJEU, 26 February 2019, Joined Cases C-115/16, C-118/16, C-119/16, C-299/16, N Luxembourg 1 & Others v Skatteministeriet, para 124, 125, 139; Joined Cases C-116/16, C-117/16, Skatteministeriet v T Danmark & Y Denmark Aps, para 97, 98, 114.
15 Helene Hayden, A rule to catch them all, Völkerrechtsblog, 2019.

On this point, this study notes that questions arise on what is the design of Article 7(2)(b) CFC rule/SAAR of the ATAD and whether Model B (transactional approach) is in compliance with the narrow Cadbury Schweppes criteria. For this reason, this study reviews in detail the definition of taxable income under Model B (transactional approach) of Article 7(2)(b) ATAD through the prism of the CJEU's two lines of jurisdiction (the Cadbury Schweppes criteria – a narrow understanding of abuse of law vs. the Halifax criteria – a broad understanding of abuse of law).

3. The CFC Income Definition under Model B (Transactional Approach)

The structure of Model B (transactional approach) under Article 7(2)(b) ATAD is comprised of five core elements. These five core elements are assimilated from other authors.[16] However, this study uses the mentioned classification of the structure of Model B (transactional approach) to examine and interpret each element of it through the application of the concepts developed by CJEU case law, the SAAR/GAAR/ATAD, and the PPT/OECD. This study examines the objective and subjective elements of the CFC rule/SAAR in conjunction with the GAAR/ATAD under the CJEU-defined two-pronged test because the GAAR/ATAD acts as backstops to the CFC rule/SAAR.

1. Model B of CFC income (transactional approach)

requires "two cumulative conditions" to exist for a CFC charge (tax) to arise: "the arrangement (1) must be a non-genuine arrangement; and (2) must have been put into place for the essential purpose of obtaining a tax advantage".[17] This requirement is in line with the analysis of the concept of abuse of EU law under the ATAD introduced initially by the advocate general in the Danish Beneficial Ownership Cases. In this regard, the advocate general, by making reference to CJEU well-established case law, identified "two mutually contingent elements" of an abuse of rights which are: (1) "wholly artificial arrangements", and (2) the "circumvention of tax laws that is also made achievable by arrangements that exist in commercial life" by suggesting that "[s]uch cases may be the more frequent" and thus explicitly covered by the ATAD.[18]

For the above reasons, this study notes that whether the mentioned two cumulative conditions exist is established by application of the CJEU-defined two-pronged test (an objective and a subjective test). As a result, the two-pronged test allows determining whether an abuse of rights exists. In other words, this study adapts a for-

---

16 Francisco Alvarez, The ATAD CFC – All Roads Lead to Cadbury Schweppes, Kluwer ITB, 2020.
17 Ibid.
18 CJEU, 01 March 2018, Case C-115/16, Opinion of Advocate General, N Luxembourg 1 v Skatteministeriet, para 62, 63, 64; Case C-116/16, Skatteministeriet v T Danmark, para 50, 51, 52.

mula "comprised of three core elements: (1) an arrangement, (2) a tax advantage, and (3) abuse" developed by some commentators for the GAAR/ATAD for the interpretation of both the CFC rule/SAAR and the GAAR in the ATAD.[19]

2. Model B of CFC income (transactional approach)

requires determining whether an arrangement under the first condition is a non-genuine arrangement which is established through the application of an objective test that is "centred on the level of activity in the CFC and tested by reference to SPF/KERT [functions] performed within the [company]". This is "a proportionate" test because only the income relevant to SPF/KERT functions carried out by the controlling company "is attributed to the controlling [jurisdiction]" in line with Article 8(2) (Computation of CFC income) of the ATAD.[20]

In Article 7(2)(b) CFC rule/SAAR of the ATAD, the objective test is referred to as "non-genuine arrangements" and defined in a narrow scope as "to the extent that the entity or permanent establishment would not own the assets or would not have undertaken the risks which generate all, or part of, its income if it were not controlled by a company where the significant people functions, which are relevant to those assets and risks, are carried out and are instrumental in generating the controlled company's income".[21] In the ATAD CFC rule/SAAR, the purpose of the objective test is to determine whether the benefits (tax advantage) obtained under specifically targeted CFC rules under Article 7(1) of the ATAD are considered abusive even though the formal requirements are met and whether obtaining the benefits in circumstances of non-genuine arrangements will be contrary to the object and purpose of CFC rules. For this reason, the objective analysis includes: (1) all persons involved in putting the arrangements in place; (2) all circumstances of the arrangements on case-by-case basis; and considers (3) the object and purpose of a relevant provision in a particular abuse situation.

In this context, Article 6(1) and (2) GAAR of the ATAD defines non-genuine arrangements in a wider scope "to the extent that they are not put into place for valid commercial reasons which reflect economic reality". In the ATAD GAAR, the purpose of the objective test is to undertake an analysis of "all relevant facts and circumstances" surrounding the arrangements and determine whether the benefits (tax advantage) obtained in these circumstances are considered abusive even though the formal conditions are fulfilled and "that defeats the object or purpose of the applicable tax law".[22] Here, "the applicable tax law" is both EU law and national laws of EU Member States. It is noteworthy that the ATAD provides for a GAAR that follows the Halifax criteria – a broad understanding of abuse of

---

19 Błażej Kuźniacki, The CJEU case-law relevant to the GAAR under the ATAD, University of Bologna Law Review, 2019.
20 Francisco Alvarez, The ATAD CFC – All Roads Lead to Cadbury Schweppes, Kluwer ITB, 2020.
21 EU Council Directive, 2016/1164 of 12 July 2016, Article 7(2)(b).
22 Ibid., Article 6(1) and (2) (GAAR).

law.²³ Both Article 6(1) and (2) GAAR and Article 7(2)(b) CFC rule/SAAR in the ATAD refer to "non-genuine" instead of "artificial" arrangements. However, some commentators take the position that, despite the ATAD's deviation from the CJEU's terminology, there is no substantial difference between "artificial" and "non-genuine" concepts.²⁴

The CJEU, in Cadbury Schweppes, developed its criteria of "wholly artificial arrangement" in order to apply a uniform abuse of law concept in different areas of tax law.²⁵ In this regard, the CJEU, in Cadbury Schweppes, laid down very similar criteria to the Emsland-Stärke and Halifax cases in which the objective test requires determining that the CFC was involved in a genuine economic activity in order to be exempted from CFC rules. For this reason, the objective test

> finding must be based on objective factors, which are ascertainable by third parties with regard, in particular, to the extent to which the CFC physically exists in terms of premises, staff and equipment" and "[i]f checking those factors leads to the finding that the CFC is a fictitious establishment not carrying out any genuine economic activity in the territory of the host [EU MS], the creation of that CFC must be regarded as having the characteristics of a wholly artificial arrangement.²⁶

Thus, these two mutually depending elements are required to exist in order to establish the non-genuine (artificial) arrangement. Moreover, the advocate general, in Cadbury Schweppes, defined the objective test as consisting of three relevant criteria: (1) "the degree of physical presence of the subsidiary in the host State"; (2) "the genuine nature of the activity provided by the subsidiary"; and, (3) "the economic value of that activity with regard to the parent [controlling] company and the entire group".²⁷

In this regard, the CJEU's ruling on Cadbury Schweppes implies that taxpayers are required to prove the genuine economic activity on the basis of objective factors that relate to the CFC, among other features, to the real substance (physical existence).²⁸

Relevantly, CJEU ruled in Cadbury Schweppes that the two-pronged test applies to determine "the existence of a wholly artificial arrangement" and opined that "in order to find that there is such an arrangement there must be [...] objective circumstances showing that, despite formal observance of the conditions laid

---

23 Helene Hayden, A rule to catch them all, Völkerrechtsblog, 2019.
24 Ashley Bergmans in Preventing Treaty Abuse, The PPT: Comparison with EU-GAAR Initiatives, 2016.
25 Michael Lang, Cadbury Schweppes' Line of Case Law from the Member States' Perspective, 2011.
26 CJEU, 12 September 2006, C-196/04, Cadbury Schweppes plc & Cadbury Schweppes Overseas Ltd, para 67, 68.
27 CJEU, 02 May 2006, C-196/04, Opinion of Advocate-General, Cadbury Schweppes plc & Cadbury Schweppes Overseas Ltd, para 111.
28 CJEU, 12 September 2006, C-196/04, Cadbury Schweppes plc & Cadbury Schweppes Overseas Ltd, Case Law IBFD.

down by Community [EU] law, the objective pursued by freedom of establishment has not been achieved".[29]

Thus, the interpretation of the concept of "wholly artificial arrangement" has been frequently debated among commentators since it was explained by the CJEU in Cadbury Schweppes. However, it can be observed that the CJEU tends to refine the concept of "wholly artificial arrangement" in recent case law. In this regard, in X GmbH, it ruled that

> the concept of 'wholly artificial arrangement' cannot necessarily be limited to merely the indications, referred to in [...] [Cadbury Schweppes criteria] [...] that the establishment of a company does not reflect economic reality, since the artificial creation of the conditions required in order to escape taxation in a [EU MS] improperly or enjoy a tax advantage in that [EU MS] improperly can take several forms [...]. However, that [wholly artificial arrangement] concept is also capable of covering [...] any scheme which has as its primary objective or one of its primary objectives the artificial transfer of the profits.[30]

Furthermore, the CJEU, in the Danish Beneficial Ownership cases, interpreted the concept of abuse of law in a wider scope compared to its previous case law, for instance, in the Halifax and Cadbury Schweppes cases, wherein the CJEU ruled that "[a] group of companies may be regarded as being an artificial arrangement where it is not set up for reasons that reflect economic reality, its structure is purely one of form and its principal objective or one of its principal objectives is to obtain a tax advantage running counter to the aim or purpose of the applicable tax law".

For this reason, the CJEU specifies that

> [t]he presence of a certain number of indications may demonstrate that there is an abuse of rights, in so far as those indications are objective and consistent". And, thus "[s]uch indications can include, in particular, the existence of conduit companies which are without economic justification and the purely formal nature of the structure of the group of companies, the financial arrangements and the loans.[31]

In this context, the CJEU explained in the Danish Beneficial Ownership cases that

> [w]hilst the pursuit by a taxpayer of the tax regime most favourable for him cannot, as such, set up a general presumption of fraud or abuse [by referring to the Cadbury Schweppes case], the fact remains that such a taxpayer cannot enjoy a right or advantage arising from EU law where the transaction at issue is purely artificial economically

---

29 CJEU, 12 September 2006, C-196/04, Cadbury Schweppes plc & Cadbury Schweppes Overseas Ltd, para 64.
30 CJEU, 26 February 2019, C-135/17, X GmbH v. Finanzamt Stuttgart – Körperschaften, para 84.
31 CJEU, 26 February 2019, Joined Cases C-115/16, C-118/16, C-119/16, C-299/16, N Luxembourg 1 & Others v Skatteministeriet, para 127, 132, 139; Joined Cases C-116/16, C-117/16, Skatteministeriet v T Danmark & Y Denmark Aps, para 100, 105, 114.

and is designed to circumvent the application of the legislation of the [EU MS] concerned.³²

In this regard, some commentators argue that the CJEU considered the concept of a "wholly artificial arrangement" in a narrow scope in Cadbury Schweppes for which "the prohibition of abuse of rights could only apply in situations deprived of any economic substance, such as letterbox companies". However, the recent CJEU case law implies that "even situations involving companies with more economic substance could constitute abuse". In other words, CJEU case law shows that an arrangement can still be abusive regardless of the amount of economic substance in a company. Thus, this commentator notes that "[t]he requirement of artificiality […] refers to the arrangements put into place, the analysis of which should reveal a reasonable proportion between the volume of economic activity and the importance of the profits that are taxable".³³

By the same token, other commentators opine that, while the CJEU considered the concept of "wholly artificial arrangements which do not reflect economic reality" in Cadbury Schweppes, its recent rulings on the Danish Beneficial Ownership cases put "the emphasis […] on the transactions […] to be considered 'economically' in order to establish whether it is purely artificial". The same commentator suggests that the CJEU "has moved away from considering the transactions in light of their 'legal substance', i.e., as an evidence-based characterisation of the transaction and its legal relations, and that [CJEU] is now instead considering the transactions in light of their 'economic substance', i.e., the commercial purpose behind the form". Thus, the CJEU refined the concept of abuse in EU law in the Danish Beneficial Ownership cases and confirmed that "it is possible to have an arrangement which is not wholly artificial in terms of legal substance, and which can still represent an abuse of EU law if it is put in place with the essential aim of obtaining a tax advantage, i.e., because it lacks economic substance".³⁴ Following on the Danish Beneficial Ownership cases, some commentators note that abuse of law could be proven, despite valid economic arguments, if one of the principal objectives of the arrangement is to obtain a tax advantage that is in contradiction with the aim or purpose of the applicable tax law. Thus, "the tax objectives may outweigh the valid economic arguments and abuse of law may apply".³⁵

---

32 CJEU, 26 February 2019, Joined Cases C-115/16, C-118/16, C-119/16, C-299/16, N Luxembourg 1 & Others v Skatteministeriet, para 109; Joined Cases C-116/16, C-117/16, Skatteministeriet v T Danmark & Y Denmark Aps, para 81.
33 Edoardo Traversa, The prohibition of abuse of rights in European Tax Law: sacrificing the internal market for the fight against BEPS? Studi Tributari Europei, 2020.
34 Susi Baerentzen, Danish Cases on the Use of Holding Companies for Cross-Border Dividends and Interest – A New Test to Disentangle Abuse from Real Economic Activity? World Tax Journal, 2020.
35 Patrick Schrievers, CJEU rules in Danish cases on beneficial ownership and treaty abuse, NovioTax, 2019.

This study concurs with the opinions of the commentators mentioned above and suggests that an assessment of the genuine character of an arrangement under the CJEU's economic substance analysis (test) to determine abusive practices may be more complex and go beyond the narrow criteria described under the Cadbury Schweppes criteria, although, it is assumed that such an assessment has to be made in conformity to the EU fundamental freedoms.

Thus, in relation to Article 7(2)(b) CFC rule/SAAR of the ATAD, a company is considered to have "non-genuine arrangements" in place when: (1) "the CFC would not own the assets or bear the risks which generate the undistributed income but for the relevant activities [SPF/KERT in EU MS]" of the controlling company undertaken in relation to those assets and risks; and (2) "it [would] be reasonable to consider that the relevant activities [SPF/KERT in EU MS of the controlling company were] instrumental in generating that income for the CFC". For the above reason, the term "arrangement" is understood to have a wide scope that includes "the various actions and activities" with a view to identify "a non-genuine arrangement". In this context, the arrangement means (1) "any transaction, action, course of action, course of conduct, scheme, plan or proposal", (2) "any agreement, arrangement, understanding, promise or undertaking whether express or implied and whether or not enforceable or intended to be enforceable by legal proceedings", and, (3) "any series of or combination of the circumstances described above". Its broad definition is regarded "to cover all types of non-genuine activities" linked to the CFC whether related to (1) "the acquisition and holding of assets by the CFC" or (2) "the management of business risks related to its assets by the CFC". In this context, the term "reasonable to consider" is regarded as "an objective test" which, based on "all the relevant facts and circumstances", would reasonably establish that "the relevant activities [SPF/KERT in EU MS] of the controlling company were instrumental in generating the income". In this regard, the term "instrumental" is referred to as "the relevant activities [SPF/KERT in EU MS]" of the controlling company that provided "a means" by which the profits (income) were received by the CFC. For this reason, "the relevant activities" are regarded as SPF/KERT functions carried out by persons in an EU Member State on behalf of the CFC which relate to: (1) "the legal or beneficial ownership of the [CFC's] assets"; or (2) "the assumption and management of the [CFC's] risks". Thus, to determine whether an arrangement is genuine, SPF/KERT functions "relevant for the income-generating assets and risks undertaken by the CFC must be taken into account".[36] For further information on the SPF/KERT analysis, the reader is referred to the section of this study on "The CFC Profits Attributable to Activities in EU Member State".

---

36   Tax and Duty Manual, CFC Rules, Part 35b-01-01, Revenue, Irish Tax and Customs, February 2021.

3. Model B of CFC income (transactional approach)

requires determining whether an arrangement was inspired by "obtaining a tax advantage" under a second condition that is established through the application of a subjective test and requires the term "obtaining a tax advantage" to carry the same meaning and interpretation for Article 7(2)(b) CFC rule/SAAR and Article 6(1) GAAR of the ATAD.[37]

With regard to the subjective test, some commentators opine that "intentions should [not] indeed play a role as an additional requirement in order to assume that an arrangement is 'wholly artificial', because [t]aking into consideration the object and purpose of a law should be a regular part of any interpretation process". For this reason, the commentator concludes that "[i]rrespective of possible intentions, attention should be paid to the object and purpose of the law under consideration", and thus "the relevance of the subjective criterion [becomes] controversial".[38] Similarly, other commentators suggest that the assessment of the taxpayer's intention under the subjective test is a debatable topic because "[a]fter all, they are driven by the most economically rational choice in the sense that they will choose the most economically efficient option if given a range of different alternatives". Thus, the same commentator argues that "the subjective element of the abuse test […] will automatically be met, because the intention to save taxes will always be there and that purpose will always be significant for the corporation".[39] Despite this debate in literature, the CJEU remains consistent in its view that the subjective test is one of the constituent elements for establishing an abuse of rights in EU law, and thus it is directly connected to the objective test.

In Article 7(2)(b) CFC rule/SAAR of ATAD, the subjective test is defined to "have been put in place for the essential purpose of obtaining a tax advantage" whereas, for Article 6(1) GAAR of the ATAD, the subjective test is referred to as "having been put into place for the main purpose or one of the main purposes of obtaining a tax advantage"[40] although it does not define the meaning of "the main purpose". Here, the purpose of the subjective test is to determine whether an arrangement was inspired by obtaining the benefits (tax advantage) of "the applicable tax law". Further, the meaning of "the main purpose or one of the main purposes" in Article 6(1) GAAR of the ATAD appears to be wider in scope compared to the meaning of "the essential purpose" in Article 7(2)(b) CFC rule/SAAR of the ATAD. In this context, the meaning of "the essential purpose" implies that the taxpayer's intention was central (principal or predominant) to the nature of the

---

37 Francisco Alvarez, The ATAD CFC – All Roads Lead to Cadbury Schweppes, Kluwer ITB, 2020.
38 Michael Lang, Cadbury Schweppes' Line of Case Law from the Member States' Perspective, 2011.
39 Susi Baerentzen, Danish Cases on the Use of Holding Companies for Cross-Border Dividends and Interest – A New Test to Disentangle Abuse from Real Economic Activity? World Tax Journal, 2020.
40 EU Council Directive, 2016/1164 of 12 July 2016, Article 6(1) (GAAR) and Article 7(2)(b) (CFC rule).

arrangement.[41] For this reason, identifying the level of that intention (purpose) is important for applying the subjective test in finding abuse of EU law.[42] On this point, some commentators note that the difference between the term "the essential purpose" under Article 7(2)(b) CFC rule/SAAR and the term "the main purpose or one of the main purposes" under Article 6(1) GAAR in the ATAD of the arrangement is "a threshold issue". Thus, this difference does not create ambiguity for the term "obtaining a tax advantage." On the contrary, this difference "indicates that the threshold requirement in [Article 7(2)(b) CFC rule/SAAR of ATAD] is higher than the threshold requirement [in Article 6(1) GAAR of ATAD]". As a result of this reasoning, the same commentator suggests that the term "the 'main' or 'one of the main [purposes]' does not need to be 'the essential purpose' and may also signal conformity with Cadbury Schweppes, as in practical terms 'essential' operates as a synonym of 'central', which is the term used in the [Cadbury Schweppes] judgment".[43]

Contrary to the mentioned opinion, this study argues that the EC showed a clear indication that it would not follow the narrow Cadbury Schweppes criteria in the ATAD by deviating from the CJEU-defined terminology of "wholly artificial arrangement solely for tax purposes" in Cadbury Schweppes[44] towards "the essential purpose of obtaining a tax advantage" in Article 7(2)(b) CFC rule/SAAR of the ATAD. The CJEU's ruling on Cadbury Schweppes implies that the intention to avoid taxation under the non-genuine (artificial) arrangement must be "the sole purpose" in order to establish an abuse of EU law.[45] Thus, this study notes that "the sole purpose" and "the essential purpose" display different meanings and thresholds.

By the same token, this study concurs with the position of the advocate general in the Danish Beneficial Ownership cases whose analysis of the concept of abuse of EU law under the ATAD in line with the recent CJEU case law implies that "it suffices if the arrangement is put in place not with the sole aim, but with the essential aim, of obtaining a tax advantage".[46] In this regard, CJEU case law, including the Halifax case etc., on the interpretation of "the essential purpose" implies that, to establish the tax avoidance intention of the taxpayer, "the essential rather than the sole purpose to avoid taxation is enough to pass the subjective part of the abusive

---

41 "Definition of essential", Oxford University Press. Available at: https://www.lexico.com/definition/essential.
42 Błażej Kuźniacki, The CJEU case-law relevant to the GAAR under the ATAD, University of Bologna Law Review, 2019.
43 Francisco Alvarez, The ATAD CFC – All Roads Lead to Cadbury Schweppes, Kluwer ITB, 2020.
44 CJEU, 12 September 2006, C-196/04, Cadbury Schweppes plc & Cadbury Schweppes Overseas Ltd, para 61.
45 Błażej Kuźniacki, The CJEU case-law relevant to the GAAR under the ATAD, University of Bologna Law Review, 2019.
46 CJEU, 01 March 2018, Case C-115/16, Opinion of Advocate General, N Luxembourg 1 v Skatteministeriet, para 63; Case C-116/16, Skatteministeriet v T Danmark, para 51.

test in the domain of [taxation]". However, in relation to Article 6(1) GAAR of the ATAD, the subjective test is already met when "at least one of the main purposes was to obtain the benefit [tax advantage]", although the arrangement might be inspired by "valid commercial reasons" among which could be tax optimization.[47]

For this reason, "the essential purpose" test under Article 7(2)(b) CFC rule/SAAR of the ATAD helps to link the subjective element of the tax avoidance intention (purpose) of the taxpayer with the objective element of the arrangement (non-genuine). Thus, for identifying the tax avoidance intention of the taxpayer under "the essential purpose" test, it requires considering what was "the decisive factor" that produced the definite result of the arrangement. In this regard, "the essential purpose" test must analyse the motive of the arrangement and determine whether securing a tax advantage was "the decisive factor" in undertaking the arrangement. The mentioned analysis will allow deciding on whether the arrangement that is put in place is liable to a CFC charge (tax). Here, when comparing "the essential purpose" test under Article 7(2)(b) CFC rule/SAAR of the ATAD against "the main purpose or one of the main purposes" test under Article 6(1) GAAR of the ATAD, it is understood that "the essential purpose" test requires a narrower interpretation. In this regard, "the essential purpose" test implies that "the essential purpose of an arrangement was to secure a tax advantage, rather than simply one of the main purposes".[48]

On this point, this study opines that the standard of "the essential purpose" under Article 7(2)(b) CFC rule/SAAR of the ATAD is neither equivalent to the standard of "the solely [only or exclusively] purpose" in line with the Cadbury Schweppes criteria nor to the standard "the main purpose and one of the main purposes" under Article 6(1) GAAR of the ATAD in line with the Halifax criteria. This study, by drawing an analogy between these criteria and provisions laid down in the ATAD, concludes that the threshold requirements for "the essential purpose" test is lower than for "the solely [only or exclusively] purpose" test (Cadbury Schweppes) and higher than "the main purpose and one of the main purposes" test (Halifax).

However, despite these threshold differences, CJEU case law implies that the term "the essential purpose" should be interpreted in line with common features of the term "the main purpose and one of the main purposes".[49] In this regard, CJEU in Cadbury Schweppes explained that it

---

47　Blażej Kuźniacki, The CJEU case-law relevant to the GAAR under the ATAD, University of Bologna Law Review, 2019.
48　Tax and Duty Manual, CFC Rules, Part 35b-01-01, Revenue, Irish Tax and Customs, February 2021.
49　Blażej Kuźniacki, The CJEU case-law relevant to the GAAR under the ATAD, University of Bologna Law Review, 2019.

requires, essentially, that the resident company show, first, that the considerable reduction in [...] tax resulting from the transactions routed between that company and the CFC was not the main purpose or one of the main purposes of those transactions and, secondly, that the achievement of a reduction in that tax by a diversion of profits within the meaning of that legislation was not the main reason, or one of the main reasons, for incorporating the CFC.[50]

On this point, this study notes that it is a well-established view that, despite the fact that CJEU did not refer explicitly in Cadbury Schweppes to "the degree of the taxpayer's intention to obtain a tax advantage, the use of the wholly artificial arrangement's [...] [formula] implies that the Court [CJEU] had in mind the sole purpose rather than the principal or one of the principal purposes".[51]

Thus, in relation to Article 7(2)(b) CFC rule/SAAR of the ATAD, a company could be considered to have "the essential purpose of obtaining a tax advantage" in place when, for instance, actions involved resulted in: (1) utilizing tax reliefs and allowances in a way that were not intended; (2) making arrangements in a way that were artificial and unrealistic; overly complex in view of their business aims; difficult to understand their structure and rationalize commercial reasons behind them; rewarded with too high benefits compared to real economic risks undertaken; and served little or no purpose other than to gain an advantage. For this reason, the term "tax advantage" is understood as (1) "a reduction, avoidance or deferral of any charge or assessment to tax, including any potential or prospective charge or assessment" and/or (2) "a refund of or a payment of an amount of tax, or an increase in an amount of tax, refundable or otherwise payable to a person, including any potential or prospective amount so refundable or payable, arising out of or by reason of an arrangement".[52]

Considering the reviews mentioned above this study concludes that the EC intended to introduce a stricter interpretation in the ATAD of the abuse of law concept under Article 7(2)(b) CFC rule/SAAR by deviating from the previously required standard of tax avoidance as "the sole purpose" towards the current standard of tax avoidance as "the essential purpose" or "the main purpose". Finally, this study opines that both the CFC rule/SAAR and the GAAR/ATAD are not in conformity with the threshold requirement of the Cadbury Schweppes criteria. The ATAD provides different thresholds between the GAAR (low) and the CFC rule/SAAR (high) because the EC does not want to give protection to any abusive practices.

---

50   CJEU, 12 September 2006, C-196/04, Cadbury Schweppes plc & Cadbury Schweppes Overseas Ltd, para 62.
51   Błażej Kuźniacki, The CJEU case-law relevant to the GAAR under the ATAD, University of Bologna Law Review, 2019.
52   Tax and Duty Manual, CFC Rules, Part 35b-01-01, Revenue, Irish Tax and Customs, February 2021.

In this context, this study concurs with the position of some commentators that the CJEU's broad Halifax-criteria is basically codified in the GAAR/ATAD. On this point, the same commentator opines that the two different standards of abuse of EU law developed by the CJEU (the Cadbury Schweppes criteria – a narrow understanding of abuse of law vs. the Halifax criteria – a broad understanding of abuse of law) may lead to legal uncertainty for taxpayers and the risk of inconsistent interpretation by tax authorities in the area of EU taxation. However, it remains to be seen whether the CJEU will follow the narrow Cadbury Schweppes criteria or whether it will likely apply a kind of blending of both the Cadbury Schweppes and the Halifax criteria in its rulings.[53] In this regard, this study notes that the practical effect of both Article 7(2)(b) CFC rule/SAAR and Article 6 (GAAR) in the ATAD on the business and investment environment in the EU, given limited guidance to date, could be assessed in the future following their application by EU Member States.

4. Model B of CFC income (transactional approach)

requires to refer to the OECD guiding principles introduced in the "OECD 2015 BEPS Final Report on Action 6 – Preventing the Granting of Treaty Benefits in Inappropriate Circumstances" and established in paragraph 9 of Article 29 of the OECD 2017 MTC for appropriate interpretation of the "obtaining a tax advantage" condition as Article 6 GAAR of the ATAD derives from the mentioned OECD documents. This is additionally because both the OECD and the EC through their GAAR concepts pursue "the same objective of tackling treaty [abuse] and other forms of abuse [of law]".[54]

In this regard, the OECD, through its MTC, introduced a GAAR based on "the principal purposes of transactions or arrangements" (PPT rule) to address forms of treaty abuse in addition to the specific limitation-on-benefits rule (LOB). The EC, from its side, has developed a GAAR concept in several instruments with the ATAD as the most recent one of which Article 6 contains a GAAR. Although the OECD identified tax treaty abuse as one of the main sources of BEPS concerns, it did not present a clear definition of what constitutes an abuse of tax treaties. However, the OECD's guiding principle states that the benefit of a tax treaty should not be granted when there is a subjective and an objective element present. Thus, under OECD's GAAR/PPT, if "one of the principal purposes of an arrangement or transaction [is to] obtain a benefit under [the treaty]", the benefit would be denied unless it is established that "obtaining the benefit [...] would be in accordance with the object and purpose of the relevant provisions of [the treaty]".[55]

---

53 Helene Hayden, A rule to catch them all, Völkerrechtsblog, 2019.
54 Francisco Alvarez, The ATAD CFC – All Roads Lead to Cadbury Schweppes, Kluwer ITB, 2020.
55 OECD Model Tax Convention (2017), Commentary on Article 29 para 170.

The GAAR introduced by Article 6 of the ATAD shows the same spirit as the GAAR/PPT introduced by the "OECD 2015 BEPS Final Report on Action 6" and the OECD 2017 MTC. The introduction of a GAAR in the ATAD was necessary "to tackle abusive tax practices" that would not be "dealt with through specifically targeted provisions [SAAR]". In this case, the GAAR serves "to fill in gaps" and its work "should not affect the applicability" of the CFC rule/SAAR in the ATAD. In fact, the interaction of the GAAR with the CFC rule/SAAR in the ATAD can involve the anti-abuse measures working together to have a stronger effect. In this regard, a GAAR threshold requirement would only subject transactions and structures that were the result of tax avoidance to the CFC rule/SAAR in the ATAD. Thus, the GAAR is designed to reinforce the CFC rule/SAAR in the ATAD and to allow EU Member States to catch all abusive tax practices.[56] In this context, the GAAR/ATAD "protects against manipulation of the conditions for exclusion" and applies if the CFC has been involved in an arrangement for which: (1) "a significant part of the CFC's business has been organised or reorganised" by, for instance, reducing the CFC's control level or reducing the associated company threshold, and (2) "the main purpose, or one of the main purposes of that (re)organisation" is to fulfil the requirements for exclusion of income.[57] The OECD mechanism works "in the same way" because its GAAR (based on the PPT) "supports and does not restrict in any way the scope or application" of the LOB rule (SAAR) in the OECD 2017 MTC.[58]

The GAAR in the ATAD is "comprised of three core elements: (1) an arrangement, (2) a tax advantage; and (3) abuse". It requires that all three core elements "must exist for GAAR to be triggered".[59] By the same token, the structure of the OECD GAAR/PPT can be interpreted. For this reason, both rules, i.e., the GAAR/PPT and the GAAR/ATAD, apply to the benefits that were obtained from using relevant instruments and resulted in a tax advantage for the taxpayer. Thus, the results triggered by the application of the GAAR/PPT and the GAAR/ATAD are similar because the legal consequence of these rules is that the benefits may not be granted. Besides, both rules contain an objective and a subjective test. Nonetheless, there are also some insignificant differences wherein the GAAR/PPT makes reference to "one of the principal purposes" and the GAAR/ATAD to "the main purpose or one of the main purposes". However, both rules mean that "it is sufficient that at least one of the purposes was to obtain the benefit" and it "need not be the sole or dominant purpose". Both rules require that, to determine a purpose in the motive test, it should derive from "having considered" [in the GAAR/PPT]

---

56 OECD Designing Effective CFC Rules, Action 3 – 2015 Final Report.
57 https://www.gov.uk/hmrc-internal-manuals/international-manual/intm200860.
58 OECD Model Tax Convention (2017), Commentary on Article 29 para 171.
59 Błażej Kuźniacki, The CJEU case-law relevant to the GAAR under the ATAD, University of Bologna Law Review, 2019.

[and "regard to" in the GAAR/ATAD] all of the relevant facts and circumstances" surrounding any arrangements on a case-by-case basis. The GAAR/PPT, in contrast to the GAAR/ATAD, states explicitly that any arrangement or transaction should result "directly or indirectly" in the benefit.[60]

In this regard, the GAAR/PPT is wider in scope and aims "to include situations where the person who claims the application of the benefits under a tax treaty may do so [regarding any arrangement, which in itself is] not undertaken for one of the principal purposes of obtaining that treaty benefit".[61] Despite the absence of the reference to "indirectly" in the GAAR/ATAD, this does not constitute an essential difference with the GAAR/PPT because this indirect link is reflected by the "to the extent" approach in the GAAR/ATAD. This study aligns with the position of other commentators that, although the GAAR/PPT does not explicitly refer to the "non-genuine" and "economic reality" test, this test is implicitly present in the GAAR/PPT.[62] However, the other position that the GAAR/PPT may give rise to concerns that the statement "it is reasonable to conclude" that "one of the principal purposes of any arrangement or transaction was [to obtain a tax] benefit" may create uncertainty for taxpayers is not necessarily true because this test is related to the objective analysis, and it scrutinizes "all the relevant facts and circumstances". Further, this study concurs with the position of the same commentator that the GAAR/PPT and the GAAR/ATAD are similar to each other and should thus be preferably interpreted in the same way.[63]

In this context, the study emphasizes that CJEU in the Danish Beneficial Ownership cases, while examining the constituent elements of abuse in EU law, ruled that the existence of a double taxation convention between an EU Member State and a third state "has no bearing on any finding of an abuse of rights" because, as a general legal principle, taxpayers cannot rely on EU law for abusive and fraudulent ends.[64]

5. Model B of CFC income (transactional approach)

requires that a GAAR (as defined by the OECD and the ATAD) does not capture "bona fide [in good faith] exchanges of goods and services, and movements of capital and persons as opposed to arrangements whose principal purpose is to secure a more favourable tax treatment". However, in order "to determine whether or not [securing a tax advantage (benefit) is] one of the principal purposes of an

---

60   OECD Model Tax Convention (2017), Commentary on Article 29 para 174, 176, 178 & 180.
61   Ibid.
62   Ashley Bergmans in Preventing Treaty Abuse, The PPT: Comparison with EU-GAAR Initiatives, 2016.
63   Ibid.
64   CJEU, 26 February 2019, Joined Cases C-115/16, C-118/16, C-119/16, C-299/16, N Luxembourg 1 & Others v Skatteministeriet, Ruling, para 2, 3; Joined Cases C-116/16, C-117/16, Skatteministeriet v T Danmark & Y Denmark Aps, Ruling, para 2.

arrangement or transaction", this triggers "an objective analysis of all the relevant facts and circumstances" as per the OECD 2017 MTC.[65]

On this point, some commentators suggest that this objective analysis appears to be in line with the objective test of the Cadbury Schweppes criteria[66] that is "based on objective factors which are ascertainable by third parties with regard, in particular, to the extent to which the CFC physically exists in terms of premises, staff and equipment". "For CFC rules, premises, staff and equipment are, inter alia, the relevant facts and circumstances".[67]

This study opines that, although the GAAR/ATAD, in general, is designed to reflect the non-genuine (artificiality) test, the recent CJEU's finding in X GmbH on economic substance analysis, which could be applied for determining abusive practices, implies that the meaning of "the concept of the wholly artificial arrangement" may be more complex, and the arrangement can take several forms that are different from those described under the Cadbury Schweppes criteria. In this regard, the CJEU ruled that "the concept of a 'wholly artificial arrangement' cannot necessarily be limited to merely the indications, referred to" situations in which (1) "the CFC physically exists in terms of premises, staff and equipment", and (2) "the CFC is a fictitious establishment not carrying out any genuine economic activity in the territory of the host [EU MS]" under the Cadbury Schweppes criteria. Thus, the CJEU stated that "the concept of the wholly artificial arrangement" may cover, "in the context of the free movement of capital, any scheme which has as its primary objective or one of its primary objectives the artificial transfer of the profits".[68] In this context, the CJEU gave some clarity in X GmbH to the concept of the non-genuine (artificial) arrangement.

Despite the CJEU refining its concept of "wholly artificial arrangement" in light of the recent case law, including the Danish Beneficial Ownership cases, this study opines that, although the GAAR/ATAD act as a backstop to the CFC rule/SAAR, the wide scope of the non-genuine (artificiality) test of the GAAR/ATAD is not designed and intended to capture bona fide arrangements because such arrangements are protected under the concept of "valid commercial reasons which reflect economic reality". By the same token, the OECD 2017 MTC illustrates this point clearly that "the provision [of GAAR] is intended to ensure that tax conventions apply in accordance with the purpose for which they were entered into", in other words, to provide benefits for "bona fide exchanges of goods and services, and movements of capitals and persons".[69]

---

65 OECD Model Tax Convention (2017), Commentary on Article 29 para 178.
66 CJEU, 12 September 2006, C-196/04, Cadbury Schweppes plc & Cadbury Schweppes Overseas Ltd, para 67.
67 Francisco Alvarez, The ATAD CFC – All Roads Lead to Cadbury Schweppes, Kluwer ITB, 2020.
68 CJEU, 26 February 2019, C-135/17, X GmbH v. Finanzamt Stuttgart – Körperschaften, para 84.
69 OECD Model Tax Convention (2017), Commentary on Article 29 para 174.

4. The Relevance of the EU Fundamental Freedoms to Model B (Transactional Approach)

In this context, some commentators take the position that, indeed, "CFC rules are inherently restrictive of the fundamental EU freedoms (particularly establishment) and [that remains] true, regardless of how 'CFC income' is defined". Further, the same commentator argues that "CFC rules can capture income that is not captured by TPR" which would generate additional revenue for the controlling jurisdiction, and thus the notion that Model B (transactional approach) Article 7(2)(b) ATAD does not restrict the EU fundamental freedoms because it relies on TPR and the SPF/KERT analysis is unconvincing. Furthermore, the same commentator, by referring to the "OECD 2015 BEPS Final Report on Action 3 – Designing Effective CFC Rules", suggests that "there is nothing preventing [EU MS] from subjecting the return allocated to a low-function cashbox to a CFC charge if the low-function cashbox is in a low tax territory". Thus, this commentator concludes that a restriction remains on the EU fundamental freedoms under Model B (transactional approach) of Article 7(2)(b) ATAD.[70]

For this reason, a proportionality test (non-discrimination) of the domestic law would require analysing "the scope and the substantive requirements protected under different [EU] fundamental freedoms". To illustrate this point, other commentators opine that "[t]he freedom of establishment will always trigger the need to scrutinise premises, people on the ground, physical offices, while the freedom to provide services or the free movement of capital may require to focus on more subtle constituencies of the arrangements, such as contracts between the companies, or the transfers of profits between companies" in conformity to the CJEU-defined wholly artificial arrangement criteria.[71]

On this point, the EC is of an opinion that Model B (transactional approach) of Article 7(2)(b) ATAD "does not engage the wholly artificial arrangement limitation" of the Cadbury Schweppes criteria, because "levying a tax on profits of foreign subsidiaries only to the extent attributable to domestic assets and activities does not pose a restriction to the freedom of establishment because it follows the same principles as those underlying the AOA concerning the attribution of profits of a foreign entity to a domestic permanent establishment".

Further, the EC, in relation to the AOA method employed in Model B (transactional approach), elaborates that:

> That approach is based on the arm's length principle. [...]. It ensures a CFC charge on the profits of a CFC but limited to those profits that have been artificially diverted away

---
70 Francisco Alvarez, The ATAD CFC – All Roads Lead to Cadbury Schweppes, Kluwer ITB, 2020.
71 Błażej Kuźniacki, The CJEU case-law relevant to the GAAR under the ATAD, University of Bologna Law Review, 2019.

from the UK, whereby the identification and quantification of such artificially diverted profits is based on a test that first identifies which SPF relevant for generating the CFC's profits are located in the UK, and subsequently subjects only that part of the CFC's profits to a CFC charge that is proportionate to the relevant SPF being located in the UK.

For the above reason, the EC in relation to the issue of infringement on the EU fundamental freedoms, clarifies that "given this effect of an SPF test, a CFC charge based on such test should in principle be compliant with the provisions in Union [EU] law concerning the freedom of establishment following the definition and explanations given to the concept of abuse by the Court [CJEU]".[72]

In the EC's view, Model B (transactional approach) of Article 7(2)(b) ATAD is not subject to a substance carve-out because this model does not restrict the freedom of establishment and thus does not engage the wholly artificial arrangement limitation of the Cadbury Schweppes criteria. Following this reasoning, the EC views that the substance carve-out is unnecessary for Model B (transactional approach).[73] In this regard, the EC explains that "it is not a mistake that Article 7(2)(a) of the Anti-Tax Avoidance Directive (the escape clause), does not apply to this second option. The reason is that the EU legislature concluded that there was no need for such an escape clause to ensure compliance with the Union [EU] freedoms for an SPF based CFC rule for the exact same reasons explained in the former recital [171]".[74]

For the reasons mentioned above, this study concurs with the position of other commentators that it is "undisputed that [...] [ATAD is] not the right instrument to (indirectly) restrict the scope of application of the [EU] fundamental freedoms by establishing new grounds for justification". Thus, the possible concern about the wide scope of the non-genuine (artificiality) test of the GAAR/ATAD is alleviated by the argument that "the (strict) proportionality test inherent in Union [EU] law" that is applicable to areas of the EU fundamental freedoms and to the GAAR/SAAR/ATAD provides adequate protection for all taxpayers.[75]

This study opines that EU Member States will most likely follow the EC's view that Model B (transactional approach) is in conformity to EU law in their judicial rulings and administrative decisions, given the fact that the EC's position presented in its decision on the issue of the UK's state aid[76] has been acknowledged by EU Member States with no reservations or objections, so far. While the CJEU's view remains to be seen, the practical interpretation of the EC's opinion could be assessed in future cases.

---

72   EC Decision, 2019/1352 of 2 April 2019 on the UK's State aid, recital 171.
73   Francisco Alvarez, The ATAD CFC – All Roads Lead to Cadbury Schweppes, Kluwer ITB, 2020.
74   EC Decision, 2019/1352 of 2 April 2019 on the UK's State aid, recital 172.
75   Helene Hayden, A rule to catch them all, Völkerrechtsblog, 2019.
76   EC Decision, 2019/1352 of 2 April 2019 on the UK's State aid, recitals, 43, 171, 172.

After having analysed the provisions of Article 7(2)(b) ATAD, this study describes Model B (transactional approach) as:

- limited to amounts generated through assets and risks which, in turn, are:
  - (a) linked to SPF/KERT functions undertaken by a controlling company in its resident EU Member State and
  - (b) calculated in accordance with the arm's length principle based on the TPR method (consistent with global standards);
- subject to a CFC charge (tax) for a portion of the CFC profits that is proportionate to relevant SPF/KERT activities of the controlling company in its resident EU Member State; and
- subject to the existence of a nexus between an EU Member State and the CFC's chargeable profits (undistributed income) for a CFC charge (tax) to arise.

For the above reasons, Model B (transactional approach) of Article 7(2)(b) ATAD:

(1) does not include a substance carve-out clause (substance escape clause) because it is based on the SPF/KERT test the application of which is in compliance with the EU fundamental freedoms;
(2) does not involve the CJEU-defined limitation clause on the wholly artificial arrangement (e.g. the freedom of establishment) under the Cadbury Schweppes criteria because it follows the same principle as the AOA; and thus,
(3) does not infringe on the EU fundamental freedoms as defined by TFEU;
(4) does not deter EU-cross border (bona fide) transactions for genuine and valid economic reasons.

Finally, Model B (transactional approach) constitutes a proportionate response to BEPS risks.

Concerning the issue of whether Article 7(2)(b) CFC rule/SAAR is in conformity with the Cadbury Schweppes criteria, this study notes that the CJEU formulated its concept in Cadbury Schweppes of a "wholly artificial arrangement" based on three criteria: (1) taxpayers can shift their genuine economic activities to other EU Member States for "the sole purpose" of avoiding taxation (wholly artificial arrangements do not exist where taxpayers conduct genuine economic activities); however, abuse of rights exists only if (2) there is no genuine economic activity conducted by taxpayers, and (3) "the sole purpose" of the non-genuine activity is to avoid taxation. Thus, grounds for restriction on the EU freedom of establishment are justified if applied only to wholly artificial arrangements intended to escape taxation.[77] In this sense, the CJEU established a narrow (strict) definition in Cadbury Schweppes of the "wholly artificial arrangement" subject to (1) "the CFC physically exists in terms of premises, staff and equipment", and (2) "the CFC is a

---

77 Błażej Kuźniacki, The CJEU case law relevant to the GAAR under the ATAD, University of Bologna Law Review, 2019

fictitious establishment not carrying out any genuine economic activity in the territory of the host [EU MS]".[78]

In conclusion, this study opines that Article 7(2)(b) CFC rule/SAAR of the ATAD is not in full conformity with the Cadbury Schweppes criteria because of three reasons: (1) the threshold requirement for "the essential purpose" standard in Model B (transactional approach) is lower than the threshold requirement for "the solely [only or exclusively] purpose" standard in the Cadbury Schweppes judgement (because these thresholds are not the same, thus the Cadbury Schweppes criterion is not met); (2) Model B (transactional approach) applies the SPF/KERT test under the AOA method (TPR covers all arrangements), thus Model B does not engage the "wholly artificial arrangement" restriction on the EU freedom of establishment under the Cadbury Schweppes criteria and, as such, it is in conformity with the TFEU (this is the other Cadbury Schweppes criterion); (3) the concept of "non-genuine [artificial] arrangements" covers non-TPR arrangements under Model B (transactional approach) when non-arm's length arrangements can be considered abusive (artificial) despite taxpayers' engagement in genuine economic activities; and the definition of "non-genuine [artificial] arrangement" in Model B (transactional approach) appears to be broader in scope than the definition of "wholly artificial arrangement" in the Cadbury Schweppes judgment (wholly artificial arrangements do not exist where taxpayers conduct genuine economic activities despite tax motives). Thus, these definitions, in light of the recent CJEU rulings, could have different implications on the interpretation of the concept of "wholly artificial arrangement".

5. The CFC Profits Attributable to Activities in EU Member State

The CFC's undistributed income (chargeable profits) under Model B (transactional approach) consists of (1) a portion of its total profits available for distribution on which (2) a CFC charge (tax) can arise that is (3) attributable to the relevant activities in EU Member States where SPF/KERT functions were instrumental in generating the CFC's profits (income), and (4) the arrangements involving those SPF/KERT functions were "non-genuine" and were "put in place for the essential purpose of obtaining a tax advantage". It is important to note that, for a CFC charge (tax) to arise, there must be a nexus between an EU Member State and the CFC's undistributed income. This nexus is established through the application of the SPF/KERT test. Thus, the definition of undistributed income is a key concept of CFC rules because a CFC charge (tax) arises only when the CFC has undistributed income.[79]

---

78 CJEU, 12 September 2006, C-196/04, Cadbury Schweppes plc & Cadbury Schweppes Overseas Ltd, para 67, 68.
79 Tax and Duty Manual, CFC Rules, Part 35b-01-01, Revenue, Irish Tax and Customs, February 2021.

In this regard, Model B (transactional approach) would require taxpayers to regularly produce FFA documentation under the TPR method wherein it includes details of their controlled (directly or indirectly) CFCs, identifies SPF/KERT functions related to control of the assets and associated risks of each CFC, and analyses how SPF/KERT functions were instrumental in generating the CFC's income. In this regard, the TPR should apply before the CFC rules. However, CFC rules can also be used after the application of the TPR to address situations that appear to be inconsistent with BEPS. In this way, CFC rules act as backstops to the TPR because CFC rules may capture some income that is not detected by the TPR and vice versa.[80]

For the above reasons, this study assimilates a methodology from one of the CFC regimes on the attribution of the CFC's profits to relevant SPF/KERT activities that provided the capability for the CFC to generate those profits in order to illustrate a basic five-step approach for the reader on how to apply the SPF/KERT method (test) under Model B (transactional approach) of Article 7(2)(b) ATAD.[81] Thus, each EU Member State may have different operating systems but, in essence, these steps must be taken in accordance with the principles set out in the OECD 2010 Report on the Attribution of Profits to PEs. In this regard, attributable profits are broadly those that (1) arise from SPF/KERT functions and (2) are situated in the EU Member State of a controlling company.

1. Identification of the CFC's relevant assets and risks

This step requires identifying the CFC's relevant assets and risks that generate the CFC's assumed total profits for the reporting period. In this regard, these assets and risks are considered together in the same way as they would be for a TPR analysis because a company's commercial activities (or parts of it) may have certain assets that share the same features and risk allocations. Thus, this step entails applying the same principles for the identification of assets and risks as required in an FFA for the TPR purpose. In this context, an FFA review of a company and its connected (associated) companies for income attribution under the AOA involves a twofold approach: (1) this method requires performing an FFA centred on a "separate and independent enterprise [entity]" approach, and (2) this method requires performing a "comparability analysis".[82]

For this reason, the first FFA method requires identifying and attributing to the PE: (1) functions, (2) risks, (3) assets, (4) capital, (5) transactions with connected (associated) companies, (6) transactions with external companies, and (7) dealings with the head office.[83] Then, the second FFA method entails an assessment of the

---

80   OECD Designing Effective CFC Rules, Action 3 – 2015 Final Report.
81   HMRC Internal Manual, UK's Tax, Payments and Customs Authority, April 2021.
     https://www.gov.uk/hmrc-internal-manuals/international-manual/intm200500.
82   OECD Report on the Attribution of Profits to PEs (2010), B-5. Summary of the two-step analysis.
83   Ibid., B-3. Step one: hypothesizing the PE as a separate and independent enterprise.

comparability of the comparable items with the help of the previously performed FFA and pricing the dealings based on an arm's length principle.[84] In this regard, "the arm's length principle means that the amount charged by one related party to another for a product or service [transaction] must be the same as would be charged between unrelated parties in comparable circumstances" in line with the OECD 2017 TP Guidelines for MNEs and TAs.[85] For the above reasons, compensation in transactions between two independent companies (enterprises) requires showing the functions that each company performs considering (1) assets used and (2) risks assumed.[86] Thus, the FFA is necessary to describe the controlled transaction and determine comparability between controlled and uncontrolled transactions or companies. In this context, the FFA needs to identify (1) the undertaken economically significant activities and responsibilities, (2) the used or contributed assets, and (3) the assumed risks by the parties to the transactions. The FFA is the most critical part of the review of the company and its connected companies (associated enterprises). In this regard, the FFA is centred on (1) "what activities the company performs" (which includes decision-making about business strategy and risks), (2) "where those activities take place", (3) "who bears what risks", and (4) "who gets what reward". Thus, the FFA helps to make a valid assessment of whether the company receives an arm's length reward. For this reason, the reward at arm's length is understood as a combination of (1) "the functions carried out", (2) "the assets employed", and (3) "the risk borne". In this regard, the meaning of the two features "the functions carried out" and "the assets employed" imply governing the amount of risk. As a result, the FFA aims at displaying an accurate and deep understanding of all three features. In this context, the purpose of the FFA is the same as defined in the OECD 2017 TP Guidelines for MNEs and TAs for transactions between connected companies (associated enterprises).[87]

2. Identification of relevant SPF/KERT functions

After having identified the relevant assets and risks, this step requires identifying SPF/KERT functions within the CFC that are relevant to (1) "the legal or economic ownership of those assets" or (2) "the assumption and management of those risks". As the term SPF/KERT functions is difficult to "capture in legislation", the meaning of the SPF/KERT is interpreted in line with the OECD 2010 Report on the Attribution of Profits to PEs. However, the OECD guidance on SPF/KERT functions is limited due to general considerations. In this regard, the term SPF/KERT functions refers to "the people functions within the enterprise [company] that contribute to value creation and, as such, should be entitled to a share of the residual profit or loss".[88]

---

84   Ibid., B-4. Step two: determining the profits of the hypothesized separate and independent enterprise based upon a comparability analysis.
85   Tax and Duty Manual, CFC Rules, Part 35b-01-01, Revenue, Irish Tax and Customs, February 2021.
86   OECD TP Guidelines for MNEs and TAs (2017), D. Guidance for applying the arm's length principle, para 1.36.
87   Ibid., D.1.2. Functional analysis.
88   Tax and Duty Manual, CFC Rules, Part 35b-01-01, Revenue, Irish Tax and Customs, February 2021.

For this reason, first, it is required to make an assumption that the CFC is regarded as if it was "a single company". Here, the identification of SPF/KERT functions follows the same principles as what would be required to attribute assets and risks to the PE of "a single company" using the AOA. In other words, this method adopts "the functionally separate entity approach" under which a PE [CFC] is treated as "a functionally separate and independent enterprise [entity]" in order to determine its business profits. Second, it requires carrying out an FFA analysis with regard to its assets, risks, and capital. The FFA attributes the mentioned features to the PE [CFC]. Here, the major reference point is viewed as to where SPF/KERT functions that are relevant to the assets and risks are performed.[89]

The OECD recognizes that SPF/KERT functions and the extent of their overlap vary between business sectors and between companies in those sectors. However, if a company has more than one relevant SPF/KERT function, then the FFA should consider each of them.[90] For the FFA purpose, both SPF and KERT functions have the same features. In this regard, the SPF is relevant to "the economic ownership of assets" or to "the assumption of risks", and the KERT is relevant to "the financial sector, specifically banking, global trading and insurance [because the relations between risks and financial assets here are intertwined]". Thus, the concept of SPF/KERT functions that involves the conduct of business functions that lead to (1) the economic ownership of assets, (2) the assumption of risks, or (3) management of those risks and assets is regarded as the basic method to attribute assets and risks to a PE [CFC] "given the absence of contractual arrangements". Here, it is understood that a company cannot conclude a legal agreement with itself as would typically be the case between independent companies.[91]

Although the OECD does not provide a definition of SPF/KERT functions, the OECD provides guidance on how to identify SPF/KERT functions relevant to the economic ownership of assets:

> The functional and factual analysis will examine all the facts and circumstances to determine the extent to which the assets of the enterprise are used in the functions performed by the permanent establishment and the conditions under which the assets are used, including the factors to be taken into account to determine which part of the enterprise is regarded as the economic owner of the assets actually owned by the enterprise. The attribution of economic ownership of assets will have consequences for both the attribution of capital and interest-bearing debt and the attribution of profit to the permanent establishment.[92]

---

89   OECD Report on the Attribution of Profits to PEs (2010), B-3. Step one: hypothesising the PE as a separate and independent enterprise.
90   Ibid., Functional and factual analysis, para 16, 17.
91   Colin Smith, Ronan Finn, Michael Douglas: The Importance of SPF in the Context of CFCs and Profit Attribution, 2019.
92   OECD Report on the Attribution of Profits to PEs (2010), Functional and factual analysis, para 18.

Further, the OECD offers guidance on how to identify SPF/KERT functions in the context of the activities of the company relevant to the assumption and management of risks which is centred on "active decision-making": "The significant people functions relevant to the assumption of risks are those which require active decision-making with regard to the acceptance and/or management (subsequent to the transfer) of those risks. The extent of the decision-making will depend on the nature of the risk involved".[93]

After having identified SPF/KERT functions under the FFA, the next step is to attribute these functions to the PE [CFC]. Here, SPF/KERT functions serve as the basis for attributing assets and risks to the PE [CFC] in accordance with where relevant SPF/KERT functions were performed in the company. With regard to CFC rules, the FFA focuses on where to attribute SPF/KERT functions in the context of controlling companies, connected companies, and CFCs rather than PEs.[94] Further, the OECD provides some indications of what it considers to be SPF/KERT functions in relation to "types of intangible assets" which include: (1) "internally developed trade intangibles", (2) "acquired trade intangibles", and (3) "marketing intangibles".[95]

3. Determining SPF/KERT functions that are carried out in an EU Member State

After having identified the relevant SPF/KERT functions, this step requires determining the extent to which (1) SPF/KERT functions are performed in EU Member States and to what extent (2) SPF/KERT functions are non-EU Member State functions. This step is the prime determiner of how to deal with the CFC. If the analysis shows that none of the SPF/KERT functions are related to an EU Member State, then a CFC charge (tax) cannot be applied. Hence, the subsequent steps for attribution of the CFC's assets and risks to an EU Member State and for determination of the CFC's undistributed income are not required to be followed-up. It is important to note that, despite the fact that the OECD recognizes SPF/KERT functions in line with usually comparable roles that require "active decision-making", the focus of a SPF/KERT analysis is not on where a particular person (function) is at the moment of making a decision. Thus, the SPF/KERT analysis needs to consider (1) "the procedures of the company", (2) "where people habitually perform the relevant functions", and in (3) "what capacity and circumstances".[96] In this regard, the OECD clarifies that SPF/KERT functions relevant to the determination of economic ownership are focused on "the active decision-making and management rather than on simply saying yes or no to a proposal" and suggests

---

93 Ibid., Functional and factual analysis, para 22.
94 Tax and Duty Manual, CFC Rules, Part 35b-01-01, Revenue, Irish Tax and Customs, February 2021.
95 Colin Smith, Ronan Finn, Michael Douglas: The Importance of SPF in the Context of CFCs and Profit Attribution, 2019.
96 https://www.gov.uk/hmrc-internal-manuals/international-manual/intm200500.

that "economic ownership may often be determined by functions performed below the strategic level of senior management".[97] Thus, the SPF/KERT analysis (test) needs to consider (1) what constitutes SPF/KERT functions and (2) at what level of the company the SPF/KERT activities are undertaken; typical examples may include: (1) "internal grade hierarchies", (2) "pay scales", (3) "frameworks of the activities and decisions undertaken in [a company] that are linked to the employees and their roles" which include "RAPID (recommend, agree, perform, input and decide) and RACI (responsible, accountable, consulted and informed) to identify those involved in active decision making".[98]

4. Attribution of the CFC's assets and risks to an EU Member State

After having established the relevant SPF/KERT functions of an EU Member State, this step requires making an assumption that these SPF/KERT functions are performed by people in a PE of the CFC in that EU Member State. Thus, this test determines the extent to which the assets and risks identified in Step 1 (Identification of the CFC's relevant assets and risks) would be attributed to that (assumed) PE in an EU Member State under the AOA. For this analysis, it is hypothetically assumed that the CFC itself carried out any SPF/KERT functions that are not related to that EU Member State (such SPF/KERT functions remain outside of the controlling jurisdiction). This method makes the attribution of assets and risks straightforward. Thus, this method allows, on the one hand, focusing on SPF/KERT functions that are assumed to be performed in the CFC's resident country (controlled jurisdiction) and, on the other hand, on those SPF/KERT functions performed in a single PE of the CFC in an EU Member State (controlling jurisdiction). It is important to note that this test focuses on the attribution of assets and risks that would determine profits attributable to a PE under the provisions of the "Business Profits" of Article 7 of the OECD 2017 MTC. In this regard, there must be a nexus between an EU Member State and the CFC's undistributed income for a CFC charge (tax) to arise. This nexus is established through the application of the SPF/KERT test based on the TPR method. Moreover, the FFA may provide grounds for justification to attribute certain assets or risks to one or the other location or both locations throughout the reporting period. However, assets and risks would remain attributed to the same location as before if the FFA displays insignificant activity in relation to the assets and risks in accordance with the provisions of the "Business Profits" of Article 7 of the OECD 2017 MTC. In this context, the OECD does not clarify situations in which the CFC may have undistributed income for acquired assets and assumed risks in previous periods. Such situations might be addressed through the comparison to situations "where a tax treaty in terms of the MTC came into force in relation to a

---
97 OECD Report on the Attribution of Profits to PEs (2010), para 87.
98 Colin Smith, Ronan Finn, Michael Douglas: The Importance of SPF in the Context of CFCs and Profit Attribution, 2019.

PE that had previously been taxed on some different basis". However, TPR documentation or other supporting evidence in relation to relevant SPF/KERT functions performed by the CFC in an EU Member States would help to address the above situations.[99]

5. Determining the CFC's undistributed income

After having attributed relevant SPF/KERT functions to an EU Member State (controlling jurisdiction), this step requires determining the CFC's undistributed income. Then, a CFC charge (tax) is raised against the CFC's undistributed income for the reporting period if none of the entity-level exemptions apply (e.g., "low profits exemption", "low profit margin exemption"). For the above reasons, the ATAD CFC rules stipulate that "the income to be included in the tax base of the taxpayer [under Model B (transactional approach) of Article 7(2)(b) ATAD is] limited to amounts generated through assets and risks which are linked to significant people functions [SPF/KERT] carried out by the controlling company. The attribution of controlled foreign company income shall be calculated in accordance with the arm's length principle".[100] For further information on computation and taxation of CFC income, the reader is referred to existing overviews.[101]

6. Conclusion

The ATAD CFC rule/SAAR is an anti-abuse measure that was enacted by the EC to prevent the artificial diversion of profits (income) from a controlling company in a high tax country (jurisdiction) to a CFC in a low or no-tax country (jurisdiction) with a view to evade or reduce their tax liability. The ATAD CFC rule/SAAR under Model B (transactional approach) of Article 7(2)(b) operates by attributing undistributed income (chargeable profits) of the CFC arising from (1) "non-genuine arrangements" put in place for (2) "the essential purpose of obtaining a tax advantage" [these two cumulative conditions must exist for a CFC charge (tax) to arise] for the controlling company in an EU Member State for taxation in which it carries out relevant SPF/KERT activities. In this case, such undistributed income forms part of the taxable income of the controlling company in its resident EU Member State. It is important to note that there must be a nexus between the EU Member State and the CFC's undistributed income for a CFC charge (tax) to arise. This nexus is established through the application of the SPF/KERT test based on the TPR method. Thus, the definition of undistributed income is a key concept of Model B (transactional approach) because a CFC charge (tax) arises only when a CFC has undistributed income. In this context, an ATAD GAAR threshold requirement would only subject transactions and structures that were

---

99   https://www.gov.uk/hmrc-internal-manuals/international-manual/intm200500.
100 EU Council Directive, 2016/1164 of 12 July 2016, Article 8(2).
101 Anca Pianoschi, Computation and attribution of income under the ATAD.

the result of tax avoidance to ATAD CFC rule/SAAR. For this reason, CJEU case law and its two-pronged test play an important role in application of the ATAD and help to interpret the key concepts with regard to abuse of law because both the CFC rule/SAAR of Article 7 and the GAAR of Article 6 in ATAD contain an objective and a subjective test similar to the GAAR/PPT in the OECD 2017 MTC. Thus, EU law requires that both SAAR and GAAR measures implemented by EU Member States specifically target the non-genuine (artificial) arrangements. In this regard, this study through the application of the CJEU-defined two-pronged test identifies that the objective test regarding the non-genuine (artificial) arrangements is defined in a narrow scope under the ATAD CFC rule/SAAR in contrast to a wider scope of the same definition under the ATAD GAAR. Thus, to determine whether an arrangement is genuine under the objective test of the CFC rule/SAAR, the SPF/KERT functions under the AOA that contribute to value creation and are relevant to the income-generating assets and risks undertaken by the CFC must be taken into account. For this reason, Model B (transactional approach) would require taxpayers to regularly produce an FFA under the TPR. However, non-arm's length arrangements may trigger a CFC rule/SAAR even if they are conducted by companies engaged in genuine economic activities. Then, the CFC rule/SAAR acts as a backstop to the TPR because CFC rules may detect some income that is not captured by the TPR and vice versa. In order to reduce administrative and compliance burdens of CFC rules, the ATAD allows EU Member States to provide exemptions for CFCs with (1) low accounting profits or (2) a low profit margin or when (3) an effective tax rate test is satisfied. At the same time, the CFC charge (tax) does not arise on undistributed income if arrangements involving SPF/KERT functions have been entered into on an arm's length basis or are subject to the TPR regime of an EU Member State. For the above reasons, the wide scope of the non-genuine test (the objective test) under Article 6 GAAR, which follows the Halifax criteria (a broad understanding of abuse of law), is designed to reinforce Article 7(2)(b) CFC rule/SAAR and allows EU Member States to catch all abusive tax practices that may escape the ATAD CFC rule/SAAR.

Next, this study identifies that the subjective test under the ATAD requires determining whether an arrangement was inspired by obtaining the benefits (tax advantage) of the applicable tax law. The subjective test will allow deciding on whether an arrangement that is put in place is liable to a CFC charge (tax). In the ATAD, the subjective test presents two different thresholds for an arrangement. Here, when comparing "the essential purpose" test (a higher threshold requirement) under Article 7(2)(b) CFC rule/SAAR of the ATAD against "the main purpose or one of the main purposes" test (a lower threshold requirement) under Article 6(1) GAAR of the ATAD, it is understood that "the essential purpose" test requires a narrower interpretation. In this regard, "the essential purpose" test implies that "the essential purpose of an arrangement was to secure a tax advantage, rather than simply one of the main purposes". However, despite these threshold differences, CJEU case law implies that this difference does not create ambiguity for the term "obtaining a tax advantage". In this regard, this study opines that the EC intended to introduce a stricter interpretation in the ATAD of the abuse of law concept under Article 7(2)(b) CFC rule/SAAR by deviating from the previously required standard of tax avoidance as "the solely purpose" towards the current standard of tax avoidance as "the essential [main] purpose".

Furthermore, this study suggests that the GAAR/ATAD and the GAAR/PPT/OECD show the same spirit and are seen as interchangeable instruments because both are designed to ensure that applicable tax laws and treaties apply in accordance with the purpose for which they were enacted; in other words, to provide benefits for bona fide exchanges of goods and services as well as movements of capitals and persons.

This study concludes that Article 7(2)(b) CFC rule/SAAR of the ATAD is not in full conformity with the Cadbury Schweppes criteria because of three reasons: (1) the threshold requirement for "the essential purpose" standard in Model B (transactional approach) is lower than the threshold requirement for "the sole [only or exclusively] purpose" standard in the Cadbury Schweppes criteria (because these thresholds are not the same, thus this standard of the Cadbury Schweppes criteria is not met); (2) the criterion of "wholly artificial arrangement" restriction of the Cadbury Schweppes criteria does not apply to Model B (transactional approach) because Model B applies the SPF/KERT test under the AOA method (the TPR covers all arrangements), thus Model B (transactional approach) is in conformity with the TFEU and does not infringe on the EU fundamental freedoms (e.g. the EU freedom of establishment); (3) the concept of "non-genuine [artificial] arrangements" covers non-TPR arrangements under Model B (transactional approach) when non-arm's length arrangements can be considered abusive (artificial) despite taxpayers' engagement in genuine economic activities; the definition of "non-genuine [artificial] arrangement" in Model B (transactional approach) appears to be broader in scope than the definition of "wholly artificial arrangement" in the Cadbury Schweppes judgment (wholly artificial arrangements do not exist where taxpayers conduct genuine economic activities despite tax motives). Thus, these definitions, in light of the recent CJEU rulings, could have different implications on the interpretation of the concept of a "wholly acritical arrangement".

On this point, this study notes that the concept of "wholly artificial arrangement" triggered some debate in literature in view of ATAD implementation. However, in absence of CJEU case law concerning the ATAD, this study takes the position that the concept of a "non-genuine (artificial) arrangement" may be considered broader in scope to include forms and arrangements that are more complex in light of the recent CJEU case law (for instance, X GmbH case, the Danish Beneficial Ownership cases). In this regard, this study argues (interprets) that the EC, by referring to the term "non-genuine arrangement" instead of the term "wholly artificial arrangement" in the ATAD, intended to show that it would not follow the strict standard of the Cadbury Schweppes criteria.

Computation and Attribution of CFC income under ATAD

Anca Pianoschi

1. Introduction
2. CFC regimes and the Anti-Tax Avoidance Directive
   2.1. Controlled foreign companies erode the taxable base and shift profits to low tax jurisdictions
   2.2. The Anti-Tax Avoidance Directive
   2.3. CFC rules, which model fits best: A, B or both?
      2.3.1. Categorical approach under Model A
      2.3.2. The substantive approach provided by Model B
      2.3.3. A third alternative?
3. What are the rules for the computation and attribution of CFC income?
   3.1. Calculation and attribution of CFC income under Model A
      3.1.1. Computation of CFC income under Model A
      3.1.2. Rules for attributing income
      3.1.3. Treatment of losses
      3.1.4. Example of calculation of CFC income according to Model A
   3.2. Computation and allocation of income under Model B
      3.2.1. Calculation and attribution of income under Model B
      3.2.2. Example of computation of CFC income under Model B
   3.3. Accounting periods
   3.4. Level of taxation
   3.5. Advantages and drawbacks of the two approaches
4. CFC rules and prevention of double taxation
   4.1. The relief for double taxation under Article 8(5), (6), and (7) of the ATAD
      4.1.1. The issue of double taxation under ATAD
      4.1.2. Treatment of actual distributions
      4.1.3. Disposal of shares
      4.1.4. Taxes paid by the CFC
   4.2. Does the ATAD provide solutions against all potential cases of double or multiple taxation?
      4.2.1. The issue of double or multiple taxation under CFC rules
      4.2.2. Double residency for the controlling parent
      4.2.3. Attribution methods
      4.2.4. Characterization of income
      4.2.5. Cascading ownership
5. Concluding remarks

1. Introduction

In recent years, controlled foreign company (CFC) legislation has gained increased importance on the global economic scene. CFC rules as anti-abuse provisions were adopted by the European Union in 2016 in the form of the Anti-Tax Avoidance Directive (ATAD or the Directive)[1].

The CFC rules included in Articles 7 and 8 of the Directive, which are built upon the work of the OECD's Action 3 of the BEPS[2] Project, require Member States to implement homogeneous measures in order to flatten out the existing legal discrepancies with respect to CFC rules and therefore *"improve resilience of the internal market as a whole against cross-border tax avoidance practices"*[3].

CFC rules are designed to prevent resident taxpayers from shifting income into a low tax jurisdiction where the CFC is located and from stripping the profit base in its residence country. According to the ATAD, the new rules should not give rise to double taxation since this would jeopardize the efficiency of the internal market. Therefore, if the same item of income gets taxed more than once, Member States should grant relief for the taxes already paid in the other Member States.

The purpose of this chapter is to critically analyse Article 8 of the ATAD from a practical perspective. The most important part of it will highlight the extent to which the provisions in Article 8 are consistent with the stated scopes and objectives of the Directive, *praesertim*, avoiding double or multiple taxation when applying the Directive, and *in genere*, whether the coveted harmonization can be achieved via the ATAD.

This chapter is divided into three main sections. The first section consists of a brief overview of the core problems tackled by CFC regimes and the corresponding mechanisms used to solve those issues. The second section will analyse in detail the rules of calculating and allocating CFC income according to first four paragraphs in Article 8. Section three will focus on the presumed prevention and relief for double taxation as provided in paragraphs 5, 6, and 7 of Article 8. Moreover, the analysis will appraise cases of double/multiple taxation not addressed by the Directive and will review whether any potential solutions to remedy those issues are available in European law and in the OECD's "soft law".

---

[1] Council Directive (EU) 2016/1164 of 12 July 2016 laying down rules against tax avoidance practices that directly affect the functioning of the internal market.
[2] OECD/G20's Base Erosion and Profit Shifting (BEPS) Project Action 3: Designing Effective Controlled Foreign Company Rules, Action 3 – 2015 Final Report.
[3] ATAD, Preamble (16).

2. CFC regimes and the Anti-Tax Avoidance Directive

2.1. Controlled foreign companies erode the taxable base and shift profits to low tax jurisdictions

In order to provide a pertinent analysis of Article 8 of the Directive regarding the computation and attribution of CFC income, it is important to understand what issues are caused by controlled foreign corporations and the remedies that CFC regimes should henceforth offer.

By generating income through a CFC and retaining the non-distributed profits in low tax jurisdictions, the controlling shareholder is killing two birds with one stone: the tax postponement of the tax on profits until actual repatriation[4] and the diversion of income to low tax jurisdictions. As a result, the taxable base of the controlling shareholder is eroded.

In general[5], CFC regimes represent instruments meant to counter tax avoidance, prevent tax deferral[6], and shifting income to low tax jurisdictions that are therefore used to avoid stripping the taxable base. In others words, CFC regimes are used as a limitation of abuse[7]. The application of CFC regimes revolves around four main questions[8]:

What are the control requirements when defining the CFC?[9]

What is the definition of low taxation[10]; do the CFC rules cover all CFCs or only those located in tax havens?

What is the definition of CFC income; is CFC legislation applicable to all income or only to specific types of income?[11]

---

4   Daniel W. Blum, 'Controlled Foreign Companies: Selected Policy Issues – or the Missing Elements of BEPS Action 3 and the Anti-Tax Avoidance Directive', (2018), 46, Intertax, Issue 4, pp. 296-312, https://kluwerlawonline.com/JournalArticle/Intertax/46.4/TAXI2018031 (accessed 31 Mar. 2020).
5   Some CFC regimes (such as the one in Brazil) are not only applicable to low taxed CFCs but to all CFCs in a worldwide income taxation regime.
6   Supra n. 2, recommendations of Action 3.
7   For an analysis of specific CFC rules that apply to all situations and not only as an anti-avoidance rule, please refer to Luis Eduardo Schoueri and Guilherme Galdino, Chapter 7: Controlled Foreign Company Legislation in Brazil, in Controlled Foreign Company Legislation (G.W. Kofler et al. eds., IBFD 2020), Books IBFD (accessed 17 Feb. 2021).
8   R.E. Krever, Chapter 1: Controlled Foreign Company Legislation: General Report in Controlled Foreign Company Legislation (G.W. Kofler et al. eds., IBFD 2020), Books IBFD (accessed 18 Feb. 2021).
9   Preparatory work for Rust Conference "Controlled Foreign Company Legislation" (2019) https://www.wu.ac.at/fileadmin/wu/d/i/taxlaw/events.main/int.events/Rust_Conferences/2019/CFC_Legislation_programme_2019.pdf (accessed 17 Mar. 2020).
10 Ibid.
11 Supra n. 9.

Do attribution rules apply to all CFC investors, or there are some thresholds that should be exceeded?[12]

Once a foreign subsidiary is deemed to be a CFC, subsequent issues regarding computation and attribution of income procedures, but also double taxation, would unequivocally arise.

2.2. The Anti-Tax Avoidance Directive

The ATAD as part of Anti-Tax Avoidance Package encompasses five measures against tax avoidance: interest limitation rule, exit taxation, general anti-avoidance rule (GAAR), CFC rules, and hybrid mismatches. The ATAD is applicable to all taxpayers that are subject to corporate income tax in one or more Member States[13]. Moreover, permanent establishments of third country resident companies that are situated in one or more Member States are also "caught" by the ATAD[14] to the extent that the PE profits are not subject to tax or are exempted from tax in the Member State of the controlling parent[15].

Prior to the time of the ATAD's enactment in 2016, almost half[16] of the Member States had CFC regimes in place[17] while some jurisdictions had substitute measures that were addressing the issue[18]. The European Commission proposal for the CFC rules was intended to fight against disparities between Member States and to comply with the EU fundamental freedoms.[19] All members of the European Union were supposed to have functional CFC legislation aligned with the provisions of the ATAD as of 1 January 2019. The implementation of the Directive by Member States should have the effect of *"strengthening the average level of protection against aggressive tax planning in the internal market"*[20]. As a result, it should create *"a minimum level of protection for national corporate tax systems against tax avoidance practices across the Union"*.[21]

According to the *de minimis*[22] nature of the Directive, Member States should not be impeded from adopting even more exigent standards in order to achieve a higher level of protection for their domestic corporate tax bases. Considering the mini-

---

12 Richard Krever, supra n.8.
13 ATAD, Article 3.
14 ATAD, Article 1.
15 ATAD, Preamble (12).
16 Belgium, Denmark, France, Finland, Germany, Greece, Hungary, Italy, Portugal, Spain, Sweden and the United Kingdom, according to Staff Working Document of the Commission Comm/2016/023 final of 28 Jan 2016, at para 22.
17 Communication from the Commission to the European Parliament and the Council ("Chappeau Communication"), Anti-Tax Avoidance Package: Next steps towards delivering effective taxation and greater transparency in the EU, 28.1.2016.
18 Austria and the Netherlands.
19 ATAD, Preamble (12).
20 ATAD, Preamble (2).
21 ATAD, Preamble (3).
22 ATAD, Article 3.

mum standards in Article 3 of the Directive that are legally binding[23] for Member States and therefore have the possibility of adopting a "*multiple solution*"[24] approach, the implementation process would probably get complicated and give rise to "*legal uncertainty and inconsistent taxation*"[25] within Member States. It would henceforth be difficult to see how the ATAD "*will lead to a higher degree of convergence than the status quo*"[26]. Having the flexibility[27] term in mind, Member States should be able to shape the specific elements of those rules in a way that fits best.

2.3. CFC rules, which model fits best[28]: A, B or both?

2.3.1. Categorical approach under Model A

The provisions of the ATAD containing CFC rules are tailored in consonance with the recommendations of OECD's Action 3 which are "*not a 'minimum standard' but are referred to as a 'best practices' approach*"[29]. The aim of Articles 7 and 8 of the Directive is to "*reattributing the income of a low-taxed controlled subsidiary to its parent company*"[30]. Subsequently, the shareholder "*becomes taxable on this attributed income in the State where it is resident for tax purposes*"[31].

Depending on the policy pursued by such a residence state, "*CFC rules may target an entire low-taxed subsidiary, specific categories of income or be limited to income which has artificially been diverted to the subsidiary*"[32]. From these three categories: (i) entire low-taxed income, (ii) specific (usually passive) categories of income, and (iii) artificially diverted income, the only option available for Member States is the third one. This is due to proportionality limitations that make the CFC rules compatible with primary EU law[33].

---

23 Article 288 of the TFEU: "*A directive shall be binding, as to the result to be achieved, upon each Member State to which it is addressed, but shall leave to the national authorities the choice of form and methods*", https://eur-lex.europa.eu/legal-content/EN/TXT/?uri=celex%3A12012E%2FTXT (accessed 17 Mar. 2020).
24 Ana Paula Dourado, 'The EU Anti Tax Avoidance Package: Moving Ahead of BEPS?', (2016), 44, Intertax, Issue 6, pp. 440-446, https://kluwerlawonline.com/JournalArticle/Intertax/44.6/TAXI2016036 (accessed 15 Mar. 2020)
25 Guglielmo Ginevra, 'The EU Anti-Tax Avoidance Directive and the Base Erosion and Profit Shifting (BEPS) Action Plan: Necessity and Adequacy of the Measures at EU level', (2017), 45, Intertax, Issue 2, pp. 120-137 (accessed 31 May 2020).
26 M. Klokar & M. Riedl, Chapter 5: Controlled Foreign Company Legislation in Austria in Controlled Foreign Company Legislation (G.W. Kofler et al. eds., IBFD 2020), Books IBFD (accessed 16 Feb. 2021).
27 Guglielmo Ginevra, supra n. 25.
28 ATAD, Preamble (3).
29 Nathalie Bravo, Sriram Govind, Rita Julien, Pedro G. Lindenberg Schoueri, 'Implementing Key BEPS Actions: Where Do We Stand?', (2017), 45, Intertax, Issue 12, pp. 852-863, https://kluwerlawonline.com/JournalArticle/Intertax/45.12/TAXI2017075 (accessed 31 May 2020).
30 ATAD, Preamble (12).
31 Ibid.
32 Ibid.
33 ATAD, Preamble (16): "*in order to ensure that CFC rules are a proportionate response to BEPS concerns, it is critical that Member States that limit their CFC rules to income which has been artificially diverted to the subsidiary*".

On a general view outside the ATAD, either all or none of the income of the controlled subsidiary may fall under the scope of the CFC income definition[34]. However, according to this approach, even if there is attributable tainted income, but it is under a certain threshold, that income will not be characterized as attributable.[35] In spite of the fact that this threshold limitation approach is suggested in Recital 12 as an option that might be considered when designing CFC rules, the ATAD is contemplating this possibility only as a non-binding option under Article 7(4).

As Model A is targeting certain categories of income that are obtained from non-genuine arrangements[36] and, as Model B is focusing on artificially diverted income situations and considering the carve out clause, Member States may only apply CFC rules to wholly artificial arrangements[37].

With regards to all of the items included in the passive income list, it should be noted that most of them can be easily created between affiliated enterprises for the purpose of stripping the taxable base in the country of residence of the parent company and also for profit shifting towards low tax jurisdictions where the CFCs are located. That could be explained by the fact that these types of income are considered geographically mobile[38] and therefore easily shifted across borders.[39]

2.3.2. The substantive approach provided by Model B

As the definition of CFC income under Model B is covered in detail in Chapter 11, "Taxable income under option 7(2)(b) of ATAD", by Jovdat Mammadov, it will be briefly discussed further on in this subsection. Subparagraph b of Article 7(2) is targeting the retained income of the controlled foreign entity or permanent establishment, *"arising from non-genuine arrangements which have been put in place for the essential purpose of obtaining tax advantage"*.

It is interesting to observe that, compared to Model A which enumerates a list of passive income, Model B refers to artificially diverted income and it would therefore be reasonable to assume it includes both active and passive income. Never-

---

34 Action 3, para. 95.
35 Ibid.
36 The ATAD, Article 7(2)(a) specifically excludes the categories of income that arise in genuine arrangements by providing the following paragraph: *"This point shall not apply where the controlled foreign company carries on a substantive economic activity supported by staff, equipment, assets and premises, as evidenced by relevant facts and circumstances"*.
37 Case C-196/04 Cadbury Schweppes plc and Cadbury Schweppes Overseas Ltd v. Commissioners of Inland Revenue.
38 OECD Action 3 para. 74, while the GILTI or "Global Intangible Low Tax Income" considers income earned by foreign affiliates of US companies from intangible assets such as patents, trademarks, and copyrights that are highly mobile.
39 Till Moser, Sven Hentschel, 'The Provisions of the EU Anti-Tax Avoidance Directive Regarding Controlled Foreign Company Rules: A Critical Review Based on the Experience with the German CFC Legislation', Intertax, 45/10 (2017) (accessed 1 Jun. 2020).

theless, activities that have real economic substance should not fall within the ambit of CFC rules. Compared to the categorical approach in Article 7(2)(a) that makes a reference to the location of the CFC in the carve out clause, the scope of the substance analysis may be construed as extending to CFCs domiciled outside the European Union[40]. The ATAD provides an option for Member States to have a wider scope of the CFC rules under Model A by not applying the economic substance carve out rule to CFCs situated in third countries. As correctly pointed out in tax literature, this option is possible due to the fact that EU primary law does not cover the situation between a parent company resident in a Member State and its subsidiary CFC that is resident in a third country. Thus, strictly in these situations, *"ATAD allows for a discriminatory treatment irrespective of whether the foreign entities carry on a substantive economic activity"*[41].

2.3.3. A third alternative?

The wording of the Directive leaves room for interpretation when suggesting Member States choose one of the two methods or even both. From a linguistic point of view, the conjunction "or" linking paragraphs a and b of Article 7(2) leads the reader to believe that there are three choices to be considered.[42] The absence of the conjunction "either" used together with "or"[43] to offer a choice between two possibilities coupled with the *de minimis* character of the Directive[44] could imply the non-mandatory idea of choosing a single method in a Member State. Moreover, the "substantive activity" carve-out clause inserted in the categorical approach denotes the fact that Model A is not a purely categorical one, but a seasoned one, with elements of substantive analysis.

Concerning the implementation of both approaches in a Member State, it is worthwhile mentioning the case of the Netherlands where the Dutch legislator considered that Model B was already applied in the Netherlands with respect to CFC rules before the ATAD. As of 2019, additional CFC rules that are (partly) based on Model A are also applicable, therefore, a hybrid system of CFC rules is applied in this country.[45]

---

40 Julia De Jong, 'Controlled Foreign Company Rules and the EU' in Limiting Base Erosion, Controlled Foreign Company Rules and the EU, Michael Lang (Ed.), Erik Pinetz and Erich Schaffer (Eds.), Series on International Tax Law, Linde, 2017 (accessed 11 Jul. 2020).
41 Ioana-Felicia Rosca, Chapter 31: Controlled Foreign Company Rules in Romania in Contrrolled Foreign Company Legislation (G.W. Kofler et al. eds., IBFD 2020), Books IBFD (accessed 17 Feb. 2021).
42 Guglielmo Ginevra, supra n. 25.
43 https://www.macmillandictionary.com/dictionary/british/or "Or": used for connecting possibilities or choices. In a list, 'or' is usually used only before the last possibility or choice (accessed 15 Mar. 2020).
44 ATAD, Article 3.
45 R.P.C. Adema, J.N. Bouwman & I.J.J. Burgers, Chapter 24: Controlled Foreign Company Legislation in the Netherlands in Controlled Foreign Company Legislation (G.W. Kofler et al. eds., IBFD 2020), Books IBFD (accessed 17 Feb. 2021).

On the contrary, some Member States like Bulgaria or Finland chose neither of the two models. Bulgaria applies a differentiated provision than Article 7(2)(a) or (b) and is considered in tax literature to have implemented the ATAD *"in the most taxpayer friendly manner, with the exception of proof matter"*[46]. In Finland, as the taxable CFC income is not divided into active and passive income or income generated by non-genuine arrangements, it is difficult to assess which model (if any) was chosen to be implemented.[47]

3. What are the rules for the computation and attribution of CFC income?

3.1. Calculation and attribution of CFC income under Model A[48]

3.1.1. Computation of CFC income under Model A

Following the same line of reasoning that was used when defining the CFC income with respect to computing and attributing CFC income, the Directive again points out the approaches mentioned previously, the categorical approach and the substantive one.

The categorical approach in Model A targets certain categories of non-distributed income of the CFC or PE that is derived from passive income. Computing the income of a CFC requires two determinations: which jurisdiction's rules should apply and whether any specific rules for computing CFC income are needed[49].

Concerning the first determination, according to Article 8(1) of the Directive, the controlled foreign corporation or permanent establishment's tainted income should be taxed in the controlling parent's jurisdiction. Therefore, under Model A, the retained income of the CFC shall be calculated according to the corporate tax rules of the Member State where the controlling shareholder is resident and not in accordance with the taxing legislation where the controlled foreign subsidiary is located. This reasoning seems to be in line with OECD's Action 3 report which recommended this option for the first determination needed for the computation of the CFC income. Alongside this option, Action 3 provided three other options when deciding which jurisdiction's rules should apply for the computation of CFC income. One option would be to use the CFC's jurisdiction's rules for the calculation of CFC income. This, however, would be inconsistent with the goals of Action 3 as such computational rules might allow less income to be allo-

---

46 I. Lazarov, Chapter 8: Controlled Foreign Company Legislation in Bulgaria in Controlled Foreign Company Legislation (G.W. Kofler et al. eds., IBFD 2020), Books IBFD, page 93 (accessed 17 Feb. 2021).
47 K. Äimä & H. Lyyski, Chapter 15: Controlled Foreign Company Legislation in Finland in Controlled Foreign Company Legislation (G.W. Kofler et al. eds., IBFD 2020), Books IBFD (accessed 17 Feb. 2021).
48 Member States that have opted for the categorical approach are: Austria, Croatia, Czech Republic, Greece, Italy, Lithuania, Poland, Portugal, Romania, Slovenia and Sweden.
49 Action 3, para. 99.

cated to the parent company. Another option would be to allow the controlling taxpayers to choose either jurisdiction's computational rules, but this may create opportunities for tax planning.[50]

The calculation of CFC income using the rules of the parent jurisdiction is considered to result in reduced administrative costs for the tax administrations[51] that would have to work with accustomed rules and regulations. On the contrary, using the CFC jurisdiction's computational rules could increase administrative burden costs and complexity as tax administrations would have to apply unfamiliar rules.[52]

Moreover, considering the fact that the parent taxpayer has to calculate the income of the controlled foreign entity under the accounting standards of its country of residency and for CFC taxation purposes under the tax accounting standards in the jurisdiction of the CFC's domicile, the compliance costs for the controlling shareholder could increase significantly.[53] This computation is needed for comparing the CFC passive income and corporate tax burden with a comparable domestic passive income and the corporate tax burden in the Member State where the controlling parent is resident. The comparison should ensure that the taxable base of the controlling parent is not reduced in the low tax jurisdiction through appropriate accounting measures.[54]

The Directive briefly provides that the CFC tainted income that is computed based on the categorical approach should be included in the tax base of the controlling shareholder in the jurisdiction of its residency. However, after computing the retained income, the Directive does not offer guidance on how to actually proceed when allocating the tainted income to the controlling shareholder[55]. This issue will be further explained in the subsequent section.

3.1.2. Rules for attributing income

From an academic, theoretical perspective and depending on the envisaged objectives, different jurisdictions can rely on a few possibilities when shaping their CFC regimes. However, in such proceedings, the existing legal infrastructure regarding the allocation of taxing rights and also the compliance with the EU fundamental freedoms must be taken into account. Therefore, in order to reach the desired outcome of including the CFC income in the taxable base of the controlling parent, states may rely on a few options: the fictitious tax transparency, the fictitious dividends, and the fictitious unlimited tax liability.

---

50 Idem., para. 100.
51 Idem., para. 101.
52 Idem., para 100(2).
53 Till Moser, supra n. 39.
54 Ibid.
55 Ibid.

Under the first approach through the fictitious tax transparency, by piercing the corporate veil,[56] the controlled foreign entity would be considered transparent for tax purposes, henceforth its income would be included in the tax base of the controlling parent. As this method disregards the CFC as a taxable entity, its income is reattributed to the resident controlling taxpayers and treated, in such a case, like a partner in a partnership. The quality of the CFC as a tax subject is henceforth negated.[57]

With the second option, i.e. the unlimited tax liability, the CFC would be treated as if it was a domestic company in the residence of the parent company. Therefore, the tax return of the CFC would be computed according to the accounting standards in the jurisdiction where the controlling parent is domiciled[58]. The CFC would be regarded as a taxable entity, but its income would be reattributed to the controlling shareholder in accordance with the domestic rules of the parent's jurisdiction. The fictitious unlimited tax liability would require, in most tax systems, a seat or place of effective management as a precondition of unlimited tax liability and could therefore raise issues.[59]

The third possibility, the deemed dividend approach[60], also regards the CFC as a taxable entity, *per se*. The CFC income is computed at the level of the controlled foreign entity under the accounting standards of the respective low-tax jurisdiction while the attribution of the profits towards the controlling resident shareholder should take the form of a fictitious dividend. The fictitious distributions would be taxed in the hands of the controlling taxpayer[61].

As the wording of the Directive refers to CFC regimes having the effect of "reattributing" the income of a low taxed controlled subsidiary to its controlling parent,[62] it would be reasonable to assume that all three theoretical approaches may be considered when implementing the ATAD within the limits of EU compliance framework.

According to Article 8(3), the income to be included in the tax base of the parent shareholder should be calculated in proportion to the controlling taxpayer's participation in the controlled subsidiary. However, this participation of the controlling taxpayer is not clarified in terms of prevalence or a tie breaker rule. This could be explained by the fact that the ATAD only sets minimum standards, and Member States can implement stricter rules. There is no doubt though, that for permanent establishments, the attribution should be 100%. It is interesting to note that, while in this article, the Directive is referring to the proportional participation

---

56 Daniel Blum, supra n. 4.
57 Till Moser, supra n. 39.
58 Ibid.
59 Ibid.
60 Daniel Blum, supra n. 4.
61 Ibid.
62 ATAD, Preamble (12).

of the controlling shareholder in the controlled entity, the control test in Article 7(1)(a) mentions the voting rights, capital ownership, and profit entitlement.

It should be pointed out that Article 8(1) is applicable in connection with Model A while Article 8(2) refers to the computation of CFC income under Model B. Given the phrasing of Article 8(2) and 8(3) of the ATAD, it seems plausible to conclude that the applicability of the latter one is valid in connection with the categorical approach under Model A. Furthermore, under the substantive approach in Model B, the income of the controlled foreign entity is calculated and attributed[63] to the controlling parent in consonance with transfer pricing rules as provided by Article 8(2).

3.1.3. Treatment of losses

Computing the CFC income requires two variables: which jurisdictional rules should apply and whether any specific rules are needed. The former variable is established by the ATAD as the parent's jurisdictional rules which should be considered when calculating the CFC income. The latter one refers to losses and limitation of offsetting losses.

By generating losses at the level of the CFC, the taxable base of the controlling shareholder could be distorted. Manoeuvring losses between controlled subsidiaries and a controlling parent may create incentives for manipulating the tax base in the parent's jurisdiction and henceforth reduce the tax burden. In order to prevent such a situation, the second sentence of Article 8(1) of the Directive states that losses of a controlled foreign subsidiary or permanent establishment "*shall not be included in the tax base*" of the parent taxpayer. The application of this measure is expected to result in combating abuse of law. It prevents companies from allowing losses generated at the level of the CFC to be compensated with the profits of the controlling company. However, the ATAD provides the option for Member States for losses to be "*carried forward, according to the national law and taken into account in subsequent tax periods*".

It is interesting to observe the way that some Member States are treating the losses of a CFC. In Austria, if the negative passive income exceeds the positive passive income, the surplus could be carried forward in subsequent tax years, but the loss offsetting cannot be higher than the passive income of the same CFC.[64] While in Finland losses of a CFC can be set off against the income of the parent company or other group companies in the following years[65], in Poland[66], loss carry forward

---

63 ATAD, Article 8(2).
64 M. Klokar & M. Riedl, Chapter 5: Controlled Foreign Company Legislation in Austria in Controlled Foreign Company Legislation (G.W. Kofler et al. eds., IBFD 2020), Books IBFD (accessed 17 Feb. 2021).
65 K. Äimä & H. Lyyski, Chapter 15: Controlled Foreign Company Legislation in Finland in Controlled Foreign Company Legislation (G.W. Kofler et al. eds., IBFD 2020), Books IBFD (accessed 17 Feb. 2021).
66 A. Wardzynski, Chapter 29: Controlled Foreign Company Legislation in Poland in Controlled Foreign Company Legislation (G.W. Kofler et al. eds., IBFD 2020), Books IBFD (accessed 17 Feb. 2021).

of a CFC is not allowed. Croatia[67] does not provide the benefit of carry forwards for CFC losses in its domestic legislation.

Another concern with respect to losses would be the inherited or imported ones incurred by the foreign entity before the date it was characterized as a CFC. However, if losses are only available for setting off against CFC profits, then *a priori* incurred losses of the CFC may not be a problem. This potential loss importation could be treated, in some countries, by domestic regulations designed to prevent tax avoidance[68], as noted in the Action 3 report.

3.1.4. Example of calculation of CFC income according to Model A

By way of illustration, take the example of a CFC subsidiary incorporated under the law of low tax jurisdiction C owned by BCo which, in turn, is owned by ACo together with DCo. A CFC is undertaking activities of developing patents and hence receiving royalties for the use of the patents that are developed and is also generating income from producing smart chips for access cards, developed in house, at the risk of ACo. In addition, the CFC is receiving dividends from a production company, PCo, located in third country T. The sales and marketing functions, but also the strategic management, are performed by ACo.

The prerequisite conditions, according to legislation in Member State A for the CFC to exist, are met. The first condition, as embedded by Article 7(1)(a) regarding the 50% control requirement, directly or indirectly, is fulfilled. The second one provided by point b) in Article 7(1) referring to the actual corporate income tax (CIT) applicable in the CFC's jurisdiction, which has to be lower than the difference between the CIT of the Member State and the CIT of the CFC, is also satisfied. Therefore, the undistributed, retained, passive income of the CFC may be included in the tax base of ACo, BCo, and possibly DCo depending on the shareholder participation.

The royalty income is generated by an active conduct business[69] as the company has a research facility that employs researchers, scientists, and engineers whose work is transposed eventually into patents. Therefore, in the case that State C would be a Member State, State A is obligated to apply the carve out clause provided in Article 7(2)(a). This provision should be construed as being mandatory for CFCs situated in Member States or EEA countries and was introduced in order to comply with the CJEU's jurisprudence[70] regarding one of the EU fundamental freedoms, i.e. the freedom of establishment.

---

67 A. Wardzynski, Chapter 29: Controlled Foreign Company Legislation in Poland in Controlled Foreign Company Legislation (G.W. Kofler et al. eds., IBFD 2020), Books IBFD (accessed 17 Feb. 2021).
68 Action 3, para. 108.
69 US: Internal Revenue Code, Title 26.
70 Till Moser, supra n. 39.

However, when applying the same reasoning towards CFCs domiciled in third countries (outside the European Union or the Economic European Area), Member States may choose not to implement this substance exemption. Although, if applied, this optional exception does not infringe the freedom of establishment, it could arguably be against another EU fundamental freedom, the only one reflected in respect with third countries, the free movement of capital. To put it shortly, if state C was a third country, for state A, it would not be mandatory to apply the aforementioned carve out clause[71] as this clause is optional for third countries.

In the example bellow, the passive income that falls within the ambit of the ATAD is comprised by royalties and dividends, totaling 1,200 (the currency is not relevant as not all Member States are using the EUR). Having at hand a third country scenario without the carve out clause applicable, even though the CFC's activities have economic substance, some of its income qualifies as passive. The attributable passive income captured by CFC rules in Member States A, B, and D would amount to 1,200.

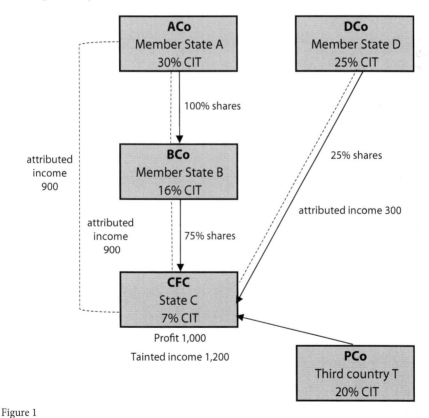

Figure 1

---

71   ATAD, Article 7(2)(a).

In a simplistic manner, the profit & loss (P&L) of the CFC in a third country scenario where the carve out clause is not applied could be computed as follows:

CFC P&L

Salaries	500	Royalties	1000
Rent for lab	100	Dividends from TCo	200
Rent for production hall	100	Resold goods	600
Prefabricated goods costs	300	Sold production	500
Magnetic cards production costs	300		
Total expenses:	1,300	Total revenue:	2,300
Profit (2,300 – 1,300)	1,000		
Retained tainted income (1,000 royalties + 200 TCo dividends)	1,200		

As seen above, the total profit of the CFC would be 1,000 (revenues minus expenses). However, the CFC tainted income to be attributed to its controlling shareholders would be 1,200, as it is comprised of 1,000 in royalties and the 200 TCo dividends. The retained passive income would be allocated to the controlling shareholders based on their participation in the CFC: 300 towards Dco (25% of 1,200) and 900 towards Bco (75% of 1,200).

It should be pointed out that, if the CFC would be located in a Member State and not a third country, the CFC income would not fall within the ambit of CFC rules as the ATAD targets only wholly artificial arrangements.

3.2. Computation and allocation of income under Model B[72]

3.2.1. Calculation and attribution of income under Model B

The computation of the income artificially diverted to the CFC, as defined in Article 7(2)(b), is comprised in Article 8(2) and refers to the substantive analysis approach. This methodology, as highlighted in the OECD's Action 3 report, is aimed at assessing whether the CFC is engaged in substantial activity and has the capacity to earn income by itself[73], or it has been established in the low tax jurisdiction for the essential purpose of availing a tax advantage[74].

Providing that the controlled foreign entity fails the principal purpose test, the income of the controlled foreign entity falls under the incidence of CFC regimes.[75]

---

72 The Member States that have opted for the substantive analysis approach are Belgium, Cyprus, Estonia, Hungary, Ireland, Latvia, Luxembourg, Malta, and Slovakia.
73 Action 3, para. 81.
74 ATAD, Article 7(2)(b).
75 Ibid.

An arrangement between the controlling parent and the CFC should be regarded as non-genuine to the extent that the CFC would not own assets or undertake the risks that generated the CFC income if it was not controlled by the parent company that actually performed the relevant functions[76]. As the Directive connects the substance analysis with the arm's length principle, it henceforth makes the liaison between non-genuine arrangements and the functional analysis of functions, assets, and risks of the controlled foreign entity[77].

The CFC income that should be included in the tax base of the controlling parent should not exceed the amounts generated through the assets and risks linked to the significant people functions carried out by that controlling parent.[78]

As there is no definition in tax literature for "significant people functions" (SPFs), the term may be interpreted according to the OECD's 2010 report on the Attribution of Profits to Permanent Establishments. The SPFs refer to the functions carried out by the enterprise that contribute to the value creation and, forthwith, should be entitled to a portion of the residual profit or loss. Under the authorized OECD approach (AOA), although a PE is not legally a separate entity *per se*, for tax purposes, the profits to be attributed to a PE are those that the PE would have earned at arm's length. This requires treating the permanent establishment as if the PE was a separate and independent entity, undertaking similar activities, under similar conditions, taking into account the functions performed, assets used, and risks assumed by the enterprise through the PE and through the other parts of the company[79]. The SPFs relevant to the assumption of risks are those that require active decision-making regarding the management of those risks.[80] Under the AOA, the attribution of risks and the economic ownership of assets will follow[81] the identification of the significant people functions relevant for the assumption or management of those risks. In other words, when the SPF relevant to the assumption or management of risks and/or to the economic ownership of assets are carried out by the PE, those risks and/or ownership of assets are attributed to the PE.

In a similar manner, when considering CFCs, the analysis will focus on the identification of SPFs performed by the controlling companies and CFCs rather than PEs. If those SPFs were instrumental[82] in generating the controlled foreign entity's income and the arrangement surrounding those SPFs was non-genuine and put in place for the essential purpose of availing tax benefits, then a CFC charge would consequently arise. Based on the controlling shareholder's nexus with respect to the CFC's activities, the determination of the amount of the artificially

---

76 Ibid.
77 ATAD, Article 8(2).
78 Ibid.
79 Attribution of Profits to PE Report (2010), para. 8.
80 Idem., para. 22.
81 Idem., para. 24.
82 ATAD, Article 7(2)(b).

diverted income has to be performed according to the arm's length principle that is dealt with in detail in the OECD's Transfer Pricing Guiding rules. The application of the rule to an arrangement or a transaction that was mentioned previously is *"based on a comparison of the conditions in a controlled transaction with the conditions that would have been made had the parties been independent and undertaking a comparable transaction under comparable circumstances"*[83].

The amount of the retained income of a controlled subsidiary that is included in the accounting profits of the parent company should be available for distribution according to the relevant SPF attributable to the controlling shareholder. The undistributed income of a controlled foreign company, for a certain accounting period, should include the distributable profits for that specific period after the deduction of the actual distributions, if any, already made for the corresponding time frame.[84]

The substantive approach under Model B captures the CFC income generated through the assets and risks that are linked to the SPFs carried out by the controlling shareholder of the CFC. Therefore, when applying the approach that was mentioned previously the following steps should be taken, assuming that the control requirements and the effective tax rate test are met:

- The principal purpose test to assess whether the essential purpose of setting up the CFC was to secure tax advantage;
- Providing that the CFC's fails the test, a functional and factual analysis has to be performed to identify the significant people functions relevant the assumption of risks and to the economic ownership of assets and capital ;
- Determination and allocation of the CFC income according to relevant SPF of the controlling shareholder based on the arm's length principle
- as envisaged by Article 9 of the Model Convention if the CFC is an entity *per se*, or
- Determination and attribution of CFC income under the OECD approach at arm's length pursuant to Article 7(2) of the MC if the CFC is not an entity *per se* but a permanent establishment of the parent shareholder to the extent that the profits of the PE are not subject to tax in the parent's Member State.

3.2.2. Example of computation of CFC income under Model B

Let us consider the CFC in Figure 2, assuming that State A is following the substantive approach. The functional analysis reveals that the sales, marketing, and strategic management, which can be seen as the "decision making functions"[85], are actually performed by the parent shareholder in State A. Besides, all activities performed in state C are undertaken on the account and risk of ACo. Therefore,

---

83 OECD Transfer Pricing Guidelines (2017), para. 1.33.
84 ATAD, Article 8(5).
85 ATAD, Preamble (12).

in the context of SPFs being carried out by ACo that are instrumental in generating the CFC's income, a CFC charge would arise. An external transfer pricing report opines that a cost plus of 5% is an appropriate remuneration for the activities undertaken by the CFC (see the profit and loss account of the CFC). In the example below, based on the functions performed, risks assumed, and assets owned, the CFC would be treated as a toll manufacturer and a contract service provider.

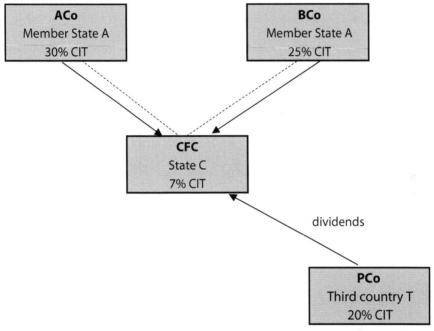

Figure 2

CFC P&L

Salaries	500	Royalties	1000
Rent for lab	100	Dividends from TCo	200
Rent for production hall	100	Resold goods	600
Prefabricated goods costs	300	Sold production	500
Magnetic cards production costs	300		
Total operational expenses:	1,300	Total operational revenue:	2,300
Operational Profit (2,300 – 1,300)	1,000		
Profit CFC (5% CPM * 1,300)	65		
Distributed profit	200		
Artificially diverted income	735		

Based on the arm's length principle and using the OECD's Transfer Pricing Guidelines, the income that was artificially diverted to the low-tax jurisdiction should be allocated to the controlling shareholder in consonance with Article 9 of the Model Convention. In the case above, that would be 735: the operational profit of 1,000 minus the relevant distribution of 200 and minus 65 which is the CFC profit that was estimated at 5% CPM over the 1,300 expenses.

Although it seems that transfer pricing rules and CFC legislation address the same income, this might not always be the case[86]. CFC rules are often referred to as "backstops" to transfer pricing rules[87]. However, CFC rules do not always complement transfer pricing rules. The OECD states that transfer pricing rules and CFC regimes do not eliminate the need for both set of rules: both are needed in order to price controlled transactions and mitigate cases of base erosion. While Article 9 would apply in all cases of intercompany transactions, CFC rules' reallocation would be only valid with respect to wholly artificial arrangements. The applicability of CFC rules would imply that the situation is artificial and the transactions at hand would be recharacterized according to transfer pricing rules. The simultaneous application of the two sets of rules seems implausible. Once transfer pricing rules "take over", CFC rules are no longer applicable as "*neither set of rules fully captures the income that the other set of rules intends to capture*"[88].

3.3. Accounting periods

According to Article 8(4) of the Directive, the accounting period for calculating and attributing the CFC income should be aligned with the tax period of the parent taxpayer. Although the OECD suggests an all-or-nothing approach for the corresponding year, some Member States[89] take into consideration only the period that a foreign entity is deemed as a CFC[90] while others[91] will embrace the whole accounting frame even if the control test was met only for a short period of time.

When the accounting years of the controlling parent and the controlled subsidiary are not coinciding, some Member States[92] opt to include only the corresponding time in the parent's taxable base (if the CFC's year ends on 30 June and the parent's year ends on 31 December, only half of the CFC income would be included in the tax return of the controlling shareholder while the rest would be

---

86 Action 3, para. 8.
87 Ibid.
88 Ibid.
89 Ireland.
90 I.M. de Groot & B. Larking, Implementation of Controlled Foreign Company Rules under the EU Anti-Tax Avoidance Directive (2016/1164), 59 Eur. Taxn. 6 (2019), Journal Articles & Papers IBFD (accessed 31Mar. 2020).
91 Hungary, starting 2020.
92 The Netherlands.

rolled out on the subsequent fiscal year[93]. Other Member States will include the undistributed income of the controlled subsidiary in the tax period of the controlling shareholder when the CFC's tax period ended.[94]

3.4. Level of taxation

As pointed out in OECD's Action 3, attribution of income raises the question of how to tax the CFC income once it is allocated to the parent shareholder.[95] The Directive sets out[96] *de minimis* standards concerning the control requirement in a foreign entity or the low tax threshold. However, although specified that the taxation of the imputed income should be levied in the country of residence of the controlling shareholder, neither Article 7 nor Article 8 specify the level of taxation that should be applied. It should be noted the imposing obligation for Members States embedded in Article 7(2), that *"the Member State of the taxpayer shall include in the tax base"*. This should be corroborated with the last phrase of Article 7(1): *"the corporate tax that would have charged in the Member State of the taxpayer means as computed according to the rules of the Member State of the taxpayer"*.

3.5. Advantages and drawbacks of the two approaches

In connection with Model A, Article 8(1) of the Directive requires for the CFC income to calculated in accordance with the provisions that are applicable in the country of residence of the controlling shareholder. Additionally, the controlled subsidiary has to compute its tax return according to the accounting standards in the low tax jurisdiction. This dual calculation can increase compliance costs for the controlling taxpayer. On the contrary, the substance analysis in Model B may increase the administrative burden and compliance costs as it may require the relevant authorities to cover a large number of companies under their CFC regimes, perform case-by-case analyses, and rely more on qualitative measures than categorical approaches.[97]. In this author's opinion, based on the analysis of other authors' considerations, Model B is able to better identify certain categories of income[98] or to attribute more accurately the ones that raise BEPS concerns compared to the categorical approach. Furthermore, a transactional approach is more likely to comply with EU law and also in consonance with the goals of Action 3 BEPS[99].

---

93 Isabella de Groot, supra n. 90.
94 Ibid.
95 Action 3, para. 119.
96 ATAD, Article 7(2)(a) and (b).
97 Action 3, para. 83.
98 Action 3, para. 81.
99 Action 3, para. 97.

The liaison between Model B and the arm's length principle could add more confidence for the tax authorities when this approach is embraced by Member States that had already been applying transfer pricing rules.[100]

Regarding the *onus probandi*, in the case of Model A, the supporting evidence process falls on the shoulders of the parent taxpayer[101] although EU law does not allow the presumption of tax avoidance unless the tax administration produces evidence, *prima facie*[102].

The substance analysis in Model B could better identify and quantify the shifted income[103] as it is able to address new business models[104] that cannot be covered by Model A. However, as the sources of passive income are not clearly defined, the controlling parent could encounter a higher level of legal uncertainty[105] as opposed to CFC regimes following Model A for which the sources of passive income are catalogued.

As an interim conclusion, this author thinks that, when implementing CFC rules according to the ATAD, each of the two models as provided by the Directive present advantages and disadvantages. However, the choice made would depend on the policies and objectives pursued by various Member States.

4. CFC rules and prevention of double taxation

4.1. The relief for double taxation under Article 8(5), (6), and (7) of the ATAD

4.1.1. The issue of double taxation under ATAD

The CFC regimes as provided by the ATAD permit Member States to tax their own residents with interest in low-taxed controlled subsidiaries as this is considered appropriate. The fact that CFC regimes require a cross border component is expected to raise issues of potential double taxation. While some cases of double taxation are addressed and (partially) solved by the Directive, others remain in suspense.

Double taxation in the context of implementing the Directive is acknowledged in the Preamble of the ATAD as a potential side effect[106]. As the application of CFC regimes may give rise to double taxation, the Directive provides rules in para-

---

100 Guglielmo Ginevra, supra n. 25.
101 Supra n. 36, para.70.
102 Guglielmo Ginevra, supra n. 25.
103 Action 3, para. 82.
104 Till Moser, supra n. 39.
105 Ibid.
106 ATAD, Preamble (5).

graphs 5, 6, and 7 of Article 8 for avoiding double/multiple taxation of the same CFC income by two or more countries. The profits subsequently distributed by a CFC as dividends, the gains obtained from the disposal of participation in a foreign entity or of the business carried out by permanent establishment, and the taxes paid by the controlled subsidiary should not give rise to double taxation. In this author's view, it is worthwhile observing, in all three paragraphs dealing with potential double taxation situations, the usage of the verb "shall" which has an imperative connotation as opposed to "might" or "may" which can both be construed as optional. Henceforth, Member States are obligated under the ATAD to prevent and grant relief in the case of double taxation occurring in the three situations previously mentioned.

4.1.2. Treatment of actual distributions

When a part of the CFC income is distributed towards the controlling shareholder and that distributed income was already taxed in the hands of the controlling parent by means of inclusion in the tax base pursuant to Article 7 of the ATAD, double taxation may arise. The Directive provides for a solution to avoid double taxation of the actual distributions already made at the level of the controlled foreign entity. Therefore, the profits distributed by the foreign entity to the controlling parent should not be taxed again in the hands of the controlling shareholders. Article 8(5) provides for a tax deduction that should be allowed for the resident controlling taxpayer towards the taxes paid by the controlled foreign entity in its domicile jurisdiction.[107]

However, most jurisdictions will provide some relief for the dividends paid by the CFC thorough the double tax treaties that are concluded and, most likely, these dividends would qualify for the participation exemption for foreign dividends.[108] Assuming that the controlling parent holds the minimum required participation and it is also the beneficial owner of the dividends,[109] the participation exemption is likely to apply, and a tax credit[110] should be granted in the jurisdiction of the parent shareholder (taking into account the maximum credit allowed). In this author's opinion, the applicability of Article 8(5) may be required only if there is no participation exemption as envisaged by Article 10 of the Model Convention or there is no bilateral treaty concluded.

---

107 The ATAD, Article 8(5): *"Where the entity distributes profits to the taxpayer, and those distributed profits are included in the taxable income of the taxpayer, the amounts of income previously included in the tax base pursuant to Article 7 shall be deducted from the tax base when calculating the amount of tax due on the distributed profits, in order to ensure there is no double taxation."*
108 OECD Model Tax Convention on Income and Capital (2017), Article 10.
109 Idem., Article 10(2).
110 Idem., Article 23A or 23B, depending on the relief method chosen in the bilateral treaty.

4.1.3. Disposal of shares

Double taxation could arise when the controlling shareholder disposes its shares in a controlled foreign entity and that controlling parent was already taxed on the income of the CFC. If any parts of the proceeds regarding the selling of the shares in the CFC were previously included in the taxable base of the controlling parent, that amount should be deducted from the tax base when computing the tax burden on those proceeds. Application of Article 8(6) should ensure there is no double taxation in such a situation.

4.1.4. Taxes paid by the CFC

Double taxation may occur when the CFC or permanent establishment pays taxes in the jurisdiction of its domicile and, afterwards, the controlling shareholder would be taxed again on the same tax base in its residency jurisdiction. Article 8(7) provides for an implementation of a credit system through deduction on the profit taxes paid at the level of the controlled foreign entity against the corporate taxes due in the controlling taxpayer's country of residence. The OECD report finds out that this is *"perhaps the most obvious situation where the application of CFC rules may lead to double taxation"*.[111]

Paragraphs 5 and 6 of Article 8 that are aimed at avoiding juridical double taxation arising from the repatriation of the profits of the CFC are in line with the recommendations of Action 3. The rule contained in paragraph 7, however, is less straightforward and poses specific issues.[112] In particular, the wording "paid by the entity" it is not very clear and does not elucidate if it refers only to the taxes paid by the CFC in its own jurisdiction. Once CFC income is attributed to the controlling shareholder, the corresponding taxes due in the residence country of parent shareholder are paid by the parent and not by the controlled subsidiary. Moreover, it does not specify if "taxes paid by the entity" could also refer to the taxes paid on the income already attributed to a controlling parent in another Member State.[113] In this author's opinion, such a scenario could, *de facto*, occur when Model A in Article 7(2)(a) is heterogeneously implemented by Member States in terms of defining participation rates in a CFC (shares, voting rights, or profit distribution). Therefore, an homogenous implementation within the European Union regarding participation in a CFC would be expected to lead to more certainty when dealing with double taxation and CFC regimes.

---

111 Action 3, para. 124.
112 Guglielmo Ginevra, supra n. 25.
113 Ibid.

4.2. Does the ATAD provide solutions against all potential cases of double or multiple taxation?

4.2.1. The issue of double or multiple taxation under CFC rules

According to the Preamble of the Directive, when the application of CFC rules gives rise to double taxation, taxpayers should get relief for the taxes paid in another Member State or a third country, as the case may be.[114] Double taxation is acknowledged to be incompatible with the internal market and addressed by the Directive through paragraphs 5, 6, and 7 of Article 8. However, the Directive does not offer solutions for preventing double/multiple taxation cases resulting from inconsistent application of the Directive due to the *de minimis* character of the ATAD at the level of different Member States. Moreover, the different interpretations that some Member States might choose to embrace could even be more problematic.

In the event of having double or multiple taxation issues resulting from the application of CFC regimes not covered by the ATAD, it is the taxpayers' responsibility to identify the correct source of law for proving relief for double taxation. The Directive covers taxpayers that are subject to corporate income tax within the European Union. Most Member States are either part of the OECD organization or are just following the principles, recommendations, and guidelines issued by the OECD. Therefore, this author thinks it would be reasonable to point out that the parent taxpayers in a double or multiple taxation circumstance not covered by the ATAD should look into the domestic legislation, double tax treaties concluded by Member States based on the OECD Model Tax Convention and EU law.

Regarding the connection between CFC rules and tax treaties, the question of whether CFC regimes are compatible with double tax treaties had been heavily debated in the international tax literature. It has been argued that the provisions contained in Article 7(1) and Article 10(5) and CFC regimes are not compatible. The prevalent opinion, but not undisputed, is that CFC legislation and tax treaties are not conflicting. This view is confirmed by the OECD in the Commentaries of Model Convention where it is affirmed that, since CFC legislation results in a state taxing its own residents, it does not conflict with tax conventions[115].

When the solution for CFC regimes sourced double taxation problems cannot be revealed by the applicable tax treaties, taxpayers may seek solutions in EU primary and secondary law: the Parent Subsidiary Directive[116], the Dispute Resolu-

---

114 ATAD, Preamble (5).
115 Commentary on Article 1, OECD Model Convention(2017), para. 81.
116 Council Directive 2011/96/EU of 30 November 2011 on the common system of taxation applicable in the case of parent companies and subsidiaries of different Member States.

tion Directive[117] or the Arbitration Convention[118]. Both Model A and Model B are compliant with EU primary law if they are applied to CFCs not engaged in genuine economic activities[119] and if CFC rules are applicable to both domestic and cross border scenarios.[120] However, as CFC rules are not intended to be applied in domestic situations, they could be considered discriminatory against taxpayers involved in cross border activities.[121] This was clarified in the landmark case Cadbury Schweppes where the Court pointed out that the *"difference in treatment creates a tax disadvantage for the resident company to which the legislation on CFCs is applicable"*[122].

The following points will touch upon cases of double/multiple taxation resulting from the application of CFC rules that are not addressed by the ATAD. Moreover, it will highlight possible answers and solutions to issues raised around those cases.

4.2.2. Double residency for the controlling parent

There may be cases when a controlling parent has a double residency quality: it was incorporated in one state and has the place of management in another country. Member States across Europe embrace either the incorporation theory[123] or the real seat[124] one. When the controlling shareholder has double residency and the doctrines followed by the residency states are conflicting, double taxation may arise in the context of CFC regimes. As the Directive does not address such a situation, in this author's opinion, a possible solution to this issue could be found in the double tax treaty, assuming there is one, concluded between the jurisdictions where the place of incorporation and the place of management/place of effective management are located.

If the bilateral tax treaty was concluded based on the 2010 MC version or older, according to Article 4(3)[125], the state of residence for a double resident taxpayer would be the place of management. Therefore, the parent shareholder would be taxed only in a state where it has its place of management.

---

117 Council Directive (EU) 2017/1852 of 10 October 2017 on tax dispute resolution mechanisms in the European Union.
118 90/436/EEC: Convention on the elimination of double taxation in connection with the adjustment of profits of associated enterprises – Final Act – Joint Declarations – Unilateral Declarations.
119 The carve out clause in Article 7(2)(a) of ATAD.
120 Guglielmo Ginevra, supra n. 25.
121 Action 3, para. 22.
122 Cadbury Schweppes case, supra n. 37, para. 45.
123 Under the incorporation theory, the corporate laws applicable to a legal entity are those of the jurisdiction in which the legal entity has been incorporated irrespective of where the entity has its real seat.
124 Under the real seat theory, the corporate laws applicable to a legal entity are those of the jurisdiction in which the entity is effectively managed.
125 Article 4 (3) of the OECD MC (2010) states that *"Where by reason of the provisions of paragraph 1 a person other than an individual is a resident of both Contracting States, then it shall be deemed to be a resident only of the State in which its place of effective management is situated."*

Whereas a double tax treaty is based on the 2017 MC version, according to the tie-breaker rule in Article 4(3)[126] of the Model Tax Convention on Income and on Capital 2017, the competent authorities shall endeavour to determine by mutual agreement the residency of the parent shareholder. Nevertheless, this fairly new rule can be implemented only if there is a mutual agreement between the two tax administrations of the states involved. It seems plausible, however, that not many states have implemented this provision, and some countries made a reservation to this rule under the MLI[127]. If there is no such agreement between the competent authorities, the parent company could lose treaty benefits[128] and subsequently be facing double taxation. This 2017 rule came into effect as a response of tax administrations to counteract the aggressive tax planning undertaken by the dual residence companies.[129]

4.2.3. Attribution methods

Pursuant to Article 8(3) of the ATAD, the income computed under Model A should be attributed to the controlling parent as a proportion to the parent taxpayer's participation in the CFC: voting rights, capital, or profit entitlement. However, the lack of a prevailing or tie-breaker rule in the ATAD regarding the participation definition due to the *de minims* character of the Directive poses difficulties when Member States apply different allocation rules. Consequently, such an ambiguity could lead to double or multiple taxation.

In the illustrative example below, if State A attributes and taxes 600 of CFC income according to the 75% capital participation, and State B allocates and taxes 640 of CFC income based on the 80% voting rights, the economic double taxation of the same 800 of CFC income in the hands of different taxpayers seems to be unavoidable. Article 8(7) of the ATAD provides a tax credit for the taxes paid by the controlled entity or permanent establishment and not for the taxes paid by controlling shareholders in their residence states. It has been debated under what provisions and to what extent states should grant relief in double taxation situations sourced in the application of CFC regimes[130].

---

126 Article 4(3) of the MC (2017) provides that: "*Where by reason of the provisions of paragraph 1 a person other than an individual is a resident of both Contracting States, the competent authorities of the Contracting States shall endeavour to determine by mutual agreement the Contracting State of which such person shall be deemed to be a resident for the purposes of the Convention, having regard to its place of effective management, the place where it is incorporated or otherwise constituted and any other relevant factors. In the absence of such agreement, such person shall not be entitled to any relief or exemption from tax provided by this Convention except to the extent and in such manner as may be agreed upon by the competent authorities of the Contracting States.*"
127 For more details about the reservations under the multilateral instrument, please refer to N. Bravo, Interpreting Tax Treaties in the Light of Reservations and Opt-Ins under the Multilateral Instrument, 74 Bull. Intl. Taxn. 4/5 (2020), Journal Articles & Opinion Pieces IBFD (accessed 19 Apr. 2021).
128 Commentary on Article 4, OECD MC (2017), para. 24.4.
129 Idem, Commentary on Article 4, para. 23.
130 Annika Soom, 'Double Taxation Resulting from the ATAD: Is There Relief?', (2020), 48, Intertax, Issue 3, pp. 273-285, https://kluwerlawonline.com/JournalArticle/Intertax/48.3/TAXI2020024 (accessed 31 Mar 2020).

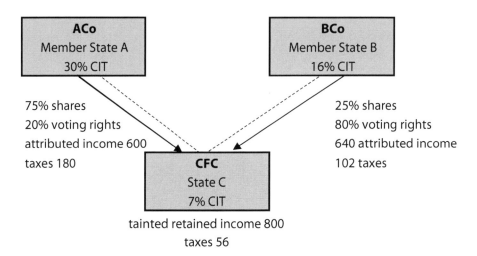

Figure 3

This author supports the idea advanced by other authors[131] that, in a case like the one above, the so-called OECD approach should be applied. It would mandate the controlling shareholder's state to grant a tax credit under Article 23B irrespective of the type of income earned by the CFC, shareholder's participation, or where the income was sourced.

4.2.4. Characterization of income

In the context of a CFC regime, under Model A, the characterization of active income as passive can be problematic from a double taxation perspective. Let us assume that we have a CFC in a third country, and the controlling shareholders are situated in two different Member States. The income of the CFC, *inter alia* royalty, is generated by an active conduct business as the company has a research facility that employs researchers, scientists, and engineers whose work is transposed eventually into patents. Besides the royalty income and the sold production revenue the CFC received dividends from PCo, a production facility in a third country T pursuant to Article 7(2)(a) of the ATAD; the CFC would be subject to CFC rules in Member State A. However, as country A has opted for Model A without the carve-out clause available for third countries, the royalty income of the CFC is catalogued as passive tainted income and therefore included in the tax base of the parent shareholder in Member State A.

---

131 Ibid.

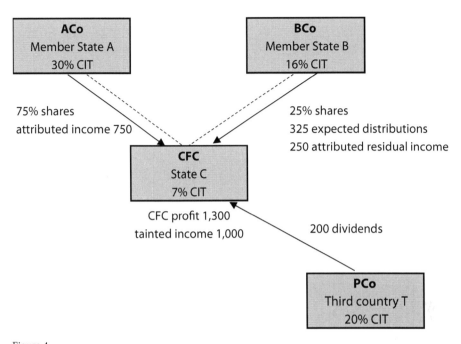

Figure 4

State B is applying Model B with the carve out clause available for third countries. Therefore, the CFC income would not fall within the ambit of CFC rules in Member State B.

However, the fact that the income generated by the CFC is recharacterized by Member State A may affect the profit base of the CFC and consequently deprive Bco of receiving the expected amount of distributed dividends by the CFC. In the example below, if part of the CFC income would not be recharacterized by Member State A as passive, the distributable profits of the CFC would be 1,300. BCo would be entitled to 25% of that amount, 325 respectively. The tainted attributed income captured by CFC rules in Member State A would be 750: 75% out of 1,000 (composed of 800 royalties and 200 dividends). Nevertheless, after being captured by CFC rules in Member State A, the distributable residual amount that would be distributed to BCo would be 25% of 550 (distributable profit 1300 minus 750 passive income ACo), instead of the expected 325.

CFC P&L

Salaries	500	Royalties	800
Rent for lab	100	Dividends from TCo	200
Rent for production hall	100	Resold goods	600
Prefabricated goods costs	300	Sold production	1,000
Magnetic cards production costs	300		
Total expenses:	1,300	Total revenue:	2,600
Profit (2,600 – 1,300)	1,300		
Retained tainted income (800 royalties + 200 TCo dividends)	1,000		

Therefore, CFC income, or parts of it, could be subject of double taxation as some amounts may be overlapping in ACo and BCo. In the context of characterization of CFC income, another element that should be highlighted and is insufficiently dealt by the ATAD is the treatment of lower-tier vehicles[132]. The dividends distributed by the production company PCo to its shareholder, the CFC, although generated by substantial economic activity, is categorized as passive and included in the taxable base of the parent shareholder ACo. In the example above, dividends distributed by the production company PCo to the CFC are assimilated as passive. Active income, taxed as such in source country T, is distributed to the controlled subsidiary CFC and acts, in this instance, as the parent of the lower-tier company. Consequently, the already taxed active income may be taxed again in the hands of the ultimate controlling shareholder as passive income. To summarize, an issue of double taxation arises in the context of mischaracterization of CFC income.

4.2.5. Cascading ownership

The Directive acknowledges the indirect control in a CFC.[133] When CFC regimes in two or more Member States are applicable on the same CFC income, double taxation could arise. CFC regimes in the ATAD do not contain clear rules providing relief with respect to taxes paid by the CFC and the CFC tax assessed on intermediate companies. Member States are not obligated to grant relief in another Member State for the taxes paid on the same CFC income.[134] However, when the application of the rules set out in the Directive gives rise to double taxation, taxpayers should receive relief through a deduction for the tax paid in another Member State or third country, as the case may be.[135]

---

132 Till Moser, supra n. 39.
133 ATAD, Article 7(1)(a).
134 Guglielmo Ginevra, supra n. 25.
135 ATAD, Preamble (5).

In the illustrative figure below[136], assume that the controlled foreign subsidiary CFC is owned by BCo in Member State B which, in turn, is controlled by ACo in Member State A together with DCo in Member State D. In a multi-tier situation[137] like this one, both Member State A and B can levy taxes on the CFC income without having the obligation of granting relief for the taxes paid in the other Member State[138]. In this author's opinion, based on other authors' considerations[139], the solution for double taxation arising as a consequence of a multi-tier structure may be found in OECD's Action 3. The report covers such a situation when it is addressed as such as it may become more common in the future for the income and profits arising in a CFC to be taxed in more than one jurisdiction.[140] In the example below, the total net taxes paid on the chain of events is 326. However, the taxes that should be calculated on the attributed income should total 230 (180 paid in state A and 50 in state B). The difference of 106 between the two amounts represents over taxation of the same CFC income as Member State A is not obligated to grant relief for the taxes already paid in Member State B.

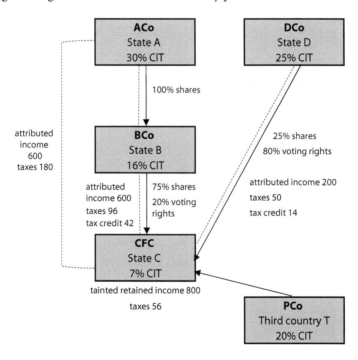

Figure 5

---

136 Guglielmo Ginevra, supra n. 25.
137 Ibid.
138 Ibid.
139 Ibid.
140 Action 3, para. 126.

A possible explanation for this kind of situation being ignored by the Directive could be the fact that multinationals are discouraged from setting up holdings to take advantage of more favourable CFC regimes.[141] It should be pointed out, however, the liaison between the ATAD and the OECD's BEPS Actions that are given a binding power through their inclusion in the Preamble of the Directive[142]. The relationship between the ATAD-BEPS Actions is emphasized in Preamble 28 of the ATAD II[143]: "*In implementing this Directive, Member States should use the applicable explanations and examples in the OECD BEPS report on Action 2 as a source of illustration or interpretation*". Following this line of reasoning, when solutions cannot be found in the text of the Directive, *mutatis mutandis*, they may be offered by BEPS Actions. In the figure above, as the CFC is owned indirectly by ACo and directly by BCo, Action 3 recommends the "hierarchy rule" to be applied: the closest resident shareholder, in this case BCo, should be given priority.

5. Concluding remarks

Taking into consideration all of the turmoil generated by the multiple attempts to regulate the CFC regimes within the European Union jurisdiction, the ATAD represents a tremendous step in fighting against tax avoidance, as such. It should be noted the importance of OECD's BEPS Actions that were the underlying framework for the Directive. Their increasing legal significance and impact was confirmed by the ATAD through their insertion in its preamble.

The enactment of the ATAD after the Cadbury Schweppes crucial case raised another sensitive issue: compatibility of CFC regimes with EU fundamental freedoms. With regard to that, the three options enumerated in Preamble 12 that might be implemented by different states should be mentioned. CFC rules may target an entire CFC, specific categories of income, or be limited to artificially diverted income. However, the only applicable option for Member States is the third one. Therefore, when opting out for Model A or B, Member States may target only income that has been artificially diverted to the controlled subsidiary. Under Model A, the non-distributed passive CFC income (such as dividends, interest, royalties, etc.) is computed and taxed in the hands of the controlling parent. Under Model B, the CFC income derived from non-genuine arrangements that have been put in place for the essential purpose of availing a tax advantage is calculated at arm's length and taxed in the hands of the controlling shareholder.

The intentions and the objectives pursued by the Directive are more than honourable: ensure "effective taxation" where profits are generated, promote a "level

---

141 Ibid.
142 ATAD, Preamble (1)-(3).
143 Council Directive (EU) 2017/952 of 29 May 2017 amending Directive (EU) 2016/1164 as regards hybrid mismatches with third countries.

playing field"[144] in the single market, and avoid double taxation when applying rules[145]. However, this author supports the idea that many features of CFC provisions create uncertainties that are contradictory to their inner scope. Moreover, it is debatable if, by denying the relief in double taxation cases as analysed in previous section, companies would be discouraged from setting up subsidiaries in low tax jurisdictions. Furthermore, it is questionable whether the coveted harmonization and the reduction of discrepancies can be achieved though *de minimis* standards as disparities "will foster again aggressive tax planning and legal uncertainty"[146]. Moreover, this author's opinion is that coherence, cohesion, and homogeneity would be key elements that are necessary for the implementation of secondary law in order to achieve desired harmonization across the European Union.

---

144 Chappeau Communication, supra n. 17.
145 ATAD, Preamble (5).
146 Ana Paula Dourado, supra n. 24.

Exceptions from the application of the CFC rules under article 7(3) and (4) of the ATAD

Hannes Hilpold

1. Introduction and scope
2. Introduction to CFC rules and exemptions
   2.1. Towards the adoption of CFC rules: BEPS Action 3 and the ATAD
3. Basic structure of CFC rules under the ATAD
   3.1. Scope of application and definition of CFC
   3.2. Methods for computing attributable income
   3.3. CFC exemptions
      3.3.1. Exemptions under the categorical approach
      3.3.1.1. Exemptions under the transactional approach
4. CFC exemptions under the categorical approach
   4.1. Brief description
   4.2. Substantive economic activities
      4.2.1. Substance factors
   4.3. Threshold exemptions
      4.3.1. Purpose and scope
      4.3.2. One-third passive income threshold
      4.3.3. Financial undertakings carve-out
   4.4. Interim conclusions on the categorical approach
5. CFC exemptions under the transactional approach
   5.1. Brief description
   5.2. De minimis thresholds
   5.3. Interim conclusions on the transactional approach
6. Comparative analysis: the impact of ATAD's CFC exceptions in different countries
   6.1. General overview
   6.2. Comparative analysis of selected countries
   6.3. Interim conclusions on the comparative analysis
7. Conclusions

1. Introduction and scope

In recent years, policy makers and practitioners around the world have paid a lot of attention to controlled foreign company (CFC) rules in consideration of the key role that such rules play in the business, economic, and financial international arenas. In particular, CFC rules play a paramount role when addressing aggressive tax planning challenges by multinational enterprises.

Following the work of the OECD/G20 on base erosion and profit shifting (BEPS) and the related recommendations concerning the design of CFC rules[1], the European Commission has decided to focus its efforts – *inter alia* – on the introduction of appropriate CFC regulation or the tightening of already existing CFC guidelines in the European Union Member States. As a result, in 2016, the anti-tax avoidance directive (ATAD) was issued[2] including minimum requirements for the design of CFC rules (Articles 7 and 8). As a consequence, the ATAD has required Member States to implement or amend accordingly the CFC regulation in their national tax systems.

In essence, CFC rules provide that shareholders should be reattributed CFCs' diverted income if they are deemed to benefit from low-tax regimes. The ATAD has basically introduced two different methods for computing attributable income together with limitations and exceptions that Member States may consider implementing in their respective domestic legislation.

The intention of this work is to provide a general overview on CFC rules according to the ATAD and particularly on the implementing peculiarities of each of the approaches envisaged thereof. The discussion will therefore focus on the exceptions from the application of CFC rules under Article 7(3) and (4) of the ATAD.

In the first chapter, following a brief outline concerning the overall structure of the ATAD's CFC rules, the author introduces the so-called "categorical" and "transactional" approaches for attributing CFC income (according to the most commonly used categorization among practitioners and legislators) as well as the related exemptions. Chapters 2 and 3 provide an in-depth examination of CFC exemptions under the two methods – Chapter 2 refers to the categorical approach whereas Chapter 3 is focused on the transactional approach and a critical analysis of the corresponding implications for the purpose of CFC rules implementation. The last chapter of the work is intended to carry out a comparative analysis of the impact of the ATAD's CFC exceptions in selected Member States to highlight the similarities and the differences in implementing legislation based on multiple and

---

[1] *Designing Effective Controlled Foreign Company Rules*, Action 3 – 2015 Final Report, OECD/G20 Base Erosion and Profit Shifting Project (Paris: OECD Publishing, 2015) http://dx.doi.org/10.1787/9789264241152-en.

[2] Council Directive (EU) 2016/1164 of 12 July 2016 laying down rules against tax avoidance practices that directly affect the functioning of the internal market, OJ L 193 (19 July 2016) p. 1.

diverse reasons. It includes the possible divergent interpretation of relevant ATAD requirements, the different degree of priority attributed to specific exceptions according to the overall national framework, and the attempt by individual countries to find a balance between protecting their domestic tax base and promoting businesses international competitiveness.

2. Introduction to CFC rules and exemptions

2.1. Towards the adoption of CFC rules: BEPS Action 3 and the ATAD

In modern times, as soon as the economy and globalization developed, the integration of national economies and markets increased substantially. This brought out the weaknesses in the current taxation rules, thus creating opportunities for base erosion and profit shifting (BEPS). One of the major risks for policy makers occurs when resident taxpayers avoid tax on their worldwide income through the use of controlled foreign companies (CFCs) in order to earn foreign source income. Therefore, taxpayers with a controlling interest in a foreign subsidiary may strip the tax base of their residence country by shifting income to a CFC. This means that CFCs may easily result in profit shifting and long-term deferral (or even avoidance) of taxation.[3] Therefore, in order to restrict or fully avert the use of CFCs as a means to defer or avoid domestic tax, several states started to adopt CFC rules. In general, the latter would target multinational corporations as they try to shift passive or similar kinds of mobile income to jurisdictions with a low-tax regime.[4]

Following the 2008 global financial crisis, base erosion and profit shifting threats gained more and more ground thus becoming of utmost relevance in the eyes of the OECD and the European Commission. Reducing BEPS risks reached the highest level among the priorities of the OECD which started work to address the

---

3   It should be also noted that, the lower the foreign country's tax rate (*e.g.* tax haven), the greater the benefit might be for residence tax purposes. Tax deferral and avoidance issues are even more noticeable in relation to passive incomes that could be more easily diverted to a foreign entity.

4   The United States was the first country to implement CFC rules in 1962 (included in Subpart F of the US Internal Revenue Code). Since then, several other countries, primarily capital-exporting countries, have enacted similar rules to protect their own tax bases. Basically, all CFC legislations replicate the tension between capital export neutrality (CEN) and capital import neutrality (CIN). Under the CEN, domestic and foreign investments should be treated equally for tax purposes on the grounds of the "worldwide" taxation principle; under the CIN, *"residents of a country should be subject to the same tax on business income earned in another country as other taxpayers carrying on business in that country"*. Accordingly, under a CEN policy, CFC rules would be applied to all of the income of all CFCs while, in countries that promote a CIN strategy, CFC rules would not be applied as foreign-source incomes would not be taxed ("territorial" principle). See Brian J. Arnold, 'The Evolution of Controlled Foreign Corporation Rules and Beyond, *Bulletin for International Taxation* Volume 73 No. 12 (2019), para 3.1. See also Ana Paula Dourado, 'The Role of CFC Rules in the BEPS Initiative and in the EU', *British Tax Review* Issue 3 (2015) p. 340 (p. 357).

Exceptions from the application of the CFC rules under the ATAD

BEPS strategies implemented by multinationals[5]. In 2015, as a result of these efforts, the OECD published fifteen final project reports[6], including the Action 3 Report[7] that contains suggestions and possible approaches to incorporate CFC rules into a Member State's legislation[8].

At the European level, following the 2010 European Council resolution[9] regarding the coordination of CFC and thin capitalization rules within the European Union as well as a result of the OECD/G20 BEPS initiative, the European institutions foresaw that the Member States would start to transpose the OECD recommendations into their disparate national laws. In order to avoid the circumstance that independent actions replicate the marked current fragmentation of the internal market, the European Council issued the anti-tax avoidance directive (ATAD)[10], which was adopted on 12 July 2016 and entered into force since 8 August 2016.

The ATAD provides for prototype *de minimis* rules that are mostly drafted to conform to the CJEU's case law relating with the EU fundamental freedoms[11]. The minimum standards provide for alternative options for the purpose of enforcement and leave a certain degree of autonomy to individual states for the implementation depending on the chosen option.

Regarding CFC rules, under Article 7 of the ATAD, the Member States are required to reattribute to a controlling taxpayer the income of foreign controlled entities or permanent establishments if these are deemed to benefit from a low-tax regime (this constitutes the minimum requirement for CFC rules). The countries are then basically given two alternative approaches for taxing the CFC's in-

---

5　OECD Action Plan on Base Erosion and Profit Shifting (OECD Publishing, 2013), http://dx.doi.org/10.1787/9789264202719-en.
6　OECD BEPS 2015 Final Reports https://www.oecd.org/ctp/beps-2015-final-reports.htm.
7　*Designing Effective Controlled Foreign Company Rules*, Action 3 – 2015 Final Report, OECD/G20 Base Erosion and Profit Shifting Project (Paris: OECD Publishing, 2015) http://dx.doi.org/10.1787/9789264241152-en.
8　The OECD BEPS Action 3 Report (para. 2) identifies the following six building blocks as basic elements for designing CFC rules: i) definition of a CFC; ii) exemptions and threshold requirements; iii) definition of CFC income; iv) rules for computing income; v) rules for attributing income; vi) rules to prevent or eliminate double taxation.
9　Council Resolution of 8 June 2010 on coordination of the controlled foreign corporation (CFC) and thin capitalization rules within the European Union, OJ C 156 (16 June 2010) p. 1–2.
10　Council Directive (EU) 2016/1164 of 12 July 2016 laying down rules against tax avoidance practices that directly affect the functioning of the internal market, OJ L 193 (19 July 2016) p. 1.
11　Among the fundamental European Union principles is non-discrimination included in Article 18 of the Treaty on the Functioning of the European Union (TFEU). Under this principle, '*any discrimination on grounds of nationality shall be prohibited*' because the political and economic union is regarded as a common market. On the basis of the non-discrimination principle, the TFEU institutes the freedom of establishment contained in Articles 49 and 56. In accordance with the right of establishment, any economic actor, person, or undertaking shall have the right to take up and pursue activities in any of the Member States without any hindrance. As a consequence, CFC rules in the European Union should be designed around these principles. See the landmark case on these issues, CJEU, 12 September 2006, C-196/04, ECLI:EU:C:2006:544, *Cadbury Schweppes plc and Cadbury Schweppes Overseas Ltd v Commissioners of Inland Revenue*.

come both of which include exceptions that reflect the CJEU's limitations on measures designed to prevent abuse of law[12].

As also suggested in the OECD BEPS Action 3 Report, countries may use exemptions and threshold requirements in order to limit the scope of their CFC rules[13]. These exceptions, as better investigated below, would help to maintain a balance between enacting targeted and effective CFC rules. Further, they would limit the administrative burden for companies that are unlikely to pose BEPS risk, or at least companies whose features and behaviours are deemed less dicey for the purpose of base erosion and profit shifting in comparison to higher-risk entities for which the chance of profit shifting is likelier.[14]

3. Basic structure of CFC rules under the ATAD

Basically, CFC legislation (both inside and outside the European Union) follows a similar pattern. Resident shareholders controlling or having a substantial interest in a foreign entity established in a country with a nil or low tax rate are taxable in their residence country on their proportionate share of all or some of the CFC's income regardless if the income is actually distributed to them. However, CFC rules do not usually apply to the income derived from legitimate commercial activities carried on by the CFC. The CFC rules under the ATAD follow an analogous pattern. Hence, their structure essentially replicates two competing policy aims: the prevention of tax avoidance and the furthering of foreign investments and competitiveness.[15]

3.1. Scope of application and definition of CFC

In general, a CFC can be defined as a low taxed foreign company (or a permanent establishment if the same is not subject to tax or is exempt in the head office's

---

12 See, *ex plurimis*, Caroline Docclo, 'The European Union's Ambition to Harmonize Rules to Counter the Abuse of Member States' Disparate Tax Legislations', *Bulletin for International Taxation* Volume 71 No. 7 (2017) p. 367; Ana Paula Dourado, 'The Role of CFC Rules in the BEPS Initiative and in the EU', *British Tax Review* Issue 3 (2015) p. 340; Guglielmo Ginevra, 'The EU Anti-Tax Avoidance Directive and the Base Erosion and Profit Shifting (BEPS) Action Plan: Necessity and Adequacy of the Measures at EU level', *Intertax* Volume 45 Issue 2 (2017) p. 120; Wolfgang Schön, 'Interpreting European Law in the Light of the OECD/G20 Base Erosion and Profit Shifting Action Plan', *Bulletin for International Taxation* Volume 74 No. 4/5 (2020) p. 286.
13 See OECD BEPS Action 3 Report, p. 33.
14 See OECD BEPS Action 3 Report, para. 50.
15 See the ATAD, Recitals 1–5. On the one hand, there is the need to prevent tax avoidance, thus realizing and improving the goals of economic efficiency and fairness as well as ensuring the good functioning of the (European) internal market. On the other hand, the unwillingness emerges of policy makers to arbitrarily affect the capability of domestic entities to invest abroad and compete in foreign markets. Based on the relevance that each jurisdiction gives to these two objectives, the scope of application and the effectiveness of CFC rules may vary by jurisdictions in the attempt to find a balance between the protection of domestic tax bases and the promotion of international competitiveness taking also into consideration the costs of compliance with and administration of the rules.

state)[16] over which the parent has control. Usually, the control test requires the entitlement, direct or indirect, to more than 50% voting rights, capital, or profits of the entity.

Regarding the scope of application, the fundamental structural aspects of CFC rules under Articles 7 and 8 of the ATAD can be identified and summarized as follows:

1. definition of a CFC and level of foreign tax on a CFC;
2. identification of the nature of the tainted income earned by a CFC;
3. attribution of the tainted income to resident shareholders[17].

In accordance with the OECD[18], the ATAD[19] suggests the use of the majority threshold of legal and economic control to define a CFC. However, it does not include situations when the controlling entity exerts a *de facto* influence regardless of the holdership of the majority of capital, profits, or voting rights.[20]

3.2. Methods for computing attributable income

Regarding the kind of revenues considered for CFC purposes, the ATAD following the OECD suggestions included in the BEPS Action 3 Report[21] and provides for two alternatives either limiting the choice to a list of selected items of income or comprising all of the CFC's income in the shareholders' profits[22].

In accordance with the first option, which is in line with the OECD's "*categorical analysis*"[23], controlling shareholders would be attributed the CFC's undistributed

---

16 Brian J. Arnold, *Bulletin for International Taxation* Volume 73 No. 12 (2019), para 3.3.1.
17 See ATAD, article 7, para. 1. The inclusion of permanent establishments in the definition of CFCs is also recommended in the BEPS Action 3, para 28: "*PEs may need to be subject to CFC rules in two circumstances. First, CFC rules should be broad enough to potentially apply to a situation where a foreign entity has a PE in another country. Second, where a parent jurisdiction exempts the income of a PE [This includes a branch as defined under domestic law that equates to a PE], the income of that PE could potentially raise the same concerns as income arising in a foreign subsidiary. Where this is the case, the parent jurisdiction could address this either by denying the exemption or by applying CFC rules to the PE.*"
18 See OECD BEPS Action 3 Report, paras. 35–39.
19 See ATAD, article 7, para. 1.
20 "*The type and level of control required by the Directive is consistent with the recommendations by the OECD – it covers both legal and economic control – except for the fact that it does not give relevance to de facto control so it does not take into account the situation where the controlling party has an effective influence over the subsidiary's business decisions without having the majority of voting rights, capital or profits. The parent company, in fact, has to hold, directly or indirectly, by itself or together with associated enterprises, more than 50% of either the voting rights or the capital of the entity, or in any case, a participation in the company which give entitlement to receive more than 50% of its profits. The determination of the level of control must be computed according to the law of the Member State of the parent company*". See Guglielmo Ginevra, *Intertax* Volume 45 Issue 2 (2017) p. 120 (p.126) and Raul Angelo Papotti/Filippo Molinari, 'La disciplina CFC alla prova della Direttiva anti-elusione dell'Unione Europea', *Corriere Tributario* 34 (2016) p. 2609 (paras. 8–9). See also OECD BEPS Action 3 Report, paras. 35–39.
21 See OECD BEPS Action 3 Report, p. 43.
22 See ATAD, article 2.
23 See OECD BEPS Action 3 Report, paras. 77–80.

passive investment income. Under this approach, the tainted income would consist of dividends, interests, capital gains, rents, royalties, sales, and services income (inter-company trading). More specifically, the first option identified in paragraph 2 of Article 7 of the ATAD indicates that

> *the Member State of the taxpayer shall include in the tax base:*
> (a) the non-distributed income of the entity or the income of the permanent establishment which is derived from the following categories:
>   (i) interest or any other income generated by financial assets;
>   (ii) royalties or any other income generated from intellectual property;
>   (iii) dividends and income from the disposal of shares;
>   (iv) income from financial leasing;
>   (v) income from insurance, banking and other financial activities;
>   (vi) income from invoicing companies that earn sales and services income from goods and services purchased from and sold to associated enterprises, and add no or little economic value".[24]

Alternatively, the taxpayer's residence country may subject all of the CFC's income to tax provided that it does not arise from genuine arrangements *"which have been put in place for the essential purpose of obtaining a tax advantage"*[25].

3.3. CFC exemptions

The scope of CFC rules may be limited through the use of threshold requirements or exemptions depending on the method chosen for the purpose of attributing the tainted income to the controlling shareholders.

Article 7 of the ATAD, which starts with the definition of CFC, introduces a general tax rate exemption according to which the rules should target low-taxed related entities. More in detail, a controlled foreign entity is a CFC if it is actually subject to a corporate tax rate that is lower than the one that would have been applied if it were resident in the controlling party's state.[26] Article 7 of the ATAD continues and categorizes additional limitations and exemptions (including *de minimis* thresholds and anti-avoidance requirements) according to two different approaches: the "categorical" approach and the "transactional" approach.[27]

---

24 ATAD, Article 7, para. 2(a). With respect to the OECD Action 3 recommendation, the ATAD actually broadens the list of passive income under the "categorical" approach as it adds income from financial leasing and income from banking and other financial activities.
25 ATAD, Article 7, para. 2(b).
26 ATAD, Article 7, para. 1(b). Further, the second subparagraph specifies that, for the purpose of *"the actual corporate tax paid"*, *"the permanent establishment of a controlled foreign company that is not subject to tax or is exempt from tax in the jurisdiction of the controlled foreign company shall not be taken into account. Furthermore the corporate tax that would have been charged in the Member State of the taxpayer means as computed according to the rules of the Member State of the taxpayer."*
27 Under each approach, the ATAD uses the types of exemptions provided by the OECD BEPS Action 3 Report. This latter identifies three types of potential CFC exemptions: i) *de minimis* threshold; ii) anti-avoidance requirement; and iii) tax rate exemption. See OECD BEPS Action 3 Report, paras. 52–71.

3.3.1. Exemptions under the categorical approach

With reference to the first approach described to compute the CFC attributable income[28], the ATAD implicitly exempts active business income as, under the categorical approach, the parent entity would be only attributed the CFC's undistributed passive income.

Moreover, the ATAD specifies that CFC rules would not be applicable in the case that the controlled foreign entity *"carries on a substantive economic activity"* using a suitable material and personal structure. That means when the CFC performs substantial activities and functions *"supported by staff, equipment, assets and premises, as evidenced by relevant facts and circumstances"*.[29] In addition, countries may also decide to not extend this substance carve-out to CFCs resident or situated in a third state that is not adhering to the EEA Agreement.[30, 31]

In order to further mitigate the effects of CFC rules, a country adopting the categorical approach may also exempt a controlled foreign entity if the amount of its annual non-distributed passive income is lower than a pre-determined threshold. Specifically, a foreign subsidiary or permanent establishment may not be treated as a CFC if its passive income amounts to one third or less of its total income.[32]

In addition, the categorical approach provides for a financial undertakings' exclusion that is intended to exempt entities operating in the financial and insurance sectors or similar. Hence, a country may choose not to treat a financial undertaking[33] as a CFC if one third or less of the relevant entity's passive income derives from transactions occurred with related parties[34].

---

28   ATAD, article 7, para. 2(a).
29   *Id.*, second subparagraph.
30   *Id.*, third subparagraph.
31   Agreement on the European Economic Area, OJ L 1 (13 January 1994) p. 3.
32   ATAD, article 7, para. 3.
33   The definition of "financial undertaking" is included in Article 2(5) of the ATAD and is valid for all of the ATAD provisions. In particular, entities such as credit institutions, insurances and reinsurances, pension institutions, alternative investment funds, and other similar financial entities are included in the definition.
34   For the purposes of the ATAD, an "associated enterprise" is defined as:
     (a) an entity in which the taxpayer holds directly or indirectly a participation in terms of voting rights or capital ownership of 25 percent or more or is entitled to receive 25 percent or more of the profits of that entity;
     (b) an individual or entity which holds directly or indirectly a participation in terms of voting rights or capital ownership in a taxpayer of 25 percent or more or is entitled to receive 25 percent or more of the profits of the taxpayer;
     If an individual or entity holds directly or indirectly a participation of 25 percent or more in a taxpayer and one or more entities, all the entities concerned, including the taxpayer, shall also be regarded as associated enterprises.
     See ATAD, Article 1(4).

3.3.1.1. Exemptions under the transactional approach

Regarding the transactional approach[35], the ATAD deliberately excludes genuine business activities. More specifically, this second option[36] explicitly defines "*non-genuine arrangements*" by referring to the typical functional approach that is adopted by the transfer pricing discipline:

> an arrangement or a series thereof shall be regarded as non-genuine to the extent that the entity or permanent establishment would not own the assets or would not have undertaken the risks which generate all, or part of, its income if it were not controlled by a company where the significant people functions, which are relevant to those assets and risks, are carried out and are instrumental in generating the controlled company's income.[37]

Therefore, the countries that intend to implement CFC rules on the basis of a "substance" (or "transactional") method, "*are expected to target situations where most of the decision-making functions that generate diverted income at the level of the CFC are carried on in the taxpayer's Member State*"[38].

Furthermore, in the case that a country would opt for the transactional approach, two additional exclusions may be implemented based on financial thresholds. Accordingly, a foreign entity or permanent establishment may be excluded if:[39]

- its accounting profits are no more than EUR 750,000 and its non-trading income amounts to no more than EUR 75,000; or
- its accounting profits amount to no more than ten percent of the operating costs for the relevant tax period.

The ATAD thus allows these supplementary safeguards in the form of *de minimis* exemptions that Member States might be willing to introduce in the respective CFC legislation. The intention underlining their application would be to reduce administrative and compliance costs. In particular, countries can exempt a controlled foreign entity with low profits or low profit margin based on the assumption that this specific circumstance should avert – or at least reduce – tax avoidance risks.[40]

---

35 ATAD, Article 7, para. 2(b).
36 The transactional approach may also be identified as a "substance analysis" according to the OECD categorization of available options for the definition of CFC income. See *Designing Effective Controlled Foreign Company Rules*, Action 3 – 2015 Final Report, OECD/G20 Base Erosion and Profit Shifting Project (Paris: OECD Publishing, 2015) http://dx.doi.org/10.1787/9789264241152-en, paras. 81–86.
37 ATAD, Article 7, para. 2(b), second subparagraph.
38 Caroline Docclo, *Bulletin for International Taxation* Volume 71 No. 7 (2017) p. 367 (p. 376–377, para. 5.4.5.).
39 ATAD, article 7, para. 4. For this purpose, "*the operating costs may not include the cost of goods sold outside the country where the entity is resident, or the permanent establishment is situated, for tax purposes and payments to associated enterprises.*" The accounting profits comprise operational profits and passive income.
40 See Caroline Docclo, *Bulletin for International Taxation* Volume 71 No. 7 (2017) p. 367 (p. 376–377, para. 5.4.5.); Guglielmo Ginevra, *Intertax* Volume 45 Issue 2 (2017) p. 120 (p.130).

4. CFC exemptions under the categorical approach

4.1. Brief description

As briefly anticipated in Chapter 1, Article 7, paragraph 2 of the ATAD suggests two alternative approaches (or a combination thereof) that Member States may apply to compute the attributable CFC income to the controlling shareholders. According to the categorical approach, a list of prescribed categories of passive income is considered for the purpose thus inherently excluding any active income derived by the CFC: (i) interest or other income generated by financial assets; (ii) royalties or other income from intellectual property; (iii) dividends and income from the disposal of shares; (iv) income from financial leasing; (v) income from insurance and financial activities; and (vi) income from inter-company trading.[41]

The European Council also introduced significant exceptions in order to limit the scope and mitigate the effects of CFC rules. In fact, the implementing country shall not apply the rules under the categorical approach if the "substantive economic activity" condition is satisfied. Precisely, it *"shall not apply where the controlled foreign company carries on a substantive economic activity supported by staff, equipment, assets and premises, as evidenced by relevant facts and circumstances"*.[42] In addition, for the purpose of the substance carve-out, the implementing state may also electively exclude CFCs that reside or are located in a third country (*"that is not party to the EEA Agreement"*).[43]

Moreover, Article 7, paragraph 3 of the ATAD allows not applying CFC rules if no more than one third of the CFC's income derives from passive income. With respect to financial entities, an exception may also apply to the extent that no more than one third of their passive income derives from transactions with the parent company or other related parties.[44]

4.2. Substantive economic activities

Regarding CFC exceptions under the categorical approach, the relevance of the expression "substantive economic activity" has to be highlighted as it denotes the CFC's capability of operating and carrying out its functions in a manner that is separate and independent from the parent company.[45] In this respect, the final version of the ATAD differs from the initial proposal[46] and defines the substance of a controlled foreign entity with a new wording. The former provision allowed

---

41 ATAD, article 7, para. 2(a).
42 *Id.*, second subparagraph.
43 *Id.*, third subparagraph.
44 ATAD, article 7, para. 3.
45 Julia de Jong, 'Controlled Foreign Company Rules and the EU' in: Erik Pinetz/Erich Schaffer (eds) *Limiting Base Erosion*, 1st edition (Vienna: Linde, 2017) p. 294 (p. 298).
46 Proposal for a Council Directive laying down rules against tax avoidance practices that directly affect the functioning of the internal market, COM/2016/026 final – 2016/011 (CNS) (28 January 2016).

the disapplication of CFC rules to Member States or countries that are party to the EEA Agreement unless they constitute entities that have been artificially established or are engaged in *"non-genuine arrangements"*.[47] Moreover, the European Council has shifted its original internal point of view, eventually moving to a more comprehensive perspective by considering those entities out of the CFC rules' perimeter that carry on a substantive economic activity with the additional possibility to not exempt third countries thus lining up the scope of exclusions with the general extent of CFC rules and the Union law.[48]

The exception based on substantial economic activities is rooted in the case law of the Court of Justice of the European Union (CJEU) on the freedom of establishment[49]. More in detail, according to CJEU's settled case law on these matters[50], specific rules are justifiable by reason of preventing tax avoidance exclusively if they are not generally provided and target explicitly "wholly artificial arrangements"[51]. Further, the CJEU has clarified that the artificiality of practices must be thoroughly assessed on a case by case basis, without *"applying predetermined general criteria"*[52].[53]

---

47 According to Article 8, paragraph 2 of the proposal for the ATAD, CFC rules shall not apply *"where an entity is tax resident in a Member State or in a third country that is party to the EEA Agreement or in respect of a permanent establishment of a third country entity which is situated in a Member State, unless the establishment of the entity is wholly artificial or to the extent that the entity engages, in the course of its activity, in non-genuine arrangements which have been put in place for the essential purpose of obtaining a tax advantage."*

48 See Julia de Jong in: Erik Pinetz/Erich Schaffer (eds) *Limiting Base Erosion*, 1st edition (Vienna: Linde, 2017) pp. 298–307.

49 The ATAD provisions are generally aimed at mitigating – if not preventing – aggressive tax planning and tax avoidance within the territory of the European Union. The rules shall also be provided in accordance with the fundamental freedoms (free movement of persons, services, and capital and the right of establishment according to the Treaty on the Functioning of the European Union), without allowing episodes of discrimination in cross-border situations. In the case of the ATAD (and, specifically, CFC) rules, which apply to transnational circumstances, restrictions of such fundamental freedoms should be carefully taken into consideration. They may be legitimate only if it is possible to provide a justification on the grounds of a justifiable and proportionate (*i.e.* legitimate) purpose that can be more precisely identified in preventing abusive conducts. See Sriram Govind/Stephanies Zolles, 'Chapter 8 – The Anti-Tax Avoidance Directive' in: Michael Lang et al (eds) *Introduction to European Tax Law on Direct Taxation*, 5th edition (Vienna: Linde, 2018), para. V.B.

50 See CJEU, 7 November 2013, C-322/11, ECLI:EU:C:2013:716, *K v Korkein hallinto-oikeus*, para. 62; CJEU, 7 September 2017, C-6/16, ECLI:EU:C:2017:641, *Eqiom SAS, formerly Holcim France SAS and Enka SA v Ministre des Finances et des Comptes publics*, para. 30; CJEU, 20 December 2017, C-504/16 and C-613/16, ECLI:EU:C:2017:1009, *Deister Holding AG, formerly Traxx Investments NV and Juhler Holding A/S v Bundeszentralamt für Steuern*, para. 60; CJEU, 12 September 2006, C-196/04, ECLI:EU:C:2006:544, *Cadbury Schweppes plc and Cadbury Schweppes Overseas Ltd v Commissioners of Inland Revenue*, para. 55; CJEU, 5 July 2012, C-318–10, ECLI:EU:C:2012:415, *Société d'investissement pour l'agriculture tropicale SA (SIAT) v État belge*, para. 40.

51 In this respect, the *Cadbury Schweppes* case put additional emphasis on the *"genuine economic activity"* – supported by effectively existing premises, staff, and equipment – that the controlled foreign entity should carry on in order for its arrangements to not be labeled as wholly artificial. See CJEU, C-196/04, ECLI:EU:C:2006:544, *Cadbury Schweppes*, paras. 54 and 67.

52 See CJEU, C-6/16, ECLI:EU:C:2017:641, *Eqiom*, para. 32. See also CJEU, Joined Cases C-504/16 and C-613/16, ECLI:EU:C:2017:1009, *Deister Holding and Juhler Holding*, para. 62.

53 See Sriram Govind/Stephanies Zolles in: Michael Lang et al (eds) *Introduction to European Tax Law on Direct Taxation*, 5th edition (Vienna: Linde, 2018), para. V.B.

The ATAD's CFC rules are in line with the mentioned case law and, in particular, with the *Cadbury Schweppes* doctrine. In this regard, the first option provided under the second paragraph of Article 7 and recital 12[54] of the ATAD seem to clearly refer to the CJEU judgement. Actually, the ATAD provisions slightly differ from the CJEU decision in the landmark *Cadbury Schweppes* case. The former, indeed, mentions a *"substantive economic activity"* rather than a *"genuine economic activity"* yet maintains the reference to *"staff, equipment, assets and premises"*.[55] Therefore, considering the term "substantive" as a synonym for "genuine" (*i.e.* broad enough for the purpose of genuineness), the ATAD provision under analysis can be regarded as being in line with the CJEU case law.[56]

4.2.1. Substance factors

Carrying on with the analysis and focusing on the elements that signal the existence of a genuine economic activity, the *Cadbury Schweppes* case mentions objective factors including, without limitation, premises, staff, and equipment. As previously noted, this list of factors is replicated in the wording of the ATAD in relation to CFC rules with the additional specification of assets.

In this respect, it should also be pointed out that some subsequent decisions (since the 2006 *Cadbury Schweppes* judgement) have broadened the scope of the definition or, at least, tried to identify items that are more specific in order to better evaluate the substance of a CFC. To this end, it is worth mentioning that, in 2014, the EFTA Court[57] ruled on the *Fred. Olsen and Others and Petter Olsen and Others* Joined Cases[58] relying on the *Cadbury Schweppes* factors but also trying to widen

---

54 "To comply with the fundamental freedoms, the income categories should be combined with a substance carve-out aimed to limit, within the Union, the impact of the rules to cases where the CFC does not carry on a substantive economic activity."
55 According to the *Cadbury Schweppes* decision, "In those circumstances, in order for the legislation on CFCs to comply with Community law, the taxation provided for by that legislation must be excluded where, despite the existence of tax motives, the incorporation of a CFC reflects economic reality. (...) That incorporation must correspond with an actual establishment intended to carry on genuine economic activities in the host Member State (...) that finding must be based on objective factors which are ascertainable by third parties with regard, in particular, to the extent to which the CFC physically exists in terms of premises, staff and equipment. If checking those factors leads to the finding that the CFC is a fictitious establishment not carrying out any genuine economic activity in the territory of the host Member State, the creation of that CFC must be regarded as having the characteristics of a wholly artificial arrangement." See CJEU, C-196/04, ECLI:EU:C:2006:544, *Cadbury Schweppes*, paras. 64–68.
56 See Sriram Govind/Stephanies Zolles in: Michael Lang et al (eds) *Introduction to European Tax Law on Direct Taxation*, 5th edition (Vienna: Linde, 2018), para. V.B. See also Mike Kollar, 'Chapter 15 – CFC rules of the Anti-Tax Avoidance Directive in light of the EU fundamental freedoms' in para. 2 'Limitations imposed on CFC legislation'.
57 The European Free Trade Association (EFTA) is the intergovernmental organisation of Iceland, Liechtenstein, Norway and Switzerland (https://www.efta.int/). The EFTA Court, based in Luxembourg, corresponds to the CJEU in matters relating to the EEA EFTA States (https://eftacourt.int/).
58 EFTA Court, 9 July 2014, Joined Cases E-3/13 and E-20/13, ECLI:EU:C:2013:716, *Fred. Olsen and Others and Petter Olsen and Others v The Norwegian State, represented by the Central Tax Office for Large Enterprises and the Directorate of Taxes*.

their interpretation. According to the decision of the EFTA Court, objective factors do not suffice for the purposes of verifying substance; the analysis of the actual activities and functions carried out by the CFC should instead be preferable[59].[60]

As a result, it should be apparent that the substance of the CFC (or, on the opposite, its artificiality) might be pointed out through various elements. In this regard, the first feature to be considered – as also outlined by the ATAD CFC provisions – would be the performance of business activities. This is because an entity that regularly carries on an active business and generates income – or at least is aimed at generating profits and is also well-structured and organized – would be automatically inferred as carrying on a genuine economic activity.[61] That is the equivalent implica-

---

[59] See EFTA Court, 9 July 2014, Joined Cases E-3/13 and E-20/13, ECLI:EU:C:2013:716, *Fred. Olsen and Others and Petter Olsen and Others v The Norwegian State, represented by the Central Tax Office for Large Enterprises and the Directorate of Taxes*, paras. 96–99: "*Accordingly, the concept of establishment under Articles 31 and 34 EEA has a specific EEA meaning and must not be interpreted narrowly. Thus, any person or entity, such as a trust, that pursues economic activities that are real and genuine must be regarded as taking advantage of its right of establishment under Articles 31 and 34 EEA. The essential feature of real and genuine business activities that constitute establishment is that a person or an entity carries on a business, such as by offering services, which are effected for consideration, for an indefinite period through a fixed establishment. A fixed establishment may be gained and maintained by such activities as settling personally in the host State, establishing the seat of management there and/or recruiting staff to perform the services that may be required from the establishment there. In contrast, an entity not carrying out any business in another EEA State, due to the extent it exists in terms of premises, staff and equipment, and whose incorporation may thus not reflect economic reality cannot invoke Articles 31 and 34 EEA due to its lack of actual economic activity (…). Whether the entity in question conducts a real and genuine economic activity cannot be answered in the abstract. It depends on the actual terms of the entity's statutes, such as, in the case at hand, the trust's deed, and the actual activities of that entity and its management. (…).*". The mentioned "EEA" denote the Agreement on the EEA, OJ L 1 (3 January 1994) p. 3–522 and EFTA States' official gazettes. Articles 31 and 34 of the EEA Agreement correspond, respectively, to articles 49 and 54 of the Treaty on the Functioning of the European Union (TFEU).
It is necessary here to also briefly point out how the reference to "*actual terms*" and "*actual activities*" may correlate to the transfer pricing principles as set forth in the 'OECD Transfer Pricing Guidelines for Multinational Enterprises and Tax Administrations' (2017) that are effectively referred to by the ATAD's CFC rules as further explored in the following of the present work.

[60] Julia de Jong in: Erik Pinetz/Erich Schaffer (eds) *Limiting Base Erosion*, 1st edition (Vienna: Linde, 2017) p. 305.

[61] "*(…) 'economic activity' must therefore be construed as meaning an* activity *likely to be carried out by a private undertaking on a market, organised within a professional framework and generally performed in the interest of generating profit. It is to be noted that this interpretation is quite different compared with the interpretation of 'economic activity' in other sectors such as competition law, where it also has the purpose of determining the scope of application of Community law. In the tax field, the concept of economic activity is based on a double criterion, not only a functional criterion relating to activity but also and above all a structural criterion relating to organisation.*" See Opinion of Advocate General Maduro, 18 May 2004, C-8/03, ECLI:EU:C:2004:309, *Banque Bruxelles Lambert SA (BBL) v Belgian State*, para. 10; CJEU, 21 October 2004, C-8/03, ECLI:EU:C:2004:650, *Banque Bruxelles Lambert SA (BBL) v Belgian State*, paras. 36–40. As regarding the concept of economic activity within the meaning of the Sixth Council Directive 77/388/EEC of 17 May 1977 on the harmonization of the laws of the Member States relating to turnover taxes – Common system of value added tax: uniform basis of assessment, OJ L 145 (13 June 1977) p. 1–40 ("Sixth Directive"), see also CJEU, 20 June 1991, C-60/90, ECLI:EU:C:1991:268, *Polysar Investments Netherlands BV v Inspecteur der Invoerrechten en Accijnzen*, para. 13; CJEU, 22 June 1993, C-333/91, ECLI:EU:C:1993:261, *Sofitam SA (formerly Satam SA) v Ministre chargé du Budget*, para. 12; CJEU, 20 June 1996, C-155/94, ECLI:EU:C:1996:243, *Wellcome Trust Ltd v Commissioners of Customs and Excise*, para. 32.

tion provided by the ATAD within the framework of the categorical approach as it is only intended to reattribute different categories of passive income to the CFC's controlling party. Accordingly, if we observe the other side of the coin, profits mainly generated by passive income would less likely suggest the carrying out of a substantive economic activity (with the exception of some financial undertakings).[62]

Secondly, for the purpose of substance under the categorical approach, the ATAD – in accordance with established case law and with the suggestions included in the OECD BEPS Action 3 Report[63] – deems the identification critical of physical factors such as staff, equipment, and premises which, on the basis of relevant facts and circumstances, should further validate the separation and functional independence of the controlled foreign entity from its parent.[64] In other words, the CFC is substantially deemed to exist and operate autonomously if supported by relevant physical and human elements.[65, 66]

---

62 Julia de Jong in: Erik Pinetz/Erich Schaffer (eds) *Limiting Base Erosion*, 1ˢᵗ edition (Vienna: Linde, 2017) p. 305–306.
63 See OECD BEPS Action 3 Report, paras. 81–86.
64 *"fixed establishment, which 'must be characterised by a sufficient degree of permanence and a suitable structure in terms of human and technical resources to enable it to receive and use the services supplied to it for its own needs'."* See Opinion of Advocate General Villalón, 25 June 2015, C-230/14, ECLI:EU:C:2015:426, *Welttimmo s.r.o. v Nemzeti Adatvédelmi és Információszabadság Hatóság*, para. 30. See also CJEU, 16 October 2014, C-605/12, ECLI:EU:C:2014:2298, *Welmory sp. z o.o. v Dyrektor Izby Skarbowej w Gdańsku*, para. 58; CJEU, 28 June 2007, C-73/06, ECLI:EU:C:2007:397, *Planzer Luxembourg Sàrl v Bundeszentralamt für Steuern*, para. 54.
65 *"In that regard, it must be remembered that Article 2(i) of the directive defines a branch of activity as 'all the assets and liabilities of a division of a company which from an organisational point of view constitute an independent business, that is to say an entity capable of functioning by its own means.' It follows that the independent operation of the business must be assessed primarily from a functional point of view – the assets transferred must be able to operate as an independent undertaking without needing to have recourse, for that purpose, to additional investments or transfers of assets – and only secondarily from a financial point of view."* See CJEU, 15 January 2002, C-43/00, ECLI:EU:C:2002:15, *Andersen og Jensen ApS and Skatteministeriet*, paras. 34–35, on the interpretation of Article 2(c) and (i) of Council Directive 90/434/EEC of 23 July 1990 on the common system of taxation applicable to mergers, divisions, transfers of assets, and exchanges of shares concerning companies of different Member States (OJ L 225, 20 August 1990, p. 1).
66 In this regard, the association of these features should also be noted and, hence, of the ATAD's provisions with the "functionally separate entity approach" introduced by the OECD for the profit allocation to permanent establishments, also known as "Authorized OECD Approach" (AOA) for which the guidelines and core principles were developed in the 2008 'Report on the Attribution of Profits to Permanent Establishments', revised in 2010. To be more specific, in 2010, the OECD replaced the "relevant business activity approach" used up to that time and implemented the AOA for the purpose of attributing profits to a permanent establishment under Article 7 of the OECD Model Tax Convention on Income and Capital. According to the AOA, permanent establishments should be treated like separate and independent enterprises for tax purposes under the fiction that the arm's length principle is applicable to the "dealings" occurring between the permanent establishment and the rest of the enterprise. Therefore, the aim of the AOA is to harmonize tax treaty rules for business profits under Article 7 of the OECD Model Tax Convention with the arm's length principle under Article 9 and the OECD Transfer Pricing Guidelines. In light of the changes to the definition of permanent establishment under Article 5 of the OECD Model Tax Convention resulting from the final report on BEPS Action 7 (*Preventing the Artificial Avoidance of Permanent Establishment Status*, Action 7 – 2015 Final Report, http://dx.doi.org/10.1787/9789264241220-en), in 2018, the OECD released 'Additional Guidance on the Attribution of Profit to Permanent Establishment' including a more detailed explanation of the AOA and some practical examples.

4.3. Threshold exemptions

4.3.1. Purpose and scope

Article 7(3) of the ATAD – consistently with the recommendations of the OECD BEPS Action 3 Report[67] – allows Member States a mere option to exclude from the application of CFC rules those entities that generate passive income for no more than one third of their total income. Furthermore, implementing states are also allowed to exclude financial undertakings if one third or less of the passive income accruing to that entity or permanent establishment stems from intercompany transactions.[68]

These two exceptions that states may decide to apply individually or simultaneously may be introduced to lower the burden of administrative and compliance costs. However, they might lead to uncertainties and differences in the Member States' implementing legislation thus inhibiting the aim to limit unilateral measures and easing the emergence of competing sets of rules at the international level.

4.3.2. One-third passive income threshold

Regarding the first of the mentioned exemptions, precisely, that relating with the one-third threshold in general[69], it would be advisable for Member States to adopt it in order to reduce administrative burdens and therefore simplify the tax administrations' duties, at least in certain circumstances. In fact, in this way, it would be *a priori* possible, on the one side, to select those CFCs that generate a considerable amount of passive income and should be further investigated to determine whether they should fall under the CFC scope. On the other side, those companies that can be deemed harmless in terms of BEPS threats should be excluded.

Implementing this first alternative may also be worthwhile to reduce compliance costs for taxpayers and increase certainty as they would have the chance to acknowledge in advance whether they will be subject to CFC legislation. It shall also be clarified that, for the purpose of the exemption under analysis, the percentage

---

67   See OECD BEPS Action 3 Report, paras. 53–59.
68   See ATAD, Article 7, para. 3: "*Where, under the rules of a Member State, the tax base of a taxpayer is calculated according to point (a) of paragraph 2, the Member State may opt not to treat an entity or permanent establishment as a controlled foreign company under paragraph 1 if one third or less of the income accruing to the entity or permanent establishment falls within the categories under point (a) of paragraph 2.*
     "*Where, under the rules of a Member State, the tax base of a taxpayer is calculated according to point (a) of paragraph 2, the Member State may opt not to treat financial undertakings as controlled foreign companies if one third or less of the entity's income from the categories under point (a) of paragraph 2 comes from transactions with the taxpayer or its associated enterprises.*"
69   This is in line with the so called "entity approach" suggested by the OECD in the BEPS Action 3 Report: "*Under the entity approach, an entity that does not earn a certain amount or percentage of attributable income or an entity that engages in certain activities will be found not to have any attributable income, even if some of its income would be of an attributable character*" (para. 95).

Exceptions from the application of the CFC rules under the ATAD

of passive income was reduced from one half to one third during the ATAD negotiations concurrently with the removal of the switch-over clause.[70]

4.3.3. Financial undertakings carve-out

Further, with regard to the second sector-specific exemption, it should be reminded that income generated by companies operating in the financial and insurance sector is usually deemed as passive due to the character of their business and the inherent nature of the services provided. As a consequence, depending on the method used to compute the attributable CFC income to the controlling shareholders, individual jurisdictions are likely to implement CFC rules using disharmonized criteria. However, as already specified, in consideration of the need for introducing an approach that is as replicable and objective as possible, it would be preferable to instead adopt coordinated criteria keeping in mind that such (passive) income actually derives from an active (financial) business. Therefore, the option made available by the ATAD provisions that also seized the recommendations of the OECD as part of the BEPS Project is welcomed.

When developing and implementing CFC legislation, the degree of risk of the relevant entity – in terms of base erosion and profit shifting – should be considered foremost. CFC rules had thus better focus on higher-risk circumstances in order to become "*more targeted and effective and also reduce the overall level of administrative burden by ensuring that certain companies are not affected by the rules*"[71].

Hence, the risk also follows of treating streams of income inappropriately that are conventionally defined as passive (because they are classified as investment type income) but essentially derived in the ordinary course of an active market-facing and customer-driven business of a financial undertaking. That is the primary reason why targeted provisions and specific exceptions are needed for entities in the financial and insurance sectors.

---

70   The switch-over clause included in Article 6 of the initial ATAD proposal was removed from the final version. The switch-over clause was targeted against the tax exemption in the European Union of some types of foreign income originated in a third country if such income had been taxed below 40 percent of the statutory tax rate that would have been charged under the applicable corporate tax system in the Member State of the taxpayer. In this respect, the Explanatory Memorandum to the Proposal (para. 5) provided that: "*Given the inherent difficulties in giving credit relief for taxes paid abroad, States tend to increasingly exempt foreign income from taxation. The unintended negative effect of this approach is that it may encourage untaxed or low-taxed income to enter the internal market and then, circulate – in many cases, untaxed – within the Union, making use of available instruments within the Union law. Switch-over clauses are commonly used against such practices. Namely, the taxpayer is subjected to taxation (instead of being exempt) and given a credit for tax paid abroad. In this way, companies are discouraged from shifting profits out of high-tax jurisdictions towards low-tax territories, unless there is sufficient business justification for these transfers.*" See also Recital 8 of the Proposal for the ATAD.
71   See OECD BEPS Action 3 Report, para. 50.

Based on the above considerations, the ATAD allows excluding those financial undertakings that engage in transactions with the controlling entity or its associated parties for less than one third of their total passive income. Along with being aligned with the BEPS recommendations[72], this optional provision calls up the exemption provided under Article 4 of the ATAD in relation to the interest limitation rule. Accordingly, financial undertakings, even if consolidated for accounting purposes, may be excluded from the scope of the limitations to the deductibility of interest[73].

More in detail, related enterprises engaging in financial and insurance businesses that are industries that could actually be conducted with a reduced number of employees and could possibly function without the use of extensive premises – that means that they require a light organization and a not significant physical presence[74] (possibly, they carry on a non-active business) – might plausibly be employed for the purpose of stripping tax bases and shifting income[75]. However, they should not undergo the ordinary approach and instead be subject to customized rules[76] on the basis of the fact that they are highly regulated sectors. These kinds of entities are usually subject to specific regulation and stringent capital requirements or constraints and need to satisfy tailored tests imposed by national and supranational regulatory bodies.

---

72 See OECD BEPS Action 3 Report, paras. 95–96.
73 See Article 4(7) of the ATAD: "*Member States may exclude financial undertakings from the scope of paragraphs 1 to 6, including where such financial undertakings are part of a consolidated group for financial accounting purposes.*" See also the Explanatory Memorandum to the Proposal for the ATAD (para. 5): "*Although it is generally accepted that financial undertakings, i.e. financial institutions and insurance undertakings, should also be subject to limitations to the deductibility of interest, it is equally acknowledged that these two sectors present special features which call for a more customised approach. This is chiefly because, contrary to other sectors of the economy, financial costs and revenues are incurred by, or accrue to, financial undertakings as part of their core trade. Given that the discussions in this field are not yet sufficiently conclusive in the international and Union context, it has not yet been possible to provide for specific rules in the financial and insurance sectors. It is however necessary to clarify that despite the temporary exclusion of these financial undertakings, the intention is to ultimately conclude an interest limitation rule of broad scope which is not subject to exceptions.*"
74 See the Communication from the Commission to the Council, the European Parliament and the European Economic and Social Committee on the application of anti-abuse measures in the area of direct taxation – within the EU and in relation to third countries, COM(2007) 785 final (10 December 2007), para. 2: "*In the context of corporate establishment there are inevitably difficulties in determining the level of economic presence and commerciality of arrangements. Objective factors for determining whether there is adequate substance include such verifiable criteria as the effective place of management and tangible presence of the establishment as well as the real commercial risk assumed by it. However, it is not altogether certain how those criteria may apply in respect of, for example, intra-group financial services and holding companies, whose activities generally do not require significant physical presence.*"
75 Structured finance and treasury functions within integrated multinational groups may actually constitute a powerful technique for BEPS.
76 See Caroline Docclo, 'The European Union's Ambition to Harmonize Rules to Counter the Abuse of Member States' Disparate Tax Legislations', *Bulletin for International Taxation* Volume 71 No. 7 (2017) p. 367 (p. 371, para. 5.2.7.).

Although these standards and requirements may have a different purpose and result, to some extent, in more flexibility, they operate at a previous stage and distinctly from the substance-based tests. They should not materially and significantly undermine the purpose or in any way weaken or challenge the effectiveness of CFC rules. Financial and insurance enterprises should therefore be treated like any other active business even though they are subject to adequate safeguards and guidance.

More in detail, a CFC for which the controlling entity is subject to regulatory controls and prudential constraints and that shall itself satisfy sector specific tests in its country of establishment should be considered as meeting the substance condition on a presumptive basis. It should therefore not be considered within the scope of CFC rules.

4.4. Interim conclusions on the categorical approach

Due to the recent and still ongoing implementation of the ATAD and, consequently, of suitable CFC rules in all Member States, it is not yet possible to assess whether the proposed categorical approach and related exceptions are apt to effectively and efficiently cover all non-genuine CFCs and associated BEPS opportunities.

However, based on all of the above, the threshold exception and the financial undertaking carve-out provided under Article 7(3) of the ATAD seem reasonable and practically viable for the purposes of an effective CFC implementing legislation. They can be electively applied prior to the substantive economic activity test thus allowing not introducing disproportionate or undue burden on businesses and focus on entities that present higher CFC risks.

5. CFC exemptions under the transactional approach
5.1. Brief description

As anticipated in paragraph 1.2.3, the ATAD provides a second option for the purposes of computing the CFC's attributable income to the controlling shareholders. According to this innovative transactional (or substance) approach, the income of the controlling foreign entity arising from genuine arrangements that have not been put in place for the essential purpose of obtaining a tax advantage shall not fall under the scope of CFC rules.[77]

The ATAD's concept of non-genuine arrangements (that reflects transfer pricing principles) is based on the fact that the CFC does not own pertinent assets nor bear risks concerning the activity that is performed whereas all of the risks are taken by the controlling entity "*where the significant people functions, which are*

---

77 ATAD, Article 7, para. 2(b). Hence, this model does contain an artificiality (or non-genuiness) test combined with a subjective test as the critical purpose shall be to obtain a tax advantage.

relevant to those assets and risks, are carried out and are instrumental in generating the controlled company's income"[78]. As a consequence, the CFC's income (or a part of it) should be attributed to the parent company in accordance with the arm's length principle.[79]

Similar to the categorical approach, the ATAD adds some practical exemptions also in relation to the transactional approach[80]. More specifically, implementing states may refrain from treating entities (or permanent establishments) as CFCs if, in the tax period concerned, the following *de minimis* thresholds are satisfied:

- accounting profits not higher than EUR 750,000 and non-trading income not higher than EUR 75,000; or
- accounting profits amounting to maximum 10% of the operating costs.

Furthermore, with respect to point (b), the country may decide to calculate the operating costs without including the cost of goods sold generated outside the CFC's tax residence country and the payments made to associated entities. However, there is no possibility to exempt financial undertakings[81].

As already clarified, these exceptions are aimed at containing – both for tax administrations and multinational groups – the overall burden of costs concerning the implementation of proper CFC rules. Additionally, this accomplishment is reached by allowing a straightforward exclusion of controlled foreign entities that pose a nil BEPS risk.

It shall be also noted that, at first sight, the two exclusions based on accounting profits may look as if they are alternative[82]; however, this would not prevent Member States from implementing both of the thresholds in their respective legislations. Moreover, they are formulated in relation to the relevant individual entity which would suggest their application on a stand-alone basis.[83] Consequently,

---

78   *Id.*, second subparagraph.
79   As clearly explained in the OECD BEPS Action 3 Report (paras. 83–84), approaches based on a transactional analysis *"typically rely on more qualitative measures than categorical analyses, and they are often included in CFC rules because they may be more accurate than a purely mechanical approach. Their inclusion, however, could lead to increased administrative and compliance burdens. This is because they require an analysis of the CFC's facts and circumstances. However, the incremental burden may be small because this analysis may be similar to that required for transfer pricing purposes. Where this analysis reveals that the CFC has insufficient substance, some or all of its profits, even after any transfer pricing adjustments, may be included in CFC income. However, substance analyses can be designed to address these concerns and to apply more mechanically while still increasing the accuracy of purely objective analyses."* Exceptions may indeed be provided.
80   ATAD, Article 7, para. 4.
81   The exemption for financial undertakings is, on the contrary, possible if the categorical approach is applied.
82   Indeed, the ATAD uses the word "or". See ATAD, Article 7, para. 4, first subparagraph.
83   See Isabella de Groot, Barry Larking, 'Implementation of Controlled Foreign Company Rules under the EU Anti-Tax Avoidance Directive (2016/1164)', *European Taxation* Volume 59 No. 6 (2019) p. 261 (p. 271).

it can be easily imagined that the implementing states' practice will vary depending on the exemptions that are applied in order to enact rules that best fit with their specific market and business environment. Member States may exercise both the excluding options, omitting some conditions or introducing additional ones, whereas other countries may not exercise either option.

5.2. De minimis thresholds

The exceptions provided under Article 7(4) of the ATAD introduce the option for Member States to set income ceilings below which the application of CFC rules is excluded thereby permitting ignoring all of the circumstances that present little economic relevance. This approach, as well as being in line with the indications of the BEPS Action 3 Report[84], is voiced in the ATAD's introductory notes. Accordingly, special tax regimes for small entrepreneurs or certain taxpayers with low profits or low margins that reasonably (as it can be substantiated on the basis of relevant facts and circumstances) do not give rise to tax avoidance risks should be legitimately exempted for the purpose of CFC rules[85].

The set thresholds look reasonable if one considers the purpose of seizing the diciest cases for base erosion and profit shifting while limiting the risk of including minor multinational groups that (possibly) pose no threats. Further, even though it might be unclear why the council chose those exact limits, they seem coherent with approaches taken in other European Union initiatives[86]. They are also consistent with the OECD threshold provided for country-by-country reporting purposes[87].

In any respect, the intention is apparently to narrow the extended scope of application of CFC rules under the transactional approach (*"non-genuine arrangements which have been put in place for the essential purpose of obtaining a tax advantage"*) exclusively to those entities that are active in the international arena

---

[84] See OECD BEPS Action 3 Report, para. 53.
[85] See Recital 12 of the ATAD: *"With a view to limiting the administrative burden and compliance costs, it should also be acceptable that those Member States exempt certain entities with low profits or a low profit margin that give rise to lower risks of tax avoidance."*
[86] Both the Proposal for a Council Directive on a Common Corporate Tax Base (CCTB) and the relaunched Proposal for Consolidation (CCCTB) published by the European Commission in October 2016, provide that the new rules will be mandatory for companies with a consolidated turnover exceeding Euro 750 million per year. See Proposal for a Council Directive on a Common Corporate Tax Base, COM/2016/685 final – 2016/0337 (CNS) (25 October 2016); Proposal for a Council Directive on a Common Corporate Tax Base, COM/2016/683 final – 2016/0336 (CNS) (25 October 2016), article 2, para. 1(c).
[87] According to the OECD BEPS Action 13 Report, the Country-by-Country Reporting requirements should apply to MNEs with annual consolidated group revenue equal to or exceeding Euro 750 million. See *Transfer Pricing Documentation and Country-by-Country Reporting*, Action 13 – 2015 Final Report, OECD/G20 Base Erosion and Profit Shifting Project (Paris: OECD Publishing, 2015) http://dx.doi.org/10.1787/9789264241480-en, paras. 51–55.

and undertake transactions of considerable value with related parties. In other words, the aim would be to consider those entities that are likelier to bump into exceptional possibilities to carry out BEPS-related transactions. The *de minimis* thresholds are also designed in order not to interfere with existing transfer pricing requirements.[88] In fact, it should be noted that the ATAD provisions are anti-avoidance rules aimed at complementing existing guidelines relating to the international tax system (such as the transfer pricing rules) rather than replace them[89].

5.3. Interim conclusions on the transactional approach

As a result of the above considerations, it would be recommendable that the transactional approach applies in such a way that merely artificially diverted profits are seized, and genuine profitable structures backed by appropriate substance are exempted.

Nevertheless, based on the variety that could emerge from adoption of the transactional approach and related exceptions, a periodic review could be considered. The review should be aimed at ensuring that the exemptions and thresholds provided are still appropriate to meet the overall policy and compliance objectives, and they do not exacerbate administrative burdens for companies. Furthermore, the periodic review should prove that the mentioned exclusions and thresholds are not disproportionate or unbalanced with respect to the benefits accruing to the relevant tax authorities. Moreover, a cautious assessment is necessary to verify if a distinction (including eventually a lowering of the thresholds) would not be preferable for smaller economies where MNEs of limited dimensions might be responsible for larger shares of commercial activities and hence for larger stakes of related tax risks which would justify equal concerns.

6. Comparative analysis: the impact of ATAD's CFC exceptions in different countries

6.1. General overview

According to the ATAD provisions, Member States should have implemented CFC rules in their national legislations by 1 January 2019. Many countries have not met this deadline, others have not precisely enforced the minimum standards

---

88   Notably, the second subparagraph of Article 7(4) of the ATAD provides as follows: *"For the purpose of point (b) of the first subparagraph, the operating costs may not include the cost of goods sold outside the country where the entity is resident, or the permanent establishment is situated, for tax purposes and payments to associated enterprises."*
89   Richard Collier, Seppo Kari, Olli Ropponen, Martin Simmler and Maximilian Todtenhaupt, 'Dissecting the EU's Recent Anti-Tax Avoidance Measures: Merits and Problems', *EconPol Policy Report* Volume 2 No. 8 (2018).

Exceptions from the application of the CFC rules under the ATAD

and, for some others, it has not been necessary to modify existing CFC regulations already in force.[90]

In this context, it may be stimulating to analyse how some individual countries have (or have not) implemented the ATAD's CFC provisions – in particular, which model for computing attributable income they established best fit their economic framework and tax system. Furthermore, identifying the respective chosen policies and the related differences (if any) – and trying to understand to what extent the ATAD is leading to homogeneous rules across the European Union, given that the ATAD itself provides options among which implementing states can choose.[91]

In general terms, some Member States have applied the categorical approach while other have chosen the transactional approach based on disparate policy considerations. More in detail, the legislator may have favoured the transactional approach as it generates lower administrative and compliance burdens, especially in the case that transfer pricing rules are already existing in the same state. Furthermore, the transactional approach would be preferable for the purpose of attracting foreign investments due to the related slighter impacts on such structures[92]. Also, selected countries have opted for a hybrid model[93] or both models[94],[95]. In the following, a comparative analysis of selected countries[96] will be performed that aims to highlight the main peculiarities, similarities, and differences of the various approaches implemented by the Member States.

6.2. Comparative analysis of selected countries

CFC rules were not in place in all Member States before the ATAD. Austria[97], for instance, did not have CFC rules but planned to implement them after the ATAD

---

90 See Isabella de Groot, Barry Larking, 'Implementation of Controlled Foreign Company Rules under the EU Anti-Tax Avoidance Directive (2016/1164)', *European Taxation* Volume 59 No. 6 (2019) p. 261. See also 'National transposition measures communicated by the Member States concerning: Council Directive (EU) 2016/1164 of 12 July 2016 laying down rules against tax avoidance practices that directly affect the functioning of the internal market', Document 32016L1164, available at https://eur-lex.europa.eu/legal-content/EN/NIM/?uri=celex:32016L1164 (accessed 17 Apr. 2021).
91 In this regard, it should be also noted that Member States are allowed to implement stricter CFC rules than the ATAD's minimum standards provided that the European Union law is respected. However, they cannot apply less severe anti-avoidance rules. See Isabella de Groot, Barry Larking, *European Taxation* Volume 59 No. 6 (2019) p. 261.
92 *E.g.*, Belgium.
93 *E.g.*, Italy.
94 *E.g.*, the Netherlands.
95 Isabella de Groot, Barry Larking, *European Taxation* Volume 59 No. 6 (2019) p. 261 (p. 265–266, para. 5.1.2).
96 For the purpose of comparative analysis, the following Member States have been selected: Austria, Belgium, Italy, Greece and Poland.
97 Martin Klokar/Mario Riedl, 'Chapter 5: Controlled Foreign Company Legislation in Austria' in: Georg Kofler/Richard Krever/Michael Lang/Jeffrey Owens/Pasquale Pistone/Alexander Rust/Josef Schuch (eds.) *Controlled Foreign Company Legislation*, 1st edition (IBFD 2020), Books IBFD (accessed 17 Feb. 2021).

was adopted. Indeed, as part of the 2018 Annual Tax Act, the Austrian legislator introduced a CFC regulation effective as of 1 January 2019, implementing the relevant ATAD provisions[98]. Likewise, Belgium[99] also introduced a CFC regulation for the first time starting from 1 January 2019[100].

Differently from Austria and Belgium, other countries had previously implemented CFC rules. Italy[101] had implemented a CFC legislation in 2000 and, in 2018, issued a new legislative decree[102] for the purpose of alignment with the ATAD provisions, including compliance with Articles 7 and 8 on CFCs. To add another example, Polish CFC rules[103] that had entered into force as of 2015 were then amended in 2017 and further in 2018 following the issue of the ATAD.

Greece[104] instead introduced CFC rules for the first time in 2013 and, in 2019, amended them to align with the relevant ATAD provisions.[105] In particular, Greece opted for the categorical approach. In this regard, it shall be noted that, along with other standard requirements (namely, control requirement and threshold of actual tax paid abroad), the Greek CFC rules provide a passive income test for the purpose of application. Specifically, Greek rules apply in the case that more than 30% of the foreign entity's net income before tax consists, *inter alia*, in passive income, which differs only slightly from the one-third threshold provided for in the ATAD[106] and applied by Polish CFC rules as well[107].

---

98 See *Jahressteuergesetz 2018*, BGBl I 2018/62 (JStG 2018).
99 Gilles Van Hulle/Jean-Philippe Van West, 'Chapter 6: Controlled Foreign Company Legislation in Belgium' in: Georg Kofler/Richard Krever/Michael Lang/Jeffrey Owens/Pasquale Pistone/Alexander Rust/Josef Schuch (eds.) *Controlled Foreign Company Legislation*, 1st edition (IBFD 2020), Books IBFD (accessed 17 Feb. 2021).
100 Belgian rules on CFC are included in the Belgian Internal Tax Code, article 185/2.
101 Raul-Angelo Papotti/Simone S. Schiavini, 'Chapter 20: Controlled Foreign Company Legislation in Italy' in: Georg Kofler/Richard Krever/Michael Lang/Jeffrey Owens/Pasquale Pistone/Alexander Rust/Josef Schuch (eds.) *Controlled Foreign Company Legislation*, 1st edition (IBFD 2020), Books IBFD (accessed 17 Feb. 2021).
102 Legislative Decree 142 of 29 November 2018, Official Gazette 300 (28 December 2018) p. 1.
103 Adrian Wardzynski, 'Chapter 29: Controlled Foreign Company Legislation in Poland' in: Georg Kofler/Richard Krever/Michael Lang/Jeffrey Owens/Pasquale Pistone/Alexander Rust/Josef Schuch (eds.) *Controlled Foreign Company Legislation*, 1st edition (IBFD 2020), Books IBFD (accessed 17 Feb. 2021).
104 Aikaterini Savvaidou, Vasiliki Athanasaki, 'Specific Anti-Avoidance Measures in Greece in the Post-BEPS and Post-ATAD Era', *European Taxation* Volume 59 No. 4 (2019) p. 169 (pp. 173–174); Vassilis Dafnomilis, 'Amendments to the Thin Cap Rule, the CFC Rule and the GAAR Following ATAD Implementation', *European Taxation* Volume 59 No. 8 (2019) p. 391 (pp. 392–393). See also Katerina Savvaidou, Vasiliki Athanasaki, 'The transposition of the ATAD into the Greek tax law', *Studi Tributari Europei* [S.l.] Volume 9 (2019), pp. 1–101–114; available at: https://ste.unibo.it/article/view/10830 (accessed 13 August 2020).
105 Article 66 of Law 4172/2013 (the New Greek Income Tax Code) and Law 4607/2019 (24 April 2019).
106 See ATAD, Article 7, para. 3, first subparagraph.
107 As explained by Explanatory Statement No. 2330 to the act implementing Polish CFC provisions. See Adrian Wardzynski in: Georg Kofler/Richard Krever/Michael Lang/Jeffrey Owens/Pasquale Pistone/Alexander Rust/Josef Schuch (eds.) *Controlled Foreign Company Legislation*, 1st edition (IBFD 2020), Books IBFD (accessed 17 Feb. 2021), para. 29.1.1.2.

Greek CFC provisions apply the substance escape provided under the ATAD's categorical approach. However, as opposed to Austria, Greece does not extend it to CFCs established in third countries outside the European Union/EEA[108]. Hence, it seems straightforward to recognize that Austria has also applied the categorical approach with a substance carve-out. More in detail, similar to the categories provided under the ATAD, Austrian CFC rules establish that only a selection of passive income could trigger them[109]; in addition, they also provide for a *de minimis* threshold[110] and a control requirement[111] in line with the ATAD.[112]

As mentioned, Austria has adopted a substance carve-out in the case that the foreign company is established both within the European Union/EEA and in a third country. Therefore, Austrian CFC rules would not apply if the foreign entity engages in substantive economic activities supported by staff, equipment, assets, and premises as evidenced by relevant facts and circumstances[113]. Compared to other countries that have implemented the same approach, the peculiarity of the Austrian substance test is that (leveraging on quantitative criteria and a non-comprehensive list of excluded activities but without clearly providing all the necessary definitions), it ought to assess whether the relevant foreign entity has the personnel and material resources *"that are in an appropriate economic relationship with the alleged economic activity"*. This means that, under Austrian CFC rules, the actual substance of the CFC economic activity shall be compared *"with the substance of such an activity that is normally reasonable from an economic point of view"*[114].

---

108 ATAD, article 7, para. 2(a), third subparagraph.
109 The list of harmful passive income follows that of the ATAD with tiny deviations regarding dividends (in order to avoid double non-taxation issues) and income from invoicing companies (to limit an otherwise excessively wide scope of the rules).
110 In accordance with ATAD, Article 7, para. 3, first subparagraph. Specifically, a controlled foreign entity does not trigger Austrian CFC rules in the case that the passive income accruing to it amounts to no more than one third of its total income.
111 In accordance with ATAD, Article 7, para. 1(a).
112 The three requirements – *de minimis* limit, controlling event, and substance carve-out – shall apply cumulatively. See Martin Klokar/Mario Riedl in: Georg Kofler/Richard Krever/Michael Lang/Jeffrey Owens/Pasquale Pistone/Alexander Rust/Josef Schuch (eds.) *Controlled Foreign Company Legislation*, 1st edition (IBFD 2020), Books IBFD (accessed 17 Feb. 2021), para. 5.2.3.
113 It should be noted that the Austrian CFC provisions reverse the burden of proof on the taxpayer. In this case, the Austrian controlling entity shall therefore bear the burden of proof and provide documentation that substantiates the CFC activities. This approach could contrast with the cooperation duty (between tax authorities and taxpayers) provided under European Union law and reiterated in the CJEU case law and Recital 12 of the ATAD. See Martin Klokar/Mario Riedl in: Georg Kofler/Richard Krever/Michael Lang/Jeffrey Owens/Pasquale Pistone/Alexander Rust/Josef Schuch (eds.) *Controlled Foreign Company Legislation*, 1st edition (IBFD 2020), Books IBFD (accessed 17 Feb. 2021), para. 5.6.2.
114 See Martin Klokar/Mario Riedl in: Georg Kofler/Richard Krever/Michael Lang/Jeffrey Owens/Pasquale Pistone/Alexander Rust/Josef Schuch (eds.) *Controlled Foreign Company Legislation*, 1st edition (IBFD 2020), Books IBFD (accessed 17 Feb. 2021), para. 5.6.2.

Additionally, Austria has also opted for the financial undertakings' exception mostly in line with the relevant ATAD provision[115]. Greece, on the contrary, has not considered the financial undertakings carve-out and has not even implemented exceptions based on accounting profit thresholds.[116] Nevertheless, it may not be excluded that new amendments to the Greek CFC legislation will follow.

Likewise, Italy has not opted for the financial undertakings' exemption in its ATAD's implementing legislation. However, what is notable about Italy is that it has introduced a very peculiar CFC system compared to the models adopted in other Member States. In fact, Italian CFC rules may be represented through a hybrid model as they include features of both approaches provided in the ATAD for attributing CFC income even though more steps towards the transactional approach have been made on the basis of the most recent amendments. More in detail, for the purpose of application of Italian CFC rules, the passive income test[117] and the effective tax rate test must first be satisfied. Then, the whole CFC income is attributed to the controlling entity and subject to tax in Italy, which seems going beyond the minimum standards of the ATAD[118].

Similarly, Poland has also deviated from the ATAD's minimum requirements, leveraging on the minimum level of the protection provision under Article 3 of the ATAD itself. Poland[119], that has basically adopted a categorical approach, applies a "full inclusion system" for the purpose of attributing CFC income as the whole income of the CFC – regardless of its nature and origin – may be included

---

115 See Section 10a, para. 8 of the Austrian Corporate Income Tax Act, in compliance with ATAD, Article 7, para. 3, second subparagraph. However, this exemption cannot be invoked by intragroup financing companies nor by captive insurance companies. See Martin Klokar/Mario Riedl in: Georg Kofler/Richard Krever/Michael Lang/Jeffrey Owens/Pasquale Pistone/Alexander Rust/Josef Schuch (eds.) *Controlled Foreign Company Legislation*, 1st edition (IBFD 2020), Books IBFD (accessed 17 Feb. 2021), para. 5.2.3.
116 Aikaterini Savvaidou, Vasiliki Athanasaki, 'Specific Anti-Avoidance Measures in Greece in the Post-BEPS and Post-ATAD Era', *European Taxation* Volume 59 No. 4 (2019) p. 169 (p. 173).
117 According to ATAD, Article 7, para. 3, first subparagraph.
118 Under the ATAD's transactional approach, only the profit actually diverted from the parent company's jurisdiction shall be attributed to the latter through assessment on a case by case basis and according to the arm's length principle. The Italian approach seems to be going beyond the ATAD's minimum requirements which is, in any case, allowed according to Recital 12 and Article 3 of the ATAD. However, as specified under Article 8(2) of the ATAD itself, "*the income to be included in the tax base of the taxpayer shall be limited to amounts generated through assets and risks which are linked to significant people functions carried out by the controlling company. The attribution of controlled foreign company income shall be calculated in accordance with the arm's length principle*". See Legislative Decree 142 of 29 November 2018, Official Gazette 300 (28 December 2018) p. 1 (pp.10–12, article 4). See also 'Audition of the General Co-Director of the Italian Association of Joint-Stock Companies before the Italian Senate' (4 October 2018) pp. 10–15.
119 Adrian Wardzynski in: Georg Kofler/Richard Krever/Michael Lang/Jeffrey Owens/Pasquale Pistone/Alexander Rust/Josef Schuch (eds.) *Controlled Foreign Company Legislation*, 1st edition (IBFD 2020), Books IBFD (accessed 17 Feb. 2021).

Exceptions from the application of the CFC rules under the ATAD

into the tax base of the Polish controlling entity[120]. Poland has also admitted a substance carve-out[121] which is another similarity with the Italian model. In fact, Italian CFC rules include a safe harbour provision in the form of a substance carve-out[122]. In this regard, it has to be noted that Italian taxpayers might also file a ruling request to the tax authorities in order to prove that "*the controlled foreign company carries on a substantive economic activity supported by staff, equipment, assets and premises*"[123]. Another characteristic of Polish CFC rules that has not been considered under other Member States' regulation is the following. Polish CFC rules apply to 27 blacklisted jurisdictions that are specifically indicated in a resolution by the Polish Ministry of Finance[124]. Moreover, the Polish CFC regulation applies to jurisdictions that have not yet ratified any agreement with Poland or the European Union concerning the exchange of tax information.[125]

As opposed to Poland and Greece, Belgium has based its internal CFC provisions on the ATAD's transactional approach[126]. Therefore, the Belgian legislator has welcomed the association with (and use of) transfer pricing principles for the purpose of CFC rules, also trusting in the assumption that this approach would help to attract foreign investments[127]. Like Poland and Italy, Belgium has also gone be-

---

120 The Polish legislator excluded the transactional approach due to the fact that it "*provides for a case-by-case factual analysis that is likely to disproportionally increase administrative burdens relative to the projected additional tax yield.*" See Adrian Wardzynski in: Georg Kofler/Richard Krever/Michael Lang/Jeffrey Owens/Pasquale Pistone/Alexander Rust/Josef Schuch (eds.) *Controlled Foreign Company Legislation*, 1st edition (IBFD 2020), Books IBFD (accessed 17 Feb. 2021), para. 29.2.4. See also Błażej Kuźniacki, 'The (In)Compatibility of Polish CFC Rules with the Constitution Pre and Post-Implementation of the EU Anti-Tax Avoidance Directive (2016/1164)', *European Taxation* Volume 58 No. 4 (2018) p. 149 (pp. 151–152).
121 In this regard, the Polish provision makes reference to the "substantial genuine economic activity" carried out by the CFC and considers objective factors to determine the degree of genuineness. See Adrian Wardzynski in: Georg Kofler/Richard Krever/Michael Lang/Jeffrey Owens/Pasquale Pistone/Alexander Rust/Josef Schuch (eds.) *Controlled Foreign Company Legislation*, 1st edition (IBFD 2020), Books IBFD (accessed 17 Feb. 2021), para. 29.1.5.
122 According to ATAD, Article 7, para. 2(a), second subparagraph.
123 See Raul-Angelo Papotti/Simone S. Schiavini, 'Chapter 20: Controlled Foreign Company Legislation in Italy' in: Georg Kofler/Richard Krever/Michael Lang/Jeffrey Owens/Pasquale Pistone/Alexander Rust/Josef Schuch (eds.) *Controlled Foreign Company Legislation*, 1st edition (IBFD 2020), Books IBFD (accessed 17 Feb. 2021), para. 20.1.5.
124 Resolution of the Polish Ministry of Finance of 28 March 2019. In this regard, it shall also be noted that European Union/EEA blacklisted jurisdictions cannot benefit from the substance carve-out.
125 See Adrian Wardzynski in: Georg Kofler/Richard Krever/Michael Lang/Jeffrey Owens/Pasquale Pistone/Alexander Rust/Josef Schuch (eds.) *Controlled Foreign Company Legislation*, 1st edition (IBFD 2020), Books IBFD (accessed 17 Feb. 2021), para. 29.1.1.3.
126 ATAD, Article 7, para. 4, first subparagraph.
127 Actually, the Belgian legislator has assumed that the transactional approach would cause less impact (*i.e.*, changes) to the existing national tax system. Furthermore, it has been stated that the transfer pricing rules will continue to prevail on CFC provisions. Although Belgium has essentially replicated the ATAD's provisions, there are minor deviations that might instill uncertainties concerning the use of the term "foreign corporation" under Belgian law and the term "entity" under Article 7 of the ATAD as well as with reference to the control requirement. See Gilles Van Hulle/Jean-Philippe Van West in: Georg Kofler/Richard Krever/Michael Lang/Jeffrey Owens/Pasquale Pistone/Alexander Rust/Josef Schuch (eds.) *Controlled Foreign Company Legislation*, 1st edition (IBFD 2020), Books IBFD (accessed 17 Feb. 2021), para. 6.2.

yond, to some extent, the ATAD's CFC rules. Belgium has indeed opted for a full inclusion of CFC income in the tax base of the parent entity without providing for the *de minimis* exceptions based on accounting profits as under Article 7(4) of the ATAD[128]. In the same way, the Netherlands has not, to date, implemented either of these exemptions[129]. However, it should be noted that this specific policy decision could undermine the country's competitiveness compared to other Member States that instead have made use of the available exceptions.

Notably, Ireland, Luxembourg, and Malta, have implemented exceptions even though with minor omissions or deviations from the ATAD. Luxembourg, for example, has implemented both exemptions based on accounting profits and has omitted the non-trading income condition; Ireland has instead reduced the low-profits threshold from EUR 750,000 to EUR 75,000[130].

6.3. Interim conclusions on the comparative analysis

Based on the above, although most of the Member States have strived and are still working to how best to conform the internal regulation with the ATAD's CFC provisions and thus accomplish their inherent objectives, there is wide evidence available to infer that Member States have implemented the rules in different and various ways. Even when opting for the same approach, the countries may have applied diverse exceptions and to different extents.

For some countries that have implemented the rules extensively, it might be advisable to think about the adoption of some exemptions as provided under the ATAD for the purposes of rationalization, effectiveness, and competitiveness of the respective tax systems and for limiting the scope of tax audits thus also improving the efficiency of competent authorities on tax avoidance issues.

To conclude, it should be also noted that, the more that CFC rules will be aligned among different countries, the lower the risk of double (non-)taxation shall and, consequently, lower risk of challenges by the tax authorities; also, limited shall be the use of court procedures or mutual agreement procedures.

---

128 ATAD, article 7, para. 2(b).
129 See Isabella de Groot, Barry Larking, 'Implementation of Controlled Foreign Company Rules under the EU Anti-Tax Avoidance Directive (2016/1164)', *European Taxation* Volume 59 No. 6 (2019) p. 261 (p. 271).
130 "*Luxembourg has implemented both, but has omitted the condition regarding non-trading income in the first option. Ireland has also implemented both but provided an alternative to the low-profits exemption that the ATAD does not provide, namely, for accounting profits of less than EUR 75,000. Malta has simply transposed both options into its implementing legislation.*" See Isabella de Groot, Barry Larking, 'Implementation of Controlled Foreign Company Rules under the EU Anti-Tax Avoidance Directive (2016/1164)', *European Taxation* Volume 59 No. 6 (2019) p. 261 (p. 271). See also Gilles Van Hulle/Jean-Philippe Van West in: Georg Kofler/Richard Krever/Michael Lang/Jeffrey Owens/Pasquale Pistone/Alexander Rust/Josef Schuch (eds.) *Controlled Foreign Company Legislation*, 1st edition (IBFD 2020), Books IBFD (accessed 17 Feb. 2021), para. 6.7.3.

7. Conclusions

Beyond the ATAD's minimum level of protection laid down against base erosion and profit shifting, the ATAD's CFC rules leave substantial leeway to Member States regarding their implementation. Consequently, the two methods provided under the ATAD for attributing the tainted income to controlling shareholders have been diversely applied by Member States. Differences in national implementation laws (or in amending provisions if CFC rules were previously existing) may derive from the decision of some legislators to rigidly adhere to the ATAD's guidelines as opposed to other policy makers' intention of deviating and adopting even stricter rules as also allowed by the ATAD itself. To this extent, CFC exceptions according to the categorical approach (Article 7(3)) or the transactional approach (Article 7(4)) have been implemented in different ways and combinations. The underlying driving force and major effort for countries is to establish a balance between the protection of their domestic tax base and the promotion of their unique and distinctive business framework at the international level thus increasing competitiveness compared to other Member States.

The critical examination and the comparative analysis carried out in this work has shown that the transactional approach might be preferable for countries that are intended to limit compliance costs and administrative burdens for companies. The categorical approach, on the contrary, would be more appropriate for deterring aggressive tax planning attempts implemented through the transfer of assets producing passive income that are more easily subject to tax optimization schemes. In order to limit the extent of CFC rules and to increase their effectiveness, Member States have mostly welcomed the use of exceptions depending on the specific approach opted for in the domestic CFC legislation. In some cases slight deviations and alternatives were introduced compared to the ATAD's rules while, in some others, the exemptions provided under the categorical and the transactional approaches were combined.

Based on the differences and the variance among Member States that have even more clearly emerged since the issue of the ATAD, it seems unlikely that a uniform set of CFC rules across all Member States will be accomplished. Therefore, countries shall be required to carefully monitor the implications of CFC rules' implementation in the coming years. It is necessary to ensure that the exceptions and the limitations that are implemented will continue to be appropriate for the purpose of challenging aggressive tax planning structures and reducing tax risks. Furthermore, countries will need to possibly adjust their choices concerning CFC rules in order to avoid overlapping with other provisions of their international tax systems and to comply with their own policy objectives without creating imbalances either domestically (between taxpayers and tax authorities) or at the international level undermining foreign investments and competitiveness with other countries.

CFC rules of the ATAD in light of the EU fundamental freedoms

Mike Kollar

1. Introduction
    1.1. The fundamental freedoms
    1.2. Secondary EU legislation
    1.3. The freedom of establishment vs the free movement of capital
        1.3.1. Substantive influence
        1.3.2. Exchange of Information
    1.4. Income attribution by the ATAD CFC rules
2. **Limitations imposed on CFC legislation**
    2.1. Cadbury-Schweppes
    2.2. X GmbH
3. **Conclusion**

1. Introduction

The first country in Europe to recognize the negative effects of international profit shifting was West Germany. By attributing income to low-tax foreign subsidiaries, internationally operating companies were able to shift income away from Germany and achieve deferral, meaning that the income was not subject to the domestic taxation until the profits were repatriated. In order to effectively counteract such practice, the German legislator, based on rules first introduced in the 1960s in the United States, developed a concept to prevent abuse beyond their borders, hence the first controlled foreign company (CFC) legislation was introduced in Europe.[1] Other countries, such as France in 1980 and the United Kingdom in 1984, followed and introduced similar legislation.[2] It is worth noting that many other EU countries such as Austria, Belgium, or the Netherlands as well as many Eastern European countries have had, until recently, no experience with CFC legislation.[3]

In 2013, the OECD in cooperation with the G20 adopted a 15-point action plan to combat base erosion and profit shifting that included, inter alia, CFC legislation.[4] Some of the participating countries had already implemented CFC rules in some form, and others were interested in introducing them which is why the Final Report on BEPS Action 3 sets out recommendations on how to structure CFC legislation that effectively tackles base erosion. The report was not meant to be a minimum standard for all participating countries but a set of building blocks for jurisdictions who wished to implement or update their existing legislation.[5] The EU decided to implement the findings of the BEPS Project by introducing the Anti-Tax Avoidance Directive of 2016 (ATAD).[6] The CFC rules included therein were largely inspired by the recommendations of the OECD.[7] The CFC rules of the ATAD aim at calculating and taxing undistributed income of controlled subsidiaries or permanent establishments in low tax jurisdictions. The conditions that must be fulfilled in order for a subsidiary to be considered a CFC is for the parent to directly or indirectly own more than 50% of the subsidiary[8] and that the effective tax rate of the state where the subsidiary/permanent establishment is situated is less than half of that in the parent state[9]. In contrast to Action 3 of the BEPS

---

1   Sebastian Dueñas, 'CFC Rules Across the world', *Fiscal Fact* (2019) p. 4.
2   Sebastian Dueñas, 'CFC Rules Across the world', *Fiscal Fact* (2019) p. 5.
3   Sebastian Dueñas, 'CFC Rules Across the world', *Fiscal Fact* (2019) p. 6.
4   Base Erosion and Profit Shifting Project (OECD/G20) of 5 October 2015 on Designing Effective Controlled Foreign Company Rules, Action 3 – 2015 Final Report, p. 3.
5   Base Erosion and Profit Shifting Project (OECD/G20) of 5 October 2015 on Designing Effective Controlled Foreign Company Rules, Action 3 – 2015 Final Report, p. 9.
6   Council Directive (EU) 2016/1164 of 12 July 2016 laying down rules against tax avoidance practices that directly affect the functioning of the internal market, OJ L 193 (19 July 2016).
7   Council Directive (EU) 2016/1164 of 12 July 2016 laying down rules against tax avoidance practices that directly affect the functioning of the internal market, OJ L 193 (19 July 2016) Preamble para 2.
8   Council Directive (EU) 2016/1164 of 12 July 2016 laying down rules against tax avoidance practices that directly affect the functioning of the internal market, OJ L 193 (19 July 2016) para 7 Sec. 1 a).
9   Council Directive (EU) 2016/1164 of 12 July 2016 laying down rules against tax avoidance practices that directly affect the functioning of the internal market, OJ L 193 (19 July 2016) para 7 Sec. 1 b).

Project, the EU's CFC legislation was drafted as a minimum standard, and all EU Member States are required to implement it.[10]

EU primary law provides the so-called four fundamental freedoms that are the essential means to form and maintain the internal market. By guaranteeing the free movement of goods, services, persons, and capital, the fundamental freedoms safeguard against restrictions on cross-border intra EU trade and thereby allow for fair competition.[11] Although direct taxation does not fall under the competence of the EU, any legislation introduced by Member States must nevertheless conform to the fundamental freedoms in order to allow the common market to function properly.[12] Any CFC legislation must therefore conform to the fundamental freedoms, which is why the BEPS Final Report on Action 3 also took the EU fundamental freedoms into account when suggesting how CFC legislation should be drafted.[13]

The research aim of this thesis is to examine whether CFC legislation as drafted in the ATAD is in line with the fundamental freedoms. Chapter 1 will provide a general overview of what the fundamental freedoms exactly are and which might be relevant for the CFC rules as included in the ATAD. Chapter 2 looks at the limits imposed on the ATAD by the case law of the Court of Justice of the European Union (CJEU) related directly to CFC legislation, most notably by the *Cadbury-Schweppes*[14], and the *X GmbH*[15] decisions. The last chapter, Chapter 3, concludes whether the ATAD CFC rules are in line with the fundamental freedoms and under which conditions this might not be the case.

1.1. The fundamental freedoms

At the heart of the EU legal systems lies the internal market which is an area allowing for the free movement of goods[16], services[17], persons[18], and capital[19], also

---

10 Council Directive (EU) 2016/1164 of 12 July 2016 laying down rules against tax avoidance practices that directly affect the functioning of the internal market, OJ L 193 (19 July 2016) Preamble para 2.
11 Haslehner Werner, 'Das Betriebsstättendiskriminierungsverbot im Internationalen Steuerrecht', *Schriftenreihe zum Internationalen Steuerrecht* (2009), p. 94.
12 CJEU, 14 February 1995, C-279/93, ECLI:EU:C:1995:31, *Finanzamt Köln-Altstadt v Schumacker*, para 21.
13 Base Erosion and Profit Shifting Project (OECD/G20) 'Designing Effective Controlled Foreign Company Rules, Action 3 – 2015 Final Report' (5 October 2015), p. 17.
14 CJEU, 12 September 2006, C-196/04, ECLI:EU:C:2006:544, *Cadbury Schweppes und Cadbury Schweppes Overseas*.
15 CJEU, 26 February 2019, C-135/17, ECLI:EU:C:2019:136, *X GmbH*.
16 Treaty on European Union and the Treaty on the functioning of the European Union 2012/C 326/01 of 13 December 2007, OJ C 326 (26 October 2012), Article 28–37.
17 Treaty on European Union and the Treaty on the functioning of the European Union 2012/C 326/01 of 13 December 2007, OJ C 326 (26 October 2012), Article 56–62.
18 Treaty on European Union and the Treaty on the functioning of the European Union 2012/C 326/01 of 13 December 2007, OJ C 326 (26 October 2012), Article 45–55.
19 Treaty on European Union and the Treaty on the functioning of the European Union 2012/C 326/01 of 13 December 2007, OJ C 326 (26 October 2012), Article 63–66.

called the fundamental freedoms. Besides the fundamental freedoms, it is important to also mention the general prohibition of discrimination on the grounds of nationality included in Article 18 of the Treaty on the Functioning of the European (TFEU) which is applicable *"without prejudice to any special provisions contained therein [TFEU]..."*. Article 18 can be viewed as a general norm, or leges generales, which is further specified in greater detail by the fundamental freedoms.[20]

The effect of the fundamental freedoms is not unrestricted on national tax law but applies only when cross-border situations with other Member States arise, as is the case with CFC legislation which requires the undistributed income of foreign subsidiaries to be included in the tax base of the parent company. Since the purpose of the fundamental freedoms is to facilitate equal treatment for parties conducting cross-border trade within the EU, they do not apply in purely domestic settings.[21] According to the fundamental freedoms, cross-border situations may not be treated less favourably than purely domestic situations unless a justifiable reason can be found. However, the fundamental freedoms do not cover situations when cross-border situations are treated more favourably than domestic ones. In purely domestic cases, tax sovereignty remains exclusively with the Member States.[22]

The free movement of goods put an end to any tariff barriers such as customs or other duties or non-tariff barriers such as quantitative restrictions to trade between EU Member States.[23] The free movement of services puts service providers within the EU on an equal footing and allows for their cross-border provision as well as their receival without restrictions. The freedom protects the right to provide, among others, insurance, banking, tourism, and broadcasting services along with digital services like software, films, and music.[24] The free movement of persons can be dissected into three specific categories which are the free movement

---

20 Haslehner Werner, 'Das Betriebsstättendiskriminierungsverbot im Internationalen Steuerrecht', *Schriftenreihe zum Internationalen Steuer-recht* (2009), p. 94.
21 Ivan Lazarov 'The Relevance of the Fundamental Freedoms for Direct Taxation' in: Michael Lang, Pasquale Pistone, Josef Schuch, Claus Staringer, *Introduction To European Tax Law On Direct Taxation* (Vienna: Linde, 2018) p. 64.
22 Patrick Orlet, 'Die unionsrechtlichen Anforderungen für CFC-Regelungen', *Steuer- und Wirtschaft International* (2018) p. 163–164.
23 Andressa Pegoraro 'Non-Discrimination under EU Law: Comparability of Corporations and Permanent Establishments' in: Kasper Dziurdź, and Christoph Marchgraber, *Non-Discrimination In European And Tax Treaty Law* (Vienna: Linde, 2018) p. 44.
24 The services can be broadly divided into three categories: (i) when the service provider crosses the boarder to provide the services in another Member State, (ii) when the recipient leaves a Member State to receive a service, and (iii) when services are provided digitally which does not required the provider nor the recipient to physically relocate; Andressa Pegoraro 'Non-Discrimination under EU Law: Comparability of Corporations and Permanent Establishments' in: Kasper Dziurdź, and Christoph Marchgraber, *Non-Discrimination In European And Tax Treaty Law* (Vienna: Linde, 2018) p. 44.

of workers, the freedom of establishment, and the right to stay in any Member State without the aim of conducting business activities. The free movement of workers constrains both the home and host Member State to treat foreign workers worse than their own nationals.[25] With respect to CFC legislation, all three of those freedoms have little relevance since they do not limit investments in other Member States and will therefore not be further discussed.

The freedom of establishment allows both individuals and companies from EU Member States to freely conduct business in any other Member State. The implication for an individual is that he can perform any activity as a self-employed person across the EU. Companies, on the other hand, are allowed to freely establish agencies, branches, or subsidiaries within the community. The free movement of capital, as the name suggests, prohibits any restrictions on the movement of capital and payments not just between Member States but also between Member States and third countries. This is important to stress since the free movement of capital is the only freedom that is applicable beyond the borders of the EU. In the realm of direct taxation, the freedom is mostly linked to real property and dividend payments.[26]

Within its jurisprudence, the CJEU decided already in the 1960s that EU law takes precedence over national provisions[27]. Since any national law, as well as the ATAD as secondary EU law, are subject to primary EU law, the fundamental freedoms must be taken into account when considering conformity with primary EU law. CFC legislation can potentially limit the freedom of establishment since part of the tax base of foreign subsidiaries or permanent establishments will be added to the tax base of the resident parent entity, in effect treating a foreign subsidiary less favourably than a purely domestic situation. As was mentioned before, in purely domestic settings, CFC rules would typically not apply. At the same time, the free movement of capital may also be limited because establishing a foreign subsidiary or permanent establishment is nothing more than a cross boarder investment that, due to CFC legislation, will be treated worse than a domestic investment. For this reason, both fundamental freedoms may potentially be affected by CFC legislation depending on the circumstances; it is therefore necessary to define the boundaries between those two freedoms or assess if, potentially, even both freedoms could be applicable at the same time, which will be further discussed in Chapter 1.3.

---

25   Ivan Lazarov 'The Relevance of the Fundamental Freedoms for Direct Taxation' in: Michael Lang, Pasquale Pistone, Josef Schuch, Claus Staringer, *Introduction To European Tax Law On Direct Taxation* (Vienna: Linde, 2018) p. 66–68.
26   Ivan Lazarov 'The Relevance of the Fundamental Freedoms for Direct Taxation' in: Michael Lang, Pasquale Pistone, Josef Schuch, Claus Staringer, *Introduction To European Tax Law On Direct Taxation* (Vienna: Linde, 2018) p. 66–69.
27   CJEU, 15 July 1964, C-6/64, ECLI:EU:C:1964:66, *Costa v E.N.E.L.*

1.2. Secondary EU legislation

Although this book's chapter is, in principle, concerned with the interplay of primary EU legislation and CFC legislation, it is important to stress that secondary EU legislation might also influence the application of CFC legislation. Due to a lack of political consensus, the area of direct taxation has been harmonized to a very little extent by secondary legislation despite the fact that it was recognized already in the 1960s that different corporate income tax systems of EU Member States have an adverse effect on the common market. The commission proposed the adoption of legislation in 1975 in order to introduce a range of acceptable tax rates from 42% to 52% and on domestic loss-carry forward and cross-border loss relief in 1984 and 1990, respectively, but all efforts failed due a lack of political consensus. A similar path seems to lie ahead for the proposal regarding a common consolidated corporate tax base that is a uniform way of calculating the tax base of taxpayers belonging to a group that operates across the EU.[28] Such legislation was first proposed in 2011 and again with slight amendments in 2016 but, due to the lack of political support, has so far failed to become EU law.[29]

On the other hand, there are also positive examples of integration in the area of taxation. Examples include the Parent-Subsidiary Directive[30], the Merger Directive[31] and the Arbitration Convention[32], which were all adopted on the same day in 1990.[33] Worth considering in respect to CFC legislation is certainly the aforementioned Parent-Subsidiary Directive in today's form[34], which is also dealing with the taxation, or rather non-taxation, of dividend income between parent companies and their subsidiaries situated in different EU Member States. The directive's objective is to exempt dividends from withholding taxes if those are paid by subsidiaries to their parent companies as well as eliminating double taxation.[35]

---

28 See here also Chapter 20 – CFC rules and CCCTB.
29 Pasquale Pistone, Rita Szudocky, 'Coordination of Tax Laws and Tax Policies in the EU' in: Michael Lang, Pasquale Pistone, Josef Schuch, and Claus Staringer, *Introduction To European Tax Law On Direct Taxation* (Vienna: Linde, 2018) p. 40–44.
30 Council Directive (EU) 90/435/EEC of 23 July 1990 on the common system of taxation applicable in the case of parent companies and subsidiaries of different Member States, OJ L 225 (20 August 1990).
31 Council Directive (EU) 90/434/EEC of 23 July 1990 on the common system of taxation applicable to mergers, divisions, transfers of assets, and exchanges of shares concerning companies of different Member States, OJ L 225 (20 August 1990).
32 Convention (EU) 90/463/EEC of 20 August 1990 on the elimination of double taxation in connection with the adjustment of profits of associated enterprises, OJ L 225 (20 August 1990).
33 Pasquale Pistone, Rita Szudocky, 'Coordination of Tax Laws and Tax Policies in the EU' in: Michael Lang, Pasquale Pistone, Josef Schuch, and Claus Staringer, *Introduction To European Tax Law On Direct Taxation* (Vienna: Linde, 2018) p. 40–41.
34 Council Directive (EU) 2011/96/EU of 30 November 2011 on the common system of taxation applicable in the case of parent companies and subsidiaries of different Member States, OJ L 345 (29 December 2011).
35 Council Directive (EU) 2011/96/EU of 30 November 2011 on the common system of taxation applicable in the case of parent companies and subsidiaries of different Member States, OJ L 345 (29 December 2011) Preamble para 3.

A company needs to hold at least 10% of the capital of its subsidiary[36] to be considered the parent company. If this is the case, the source state is bound not to tax dividend distributions within the EU[37] while the resident state has to either exempt such income or, in the case that it decides to tax, allow for a deduction for all levied lower tier corporate taxes.[38]

The Parent-Subsidiary Directive, therefore, either exempts or credits profits against the tax already paid at the level of the parent company as opposed to CFC rules that shift the retained profits of the subsidiary to be taxed at the level of the parent company. This may lead to conflicts in situations in which the Parent-Subsidiary Directive and CFC legislation are applicable simultaneously, e.g. CFC rules require undistributed income to be taxed at the level of the parent whereby the conditions for exempting such income (if it were really distributed) would be met under the Parent-Subsidiary Directive. According to *Orlet*, it is worth noting that, since the Parent-Subsidiary Directive and the ATAD are equivalent in strength, the CFC resident state must follow the former and grant relief for the taxes levied since the Parent-Subsidiary Directive is, despite its wording, also applicable to fictitious dividend distributions.[39]

1.3. The freedom of establishment vs the free movement of capital

At first glance, one might suspect that only the freedom of establishment is possibly at stake, since CFC legislations in general aims at curbing the transfer of profits to subsidiaries located in states with more favourable taxation. In contrast to purely domestic situations, CFC rules may restrict the freedom of establishment because retained profits of establishment or subsidiaries in low-taxed Member States are added to the parent company which leads to a worse treatment of a foreign subsidiary compared to a purely domestic situation. The ATAD itself specifically states a 50% control threshold[40] which is a strong indicator for the application of the freedom of establishment, but it is important to point out that this legislation shall be viewed as only a minimum level of protection for Member States

---

36   Council Directive (EU) 2011/96/EU of 30 November 2011 on the common system of taxation applicable in the case of parent companies and subsidiaries of different Member States, OJ L 345 (29 December 2011) Article 3 para 1 letter a) point (i).
37   Council Directive (EU) 2011/96/EU of 30 November 2011 on the common system of taxation applicable in the case of parent companies and subsidiaries of different Member States, OJ L 345 (29 December 2011) Article 5.
38   Council Directive (EU) 2011/96/EU of 30 November 2011 on the common system of taxation applicable in the case of parent companies and subsidiaries of different Member States, OJ L 345 (29 December 2011) Article 4 Sec. 2.
39   Patrick Orlet, 'Die unions-rechtlichen Anforderungen für CFC-Regelungen', *Steuer und Wirtschaft International* (2018) p. 163.
40   Council Directive (EU) 2016/1164 of 12 July 2016 laying down rules against tax avoidance practices that directly affect the functioning of the internal market, OJ L 193 (19 July 2016) Article 7 Sec. 1 a).

meaning that they are free to implement a lower control threshold if they see the need. This is expressed in the explanatory notes of the ATAD reading *"In order to ensure a higher level of protection, Member States could reduce the control threshold..."*[41]. Therefore, it is not only the freedom of establishment that needs to be considered but also the free movement of capital. The latter freedom extends to all shareholdings regardless of the level of influence, hence also portfolio investments which do not fall within the scope of the freedom of establishment. Therefore, smaller investors could also rely on the protection of the free movement of capital if their foreign investments are treated worse than their domestic investments.[42]

The CJEU in its earlier decisions took the position that more than one of the freedoms can be applied to a particular situation[43], but more recent case law suggests that the court tends to apply the "center of gravity" view which says that, despite that more fundamental freedoms could be applicable simultaneously, freedoms that are only ancillary will not be further inspected, meaning that only one freedom is being considered by the court.[44] To determine which of the two freedoms is applicable, it is necessary to determine if the legislation was intended to apply to all shareholders or only shareholders with substantive influence on the decisions of the other company[45]. Whenever the legislation requires substantive influence, the freedom of establishment needs to be considered; if the opposite is true, it is the free movement of capital. If this distinction is not expressly made by the legislation in question, two situations must be contrasted which are (i) intra-EU and (ii) third countries. In intra-EU scenarios, the logic is the same as if the legislation specifically stated what kind of shareholding is required, meaning that, as long as the shareholder has substantive influence over the company in the individual case at hand, the freedom of establishment is at stake[46] except if the legislation is more closely connected to the free movement of capital[47]. In third country scenarios in which the disputed legislation not only applies exclusively to shareholders with substantive influence, one can rely on the free movement on capital also in situations where a substantive influence is given.[48] In spite of that, the previously mentioned steps should never lead to a disguised expansion of the freedom of establishment to third country scenarios where the purpose of the legislation is closely linked to market access[49]. To sum up, the CJEU is distinguishing between simple

---

41 Council Directive (EU) 2016/1164 of 12 July 2016 laying down rules against tax avoidance practices that directly affect the functioning of the internal market, OJ L 193 (19 July 2016) Preamble para 12.
42 Martin Klokar, 'Die österreichische Hinzurechnungsbesteuerung (CFC-Regime) und das Unionsrecht', *Steuer und Wirtschaft International* (2020) p. 72.
43 CJEU, 18 November 1999, C-200/98, ECLI:EU:C:1999:566, *X and Y*, para 30.
44 CJEU, 8 June 2017, C-580/15, ECLI:EU:C:2017:429, *Van der Weegen and Others*, para 25.
45 CJEU, 20 December 2017, C-504/16, ECLI:EU:C:2017:1009, *Deister Holding*, para 78.
46 CJEU, 11 September 2014, C-47/12, ECLI:EU:C:2014:2200, *Kronos International*, para 35; CJEU, 20 December 2017, C-504/16, ECLI:EU:C:2017:1009, *Deister Holding*, para 81.
47 CJEU, 23 January 2014, C-164/12, ECLI:EU:C:2014:20, *DMC*, paras. 28–38.
48 CJEU, 24 November 2016, C-464/14, ECLI:EU:C:2016:896, *SECIL*, para. 41.
49 CJEU, 24 November 2016, C-464/14, ECLI:EU:C:2016:896, *SECIL*, para. 43.

"capital movements" and full "market access" which is crucial regarding CFC legislation since the free movement of capital extends to third countries while the freedom of establishment does not. In the end, the purpose of the legislation is the decisive factor[50] for determining which fundamental freedom is relevant.[51]

It is important to note that some scholars also have contrasting views and that, whenever a third country scenario is being considered and the taxpayer can, for obvious reasons, not rely on the freedom of establishment, it should be possible to rely on the free movement of capital despite the purpose of the legislation. *Pistone* considers capital liberalization extending beyond EU boarders to be justifiable since the free movement of capital protects the capital itself and not the investee/investor or any person disposing over the capital.[52] Other scholars, such as *Stahl*, consider that such a wide interpretation of the free movement of capital would inevitably extend the other freedoms to third states *"through the back door"* which was supposedly not their original purpose.[53]

1.3.1. Substantive influence

To distinguish between mere capital movements and market access, it is necessary to determine what constitutes a substantive influence of a shareholder. Settled case law of the CJEU confirms that shareholdings of more than 50% are sufficient to constitute a substantive influence[54]. In addition, the CJEU confirmed the applicability of the freedom of establishment even to shareholdings of 34% in *SGI*[55] and 25%,, respectively in the decisions *Lasertec*[56] and *Scheunemann*[57]. It is unclear if a lower shareholding is sufficient to trigger the freedom of establishment, but the CJEU took the position in the cases *Test Claimants in the FII Group Litigation*[58], *Kronos*[59], and *Itelcar*[60] that a 10% shareholding is too low to be regarded as substantive and therefore the freedom of establishment is not applicable in such cases.[61]

---

50   CJEU, 10 February 2011, Case C-436/08 and C-437/08, ECLI:EU:C:2011:61, *Haribo Lakritzen Hans Riegel and Österreichische Salinen AG*, para. 35.
51   Ivan Lazarov 'The Relevance of the Fundamental Freedoms for Direct Taxation' in: Michael Lang, Pasquale Pistone, Josef Schuch, Claus Staringer, *Introduction To European Tax Law On Direct Taxation* (Vienna: Linde, 2018) pp. 69–71.
52   Sergey Bezborodov, 'Freedom of Establishment in the EC Economic Partnership Agreements: in Search of its Direct Effect on Direct Taxation', *INTERTAX* (2007) p. 668 and p. 672.
53   Sergey Bezborodov, 'Freedom of Establishment in the EC Economic Partnership Agreements: in Search of its Direct Effect on Direct Taxation', *INTERTAX* (2007) p. 672.
54   CJEU, 13 April 2000, C-251/98, ECLI:EU:C:2000:205, *Baars*, para 21.
55   CJEU, 21 January 2010, C-311/08, ECLI:EU:C:2010:26, *SGI*, para. 34.
56   CJEU, 10 May 2007, C-492/04, ECLI:EU:C:2007:273, *Lasertec*, para. 20.
57   CJEU, 19 July 2012, C-31/11, ECLI:EU:C:2012:481, *Scheunemann*, para. 25.
58   CJEU, 12 December 2006, C-446/04, ECLI:EU:C:2006:774, *Test Claimants in the FII Group Litigation*, para 58
59   CJEU, 11 November 2014, C-47/12, ECLI:EU:C:2014:2200, *Kronos International*, para. 55.
60   CJEU, 3 October 2013, C-282/12, ECLI:EU:C:2013:629, *Itelcar*, para 22.
61   Patrick Orlet, 'Die unions-rechtlichen Anforderungen für CFC-Regelungen', Steuer und Wirtschaft International (2018) p. 166.

In addition to simple percentages, the CJEU stated, e.g. in the decision *SGI*[62], that *"Such holdings [more than 34%] are, in principle, capable of giving SGI "definite influence"...".* Spies highlights that percentages as such are therefore only an indication of which freedom might be applicable but are, by themselves, not sufficient.[63] The CJEU continues by stating that *"Moreover ... there are links between those companies at management level"*,[64] which suggests that dependencies on the management level can also influence whether a definitive influence is given or not. This could also be observed in the case *Columbus Container*[65] for which the court decided that, despite the fact that only a 10% shareholding existed, family ties between shareholders were strong enough to substantiate the application of the freedom of establishment. Such tests of factual control were performed by the court only in cases of rather low shareholdings; in cases of higher shareholdings, the court automatically assumed that the control is sufficient to constitute substantial influence and thereby applied the freedom of establishment without turning to such a test.[66]

The ATAD, by default, requires a 50% shareholding[67] which means that, primarily, the freedom of establishment is to be considered. Only under certain circumstances, such as when Member States decide to lower this threshold[68], might the free movement of capital become relevant. For the purposes of further analysis, there is no difference between the freedom of establishment and the free movement of capital, i.e. the assessment of the violation of the freedoms is the same; the only difference lies in third-country aspects. The following chapters will therefore refer to both freedoms, but any peculiarities concerning third-country situations will be addressed when appropriate.

1.3.2. Exchange of Information

Another aspect that needs to be considered is that, in third country situations without a framework for the exchange of information, one cannot rely on the protection of the free movement of capital. The reason is that tax authorities cannot request necessary information in order to access whether a business is genuine. A lack of information exchange can therefore limit the protection of the free movement of capital.[69]

---

62 CJEU, 21 January 2010, C-311/08, ECLI:EU:C:2010:26, SGI, para 35.
63 Karoline Spies, 'Die Kapitalverkehrsfreiheit und Kapitalbeteiligungen in der EuGH-Rechtsprechung', *Steuer und Wirtschaft International – Tax and Business Review* (2011).
64 CJEU, 21 January 2010, C-311/08, ECLI:EU:C:2010:26, SGI, para 35.
65 CJEU, 6 December 2007, C-298/05, ECLI:EU:C:2007:754, *Columbus Container Services*, para 14 and 31.
66 Karoline Spies, 'Die Kapitalverkehrsfreiheit und Kapitalbeteiligungen in der EuGH-Rechtsprechung', *Steuer und Wirtschaft International – Tax and Business Review* (2011).
67 Council Directive (EU) 2016/1164 of 12 July 2016 laying down rules against tax avoidance practices that directly affect the functioning of the internal market, OJ L 193 (19 July 2016) para 7 Sec. 1 a).
68 Council Directive (EU) 2016/1164 of 12 July 2016 laying down rules against tax avoidance practices that directly affect the functioning of the internal market, OJ L 193 (19 July 2016) Preamble para 12.
69 CJEU, 26 February 2019, C-135/17, ECLI:EU:C:2019:136, *X GmbH*, para 95.

This does not concern the freedom of establishment which is only applicable within the EU since Member States can rely on the Mutual Assistance Directive[70] that was introduced already in 1977 and gave them the possibility to request information on tax matters from each other. The directive was meanwhile repealed in 2011 with the introduction of the currently in force Directive on Administrative Cooperation[71] that went even beyond the mere exchange of information on request by allowing for an automatic exchange of information with respect to certain tax and financial information.[72] The aim of those directives was always to tackle tax evasion in the EU which is why the CJEU never accepted a lack of information as a sufficient reason to limit the fundamental freedoms in a pure EU context[73] despite difficulties that arise in practice. In a third country scenario, the directive cannot be relied on, but one must keep in mind the numerous agreements of exchange of information that have been signed by individual Member States with third states[74] to facilitate such an exchange as well as the automatic exchange of information framework of the OECD. Due to the large information exchange network, it will become increasingly difficult in the future to limit the free movement of capital towards third states since it is the only freedom applicable outside the EU.[75]

1.4. Income attribution by the ATAD CFC rules

Since the aim of the thesis is to analyze whether CFC rules, particularly as included in the ATAD, conform to the fundamental freedoms, it is necessary to have a closer look at the conditions under which the ATAD requires income to be attributed to the parent company. When implementing the directive, tax administrations can choose either of two options, i.e. the categorical approach[76] and the non-genuine arrangement approach[77]. Both include taxable income of the con-

---

70 Council Directive (EU) 77/799/EE of 19 December 1977 concerning mutual assistance by the competent authorities of the Member States in the field of direct taxation and taxation of insurance premiums, OJ L 336 (27 December 1977).
71 Council Directive (EU) 2011/16/EU of 15 February 2011 on administrative cooperation in the field of taxation and repealing Directive 77/799/EEC, OJ L 064 (11 March 2011).
72 Michael Schiller, Karoline Spies, Sabine Zirngast, 'Mutual Assistance in Direct Tax Matters' in: Michael Lang, Pasquale Pistone, Josef Schuch, Claus Staringer, *Introduction to European tax law on direct taxation* (Vienna: Linde, 2018) p. 257.
73 CJEU, 28 January 1986, C-270/83, ECLI:EU:C:1986:37, *Commission v France (Avoir Fiscal)*.
74 E.g. Agreement between the Government of Bermuda and the Government of the French Republic for the exchange of information relating to tax matters from 8 October 2009 or the Agreement between the Government of The Kingdom of Sweden and the Government of The Kingdom of Bahrain for the exchange of information relating to tax matters from 14 October 2011.
75 Ivan Lazarov 'The Relevance of the Fundamental Freedoms for Direct Taxation' in: Michael Lang, Pasquale Pistone, Josef Schuch, Claus Staringer, *Introduction To European Tax Law On Direct Taxation* (Vienna: Linde, 2018) p. 95.
76 Council Directive (EU) 2016/1164 of 12 July 2016 laying down rules against tax avoidance practices that directly affect the functioning of the internal market, OJ L 193 (19 July 2016) Article 7 para 2 letter a).
77 Council Directive (EU) 2016/1164 of 12 July 2016 laying down rules against tax avoidance practices that directly affect the functioning of the internal market, OJ L 193 (19 July 2016) Article 7 para 2 letter b).

trolled entity or permanent establishment in the low tax jurisdiction and add it to the tax base of the controlling company whereby the tax base is calculated based on the tax law of the controlling entity's state.[78]

The categorical approach lists specific types of passive income such as interest, royalties, dividends etc. that are subject to the rule provided that the controlled entity does not have enough substance (staff, equipment, assets, and premises) to support its business activity. In third country situations, Member States may refrain from applying the substance requirement, i.e. substance carve-out, and always subject the passive income listed to CFC legislation.[79] In addition, this approach excludes losses of the controlled entity or permanent establishment and requires that those shall be taken into account in subsequent periods by the controlled company/permanent establishment.[80]

By contrast, the non-genuine arrangement approach requires that non-distributed income that arises from non-genuine arrangements that were set up in order to obtain a tax advantage[81] shall be included in the tax base of the controlling company. The amount that is considered to be non-genuine depends on the actual functions performed and risks assumed by the controlling entity and must correspond to its scope of duties.[82]

Comparing the two options, it appears that only the categorical approach has a substance carve out but, since the non-genuine arrangement approach applies by definition only to situations that are "not genuine" and lacking in substance, such a carve out is unnecessary.[83]

2. Limitations imposed on CFC legislation

In general, the CJEU follows a four-step approach in order to arrive at its decision of whether a certain provision of national law or, in the case of the ATAD EU secondary law, is limiting the fundamental freedoms. First, it must be established if the provision in question is within the scope of the fundamental freedoms which is only the case if there is an entitled person (natural or legal) and a cross boarder

---

78 Council Directive (EU) 2016/1164 of 12 July 2016 laying down rules against tax avoidance practices that directly affect the functioning of the internal market, OJ L 193 (19 July 2016) Article 7 para 2.
79 Council Directive (EU) 2016/1164 of 12 July 2016 laying down rules against tax avoidance practices that directly affect the functioning of the internal market, OJ L 193 (19 July 2016) Article 7 para 2 letter a).
80 Council Directive (EU) 2016/1164 of 12 July 2016 laying down rules against tax avoidance practices that directly affect the functioning of the internal market, OJ L 193 (19 July 2016) Article 8 para 1.
81 Council Directive (EU) 2016/1164 of 12 July 2016 laying down rules against tax avoidance practices that directly affect the functioning of the internal market, OJ L 193 (19 July 2016) Article 7 para 2.
82 Sabine Kirchmayr 'Hinzurechnungsbesteuerung' in: Sabine Kirchmayr, Gunter Mayr, Klaus Hirschler, Georg Kofler, *Anti-BEPS-Richtlinie: Konzernsteuerrecht im Umbruch?* p. 105 (Vienna: Linde, 2017).
83 Francisco E. Alvarez, 'The ATAD CFC – All Roads Lead to Cadbury Schweppes', *Kluwer International Tax Blog* (2020).

element.[84] The second step is to assess whether the fundamental freedoms are restricted by looking at the treatment of the same situation in a purely domestic setting and whether the treatment of the cross-border situation would be equal or worse.[85] Thirdly, if the cross-border situation is treated worse, it must be determined whether such treatment can be justified. The CJEU accepts only a few justifications that aim at protecting higher goals of public interest; in the realm of direct taxation, this can be, e.g. measures that limit tax avoidance[86] or protect the cohesion of the tax system[87]. Lastly, the measure must conform to the requirement of proportionality meaning that the legislation shall not exceed what is necessary to achieve the objective.[88]

The fundamental freedoms are limited whenever a domestic situation is treated differently from a cross-border situation which holds true for both the transactional and the non-genuine approach since the ATAD CFC legislation does not apply in purely domestic settings. Local investment is treated differently from an investment in another EU Member State because holding a decisive influence in a domestic entity is treated differently from holding a decisive influence in an entity established in another Member State. For CFC legislation to fall under the scope of the fundamental freedoms, it is necessary that the treatment is not only different from a purely domestic situation but to the disadvantage of the shareholder in cross boarder situations. In a purely domestic investment case, the shareholder can take advantage of deferral, i.e. the income will be taxed only once it is distributed whereby, in a cross boarder situation when CFC rules apply, the income will be taxed immediately leading to a cash flow disadvantage. In addition, in cross boarder situations, the shareholder also bears a greater administrative burden as the income calculated by foreign tax law must be converted based on domestic rules in order to determine which proportion of the income is subject to taxation in the shareholder's state. Shareholders investing domestically suffer none of those consequences which means that the fundamental freedoms are clearly being limited by CFC legislation.[89]

---

84 Ivan Lazarov 'The Relevance of the Fundamental Freedoms for Direct Taxation' in: Michael Lang, Pasquale Pistone, Josef Schuch, Claus Staringer, *Introduction To European Tax Law On Direct Taxation* (Vienna: Linde, 2018) p. 64.
85 Ivan Lazarov 'The Relevance of the Fundamental Freedoms for Direct Taxation' in: Michael Lang, Pasquale Pistone, Josef Schuch, Claus Staringer, *Introduction To European Tax Law On Direct Taxation* (Vienna: Linde, 2018) p. 75.
86 E.g. CJEU, 20 December 2017, C-504/16, ECLI:EU:C:2017:1009, *Deister Holding* and CJEU, 7 September 2017, Case C-6/16, ECLI:EU:C:2017:641, *Eqiom and Enka*.
87 E.g. CJEU, 28 January 1992, Case C-204/90, ECLI:EU:C:1992:35, *Bachmann* and CJEU, 28 January 1992, Case C-300/90, ECLI:EU:C:1992:37, *Commission v Belgium*.
88 Ivan Lazarov 'The Relevance of the Fundamental Freedoms for Direct Taxation' in: Michael Lang, Pasquale Pistone, Josef Schuch, Claus Staringer, *Introduction To European Tax Law On Direct Taxation* (Vienna: Linde, 2018) p. 97.
89 Patrick Orlet, 'Die unionsrechtlichen Anforderungen für CFC-Regelungen', *Steuer und Wirtschaft International* (2018) p. 168.

After it has been established that the fundamental freedoms are limited by the CFC legislation included in the ATAD and by CFC rules, in general, it is necessary to have a closer look at whether such a restriction is justified. The preamble of the ATAD states that *"the current political priorities in international taxation highlight the need for ensuring that tax is paid where profits and value are generated"*[90]. This underscores the already mentioned purpose of the introduced CFC legislation which is primarily combating tax evasion. This is not a surprise since the ATAD was drafted after the reports on BEPS Action 3 which dealt with countering offshore structures that shift income to low tax jurisdictions.[91]

If national legislation or secondary EU legislation implemented into national law was designed to prevent the abuse of the tax systems, a restriction of the fundamental freedoms may be warranted under certain circumstances according to case law of the CJEU.[92] Although the ATAD is rather recent legislation that was only enacted 12 July 2016, the CJEU dealt with CFC legislation already in the past since some Member States had CFC legislation already before the ATAD was introduced. This chapter examines the presumably most influential decision in this respect, namely, the judgment on the *Cadbury-Schweppes* case[93], and the more recent *X GmbH*[94] decisions of the CJEU that offer isight into what CFC legislation needs to fulfil in order to comply with EU primary law.

2.1. Cadbury-Schweppes[95]

Facts and subject matter of the dispute

Under UK foreign tax law, the profits of a subsidiary are added to the profits of a UK company holding more than 50% of the shares of the subsidiary and taxed at the level of the parent company if the foreign tax rate is less than 75% of the rate applicable in the United Kingdom. The tax paid abroad by the subsidiary is credited against this. The addition is waived if it can be shown that the main aim of this arrangement is not to avoid UK taxation (so-called motive test). The British parent company (CSO) of the Cadbury-Schweppes Group set up two subsidiaries in Ireland whose task was to raise funds for the entire group. As both companies are based in the particularly low-taxed International Financial Services Centre

---

90 Council Directive (EU) 2016/1164 of 12 July 2016 laying down rules against tax avoidance practices that directly affect the functioning of the internal market, OJ L 193 (19 July 2016) Preamble para 1.
91 Base Erosion and Profit Shifting Project (OECD/G20) of 5 October 2015 on Designing Effective Controlled Foreign Company Rules, Action 3 – 2015 Final Report.
92 E.g. CJEU, 16 July 1998, C-264/96, ECLI:EU:C:1998:370, *Imperial Chemical Industries v Colmer*; CJEU, 21 November 2002, C-436/00, ECLI:EU:C:2002:704, *X and Y v Riksskatteverket*; CJEU, 11 March 2004, C-9/02, ECLI:EU:C:2004:138, *de Lasteyrie du Saillant*.
93 CJEU, 12 September 2006, C-196/04, ECLI:EU:C:2006:544, *Cadbury Schweppes und Cadbury Schweppes Overseas*.
94 CJEU, 26 February 2019, C-135/17, ECLI:EU:C:2019:136, *X GmbH*.
95 CJEU, 12 September 2006, C-196/04, ECLI:EU:C:2006:544, *Cadbury Schweppes und Cadbury Schweppes Overseas*.

(IFSC) in Dublin, their profits were taxed at only 10%. The British tax authorities considered the above-mentioned conditions for supplementary taxation to be fulfilled and increased the corporation tax payable by the parent company accordingly. Cadbury Schweppes brought an action against this decision and claimed that the British rules on supplementary taxation violated the freedom of establishment. The competent British court therefore referred the question of whether the fundamental freedoms preclude the British CFC legislation to the ECJ for a decision.

The decision of the CJEU

The substantive scope of the freedom of establishment was met since CSO, a resident of the United Kingdom, owned two subsidiaries in Ireland, meaning that a cross-border element was present which is a prerequisite for any freedom to be applicable. Companies having their seat within the community are to be treated in the same way as domestic companies with respect to the freedom of establishment.[96]

As discussed before in Chapter 1.3.1, a 50% shareholding is considered enough by case law to be regarded as a substantive influence for the freedom of establishment to be applicable which is why the court only examined the application of the freedom of establishment.[97] According to the court, any restriction of the free movement of services or the free movement of capital are only unavoidable consequence of the restriction of the freedom of establishment which therefore does not warrant a separate examination of those freedoms.[98]

The CJEU ruled that the freedom of establishment is restricted if the addition of foreign profits is differentiated according to the tax rate in the country where the subsidiary is domiciled.[99] This could discourage companies from establishing subsidiaries in countries with low taxation levels. However, the restriction is justified only when *"the specific objective of such a restriction must be to prevent conduct involving the creation of wholly artificial arrangements which do not reflect economic reality, with a view to escaping the tax normally due on the profits generated by activities carried out on national territory"*.[100]

The mere aim of the company to minimize its tax burden by taking advantage of the different rates of corporate income tax existing in other Member States does

---

96   CJEU, 12 September 2006, C-196/04, ECLI:EU:C:2006:544, *Cadbury Schweppes und Cadbury Schweppes Overseas, para 30.*
97   CJEU, 12 September 2006, C-196/04, ECLI:EU:C:2006:544, *Cadbury Schweppes und Cadbury Schweppes Overseas, para 31.*
98   CJEU, 12 September 2006, C-196/04, ECLI:EU:C:2006:544, *Cadbury Schweppes und Cadbury Schweppes Overseas, para 33.*
99   CJEU, 12 September 2006, C-196/04, ECLI:EU:C:2006:544, *Cadbury Schweppes und Cadbury Schweppes Overseas, para 37.*
100 CJEU, 12 September 2006, C-196/04, ECLI:EU:C:2006:544, *Cadbury Schweppes und Cadbury Schweppes Overseas, para 55.*

CFC rules of the ATAD in light of the EU fundamental freedoms

not in itself justify the presumption that the arrangement is abusive.[101] In addition to this subjective element, objectively verifiable criteria must be added.[102] Only if the controlled foreign company is a fictitious establishment that is *"not carrying out any genuine economic activity in the territory of the host Member State, the creation of that CFC must be regarded as having the characteristics of a wholly artificial arrangement"*.[103] This applies in the case of subsidiaries that are *"letterbox"* or *"front"* subsidiaries.[104] In addition, the court states that general, irrefutable presumptions of abuse are disproportionate as opposed to rebuttable presumptions that allow for an individual review.[105]

The CJEU leaves it to the national court to decide whether the exception to the "motive test" provided for in UK foreign tax law can be interpreted as meeting those requirements. If necessary, the information necessary for the authorities to examine the objective criteria can rely on the information exchange possible through the Mutual Assistance Directive.[106]

2.2. X GmbH[107]

Facts and subject matter of the dispute

In the dispute, the German limited liability company X GmbH held a 30% stake in the Swiss joint stock company Y AG. Y AG concluded so called debt assignment contracts with Z GmbH, a company managing sports rights in Germany, for which it received profit participation rights.[108] Under the German Foreign Tax Act, such income from profit participation was considered to be passive and falling under German CFC rules which is why the German tax administration included it in the taxable income of X GmbH (in proportion to the company's stake in the Swiss Y AG). German CFC legislation usually requires a holding of at least 50% in a foreign company in order for that company to be considered to be controlled but, in the case that foreign subsidiaries generate passive income, a 1% shareholding is already sufficient to trigger CFC rules.[109]

---

101 CJEU, 12 September 2006, C-196/04, ECLI:EU:C:2006:544, *Cadbury Schweppes und Cadbury Schweppes Overseas, para 38*.
102 CJEU, 12 September 2006, C-196/04, ECLI:EU:C:2006:544, *Cadbury Schweppes und Cadbury Schweppes Overseas, para 67*.
103 CJEU, 12 September 2006, C-196/04, ECLI:EU:C:2006:544, *Cadbury Schweppes und Cadbury Schweppes Overseas, para 68*.
104 CJEU, 12 September 2006, C-196/04, ECLI:EU:C:2006:544, *Cadbury Schweppes und Cadbury Schweppes Overseas, para 68*.
105 CJEU, 12 September 2006, C-196/04, ECLI:EU:C:2006:544, *Cadbury Schweppes und Cadbury Schweppes Overseas, para 70*.
106 CJEU, 12 September 2006, C-196/04, ECLI:EU:C:2006:544, *Cadbury Schweppes und Cadbury Schweppes Overseas, para 71*
107 CJEU, 26 February 2019, C-135/17, ECLI:EU:C:2019:136, *X GmbH*
108 CJEU, 26 February 2019, C-135/17, ECLI:EU:C:2019:136, *X GmbH*, para 9
109 CJEU, 26 February 2019, C-135/17, ECLI:EU:C:2019:136, *X GmbH*, para 4–5.

Since X GmbH disagreed with this decision, the competent German court decided to refer three question to the CJEU. In its first and second question, the CJEU was asked whether CFC legislation restricting the free movement of capital with respect to third states can be justified by Article 64(1) of the TFEU (stand-still clause)[110], taking into account that the legislation was substantially amended, but the changes were never implemented[111]. The third question referred to whether Article 63 of the TFEU (free movement of capital) is prohibiting CFC legislation that subjects income of a company in a third state owned by only 1%.[112]

The decision of the CJEU

The first two questions referred to the stand-still clause that allows Member States to restrict the free movement of capital toward third states if they had legislation in place limiting direct investment before 1993[113], i.e. before the introduction of the single market. The situation was specific since Germany already had CFC rules at that time, but the threshold was lowered in subsequent years from 10% to 1% which is why the court was asked whether the stand-still clause is still applicable. The court decided that the German CFC legislation had not changed, in essence, despite being widened to also include portfolio investments which is why the stand-still clause may be applied in this regard.[114] The second question referred to a substantial change in German CFC legislation that occurred in 2000 but, before taxpayers had to apply the amended legislation, it was retroactively repealed and legislation in the spirit of the one before 1993 was reintroduced. The court held that, unless the applicability of the law was only deferred which is for the German national court to determine, the restriction of the stand-still clause is applicable.[115]

The third question related to whether the company could take advantage of the protection of the free movement of capital. Since German CFC legislation was applicable to both portfolio investments and direct investments due to its low threshold of only 1%, the legislation was, besides the freedom of establishment, also potentially subject to the free movement of capital. Considering that Y AG was a resident of Switzerland, the freedom of establishment was not an option but, as was already confirmed by previous case law[116], X GmbH could rely on the free movement of capital.[117]

---

110 Before 1993, the German CFC legislation applied, in essence, only to direct investments but was later extended to cover also shareholdings of less than 10%.
111 The changed legislation came into effect but was never applied in practice since it was converted to its previous form before affecting taxpayers.
112 CJEU, 26 February 2019, C-135/17, ECLI:EU:C:2019:136, *X GmbH,* para 24.
113 Treaty on European Union and the Treaty on the functioning of the European Union 2012/C 326/01 of 13 December 2007, OJ C 326 (26 October 2012) Article 64 para 1.
114 CJEU, 26 February 2019, C-135/17, ECLI:EU:C:2019:136, *X GmbH,* para 33–34.
115 CJEU, 26 February 2019, C-135/17, ECLI:EU:C:2019:136, *X GmbH,* para 51.
116 CJEU, 12 December 2006, C-446/04, ECLI:EU:C:2006:774, *Test Claimants in the FII Group Litigation,* para 99.
117 Alexander Rust, 'Germany II: Bechtel & Bechtel (C-20/16), X (C-135/17) and EV (C-685/16)' in: Michael Lang, Pasquale Pistone, Alexander Rust, Josef Schuch, Claus Staringer, Alfred Storck, *CJEU – Recent developments in direct taxation 2017,* (Vienna: Linde, 2018) p. 99.

The German Government argued that there was no restriction on the free movement of capital since holding a share in a German company and holding a share in a company established in a third state with a low level of taxation, where Germany has no taxing right, are not comparable situations.[118] The CJEU pointed out that the free movement of capital would be deprived of all meaning *"if it were accepted that situations are not comparable solely because the investor in question holds shares in a company established in a third country, when that provision specifically prohibits restrictions on cross-border movements of capital".*[119]

German CFC legislation for passive income was triggered after the conditions for it were met with no option for the taxpayer to provide proof that the arrangement was genuine. This was seen by the court as going beyond what is necessary to attain the objective.[120]

The court therefore decided that the German CFC legislation was limiting the free movement of capital. It is important to highlight that the court granted the protection of the free movement of capital in third country situations (the option to prove that the arrangement is genuine) only in cases when a legal framework of information exchange is in place;, see here also Chapter 1.3.2.[121] In other words, if there was no double tax treaty or another agreement on exchange of information relating to tax matters between Germany and Switzerland, the court would not have granted the protection of the free movement of capital.

3. Conclusion

The decision on the *Cadbury Schweppes* case[122] highlighted that it is important to distinguish between situations with economic substance, e.g. a subsidiary performing real business activities in a EU Member State with a lower tax burden, from situations with no economic substance for which the arrangement was only put in place to formally comply with legislation.[123] In its ruling, the CJEU laid down the conditions under which Member States may add profits of controlled foreign corporations to the tax base of their residents from low-tax jurisdictions in line with primary EU law. Based on this decision, whenever the freedom of establishment is applicable, i.e. in an intra EU situation, CFC legislation may only be applied if no *"genuine economic activity"*[124] is carried out. This is reflected in

---

118   CJEU, 26 February 2019, C-135/17, ECLI:EU:C:2019:136, *X GmbH*, para 63.
119   CJEU, 26 February 2019, C-135/17, ECLI:EU:C:2019:136, *X GmbH*, para 68.
120   CJEU, 26 February 2019, C-135/17, ECLI:EU:C:2019:136, *X GmbH*, para 88.
121   CJEU, 26 February 2019, C-135/17, ECLI:EU:C:2019:136, *X GmbH*, para 95.
122   CJEU, 12 September 2006, C-196/04, ECLI:EU:C:2006:544, *Cadbury Schweppes und Cadbury Schweppes Overseas*.
123   Sabine Kirchmayr 'Hinzurechnungsbesteuerung' in: Sabine Kirchmayr, Gunter Mayr, Klaus Hirschler, Georg Kofler, *Anti-BEPS-Richtlinie: Konzernsteuerrecht im Umbruch?* (Vienna: Linde, 2017) p. 115.
124   CJEU, 12 September 2006, C-196/04, ECLI:EU:C:2006:544, *Cadbury Schweppes und Cadbury Schweppes Overseas, para 68*.

the substance carve out of Article 7 section 2 of the ATAD reading that CFC legislation *"shall not apply where the controlled foreign company carries on a substantive economic activity supported by staff, equipment, assets and premises, as evidenced by relevant facts and circumstances"*.[125] It is interesting to point out the wording of the ATAD's substance carve-out is referring to *"substantive economic activity"* as opposed to *"genuine economic activity"* which is the wording used in the *Cadbury Schweppes* decision. According to scientific literature, despite the slight deviation, the meaning should be considered identical and therefore, in this respect, in line with primary EU law.[126]

The ATAD provides that Member States may refrain from applying the substantive economic activity carve-out[127] when the controlled company is located in a third (non-EEA) state. The disadvantageous treatment of third countries does not infringe the freedom of establishment because the freedom of establishment does not extend towards third states and is therefore in line with primary EU law.

As was discussed in Chapter 1.3., the decisive factor for determining whether the freedom of establishment or also the free movement of capital is applicable depends on the objective of the legislation. The free movement of capital might therefore become relevant in the case that the threshold for the applicability of CFC legislation would be lowered to also apply to portfolio investments. This is possible because the ATAD is drafted as a minimum standard, and Member States are free to lower the threshold if they see the need.[128] In addition, in third country situations, the substance carve-out can be omitted.[129] In theory, Member States could therefore opt for implementing CFC legislation in such a way that (i) the threshold for the application would be lowered and also become applicable to portfolio investments while, at the same time, (ii) refraining from applying the substance carve out to third countries whereby (iii) an information exchange mechanism for tax matters through a double tax treaty or other means would be in place with third countries. Not applying the substance carve-out to third countries under such circumstances would be a de-facto irrebuttable presumption that any activity performed in those third states is considered non-genuine. As was confirmed in the *X-GmbH* decision, this would be prohibited by the free movement of capital.[130]

---

125 Council Directive (EU) 2016/1164 of 12 July 2016 laying down rules against tax avoidance practices that directly affect the functioning of the internal market, OJ L 193 (19 July 2016) Article 7 para 2.
126 Martin Klokar, 'Die österreichische Hinzurechnungsbesteuerung (CFC-Regime) und das Unionsrecht', *Steuer und Wirtschaft International* (2020) p. 77.
127 Council Directive (EU) 2016/1164 of 12 July 2016 laying down rules against tax avoidance practices that directly affect the functioning of the internal market, OJ L 193 (19 July 2016) Article 7 para 2 letter b).
128 Council Directive (EU) 2016/1164 of 12 July 2016 laying down rules against tax avoidance practices that directly affect the functioning of the internal market, OJ L 193 (19 July 2016) Preamble para 12.
129 Council Directive (EU) 2016/1164 of 12 July 2016 laying down rules against tax avoidance practices that directly affect the functioning of the internal market, OJ L 193 (19 July 2016) Article 7 para 2 letter a.
130 CJEU, 26 February 2019, C-135/17, ECLI:EU:C:2019:136, *X GmbH*, para 95.

CFC rules of the ATAD in light of the EU fundamental freedoms

It can therefore be concluded that, in general, CFC legislation as included in the ATAD is in line with the fundamental freedoms but, in specific circumstances as described in the previous paragraph (i.e. third country scenario, CFC rules applicable not just to direct investments but also portfolio investments, no substance carve-out, exchange of information for tax matters in place), the free movement of capital could be breached. If a Member State was to implement the ATAD in such a way, the fundamental freedoms as primary EU law take precedence over national legislation.[131] The CJEU clearly stated that *"the law stemming from the treaty, an independent source of law, could not because of its special and original nature, be overridden by domestic legal provisions"*[132] and courts are obligated not to apply national provisions that conflict with EU law.[133] The fact that the ATAD allows Member States to lower the default control threshold of 50% should not be mistaken to mean that the directive itself is not in line with primary EU law; only a far-reaching implementation of the directive into national legislation could constitute a breach of the free movement of capital. In order to avoid such situations, the ATAD could be amended by making the substance carve-out also mandatory for third country situations. Another option would be to disallow Member States from introducing a holding threshold of less than 25% since, based on Chapter 1.3.1, such a holding is still considered to be substantive, and the ATAD's CFC rules would therefore always be subject only to the freedom of establishment.

---

[131] Łukasz Adamczyk, Alicja Majdańska 'The Sources of EU Law Relevant for Direct Taxation' in: Michael Lang, Pasquale Pistone, Josef Schuch, Claus Staringer, *Introduction To European Tax Law On Direct Taxation* (Vienna: Linde, 2020) p. 3.
[132] CJEU, 15 July 1964, C-6/64, ECLI:EU:C:1964:66, *Costa v E.N.E.L.*
[133] CJEU, 9 March 1978, Case C-106/77, EU:C:1978:49, *Simmenthal*, para 21.

CFC selected issues

CFC legislation and application of tax treaty law (particular focus on Savings Clause of Article 1(3) OECD MC)

Dawid Widzyk

1. **Interactions between national regulations on tax avoidance and tax treaty law**
   1.1. International tax law and the avoidance of taxation problem
   1.2. General principles of tax treaty law
   1.3. Analysis of the OECD Commentary from the year 2000 and 2003 in the context of national anti-abusive measures
2. **CFC rules and the international tax treaty principles**
   2.1. Basic principles of CFC taxation
       2.1.1. Examples of policies connected to CFC rules
       2.1.2. Notes on how CFC rules operate
   2.2. Examples of positions towards CFC compatibility with the treaty law
       2.2.1. Notes on the separate entity approach
       2.2.2. Pre-2003 positions on using treaty allocation rules in reconcilig CFC compatibility with treaty law
       2.2.3. Court rulings concerning CFC and tax treaty interactions
3. **Notes on the savings clause**
   3.1. Savings clause and the issue of CFC compatibility with the treaties
   3.2. Does the savings clause only have a clarifying nature?
4. **Summary of conclusions**

1. Interactions between national regulations on tax avoidance and tax treaty law

1.1. International tax law and the avoidance of taxation problem

The problem of taxation avoidance has been subject to discussions between practitioners and scholars for a significant number of years.[1] One of the methods that could help stand against more aggressive forms of tax avoidance is implemented through national rules such as the CFC principles.[2]

An element in the discussions on preventing tax avoidance concern the level to which national measures such as CFC rules may intervene into the already established tax treaty context. Different states seem to present various opinions about this issue. There are also different views about the interactions between treaty law and national law.[3] The main question, typically, is if national law can interfere with tax treatment of bilateral, cross-border events to prevent aggressive tax avoidance irrespective of the established order of treaty law. From this perspective, the relation between international tax conventions law and local law should be analysed. This relation may sometimes require a complex analysis on the ‚hierarchy of the two legal frameworks, the scope of the applicable laws and the aim achieved. One should take into consideration the possible differences between applying a monism and dualism approach.[4] For the sake of explaining how these two different approaches vary, both of them will now be analyzed in more detail.

---

[1] For an in depth analysis of the issues regarding tax avoidance, please note the recent extensive literature by M. Lang, P. Pistone, A. Rust, J. Schuch, C. Staringer, ‚Base Erosion and Profit Shifting (BEPS): the proposals to revise the OECD Model Convention', Linde, 2016; M. Lang, ‚CFC Regulations and Double Taxation Treaties', IBFD, 2003; B.J. Arnold, ‚Tax Treaties And Tax Avoidance: 2003 Revisions to the Commentary to the OECD Model', Bulletin – Tax Treaty Monitor, IBFD, 2004; Daniel W. Blum, ‚Controlled Foreign Companies: Selected Policy Issues – or the Missing Elements of BEPS Action 3 and the Anti-Avoidance Directive', Intertax, 2018; A.P. Dourado (ed.), ‚Tax Avoidance Revisited in the EU BEPS Context', EATLP International Tax Series, IBFD, 2017; D. Weber, ‚Tax Avoidance and the EC Treaty Freedoms: A Study of the Limitations under European Law to the Prevention of Tax Avoidance', Kluwer Law International, Eucotax Series, 2005.

[2] G. Kofler and Isabel Verlinden in 'Unlimited Adjustments: Some Reflections on Transfer Pricing, General Anti-Avoidance and Controlled Foreign Company Rules, and the "Saving Clause"' (Bulletin For International Taxation, April/May 2020, p. 270).

[3] As an example, as mentioned in the article by Pierre-Jean Douvier and Dali Bouzoraa, ‚What's Going On In France, Court of Appeals Confirms Incompatibility of CFC Rules with Tax Treaties, Decision of the Court of Appeals of Paris of 30 January 2001', the Paris Court of Appeals stood against direct applicability of national anti-avoidance rules in cases for which the respective treaty literally did not allow such a possibility. However, there are also examples of positions by which the treaty law does not generally stand against national anti-avoidance measures. One of such examples is the position of the UK Court in the case *Bricom Holdings Ltd v Inland Revenue Commissioners* (judgment from 1997; source: https://library.croneri.co.uk/cch_uk/btc/1997-btc-471 (accessed 18 April 2021).

[4] These issues were analysed by B.J. Arnold, ‚Tax Treaties And Tax Avoidance: 2003 Revisions to the Commentary to the OECD Model', Bulletin – Tax Treaty Monitor, IBFD, 2004, p. 249–252.

According to some authors, within the system referred to as the *"monist"* system, the legal order of a given country is integrated with the legal principles coming from international treaties.[5] As an example of a monist system, Poland applies the rules of international treaties directly in its legal system without a requirement to implement a specific act of law under its national system.[6] As noted in the legal literature, within a monist legal system, the rules coming from treaty law generally constitute source for binding regulations already implemented into and treated as principal to local law.[7]

On the other hand, according to a definition from literature, in a system referred to as *"dualist"*, the treaty law and the local law should be viewed as distinct.[8] Also, as stated in the literature, the binding effect of the treaty law in such a model comes from a direct regulation of local law allowing for the applicability of the treaty rule.[9]

An example of a dualist legal system is the United Kingdom.[10] In accordance with this system, only when a specific introductory local act of law is implemented through standard parliamentary measures are the UK courts of law entitled to base their respective rulings on the rules of tax conventions.[11]

According to the literature, for the bigger part of relevant countries, an argument can be made on the primacy of treaty principles in respect to national tax law.[12] This is because, in a dualist system, as already explained, international treaties should be implemented through national legal measures.[13]

Within this thesis, the considered question is how exactly tax treaties correlate with national laws and to what extent treaty law could disallow or limit applicability of anti-avoidance measures coming from the national law.[14] The issue of interactions between national anti-avoidance measures and treaty law should also be viewed from the perspective of the historical review of the Commentary to the

---

5   This analysis has been performed by Carolyn A. Dubay in ‚General Principles of International Law: Monism and Dualism', source: http://www.judicialmonitor.org/archive_winter2014generalprinciples.html. (accessed 11 April 2021).
6   (although, in almost all other cases, for the law to be binding, a separate act of law called „*ustawa*" [EN: „*act of law*"] needs to be introduced through parliamentary measures).
7   Supra n. 5.
8   This position was given by Madelaine Chan in ‚Monism and Dualism in International Law, Source: https://www.oxfordbibliographies.com/view/document/obo-9780199796953/obo-9780199796953-0168.xml accessed 18 April 2021).
9   Supra n. 8.
10 'European Scrutiny Committee – Tenth Report The EU Bill and Parliamentary Sovereignty' Source: https://publications.parliament.uk/pa/cm201011/cmselect/cmeuleg/633/63304.htm (accessed 19 Aprill 2021).
11 Supra n. 10.
12 Supra n. 4, p. 244.
13 Supra n. 8.
14 These issues were also referenced in supra n. 4, p. 244-260.

relevant Model Convention published by the OECD.[15] This is due to the fact that the model commentary provides clarity on how established treaty principles (concerning the taxation rights allocation or recognition of a taxable person) relate to the national legislation aimed against tax avoidance.[16] It is essential to state that the standpoint of the OECD on compatibility of local rules against tax avoidance with the treaty law has changed[17] which confirms the necessity of analyzing especially the 2000 and 2003 versions of the OECD Model.

In this thesis, an emphasis will be put on mutual interactions of tax treaty law and national measures against tax avoidance (including CFC rules). An essential question to address is the following: do the CFC rules interfere with the order of international tax law established in bilateral conventions, or are these rules systematically, principally in line with the treaty order? One can also reverse this question and consider if treaty principles may limit the applicability of CFC provisions.

1.2. General principles of tax treaty law

Before analysing in detail various mutual interactions between CFC rules and bilateral tax treaties, it seems necessary to firstly summarize certain basic principles of tax treaty law as established prior to recent changes (such as the OECD's BEPS).[18] As noted in the literature, tax treaties principally aim to stand against obstructions and disadvantages to international trade and investment.[19] For this purpose, the OECD's model provides guidance and summarizes basic principles concerning the allocation of taxation rights between respective signatory states (which agree to bilateral treaties in order to enable the proper taxation rights allocation and to disallow double taxation).[20] According to the OECD, the Model Convention is *"(...) a model for countries concluding bilateral tax conventions, plays a crucial role in removing tax related barriers to cross border trade and investment"*.[21] The preamble of the 2017 version of the model confirms that the convention is also aimed at disallowing evasion of tax and at disallowing the avoidance of tax (which suggests that double taxation is now not the only concern of the model).[22]

---

15 OECD (2017), Model Tax Convention on Income and on Capital: Condensed Version 2017, OECD Publishing, Paris, https://doi.org/10.1787/mtc_cond-2017-en.
 Source: https://read.oecd-ilibrary.org/taxation/model-tax-convention-on-income-and-on-capital-condensed-version-2017_mtc_cond-2017-en#page9 (accessed 22 April 2021).
16 Supra n. 15.
17 Supra n. 4, p. 244–260.
18 More information on the BEPS initiative can be found at: https://www.oecd.org/tax/beps/ (accessed 23 February 2021).
19 Michael J. McIntyre in ‚Legal Structure of Tax Treaties', p. 1 source: https://iatj.net/content/congresses/amsterdam2013/LegalStructureofTaxTreaties.-M.McIntyre.pdf (accessed 18 April 2021).
20 Supra n. 15.
21 Supra n. 15.
22 Supra n. 15.

As confirmed in the literature, the basic principles of tax treaty law were based on respective countries entitlement (or obligation) to: a) apply taxation on relevant proceeds in the country where the income emerges, b) apply taxation in the residency country of a specified person (or entity), on the basis of including for taxation the whole income reported on a worldwide basis, and c) provide for effective avoidance of double taxation with the relief method to be enabled in the residency country due to tax being collected at source.[23] The allocation rule for taxation rights suggested by the model that is relevant in respect to CFC taxation concerns taxing rights on dividends and on generic income of an enterprise (a so called *"business income"*).[24] These rules will now be briefly summarized with the use of examples taken from the 2017 version of the model convention.

Taxation rights allocation concerning dividends is dealt with in Article 10 of the OECD Model (version from 2017).[25] According to the structure of Article 10, as proposed for the allocation of taxation rights on payments from company profits (dividends), there are two principal rules. According to the first set of rules stipulated in paragraph 1 of the article, dividends settled by a company having residency in state A to the person (taxpayer) residing in state B may come under taxation in state B (residency state). However, paragraph 2 allows collecting tax according to a specified rate[26] also in the source country.[27]

Other important allocation rules coming directly from the OECD Model and relevant from the perspective of CFC taxation are found in Article 7 of the model *(Business Profits)*.[28] In summary, according to the Model's Commentary on Article 7 (paragraph 1), profits allocable to a specific enterprise of a given state should, in principle, come under taxation only in this state.[29] However, according to the indicated paragraph, taxation in the country of localization of a permanent establishment (PE) is possible.[30] Subsequent rules in paragraphs 2 and 3 provide for more clarity on how the allocation of respective PE profits should be performed.[31] Article 5 of the model relevantly defines a PE.[32] In a very concise summary, a PE is determined as a place to perform business; having a solidified, material character; and aimed at performing either a part or the whole business activity of an enterprise (a PE may have, for example, a

---

23 G. Kofler and Isabel Verlinden in 'Unlimited Adjustments: Some Reflections on Transfer Pricing, General Anti-Avoidance and Controlled Foreign Company Rules, and the "Saving Clause"' (Bulletin For International Taxation, April/May 2020, p. 271).
24 Supra n. 15.
25 Supra n. 15.
26 The OECD Model gives the rates of 5% and 15% relevant for two separate cases differentiated by the percentage of shares held in the paying entity by the owner.
27 Supra n. 15.
28 Supra n. 15.
29 Supra n. 15.
30 Supra n. 15
31 Supra n. 15.
32 Supra n. 15.

character of an office or a branch).³³ The allocation through Article 7 implements a basic rule according to which business-related profits of a given enterprise may not come under taxation in the state other than the enterprise's residency state unless a PE is operated in the other state or unless respective profits can be treated as coming under other specific articles of the relevant treaty (other allocation rules).³⁴

The reason why the allocation rules for dividends and for business profits have been summarized above is that CFC principles often interact with these two sets of rules.³⁵ This is mostly because dividends taxation and business profits taxation may be connected to companies' taxation in the international context (which is the scope covered by CFC rules).³⁶

As confirmed above, the treaties based on the OECD Model provide allocation rules for different types of income that may be relevant from the perspective of CFC rules. Irrespective of a specified allocation, on a more generic note, the analysis on how treaty law interacts with the CFC rules (or – more broadly – with national anti-avoidance measures) is important. From the perspective of mutual interconnections between treaty law and CFC principles, a historical analysis of Article's 1 Commentary will now be performed in order to assess if the OECD's position changed in this respect.

1.3. Analysis of the OECD Commentary from the year 2000 and 2003 in the context of national anti-abusive measures

As indicated in the legal literature, the 2003 OECD Model Commentary included changes to Commentary to Article 1, and the regarded changes concerned the use of tax treaty principles in an improper manner.³⁷ The model's 2003 version referred to the practices of using tax treaties for tax-avoidance purposes.³⁸

---

33 Supra n. 15.
34 Supra n. 15.
35 These issues were referenced in A.W. Oguttu in ‚Resolving the conflict between ‚controlled foreign company' legislation and tax treaties: a South African perspective', source: JSTOR htps://about.jstor.org/terms (accessed 19 April 2021).
36 Supra n. 35.
37 Juan Jose Zornoza Perez and Andres Baez in ‚The Revisions to the Commentary to the OECD Model on Tax Treaties and GAARs: A Mistaken Starting Point', published in Tax Treaties: Building Bridges Between Law and Economics' (edited by Michael Lang, Pasquale Pistone, Josef Schuch, Claus Staringer, Alfred Storck and Martin Zagler), p. 130.
38 In the 2003 version of the OECD Model Tax Convention, within the Commentary to Article 1, there was a statement in par. 7.1 confirming that the actions aimed at abusing specific tax law of a given treaty signatory state can be dealt with by the application of domestic law or domestic jurisprudential principles of a relevant state. The tax avoidance and countering measures were mentioned in the Commentary to Article 1. In the subsequent sentence, the commentary states that the relevant state "(...) State is then unlikely to agree to provisions of bilateral double taxation conventions that would have the effect of allowing abusive transactions that would otherwise be prevented by the provisions and rules of this kind contained in in its domestic law".

As stated in the literature, the better part of the Member States from the OECD were positive towards solutions from national law, standing against improper tax avoidance.[39] However, according to the scholars, only since the 2003 version of the commentary was there a clear confirmation that CFC rules are aligned with treaty law principles.[40]

The author of this thesis will now demonstrate how the position in the Model Commentary to Article 1 has changed. Below, the wording of the Commentary to Article 1, paragraph 7 (as taken from the 2000 OECD Model) is summarized and presented. According to the mentioned paragraph 7, double tax avoidance conventions are aimed at promoting services exchanges, goods exchanges, capital movement, and persons movement through standing against double taxation but not allowing tax evasion or tax avoidance.[41] Further, we read the following passage.

> 7. (...) True, taxpayers have a possibility, irrespective of double taxation conventions, to exploit differences in tax levels between States and the tax advantages provided by various countries' taxation laws, but it is for the States concerned to adopt provisions in their domestic laws to counter such manoeuvres. Such States will then wish, in their bilateral double taxation conventions, to preserve the application of provisions of this kind contained in their domestic laws."[42]

As shown above, paragraph 7 to the Commentary to Article 1 from the 2000 version of the model explicitly confirms that the states aiming to enable provisions in their national laws oriented at standing against improper exploitations of different taxation levels in different countries should make sure that the application of such provisions is allowed by the respective treaties they conclude.[43]

It should now be stated that the model commentary from the year 2003 contains a different version of paragraph 7 of the commentary to Article 1[44]: *"7. The principal purpose of double taxation conventions is to promote, by eliminating international double taxation, exchanges of goods and services, and the movement of capital and persons. It is also a purpose of tax conventions to prevent tax avoidance and evasion."*[45]

The above comments are based on OECD (2003), Model Tax Convention on Income and on Capital: Condensed Version 2003, OECD Publishing, Paris, https://doi.org/10.1787/mtc_cond-2003-en. Source: https://read.oecd-ilibrary.org/taxation/model-tax-convention-on-income-and-on-capital-condensed-version-2003_mtc_cond-2003-en#page48 (accessed 18 April 2021), p. 52–53.

39 This position was given in M. Lang, H. Aigner, U. Scheurle and M. Stefaner in ‚CFC Legislation, Tax Treaties and EC Law', Eucotax Kluwer Law International; Illustrated edition (May 21, 2004), p. 29.
40 Supra n. 39.
41 OECD (2000), *Model Tax Convention on Income and on Capital: Condensed Version 2000*, OECD Publishing, Paris, https://doi.org/10.1787/mtc_cond-2000-en. Source: https://read.oecd-ilibrary.org/taxation/model-tax-convention-on-income-and-on-capital-condensed-version-2000_mtc_cond-2000-en. p. 55 (accessed 18 April 2021).
42 Supra n. 41.
43 Supra n. 4, p. 246.
44 OECD (2003), *Model Tax Convention on Income and on Capital: Condensed Version 2003*, OECD Publishing, Paris, https://doi.org/10.1787/mtc_cond-2003-en, p. 52.
45 Supra n. 44, p. 52

CFC rules and application of tax treaty law (focus on Savings Clause)

As can be seen, since the 2003 update, the purpose of the treaties has been expanded because the commentary references both the matters of *"tax avoidance"* as well as *"tax evasion"*. According to the updated commentary, as it is stated in paragraph 9.5 of Article 1 Commentary, although it is not allowed to assume too swiftly that the relevant taxpayer introduces a specific transaction for abusive purposes, the *"guiding principle"*[46] is that double tax treaty convention's benefits should be disallowed in the case in which the basic purpose of introducing a specified event was to receive a more beneficial tax position or treatment.[47] The additional condition here is also that the granting of specified benefits would stand against the substantial principles of the treaty regulations (referred to as the "object" and the "purpose").[48]

According to the above, since 2003, there has been a general position of the OECD that treaties cannot be interpreted in contradiction to anti-avoidance principles even if these principles come directly from national law.[49] In reference to this, as argued by scholars, the OECD was initially not willing to implement a literal rule standing against tax abuse, but its position changed while the process of expansion of tax treaties connections between more and more countries was developing.[50]

In this instance, it now seems important to cite par. 7.1 to the updated Article 1 Commentary from the 2003 Model.[51] This citation is provided below.

> 7.1. Taxpayers may be tempted to abuse the tax laws of a State by exploiting the differences between various countries' laws. Such attempts may be countered by provisions or jurisprudential rules that are part of the domestic law of the State concerned. Such a State is then unlikely to agree to provisions of bilateral double taxation convention that would have the effect of allowing abusive transactions that would otherwise be prevented by the provisions and rules of this kind contained in its domestic law. Also, it will not wish to apply its bilateral conventions in a way that would have that effect."[52]

As indicated hereby, the wording of paragraph 7 of the commentary to Article 1 has changed, and the new version of this article now does not state that the only way to enable standing against the improper use of the treaties would be by making reservations in the treaty itself for the sake of applying national anti-abuse measures.[53]

---

46 This exact wording is used in par. 9.5 of the Commentary to Article 1) supra n. 44, p. 54.
47 Supra n. 44, p. 54.
48 Supra n. 44, p. 54.
49 Supra n. 4, p. 260.
50 This position was stated by David G. Duff in, Tax Treaty Abuse and the Principal Purpose Test – Part I', Allard School of Law at the University of British Columbia, p. 638–639.
51 Supra n. 44.
52 Supra n. 44, p. 52.
53 Supra n. 4, p. 247–249.

Importantly, according to paragraph 9.1. of the 2003 commentary to Article 1, there is a question "(...) whether the benefits of tax conventions must be granted when transactions that constitute an abuse of the provisions of these conventions are entered into (...)".[54] Another question raised in Article 1 paragraph 9.1. of the 2003 commentary is if national laws and rules coming from the local court practice of a given state aimed at disallowing abusive transactions stand against treaty law.[55] The commentary makes a note that both of the above questions are connected in the case of some states because the answer to the question about the granting of benefits of the convention relates to the answer about the applicability of local measures standing against tax avoidance.[56]

Further, paragraph 9.2. the commentary provides an example of a state for which the abuse of the treaty law is, at the same time, the abuse of domestic law.[57] According to the commentary, *"(...) to the extent these anti-avoidance rules are part of the basic domestic rules set by domestic tax laws for determining which facts give rise to a tax liability, they are not addressed in tax treaties and are therefore not affected by them"*.[58] According to scholars, the OECD confirmed in the 2003 commentary that, for dualist states, the treaty law does not stand against the application of national anti-avoidance measures if these rules help determine the facts on which the general basis for a tax liability is assumed.[59]

A different case is made for countries viewing the respective abuses that are aimed against treaty law (as indicated in the Commentary to Article 1, paragraph 9.3).[60] According to the commentary, such states usually take the position that the very construction of the tax treaty allows not taking into consideration the abusive legal event. This is the case for legal events principally implemented for the sake of receiving the treaty's protection, the right to a specified tax rate or a specific allocation. The above is relevant if these benefits are not intended by the very structure of the treaty.[61]

As provided for in the literature, although the 2003 commentary differentiated between the monist and dualist legal systems in the commentary to Article 1 (paragraph 9.2. and 9.3, respectively), the answer for both cases was that the abusive transactions may be challenged – either by local means or by means of interpreting the convention (depending on the type of a legal system and the method used).[62]

---

54 Supra n. 44, p. 53.
55 Supra n. 44, p. 53.
56 Supra n. 44, p. 53.
57 Supra n. 44, p. 53.
58 Supra n. 44, p. 53.
59 Supra n. 4, p. 246.
60 Supra n. 44, p. 53.
61 Supra n. 44, p. 53.
62 Supra n. 4, p. 247.

The above issues are connected with CFC legislation and its applicability in the specific treaty context. In the legal literature, it is confirmed that CFC rules are purposed to stand against income transfers aimed at tax avoidance that are typically performed in jurisdictions with low taxation.[63] CFC rules are implemented for the sake of protecting a given country's tax base through disallowance of transferring specified income to companies in foreign countries.[64]

Irrespective of how CFC rules are structured from a technical standpoint (which will be summarized in further sections of this thesis), it is important to ask the question: what was the exact position of OECD on the matter of applicability of national measures standing against abuse of tax law (such as CFC measures) in the international situations covered by double tax avoidance treaties? As an answer to these issues, according to the OECD, CFC regulations do not stand against treaty law irrespective of whether the situation of a monist or a dualist legal system is being analyzed[65] because CFC rules constitute the basic set of rules aiming at establishing facts that trigger tax liability and that these types of national tax rules do not interfere with treaty law.[66]

2. CFC rules and the international tax treaty principles
2.1. Basic principles of CFC taxation

Before discussing the interactions between CFC rules and the international legal order based on double tax avoidance treaties, it seems necessary to present general principles of CFC taxation.

As stated in the literature, rules concerning taxation of CFCs have originated from laws of the United States.[67] At the moment of preparing this thesis, CFC regulations may be considered as quite widely used within legal frameworks of many countries.[68] According to BEPS Action 3: 2015 Final Report, at the date of Report 30, involved states had already implemented the CFC rules.[69]

---

63 Sara Andersson, ‚CFC rules and double tax treaties, The OECD and UN model tax conventions, Paper within International Tax Law', August 2006, p. 12. https://www.diva-portal.org/smash/get/diva2:4297/fulltext01.pdf (accessed 18 April 2021).
64 Supra n. 2, p. 272.
65 Supra n. 4, p. 247.
66 This is suggested by the wording of par. 22.1 of the Commentary to Article 1 of the Model Convention from 2003, supra n. 44, p. 63.
67 Supra n. 2, p. 270.
68 A. Prettl, 'Profit Shifting & Controlled Foreign Corporation Rules – The thin bridge between corporate tax systems', February 2018, p. 1 (Abstract) source: https://papers.ssrn.com/sol3/papers.cfm?abstract_id=3102553 (accessed 22 April 2021)
69 OECD (2013), *Action Plan on Base Erosion and Profit Shifting*, OECD Publishing, http://dx.doi.org/10.1787/9789264202719-en
p. 9 source: https://read.oecd-ilibrary.org/taxation/designing-effective-controlled-foreign-company-rules-action-3-2015-final-report_9789264241152-en#page14.

As indicated by scholars, CFC regulations are applicable in respect to a specified type of income obtained through subsidiary entities situated abroad and are used in relation to the domestic entity owning the indicated subsidiary.[70] According to the legal literature, CFC rules typically have a common, similar scheme based on the determination of the level of control.[71] CFC rules also operate on the conditions relating to a minimal tax threshold and passive income threshold.[72] As to the minimal tax threshold, typically the foreign CIT should be above a specified percentage for the sake of CFC rules not to apply.[73] Sometimes, the reference to effective corporate tax in a foreign country is made within CFC rules.[74] As to the passive income threshold, the reception of this type of income by a CFC usually only triggers application of CFC rules in the case that the passive income is relatively high (percentage-wise) in reference to the CFC's total income.[75] According to the legal literature, for CFC rules to apply, the below mentioned elements should be in place: a) a foreign company should be existing, b) there should be some level of control of such a company by residents of a specified state, and c) the profit of such a foreign company should be assumed as received for the sake of tax avoidance.[76]

2.1.1. Examples of policies connected to CFC rules

In this part of the paper, the author will aim to summarize the main policies connected to CFC rules.

According to some scholars, as a result of struggle of various governments in having to deal with less and less tax-related revenue due to multinational entities utilizing various mechanisms of shifting of profit abroad, the OECD proposed to introduce CFC rules through a relevant BEPS Action Plan.[77] As a result, a significant number of countries implemented CFC rules and, in reaction to this, the financial and actual business actions of multinational entities have changed.[78] In the EU, CFC rules have been included in the respective national rules through the implementation of the ATAD Directive.[79]

---

70 A. Kristina Zvinys, 'CFC Rules in Europe', source: https://taxfoundation.org/controlled-foreign-corporation-rules-cfc-rules-in-europe-2020/ (accessed 17 April 2021).
71 Supra n. 70.
72 Supra n. 68, p. 10.
73 Supra n. 68, p. 10.
74 Supra n. 68, p. 10.
75 Supra n. 68, p. 10.
76 M. R. Pinskaya, N. I Malis, N. S. Milogolov, 'Rules of Taxation of Controlled Foreign Companies: A Comparative Study, Asian Social Science, vol. 11, No. 3; 2015, p. 275.
77 A. Haufler, M. Marda, and D. Schindler in 'Optimal Policies Against Profit Shifting: The Role of Controlled-Foreign-Company Rules', p. 23–24, source: htpps://epub.ub.uni-muenchen.de/27745/1/Haufler_Profit.pdf (accessed 17 April 2021).
78 Supra n. 69.
79 Council Directive (EU) 2016/1164 of 12 July 2016 laying down rules against tax avoidance practices that directly affect the functioning of the internal market, Source: https://eur-lex.europa.eu/legal-content/PL/ALL/?uri=uriserv:OJ.L_.2016.193.01.0001.01.ENG (accessed 18 April 2021).

There are different policies that stand behind the implementation of CFC rules in different countries. However, according to the OECD Action 3: 2015 Final Report, there should be some common aspects of policies applied in reference to CFC rules.[80] The report confirms that, typically, countries use CFC rules to disallow the transfer of relevant proceeds from the place where the parent is situated.[81] On the other hand, the report also states that the effect of a deferral of taxation for a longer period may also be an issue.[82] The report states in subsequent points that CFC rules are mainly aimed at being used as preventive rules rather than rules aimed at collecting the tax of a subsidiary entity.[83] The revenue protection aspect is also mentioned in the report.[84] Finally, it confirms that the purpose of CFC rules may be used for amending the behaviour of taxpayers.[85] The CFC preventive aspect certainly has some significance as it may influence the decisions of taxpayers on setting-up a company abroad.[86] The OECD Action 3 Report also indicates that the taxation in source countries may be expanded through the limitation or even disallowance of specified tax benefits structured around switching of income to tax jurisdictions with low taxation systems.[87]

In the legal literature, we can read that CFC rules stand against postponing of taxation until the moment of the distribution of income.[88] According to this literature, CFC rules also aim to switch specific payments back to the shareholder by adding respective income to his tax base.[89] As mentioned by scholars, for countries applying a territorial basis tax system, the anti-deferral aspect is not as important as protecting the tax base from erosion.[90]

As noted in the OECD Action 3 Report, one of the elements of properly implementing CFC rules is aligned with preventing double taxation.[91] The report suggests that double taxation may be the result of implementing CFC regulations because these effectively allow for taxation in the residency state of the parent entity.[92]

---

[80] ‚Designing Effective Controlled Foreign Company Rules; Action 3: 2015 Final Report', p. 13, source: https://www.oecd-ilibrary.org/docserver/9789264241152-en.pdf?expires=1617387853&id=id&accname=guest&checksum=2F9E475E88C412963DFE4318B96E8800 (accessed 17 April 2021).
[81] Supra n. 80.
[82] Supra n. 80.
[83] Supra n. 80.
[84] Supra n. 80.
[85] Supra n. 80.
[86] Supra n. 77.
[87] Supra n. 80.
[88] D.W. Blum, ‚Controlled Foreign Companies: Selected Policy Issues – or the Missing Elements of BEPS Action 3 and the Anti-Avoidance Directive', Intertax, 2018, p. 297.
[89] Supra n. 88.
[90] V. Myrizakis, 'The Post-ATAD era in the EU: The impact of the new CFC rules', Tilburg University, 2018–2019, p. 7.
[91] Supra n. 80 p. 13.
[92] Supra n. 80, p. 13.

2.1.2. Notes on how CFC rules operate

Within this chapter, elemental principles of how CFC rules operate will be summarized. On this matter, the already mentioned BEPS Action 3 Report goes in detail through the rules of defining a CFC, exemption requirements, respective threshold conditions, income definitions and principles on computation, as well as rules on attributing the relevant income.[93] These basic rules will now be summarized in a generic manner. The respective summary will relate to the definition of a CFC, main threshold considerations, and some income definition aspects.

In relation to the CFC definition aspect, the OECD BEPS Action 3 Report suggests that the definition is broad and aims at defining various entities, including companies and other corporate objects.[94] It also suggests that the definition should relate to transparent entities and should not exclude situations with PEs.[95]

There is also an important aspect of control. The report, describing various types of control, differentiates between legal control (voting rights and other corporate rights), economic control, and factual control.[96] Further parts of the report concern the percentages of various forms of control.[97] It assumes that a more than 50 percent level of economic control or legal control should trigger CFC rules application with the possibility of lowering this threshold to even below 50 percent.[98] The report also confirms that, in the case of different entities holding together the specified level of legal or economic control in a CFC, the percentages of control should be calculated together for the sake of confirming if the control threshold has been met.[99]

As to the tax rate element, the result that the OECD is seeking would be to subject the CFC's to taxation in only the residence state if these CFCs operate in jurisdictions where the comparable tax rate is substantially lower.[100] As the report states, this result can be effected by three methods: a) by setting the amount under which CFC rules are not applicable, b) by focusing on the scenarios in which a clear tax avoidance element of the transaction is visible or c) by implementing an exemption from CFC rules related to the tax rate through applying CFC regulations to companies residing in countries having a low rate of corporate taxation (in reference to the CIT in the state of the CFC's owner).[101] The report contains a general

---

93   Supra n. 80, p. 5.
94   Supra n. 80, p. 21.
95   Supra n. 80, p. 21.In Poland, according to the current state of law, in line with the OECD recommendations, a CFC can not only be a company but also another legal entity controlled by the resident taxpayer, such as the private foundation or a trust. The ATAD Directive seems to not go that far in defining the CFC so the compatibility with the directive of Polish CFC law may be questionable.
96   Supra n. 80, p. 24.
97   Supra n. 80, p. 26–28.
98   Supra n. 80, p. 26–28.
99   Supra n. 80, p. 26–28.
100 Supra n. 80, p. 33.
101 Supra n. 80, p. 35.

recommendation according to which countries should agree not to apply CFC principles if the tax rate of a CFC is not much different from the tax applied in the residency jurisdiction.[102]

When it comes to the definition of the income of a CFC, the report states that countries should be allowed to make their own decisions in designing the rules for defining the income coming under CFC regulations (which is sometimes referred to as *"tainted"*).[103] The report subsequently provides examples of the types of income that could trigger CFC applicability and lists: a) income from company profits, b) interest income, c) income related to insurance services, d) royalty payments and other similar income and, finally, e) sales and services proceeds.[104]

According to Article 7 of the ATAD Directive through which various EU Member States introduced the CFC principles, a relevant Member State shall view a given entity (or a PE of such entity) as a CFC in the case that: a) in the entity (or in a PE of such), the relevant taxpayer has (separately or together with connected partner(s)) control[105] referred either to the rights to vote or to holding in the respective capital and b) the corporate taxation of an entity or a relevant PE is *„(...) lower than the difference between the corporate tax that would have been charged on the entity or permanent establishment under the applicable corporate tax system in the Member State of the taxpayer and the actual corporate tax paid on its profits by the entity or permanent establishment."*[106] Paragraph 2 to Article 7 of the ATAD lists types of income of a specified CFC that should come under taxation for the taxpayer from the residency Member State.[107] As to the computation rules, as stipulated in Directive's Article 8, respective income from Article 7 paragraph 2 should be added to the taxable base of the shareholder of a CFC within the use of corporate taxation principles of the residency Member State of such shareholder (with losses only being able to be settled in future periods).[108] The respective income allocable to the taxpayer in the residency Member State should be calculated accordingly to the level of control held by such taxpayer in a CFC.[109]

---

102 Supra n. 80, p. 35.
103 Supra n. 80, p. 43.
104 Supra n. 80, p. 43.
105 Of a direct nature or through intermediary entities.
106 Council Directive (EU) 2016/1164 of 12 July 2016 laying down rules against tax avoidance practices that directly affect the functioning of the internal market.
     Source: https://eur-lex.europa.eu/legal-content/PL/ALL/?uri=uriserv:OJ.L_.2016.193.01.0001.01.ENG (accessed 18 April 2021).
107 These consist of interest or other financial-type income, royalties, passive income from company profit payments, income from trading of financial instruments, income related to financial services (including insurance and banking services), as well as invoicing proceeds in relationships with associated parties relating to transactions that bear insignificant business value. The directive also targets the income that is not distributed and comes from the arrangements that have little or no real substance and cannot be regarded as genuine. Supra n. 106.
108 Supra n. 106.
109 Supra n. 106.

2.2. Examples of positions towards CFC compatibility with the treaty law

2.2.1. Notes on the separate entity approach

The analysis of CFC rules is incomplete without providing some notes on the treatment of a corporation as having specifics of a legally distinguished entity and as a distinguished taxpayer (both in the view of the treaty law as well as the domestic law).

On this note, D.W. Blum mentions a problematic possibility of creating a foreign entity and postponing relevant taxation to the future by allocating the income to this entity and not paying out the income to the relevant shareholder.[110] According D.W. Blum, a separate status as a taxpayer for new companies that are being set-up in foreign jurisdictions was quite commonly accepted.[111]

As noted by scholars, the rule of assuming that a company is a specified person in the view of respective regulations seems to be reflected in the practice.[112] In relation to this issue, according to B.J. Arnold, *"(...) source countries impose tax on the income of resident corporations, not on their non-resident controlling shareholders, and residence countries did not tax the income earned by foreign-resident subsidiaries of resident parent corporations."*[113] However, in relation to the basic operation of CFC rules, B.J. Arnold states that one of the elements of this process is the actual ignoring of the separate status of the CFC as both the legal entity and as a taxpayer which effects the taxation of the owners in respect to the income actually obtained by the CFC.[114]

Summarizing the above, it seems logical to assume that, because the CFC is usually a company from another country, a principal assumption should be that such a company actually exists. However, this assumption can be challenged by one of the methods of operation of CFC rules called *"piercing the corporate veil"*.[115] In relation to the issues of tax avoidance, some scholars give a position according to which a relevant company should be treated as a *"juridical person"* recognized as a taxpayer under local law, and only then may the relevant share-

---

110 Supra n. 88, p. 297.
111 Supra n. 88, p. 299.
112 J. Sasseville, 'International and EC Tax Aspects of Groups of Companies, EC and International Tax Law Series – Volume 4, Chapter 6, Treaty Recognition of Groups of Companies', source: https://www.ibfd.org/sites/ibfd.org/files/content/pdf/International_EC_Tax%20Aspects_Groups_%20Companies_sample-excerpt.pdf (accessed 17 April 2021).
113 Brian J. Arnold in 'The Evolution of Controlled Foreign Corporation Rules and Beyond' (Bulletin For International Taxation, December 2019, p. 640).
114 Supra n. 113, p. 634.
115 Supra n. 88, p. 297.

holder assume that the transfer of assets will effect avoiding the resident tax.[116] In this example, through the application of CFC rules, domestic shareholders come under taxation on the relevant income being assigned to them through their share in the CFC.[117]

As of the date of this thesis, according to the legal literature, it is rather commonly accepted that the residence countries are entitled to tax their own resident taxpayers without considering other states' attribution rules.[118] From this perspective, we could observe an interesting development initiated by the OECD which has tried to convince its members to input into their tax agreements the regulation referred to as "savings clause".[119] The analysis on the savings clause will be performed in Chapter 3 of this thesis.

2.2.2. Pre-2003 positions on using treaty allocation rules in reconcilig CFC compatibility with treaty law

According to the literature, CFC rules were not always regarded as being aligned with treaty law.[120] As an example, in the paper from 2009, we can read as follows: „(...) *the validity of CFC legislation has been questioned on the basis that it contradicts some of the basic principles of double taxation treaties entered into by the countries concerned*".[121] One example given by scholars regards the potential issue of Article 7(1) of the model not being compatible to the regulations on CFCs.[122] The relevant position in the literature is that Article 7 is centered around limiting the source country jurisdiction in relation to profits of a non-resident's PE whereas CFC legislation does not refer to source country taxation but rather refers to conditions centered around the residency of the shareholder.[123] Additionally, there is an assumed conflict of the model's Article 10(5) concerning dividends and CFC regulations because this article disallows the taxation of undistributed profits of a non-resident company even if such have arisen in the mentioned source country.[124] However, the very characterization of CFC income as *"tainted"* should make the CFC rules not contradictory to treaty allocation rules.[125]

---

116 Supra n. 63, p. 12.
117 Supra n. 63, p. 12.
118 Supra n. 88, p. 308, as followed by Rust, *supra* n. 17, at 11.
119 Supra n. 15.
120 See Pierre-Jan Douvier and Dali Bouzoraa, ‚What's Going On In France, Court of Appeals Confirms Incompatibility of CFC Rules with Tax Treaties, Decision of the Court of Appeals of Paris of 30 January 2001', p. 184.
121 Supra n. 35, p. 74, 76 and 80–81.
122 Supra n. 35, p. 74, 76 and 80–81.
123 Supra n. 35, p. 74, 76 and 80–81.
124 Supra n. 35, p. 74, 76 and 80–81
125 Supra n. 35, p. 74, 76 and 80–81.

2.2.3. Court rulings concerning CFC and tax treaty interactions

In jurisprudence, there are some examples of rulings confirming that CFC regulations are generally compatible with those of the tax conventions.[126] There are also rulings standing against this assumption.[127]

An example of a ruling confirming compatibility between CFC rules and treaty law was the ruling in the case *"A Oyj Abp"*.[128] According to the legal literature, in this ruling, Article 7(1) of the relevant convention from 1976 was referenced, and the ruling confirmed that the treaty does not disallow taxation in Finland (such taxation relating to the local company being the shareholder).[129] An important element of the case was the qualification of respective income to the category of business profits and, because of this, Article 7 of the respective convention has been used.[130] According to the court, the convention's purpose allows assuming that CFC taxation principles are aligned with the treaty.[131] The court also confirmed that OECD-based treaties do not stand against economic double taxation and that treaties are not against implementation of local anti-avoidance regulations.[132]

Another example of a ruling confirming compatibility of the tax treaty law with CFC rules is the ruling in the case *"Bricom Holdings Ltd v Inland Revenue Commissioners"* (judgment from 1997).[133] The respective case concerned an appeal to the higher court in the United Kingdom against a decision based on which interest income received by a foreign controlled company was to be included in the income of its shareholders under the treaty between the United Kingdom and the Netherlands.[134] The court dismissed the argument that treaty exemption interest income

---

126 See rulings:
  1.) Finnish Supreme Administrative Court's ruling of 20 March 2002 in the case A Oyj Abp [Case. No. KHO:2002:26], Source: Judgement of 14 20 March KHO: 2002:26, International Tax Law Reports 2002, No. 4, pp. 1009 et seq. 20 March 2002.
  2.) Bricom Holdings Ltd. v. Commissioners of Inland Revenue, (1997) STC 1179 Source: P. Morton & L. Sykes, IFA Cahiers 2010 – Volume 95A. Tax Treaties and Tax Avoidance: Application of Antti-Avoidance Provisions 805, 810 et seq., United Kingdom.
127 See a ruling: Société Schneider Electric, 28 June 2002, Conseil d'Etat No. 232,276, Source: International Tax Law Reports, 2002, at 1077.
128 Finnish Supreme Administrative Court's ruling of 20 March 2002 in the case A Oyj Abp [Case. No. KHO:2002:26], Source: Judgement of 14 20 March KHO: 2002:26, International Tax Law Reports 2002, No. 4, pp. 1009 et seq. 20 March 2002.
129 See B. Kuźniacki in 'Tax Treaty Interpretation by Supreme Courts: Case Study of CFC Rules', RDTI Actual 01, IBDT Instituto Brasileiro De Direito Tributario, p. 164–165 and M. Lang in ‚CFC Regulations and Double Taxation Treaties', Bulletin – Tax Treaty Monitor, February 2003, p. 51.
130 Supra n. 129.
131 Supra n. 129.
132 Supra n. 129.
133 Bricom Holdings Ltd v Inland Revenue Commissioners. [1997] BTC 471 of 25 July 1997.
  Source: P. Morton & L. Sykes, IFA Cahiers 2010 – Volume 95A. Tax Treaties and Tax Avoidance: Application of Antti-Avoidance Provisions 805, 810 et seq., United Kingdom.
  This case was analyzed in D. Sandler, ‚Tax Treaties and Controlled Foreign Company Legislation: Pushing the Boundaries', Kluwer Law International, Second Edition: 2, p. 208–210.
134 Supra n. 133.

applies directly and precludes CFC rules.¹³⁵ At the same time, the court confirmed general conformity between CFC regulations and the law of tax conventions.¹³⁶ Although the court confirmed that the United Kingdom does not allow implementing double tax convention principles directly and that such principles must first be introduced in the form of a local law implementation act, it did not dispute the fact that both CFC rules and the treaties exist in mutual coherence.¹³⁷

The jurisprudence on the interaction between CFC rules and treaty law has been discussed in recent tax literature.¹³⁸ As indicated in the literature, a different result than the one summarized in the cases mentioned above was given in the French ruling in the matter referenced as the *"Schneider"* case.¹³⁹ The case concerned the relevant treaty's Article 7.¹⁴⁰ The court decided that the relevant treaty did not contain any specific rule that would allow the applicability of local CFC laws of France, therefore, the application of such rules constitutes a violation of the treaty's Article 7.¹⁴¹ According to the court, the general aim at standing against tax evasion or avoidance cannot constitute an argument for breaching literal rules of the tax convention.¹⁴² For the sake of applying local anti-avoidance rule, a reflecting provision should be included in the treaty, as the Court suggested.¹⁴³

3. Notes on the savings clause

3.1. Savings clause and the issue of CFC compatibility with the treaties

The discussion on the correlation between the savings clause and CFC regulations is very much connected to the broader issue of compatibility of tax treaty law with national anti-abusive provisions.

The savings clause comes from the general policy on concluding tax conventions as applied to by the United States.¹⁴⁴ In literature, it is often confirmed that the

---

135 Supra n. 133.
136 Supra n. 133.
137 Supra n. 133.
138 See M. Lang in ‚CFC Regulations and Double Taxation Treaties', Bulletin – Tax Treaty Monitor, February 2003, p. 51, as well as. Dora Brajdic in 'Are CFC Rules In Need Of Redesigning?' Tilburg University, 2018/2019, p. 36.
139 Supra n. 138.
140 Supra n. 138 (the convention was concluded between France and Switzerland).
141 Supra n. 138.
142 Supra n. 138.
143 Supra n. 138.
144 This is confirmed by G. Kofler in ‚Some reflections on the ‚Savings clause', INTERTAX Volume 44, Issue 8 & 9, 2016 Kluwer Law Internaional BV, Netherlands, p. 576. Source: https://www.jku.at/fileadmin/gruppen/150/Team/Georg_Kofler/Aufsaetze_in_Fachzeitschriften/Intertax_Saving_-Clause_185.pdf (accessed 22 April 2021).

savings clause is aimed at retaining the possibility of taxing own residents or citizens by a given contracting state almost as in the case in which there would be no tax treaty to apply.[145] Therefore, it can be assumed that the savings clause, by its nature, is generally aimed at allowing the retaining of rights of taxation for the state of residency.[146, 147] The savings clause has been entered into OECD documents through Article 11 of the MLI.[148] and within the 2017 OECD Model.[149] As to the practical effect of the savings clause, this may be limited, for example, due to the fact that some signatories to the MLI decided to object to it.[150] In any case, due to the insertion of the savings clause into the 2017 OECD Model, the relevance of the clause may increase in the future.

According to the model convention (version from 2017), Article 1(3) states as follows: "This Convention shall not affect the taxation, by a Contracting State, of its residents except with respect to the benefits granted under paragraph 3 of Article 7, paragraph 2 of Article 9 and Articles 19, 20, 23 [A] [B], 24, 25 and 28."[151]

In reference to the savings clause, in the 2017 Model Commentary, we read these remarks to Article 1 paragraph 3 of the model: "In some limited cases (…) it has been argued that some provisions could be interpreted as limiting a Contracting State's right to tax its own residents in cases where this was not intended (…)."[152] In the literature, it is argued that the savings clause only clarifies that the double tax avoidance treaties do not stand against rules similar to CFC principles.[153] Referencing the above issues, the commentary later confirms that there is a general rule allowing taxation of a country's own residents unless it is clearly stipulated otherwise (at the same time mentioning the situations by which such taxation is not

---

145 Elizabeth V. Zanet, Galia Antebi and Neha Rastogi in ‚Income Tax Treaties V. Domestic Law: An International Look at the Current Score', source: http://publications.ruchelaw.com/news/2016-06/Tax_Treaty_Saving_Clause.pdf (accessed 18 April 2021).
146 Supra n. 144, p. 575.
147 According to L. Parada, the savings clause „(…) encouraged the United States to preserve ist rights to tax its non-resident citizens, especially when tax treaties threat to limit such rights". The above arguments were summarized by Leopoldo Parada in ‚The OECD „Saving Clause" An American-Tailored Provision Made to Measure The World' (Rivista Di Diritto Finanziario E Scienza Delle Finanze, Anno LXXVIII Fasc. 1 – 2019, p. 21 and 22).
148 Multilateral Convention to Implement Tax Treaty Related Measures to Prevent BEPS. Source: https://www.oecd.org/tax/treaties/multilateral-convention-to-implement-tax-treaty-related-measures-to-prevent-beps.htm (accessed 18 April 2021).
149 Supra n. 15.
150 An example of reservations on the savings clause has been given in Loyens & Loeff – Margriet Lukkien, Charlotte Kies and Fabian Sutter, ‚Overview: MLI choices made by the Netherlands, Belgium, Luxembourg and Switzerland'.
source: https://www.lexology.com/library/detail.aspx?g=d02f2c31-ccc3-420f-80f6-319c2e618100 (accessed 18 April 2021).
The article shows that, out of 4 indicated countries, only Belgium opted-in on the savings clause.
151 Supra n. 15.
152 Supra n 15, p. 59 and 78.
153 This position was stated in V. Chand, 'Should States Opt for the Saving Clause In the Multilateral Instrument?' (Tax Notes International, May 22, 2017, p. 691).

possible due to a specific treaty rule).[154] The commentary suggests only a clarifying nature of the savings clause also in the context of the regulations on CFC's.[155]

Importantly, a savings clause was mentioned in the BEPS Action 6 Report.[156] According to it, the clause is constructed to confirm the relevant state's taxing rights aimed at taxing its own residents irrespective of other convention's principles with the exception of specified ones.[157]

3.2. Does the savings clause only have a clarifying nature?

The important question is if the savings clause, as introduced to the model, should be viewed as only of a clarifying nature in relation to applicability of local measures against the avoidance of taxation.[158] According to the legal literature, OECD's Action 6 implemented the clause for the purpose of explicitly indicating that the rules of the treaty cannot have an effect of limiting the residency state in applying taxation to its own residents.[159] According to V. Chand, *"to avoid specific recurring controversies, it may be wise for both the majority and the minority to adopt a treaty provision clarifying that treaties do not prevent the application of CFC-type rules and do not prevent the application of residence state income attribution rules."*[160] However, it is further argued by this author that, potentially, the introduction of the savings clause to the OECD Model could strengthen the arguments according to which the previously assumed direct applicability of the local anti-avoidance regulations (such as CFC rules) is not proper.[161] Some scholars therefore believe that, possibly, relevant courts could question the clarifying nature of the savings clause.[162]

In respective legal literature, it is also argued that, because a tax treaty should be viewed as a specific agreement aimed at restricting applicability of local law, it was assumed in the past that the use of domestic anti-avoidance regulations permitting residence country taxation stands against treaty law.[163] Therefore, as pro-

---

154 Supra n. 15, p. 59 and 78.
155 Supra n. 15, p. 59 and 78.
156 OECD (2015), *Preventing the Granting of Treaty Benefits in Inappropriate Circumstances, Action 6 – 2015 Final Report*, OECD/G20 Base Erosion and Profit Shifting Project, OECD Publishing, Paris, https://doi.org/10.1787/9789264241695-en.
p. 86. Source: https://read.oecd-ilibrary.org/taxation/preventing-the-granting-of-treaty-benefits-in-inappropriate-circumstances-action-6-2015-final-report_9789264241695-en.
157 Supra n. 156.
158 Supra n. 15, p. 59 and 78.
159 Supra n. 153, p. 690–691.
160 Supra n. 153, p. 690–691.
161 Supra n. 153, p. 690–691.
162 Supra n. 153, p. 690–691.
163 These arguments were provided by Mrs. Annett Wanyana Oguttu in, Should Developing Countries Sign the OECD Multilateral Instrument to Address Treaty – Related Base Erosion and Profit Shifting Measures?', Center for Global Development, p. 2.

vided for in the literature, in order to enable the possibility of taxing their own residents, respective states implement the saving clause into their double taxation conventions.[164] As to the recent effects of the saving clause, it is indicated in the literature that the clause is not viewed by BEPS as a *"minimum standard"* and, therefore, while applying MLI, a relevant signatory is allowed to not implement the entirety of Article 11 in its tax treaties.[165]

4. Summary of conclusions

According to the OECD, national regulations on taxation of CFC income do not interfere with general allocation rules and other principles of double tax avoidance conventions. This conclusion could be viewed as an established position of the OECD at least since the publication of the 2003 Commentary to the Model Convention. Therefore, in the case that relevant CFC rules relate only to an anti-abusive purpose, it seems rational to argue that these rules do not interfere with the order of tax treaty law. This is because the OECD confirmed that the principles of international double tax treaties are generally against abusive tax avoidance and that double tax conventions should disallow such avoidance (because it is a part of their purpose).

However, the above position was not always clear. As already noted, CFC concepts that were created as a reaction to the abuse of foreign structures and to problems of eroding the taxable base in the residency state were often inspired by solutions coming strictly from domestic law. These mechanisms were based on assigning the dividend or ignoring the foreign company's separate legal existence. CFC rules were argued by various courts and tax scholars as going against the model's Articles 7 and 10.

Problems concerning compatibility between CFC rules and the treaty law may be the result of different origins of tax treaty law and domestic anti-abuse regulations. The savings clause could potentially become the bridge binding together these two very different sets of rules. As of now, there are still some disputes if the savings clause only clarifies the already established principle on the compatibility of CFC and treaty law. There are arguments made that the rule allowing to tax the residents is established only by the implementation of the savings clause to the respective treaty. In any case, this instrument can be viewed as a reasonable solution to help make the CFC rules more formally aligned with treaty law.

There are arguments that the saving clause only has a clarifying nature because the OECD confirms that most of the national regulations standing against tax avoidance do not interfere with double tax treaties principles. On the other hand,

---

164   Supra n. 163.
165   Supra n. 163.

because the MLI does not view the clause as a BEPS *"minimum standard"*, it is not obligatory to implement the clause within double tax conventions through MLI measures.

Nevertheless, the aim of introducing a saving clause into double tax treaties still deserves credit. In the case that the saving clause implementation is more widely accepted, it is possible that it will become a standard for the sake of preserving the taxing rights of the residency state and applying domestic rules for that cause.

The relationship between CFC rules and general anti-avoidance rules

Rodrigo Saavedra Zepeda

1. Introduction
2. Relationship between CFC rules and domestic GAARs
    2.1. Preventing avoidance and ensuring tax collection through controlled foreign company rules
        2.1.1. CFC rules as a type of SAAR
        2.1.2. CFC regimes under the Anti-Tax Avoidance Directive
    2.2. General anti-avoidance approaches
        2.2.1. GAARs in general
        2.2.2. GAARs according to the Anti-Tax Avoidance Directive
    2.3. The relationship between CFC rules and GAARs within domestic legal systems
        2.3.1. General considerations on the relationship between CFC rules and GAARs
3. Relationship between CFC rules and GAARs laid down in tax treaty law
    3.1. The right of states to protect their tax bases from the improper use of tax treaties
    3.2. The principal purpose test in the OECD Model Convention
    3.3. The interplay of CFC rules and general anti-avoidance provisions in tax treaties
4. Final remarks

1. Introduction

General anti-avoidance rules (GAAR) are general instruments conceived to cover all forms of abusive arrangements with regards to all existing tax-related laws within a legal system. GAARs have a broad scope of application; so broad that it might overlap and conflict with that of one or more specific anti-avoidance rules (SAAR). This chapter examines the interplay or conflict between controlled foreign company (CFC) legislation and GAARs either forming part of domestic law or tax treaty law because *"the relationship between domestic anti-abuse rules and double taxation treaties is a complex and unsettled issue."*[1] Whether a transaction or scheme triggers a CFC rule, a domestic or treaty GAAR or more than one norm; whether a conflict of norms or divergence arises; and how such a case should be handled are unresolved issues that deserve attention.

Therefore, Section 2 analyses the different domestic approaches available to states in countering tax avoidance, emphasizing on CFC rules, general anti-avoidance rules and doctrines, and their relationship within domestic legal systems. Section 3 is concerned with tax treaty general anti-avoidance rules i.e. the principal purpose test, the standards for their application, their interplay with CFC rules, and the use of international law to solve potential conflicts of norms.

2. Relationship between CFC rules and domestic GAARs

2.1. Preventing avoidance and ensuring tax collection through controlled foreign company rules

2.1.1. CFC rules as a type of SAAR

A somewhat common phenomenon in international taxation throughout the years has been the use of foreign base companies in low-taxed jurisdictions to allow its shareholders to defer taxation on the income generated abroad until its repatriation, resulting in an intentional erosion of the tax base of their country of residence. The real issue is two-fold: a) the recognition of the foreign base company as an independent taxpayer, allowing the attribution of income to it and theoretically being subject to tax in a different jurisdiction; and b) the separate system of taxation[2] permitting shareholders to indefinitely defer the distribution of dividends, keeping the income away from the tax authorities in their country of residence, and making second-tier taxation highly unlikely. As considered by Rosenbloom, *"[r]espect for the corporation as an entity separate from its controlling*

---

1   Adolfo J. Martín Jiménez, 'Domestic Anti-Abuse Rules and Double Taxation Treaties: a Spanish Perspective – Part I', *Bulletin for International Taxation* (2002) p. 542 (p. 542).
2   According to which a company is taxed on its profits and then the shareholders are also taxed upon actual distribution.

shareholders leads to difficult questions about when income enters or leaves corporate solution".[3]

In 1962, the United States cleverly adopted the 'foreign personal holding company', a specific anti-avoidance rule through which profits generated by a 'controlled foreign company' would be regarded as dividends paid to its US shareholders and consequently taxed even without waiting for an actual distribution to take place.[4] Although that very first version of CFC rules exclusively addressed tax deferral and, interestingly, it was not originally conceived as an anti-avoidance measure,[5] its effectiveness influenced the OECD/G20 Base Erosion and Profit Shifting Project (BEPS Project).

The relevance of CFC rules as a SAAR became evident for OECD members in the report on Action 3 of the BEPS Project which exclusively addressed the design of effective CFC rules in search for consistency, certainty, and predictability in their adoption. With regards to non-OECD countries, Action 6 concerning the identification of treaty abuse and its prevention, has been more far-reaching for it is part of the Inclusive Framework on BEPS.[6] A considerable number of countries have introduced a CFC regime because it has proven to be highly effective and because it protects their own tax base from the undesirable effects of the *"conceptual deficiencies of two-tiered corporate tax systems".*[7]

The narrow scope of a CFC rule allows addressing precise fact-patterns of abusive behaviour,[8] and it is triggered automatically when a foreign company matches the definition and the criteria for its application. The final report on Action 3 of the BEPS Project analyses the pertinent policy considerations and sets out a series of detailed recommendations on how to design effective CFC rules in the form of building blocks, covering: definition of CFC, control threshold, level of taxation, type, and computation and attribution of income as well as how to ensure that they do not result in double taxation.[9] Nevertheless, the design choices overlook a

---

[3] H. David Rosenbloom, 'From the Bottom Up: Taxing the Income of Foreign Controlled Corporations', *Brooklyn Journal of International Law* (2001) p. 1525 (p. 1534).

[4] US: Internal Revenue Code, Title 26, Subtitle A, Chapter 1, Part III, Subpart F – Controlled Foreign Corporations, Sections 951-65; Daniel W. Blum, 'Controlled Foreign Companies: Selected Policy Issues – or the Missing Elements of BEPS Action 3 and the Anti-Tax Avoidance Directive' *Intertax* (2018) p.296 (p. 297).

[5] Richard Krever, 'Controlled Foreign Company Legislation: General Report' in: Georg Kofler/Richard Krever/Michael Lang/Jeffrey Owens/Pasquale Pistone/Alexander Rust/Josef Schuch (eds.) *Controlled Foreign Company Legislation*, Vol. 17 (Vienna: IBFD, 2020) p. 3 (p.3).

[6] According to the update of February 2021, 139 countries are part of the Inclusive Framework on BEPS.

[7] Daniel W. Blum, *Intertax* (2018) p. 300; Richard Krever in: Georg Kofler/Richard Krever/Michael Lang/Jeffrey Owens/Pasquale Pistone/Alexander Rust/Josef Schuch (eds.) *Controlled Foreign Company Legislation*, Vol. 17, p.6.

[8] Adolfo J. Martín Jiménez, 'Domestic Anti-Abuse Rules and Double Taxation Treaties: A Spanish Perspective – Part II', *Bulletin for International Taxation* (2002) p. 620 (p. 620).

[9] OECD (2015), *Designing Effective Controlled Foreign Company Rules, Action 3 – 2015 Final Report*, OECD/G20 Base Erosion and Profit Shifting Project, OECD Publishing, Paris, pp. 9–10.

key question pointed out by *Blum*, referred to as 'technical operationalization of CFC regimes': "*how to technically achieve the income inclusion in the state of residence of the controlling shareholder.*"[10] The question is extremely relevant because CFC rules must fit in a pre-existent legal system, i.e. one that already has mechanisms to allocate taxing rights and, in some cases, to prevent tax avoidance. There are four approaches to achieve income inclusion:

(1) To tax the 'fair value' of the shares which tackles the second-tier taxation by targeting shareholders' increase in wealth as the value of the shares of the controlled foreign company increases.[11]
(2) To pierce the corporate veil approach which provides a solution for income attribution by treating the controlling shareholder of the foreign company as a partner in a partnership and a transparent entity, disregarding the CFC as a taxable person.[12]
(3) To reattribute the income of the CFC which does respect the separate personality of the foreign entity but domestically attributes its income to the controlling shareholder based on its own legislation.[13] This approach is limited in scope as tax treaties restrict domestic income attribution.[14]
(4) The deemed dividend approach which, again, triggers taxation at the second tier by deeming a dividend distribution. Even if the legal personality of the CFC is recognized, the issue of deferral is overcome by taxing the deferred income as if it had been repatriated.

2.1.2. CFC regimes under the Anti-Tax Avoidance Directive

Among Member States to the European Union (EU), before the ATAD, CFC legislation varied widely from country to country in the same way that direct taxes are quite dissimilar among them. Generally, CFC rules restricted the exercise of fundamental freedoms to nationals from EU Member States. Such a restriction came in the form of discrimination against the domestic shareholder who was obligated to pay taxes on profits earned by an independent and sometimes extra-EU entity. The implementation of CFC legislation constituted an infringement of fundamental freedoms. On whether CFC rules constituted a justifiable restriction, the CJEU considered that the objective to combat abuse could be regarded as valid justification in as much as the measure concerned targeted solely "wholly artificial arrangements".[15]

---

10 Daniel W. Blum, *Intertax* (2018) p. 307.
11 Alexander Rust, 'CFC Legislation and EC Law', *Intertax* (2008), p. 492 (p. 493).
12 Alexander Rust, *Intertax* (2008), p. 496.
13 Daniel W. Blum, *Intertax* (2018) p. 307.
14 Alexander Rust, *Intertax* (2008), p. 493.
15 CJEU, 16 July 1998, C-264/96, ECLI:EU:C:1998:370, Imperial Chemical Industries plc (ICI) v Kennet Hall Colmer (Her Majesty's Inspector of Taxes), para. 26; Michael Lang, CFC Legislation, Tax Treaties and EC Law, p. 44.

Given that the main objective of CFC rules is to tackle profit shifting, the freedom of establishment is at issue. According to *Lang*, influence on management seems to be necessary for the right of establishment to be applicable.[16] For example, a resident corporation in any EU Member State transferring profits to its subsidiaries abroad would be under scrutiny. If CFC legislations were to apply to participations that do not grant influence on management, the free movement of capital would be at stake.[17] Furthermore, the latter would prohibit restrictions and discrimination of investments in third countries. However, as recognized by the CJEU in *X-AB & Y-AB* and other cases, the free movement of capital is implicit in the right of establishment.[18]

In *Cadbury Schweppes* and *Test Claimants in the CFC and Dividend GLO*, the CJEU analysed whether a company's CFC constituted abuse through the lens of the United Kingdom's CFC rule. In that regard, the subjective element, i.e. the intention to obtain a tax advantage, was deemed insufficient to qualify a practice as abusive. An objective analysis was required for the qualification, specifically on the satisfaction of the fundamental elements of a company's existence, i.e. premises, staff, and equipment. The court developed a minimum standard requiring states implementing anti-abuse measures to counter only wholly artificial transactions for which the principal purpose was to avoid taxation, meaning that genuine activities reflecting economic reality were lacking.[19]

The ATAD developed from that minimum standard to provide a harmonized new type of CFC rules that are fully compliant with the requirements developed by the CJEU. However, upon the improbability of all Member States to agree on a one-size-fits-all solution, the ATAD includes two CFC options, leaving a little discretion to the implementing state.

Firstly, a criterion set in the ATAD for the application of CFC rules is that a resident in a Member State must exercise control over a foreign entity. Moreover, the resident must have control over a certain threshold. According to Article 7(1)(a), a CFC is an entity or a permanent establishment (PE) in which a taxpayer of a Member State, individually or in connection with associated enterprises: a) holds a direct or indirect participation of more than 50% of the voting rights; b) owns directly or indirectly more than 50% of capital; or c) is entitled to receive more than 50% of its profits.

---

16 Michael Lang, *CFC Legislation, Tax Treaties and EC Law* (The Hague: Linde/Kluwer Law International, 2004) p. 40; Consolidated versions of the Treaty on European Union and the Treaty on the Functioning of the European Union (TFEU) (2016) OJ C202/1, Article 49.
17 Consolidated versions of the Treaty on European Union and the Treaty on the Functioning of the European Union (TFEU) (2016) OJ C202/1, Article 63.
18 CJEU, 18 November 1999, C-200/98, ECLI:EU:C:1999:566, X AB and Y AB v Riksskatteverket, para. 30.
19 CJEU, 12 September 2006, C-196/04, ECLI:EU:C:2006:544, Cadbury Schweppes plc, Cadbury Schweppes Overseas Ltd v Commissioners of Inland Revenue, paras. 64-67; CJEU, 3 October 2013, C-282/12, ECLI:EU:C:2013:629, Itelcar – Automóveis de Aluguer Lda v Fazenda Pública; Daniel W. Blum, *Intertax* (2018) p. 310.

Interestingly, the liability created or extended by paragraph 1 is objective and does not take into account those PEs that are either not subject to tax or exempt from tax in the Member State of the taxpayer.

The control requirement in Article 7(1)(a) deviates considerably from the typical CFC legislation. As noted by *Schönfeld*, the ATAD focuses on related parties exercising control rather than on a control threshold regardless of the connection between the parties, like the original Subpart F regulations in the United States used to do.[20]

Secondly, pursuant to Article 7(1)(b), the CFC must be taxed below 50% of the corporate tax that would have been charged on the CFC under the tax law of the Member State of the taxpayer. To the extent that there is no harmonization in taxation laws among Member States, a CFC may qualify as low-taxed under the scope of one Member State while escaping the threshold in other Member States.

Thirdly, Article 7(2) provides a set of alternatives for Member States to determine whether the CFC income is artificial either based on a list of items of passive income (option A) or by performing a 'principal purpose' test over the transactions (option B). At the end of the categories of income listed under option A, there is a carve out requiring staff, equipment, assets, and premises to evidence that the economic activity is 'substantive' which seems to exceed the *Cadbury Schweppes* test requiring "genuine economic activities".[21] It could be seen as an example of semantics but clearly 'genuine' and 'substantive' are not always interchangeable. Therefore, to avoid inconsistencies with primary law that would generate uncertainty, the so-called 'carve out' in the second sentence of Article 7(2) should be interpreted in the light of the case law.[22]

Lastly, Article 7(3) provides a threshold on passive income for subsidiaries or permanent establishments to be regarded either as a CFC or as legitimate direct investments. In this respect, the CJEU recently clarified that such a restriction is only permissible under EU law to the extent that the taxpayer in question is granted the opportunity to demonstrate, without undue administrative constraints, that the investment follows economic reasons.[23]

The case law of the CJEU has certainly guided the process of shaping domestic anti-abuse or substance over form rules, particularly with regards to the determination of intent and its relevance. It has led to '*taxation according to economic reality rather than pursuant to legal form*'.[24]

---

20   Jens Schönfeld Bonn, 'CFC Rules and Anti-Tax Avoidance Directive', *EC Tax Review* (2017) p. 145 (p. 146).
21   CJEU, 12 September 2006, C-196/04, ECLI:EU:C:2006:544, Cadbury Schweppes plc, Cadbury Schweppes Overseas Ltd v Commissioners of Inland Revenue, para. 68.
22   Jens Schönfeld Bonn, *EC Tax Review* (2017) p. 150.
23   CJEU, 26 February 2019, C-135/17, ECLI:EU:C:2019:136, X-GmbH v Finanzamt Stuttgart – Körperschaften, para. 95; Consolidated versions of the Treaty on European Union and the Treaty on the Functioning of the European Union (TFEU) (2016) OJ C202/1, Articles 63(1) and 64.
24   Stef van Weeghel, *The Improper Use of Tax Treaties – With Particular Reference to the Netherlands and the United States*, (The Hague: Kluwer Law International, 1998) p. 102.

2.2. General anti-avoidance approaches
2.2.1. GAARs in general

A general anti-avoidance approach, broader and more flexible than specific approaches, grants the states a tool for unrestricted future use, covering any kind of tax avoidance strategies, from existing to yet unidentified or inexistent.

There is divergence in the doctrine that shapes the approach, so it may vary considerably from one country to the next. In academia, they are classified in the following groups: *"sham, legally ineffective transactions, substance over form, abuse of law, fraus legis (abuse of rights)"*.[25]

Regarding the form, a GAAR is typically shaped as domestic legislation or developed as a judicial principle. The use of the latter type was widespread for decades, however, very few countries nowadays rely exclusively on a judicial doctrine. Rare exceptions, like the United States, value certainty and are persistently opposed to the idea of building their anti-avoidance measures over broad doctrines or GAARs. Thus, they've developed *"rules which do not turn on taxpayer intent but on broad categories of transactions"*[26] and a complex set of judicial doctrines to counter avoidance; Switzerland still trusts the cumulative criteria developed by the Federal Supreme Court *"to counter undesired aggressive tax planning schemes."*[27]; Russia has a comprehensive and systematic anti-abuse tool introduced by the Supreme Arbitration Court through Plenary Ruling No. 53;[28] or Norway that has developed a tax GAAR as part of a system that also prevents the circumvention of other types of legislation that assesses the purpose and consequences of transactions.[29] A statutory GAAR, on the other hand, should be understood as a general and simplified legal provision that allows the tax authority to determine and/or assess tax liability against a taxpayer.[30]

---

25 Stef van Weeghel, 'General Report' in: International Fiscal Association *Cahiers de Droit Fiscal International*, Volume 95a (Roma: IFA Cahiers, 2010), p. 22.
26 John Tiley, Erik M. Jensen, The Control of Avoidance: The United States Alternative, Case Western University School of Law, Faculty Publications (2006), p. 162; US: Internal Revenue Code, Sections 482; Health Care and Education Reconciliation Act of 2010, Section 7701(o).
27 Stefano Bernasconi/Basil Peyer in: International Fiscal Association (eds.) *Cahiers de Droit Fiscal International*, Volume 105, (The Hague: Kluwer Law International, 2020) p. 800; Decision of the Federal Supreme Court 2A.239/2005.
28 Vladimir Tyutyuryukov, 'Chapter 27: Russia' in: Georg Kofler/Richard Krever/Michael Lang/Jeffrey Owens/Pasquale Pistone/Alexander Rust/Josef Schuch (eds.) *Controlled Foreign Company Legislation*, Vol. 17 (Vienna: IBFD, 2020), p. 543 (section 27.1.1); Ruling of the Plenum of the Supreme Arbitration Court of the Russian Federation dated 12 October 2006 No. 53 "On assessment by the Arbitration Courts of the justified nature of the tax benefit obtained by a taxpayer".
29 Ingebjørg Vamråk, 'Chapter 23: Norway; in: Georg Kofler/Richard Krever/Michael Lang/Jeffrey Owens/Pasquale Pistone/Alexander Rust/Josef Schuch (eds.) *Controlled Foreign Company Legislation*, Vol. 17 (Vienna: IBFD, 2020) p. 473 (section 23.2).
30 Christophe Waerzeggers, Cory Hillier, 'Introducing a general anti-avoidance rule (GAAR) – Ensuring that a GAAR achieves its purpose', Tax Law IMF Technical Note 2016/1, IMF Legal Department, p. 2.

In its applicability, a GAAR is not self-executing; it depends on the intervention of the tax authority. However, the high degree of flexibility calls for an equivalent degree of caution. Otherwise, its application could result in inconsistencies, treating similar schemes in different manners, i.e. applying the law differently to taxpayers in similar circumstances. The described risk places utmost importance on the judgment and capabilities of the tax authority whose interpretation carries an enormous responsibility. Their intervention is essential for assessing whether a taxpayer has obtained a tax benefit through an arrangement or transaction aimed solely or predominantly to attain it.

The consequence of identifying an abuse of law must be a re-evaluation of the dealings at issue.[31] Additionally, whatever its form and underlying doctrine, for a GAAR to transcend the re-evaluation, it must identify that the sole or main purpose of the transactions it targets is avoiding taxes and that it transgresses the object and purpose of the applicable tax law.[32] Although, by referring to 'purpose' rather than 'intent', lawmakers attempt to eliminate any trait of subjectivity from tax law, most avoidance thresholds necessary to trigger a GAAR are not sufficiently high. They allow tax authorities to overlook the commercial goal of transactions even if they are valid and go beyond irrational schemes with the sole purpose of obtaining tax benefits. GAARs have been highly criticized because they allow tax authorities to focus on the steps undertaken by taxpayers to mitigate taxation rather than on the potential artificiality, undue complexity, and circularity or lack of business reality of the transactions.[33] Additionally, even the burden of proof, which is essential for determining the objectivity of a measure, is sometimes shifted to the taxpayer who must demonstrate commercial reasons, automatically lowering the threshold for its application. The discretion in its application may deter investors who appreciate certainty and predictability with regards to the tax consequences in the host country.

Despite the fact that tax authorities are required to conduct their assessments objectively, many dealings may reduce tax liability and thus fall within the scope of the category of 'tax advantageous' without being artificial transactions. Again, flexibility and discretion may easily degenerate into uncertainty. Ergo, artificiality, undue complexity, and circularity or lack of business reality are non-cumulative criteria that must be carefully analysed, and it should be sufficient for one to be met for a transaction to be considered tax avoidance. To ensure the effective-

---

31 Richard Krever, 'General Report: GAARs' in: Michael Lang/Jeffrey Owens/Pasquale Pistone/Alexander Rust/Josef Schuch/Claus Staringer (eds.) *GAARs – A Key Element of Tax Systems in the Post-BEPS Tax World'*, (Vienna: IBFD, 2016) p. 1 (p. 4).
32 Stef van Weeghel, in: International Fiscal Association *Cahiers de Droit Fiscal International*, Volume 95a, p. 22.
33 Richard Krever, in: Michael Lang/Jeffrey Owens/Pasquale Pistone/Alexander Rust/Josef Schuch/Claus Staringer (eds.) *GAARs – A Key Element of Tax Systems in the Post-BEPS Tax World'*, pp. 8–9.

ness of a GAAR, the International Monetary Fund identified the following conditions as highly desirable[34]:

- The target of an anti-tax avoidance policy should be clearly set in artificial or abusive arrangements.
- The scope of the possible tax benefit obtained should be prescribed in law.
- The substance of a suspected arrangement should be carefully considered in the assessment of the purpose.
- The causality link should be demonstrated.
- The taxpayer should have the opportunity to demonstrate the genuineness of a suspected transaction but not bear the *onus*.

Based on those considerations, the complexity in designing an effective GAAR lies in making sure that all genuine commercial transactions will succeed at passing the test when they are analysed. According to *Martín Jiménez*, every GAAR should be available to tackle forms of behaviour analogous to those envisaged by specific anti-abuse clauses but that were and could not be foreseen at the time of their drafting.[35] Two notable attributes of a general rule are its pre-emptive character against tax avoidance to ensure tax collection and its deterrent effect that helps prevent tax avoidance and not merely deal with it after its materialization, as opposed to SAARs. Also, if statutory, it provides a legislative definition of tax avoidance.

2.2.2. GAARs according to the Anti-Tax Avoidance Directive

In the European Union, taxpayers can structure their businesses so as to benefit from the tax advantages available in different legal systems and *"limit their tax liability"*.[36] However, the arrangements they enter into cannot have the obtention of tax benefits to the detriment of the applicable tax law as their main purpose. That has been confirmed by the CJEU in various rulings, particularly in *Kofoed*[37] when it confirmed the principle on the prohibition of abuse of rights as part of community law.

The BEPS Project paved the way for the harmonization of corporate tax avoidance among EU Member States and, in doing so, included a GAAR in the ATAD following the recommendations on Action 6.[38] This measure represents a backstop for the applicability of the specific measures in the ATAD and a legitimizing

---

34 Christophe Waerzeggers, Cory Hillier, 'Introducing a General Anti-Avoidance Rule (GAAR)', pp. 2–9.
35 Adolfo J. Martín Jiménez, *Bulletin for International Taxation* (2002) p. 621.
36 CJEU, 14 December 2000, C-110/99, ECLI:EU:C:2000:695, Emsland-Stärke GmbH v. Hauptzollamt Hamburg-Jonas, paras. 52–53; CJEU, 21 February 2006, C-255/02, ECLI:EU:C:2006:121, Halifax plc, Leeds Permanent Development Services Ltd and County Wide Property Investments Ltd v. Commissioners of Customs & Excise, paras. 73–75.
37 CJEU, 5 July 2007, ECLI:EU:C:2007:408, Hans Markus Kofoed v Skatteministeriet [2007] CJEU C-321/05, para. 38.
38 OECD (2015), *Preventing the Granting of Treaty Benefits in Inappropriate Circumstances, Action 6, 2015 – Final Report*, OECD Publishing, Paris, pp. 54–72.

measure for the CJEU to define abuse and determine the scope of domestic tax avoidance measures.

According to Article 6, the GAAR tests three cumulative criteria: artificiality, motive, and the defeat of the object and purpose of corporate tax law. The standard is overall developed from *Cadbury Schweppes*. The first and second elements are both inferred from verifiable objective facts even though the case law of the CJEU supports the position that a non-tax purpose of an arrangement is not sufficient to render an anti-avoidance measure inapplicable which reduces the objectivity in the determination of intent. Finally, the defeat of the object and purpose of corporate tax law requires a specific analysis in the context of the Member State at issue and aims at preventing that a tax-avoidance scheme benefits from mismatches created in the interaction between the domestic laws of two or more jurisdictions. According to Article 6(3), if the criteria are met, the concerned dealing is ignored and subject to tax in accordance with national law.

A peculiarity of EU law is that, based on the case law of the CJEU according to which the Member State bears the burden to prove abuse in every particular case, the taxpayer is guaranteed an opportunity to demonstrate commercial justification.[39]

2.3. The relationship between CFC rules and GAARs within domestic legal systems

2.3.1. General considerations on the relationship between CFC rules and GAARs

States have at their disposal several tools to counter tax avoidance. As presented above, a comprehensive and effective CFC rule has the potential of reducing the incentive to shift profits from a market country into a low-tax jurisdiction.[40] However, it could also lead to double taxation on the CFC income. Rather, a GAAR allows for the identification of artificial schemes aimed at avoiding tax that could have circumvented the CFC criteria. Nonetheless, past the stage in which a country adopts an anti-abuse approach, the discussion should not be centred around which measure is best equipped to identify certain artificial arrangements but how both can coexist in order to provide certainty at a wider scale.

Both CFC rules and GAARs impose restrictions that aim to modify certain behaviours. They have been used as deterrents for tax avoidance. Upon their imple-

---

39 Daniël Smit, 'The Anti-Tax Avoidance Directive (ATAD)' in: Peter J. Wattel/Otto Marres/Hein Vermeulen (eds.) Terra/Wattel – European Tax Law, vol. 1 (The Netherlands: Kluwer Law International B.V., 2019) p. 485 (p. 536).
40 Daniël Smit, in: Peter J. Wattel/Otto Marres/Hein Vermeulen (eds.) Terra/Wattel – European Tax Law, p. 512.

mentation, the concerned state expects to reduce harmful practices. To qualify transactions as abusive, a state broadly needs to identify artificiality, undue complexity, and circularity or lack of business reality.

If analysed through the lens of Action 3 of the BEPS Project, while the initial objective for adopting CFC rules was to tackle tax avoidance at residence by taxpayers who divert income to their controlled foreign companies in low or no-tax jurisdictions, it has evolved into ensuring that deferred income, either active or passive, is taxed at residence if not subject to appropriate taxation in the source state. Additionally, a CFC can protect a country's tax base: i) by the need to ensure taxation of the controlling shareholder; ii) by ensuring source taxation with respect to cross-border base eroding payments; and iii) by ensuring source taxation with respect to the shareholders of the controlling company.

In contrast, the first and essential consequence of the application of a GAAR is typically the denial of the tax saving obtained through the specific abusive scheme. A GAAR allows a *"margin of appreciation"*,[41] as Cunha portrays it, since it is not possible to predict every possible form of business transaction or investment vehicle. This unusual characteristic of tax laws regulating unforeseen future scenarios justifies the existence of GAARs.[42]

Conflict of norms between a domestic CFC rule and a domestic GAAR must be prevented through the application of general principles of law, *lex specialis derogate legi generali*. In the operationalization of a domestic CFC rule as opposed to a domestic GAAR for which a taxpayer satisfies the CFC criteria, it automatically triggers its application. Therefore, a CFC rule constitutes a special norm that overrides the application of a general norm i.e. a GAAR.[43] Both the OECD and UN Models confirm the latter approach by including in their respective commentaries that "[t]*ax authorities seeking to address the improper use of a tax treaty may first consider the application of specific anti-abuse rules included in their domestic tax law*"[44] Also, to a lesser extent but still relevant in the post-BEPS era, even if a GAAR was later enacted, it would not override an existing special rule unless expressly stated.[45]

---

41 Rita C. Cunha, 'BEPS Action 6: Uncertainty in the Principal Purpose Test Rule', *Global Taxation* (2016), p. 186 (p. 187).
42 John Prebble, Q.C., 'Kelsen, the Principle of Exclusion of Contradictions, and General Anti-Avoidance Rules in Tax Law' in: Monica Bhandari (ed.) *Philosophical Foundations of Tax Law* (Oxford: Oxford Scholarship Online, 2017). p. 2.
43 Lex specialis derogat legi generali.
44 United Nations Committee of Experts on International Cooperation in Tax Matters (UN), 'Note by the Coordinator of the Subcommittee on "Improper use of treaties: Proposed amendments" of 17 October 2008 (E/C.18/2008/CRP.2) p. 6; Commentary on Article 1 of the OECD Model Tax Convention on Income and on Capital (2017) para. 68; Commentary on Article 1 of the UN Model Double Taxation Convention (2011) para. 12.
45 Lex posterior generalis non derogat legi priori speciali.

In short, as identified by the United Nations Committee of Experts on International Cooperation in Tax Matters (UN Tax Committee), complex avoidance schemes require complex rules to tackle them.[46] Following that reasoning, exit taxes, thin capitalization, transfer pricing, dividend stripping, anti-conduit, and certainly CFC rules are widely known and used to prevent specific transactions or arrangements. Nevertheless, specific rules are generally easier to circumvent due to their narrow scope. Thus, relying exclusively on specific rules may unnecessarily expose a state to abuse. Hence, it seems reasonable for states to consider complementing their toolkit with a GAAR, as it is broader and more flexible, to be applicable to transactions that, although artificial, manage to bypass CFC rules.

3. Relationship between CFC rules and GAARs laid down in tax treaty law

3.1. The right of states to protect their tax bases from the improper use of tax treaties[47]

Tax treaties primarily aim at preventing juridical double taxation among the concerned parties by imposing a series of limitations on domestic laws. However, they also prevent the creation of opportunities for double non-taxation and have an ancillary purpose of eliminating or reducing tax avoidance.[48] In particular, tax treaties increase legal certainty and reflect a sense of interstate economic cooperation by removing obstacles for trade and investment flows.

While taxpayers are free to choose the most appropriate vehicle to conduct their affairs, sometimes certain taxpayers make use of cross-border business transactions or investment strategies to fall under the scope of tax treaties. They do so in order to reduce their tax liability, even without an actual connection to any contracting party.[49] Such use of tax treaties is improper, and the transactions qualify as tax avoidance[50] which seems easier to exemplify than to define.[51]

---

46 United Nations Committee of Experts on International Cooperation in Tax Matters (UN), 'Note by the Coordinator of the Subcommittee on "Improper use of treaties: Proposed amendments" of 17 October 2008 (E/C.18/2008/CRP.2) p. 10.
47 Brian J. Arnold, 'An overview of the issues involved in the application of double tax treaties' in: Alexander Trepelkov, Harry Tonino and Dominika Halka (eds.) United Nations Handbook on Selected Issues in Administration of Double Tax Treaties for Developing Countries (New York: United Nations, 2013) p. 1 (p. 46).
48 Adolfo J. Martín Jiménez, *Bulletin for International Taxation* (2002) p. 545.
49 Stef van Weeghel, *The Improper Use of Tax Treaties – With Particular Reference to the Netherlands and the United States*, p. 95.
50 Stef van Weeghel, *The Improper Use of Tax Treaties – With Particular Reference to the Netherlands and the United States*, p. 3.
51 Rebecca Prebble, John Prebble QC, 'Does the Use of General Anti-Avoidance Rules to Combat Tax Avoidance Breach Principles of the Rule of Law?' *Saint Louis University Law Journal* (2010) p. 5.

The principle of the prohibition on the abuse of rights is internationally recognized. As presented by *Martín Jiménez*,[52] that principle sets a limit to the exercise of the rights and obligations assigned by tax treaties to both, state parties and taxpayers.[53] It means that, as subjects of international law with respect to tax treaties, they are both bound by the principle of *pacta sunt servanda*. Consequently, states and taxpayers shall exercise their rights in a reasonable manner and in good faith, refraining from acts contrary to the object and purpose of a treaty.[54] Therefore, if a taxpayer, placing personal interests over social, chooses to exercise a right accorded by a tax treaty with the intention of reducing or avoiding a tax liability, it can be reasonably inferred that such an act or transaction was not performed in good faith but with the motive of causing harm thus it triggers responsibility.[55] In brief, abuse of a tax treaty provision results in an abuse of domestic law.

Now, turning to the facts, not long after the entry into force of the first double tax treaty mirroring the Model Tax Convention on Income and on Capital of the Organisation for Economic Co-operation and Development (OECD Model Convention), states identified practices favouring tax evasion or avoidance. Before the BEPS Project, the idea of including a general anti-avoidance rule in a tax treaty seemed eccentric. In 2003, the OECD incorporated an abuse-threshold in the Commentary on Article 1 of the Model Convention, i.e. the 'guiding principle'.[56] The consequence of its application was the denial of treaty benefits to any taxpayer improperly using a tax treaty. The UN Committee endorsed the approach and incorporated it into the UN Model Convention as well in the form of a general test attempting to maintain the *"balance between the need to prevent abuses and the need to ensure that countries respect their international obligations and provide legal certainty"*.[57]

---

52 See AB Report, United States — Import Prohibition of Certain Shrimp and Shrimp Products [1998] Appellate Body, World Trade Organization WT/DS58/AB/R 61–62; Case Concerning Certain German Interests in Polish Upper Silesia (Germany v Poland) Perm Court Int Justice PCIJ (Permanent Court of International Justice, PCIJ Series A – No 7) 30,37; Case of the Free Zones of Upper Savoy and the District of Gex [1932] PCIJ Series A/B 46, Perm Court Int Justice PCIJ 167 167; Nottebohm Case (second phase) [1955] Int Court Justice ICJ (ICJ Reports 1955, p 4) 53–54 at para. 51; Case Concerning the Barcelona Traction, Light and Power Company, Limited (Belgium v Spain) Second Phase (1970) Second Phase Int Court Justice ICJ 3 (Judgment, ICJ Reports 1970) 17; Case Concerning Fisheries Jurisdiction (United Kingdom v Iceland) 'Memorial of the Merits of the Dispute Submitted by the Government of the United Kingdom' [1972] Int Court Justice ICJ (ICJ Pleadings (Vol1)) 318 at paras. 153–154.
53 Malcolm N. Shaw, International Law (Cambridge: Cambridge University Press, 2014) pp. 188-189; PCIJ (Permanent Court of International Justice), 3 March 1928, P.C.I.J. Series B – No. 15, Jurisdiction of the Courts of Danzig (Advisory Opinion), pp. 17–19.
54 United Nations, Vienna Convention on the Law of Treaties (1969), United Nations Treaty Series, vol. 1155 p. 331 (Article 26); Adolfo J. Martín Jiménez, *Bulletin for International Taxation* (2002) p. 546.
55 Michael Byers, 'Abuse of Rights: An Old Principle, A New Age' *McGill Law Journal* (2002) p. 389 (pp. 395–397); Stef van Weeghel, *The Improper Use of Tax Treaties – With Particular Reference to the Netherlands and the United States*, p. 96.
56 Brian J. Arnold, 'in: Alexander Trepelkov, Harry Tonino and Dominika Halka (eds.) United Nations Handbook on Selected Issues in Administration of Double Tax Treaties for Developing Countries. p. 49.
57 Commentary on Article 1 of the UN Model (2011) paras. 24, 34-37.

According to *van Weeghel*,[58] Belgium was the pioneer in shaping the tax treaty GAAR. In the early twenty-first century, its draft model convention included a provision that would deny treaty benefits to a resident or person connected to a resident whose main purpose was to obtain those benefits. However, it was an almost non-operative provision as it was rarely part of the actual text of the treaties in force. Some other states followed suit, including Portugal, China, Mexico, and Israel.[59] However, those scattered examples were far from uniform or consistent.

Those initial efforts were taken into account when shaping the response to treaty shopping at the core of the OECD and the United Nations. However, instead of structuring a general anti-abuse clause, the efforts focused on the inclusion of the term 'beneficial owner', the guiding principle, and the so-called limitation on benefits clause (LOB) which is a specific anti-avoidance provision widely used by the United States.[60] After that, it took the OECD more than a decade to consider the inclusion of a GAAR in the model convention. Eventually, when suggested in the final report on Action 6 of the BEPS Project, the treaty GAAR was designed only as a complement to the guiding principle and the LOB.[61] The result is that both the United Nations and OECD Model Conventions incorporate a guiding principle delineating the limits of what constitutes treaty abuse. Its operational relevance, as clarified by the BEPS Project and the 2017 OECD Commentary, is that the benefits of a tax treaty should not be granted to taxpayers using transactions with the main purpose of obtaining a more favourable tax treatment.

3.2. The principal purpose test in the OECD Model Convention

The Final Report on Action 6 of the BEPS Project aims at ending treaty shopping completely. To do so, it was agreed by OECD/G20 countries that a minimum standard would be set for countries to adopt provisions capable of addressing treaty shopping. The minimum standard that was developed consists of two elements: a) an express statement on non-taxation comprising treaty shopping arrangements; and b) the adoption of one of the three available methods of addressing treaty shopping.[62] Two out of the three options to choose from include a GAAR in the OECD Model Convention, the Principal Purpose Test (PPT), in the form of a treaty provision, drafted as follows:

---

58 Stef van Weeghel, in: International Fiscal Association *Cahiers de Droit Fiscal International*, Volume 95a, p. 46.
59 Stef van Weeghel, in: International Fiscal Association *Cahiers de Droit Fiscal International*, Volume 95a, p. 47.
60 Stef van Weeghel, 'A Deconstruction of the Principal Purpose Test', *World Tax Journal* (2019), p. 6
61 See Chapter on "The relationship between CFC rules and other SAARs".
62 OECD (2019), *Prevention of Treaty Abuse – Peer Review Report on Treaty Shopping: Inclusive Framework on BEPS: Action 6*, OECD/G20 Base Erosion and Profit Shifting Project, OECD Publishing, Paris.

> Notwithstanding the other provisions of this Convention, a benefit under this Convention shall not be granted in respect of an item of income or capital if it is reasonable to conclude, having regard to all relevant facts and circumstances, that obtaining that benefit was one of the principal purposes of any arrangement or transaction that resulted directly or indirectly in that benefit, unless it is established that granting that benefit in these circumstances would be in accordance with the object and purpose of the relevant provisions of this Convention.[63]

The objective of the PPT is to tackle treaty shopping by assessing transactions to seek for substance and, if absent, qualifying business operations as artificial in order to prevent taxpayers from exploiting legal forms to avoid their tax liabilities. Therefore, it is meant to have interpretative value. However, it does not provide a test for economic substance, i.e. genuine economic activity.

Also, in its application, a treaty benefit may be denied if it can be reasonably inferred from the objective facts and circumstances that obtaining such a benefit was 'one of the principal purposes' of the arrangement. Nonetheless, the OECD does not propose any guidance on the proper identification of the principal purpose.[64] By failing to provide objective criteria to distinguish 'principal' from 'secondary purposes', the PPT fails to establish a standard that is sufficiently clear, precise, and predictable to comply with the principles of legality and legal certainty.[65]

Instead, the PPT provides for an intermediate threshold test based upon a double subjective and objective test that has proven hugely problematic.[66] *Lang* questions the relevance of the former concerning the motive of the taxpayer because it is practically impossible to prove the intention with objective facts. The text of the clause refers to 'reasonableness' as the standard which would probably require tax administrations to prove that a tax benefit was obtained through a transaction and that would suffice for it to amount to abuse. Although in common law systems that might constitute a desirable standard, sets a far from ideal framework for abuse in civil law systems. However, contrary to the text, the OECD Commentary clarifies that there must be "*clear evidence that the treaties are being abused*"[67]. *De Broe* and *Luts* still consider that the PPT sets a low threshold for determining abuse.[68]

---

[63] OECD Model Tax Convention on Income and on Capital (2017) Article 29(9).
[64] CJEU, 26 February 2019, C-116/16 and C-117/16, ECLI:EU:C:2019:135, Skatteministeriet v. T Danmark and Y Denmark, paras, 69–73.
[65] Rita C. Cunha, *Global Taxation* (2016), p. 187.
[66] Andrés Báez Moreno, 'GAARs and Treaties: From the Guiding Principle to the Principal Purpose Test. What Have We Gained from BEPS Action 6?', *Intertax* (2017) p. 432 (p. 446); Michael Lang, 'BEPS Action 6: Introducing an Antiabuse Rule in Tax Treaties', *Tax Notes International* (2014) p. 655 (p. 658).
[67] Commentary on Article 1 of the OECD Model Tax Convention on Income and on Capital (2014), para. 22.2.
[68] Luc De Broe and Joris Luts, 'BEPS Action 6: Tax Treaty abuse', *Intertax* (2015) p. 122 (p. 131).

Interestingly, no reservations were raised by OECD Members with respect to Article 29(9) of the 2017 Model Convention, and only Indonesia recorded a position as a non-OECD country, reserving its right to address it through bilateral negotiations. The PPT was even incorporated into Article 7(1) of the MLI exactly as included in the 2017 OECD Model Convention.

3.3. The interplay of CFC rules and general anti-avoidance provisions in tax treaties

In the analysis at issue, a state has the right to choose the most appropriate measure or set of measures to prevent abuse of law. Assuming a state introduces a CFC rule domestically and it concludes tax treaties with other states, both norms operate in parallel but each of them within a different juridical order and the eventual conflict of obligations is solved by identifying which sphere is affected in a specific factual situation.[69] The legal tradition of each state and the status international agreements occupy within its legal system would play a key role in preventing a conflict of norms.[70] Most countries adopt constitutional measures that help prevent potential conflicts by ensuring that treaties will override domestic law. That is coherent with Article 27 of the Vienna Convention on the Law of Treaties according to which a state party to an international agreement is not in the position to justify a failure to comply with its international obligations based on domestic provisions.[71] This does not mean that a treaty is hierarchically superior but rather that, in the sphere of international obligations, internal law has no applicability. As expressed in the Commentary on Article 1 of the OECD Model "*where the application of provisions of domestic law and of those of tax treaties produces conflicting results, the provisions of tax treaties are intended to prevail.*"[72]

However, contradictions and overlaps between CFC rules and tax treaty provisions might arise in the application of treaty provisions. However, countries should not be entitled to bypass their obligations to respect the allocation of rights under tax treaties by qualifying legitimate transactions as abusive and applying domestic laws allegedly constituting anti-abuse rules to override treaty provisions.[73] As early as 1989, the OECD took the initiative to call the attention of its

---

69 Malcolm N. Shaw, *International Law*, p. 94; Klaus Vogel in: Guglielmo Maisto (ed.), *Tax Treaties and Domestic Law*, (Vienna: IBFD, 2006) p. 1 (p. 3); Gerald Fitzmaurice K. C. M. G., Q.C., Sir, 'The General Principles of International Law Considered from the Standpoint of the Rule of Law (vol. 92)' in: *Collected Courses of the Hague Academy of International Law* (1957-II), p. 71.
70 Brian J. Arnold, in: Alexander Trepelkov, Harry Tonino and Dominika Halka (eds.) United Nations Handbook on Selected Issues in Administration of Double Tax Treaties for Developing Countries p. 3; Klaus Vogel in: Guglielmo Maisto (ed.), *Tax Treaties and Domestic Law*, pp. 4–5.
71 United Nations, Vienna Convention on the Law of Treaties (1969), United Nations Treaty Series, vol. 1155 p. 331 (Articles 26, 27).
72 Commentary on Article 1 of the OECD Model (2017), para. 70.
73 Commentary on Article 1 of the UN Model Double Taxation Convention (2011) para. 24.

member countries to the fact that domestic legislation conflicting with tax treaty provisions was becoming an alarming phenomenon and recommended consultations either bilaterally or multilaterally to address it.[74]

In 2017, the OECD Commentary clarified the role of domestic provisions in countering treaty abuse and recognized their importance by incorporating Article 1(3) into the 2017 OECD Model. This is the so-called 'saving clause' pursuant to which tax treaties do not prevent the application of specific domestic law provisions that would prevent certain abuses of domestic law.[75] Its applicability is not restricted to tax avoidance, rather, it is designed to prevent all unintended restrictions to residence taxation.[76] Additionally, the saving clause takes precedence over other treaty provisions except for the specific exceptions listed at the end of Article 1(3) of the 2017 OECD Model.

An intended effect of the OECD in introducing the saving clause is to put an end to the discussion on whether domestic CFC regimes are compatible with a state's international obligations under a treaty. The ultimate goal is to achieve tax treaty consistency of domestic anti-avoidance rules and, as *Martín Jiménez* stressed, a specific clause in domestic law can be applied in a treaty context only if the treaty, when properly interpreted, admits the application of the clause.[77] In general, no issues should arise if a CFC regime coexists with a treaty GAAR because they both aim at altering the profit attribution that would otherwise be applicable under the tax convention, resulting in a state being able to tax its own residents.

As noted by *Kofler*,[78] a number of scholars and institutions consider that Articles 7(1) and 10(5) of the OECD Model and their respective commentaries already restrict the application of CFC rules, but the outcome of their application is still dependent on the approach used by the CFC regime to achieve income inclusion. The saving clause, by providing that a state is able to tax its own residents as it deems appropriate and is not bound by the other state's attribution of income,[79] avoids any doubt regarding the compatibility of CFC legislation with the allocation rules.

Finally, relevant in the context of the European Union, *Blum* expressed with regards to the construction of a CFC rule that a *"CFC regime should be drafted in a way that neither interferes with the allocation of taxing rights between the source and the residence state, nor with obligations enshrined in EU law"*[80]. The obligation

---

74 OECD 'Recommendation of the Council concerning Tax Treaty Override' adopted on 2 October 1989, OECD/LEGAL/0253.
75 Luc De Broe and Joris Luts, 'BEPS Action 6: Tax Treaty abuse', *Intertax* (2015) p. 138; Commentary on Article 1 of the UN Model Double Taxation Convention (2017) paras. 66–81.
76 Georg Kofler, 'Some Reflections on the 'Saving Clause'', *Intertax* (2016) p. 574 (p. 575).
77 Adolfo J. Martín Jiménez, *Bulletin for International Taxation* (2002) p. 621.
78 Georg Kofler, *Intertax* (2016) p. 583.
79 Daniel W. Blum, *Intertax* (2018) p. 308.
80 Daniel W. Blum, *Intertax* (2018) p. 308.

to ensure consistency between national legislation and concluded tax treaties and that they all ensure that the objectives of the ATAD are fulfilled falls upon EU Member States. Nonetheless, it is worth highlighting that, even though both the ATAD CFC rule and the PPT target artificial arrangements for their potential to avoid taxation, the former does not interfere with the latter. All arrangements reflecting economic reality escape from the applicability of the CFC and could only be subject to tax through the denial of treaty benefits by applying the PPT.[81]

4. Final remarks

Controlled foreign company regimes are considered as specific anti-avoidance measures for their potential to target artificial arrangements based on a precise fact-pattern and predetermined legal consequences. Additionally, both CFC rules and GAARs impose restrictions that aim to modify certain behaviours.

From the author's perspective, tax avoidance and abuse would be best addressed through a combination of specific and general anti-avoidance rules both domestically and as part of tax treaties. However, the highest level of protection is achieved by states focusing their efforts on designing effective specific anti-avoidance measures.

Conflict of norms between a domestic CFC rule and a domestic GAAR must be prevented through the application of general principles of law e.g., *lex specialis derogate legi generali*, and *lex posterior generalis non derogat priori specialis*. In the rare event of conflict between the provisions of tax treaties and domestic legislation, the provisions of tax treaties must prevail in the application of Article 27 of the Vienna Convention on the Law of Treaties.

As a general rule, states remain sovereign to choose their own perspective and to define the relationship between tax treaties and anti-avoidance rules and certainly the status of tax treaties in domestic legal systems.

---

81 CJEU, 12 September 2006, C-196/04, ECLI:EU:C:2006:544, Cadbury Schweppes plc, Cadbury Schweppes Overseas Ltd v Commissioners of Inland Revenue, para. 65; CJEU, 23 April 2008, C-201/05, ECLI:EU:C:2008:239, The Test Claimants in the CFC and Dividend Group Litigation v Commissioners of Inland Revenue, para. 79.

Common Corporate (Consolidated) Tax Base and CFC-Rules

Niki Mitrakou

1. **Overview**
2. **European Commission's CC(C)TB proposal**
    2.1. The 2011 CCCTB proposal and its 2016 relaunch
    2.2. Objectives, opportunities, and challenges of the CCCTB proposal
        2.2.1. Enhanced cooperation as an answer to the CCCTB's obstacles
        2.2.2. Application of the proposed CCCTB rules to EU Member States
3. **Introduction of CFC rules in a variety of legislative instruments**
    3.1. The CFC regime within the CCCTB proposal
    3.2. Application of the proposed CCCTB CFC rules to EU Member States
    3.3. Provision within the ATAD I for another set of CFC rules
    3.4. Interaction between the CCCTB's and the ATAD's I CFC rules and potential implications of parallel application
4. **Conclusions**

1. Overview

The chapter at hand examines the common corporate (consolidated) tax base (hereafter CC(C)TB) proposal initiated and proposed by the European Commission and focuses particularly on the controlled foreign companies (hereafter CFC) rules included therein, comparing this set of CFC rules to the one inserted in the EU 2016/1164 Anti-Tax Avoidance Directive (hereafter ATAD I). The author intends to analyse Articles 7 and 8 of ATAD I and Articles 59 and 60 of the 2016 CC(C)TB proposal seeking to investigate the reasons why two different sets of CFC regimes are introduced in two different legislative tools by comparing the two set of rules and identifying their similarities and differences. Moreover, the author wishes to elaborate further on the possible reasons behind the persistent effort of the European Commission to uproot the erosion of the European tax bases and profit shifting by adopting almost identical CFC rules through two different legislative instruments. The potential conflicts will be presented that may arise in the case of a simultaneous application of both rules. Concluding, some suggestions and proposals are given for the eradication of the mismatches in the case that the CCCTB proposal gets approved and transposed into the national legislations.

2. European Commission's CC(C)TB proposal

The CCCTB[1] has been identified as an initiative of a significant importance in the context of the Europe 2020 Strategy and has been mentioned in a series of major policy European documents aiming to remove obstacles of the single market and stimulate growth, investments, and employment within the European Union (hereafter EU). The Lisbon Strategy, the previous development plan launched by the European Council in March 2000, aimed to establish the EU as "*the most competitive and dynamic knowledge-based economy in the world capable of sustainable economic growth with more and better jobs and greater social cohesion*"[2] by 2010. The reformation of the corporate tax system and the creation of a more competitive and coherent internal market without tax obstacles, tax fraud, and tax evasion were some of the goals of the Lisbon Strategy. However, most of these goals were not achieved in the settled timeframe and, consequently, the Lisbon Strategy was succeeded by the Europe 2020 Strategy[3]. The introduction of the CCCTB[4] in both

---

1 Article 115 TFEU constitutes the legal base for the CCCTB, i.e. *the Council shall, acting unanimously ... issue directives for the approximation of laws, ... as directly affect the establishment or functioning of the internal market.*
2 European Commission, *Working together for growth and jobs – a new start for the Lisbon Strategy*, COM (2005) 24, at 3.
3 Communication from the Commission, *EUROPE 2020 – A strategy for smart, sustainable and inclusive growth* – COM (2010) 2020, 3.3.2010.
4 The actual technical work on the CCCTB started in 2004 with the creation of a Commission Working Group to work and progress on the EU's CCCTB and continued quite fast as more than 50 working papers have been drafted in this regard.

aforementioned strategies constituted a major priority for the commission and is considered to be the most *"instrumental long-term solution to the current problems, leading to greater efficiency, transparency and simplicity of corporate taxation"*.[5] Nevertheless, it took many years for the commission to develop its CCCTB proposal into a directive that was first launched in 2011 and was relaunched in 2016. In the European Commission's 2015 communication on the Action Plan for a Fair and Efficient Corporate Tax System, the European Commission (hereafter EC) proposed a step-by-step approach with the first step being the adoption of the ATAD I in July 2016[6] followed by the Common Corporate Tax Base (hereafter CCTB) as second, and the CCCTB as a third step. Nevertheless, *apart from the adoption of the wide-ranging proposal*, the CCCTB has not yet been approved and transposed into EU's binding law[7] in comparison to the ATAD I which became hard law in 2018.

The main reason behind the fact that it takes so long to reach a common agreement in reference with the CCCTB scheme relates mostly to the tax sovereignty of the Member States with respect to direct taxation. Many states were of the opinion that a common definition and the consolidation of the EU corporations' tax base would limit their sovereign taxing rights and would infringe Articles 113 and 115 of TFEU that stipulate that the EU has competences only with regard to indirect taxation and harmonization of tax laws subject to the members' unanimous consent. Taking all of this into consideration, there is no doubt that the CCCTB is a long and still ongoing *radical and ambitious*[8] project that requires *"tremendous political will* and *which is often threatened to be watered down by political compromises"*.[9]

In contrast to those who disapprove and are reluctant towards the CCCTB, the EC and the industry along with many multinational enterprises (hereafter MNE) warmly support the CCCTB proposal mostly due to its consolidation scheme. The latter are of the opinion that by *"freeing companies from compliance with intra-group transfer-pricing rules and allowing an immediate profit and loss consolidation, a consolidated tax base shall make Europe a highly attractive area to do business"*.[10]

---

5   Bersani, *Draft report on companies and taxation in the European Union: a common consolidated corporate tax base and home state taxation for SMEs*, 2004/2232 (INI), at 9.
6   Council Directive (EU) 2016/1164, Anti-Tax Avoidance Directive I.
7   S. Khan, *Re-Launch of a Proposal for a Common Consolidated Corporate Tax Base (CCCTB) in the EU: A Shift in Paradigm*, Legal Issues of Economic Integration, May 2018, pg. 294.
8   U. Schreiber, *Evaluating the Common Consolidated Corporate Tax Base*, (Berlin, Heidelberg: Springer, 2008) pg.125.
9   J. Barenfeld, *A common consolidated corporate tax base in the European Union – A beauty or a beast in the quest for tax simplicity* (Bulletin for international taxation, 2007), pg. 268.
10 M. Aujean – M.P Hoo/Taj, *An outline of the CCCTB and some focal points*, 2011.

2.1. The 2011 CCCTB proposal and its 2016 relaunch

In the footsteps of globalization, the number and complexity of the various different tax systems across the EU gave birth to the idea of the CCCTB, a single set of rules, aiming to simplify the computation of taxable income for businesses operating within the EU. Nowadays, corporations often operate in more than one jurisdiction across the EU, hence face multiple and complex tax regimes in several countries. A MNE may, for example, deal with up to 27 different tax jurisdictions that often include overlapping elements or loopholes able to lead either to a more burdensome taxation or to double taxation of the same profits or even to tax evasion and profit shifting. Due to these complexities and the subsequent potential mismatches, it is believed that the establishment of the CCCTB as a new, harmonized, common tax system could provide simplicity and constitute a tool against the phenomena of base erosion and profit shifting, hereafter BEPS, within the EU[11].

The EC announced its first directive proposal for the CCCTB in March 2011 aiming to introduce a single set of rules for **i)** calculating the corporate tax base within the EU, **ii)** consolidating the tax bases of all of the EU operating companies, and **iii)** implementing a formulary apportionment, hereafter FA, able to proportionally attribute the net profits of a group to all of the Member States involved. However, the first CCCTB proposal, despite its innovation and significance, proved to be too ambitious for the Member States to agree on it in one go. Many discussions took place in the Council of EU with regards to that first CCCTB proposal, and the Member States proposed several changes while the United Kingdom and Ireland were strongly opposed to it. For the adoption though of a directive, the unanimous consensus of all Member States is required, and it seems that this consent could not be easily reached at that point of time due to the hesitation of some Member States that argued that severe budgetary implications will arise. Nevertheless, that reluctance in conjunction with the strong demand for the CCCTB's benefits constituted the main reasons behind the rebooting of the CCCTB proposal in 2016 which then included the key provision of an implementation through a more manageable process, i.e. through a two-steps approach.

The relaunched directive proposal provides a two-phase implementation with the first step being the CCTB, i.e. the establishment of standardized rules simply on how to calculate a company's taxable profits. At this first stage, the allocation between Member States remains on the traditional basis of residence, permanent establishment (hereafter PE), and the transfer pricing rules (hereafter TP)[12]. The

---

11 BEPS is defined as: *tax planning strategies that exploit gaps and mismatches in tax rules to make profits „disappear" for tax purposes or to shift profits to locations where there is little or no real activity but the taxes are low resulting in little or no overall corporate tax being paid.*

12 D. Neidle, *The relaunched CCCTB*, (Tax Journal, 2016), https://www.taxjournal.com/articles/relaunched-common-consolidated-corporate-tax-base-03112016.

second step, *"after a consensus on the calculation of the tax base is reached"*[13], is the automatic transition to the CCCTB for which the consolidation of a company's profits and losses[14] is requested with the subsequent allocation of the net profits to the individual Member States using the FA by estimating the following elements: **i)** employees/labour, **ii)** assets, and **iii)** sales in each Member State.

A further amendment in the relaunched proposal is its mandatory character for the large group of companies. The 2011 CCCTB proposal was optional for all companies while, with the 2016 proposal, the CCCTB becomes mandatory for groups with a global turnover exceeding EUR 750 million and remains optional for the rest of the companies under certain conditions (voluntary opt in)[15]. The reason of this meaningful amendment is the need to bring the MNEs under the CCCTB's mandatory scope as they undoubtedly have the greatest capacity to tax plan by creating complicated tax structures in order to avoid taxes and shift their profits to low tax jurisdictions.

2.2. Objectives, opportunities, and challenges of the CCCTB proposal

This section aims to provide a brief explanation of what are considered to be the benefits of implementing CCCTB as well as to accurately estimate the challenges along with the opportunities that the CCCTB may generate. With the implementation of the CCCTB, EU companies will be enabled to file a single tax return for all of their activity within the EU through one tax authority, i.e. one-stop-shop, instead of filing a tax return in each country where they operate[16]. It is undoubtful that businesses operate nowadays in cross border environments, a fact that often leads to tax uncertainty and a high amount of compliance costs. In this respect, the CCCTB could constitute a tool to confront the complications occurred by the increasing mobility of both taxable income and taxpayers. Therefore, the objective of the CCCTB's implementation is to establish a common way to compute the profits and losses of EU based corporations in a way that is able to mitigate the risks of potential tax fraud and profit shifting. It is believed that the CCCTB could eliminate the existing complex tax regimes and replace them by one single set of rules, achieving a more transparent EU corporate taxation. Hence, the commission is of the opinion that the CCCTB's adoption

---

13   EU: CCCTB, *What businesses should know about Europe's CCCTB*, (International Tax Review, 2014) pg. 12.
14   Consolidation: All profits and losses from companies of a group in different Member States are added up to reach a net profit or loss for the group's entire EU activity.
15   Art. 2 par. 1 and 3 of COM (2016) 685 final 2016/0337 (CNS) Proposal for a Council Directve on a Common Corporate Tax Base.
16   J. Barenfeld, *A common consolidated corporate tax base in the European Union – A beauty or a beast in the quest for tax simplicity*, pg. 269.

will promote the single market by reducing tax compliance costs for corporations operating in several EU states.[17]

The consolidation element from its end targets allowing companies to offset losses in one Member State against profits in another that could incentivise small and medium sized companies and start-ups to expand their business. Additional opportunities of the CCCTB could be, according to tax experts, the elimination of the TP requirements which are often considered to constitute an important vehicle to shift profits[18] and the elimination of the need to consult double tax treaties to ensure net taxation within the EU. It must be highlighted, though, that such TP requirements will only be abolished between associated enterprises within the EU, being part of the CCCTB either mandatorily or due to their opt-in choice. However, TP rules will still be implemented for intercompany transactions with third countries' entities taking into consideration that the CCCTB affects and facilitates only the EU based legal entities.

It is noteworthy that the CCCTB only aims to align the tax bases throughout the EU, and it still leaves the tax rate that constitutes one of the main elements of the states' tax sovereignty untouched. There is no intention to harmonize tax rates as each state's *tax rate is instrumental in having sound tax competition among the EU and thus stimulate efficiency.*[19] Thus, the CCCTB wishes to create more transparency with regard to the effective corporate tax situation by creating fairer tax competition within the EU[20], and it will not interfere with financial accounts, therefore, the Member States will maintain their national rules on financial accounting, and the CCCTB will not affect the preparation of such annual and/or consolidated accounts.

Challenges and risks, however, are inherent to the CCCTB proposal, and several objections have been raised for its approval. First of all, it is argued that, even with the CCCTB, certain issues will still be determined under national law such as, for example, the passive foreign income which could be taxed according to the domestic rules[21]. Certain Member States are opposing the CCCTB arguing that they will lose part of their tax revenues while an increase in internal costs may be created due to the compliance with the more stringent legislation of the CCCTB Di-

---

17 According to figures from the Commission Impact Assessment for the 2011 CCCTB proposal, *it is estimated that the CCCTB could save businesses across the EU EUR 0.7 billion per year in compliance costs and reduce the costs of cross-border expansion by around 62%.*
18 *Transaction-by-transaction pricing based on the arm's length principle may no longer be the most appropriate method for profit allocation* according to the supporters of the CCCTB Directive.
19 European Commission, *Implementation of the Community Lisbon Programme – Communication from the Commission to the Council and the European Parliament*, 2005, at 5.
20 Tax rates' differentiation allows tax competition to be maintained in the internal market and fair tax competition based on rates offers more transparency and allows Member States to consider both their market competitiveness and budgetary needs in fixing their tax rates, EC 16.03.2011 COM (2011) 121 final, 2011/0058 (CNS) – CCCTB proposal.
21 European Commission, *The territorial scope of the CCCTB*, CCCTB/026/WP (2006), at 6.

rective.[22] An indirect incentive could be considered to be given to MNEs to dismantle their business by transferring it to non-EU countries, a fact that is able to lead to loss of the EU's competitiveness and of potential investments.

Moreover, the proposal stipulates that the CCCTB will be mandatory for MNEs with consolidated turnover exceeding EUR 750 million within a financial year which automatically means that two different corporate tax systems may coexist, i.e. one for MNEs falling under the mandatory scope and one for those not exceeding it. At this stage, it cannot be predicted with certainty whether smaller companies with revenues not reaching the EUR 750 million threshold will continue to be taxed under the arm's length principle or would opt into the CCCTB system. Therefore, opposers of the CCCTB are concerned that it may produce a two speeds EU tax system that will be contrary to the CCCTB's desired effect.[23]

2.2.1. Enhanced cooperation as an answer to the CCCTB's obstacles

As mentioned previously, it is not easy to reach a unanimous consensus on the CC(C)TB Directive as some Member States fear that the establishment of a common EU tax base may open the path to an indirect tax rate's harmonization that is able to indicate the end of their tax sovereignty. Faced with this reasoning and due to the potential of a long intermediary phase that is able to jeopardize the CC(C)TB itself, the commission may consider the possibility of enhanced cooperation[24] as an alternative tool to move forward in the case that the relaunched CC(C)TB proposal does not get easily approved.

According to Article 20 TEU, those

> Member States which wish to establish enhanced cooperation between themselves within the framework of the Union's non-exclusive competences may make use of EU institutions and exercise those competences by applying the relevant provisions of the Treaties, subject to the limits and in accordance with the detailed arrangements laid down in this Article and in Articles 326 to 334 of the TFEU.

These articles give permission to a limited number of Member States to implement the CCCTB among themselves while the rest of the states maintain the right to join the scheme at a later stage.[25] Enhanced cooperation namely permits a min-

---

22 G. Cacavello, *The CCCTB is not the corporate tax reform the EU needs*, Epicenter.
23 R. Offermanns, S. Huibregtse, L. Verdoner and J. Michalak, *Bridging the CCCTB and the Arm's Length Principle – A Value Chain Analysis Approach*, (IBFD, 2017), pg.470.
24 Since the Treaty of Amsterdam (1997), enhanced cooperation constitutes a special element of EU law encouraging further harmonization by offering solace whenever it is impossible to achieve further integration to realize a much desired EU goal, Prof. Dr. H.T.P.M. van de Hurk, *The CCCTB: A desirable alternative to a flat EU CIT* (IBFD, 2011), pg. 263.
25 J. Barenfeld, *A common consolidated corporate tax base in the European Union – A beauty or a beast in the quest for tax simplicity*, pg. 260.

imum of nine Member States to implement a measure which otherwise would need unanimity and constitutes another process via which the CCCTB could be introduced into EU law.[26] Enhanced cooperation may be initiated if a common agreement remains utopian and in the case that the hesitation of some Member States obstruct the EU's goals. This is because it enables the participating states to organize greater cooperation on a subject than initially provided for by the treaties.[27]

It is, however, believed that the Member States should not opt yet for the enhanced cooperation scheme, as this shall be considered as a last resort option[28], and efforts should be continued towards a common approval of the CCCTB Directive. Enhanced cooperation cannot arise from scratch as it has to follow a commission proposal that has not succeeded to reach agreement through the usual legislative cycle. Even if enhanced cooperation is a last resort measure, it constitutes *"undoubtedly a tool that allows to overcome legislative paralysis due to the unanimity requirement"*[29].

The two biggest EU economies, France and Germany, are strongly pushing towards the approval of the relaunched CCCTB and have further announced their mutual commitment to introduce and apply a CCTB system as from 2019, including a common tax rate for companies located in their territory. No consolidation requirement is required under such agreement, i.e. each country will keep the tax revenues generated locally, and each country's profit calculation would follow similar standard rules. Additionally, the joint proposal provides for a corporate tax harmonization among the EU Member States according to which the scope of the CCTB Directive should be extended and be compulsory for all companies subject to corporate tax irrespective of their legal form and size.[30]

2.2.2. Application of the proposed CCCTB rules to EU Member States

The relaunched CCCTB proposal provides a single set of rules for the calculation of the corporate tax base that is mandatory for corporate groups with a consolidated turnover exceeding EUR 750 million per financial year. Companies that do not reach such a threshold retain the possibility to opt into the system. Under the first phase, i.e. CCTB, companies still have to file a separate tax return in all Member States where they have a taxable presence while, in the second phase, i.e. the

---

26   P. Cussons, *CCCTB: It's on the Horizon* (International Tax Review, vol. 19, nr 1, 2008), pg. 21.
27   J. Lamotte, *New EU tax challenges and opportunities in a CC(C)TB world: Overview of the EU Commission Proposal for a draft Directive for a CCCTB*, (IBFD, European Taxation June 2012), pg. 279.
28   Title IV of TEU, Provisions on Enhanced Cooperation art. 20, par. 2.
29   https://www.europarl.europa.eu/doceo/document/A-8-2019-0038_EN.html.
30   R. Ortmann and C. Sureth, *Can the CCCTB alleviate tax discrimination against loss-making European multinational groups?* (WU Research Paper, No. 2014-08), pg. 3.

CCCTB, a single tax return shall be filed with the principal tax authority, namely, that of the parent company. The profits will not be taxed in the source state as companies in the second phase may offset losses in one state against profits in another which shall facilitate companies operating across the single market.

With regards to the optionality of the CCCTB, all of the companies residing in the EU may opt for applying the CCCTB rules. The same applies for eligible companies not residing in the EU that are, however, able to opt in for their PEs established within the EU. The companies' option to enter into the CCCTB is valid for five years and can be automatically renewed for successive periods of three years unless notice to the contrary is given.[31]

The CCCTB rules define the tax base but not the methodology for adjusting the accounts to arrive at it as there is no formal link between it and accounting standards like the IAS/IFRS. However, the work for defining the tax base has made constant reference to IAS/IFRS and, unless uniform treatment is explicitly provided, the CCCTB's tax base shall be computed by reference to the general principles provided in the CCCTB Directive.[32] That said, the CCCTB's tax base is calculated as follows: revenues minus the exempt revenues, minus any deductible expenses or any other deductible items, minus depreciation of fixed assets, minus any allowance for growth and investment (AGI), minus any R&D expenses. CCCTB losses are eligible for carry forward indefinitely in contrast to loss carry back which is not allowed. As to the consolidation scheme, a two-part test determines the entitlement to participation in the group. The deciding factors are control, i.e. a percentage higher than fifty percent (50%) of voting rights and either ownership at a percentage higher of seventy five percent (75%) of capital or rights to profits at a percentage higher than seventy five (75%) of rights giving entitlement to profit. Furthermore, EU located branches of third countries' corporations are treated as individual group members in the allocation of their apportioned share and their inbound and outbound payments.[33] Both requirements should be met throughout the financial year and for an unlimited period of nine months, otherwise, the company shall leave the group.

Meeting the above requirements leads to the elimination of the intragroup transactions. No withholding tax shall be levied to such transactions and, as mentioned previously, the tax base will be shared through the FA and its three equally weighted factors to compute the taxing entitlement of each Member State.

---

31   Proposal for a Council Directive on a Common Consolidated Corporate Tax Base, Art. 2- Scope.
32   The 2012 KPMG guide to the CCCTB, pg. 73–77.
33   The 2012 KPMG guide to the CCCTB, pg. 73–77.

3. Introduction of CFC rules in a variety of legislative instruments

The following chapter presents the main features and goals of controlled foreign company (CFC) rules and elaborates on their incorporation within the CCCTB proposal. Moreover, the reason why CFC rules are provided **i)** in most of the EU national legislations, **ii)** in the CCCTB proposal, and **iii)** in the ATAD I[34] are going to be investigated, exploring in parallel any differences between those three different sets of CFC rules and any conflicts that their parallel/simultaneous application may provoke.

To begin with, a CFC is a corporate entity registered and conducting business in a country that is different than the residency of its controlling owner. Its control is defined according to the percentage of shares owned by foreign citizens. The reason behind the creation and adoption of CFC rules stems from the fact that many countries do not normally tax the shareholder of a corporation on the corporation's income until the income gets repatriated by way of distributions to the shareholder.[35] Many companies, taking advantage of that, formed offshore companies in low tax jurisdictions by subsequently shifting their profits there either as investment (equity) or as passive income (interest, rents, and royalties). In that way, they succeeded to defer due taxes until a dividend distribution would take place. Therefore, shareholders were generating income via foreign entities by deferring taxation until the income's actual repatriation and, hence, the CFC regime implies taxing the resident shareholder on its pro rata share of some or even all of the undistributed CFC's income.[36] As a result, the introduction of CFC occurred as a special anti-tax avoidance rule (hereafter SAAR)[37]. Additionally, CFC rules being an anti-deferral regime intend to cause current taxation to mitigate the potentiality of artificial profit shifting and to eradicate distortions associated with cross border transactions and the subsequent loss of revenues for the high tax jurisdictions. In other words, the introduction of CFC rules was justified by the need to ensure taxation of the controlling shareholder as a resident and to ensure source taxation with respect to cross-border base eroding payments.[38] The CFC rules are namely seen as an indispensable anti-avoidance provision ensuring the international tax

---

34 *The OECD BEPS initiative, in its effort to enhance the coherence of the corporate income tax, has devoted an entire BEPS Action to the topic of Designing Effective Controlled Foreign Company Rules,* D. Blum, *Controlled Foreign Companies: Selected Policy Issues – or the missing elements of BEPS Action 3 and the Anti-Tax Avoidance Directive* (Kluwer Law International, 2018) Volume 46, issue 4.
35 L. Ostorero, *Historical background to CFC-rules and policy considerations,* Chapter 1.
36 M. Lang, *CFC Legislations, Tax Treaties and EC law* (2004 Kluwer Law International), p.97.
37 SAARs are targeted legislation that remove or reduce the tax effect of certain transactions, e.g. a) Interest Limitation Rules, b) CFC, c) Exit Taxation, d) Hybrid Mismatch Rules, e) Diverted Profit Tax and e) Digital Service Tax.
38 D. Blum, *Controlled Foreign Companies: Selected Policy Issues – or the missing elements of BEPS Action 3 and the Anti-Tax Avoidance Directive* (Kluwer Law International, 2018).

neutrality by the establishment of a defensive measure against those low tax jurisdictions that undertake harmful tax competition. They are also a tax policy against the erosion of the countries' tax base and the complicated TP rules.[39]

Additionally, the fact that three layers of CFC rules currently exist is remarkable, i.e. **i)** the national CFC rules that had been adopted by several Member States prior to the approval of the ATAD I; **ii)** the CFC rules provided within Article 59 of the CCCTB Directive proposal (not yet in force, though); and **iii)** the CFC rules adopted in virtue of the transposition of the ATAD I in EU law. This fact makes clear that the tools established by the EU institutions to counterbalance tax avoidance are no longer limited. Having said that, the intention of the following sections is to understand why several different legislative instruments aimed to insert CFC rules into EU tax law, to compare those different sets of rules, and explore the conflicts that may arise in the case of a parallel application.

3.1. The CFC regime within the CCCTB proposal

Prior to the introduction of the CFC rules in the 2011 CCCTB proposal, several countries,[40] among others, the United States, the United Kingdom, and Germany, had already introduced CFC rules in their national tax legislation. The aim was to circumvent tax driven foreign investments and minimize the transfer of their capital to low tax jurisdictions.[41] National CFC provisions were not identical as different thresholds and technical details were introduced in each national tax system according to each country's needs. However, the policy background, the main structure, and the underlying objectives did not vary substantially. The variations related mostly to the ownership requirements, the activities, and the type of CFC income as some countries were distinguishing between passive and active income. Furthermore, the Member States had several options when it came to deciding on how to define a low taxation regime, ranging from objective criteria, e.g. a jurisdictional approach, to a system of designated countries, or a combination of both. Furthermore, there are different approaches on how to tax the shareholders on the undistributed income[42]. The first mechanism is the piercing the corporate veil which does not treat CFCs as separate taxable entities, disregards them, and attributes the CFC income directly to the shareholders.[43] Another mechanism is the deemed dividend approach that deems the CFC's deferred or diverted income to be distributed to its shareholders on a current basis even with-

---

39 *Fee Position Paper on Controlled Foreign Company Legislations in the EU*, April 2002, issued by the European Federation of Accountants (FEE), pg. 5.
40 DE adopted its CFC rules in 1972, FR in 1980, UK in 1984, SE in 1990, NO in 1992, FL in 1995 etc.
41 In contrast, EU holding jurisdictions (e.g. Lux, BE, and NL) did not have CFC rules until the approval of the ATAD I.
42 I.U. Skreblin, *Different Approaches to the application of CFC rules*, Chapter 2.
43 Such tax treatment is equated to a pass-through tax treatment.

out any actual profit distribution to the shareholder.[44] Subsequently, the benefit of deferral or profit diversion vanishes as the income is taxed immediately in the shareholders' hands as if it had already been distributed. It is difficult to understand which approach is endorsed by the CCCTB's CFCs as, under both methods, the CFC income gets included in the shareholder's tax base.

In the years that followed, it became obvious that a common approach should be implemented and that the lack of uniformity of the national CFC rules would indicate that the results to counter tax avoidance would differ from country to country. Bearing in mind the fact that many Member States had national CFC rules, it was questionable if the states would support the introduction of the common CFC rules in the CCCTB proposal. As the individual CFC rules were not aligned, it was considered of high importance to harmonize the anti-abuse provisions within the CCCTB, otherwise, the harmonization would not be properly ensured and would lack its main economical purpose. This may be one of the reasons that the EU Commission realized the need to introduce CFC rules in both the ATAD I and the CCCTB to create symmetry within EU and to effectively preserve the cohesion of the tax systems. Moreover, national CFC rules operated to curb tax deferral on passive income derived by foreign corporations situated in low tax jurisdictions. In the area of the SAARs, if left to the individual action of the Member States, it would raise the risk of inconsistent provisions and undesirable complication of the CCCTB.[45] Consequently, the decision taken by the EU legislative bodies was that the CFC, along with the provisions on hybrid and tax residency mismatches provisions, should be foreseen in the CCCTB Directive[46]. Therefore, the CFC rules were introduced in the 2011 and 2016 CCCTB Directive proposals to protect the domestic tax bases.

Within the EU itself, national and the ATAD's CFC provisions would become redundant for those entities falling within CCCTB's scope and being subject to CCCTB's CFC rules. However, with regard to third countries, CFC legislation will still be relevant and necessary as *"Member States will remain vulnerable to geographical income shifting using low-tax third countries"*.[47] Under other circumstances, the members would have lost an important anti-abuse shield, and it was therefore that both CCCTB proposals took into account the CFC legislation as an anti-abuse tool able to protect the CCCTB. As a result, CFC rules were introduced with Articles 82, 59, 60, and 73 in each CCCTB proposal, respectively. The aim was to *reattribute the income of a low-taxed CFC* to its parent company, which is

---

44 A. Rust, *CFC legislation and EC Law*, Intertax, Vol. 36, 2008, p. 492.
45 E.A.G.Ali, *The International aspects of the European CCCTB and their interaction with third countries*, Brunel University, May 2013, pg. 182.
46 The EU Commission, the EU Parliament and the Council of EU are the three central legislative institutions of the EU, often referred to as the EU's *institutional triangle*.
47 S. Clifford, *Taxing multinationals beyond borders: Financial and locational responses to CFC rules* (Journal of Public Economics Vol. 173, 2019), pg. 58.

subject to tax on such attributed, undistributed, income in the Member State where it is resident for tax purposes.[48] The CCCTB's CFC regime further strengthens the principle of the substance over form and, consequently, the restriction of using interposed entities assisting in the enforcement of the anti-abuse provision.[49]

More precisely, under the CCCTB proposal, the CFC rules are limited to the entities and PEs located in third countries as the rest, i.e. the ones located in the EU, are commonly taxed in accordance with the CCCTB legislation and the FA scheme. In the timeframe, though, where only the first phase of the 2016 CCCTB is implemented, the CFC rules may still be applicable within the EU as the common way to form the taxable base does not prevent countries from establishing CFCs in other EU countries. If the consolidation phase also takes place, then it is not important if CFC applies between EU countries as only one tax base will exist and profits will be allocated according to the FA. Consolidation is undoubtedly the most far-reaching component and it is this that it seems to create major budgetary and administrative burdens for taxpayers and tax authorities, leading to some Member States' hesitation to approve the CCCTB Directive.

3.2. Application of the proposed CCCTB CFC rules to EU Member States

The application of CFC rules may lead to practical difficulties when analysing an EU company that constitutes part of a CCCTB group. Article 59 of the CCCTB proposal prescribes the conditions triggering the application of CFC rules whereas Article 60 specifies the way to calculate the tax base. The CCCTB, in contrast to BEPS, has not provided extensive recommendations or clarifications for what should be attributable in the taxable base of a parent company and/or of a CFC. In this regard, one may conclude that the CCCTB is insufficient for addressing how the elimination of double taxation could occur.

Nevertheless, in accordance with the carve out rule of Article 52 (2), the CFC rules should not be applied in the case of a third country being party to the European Economic Area Agreement (hereafter EEAA) or in the case of an agreement on the exchange of information (hereafter AEoI) comparable to the exchange of information on request provided in the Mutual Assistance Directive. This provision constitutes an escape clause and a waiver of CFC rules that are limited to third countries being party of EEA or having AEoI. It shall not be considered as discriminatory as the reasoning behind this is the need to counteract tax avoid-

---

48 Loyens&Loeff, *The CCTB and CCCTB proposals: Huge Impact Expected for Company Taxation*, Nov. 2016, Special Edition, pg. 11.
49 G. Maisto and P. Pistone, *A European Model for member states' Legislation on the taxation of the controlled foreign subsidiaries – Part 1*, IBD (2008), pg. 505.

ance that is confronted by such agreements. This is a fact that indicates that such companies have been set up for *valid* commercial reasons and reflect economic reality.[50] Therefore, to avoid a potential claim of discriminatory treatment of companies located in third countries, the provisions mentioned above have been inserted in the CCCTB's CFC rules. Second, with regard to PEs, CFC rules do not apply if the CFC income does not constitute more than one third of the total income of the controlling company. The CFC income that will be included in the CCCTB shall be calculated based on the general rules of the CCCTB directive in proportion to the entitlement of the taxpayer to share the profits of the CFC.

As to the material scope of the CCCTB's CFC rules, they should be applied by the Member State to the entity or PE whose profits are not subject to tax or are tax exempt in the Member State where the entity is tax resident or the PE is situated. This applies if the following conditions are cumulatively met: **a)** the taxpayer by itself or together with associated enterprises[51] directly or indirectly holds more than 50% of the capital or the voting rights or is entitled to receive more than 50% of the profits of an entity and **b)** the actual corporate tax paid by the entity or PE is lower than the difference between the corporate tax that would have been charged on the entity or PE under the CCCTB rules and the actual corporate tax paid on those profits. To put it simpler, the CFC rules apply if the actual CIT paid by the CFC is less than half of the CIT that would have been paid in the Member State of the taxpayer.[52]

Moreover, the foreign income that will be included in the taxpayer's tax base should be calculated according to the CCCTB rules. The losses of a CFC or PE should not be included in the tax base but should be carried forward to reduce the CFC income in the coming years. In the case that a CFC distributes profits that have already been calculated and included in the taxpayer's tax base pursuant to the CFC legislation, and the taxpayer is liable to tax on those profits, the CFC income previously included in the tax base should be deducted from the tax base when calculating the taxpayer's tax liability on the distributed profits. This is how to prevent that the CFC income is taxed twice in the hands of the same taxpayer.[53]

It is evident that, in the case of adoption of the CCCTB, its CFC rules will be implemented uniformly as common legislation while the national CFC rules, most of which were implemented by the ATAD, will only be apply to those undertakings that do not fall under CCCTB's scope. This is, namely, the undertakings with third countries and low tax jurisdiction outside of the EU. Tax exemptions will

---

50 C-196/04 Cadbury Schweppes, par. 67 states that the factors that need to be considered for testifying the existence of economic reality are a) staff, b) equipment, and c) premises.
51 Associated enterprises are determined on the basis of a direct or indirect participation in terms of voting rights or capital ownership exceeding 20% or the possibility to exercise significant influence on the management of the entity.
52 Loyens&Loeff, *The CCTB and CCCTB proposals: Huge Impact Expected for Company Taxation*, pg. 11.
53 Loyens&Loeff, *The CCTB and CCCTB proposals: Huge Impact Expected for Company Taxation*, pg. 12.

apply to the income already taxed under the CFC rules as a way to prevent double taxation. This means that dividend distributions will be exempted by the CFC up to the extent that the profit corresponds to income already taxed under the CFC rules. The same goes for the proceeds from disposals of shares in the CFC that will be exempted up to the amount of undistributed income that has already been taxed under the CFC legislation.

3.3. Provision within the ATAD I for another set of CFC rules

This chapter provides insights into the impact and the implementation of the CFC rules in the EU Anti-Tax Avoidance Directive 2016/1164. The ATAD I, which constitutes part of a package presented by the EU Commission in January 2016, was adopted by the ECOFIN Council in July 2016.[54]

The 2011 CCCTB proposal that contained, for the first time, CFC rules aiming to be commonly established within the EU, did not manage to be approved. Therefore, the commission decided to also enact them within the ATAD as the ATAD seemed to be easier to get approved by all Member States, as indeed happened, and hence CFCs rules are now introduced in all EU legislations. The main aim of the ATAD I, which was transposed to all EU national legislations by December 2018, was to provide a minimum level of protection for the internal market and to ensure a harmonized and coordinated approach to the implementation of the OECD BEPS Project.[55] The ATAD I provides a minimum harmonization in the frame of the CFC legislation by allowing the EU Member State where the parent company is located to tax certain profits that the company would shift to another country that imposes low or even zero tax and to combat that way against aggressive tax planning within the internal market. In a case where a country had already adopted national CFC rules prior to the approval of the ATAD, and if the national CFC rules had stricter provisions and higher thresholds than the ATAD's, then the national CFC shall be applied. This is because the ATAD's CFC rules consist simply of the minimum standard that needs to be established within the EU.

The ATAD's CFC rules attribute the undistributed income of a foreign company or a PE to a domestic parent company so that such income will be included in the taxable income of the domestic taxpayer.[56] This means that CFC rules have a double function. They prevent the ability to defer actual taxation at the level of the controlling shareholder until its actual distribution. They also prevent the base erosion of the tax base of the residence state of the controlling shareholder.

---

54 https://data.consilium.europa.eu/doc/document/ST-10672-2016-INIT/en/pdf.
55 https://www2.deloitte.com/content/dam/Deloitte/global/Documents/Tax/dttl-tax-eu-anti-tax-avoidance-directive-implementation-of-controlled-foreign-company-rules.pdf.
56 O. Bokan, *CFC definition under the Anti-Tax Avoidance Directive*, Chapter 10.

According to the ATAD's Article 7, the following conditions should be met in order to treat an entity or a PE as a CFC, i.e. **a)** the taxpayer by itself or together with its associated enterprises shall hold a direct or indirect participation of more than 50% of the voting rights or of capital or is entitled to receive more than 50% of the entity's profits and **b)** the actual corporate tax rate paid on its profits is lower than the difference between the corporate tax that would have been charged on the entity or PE under the applicable corporate tax system in the Member State of the taxpayer and the actual corporate tax paid on its profits by the entity or PE.

3.4. Interaction between the CCCTB's and the ATAD's I CFC rules and potential implications of parallel application

Some Member States already had CFC rules before the implementation of the ATAD I. As a consequence, the states that already had rules in the areas covered by the ATAD I had to amend them only to the extent that they did not meet the minimum prescribed by the ATAD. However, the rules which were stricter did not need to be modified and remained so according to each state's will. In contrast, if a state does not have national CFC rules at all, it needs to introduce rules that give effect to the ATAD's CFC legislation.

It is evident that the CCCTB's and the ATAD's CFC rules contain the same thresholds and economic requirements to activate their application. This is despite the fact that the wording is not identical and some paraphrasing has taken place as it would not be understandable to have varying degrees of control in the two CFC regimes. However, then what are the distinct elements of the two regimes, and what are their main differences? There shall be some, otherwise, it would show negligence from the EU's side to approve and apply two different and inconsistent set of CFC rules within different legislative tools that, however, seem identical.

First of all, the objectives of the CCCTB and the ATAD slightly differ from each other. The CCCTB's primary goal is to establish a common corporate tax base while the ATAD I serves more as an anti-tax avoidance tool. This is visible from the wording selected in which, in the ATAD I, tax avoidance is noted as one of the main purposes while, in the CCCTB, it is its essential purpose. Additionally, the CCCTB has a limited scope, and it applies only to legal entities and, more precisely, to **i)** those who have a turnover exceeding EUR 750 million or **ii)** to those who opt in for the establishment of a CCCTB. The ATAD I, from the other side, applies to corporate legal entities and to individual taxpayers. It should be noted that, whereas the ATAD is a minimum standards directive, the CCTB and the CCCTB proposals are far more prescriptive.

To make the interaction of the CFC legislation in the CCCTB Directive and the ATAD clear, one should comprehend that the CCCTB Directive includes rules able to address some of the fundamental actions of the OECD initiative against BEPS for which actions have been incorporated in the form of minimum standards in the adopted ATAD. It should, though, be expected that the CCCTB incorporates the anti-tax avoidance elements of the ATAD within the new legal context, *"meaning that the norms should be part of a common EU-wide corporate tax system and lay down absolute rules, rather than minimum standards"*.[57] Both the CCCTB Directive and the ATAD with the incorporated CFC rules aim to contribute to the same wider object, i.e. the elimination of tax obstacles that impede the proper functioning of the EU market and make the EU tax system more robust and resilient to aggressive tax planning. On the one part, however, the CCCTB tries to achieve this goal by eliminating the mismatches and the distortions caused by the interaction of 27 different tax systems. It attempts to do so by harmonizing the corporate tax base and by attributing income to where the real economic activity and value is created through the established FA. The ATAD, on the other part, constitutes a tool aiming to tackle BEPS and to make the EU market more sustainable and resistant to tax planning by removing the barriers to the smooth functioning of the internal market. Both directives, though, stipulate and include CFC rules in their provisions as a SAAR. This is because there is a wish to reattribute the income of low-taxed controlled subsidiaries to their parent company in an effort to discourage profit shifting and to curb any abusive practices of a cross-border nature.

As described above, situations may arise for which the CFC regime overlaps with the national CFC regime. This would constitute a potential risk of double taxation since the income of the CFC will be taxed both by the company and the individual shareholder. Such situations though should not be left to the national legislators without any coordination as there is the risk of creating *inconsistent provisions able to affect the CCCTB*[58] and distort the single European market due to mismatches. As small differences have been noticed between the two different sets of rules, the author's recommendation would be the initiation of a third draft of the CCCTB proposal. It would make the CFC rules along with other similar SAARs more robust, and they will not present differences with the already established CFCs rules of the ATAD I. Another suggestion would be to eliminate and delete from the existing CCCTB proposal the references made to SAARs already well documented under the ATAD I and established in the Member States so that the CCCTB focuses mostly on its main scope that is nothing other than the implementation of a common corporate consolidated EU tax base. Otherwise, clarifications shall be provided to the EU's tax authorities as to what they are supposed to implement in the case that both CFC rules are applicable.

---

57 https://ec.europa.eu/taxation_customs/sites/taxation/files/com_2016_685_en.pdf.
58 Working Document, International aspects in the CCCTB, CCCTB/WP/019 (18 November 2015), par. 43.

4. Conclusions

The 2011 proposal for the CCCTB Directive, relaunched in 2016, has not been approved so far, and it does not even seem likely to obtain such agreement any time soon. On the contrary, the ATAD, by introducing a pragmatic approach and setting out specific initiatives, took effect prior to the CCCTB and introduced, in 2016, a minimum level of protection for all Member States' corporate tax systems. Articles 8 and 9 of the ATAD relating to the implemented CFC rules, were also already foreseen in the CCCTB proposal despite the fact that the wording was slightly different. CFCs are generally considered to be in line with the outcome of Action 3 of the OECD/G20 BEPS Project. While the CFC regime within the ATAD I is clear and seems to fulfill the objectives set therein, within the CCCTB, the CFC rules are not that watertight and well explained. This is maybe because the main objective of the CCCTB is the establishment of a common tax base within the EU, and the CFC rules simply play a supportive and ancillary role to the main goal. The CCCTB aims to offer a holistic approach to the problem of tax avoidance. Therefore, it is important to ensure that, in the shorter term, the 27 national corporate rules are coordinated and effectively address aggressive tax planning and this is what the ATAD I succeeded in doing. However, in the case of a future CCCTB approval, it seems that the Member States will not be certain which CFC rules shall be applied towards the third states, i.e. the CFC predicted in the ATAD I that are already applicable or the new CFC rules that will be predicted in the CCCTB Directive. It is hence of high importance that clarifications are provided on the interaction between the different sets of CFC rules.

Last, but not least, the CCCTB is a very ambitious project. If adopted, it will dramatically change the EU's corporate taxation. Thus, the fact that a potential adoption of the CCCTB might cause serious interpretational issues is of high importance. The application of its rules as well as their interplay with the ATAD's rules will need to be clarified by the commission because many questions will be raised which, at the moment, are far from being resolved or clarified.

CFC Rules and Global Minimum Tax

Benjamin Florian Vlasich

1. **Preamble/Introduction**
2. **Limitation of CFC Rules**
    2.1. CFC Rules in the U.S. and the European Union
    2.2. Limitation of CFC Rules
    2.3. The Harmful Race to the Bottom
3. **Global Minimum Tax the GloBE**
    3.1. BEPS Pillar One and Pillar Two Timeline
    3.2. The GloBE Proposal
        3.2.1. Multinational Enterprise Group (MNE Group)
        3.2.2. Constituent Entity
        3.2.3. Covered Taxes
        3.2.4. Effective Tax Rate
        3.2.5. GloBE's Tax Base
        3.2.6. Income Inclusion Rule
        3.2.7. Switch over Rule
        3.2.8. Subject to Tax Rule
        3.2.9. Undertaxed Payments Rule
        3.2.10. Rule order of Instruments
    3.3. The technical implementation into domestic law and international tax treaties of the GloBE instruments
        3.3.1. Peculiarities and differences between GloBE and CFC rules
        3.3.2. Limitation of the GloBE Proposal and Future Perspectives
4. **Conclusion**

1. Preamble/Introduction

The Organisation for Economic Co-operation and Development (OECD) together with the G20 created the Inclusive Framework, in 2016, in order to address the still remaining and new issues regarding Base Erosion and Profit Shifting (BEPS). The time this thesis was written, the Inclusive Framework consisted of 139 countries and 14 observing organisations, developing and designing cooperatively a new set of rules and instruments. The existing CFC rules, worldwide, may be partly harmonized, as in the European Union (EU), but they are always unilateral, which is an inherent flaw. The Inclusive Framework is confident in achieving a greater tax fairness around the world while creating beneficial effects both for developed and undeveloped countries, with a unified – a multilateral approach.

This thesis focuses on the development of the Inclusive Framework on the GloBE (Global Anti-Base Erosion) proposal on Pillar Two regarding a "Global Minimum Tax". After this introduction (Chapter 1), Chapter 2 will illustrate the existing CFC rules and their limitations as well as flaws, including the still remaining issues and problems of international taxation that the CFC regimes could not solve entirely. The harmful race to the bottom will be described in detail, taking into account worldwide data on corporate income tax rates. Chapter 3 starts with the history of the GloBE proposal, followed by the important mechanics and details of the Report on Pillar Two Blueprint from October 2020. The GloBE will be summarized, the 4 main instruments will be illustrated including a brief critical account. It will then provide a comparison between existing CFC regimes and the GloBE, followed by the limitations and future perspectives of the GloBE proposal. Chapter 4 presents the concluding comments.

For the GloBE proposal, the effective implementation into a diverse international legal framework is the key to introducing new interlocking rules, as well as the commitment and execution of the states being a critical task. The European fundamental freedoms, the existing bilateral double tax treaties, the respective national tax rules including already existing CFC regimes all need to be respected when to setting out rules that not only function, but rules that are legally binding, efficient and are comprehensive in order to fulfil the BEPS-targets.

2. Limitation of CFC Rules

2.1. CFC Rules in the U.S. and the European Union

The first CFC (Controlled-Foreign-Company) rule was introduced in the United States of America. The ratification of Subpart F in 1962 was deemed to be the first CFC rule worldwide. The CFC- regime was designed to prevent U.S. citizens and resident individuals, as well as corporations from using foreign entities to artificially defer taxable income.[1]

---

1 Sebastian Duenas, CFC Rules Around the World, Tax foundation 2019, p. 2.

In 2017, the Tax Cuts and Jobs Act of the United States (TCJA), introduced two rules in addition to the existing Subpart F CFC-Rules[2], namely GILTI (Global Intangible Low Taxed Income) and BEAT (Base Erosion Anti-Abuse Tax). GILTI serves as an extension to the already existing CFC-regime in the United States (U.S.),[3] adding much more complexity to the already extensive Subpart F rules. The principle of GILTI is based on an objective mechanism, as generated income over a certain percentage, calculated from CFC's assets, is deemed to be intangible income, and has to be added to the U.S. tax base. Therefore, it is possible that the so called "tested" income is not generated from intangible or passive income and is deemed to be taxable income in the U.S.[4]

The BEAT is considered as the "mirror rule" to GILTI.[5] The aim of the BEAT is intended to tax companies with over USD 500 Million revenue that significantly reduces their U.S. tax base by making payments to foreign CFC entities.[6] Even with blending out the complexity and the partial inaccuracy of GILTI and BEAT, a unilateral approach is not sufficient, as the mechanics used in order to achieve the set out goals, are often pointless, in particular with the high grade of mobility of the digitalized economy. Moreover, the mechanics of GILTI and BEAT may create double taxation when both regimes apply.[7]

Outdated international tax rules in evolving markets were reasons among others for the report Addressing Base Erosion and Profit Shifting released by the OECD (Organisation for Economic Co-operation and Development) and the G20 countries, in February 2013. Setting out a 15-point Action plan, in particular BEPS (Base Erosion and Profit Shifting) Action 3, provided recommendations for the implementation or improvement of CFC regimes, in order to create coherence in the domestic rules that affect cross-border economic activities, while improving certainty and transparency for all stakeholders.[8] The work of the OECD together with the G20 countries led to the establishment of the Inclusive Framework, in the year 2016,[9] consisting of 139 countries and 14 observing organisations today. For the members of the EU, the BEPS Action 3 plan led to the Anti-Tax Avoidance Directive (ATAD) EU 2016/1164. It introduced five anti-abuse measures, including rule number 4, which is the CFC-rule that had to be embedded in every European country and taken into action, until January 2019.[10]

---

2   Sebastian Duenas, CFC Rules Around the World, Tax foundation 2019, p. 6.
3   Mindy Herzfeld, Can GILTI + BEAT = GLOBE?, INTERTAX Volume 47, Issue 5, p. 505, par. 1.2.
4   Daniel W. Blum, The Proposal for a Global Minimum Tax: Comeback of Residence Taxation in the Digital Era?: Comment on Can GILTI +BEAT = GLOBE?, Intertax, Kluwer Law International 2019,Volume 47, Issue 5., p. 516, par. 2.1.1.
5   Mindy Herzfeld, Can GILTI + BEAT = GLOBE?, INTERTAX Volume 47, p.510, par. 2.2.
6   Mindy Herzfeld, Can GILTI + BEAT = GLOBE?, INTERTAX Volume 47, p. 511, par. 2.2.
7   Mindy Herzfeld, Can GILTI + BEAT = GLOBE?, INTERTAX Volume 47, p. 513, par. 2.2.
8   OECD 2020, Tax Challenges Arising from Digitalisation – Report on Pillar Two Blueprint, p. 3.
9   OECD (2020), Tax Challenges Arising From Digitalisation – Report on Pillar One Blueprint. p.3.
10 Deloitte (2020), EU Anti Tax Avoidance Directive, Implementation of interest expense limitation rule, p. 1.

The CFC Rules of the ATAD are minimum standards.[11] Countries like Austria for instance, implemented and enforced their first CFC Rule for business years starting from the 1st January 2019.[12] The type of income covered by the ATAD is passive income. Passive income or synonymously intangible income is generated in its essence by income out of interests, licenses, dividends, and royalties.

2.2. Limitation of CFC Rules

In its essence, CFC rules may be considered as prophylactic rules that prevent profit shifting and base erosion from resident taxpayers in one country to controlled foreign companies in low or no tax countries.[13] While, the main purpose of CFC rules may be clear, the scope and the details of the mechanics of the different CFC rules worldwide vary. One characteristic most of the existing CFC rules have in common is the limitation on the type of income that is generated. This is due to the fact that CFC rules basically only focus on passive income.[14]

Another limitation is that unilateral approaches, like the U.S., or even harmonized CFC approaches in the EU, are only able to address a certain number of base erosion and profit shifting by multinational companies. By combining overlapping and diametrically working rulings that partly work against the overall idea and targets, a success can not be granted.[15]

The digitalization of the economy makes it very easy for a company to set up a new branch, subsidiary or to even shift their headquarters. With different states and different unilateral approaches in CFC rulings, combined with the motivation of countries to attract new companies, multinational companies may always be one step ahead. In addition to that, every new CFC rule increases the risk of double taxation as well as the bureaucracy, and this can be seen as obstacles for international trading, as well as a limitation of the efficiency of CFC rules per se. Double non-taxation is another issue that is, presently, not entirely solved by CFC regimes.

While existing CFC rules have limitations, they may still work partly as a Blueprint for the GloBE. However, the U.S. CFC law, for example, is based on a diverse number of additional laws that would need to be implemented in order to work as such. In addition, the criticism regarding GILTI and BEAT, especially the overlap between these two regimes that lead to a double taxation in certain cases,

---

11 Deloitte (2020), EU Anti Tax Avoidance Directive, Implementation of interest expense limitation rule, p. 1.
12 Section 10a Austrian Corporate Income Tax Act.
13 Brian J. Arnold, The Evolution of Controlled Foreign Corporation Rules and Beyond, Bulletin for International Taxation, (Amsterdam: IBFD, 2019), p. 633, cap. 3.1.
14 Brian J. Arnold, The Evolution of Controlled Foreign Corporation Rules and Beyond, Bulletin for International Taxation, (Amsterdam: IBFD, 2019), p. 642, p. 6.1.
15 Daniel W. Blum, The Proposal for a Global Minimum Tax: Comeback of Residence Taxation in the Digital Era?: Comment on Can GILTI +BEAT = GLOBE?, Blum p. 518, par. 2.1.2.

are points that the Inclusive Framework has to refrain from copying.[16] Furthermore, as one of the targets of the CFC rules is to hinder or discourage multinationals to take advantage of patent boxes, the U.S. introduced the FDII (Foreign-Derived Intangible Income) together with GILTI and BEAT. The FDII creates a preferential tax regime for intangible income that may be considered as a counterpart to GILTI and BEAT.[17]

This being said, a fact that should act as role model for the Inclusive Framework is the fact to combine different instruments. However, combining different systems requires a clearly defined ruling to prevent taxpayers from unequal treatment and/or double taxation, and finally, an unproportionate increase in bureaucracy.

2.3. The Harmful Race to the Bottom

The harmful race to the bottom of tax rates may be an indicator for bias and ineffectiveness of existing tax systems including CFC-rules. The harmful race to the bottom is defined as the pursuit of developed, as well as underdeveloped countries to lower their taxes to be considered more attractive for the tax planning of multinational companies. As a result, governments will increase taxes on less mobile bases like labour or consumption.[18]

During the last years, European countries have lowered their corporate income tax rates considerably. The average corporate income tax rate, and as a result, the effective average tax rates for large corporations, have decreased from 22,7% in 2006 to 19,7% in 2019:

a decrease by 13% in 13 years.[19] Note that the lowering of corporate income tax is neither an isolated European nor a western country phenomenon with corporate income tax rates declining, since the year 1980.

In 1980, average corporate tax rate, worldwide, was around 40%, whereas in 2020, the average CIT was around 24%.[20] Developed and/or western countries are, in particular, nations that have lowered their corporate income taxes.[21] Furthermore, within the last decades, the European countries almost halved their average corporate income tax and the Asian countries and the North American countries more drasticly.

16　Daniel W. Blum, The Proposal for a Global Minimum Tax: Comeback of Residence Taxation in the Digital Era?: Comment on Can GILTI +BEAT = GLOBE?, Intertax, Kluwer Law International 2019,Volume 47, Issue 5, p. 522, par. 3.
17　Daniel W. Blum, The Proposal for a Global Minimum Tax: Comeback of Residence Taxation in the Digital Era?: Comment on Can GILTI +BEAT = GLOBE?, Blum p. 518, par. 2.1.2.
18　OECD (2019), Addressing the tax challenges of the Digitalisation of the economy, Public Consultation Document, p. 24, cap 3.1 par. 90.
19　Report project for EU Commission DG TAXUD, Section C of ZEW (2019), Data on Taxation, Effective Average Tax Rates for large corporations in non-financial sector.
20　Elke Asen, TAX FOUNDATION (2019), Corporate Tax Rates around the World, 2019, No- 679, p.1.
21　Elke Asen, TAX FOUNDATION (2019), Corporate Tax Rates around the World, 2019, No- 679, p.10.

The lowest average decrease, in corporate income tax, may be seen in South America. The average CIT, in the 1980, was around 36% compared to the G7 countries, in the 1980, with an average CIT of 50%, this figure was low. Today, the average corporate income tax in South America is around 27%, which is considered as definitely above the global average rate of around 24%. Nonetheless, almost all countries in the world lowered their CIT's over the last four decades.[22] The lowering of corporate income taxes may be seen as an indicator for global changes and bias of the economy, as the lowering of the CIT is a rather blunt and not effective unilateral measure. Seemingly, to a unilateral CFC approach, the overall effects are limited.

3. Global Minimum Tax the GloBE

3.1. BEPS Pillar One and Pillar Two Timeline

After the worldwide financial crisis starting in the year 2008 and 2009, the G20 leaders decided to take measures in order to prevent the global economy from a similar economic crisis in the future. Therefore, the exchange of information was key for more transparency in the financial markets. More transparency will lead to a higher level of protection against bad business practices, fraudulent behaviour and last but not least aggressive tax planning by multinational enterprises.[23] In September 2013, together with the OECD and other international stake holders, the G20 leaders endorsed the BEPS Action Plan. The 15 reports of the BEPS package were agreed upon, in Antalya in November 2015, by the OECD members as well as the G20 leaders.[24] The Inclusive Framework was established in 2016, with the great advantage being that it included an increasing number of countries, while not excluding developing countries.[25] This broadens the acceptance of the treaties and should prevent legal difficulties, as more jurisdictions are involved.

The right to "tax back" was proposed by the Inclusive Framework, in 2019, to effectively close the still existing loopholes and gaps in the globalized and artificially architected world of multinational companies. The measures and instruments of Pillar Two are planned to go further than other rules worldwide.[26]

As stated above the BEPS Action plan consists of 15 reports on different actions. BEPS Action 1 is specifically addressing the tax challenges of the digital economy

---

22 Elke Asen, TAX Foundation (2019), Corporate Tax Rates around the World, 2019, No- 679, p.10–11.
23 OECD/G20 (2017), Harmful Tax Practices- Peer Review Reports on the Exchange of Information on Tax Ruling, pp. 17–19
24 OECD/G20 (2017), Harmful Tax Practices- Peer Review Reports on the Exchange of Information on Tax Ruling, p..3.
25 OECD (2020), Tax Challenges Arising From Digitalization – Report on Pillar Two Blueprint. p. 3.
26 OECD (2020), Tax Challenges Arising From Digitalization – Report on Pillar Two Blueprint. p. 3.

and is divided into two Pillars. The TFDE (Task Force on the Digital Economy) presented the split of BEPS Action 1 into two Pillars, in January 2019.[27]

Then, in May 2019, the Programme of Work (PoW) for Addressing the Tax Challenges of the Digitalisation of the Economy was presented by the Inclusive Framework.[28]

Sharing the same history, Pillar One and Pillar Two have many touching points. However, Pillar One is focusing on rules that need to be implemented in order to tax global interacting multinational digital companies at the point of sale, following the nexus approach and other rules for profit allocation. Thus, the core of Pillar Two is the GloBE proposal.[29]

With Pillar One, the Inclusive Framework proposed a "Unified Approach" based on the Action 1 Report of the OECD/G20.[30] This approach grants taxing rights to countries and jurisdiction, where multinational companies generate high amounts of revenue and profits without being liable to paying taxes.[31]. By contrast to Pillar One, the Pillar Two GloBE's instruments are not designed to be limited to the highly digitalized economy. Critics say that Pillar One and Pillar Two could be interpreted as following different directions, as Pillar One tries to tax income at the level of the source country and Pillar Two at the level of the resident country.[32]

However, Pillar One and Two measures are designed to have intersecting mechanisms seeking to result in a mutually reinforcing effect, due to the Inclusive Framework.[33]

3.2. The GloBE Proposal

Based on the OECD Secretariat's update, on the 31st January 2020, on the status of Pillar Two, which illustrated technical aspects of Pillar Two's GloBE, four supplementary instruments were suggested. The Income Inclusion Rule (IIR), the Switch-over Rule (SoR), the Subject to tax rule (STTR) and the Under-taxed payment rule (UTPR). These instruments were established to prevent Base Erosion and Profit Shifting (BEPS).[34]

---

27 OECD (2019), Addressing the Tax Challenges of the Digitalisation of the Economy- Policy Note, OECD Publishing Paris p. 1, par. 1.2.
28 OECD (2019), Global Anti-Base Erosion Proposal ("GloBE") – Pillar Two, Public consultation document, OECD Publishing, Paris p. 3.
29 OECD (2019), Global Anti-Base Erosion Proposal ("GloBE") – Pillar Two, Public consultation document, OECD Publishing, Paris p. 3.
30 OECD (2020), Tax Challenges Arising From Digitalisation – Report on Pillar One Blueprint. p.10, par. 2 5.
31 OECD (2020), Tax Challenges Arising From Digitalisation – Report on Pillar One Blueprint. p.11, par. 6.
32 Michael P. Devereux, The OECD Global Anti-Base Erosion ("GloBE") proposal, Oxford University Centre for Business Taxation, January 2020, p. 2, par. 3.
33 OECD (2019), Programme of Work to Develop a Consensus Solution to the Tax Challenges Arising from the Digitalisation of the Economy, OECD Publishing, Paris. p. 6, par. 8.
34 OECD (2020), Statement by the OECD/G20 Inclusive Framework on BEPS on the Two-Pillar Approach to Address the Tax Challenges Arising from the Digitalisation of the Economy, OECD Publishing Paris, Annex 2.

With the Blueprint of Pillar Two, released in October 2020 by the OECD Secretariat, the definition and the mechanics, as well as the interaction and the ranking of the instruments, were presented in detail.[35] Essentially, there are four instruments where the IIR and the UTPR use a common tax base and similar calculations and the same definition of taxes covered.[36] The four instruments are designed to be interlocking, the main instrument designed is the IIR supported by the UTPR, which provides a main function as a backstop in case the IIR is not allowed to tax.[37] The Subject to Tax Rule (STTR) complements the IIR and the UTPR by denying specific treaty benefits; for example, certain deductible intragroup payments to low tax jurisdiction.[38] In addition to the IIR, the Switch-Over Rule (SoR) is designed, in certain events, to provide a switch from the exemption method to the credit method, in cases where the exemption method is mutually agreed in the existing double tax treaty between the source jurisdiction and the resident jurisdiction, and thus effectively supports the IIR. As otherwise an agreed exemption method would hinder the IIR to work[39]

Before describing the GloBE Instruments in detail, certain important terminology have to be explained, such as: the Multinational Enterprise Group (MNE Group), Constituent Entity, Effective Tax Rate (ETR), GloBE's Tax Base and the Covered Taxes.

3.2.1. Multinational Enterprise Group (MNE Group)

The definition of an MNE Group, and the calculation of the revenue of an MNE Group, is key for the GloBE Instruments. Only groups of companies that exceed a yearly revenue of EUR 750 million are considered to be MNE Groups under the definition of Pillar Two. An MNE group consists of different entities in different jurisdictions.[40] The calculation of the revenue of the MNE group will be made using the "Consolidated Revenue Threshold", computing the group revenue for the fiscal year of the parent company based on financial accounts in accordance with the accounting standards of the parent company.[41] The threshold of EUR 750 Million is identical with the threshold for Multinational Groups under Pillar One and the BEPS Action 13 Country-by-Country Reporting (CbCR), provides synergies with the CbCR rules.[42]

---

35 OECD (2020), Tax Challenges Arising From Digitalization – Report on Pillar Two Blueprint.
36 OECD (2020), Tax Challenges Arising From Digitalization – Report on Pillar Two Blueprint. p. 112, par. 412–413.
37 OECD (2020), Tax Challenges Arising From Digitalization – Report on Pillar Two Blueprint. p.14, par. 8–9.
38 OECD (2020), Tax Challenges Arising From Digitalization – Report on Pillar Two Blueprint. p.14, par. 11.
39 OECD (2020), Tax Challenges Arising From Digitalization – Report on Pillar Two Blueprint. p. 121, par. 453–455.
40 OECD (2020) Tax Challenges Arising From Digitalization – Report on Pillar Two Blueprint. p. 40, cap. 2.4.
41 OECD (2020) Tax Challenges Arising From Digitalization – Report on Pillar Two Blueprint. p. 15, par 14.
42 OECD (2020) Tax Challenges Arising From Digitalization – Report on Pillar Two Blueprint. p. 41, par. 119.

3.2.2. Constituent Entity

The next important term is "Constituent Entity". It defines any separate business unit of an MNE Group that is to include in the consolidated financial statement of an MNE Group and any permanent establishment of any separate business unit. In addition, a Constitute Entity is also a separate business unit that is not in the consolidated financial statement solely on size and material grounds.[43] The term "Ultimate Parent Entity" (UPE) defines the constituent entity that owns directly or indirectly sufficient interest on the other constituent entities of the MNE Group, and no other constituent entity holds interests on the UPE.[44]

3.2.3. Covered Taxes

Another essential term for the usage of the GloBE instruments is the definition of the "Covered Taxes". The attributable income of a constituent entity is taxed by the jurisdiction that has the taxing right over this entity. All taxes paid by the entity, include taxes on income or profit depending on the jurisdiction, as well as taxes imposed in lieu of a general income tax, taxes on retained earnings, or corporate equity as well as taxes for distributed profits.[45] By contrast to covered taxes, there are specifically non-covered taxes listed in the Blueprint of Pillar Two. In general, the taxes that are levied on sold products or services are not covered, such as consumption- or sales tax or VAT. Furthermore, duties and excise taxes are considered to be non-covered taxes. In addition, payroll taxes and social security contributions, as well as property taxes, are considered as non-covered taxes.[46]

3.2.4. Effective Tax Rate

The "Effective Tax Rate" (ETR) for MNE Groups and every constituent entity is a critical and important point. Only if the ETR is below a defined threshold (agreed minimum rate), it will determine if the instruments of the GloBE are triggered or not. The calculation of the ETR is defined by dividing the amount of covered taxes by the amount of income of the respective constituent entity of the jurisdiction.[47] The divisor of the previous simplified division is the "GloBE`s Tax Base", which is an adjusted tax base originated from the profit or loss before taxes of the respective constitute entity.[48] On a jurisdictional basis, a blending has to be made, and the income and taxes paid of every constituent entity is calculated in respect of consolidated adjustments made on entities level.[49]

---

43 OECD (2020) Tax Challenges Arising From Digitalization – Report on Pillar Two Blueprint. p. 24 par. 42.
44 OECD (2020) Tax Challenges Arising From Digitalization – Report on Pillar Two Blueprint. p. 24 par. 42.
45 OECD (2020) Tax Challenges Arising From Digitalization – Report on Pillar Two Blueprint. p. 46 par. 128.
46 OECD (2020) Tax Challenges Arising From Digitalization – Report on Pillar Two Blueprint. p. 50–51, cap. 3.2.8.
47 OECD (2020) Tax Challenges Arising From Digitalization – Report on Pillar Two Blueprint. p. 45, par. 127.
48 OECD (2020) Tax Challenges Arising From Digitalization – Report on Pillar Two Blueprint. p. 51, chap. 3.3.
49 OECD (2020), Tax Challenges Arising From Digitalization – Report on Pillar Two Blueprint. p.72, par. 248.

3.2.5. GloBE's Tax Base

The GloBE Tax Base is one of the most important definitions of Pillar Two, as it influences the "trigger-mechanism" as a divisor of the ETR. Then again, it reveals uncertainty, or the vastest area of definitions needed. The fundamental proposed rule regarding the calculation of the GloBE's tax base is, that the financial standard in order to calculate the tax base for the MNE Group, is always the financial accounting standard used by the parent company for preparing the consolidated financial statements. The acceptable accounting standards are IFRS and any equivalent financial accounting standard. An example for acceptable accounting standards is the accounting standards of countries like Canada, Japan, Singapore, Republic of China and the United States. In addition, the GloBE's tax base can also be permitted to be calculated by the UPE's tax jurisdiction accounting standards for financial reporting purposes, as long as the standard will not result in a competitive misuse in the application of the GloBE rules.[50] Before the disclosure of the Blueprint, critics pointed out that IFRS (International Financial Reporting Standards) may be a starting point and by introducing appropriate adjustments, the GloBE's proposal would have the best chance to succeed.[51]

The author's perspective, the topic of the computation of the tax base is a very critical point because of the presence of different accounting standards and different tax laws within jurisdictions of an MNE. In addition to intra group businesses the risk of miscalculation due to adjustments is further increased. Experts stated that a uniform determination of the tax base would decrease compliance and administrative costs, while making mutual assistance between tax authorities more efficient.[52] This is one of the pursuit targets of the Inclusive Framework.

3.2.6. Income Inclusion Rule

The IIR is an instrument that functions undoubtedly in its essence, similar to existing CFC rules worldwide. The basic mechanic is comparable with CFC mechanics, as foreign income from controlled entities under certain conditions has to be taxed on the level of the parent company.[53] The IIR provides the UPE in the parent's jurisdiction with the obligation to pay taxes over generated profits, that are taxed under an agreed minimum tax in a low-tax jurisdiction.[54] The taxation of foreign in-

---

50 OECD (2020) Tax Challenges Arising From Digitalization – Report on Pillar Two Blueprint. p. 51, chap. 3.3.
51 Joachim Englisch, Johannes Becker, World Tax Journal, 2019 (Volume 11), No. 4, United States/EEA/European Union/G20/OECD/International – International Effective Minimum Taxation – The GloBE Proposal, p.15, par 3.2.4.2.
52 Pasquale Pistone, Joao Felix Pinto Nogueira, Betty Andrade, Alessandro Turina, OECD – The OECD Public Consultation Document "Global Anti-Base Erosion (CloBE) Proposal – Pillar Two": An Assessment, Bulletin for International Taxation, Volume 74 (2020), p. 13, chap 2.3.1.
53 OECD 2020, Tax Challenges Arising from Digitalisation – Report on Pillar Two Blueprint, p 112, par. 411.
54 OECD 2020, Tax Challenges Arising from Digitalisation – Report on Pillar Two Blueprint, p 112, par. 410.

come from controlled foreign companies on the level of the parent company is the basic mechanic of a CFC rule. This mechanic is now used for the IIR.

The calculation has two levels. Firstly, with jurisdictional blending, an overall tax base, is calculated for the individual potential low-tax jurisdiction. Therefore, a calculation for every jurisdiction having one or more constituent entities is made. In fact, it does not matter how many constituent entities are directly or indirectly held by the UPE, all covered taxes have to be divided by the overall generated profit in the individual jurisdiction, in order to calculate the ETR. Resulting in the conclusion that the jurisdiction where constituent entities are based, is a low-tax-jurisdiction, or not. In the event the jurisdiction, where constituent entities are based, is eventually considered a low-tax jurisdiction, a "top-up tax" has to be calculated. This top-up tax is calculated on the level of each constituent entity in the low tax jurisdiction that needs to be paid in order to top-up to the minimum agreed tax rate; that is, a top-up to the global minimum tax rate.[55] Secondly, the liability to pay the top up tax amount is allocated to the parent entity. The amount of equity, respective shares owned by the UPE, is respected. Therefore, directly or indirectly held shares of each constituent entity, in the low tax country and the calculated top-up tax, is attributed proportionally to the UPE.[56]

In the event that the IIR is not implemented in the jurisdiction, where the UPE is situated, the IIR can not be triggered. This potential threat has been addressed by critics. Basically, all important developed countries have to incorporate the rule into domestic law.[57] In the event the UPE did not implement the IIR, the nearest constituent entity that has an IIR introduced, is liable for a potential top-up tax: this is called the "top-down approach".[58] This mechanic tries to make the IIR effective even in the event that the UPE has not implemented the IIR, possibly because the UPE is not in a jurisdiction included in the Inclusive Framework.

Critics confirmed that the IIR shares many similarities with existing CFCs, and proposed that instead of implementing a new set of rules, the existing CFC rules worldwide should be effectively harmonized and extended.[59] Notwithstanding critics also arguing that the IIR may be the only way to implement a simultaneous CFC rule internationally.[60] Even so, the Inclusive Framework stated: to "explore" the development of rules to preserve integrity of the GloBE rules in connection with a decrease of compliance costs and bureaucracy, also in respect of the IIR.[61]

---

55 OECD 2020, Tax Challenges Arising from Digitalisation – Report on Pillar Two Blueprint, p 112, par. 412.
56 OECD 2020, Tax Challenges Arising from Digitalisation – Report on Pillar Two Blueprint, p 113, par. 415.
57 Johannes Becker, Joachim Englisch, Internationale Mindestbesteuerung von Unternehmen, p. 646.
58 OECD 2020, Tax Challenges Arising from Digitalisation – Report on Pillar Two Blueprint, p 113, par. 417.
59 Brian J. Arnold, The Evolution of Controlled Foreign Corporation Rules and Beyond, Bulletin for International Taxation, (Amsterdam: IBFD, 2019). p. 631, cap.1, par. 2.
60 Brian J. Arnold, The Evolution of Controlled Foreign Corporation Rules and Beyond, Bulletin for International Taxation, (Amsterdam: IBFD, 2019). p. 646, cap 6.3.2., par. 7.
61 OECD (2020), Tax Challenges Arising From Digitalization – Report on Pillar Two Blueprint. p.117, par. 431.

As an example of this effort, an important IIR detail is the jurisdictional blending, as it simplifies the calculation of the UPE by blending all income and taxes of an individual jurisdiction irrespective of the number of constituent entities or if they are held directly or indirectly by the UPE.[62] By contrast to existing CFC rules, all covered taxes and covered income is being considered in the calculations of the IIR, while existing CFC rules worldwide only consider passive income or income from intangibles. However, an extension of the scope of income of existing CFCs to all income generated by CFC remains a valid option for critics.[63]

3.2.7. Switch over Rule

The Switch over Rule (SoR) is a well-known instrument with regards to international tax treaties that has been proposed by the Pillar Two GloBE proposal. It is important to note that in order to have the SoR work efficiently, the Inclusive Framework states that in the event the parent company receives income from a PE (Permanent Establishment) jurisdiction and the parent jurisdictions exempts the profit of the PE. The PE's income has to be allocated to the PE's jurisdiction to accurately calculate the jurisdictional income tax base and eventually ETR.[64] The reason for this is that otherwise potentially low taxed income from PE's could be blended with high tax income in the parent's jurisdiction.[65]

Furthermore, the SoR is developed to then permit the resident state, this is the jurisdiction where the parent company is located, to switch from an existing exemption method agreed in the applicable double tax treaty with the low-tax jurisdiction, to the credit method.[66] The scope of the SoR may cover foreign subsidiaries, as well as foreign permanent establishments.[67] Without the SoR, the IIR would be useless in case of an mutually agreed exemption method between the source and the resident state, as due to the domestic law of the foreign PE or subsidiary, possibly no taxes are levied in the domestic country, resulting in a double non taxation. Consequently, the SoR ensures that foreign branches, as well as subsidiaries and immovable property situated in the source state, are being taxed in the resident state in case the IIR is triggered.[68] In addition, the SoR is especially

---

62 OECD (2020), Tax Challenges Arising From Digitalization – Report on Pillar Two Blueprint. p.115, par. 423.
63 Brian J. Arnold, The Evolution of Controlled Foreign Corporation Rules and Beyond, Bulletin for International Taxation, (Amsterdam: IBFD, 2019). p. 646, cap 6.3.2., par. 6.
64 OECD (2020), Tax Challenges Arising From Digitalization – Report on Pillar Two Blueprint. p.121, par. 453.
65 OECD (2020), Tax Challenges Arising From Digitalization – Report on Pillar Two Blueprint. p.121, par. 454.
66 OECD (2020), Report to G20 Finance Ministers and Central Bank Governors, Riyadh, Saudi Arabia February 2020, OECD Publishing, Paris, p. 49, par. 14–15.
67 OECD (2020), Tax Challenges Arising From Digitalization – Report on Pillar Two Blueprint. p.121, par. 455.
68 OECD (2020), Statement by the OECD/G20 Inclusive Framework on BEPS on the Two-Pillar Approach to Address the Tax Challenges Arising from the Digitalisation of the Economy, Annex 2. P. 29, par. 114.

effective in the event where the source state defines the income of a branch or subsidiary differently from the resident state. Therefore, in the event of a hybrid mismatch, the SoR prevents from aggressive tax planning via profit shifting.

3.2.8. Subject to Tax Rule

The Subject to Tax Rule (STTR) can be defined as a complement to the undertaxed payment rule. The STTR addresses cross-border BEPS-structures of MNEs, where intragroup payments are used to distort the tax base in the residence via intragroup payments to low tax countries, under existing tax treaty protection.[69] In addition, the STTR is proposed to function in cases where gains are shifted from the jurisdiction of the source country to the residence jurisdiction.[70] The covered payments in a MNE group are interests, royalties, franchise fees, insurance premiums, financing fees or rent for moveable property and similar payments;[71] that is, transactions that may be already covered by existing CFC rules. These transactions and payments have to be agreed upon between "Connected Persons". Connected persons are considered as persons or enterprises when one participant possesses directly either the majority of voting power or more than 50% of the shares.[72] The trigger mechanism is comparable with the IIR if the jurisdiction of the payee taxes the covered payments below the nominal tax rate, the difference to the nominal rate has to be topped up in the payer's jurisdiction otherwise a withholding tax can be imposed.[73]

Noteworthy, in the event these covered payments are forming a part of the income of the permanent establishment in the source state, these payments are excluded from the STTR. Likewise, where the covered payments are used to form a part of the business property in the source jurisdiction, they are out of the scope of the STTR, as this income is to be taxed in the source country.[74] Furthermore, covered payments are excluded that are only low return payments. Low return payments are for example cost plus agreements, where the profit is only marginal.[75]

---

69 OECD (2020), Tax Challenges Arising From Digitalization – Report on Pillar Two Blueprint. p.150, par. 566–567.
70 OECD (2020), Tax Challenges Arising From Digitalization – Report on Pillar Two Blueprint. p.150, par. 569.
71 OECD (2020), Tax Challenges Arising From Digitalization – Report on Pillar Two Blueprint. p.155, par. 589–591.
72 OECD (2020), Tax Challenges Arising From Digitalization – Report on Pillar Two Blueprint. p.153, cap. 9.2.2.
73 OECD (2020), Tax Challenges Arising From Digitalization – Report on Pillar Two Blueprint. p.163, par. 637.
74 OECD (2020), Tax Challenges Arising From Digitalization – Report on Pillar Two Blueprint. p.155, par. 593.
75 OECD (2020), Tax Challenges Arising From Digitalization – Report on Pillar Two Blueprint. p.158, par. 613.

The STTR may lead to an over-taxation, as the top up tax will be applied to the gross amount of the individual covered payment. Therefore, a limitation of the trigger rate, as well as the maximum top up, is under discussion. Even with a limitation, the over taxation is likely, especially in the event where the source jurisdiction applies a withholding tax.[76] Moreover, extensions to the STTR, further exclusions and additional mechanisms are under discussion. The STTR is likely to violate the pursuit targets of the GloBE proposal, as double and over taxation can not be fully mitigated.

3.2.9. Undertaxed Payments Rule

The Undertaxed Payments Rule (UTPR) and the IIR pursue similar targets, while the underlying mechanics are different. The UTPR is a backstop to the IIR and taxes intra group base-eroding payments. This backstop to the IIR potentially decreases the motivation for adjustments to lower the top up tax for a constituent entity in a low-tax country.[77] This back stop mechanism indicates clearly that the IIR has priority over the UTPR. On the one hand, the UTPR is effective, in a case where a constituent entity of a low tax jurisdiction tries to lower the tax base, while not respecting the arm's lengths principle, as an example. On the other hand, in a case where the jurisdiction of the UPE has not implemented an IIR, the subsequent next jurisdiction of a constituent entity that has implemented an IIR, taxes the low tax constituent entity. In the case where this constituent entity holds less shares than the UPE, thus would only receive a partially top up tax, the UTPR is designed to tax the part of the top up tax that would otherwise be lost.[78]

The UTPR uses the same methods of calculation as the IIR in order to calculate the ETR and the top-up tax.[79] Whereas, with the IIR, the UPE or the next following entity is allowed to tax a potential low tax constituent entity, a UTPR-taxpayer consists of one or more constituent entities situated in one jurisdiction and is enabled by domestic law, if the UTPR rule is implemented, to tax a calculated top-up tax.[80] Note, the domestic law that operates the UTPR is not dictated by the GloBE rules. Therefore, the design of the rule will depend on the existing domestic tax system.[81]

---

76 OECD (2020), Tax Challenges Arising From Digitalization – Report on Pillar Two Blueprint. p.167, par. 661–662.
77 OECD (2020), Tax Challenges Arising From Digitalization – Report on Pillar Two Blueprint. p.124, par. 457
78 OECD (2020), Tax Challenges Arising From Digitalization – Report on Pillar Two Blueprint. p.125, par. 460.
79 OECD (2020), Tax Challenges Arising From Digitalization – Report on Pillar Two Blueprint. p.126, par. 467.
80 OECD (2020), Tax Challenges Arising From Digitalization – Report on Pillar Two Blueprint. p.136, par. 517–518.
81 OECD (2020), Tax Challenges Arising From Digitalization – Report on Pillar Two Blueprint. p.136, par. 519.

The UTPR has the potential to create negative effects that need to be avoided through a careful implementation and definition of the rule. The aim is to avoid effects of double taxation and the taxation over the economic profit. The importance to define the way the profit is calculated is essential. Ultimately, a different calculation of profit, as well as a different way of calculating the taxation may result in an excess taxation of the economic profit through double taxation.[82]

3.2.10. Rule order of Instruments

The 4 described GloBE instruments are designed to work in an interlocking manner. The order of the instruments is important, ultimately to grant tax certainty and an effective co-ordination between the different instruments.[83]

The STTR is prior to all other instruments. The IIR is the second instrument followed by the UTPR as a backstop. The SoR complements the IIR rule, as it enhances the IIR to work in cases where the parent jurisdiction has an exemption over the income of a permanent establishment.[84] Thus, the order complements and a ranking for the SoR is, therefore, not given. According to the OECD Report on Pillar Two Blueprint, dated October 2020, the suggested order is STTR, IIR then UTPR.

The reason the STTR precedes the IIR is in the case the STTR is being executed and taxes as covered payment from a source jurisdiction with a top-up tax. Subsequently, this top up tax is taken into account, calculating the ETR under the jurisdictional blending approach at the level of the payee jurisdiction.[85] Therefore, the STTR has to precede the IIR, as the IIR needs to consider the STTR corrections as covered taxes in their calculation of the ETR.

As the rules are complex and the interaction as well as the vast number of possible different economic and legal cases are numerous, the Inclusive Framework will establish model legislation and further guidance in addition to a multilateral convention.[86]

The Inclusive Framework is flexible regarding the time or order of the implementation of the different rules. The IIR may be implemented first and after some time the UTPR should eventually follow.[87] This may be a sign for the overall

---

[82] OECD (2019), Addressing the Tax Challenges of the Digitalisation of the Economy, p. 27, par. 105.
[83] OECD (2020), Tax Challenges Arising From Digitalization – Report on Pillar Two Blueprint. p.171, par. 668.
[84] OECD (2020), Tax Challenges Arising From Digitalization – Report on Pillar Two Blueprint. p.122, par. 456.
[85] OECD (2020), Tax Challenges Arising From Digitalization – Report on Pillar Two Blueprint. p.171, par. 671.
[86] OECD (2020), Tax Challenges Arising From Digitalization – Report on Pillar Two Blueprint. p. 177, par. 697.
[87] OECD (2020), Tax Challenges Arising From Digitalization – Report on Pillar Two Blueprint. p.177, par. 698.

awareness that the instruments and the order of rules are at this point roughly created; however, in order to have them implemented in every jurisdiction and by respecting all pursuit targets, it will take more time and may be a step-by-step approach.

3.3. The technical implementation into domestic law and international tax treaties of the GloBE instruments

The setup of measurements and rules, as described in the former paragraphs, will be agreed, and taken into action by implementation into domestic law. In combination with either an amendment of the existing double tax treaties between the individual countries or by an MLI (Multilateral Convention to Implement Tax Treaty Related Measures to Prevent Base Erosion and Profit Shifting).[88] The MLI should be an agreed international mandatory set of rules that coexists with already existing tax treaties. The existing limits of the MLI can not be adapted towards the regulation of the GloBE,[89] therefore, the Inclusive Framework must develop provisions to be included in a new multilateral convention. These provisions should combine the most important elements of the GloBE instruments with all important mechanics and calculations.[90] Thus, the provisions of the multilateral convention together with the model legislation may increase the pace as well as the efficiency of the realization. A periodical revision of the MLI is recommended by experts.[91]

Furthermore, a coordination or ordering rule to avoid the risk of economic double taxation must be implemented.[92] The IIR and UTPR have to be implemented in domestic law, a model legislation will be established in order to coordinate the international implementation, while having the same standards. As already mentioned above, the jurisdiction may be given the right to stagger the instruments, meaning that instruments can be introduced step by step.[93]

Within the EU, a directive comparable with the ATAD I and II directive, may be released with a given due date in order to have every member state of the EU implement the set of rules within their jurisdiction. The harmonization within the

---

88 OECD (2020), Tax Challenges Arising From Digitalization – Report on Pillar Two Blueprint. p. 173, par. 677.
89 Pasquale Pistone, Joao Felix Pinto Nogueira, Betty Andrade, Alessandro Turina, OECD – The OECD Public Consultation Document "Global Anti-Base Erosion (CloBE) Proposal – Pillar Two": An Assessment, Bulletin for International Taxation, Volume 74 (2020), p. 12, chap 2.2.4.
90 OECD (2020), Tax Challenges Arising From Digitalization – Report on Pillar Two Blueprint. p. 178, par. 705–706.
91 Pasquale Pistone, Joao Felix Pinto Nogueira, Betty Andrade, Alessandro Turina, OECD – The OECD Public Consultation Document "Global Anti-Base Erosion (CloBE) Proposal – Pillar Two": An Assessment, Bulletin for International Taxation, Volume 74 (2020), p. 13, chap 2.2.4.
92 OECD (2019), Addressing the Tax Challenges of the Digitalisation of the Economy, p. 29, par 109.
93 OECD (2020), Tax Challenges Arising From Digitalization – Report on Pillar Two Blueprint. p. 177, par. 697–699.

EU will may strengthen the rules itself. In addition to that, a harmonisation will simplify the implementation of the set of rules at least for 27 countries and for more than 400 million people. Furthermore, with regards to the Court of Justice of the European Union (CJEU), the expected CJEU cases will be lower compared to an unharmonized approach within the EU. Even if the harmonization within the EU will be fulfilled, the CJEU will most likely face court cases regarding fundamental freedoms with third countries, especially regarding capital neutrality. The new instruments are potentially violating the import neutrality of capital, for instance in the event where multinational companies sell products or services to a nation where the effective tax rate is below the threshold. The consequence of the instruments would potentially be that the services and supply coming from outside of the country are discriminated, compared to the companies providing services inside the country, as mentioned in the public comments received on the possible solutions to the tax challenges of digitalisation.[94]

In case of disputes, the STTR and the SoR are treaty rules that could be enclosed into existing double tax treaties. A mutual agreement procedure in order to settle disputes regarding these instruments could be initiated by the taxpayer, as all Inclusive Framework members should have implemented a mutual agreement procedure (MAP) Article 25 (1–3) in their tax treaties.[95]

3.3.1. Peculiarities and differences between GloBE and CFC rules

The GloBE proposal has new peculiarities and instruments as well as mechanics that are already known from existing CFC rules. Critics state that the IIR itself is "hardly distinguishable" from existing CFC regimes.[96] With focus isolated on the IIR, this may be correct. However, the definition of income used by most CFC regimes and the income in the GloBE proposal differ. The aim of the Inclusive Framework is to cover income under a broad scope. Therefore, every income directly attributed to a constituent entity is added to the income if taxed at a low rate or even with 0%.[97] By contrast to other CFC regimes that mostly tax only passive income, this is generally income from intangibles, unless deriving from active businesses.[98] Consequently, the type of covered income is one of the main differences between IIR and existing CFC rules.

---

94 Joachim Englisch, Johannes Becker, World Tax Journal, 2019 (Volume 11), No. 4, United States/EEA/European Union/G20/OECD/International – International Effective Minimum Taxation – The GloBE Proposal, p. 8, par 2.2.7.
95 OECD (2020), Tax Challenges Arising From Digitalization – Report on Pillar Two Blueprint. p. 178, par. 710.
96 Johanna Hey, GloBE: Wo We Need a Super-CFC?, Intertax, Vol 49, 2021, p. 1, par 2.
97 OECD (2020), Tax Challenges Arising From Digitalization – Report on Pillar Two Blueprint. p. 54, par. 154.
98 Brian J. Arnold, The Evolution of Controlled Foreign Corporation Rules and Beyond, Bulletin for International Taxation, (Amsterdam: IBFD, 2019), p. 637, cap. 3.3.4.

Another main difference is that existing CFC regimes are focusing on the controlled foreign company itself, a "per-entity" basis, whereas, the GloBE focuses on a jurisdictional basis, potentially blending dozens of different constituent entities within one jurisdiction together, in order to determine the tax base, the income and the ETR.[99] In addition, the difference between CFC rules and the GloBE is also the tax rate itself, or the calculation of the tax rate. According to Pascal Saint-Amans, the director of the centre for tax policies at the OECD the minimum tax rate or effective tax rate will be around 12,5%.[100] According to the examples of the Blueprint, the minimum tax rate will be 10–12% depending on the example.[101] In the case of the UTPR, the minimum tax may be even set to an even lower level.[102] By contrast, for instance, the U.S. CFC's minimum tax rate in the GILTI calculation is 13,125%, below this rate the rule is triggered. Basically, the applicable rate is 10,5% , which is half of the U.S. statutory rate of 21%, but as the foreign taxes creditability is limited to 80% an effective triggering tax rate of 13.125% is applicable.[103]

The isolated view or a statement about a minimum tax rate is not sufficient in order to define the eventual effective tax rate, multiple factors will need to be defined and agreed upon. However, by contrast to existing CFC Rules, the GloBE proposal intends to use a fixed ETR rather than a percentage of the for instance parents' jurisdiction's CIT rate or a range or corridor of CIT rates.[104] By using a fixed percentage instead of a percentage of the parent jurisdiction's CIT, significant variations and differences between countries are hindered, resulting in a better coordination with the undertaxed payment rule and seemingly the prevent of over taxation.

Overall, a fixed percentage is the simplest option, while providing greater transparency, in the opinion of the Inclusive Framework.[105] By contrast, critics would prefer a mechanism that is based on the CIT of the residence jurisdiction. They point out that the deficiency of assuming that a minimum tax rate would completely prevent base erosion is invalid, as it would only potentially limit the amount of base erosion

---

99 Johanna Hey, The 2020 Pillar Two Blueprint: What Can the GloBE Income Inclusion Rule Do That CFC Legislation Can't Do?, Intertax, Vol 49, 2021, p. 10, cap 4.2.
100 C. Taylor Irish Times 30.07.2019 C. Taylor: Time for 'aggressive tax behaviour' is over, https://www.irishtimes.com/business/economy/time-for-aggressive-tax-behaviour-is-oversays-oecd-reform-director-1.3970058 (22.8.2019).
101 OECD (2020), Tax Challenges Arising From Digitalization – Report on Pillar Two Blueprint. p. 187 example 3.3.6B.
102 OECD (2020), Tax Challenges Arising From Digitalization – Report on Pillar Two Blueprint. p. 131, par. 491.
103 Daniel W. Blum, The Proposal for a Global Minimum Tax: Comeback of Residence Taxation in the Digital Era?: Comment on Can GILTI +BEAT = GLOBE?, Blum p. 517, par. 2.1.2.
104 OECD (2019), Programme of Work to Develop a Consensus Solution to the Tax Challenges Arising from the Digitalisation of the Economy, pp. 27 28, par. 64 -67.
105 OECD (2019), Programme of Work to Develop a Consensus Solution to the Tax Challenges Arising from the Digitalisation of the Economy, pp. 27–28, par. 65 67.

to the agreed minimum tax rate.[106] Consequently, the applicable tax rate may be seen as a "key difference" between existing CFCs and the GloBE.[107]

By contrast to the proposed multilateral approach of the GloBE proposal, the existing CFCs worldwide are unilateral approaches: partly harmonized in the EU but still unilateral. However, even with harmonization, the CFC rules differ from country to country as the E.U. mostly sets minimum standards and not fixed standards for every E.U. member states.

Another main difference between existing CFCs and the GloBE instruments is that the GloBE has only a limited scope due to the threshold of EUR 750 million, addressing and focusing mainly on MNEs; whereas, the existing CFC rules worldwide have thresholds that are mostly below EUR 1 million. This makes it very unlikely that the existing CFC regimes will be abolished.[108] Surprisingly, the Blueprint of the GloBE proposal does not address the issue of existing CFC rules, and the potential problems arising with the co-existence.[109]

3.3.2. Limitation of the GloBE Proposal and Future Perspectives

The limitation of the GloBE proposal or the instruments proposed in the Blueprint of the Inclusive Framework on BEPS, are heavily dependent on the way they are implemented within the jurisdictions. Due to critics, the global minimum tax will most likely add more complexity to the world of international taxation, while increasing the costs and administrative burden for the taxpayer, as well as the authorities.[110]

Even if it is agreed by all the states of the Inclusive framework in the proposed way, critical details will still have to be considered and determined. The fast-evolving digital economy may find new loopholes to artificially create expenses and promote base erosion and profit shifting. In addition, the instruments are only targeting multinational companies. The thresholds that may be agreed on are a group revenue of EUR 750 million or more[111], which will set an inherent and compelling limitation to the Global Minimum Tax, underlining the importance and disclosing the co-existing of CFC rules for companies with lower overall revenue.

---

106 Brian J. Arnold, The Evolution of Controlled Foreign Corporation Rules and Beyond, Bulletin for International Taxation, (Amsterdam: IBFD, 2019). p.645, par 2.
107 Johanna Hey, GloBE: Wo We Need a Super-CFC?, Intertax, Vol 49, 2021, p. 1, par. 6.
108 Johanna Hey, GloBE: Wo We Need a Super-CFC?, Intertax, Vol 49, 2021, p. 2, par. 2.
109 Johanna Hey, The 2020 Pillar Two Blueprint: What Can the GloBE Income Inclusion Rule Do That CFC Legislation Can't Do?, Intertax, Vol 49, 2021, p. 10, cap 4.1.
110 Joachim Englisch, Johannes Becker, World Tax Journal, 2019 (Volume 11), No. 4, United States/EEA/European Union/G20/OECD/International – International Effective Minimum Taxation – The GloBE Proposal, p.8, par 2.2.8
111 OECD (2020), Report to G20 Finance Ministers and Central Bank Governors, Riyadh, Saudi Arabia, par. 35.

Another natural limitation is the number of member states in the Inclusive Framework. Even if more than 65% of the world's nations are part of the Inclusive Framework, there are countries that are not part of this process. Countries like Guatemala, Kuwait, Marshall Islands and Vanuatu are not taking part in the negotiations.[112]. Even the countries of the Inclusive Framework could potentially not implement the instruments effectively within the jurisdiction[113], by intention or even unintentionally. By contrast, the UTPR is designed to be applicable in jurisdictions even if the jurisdiction did notimplement any GloBE instruments. Therefore, the GloBE instruments as proposed are not limited to the Inclusive Framework´s jurisdictions exclusively. A need for coordination between the existing CFCs rules, as well as the new GloBE rules, is essential.

A limitation in the opinion of critics is that the GloBE instruments can not completely eliminate the competition between low tax countries. Even if the race to the bottom may be stopped.[114] This criticism can be followed, as low-tax countries will have to compensate the MNEs somehow, as otherwise, the MNEs will most likely leave the jurisdiction by closing the constituent entity. Essentially, the only reason of setting up a subsidiary or branch in a low-tax country is to save taxes. If this advantage is lost and not compensated, MNEs have no reason to uphold the entity anymore.[115] Furthermore, critics say that, Pillar Two may be seen as an ultimatum from a few powerful countries to either have the developing countries raise their tax rate to a minimum, otherwise, the developed countries will do that for them, taking the advantage of low tax countries to attract business investments through lower tax rates.[116] Moreover, critics stated that the GloBE proposal is not "incentive compatible", in the event that some countries will either not agree with the proposal or will defect from the agreed instruments to create business opportunities.[117] This is a valid critique and a topic the Inclusive Framework will have to address in detail. The issue is clear, with low-tax countries losing their business due to a lack of incentives for MNEs, either a compensation in the form of money or other contributions have to be developed for these jurisdictions.

---

112 OECD (2020), Report to G20 Finance Ministers and Central Bank Governors, Riyadh, Saudi Arabia February 2020, OECD Publishing, Paris, page 71. Annex E.
113 Brian J. Arnold, The Evolution of Controlled Foreign Corporation Rules and Beyond, Bulletin for International Taxation, (Amsterdam: IBFD, 2019). p. 645, par. 4.
114 Vikram Chand (2020), Kluwer International Tax Blog, International Tax Competition in light of Pillar II of the OECD Project on Digitalization, http://kluwertaxblog.com/2020/05/14/international-tax-competition-in-light-of-pillar-ii-of-the-oecd-project-on-digitalization/.
115 Brian J. Arnold, The Evolution of Controlled Foreign Corporation Rules and Beyond, Bulletin for International Taxation, (Amsterdam: IBFD, 2019). p. 648 par1 last sentence.
116 Brian J. Arnold, The Evolution of Controlled Foreign Corporation Rules and Beyond, Bulletin for International Taxation, (Amsterdam: IBFD, 2019). p. 648 par 5.
117 Michael P. Devereux, The OECD Global Anti-Base Erosion ("GloBE") proposal, Oxford University Centre for Business Taxation, January 2020, p.19, par.2.

Another critique is the possible inherent limitation with the proposed excluded entities. Taxing profits from entities that are in most jurisdiction not liable to tax seems logical and conclusive. In reality, it reveals options for tax planning in order to circumvent the GloBE rules. For instance, an investment fund could be used as an otherwise taxable UPE to split an MNE into two MNEs below the EUR 750 million threshold, resulting in an escape from the GloBE doctrine.[118] The Inclusive Framework stresses that further definition, especially for Investment funds and special purposes vehicles of investment funds, have to be defined.[119]

The effectiveness and the acceptance of the economy is, in the author's mind, heavily dependent on the amount of bureaucracy, as well as the complexity of the rules. The best way is to use already existing data from the CbCR in order to calculate the ETR, as well as the GloBE's tax base. Furthermore, thresholds, carve-outs and de minimis rules have to be designed more comprehensively in order to create a more holistic effect and to minimize the administrative burden. Moreover, the existing CFC rules have to be respected as the GloBE instruments are not going to make CFC regimes obsolete per se, and a coordination between the rules has to be implemented.

4. Conclusion

The GloBE-Proposal can be considered as an historical development in the history of multinational coworking and international negotiations. Presently, the Inclusive Framework consists of 139 countries. Different countries from all over the world with a different history, economy, and development status are working together to potentially create more tax- and economical fairness. The disclosed Blueprint in October 2020 leaves room for interpretation regarding the final specifics of the mechanics, despite providing a very comprehensive, extensive and well elaborated set of rules.

Overall, the GloBE proposal and the designed instruments, especially the IIR, are based on already existing CFC mechanics. By contrast to existing CFC regimes, the scope of the GloBE instruments is broader, and they are intended to work not only unilateral. The challenge to implement this spectrum of different rules in domestic law, as well as multilaterally, will have to be considered as revolutionary. The implementation of the GloBE instruments will not abolish the existing CFC rules, as the thresholds and the scope of the unilateral CFCs are different. As a consequence, a co-existence of GloBE and CFC rules will have to be the result, leading to potentially even more bureaucracy and complexity paired with an increase of potential double taxation.

---

118 OECD (2020), Tax Challenges Arising From Digitalization – Report on Pillar Two Blueprint. p. 183, example 2.4.3.
119 OECD (2020), Tax Challenges Arising From Digitalization – Report on Pillar Two Blueprint. p. 35, par. 83.

At the time this thesis is written, the outcome of the GloBE is uncertain even though the stakeholders and OECD officers are highly motivated to agree on technical specifics and to make decisions in summer 2021. Perhaps the Corona-pandemic is an opportunity instead of a hurdle for this global project.

Interaction of CFC rules and transfer pricing rules

Francesco Grieco

1. Introduction
2. Comparison between CFC and Transfer Pricing rules
    2.1. Purposes of the rules
        2.1.1. Transfer pricing and protection of a sourcing state
        2.1.2. CFC and restoring the tax powers of a parent company's residence state
    2.2. Addressing substance
        2.2.1. Transfer pricing and substance – Functional alignment
        2.2.2. CFC and substance – Control operated by the owner
    2.3. Allocation rule
        2.3.1. Transfer pricing – The arm's length principle
        2.3.2. CFC – subject income
        2.3.3. Subjectivity of the rules
3. CFC regulations as a backstop to transfer pricing rules
    3.1. Tax effective transfer pricing structures
        3.1.1. Invoicing company
        3.1.2. IP box structure
        3.1.3. Double sandwich structure
        3.1.4. Cash box for leasing of assets
        3.1.5. Parent company in a low-tax jurisdiction
    3.2. Limiting transfer pricing manipulation
4. Overlapping CFC and Transfer Pricing rules
    4.1. Reasons why both sets of rules are needed
    4.2. Cases in which CFC and transfer pricing rules can coexist
    4.3. Cases in which CFC and transfer pricing rules cannot be consistently applied
    4.4. Open issues
        4.4.1. Rule hierarchy
        4.4.2. Double taxation
        4.4.3. Allocating losses
5. Conclusions

1. Introduction

Within literature on controlled foreign corporations (CFC), it has been largely discussed i) whether or not the CFC rules could work as a backstop to transfer pricing rules in cases in which transfer pricing rules had been manipulated leading to base erosion and profit shifting; 2) whether or not CFC rules would be really needed if transfer pricing was set correctly.

By reviewing the most frequently applied transfer pricing structures, this paper analyses i) whether or not CFC rules can really be a backstop for transfer pricing rules, ii) whether both of these two sets of rules are needed, and iii) whether applying both sets of rules could lead to double taxation.

2. Comparison between CFC and Transfer Pricing rules

This section aims to briefly compare both transfer pricing rules and CFC rules when applied individually.

2.1. Purposes of the rules

2.1.1. Transfer pricing and protection of a sourcing state

The transfer pricing scope is broad and involves all jurisdictions where multinational enterprises are active as long as they have transfer pricing rules.

The purposes of transfer pricing rules are the following:

- Reconciling the legitimate taxation rights of states in respect of income and expenses raised in their territory;
- Avoiding that two or more states levy taxation on the same income.

The protection of the sourcing state within the purposes above is granted by restoring the market forces that would incur within transactions between independent enterprises[1], leading to a relevant adjustment to be imposed by the tax administration[2].

Within the above, transfer pricing rules are particularly applicable to avoid phenomena in which profit is shifted by overpricing or low-pricing intercompany transactions[3].

---

[1] OECD Transfer Pricing Guidelines for Multinational Enterprises and Tax Administrations (2017), para. 1.1.
[2] OECD Model Tax Convention on Income and on Capital (2017), Article 9.
[3] Mitchell A. Kane, Milking versus Parking Transfer Pricing and CFC Rules, *Tax Law Review, International Taxation 66* (2012), p. 488.

2.1.2. CFC and restoring the tax powers of a parent company's residence state

The purpose of CFC rules are the following:

- Restoring the taxation rights of the state where the owner operates its control over the CFC;
- Limiting the risk that taxpayers with a controlling interest in a foreign subsidiary can strip the tax base of their country of residence and, in some cases, other countries by shifting income into a CFC.
  CFC rules tax parent companies on the basis of the income, either partial or total, of some or all their foreign subsidiaries and target preventing the shifting of profit outside the parent company's jurisdiction or from the parent's company jurisdiction and other tax jurisdictions[4].

It is worth noting that the scope of CFC rules only aims at restoring the taxing rights of one jurisdiction, i.e. the one of the parent company. They are particularly valid for avoiding profit shifting operated by strategically settling companies in low tax jurisdictions, e.g. holding companies[5].

2.2. Addressing substance

2.2.1. Transfer pricing and substance – Functional alignment

For as long as transfer pricing rules have been introduced, most of the discussion on these rules has been about aligning taxation rights and contribution of sourcing states in terms of functions performed, assets used, and risks assumed. Recently, this approach has been further strengthened with stressing the concept of alignment between taxation and value creation[6].

Within the provisions of BEPS Actions 8–10[7], this alignment should be based on a functional analysis seeking to identify economically significant activities, responsibilities and actions taken, assets used, and risks assumed by the entities belonging to the group of companies with particular attention on their role in terms of decision making and strategy. Below, this analysis of functions, assets, and risks is referred as the FAR analysis. This should start with an analysis on how the value is created as a whole and how each entity contributes to the creation of this value.

---

4   OECD/G20 Base Erosion and Profit Shifting Project: Designing Effective Controlled Foreign Company Rules, Action 3: 2015 Final Report (2015), para. 1.1.
5   Mitchell A. Kane, Milking versus Parking Transfer Pricing and CFC Rules, *Tax Law Review, International Taxation 66* (2012), p. 488.
6   OECD/G20 Base Erosion and Profit Shifting Project: Aligning Transfer Pricing Outcomes with Value Creation, Action 8–10: 2015 Final Report (2015).
7   OECD/G20 Base Erosion and Profit Shifting Project: Aligning Transfer Pricing Out-comes with Value Creation, Action 8–10: 2015 Final Report (2015), para 1.51.

Interaction of CFC rules and transfer pricing rules

When the value creation chain is outlined, this should be reflected within the application of relevant transfer pricing methods.

When properly applied, the effects of this functional alignment would be that arranging transfer prices is neutral against arranging prices for the same products or services with third parties.

Given the above, while looking at intercompany transactions, transfer pricing focuses on a "form of solidarity" within related entities[8] that found its expression in their conjoint contribution to the group's value creation.

2.2.2. CFC and substance – Control operated by the owner

CFC rules recognize that there is a driver to allocate a minimum income to the state where the controlling entity is resident. When these entities have significant influence on their foreign controlled entities, they should gain a return from their investing and operating control over the latter. They should also determine the amount sourced by controlled entities to be incorporated within the owner's income.

Different approaches are used by jurisdictions when implementing their own CFC rules. Some may opt to fully recognize the investor role of the parent company while others may target some forms of income that may be easily separated by the underlying value creation to obtain a reduction in tax, e.g. royalties and interest expenses[9].

Given the above, while seeing intercompany transactions by looking at solidarity within group companies within the value creation, CFC income is subjected to CFC rules that carve out income that is genuinely derived from business activities[10].

For most countries, CFC rules tax parent companies based on some or all of the income of some or all the foreign companies that is used either to shift income from the parent company jurisdiction or from the parent and other tax jurisdictions[11].

---

[8] Georg W. Kofler and Isabel Verlinden, 'OECD/International – Unlimited Adjustments: Some Reflections on Transfer Pricing, General Anti-Avoidance and Controlled Foreign Company Rules, and the "Saving Clause"', *Bulletin for International Taxation 74* (2020), p. 272.

[9] OECD/G20 Base Erosion and Profit Shifting Project: Designing Effective Controlled Foreign Company Rules, Action 3: 2015 Final Report (2015), para 74.

[10] Georg W. Kofler and Isabel Verlinden, 'OECD/International – Unlimited Adjustments: Some Reflections on Transfer Pricing, General Anti-Avoidance and Controlled Foreign Company Rules, and the "Saving Clause"', *Bulletin for International Taxation 74* (2020), p. 272.

[11] OECD/G20 Base Erosion and Profit Shifting Project: Designing Effective Controlled Foreign Company Rules, Action 3: 2015 Final Report (2015), para 1.1.1.

2.3. Allocation rule

2.3.1. Transfer pricing – The arm's length principle

Within the transfer pricing guidelines released by the OECD, transfer prices should be arranged in line with the arm's length principle[12]. The arm's length principle is based on the concept that commercial and financial relations between independent enterprises are determined by market forces. These forces determine prices that are acceptable by both independent parties and would allow both parties to have the greater benefit from the transaction, possibly leading to greater profits, that will be accepted by the tax authorities to which the parties belong[13].

Within the OECD Model Convention, which is also reproduced by the UN Model Convention, the arm's length principle is described as per the statement below:

> [Where] conditions are made or imposed between the two [associated] enterprises in their commercial or financial relations which differ from those which would be made between independent enterprises, then any profits which would, but for those conditions, have accrued to one of the enterprises, but, by reason of those conditions, have not so accrued, may be included in the profits of that enterprise and taxed accordingly[14, 15].

In substance, according to the arm's length principle, all intercompany transactions arranged within related entities should occur and be priced under the same condition as they have been arranged within unrelated parties.

From a practical view, this means that income is allocated to source states based on benchmarking against independent comparable parties or transactions under similar circumstances. In addition, in order to compare the controlled and uncontrolled transactions that are actually comparable, the key is to treat the associated enterprises as separate entities (separate entity approach)[16].

---

12   OECD Transfer Pricing Guidelines for Multinational Enterprises and Tax Administrations (2017), chap. 1.
13   Jérôme Monsenego, *The Key to Understanding Transfer Pricing – The Arm's Length Principle*, Chapter 3 in *Introduction to Transfer Pricing*, (Alphen aan den Rijn: Wolters Kluwer, 2015) p 22.
14   OECD Model Tax Convention on Income and on Capital (2017), Article 9(1).
15   A similar wording is contained within the UN Tax Model Convention, as per the following: *"Where: (a) an enterprise of a Contracting State participates directly or indirectly in the management, control or capital of an enterprise of the other Contracting State, or (b) the same persons participate directly or indirectly in the management, control or capital of an enterprise of a Contracting State and an enterprise of the other Contracting State, and in either case conditions are made or imposed between the two enterprises in their commercial or financial relations which differ from those which would be made between independent enterprises, then any profits which would, but for those conditions, have accrued to one of the enterprises, but by reason of those conditions, have not so accrued, may be included in the profits of that enterprise and taxed accordingly"*. United Nations Model Double Taxation Convention between Developed and Developing Countries (2017), Article 9(1).
16   Jérôme Monsenego, *The Key to Understanding Transfer Pricing – The Arm's Length Principle*, Chapter 3 in *Introduction to Transfer Pricing*, (Alphen aan den Rijn: Wolters Kluwer, 2015) p 21.

2.3.2. CFC – subject income

Within the CFC rules, a methodological approach to determine the income to be allocated to the controlling entity is given by the OECD's BEPS Action 3 as per the following:

- Defining a CFC (including definition of control).
- Determining CFC exemptions and threshold requirements
- Defining CFC income
- Computing income
- Attributing income[17]

In substance, CFC rules determine whether an entity should be deemed as a CFC and how the income to be allocated to the parent company should be computed and attributed.

The nature of the income of the CFC to be attributed to its parent shareholder is particularly important for policy makers to meet the scope for which the rules had been implemented[18]. In this regard, three options are identified:

- The first option is that CFC rules only target certain tainted income. This is the case of CFCs in most countries[19], and it is commonly referred to as "partial inclusion system". Generally, tainted income includes passive income (e.g. dividends, interest, royalties, and capital gains depending on the relevant applicable law). Business income is usually considered passive if the following conditions are met:
  - It is derived by a CFC from the residence country;
  - It comes from related-party transactions; and
  - It comes from transactions outside the country in which a CFC is resident.[20]
- The second option is that CFCs target non-distributed income arising from non-genuine arrangements. An arrangement is defined as non-genuine if the CFC would not have owned assets and not assumed risks if it was not controlled by the parent company that has significant people functions that are relevant for owning these assets and assuming these risks. The income to be allocated to the CFC should then be limited to the people functions it performed based on the arm's length principle;
- The third option is that CFC rules can apply to the whole income of the CFC regardless of its character, as in the case of Brazilian and Swedish CFC rules. This is commonly referred as a "full inclusion system". According to the OECD, full-inclusion systems prevent long-term deferral of taxation[21].

---

17 OECD/G20 Base Erosion and Profit Shifting Project: Designing Effective Con-trolled Foreign Company Rules, Action 3: 2015 Final Report (2015), p. 6.
18 Brian J. Arnold, *The Taxation of Controlled Foreign Corporations: A Comparative Analysis* (Canadian Tax Foundation, 1986). pp. 487–495.
19 Brian J. Arnold, OECD/International – The Evolution of Controlled Foreign Corporation Rules and Beyond, Bulletin for International Taxation 73 (2019), p. 637.
20 Brian J. Arnold, OECD/International – The Evolution of Controlled Foreign Corporation Rules and Beyond, Bulletin for International Taxation 73 (2019), p. 637.
21 OECD/G20 Base Erosion and Profit Shifting Project: Designing Effective
Controlled Foreign Company Rules, Action 3: 2015 Final Report (2015), para 75.

The first two options are the ones included within the ATAD, namely, as Model A and Model B[22]. Within all methods, CFC rules omit the separate entity and "pierce the corporate veil", i.e. they give the right to the parent company's country to tax all of the profit from the multinational business, including that arising from foreign subsidiaries[23].

2.3.3. Subjectivity of the rules

Given the above, it is important to notice how transfer pricing rules are open to economic and valuation considerations that may lead to divergent tax effects and, in some cases, to manipulation. On the other hand, CFC rules apply in a mechanical fashion.[24]

This characteristic makes both sets of rules not interchangeable, and CFC rules may be needed to adress situations in which transfer pricing had been set in a way that is either structured in line with the recommendations of BEPS Actions 8–10 and still trigger base erosion and profit shifting.[25]

3. CFC regulations as a backstop to transfer pricing rules

Parent companies and their CFCs are related parties, and their transactions fall within the scope of transfer pricing. Therefore, it had been largely discussed whether CFC rules may act as a limitation or eventually a replacement for transfer pricing and vice versa.

Within this context, CFC rules are often intended as a backstop to transfer pricing rules[26] or even exclusionary to transfer pricing[27].

---

22 (EU) 2016/1164.
23 Conrad Turley, Mario Petriccione and David Chamberlain, *A New Dawn for the International Tax System: Evolution from past to future and what role will China play?* (Amsterdam: IBFD, 2017) pp. 406–410.
24 OECD/G20 Base Erosion and Profit Shifting Project: Designing Effective Controlled Foreign Company Rules, Action 3: 2015 Final Report (2015), para 9.
25 OECD/G20 Base Erosion and Profit Shifting Project: Designing Effective Controlled Foreign Company Rules, Action 3: 2015 Final Report (2015), para 9.
26 Michael McIntyre, Australian Measures to Curb Tax Haven Abuses: A United States Perspective, *Australian Tax Forum* (1988); OECD The Deferral of Income Earned Through US Controlled Foreign Corporations: A Policy Study (Treasury Department Office of Tax Policy, 2000); HMRC, Tackling Aggressive Tax Planning in the Global Economy: UK Priorities for the G20-OECD Project for Countering Base Erosion and Profit Shifting, para 3.7 (2014); J. Clifton Fleming Jr., Robert J. Peroni, Stephen E. Shay, Worse than Exemption, Emory Law Journal 59 1 (2009); Bret Wells & Cym Lowell, Tax Base Erosion: Reformation of Section 482's Arm's Length Standard, 15 Florida Tax Review 737 (2014); Stephen E. Shay, J. Clifton Fleming, Jr. & Robert J. Peroni, Getting Serious About Cross-Border Earnings Stripping: Establishing an Analytical Framework, *NC Law Review* 673 (2015); Ana P. Dourado, The Role of CFC Rules in the BEPS Initiative and in the EU, *British Tax Review* 347 (2015); Kate Ramm, Designing Effective Controlled Foreign Company Rules, Action 3 – 2015 Final Report, *International Tax Review* (2015).
27 EY Corporate Tax Association Submission on the Review of Foreign Income Accruals Tax Rules 22 (2007).

Kane (2013) argued that deeming CFC rules as a backstop to transfer pricing rules is an "instance of redundancy"[28]. This is because defining CFC rules as a backstop for transfer pricing mismatches and narrows the purpose of CFC rules themselves. Indeed, including non-arm's-length amounts of profits to the taxable income is not the main purpose of CFC rules. Then, parent jurisdictions have often seen CFC rules as a way to capture income that had been missed in cases when transfer pricing was not set correctly[29].

The OECD follows this approach, stating that the term "backstop" is misleading when referring to CFC rules. Indeed, CFC rules may target the same income as transfer pricing rules from time to time, but neither CFC rules nor transfer pricing rules fully capture the income that the other set of rules is intended to capture and are not interchangeable. Consequently, none of these sets of rules eliminates the need for the other one[30].

This argument is being analysed in the next section by looking at some practical examples.

3.1. Tax effective transfer pricing structures

Several multinationals had been accused of having used tax effective transfer pricing structures to artificially reduce their tax liabilities[31], raising countries' concerns.[32] Within the below, the most common transfer pricing structures are analysed.

3.1.1. Invoicing company

The invoicing model works by settling an invoicing company in a low-tax state to invoice third parties.

---

28 Mitchell A. Kane, Milking versus Parking Transfer Pricing and CFC Rules, *Tax Law Review, International Taxation 66* (2012), p. 488.
29 OECD/G20 Base Erosion and Profit Shifting Project: Designing Effective. Controlled Foreign Company Rules, Action 3: 2015 Final Report (2015), para 8.
30 OECD/G20 Base Erosion and Profit Shifting Project: Designing Effective. Controlled Foreign Company Rules, Action 3: 2015 Final Report (2015), para 8.
31 Huanyu Ouyang and James G. S. Yang, Current Developments in International Taxation, *International Tax Journal 45-5* (2019); Edward D. Kleinbard, 2013. Through a Latte, Darkly Starbucks's Stateless Income Planning, *Tax Notes* (2013), pp. 1515–1535; Larissa S. Kyj and George C. Romeo, Microsoft's Foreign Earnings Tax Strategy, *Issues in Accounting Education 30* (2015), pp. 297–310.
32 Elena Burkadze, Interaction of Transfer Pricing Rules and CFC Provisions. *International Transfer Pricing Journal 23* (2016), p. 367.

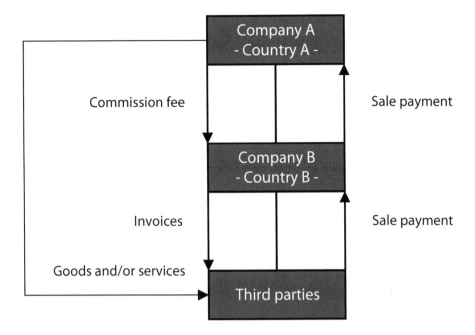

The elements of the structure are the following:

- Company A is the parent company of the multinational group; it is organized in Country A and operates all of the business except invoicing the customers. As the latter function is performed by Company B, Company A remunerates Company B by paying a commission fee.
- Company B is a subsidiary of Company A and is resident in Country B. It receives the commission fee from Company A for its activity of invoicing.

The procedure according to which the base erosion and profit shifting works in absence of CFC rules is manipulating transfer pricing in order to overprice the remuneration of the invoicing company. In this context, CFC rules may easily be able to catch profits diverted to Country B in the case of a full-inclusion system.

3.1.2. IP box structure

Since IP assets are highly mobile, the income from these assets can be diverted from the jurisdiction where the assets had been created quite easily, creating sort of "IP boxes" within certain jurisdictions, especially those charging lower taxes on profits made from IP exploitation.[33]

---

33 E.g. patent box regimes.

Interaction of CFC rules and transfer pricing rules

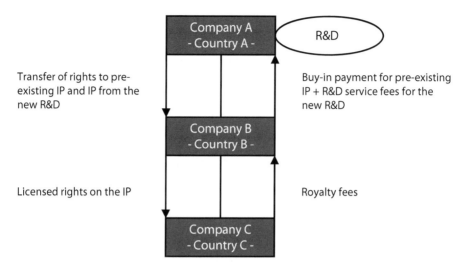

The elements of the structure are the following:

- Company A is the parent company of a multinational group; it is organized in Country A, and it developed the technology and intangibles that form the basis of its business. It licenses or transfers the IP to Company B under a cost-sharing or cost contribution arrangement. Under the agreement, Company A transfers to Company B the previously developed IP. Under the agreement, Company B makes a buy-in payment for the IP transferred by Company A to Company B. Furthermore, both of the participants of the cost-sharing agreement agree to share the costs of further development in accordance with the anticipated benefits to be obtained from the developed technology.
- Company B is organized in Country B which is a tax haven or has special tax regimes for IP. It sublicenses the intangibles to Company C in Country C.
- Company C is a resident of Country C and is an operating company.

The procedure according to which the base erosion and profit shifting works in absence of CFC rules is the following:

- Company C is entitled of a minimum routine return from its operations which can eventually be reduced due to transfer pricing manipulation and subjectivity. The residual profit is paid to Company B in form of royalty fees[34].
- Company B pays low taxes in Country B because it is a tax haven or has special regimes for levying taxes on the income from IP. Furthermore, if both Company B and Company C are tax residents within the European Union and the

---

34 Furthermore, no withholding tax can be levied on the royalty fee paid by Company B to Company D if Country B is a Member State of the European Union and Company B applies the EU Interest and Royalty Directive (2003/49/EC).

Royalty Directive is applicable, if Company B owns more than 25% of the shares of Company C, an exemption of royalties and interests in the participation may be applied;
- Transfer pricing rules may not be able to catch all of the return to be earned by Company A from its contributing the intangibles due to the cost sharing agreement or cost contribution arrangement. Consequently, in the long term, Company A would be subjected to taxation only for the return earned from providing R&D services to Company B.

This structure raises several challenges for tax purposes, such as the following:
- IP income can be exploited and distributed in several ways, it is easy to manipulate, and may either be considered passive or active income depending on how the CFC rules had been implemented.
- Often, IP assets are unique, and it is hard or impossible to find proper comparables. The cost base of the assets may not be a good measure of the value they can generate.
- It is not so easy to separate the income from the IP from the income earned by associated parties from their operating businesses.

Then BEPS concerns arise from the fact that CFC rules may be able to catch profits diverted to Country B only if they are set in a way to include the relevant payments within the attributable income[35]. Therefore, CFC rules may be able to capture profits from the new intangibles developed by the CFC that would not be taxable within transfer pricing rules[36].

It is important to note that CFC rules with a full inclusion system may leave less room for manipulation than CFC rules with a partial inclusion system.

3.1.3. Double sandwich structure

The double sandwich structure described by the OECD[37] as "e-commerce structure" is often referred to as "Double Irish with a Dutch sandwich"[38] when it involves these jurisdictions, and it is known for having tax structures used by US MNEs to lower their tax liabilities.

---

35 OECD/G20 Base Erosion and Profit Shifting Project: Designing Effective. Controlled Foreign Company Rules, Action 3: 2015 Final Report (2015), para 78.
36 Jens Wittendorff, International – Valuation of Intangibles under Income-Based Methods – Part II, *International Transfer Pricing Journal 17-6* (2010), p. 400.
37 Elena Burkadze, Interaction of Transfer Pricing Rules and CFC Provisions. *International Transfer Pricing Journal 23* (2016), pp. 367–369.
38 Michael Butler and Mathew Brittingham, International – OECD Report on Base Erosion and Profit Shifting: Search for a New Paradigm or Is the Proposed Tax Order a Distant Galaxy Many Light Years Away?, *International Transfer Pricing Journal 20-4* (2013), pp. 240–242.

Interaction of CFC rules and transfer pricing rules

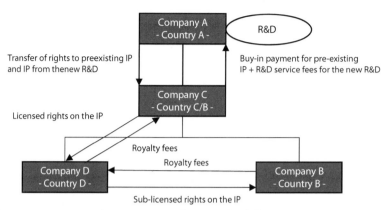

The basic structure can be summarized as per the following:

Company A is the parent company of a multinational group; it is organised in Country A, and it developed the technology and intangibles that form the basis of its business. It licenses or transfers the IP to Company C under a cost-sharing or cost contribution arrangement. Under the agreement, Company A transfers to Company C the IP previously developed. Company C makes a buy-in payment for the IP transferred by Company A to Company C. Furthermore, both of the participants of the cost-sharing agreement agree to share the costs of the further development in accordance with the anticipated benefits to be obtained from the developed technology[39].

- Company C is registered in Country B where it is a tax resident but is managed and organized in Country C, a tax haven. It sublicenses the intangibles to Company D in Country D.
- Company D is a resident of Country D and sublicenses the intangibles to Company B in Country B;
- Company B is an operating company in Country B.

The procedure according to which the base erosion and profit shifting works in absence of CFC rules is the following:

- Company B's is entitled of a minimum routine return from its operations that can eventually be reduced due to transfer pricing manipulation and subjectivity. The residual profit is paid to Company D in the form of royalty fees[40].
- Company D's contribution to the royalty flow is minimum and, by applying the arm's length principle, it is compensated according to its contribution to the value creation[41].

---

39   Elena Burkadze, Interaction of Transfer Pricing Rules and CFC Provisions. *International Transfer Pricing Journal 23* (2016), pp. 367–369.
40   Furthermore, no withholding tax can be levy on the royalty fee paid by Company B to Company D if Country B is a Member State of the European Union and Company B applies the EU Interest and Royalty Directive.
41   Likely, no withholding tax would be levied by Country D within its domestic law.

- Company C does not pay any taxes in Country B because it is not present therein, it is managed and operates in Country C, and has no income sourced in Country B. It does not pay taxes in Country C as well because Country C is a tax haven or acts as if it was regarding royalty payments.
- Transfer pricing rules may not be able to catch all of the return to be earned by Company A from contributing the intangibles due to the cost sharing agreement or cost contribution arrangement.[42]

On the one hand, CFC rules with partial inclusion systems may not be able to fully capture income from TP manipulation within this structure. In fact, if Company A has filed a check-the-box election for Company D and Company B, the royalty transactions will be deemed as not existing and will not be included within the CFC tainted income[43]. Then, as a result of the check-the-box regime, or an hybrid mismatching, Company C can be disregarded for State A tax purposes. Then, State A would only see Company B deriving the active income, and this is usually exempt under CFC rules that are in place in most countries as it would be considered as active income.

On the other hand, a CFC with a full inclusion system may capture the income from TP manipulation. The OECD itself considers CFC rules with a full inclusion system to be the most complete example of the backstop effect.

3.1.4. Cash box for leasing of assets

The example case assumes the following:

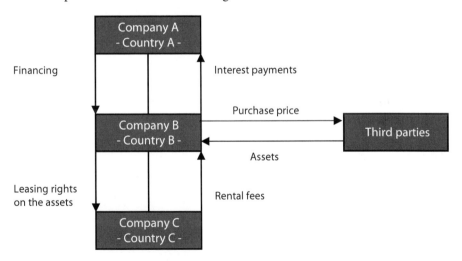

---

42 Michael Butler and Mathew Brittingham, International – OECD Report on Base Erosion and Profit Shifting: Search for a New Paradigm or Is the Proposed Tax Order a Distant Galaxy Many Light Years Away?, *International Transfer Pricing Journal* 20-4 (2013), pp. 240–242.
43 Elena Burkadze, Interaction of Transfer Pricing Rules and CFC Provisions. *International Transfer Pricing Journal* 23 (2016), pp. 367–377.

- Company A is established and a tax resident in State A.
- Company B is established and a tax resident in State B, a low tax jurisdiction, and is a wholly owned subsidiary of Company A. The latter finances it with capital. Company B purchases an asset and leases it to Company C under an operating lease agreement. In this regard, Company B performs only investment functions and assumes the inherent risks.
- Company C is established and a tax resident in State C and is a wholly owned subsidiary of Company B. It operates as an operating company and performs most of the operations for which the asset is used.

The procedure according to which the base erosion and profit shifting works in absence of CFC rules is the following:

- The transfer pricing is manipulated in a way that Company C pays high leasing fees, and its overall return from its operation is pretty low. Within this structure, even though C is the operating company and performs most of functions for which the asset is used, its taxable profits in State C may be low due to the lease it has to pay to Company B.
- Company B has low taxation in Country B,
- leading to an accumulation of tax-free income therein[44].

Within a partial inclusion system, CFC rules may be avoided by using hybrid structures. As an example, if Country A disregarded Company C due to a check-the-box regime, Country A would only see Company B achieving the active income, and this may be exempt under the CFC rules in most jurisdictions.

CFC rules with a full inclusion system may instead be able to catch the income collected in the cash box[45, 46].

3.1.5. Parent company in a low-tax jurisdiction

It happens that some multinational companies set their parent entity within a low-tax jurisdiction.

Within the example below, as an effect of an acquisition or restructuring, relevant intangibles are shifted to the parent company of the multinational group in a low-tax jurisdiction.

---

[44] Eventually, if State C and State B have a tax treaty that is consistent with the OECD Model Convention, the lease payments would not be subject to withholding tax and not be taxed in State C.
[45] Elena Burkadze, Interaction of Transfer Pricing Rules and CFC Provisions. International Transfer Pricing Journal 23 (2016), p. 375.
[46] BEPS Actions 8–10 on interest expenses also target restoring the taxable income in Country C. Also refer to Filip Majdowski and Katarzyna BronzewskaRevolutionary Changes to the Arm's Length Principle under the OECD BEPS Project Have CFC Rules Become Redundant, Intertax 46 (2019), pp. 210–214.

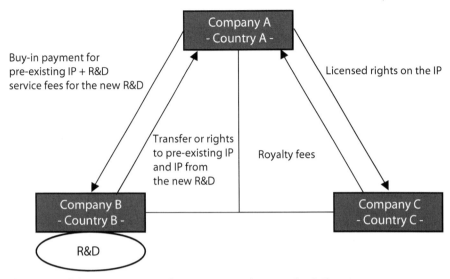

Elements of the structure can be summarized as per the following:

- Company B is resident in Country B and is the entity that originally developed the technology and intangibles that form the basis of its business. It licenses or transfers the IP to the parent company, Company A, under a cost-sharing or cost contribution arrangement. Under the agreement, Company B transfers to Company A the IP previously developed. Under the agreement, Company A makes a buy-in payment for the IP transferred by Company B to Company A. Furthermore, both of the participants of the cost-sharing agreement agree to share the costs of further development in accordance with the anticipated benefits to be obtained from the developed technology.
- Company A is the parent company of the multinational group; it is organized in Country A[47]. It licenses the intangibles to Company C in Country C.
- Company C is an operating company in Country C.

The procedure according to which the base erosion and profit shifting works in absence of CFC rules is the following:

- Company C is entitled to a minimum routine return from its operations that can be eventually reduced due to transfer pricing manipulation and subjectivity. The residual profit is paid to Company A in the form of royalty fees[48].
- Company A pays low taxes in Country A.

---

47   Elena Burkadze, Interaction of Transfer Pricing Rules and CFC Provisions. International Transfer Pricing Journal 23 (2016), pp. 367–369.
48   Furthermore, no withholding tax can be levied on the royalty fee paid by Company B to Company D if Country B is a Member State of the European Union and Company B applies the EU Interest and Royalty Directive.

- Transfer pricing rules may not be able to catch all of the return to be earned by Company B from its contributing the intangibles due to the cost sharing agreement or cost contribution arrangement.

In this case, CFC rules cannot limit transfer pricing manipulation as the latter falls out of the scope of CFC rules, and none of the sets of rules would be able to restore the taxing rights of Country B.

3.2. Limiting transfer pricing manipulation

The transfer pricing structures analysed above had been set with the following characteristics:

- Creating a structure that allows the allocation of income to a different jurisdiction;
- Creating a FAR analysis tailored to reduce or increase the contribution of group companies to the value creation;
- Allocating income based on the altered analysis of functions, risks, and assets.

In this sense, CFC rules may be applied with the following effects:

- CFCs can challenge the creation of artificial structures unless they make use of check-the-box regimes or other schemes to make income not subject to CFCs;
- Groups still have advantages with tailoring their FAR analyses, especially to justify transactions within sister companies;
- CFCs could have an impact on the allocation of income according to the rules and the hierarchy given by jurisdictions.

4. Overlapping CFC and Transfer Pricing rules
4.1. Reasons why both sets of rules are needed

The reasons why CFC rules and transfer pricing legislation do not eliminate the need for each other[49] include:

- Different types of CFC legislation;
- CFC legislation restores the taxation right of the parent company's jurisdiction only;
- Multinational enterprises might be based in a jurisdiction without CFC legislation;
- CFC legislation is applicable to the relationship between the parent company and its subsidiaries. Therefore, it does not apply to the relationship between sister companies.

---

49 There are some authors thinking that appropriate transfer pricing rules would take away most of the needs for CFC rules, e.g. see EBIT European Business Initiative on Taxation, 2015. Comments on the OECD Public Discussion Draft on BEPS Action 3 Strengthening CFC Rules, p. 6.

4.2. Cases in which CFC and transfer pricing rules can coexist

CFC and transfer pricing rules can coexist in all of the following cases:

- Foreign-to-foreign transfer pricing manipulation
- Exceeding profit
- Proper valuation of the contribution of the shareholders in term of assets and risks
- Proper valuation of the options realistically available for the shareholders and not only the arm's length principle
- Situations in which any concerns arising from double taxation can be solved[50].

4.3. Cases in which CFC and transfer pricing rules cannot be consistently applied

CFC and Transfer Pricing rules cannot be mechanically applied conjointly in the following cases:

- Foreign-to-foreign TP manipulation as the CFC rules only apply to a parent company's jurisdiction;
- Losses
- Lack in valuing the contribution given by the shareholder
- Lack in considering the options realistically available
- Different hierarchy of rules

4.4. Open issues

4.4.1. Rule hierarchy

As per the OECD recommendation[51], transfer pricing rules should apply before CFC rules even though there are cases in which applying CFC rules before transfer pricing rules would be in line with the BEPS Action Plan.

In addition, it is worth noting that a change of residence is enough to avoid CFC rules while transfer pricing rules would be still applicable.

---

50 In this regard, relevant suggestions are provided by the OECD, please refer to OECD/G20 Base Erosion and Profit Shifting Project: Designing Effective Controlled Foreign Company Rules, Action 3: 2015 Final Report (2015), para 74.
51 OECD/G20 Base Erosion and Profit Shifting Project: Designing Effective Controlled Foreign Company Rules, Action 3: 2015 Final Report (2015), para 9.

4.4.2. Double taxation

Double taxation may arise at least in four situations:

- Firstly, double taxation may arise in cases when CFC income is also subjected to corporate taxes in a CFC's jurisdiction;
- Secondly, double taxation may also arise in the case that a parent company in State A has a subsidiary in State B that, in turn, has a subsidiary in State C, and both CFC rules of State A and B are applicable. In this case, the application of CFC rules could be limited to the transfer of income out of that jurisdiction, but this measure would also limit the effectiveness of CFC rules. In particular, with reference to the recommendation of the OECD to opt for a full inclusion system, it is recommended that jurisdictions find a way according to which only one of them has right to levy taxes based on CFC rules on the same income.[52]
- Thirdly, double taxation may arise in the case that the CFC distributes dividends out of income attributed to its shareholders under the CFC rules;
- Fourthly, double taxation may arise in cases when a transfer pricing adjustment has been made within two jurisdictions and the CFC charge arises in a third jurisdiction[53].

According to the OECD, in cases when the interaction of CFC rules and transfer pricing rules could give rise to double taxation issues, it is important that countries' rules contain provisions to eliminate any double taxation that would otherwise result[54]. In this regard, the issue is understanding which jurisdiction should provide the relief from double taxation and in what amount. If the transfer pricing adjustment is made in accordance with the arm's length principle, it is reasonable that the country providing the relief is the same as that applying the CFC rules.

4.4.3. Allocating losses

Recognizing the time value of money, MNEs may have the incentive to transfer profits to a loss-making company (either parent company or other related entities) in order to make early use of losses and defer taxes to a later time and have a tax efficient outcome.

---

52 Richard J. Vann, Taxing International Business Income Hard-Boiled Wonderland and the End of the World, *World Tax Journal* 2-3 (2010), p. 341.
53 OECD/G20 Base Erosion and Profit Shifting Project: Designing Effective Controlled Foreign Company Rules, Action 3: 2015 Final Report (2015), para 122.
54 OECD/G20 Base Erosion and Profit Shifting Project: Designing Effective Controlled Foreign Company Rules, Action 3: 2015 Final Report (2015), notes. p. 69.

Then, even if the parent company's jurisdiction has CFC rules, these would not be able to contrast the mismatching. This scope can only be covered by effective transfer pricing rules[55].

5. Conclusions

By reviewing the most frequently applied transfer pricing structures, the paper confirms that CFC rules may have a backstop effect to transfer pricing structures but, as suggested by the OECD[56], this effect is greater and more durable in cases when CFC rules opt for a full inclusive system.

However, the scope of CFC rules is restoring the taxation rights of the parent company and their role is broader than backstopping transfer pricing rules.

In addition, the backstopping function does not work in all cases that transfer pricing is manipulated in order to have a tax benefit. Then, both sets of rules are needed.

The application of both sets of rules, however, may lead to double taxation. In this regard, the country to provide the relief from double taxation is the country applying the CFC legislation.

---

55 Elena Burkadze, Interaction of Transfer Pricing Rules and CFC Provisions. *International Transfer Pricing Journal 23* (2016), p. 375.
56 OECD/G20 Base Erosion and Profit Shifting Project: Designing Effective Controlled Foreign Company Rules, Action 3: 2015 Final Report (2015), para 74., para 75.

Balance between effective CFC rules and compliance burdens

Lýdia Gregorová

1. Introduction
2. Compliance costs of taxation and their relationship with the complexity of tax systems
3. Complexity of CFC rules
   3.1. Disproportionate requirements in the burden of proof
   3.2. Causes of complexity of CFC rules
      3.2.1. Classification of income
      3.2.2. Attribution of income
      3.2.3. Control
      3.2.4. Scope of application
   3.3. Increase of compliance burdens
4. Methods and tools to decrease the compliance burden
5. CFC rules under the ATAD
   5.1. Model A
   5.2. Model B
   5.3. The categorical approach
6. Conclusion

1. Introduction

This chapter analyses the balance between CFC rules and the related compliance and administration costs. Compliance costs are the costs that taxpayers absorb due to the need to meet regulation requirements. These costs mostly contain human resources, IT system costs, and consultation fees. In recent years, there is more focus on compliance costs due to their rising trend. This increase of compliance is caused by the need of tax administrations to be one step ahead of some taxpayers who try to avoid paying the taxes.

This paper identifies connections between compliance and administration costs resulting from the complexity of tax legislation with a focus on CFC legislation. It walks through survey results on the complexity of tax systems and the status of CFC rules in terms of overall complexity. Furthermore, this paper goes through tax complexity and illustrates the complexity index, i.e. the impact of the countries' decisions on their CFC legislations. It goes through categories of income, mainly focusing on passive income. The document also walks through analyses that can be used by countries. The paper gives an overview of the advantages and disadvantages of each of these analyses. It also indicates differences between levels of controls that countries can choose from and compares the complexity of the global, jurisdictional, and transactional approaches.

In general, the application of CFC rules requires the balancing of taxation of foreign income and the competitiveness of countries when attracting multinational enterprises.[1] Among others, the importance of this topic is displayed in the third OECD policy consideration that focuses on the limitation of administrative and compliance burdens. Against this backdrop, the chapter addresses the interrelation between complex tax systems, tax evasion, and the competitiveness of countries.

In particular, the compliance costs are relevant for the countries themselves that have to balance between, on the one side, ensuring that they have enough funding for their programs and working on decreasing of tax evasion and, on the other side, creating a comprehensive set of rules that are also causing administration costs. Likewise, this topic is relevant for taxpayers as they are affected by the compliance costs and have to consider them in their decisions. It can be observed that, in recent years, big corporations are increasingly focusing on the tax costs of their investments. This trend can be still observed as many corporations created shared services centers for their compliance work trying to decrease their costs through countries with lower personnel costs and centralization of the work. Perhaps influenced by the fact that they are subject to the public closely looking at their ac-

---

[1] 'Oecd_discussion_draft_beps_action_3_strengthening_cfc_rules.Pdf', 8, accessed 25 February 2020, https://research.ibfd.org/collections/oecd/pdf/oecd_discussion_draft_beps_action_3_strengthening_cfc_rules.pdf.

tivities, most of the big corporations are trying to comply and not to draw too much public attention. Even though both parties of this relationship are aiming for different goals, both compliance and administration costs have a direct influence on them, so it is the goal of both sides to decrease the costs or at least not to increase them significantly.

2. Compliance costs of taxation and their relationship with the complexity of tax systems

To begin with, it is important to define what is complexity of a tax system. Many authors focus on this topic in their research either in connection with tax reforms or the competitiveness of tax regimes. *William G. Gale* and *Jane Holtzblatt* define the complexity of a tax system as the *"sum of compliance costs – which are incurred directly by individuals and businesses – and administrative costs – which are incurred by government. Compliance costs include the time taxpayers spend preparing and filing tax forms, learning about the law, and maintaining record-keeping for tax purposes"*.[2] Following this definition, the level of complexity is influenced by the *"tax base, tax rate, allowable deductions, exemptions and credits"*.[3]

Another definition of compliance costs by Chris Evans is "the costs incurred by taxpayers, or third parties such as businesses, in meeting the requirements laid upon them in complying with a given structure and level of tax".[4] He defines typical compliance costs as:

- the time needed for the preparation of returns which should also include the time of person preparing the return getting updated on legislation changes;
- the fees to professional advisors;
- the costs of equipment needed for the completion of returns such as computers, software, and travel costs; and
- the psychological costs such as frustration and stress that are usually not taken into consideration in surveys but can have a big impact on taxpayers.[5]

On top of the above costs, it is likely that, in upcoming years, also costs for developing automation applications and software would be included as taxpayers will have to keep pace with tax administration requirements in order to deliver data and information in real life time.

---

2   'Gale and Holtzblatt – 2002 – The Role of Administrative Issues in Tax Reform S.Pdf', 3, accessed 17 April 2020, https://www.brookings.edu/wp-content/uploads/2016/06/20001205.pdf.
3   'Gale and Holtzblatt –2002 – The Role of Administrative Issues in Tax Reform S.Pdf', 4, accessed 17 April 2020, https://www.brookings.edu/wp-content/uploads/2016/06/20001205.pdf.
4   Christopher Evans, 'Taxation Compliance and Administrative Costs: An Overview', Tax Compliance Costs for Companies in an Enlarged European Community, 1 January 2008, 447–68.
5   Evans, 451.

Some countries like the United States even use models to estimate the compliance costs. The result of study done in 2013 estimated that US taxpayers spent 1.8 billion hours and USD 28.3 billion in 2010 in preparation and filing returns. The average time per taxpayer was 12.5 hours and USD 198 in cash. The numbers did vary depending of the size of the company.[6] The Internal Revenue Service (IRS) even invested into a new methodology on compliance cost modeling. The methodology brings the result in money as it monetizes the time invested in the preparation of the return.[7] The fact that the IRS invests into this methodology and into the survey shows how important compliance and administration costs are.

Compliance costs are also affected by the CFC rules implemented by the countries. For instance, in Belgium, the approach to CFC rules is to tax CFCs in low tax jurisdictions. However, as a low tax rate is determined by the ETR, taxpayers have to recalculate their tax base based on domestic tax legislation which would increase the compliance costs.[8] Other taxpayers that have to recalculate their tax base due to the ETR are the Japanese. This has to be done on annual bases. On top of this requirement, the Japanese legislator adopted the de facto test that also increases compliance costs.[9]

By contrast, Korean CFC legislation has a bigger scope, and it covers both active and passive income, and the structure of the CFC regime is generally complex. Another layer of complexity is added with exceptions and further exceptions to exceptions. This is also impacting the increase of compliance costs.[10]

As discussed in this chapter, the costs of compliance are determined by various factors. The main ones are the complexity of the tax system as well as the rules, requirements, and certainty. Even though it is difficult to measure, complexity increases the costs in the matter due to the additional time that is taken for the preparation of tax returns, software license fees, tax and accounting employee costs, and tax advisors fees. It is also important to consider the administration cost of tax authorities.

The complexity of tax systems of countries is measured by a "Tax Complexity Index" that is the result of the Global MNC Tax Complexity Project of LMU Munich and the Paderborn University in Germany. It is prepared on the basis of information provided by multinational corporations regarding corporate income tax systems in different countries. The information is collected from a survey of tax service companies and tax consultants. The index scale goes from not com-

---

6 '4.6.2 – How Costly Is Complexity.Pdf', accessed 15 August 2020, http://www.taxpolicycenter.org/sites/default/files/briefing-book/4.6.2-how_costly_is_complexity.pdf.
7 George Contos et al., 'Taxpayer Compliance Costs for Corporations and Partnerships: A New Look', n.d., 16.
8 Lang et al., *Controlled Foreign Company Legislation*, 104.
9 Lang et al., 17:293.
10 Lang et al., 17:504.

plex to overly complex taking into consideration tax regulations and tax systems.[11] The latest published index is from 2016. This index is formed by components such as minimum tax, CFC rules, depreciation, dividends, and statutory tax rates. With a total of 1, the CFC rules weight is determined by 0,052 (5.2 %) along with other 15 components.

The survey, in which 100 countries have been examined, shows that there is certain proportionality between CFC rules and the overall tax complexity. However, there are some components with a higher impact than a CFC, for instance, transfer pricing. The graph below, which is based on data available in 2016, shows the sample of the countries and their allocation of complexity relating to CFC rules and also to the overall tax complexity. Despite the fact that a CFC has a lower impact than some of the other components, complexity of CFC legislation might still have a strong link to the overall tax complexity of a country`s corporate income tax system as faced by multinational corporations. For example, countries like Costa Rica, Jersey, Hong Kong, and Laos have no CFC legislation implemented, and their score on tax complexity is generally low. On the other side of the scale, there are countries such as Russia, Brazil, Italy, and Chile with complex CFC legislation, and they achieve a high score with regard to tax complexity. This might indicate the link between CFC regulations and the general perception of tax complexity.

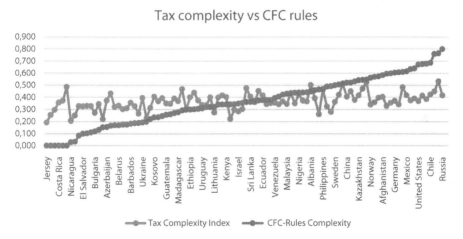

Source: Graph based on information on https://www.taxcomplexity.org/

From the legislators' perspective, it is challenging to balance the various goals that they are trying to achieve mostly because they are not all in direct correlation and sometimes even contradictory. The main goals are the decrease of tax evasion, de-

---

11 'Tax Complexity Index', accessed 18 May 2020, https://www.taxcomplexity.org/.

crease of compliance burdens and costs of administration, and the increase of competitiveness of the country when attracting investors. The relationship of these goals is illustrated in the graph below.

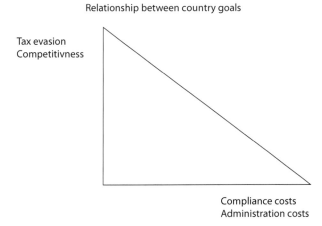

In this context, a study[12] was conducted on "Paying taxes and compliance burden" which analyses how the tax administration practice impacts compliance burden for businesses. The findings of this study are summarized as follows: *"[C]omplicated or ambiguous tax rules increase the compliance burden for business and stable tax rules can help reduce the complexity. Where tax rules are complicated, the approach of the tax authorities in issuing helpful guidance notes is important and also consistent application of the rules can help build taxpayer trust in the tax system."*[13] As a result of the study, nearly half of the economies consider their rules simple, and another half lean more towards being complicated. Complexity also raises the time needed to comply with the rules; in terms of complex rules, it can raise, in average, by even 97 hours of time dedicated to preparation.[14] Concerning the first finding regarding complex tax rules, it is helpful if rules are simple and the tax authority gives sufficient guidance on them. Consistent with the result of the study is the statement from *Chris Lenon*: *"It's about governments being consistent, so that businesses have a certainty about the position, and it's about building an atmosphere of trust between tax administrations and tax payers."*[15]

Countries encounter difficulties striking the right balance between the minimization of taxes and the complexity of tax systems. To illustrate, for instance, Australia introduced the "foreign investment fund" anti-deferral regime to cover the

---

12 'Paying Taxes. The Compliance Burden.Pdf', PWC study, accessed 22 May 2020, https://www.pwc.com/gr/en/publications/assets/paying-taxes-the-compliance-burden.pdf.
13 'Paying Taxes. The Compliance Burden', n.d., 10.
14 'Paying Taxes. The Compliance Burden.Pdf', 15.
15 'Paying Taxes. The Compliance Burden.Pdf', 39.

taxation of foreign income even in cases in which the requirement of control is avoided by splitting ownership between more than five persons. The application of the provision was found too complex because it caused high compliance costs and disturbed the competitiveness of Australia for investors. In 2010, it was replaced to achieve more simplicity.[16] The treasury introduced foreign investment fund rules to achieve the decrease of complexity.[17] By contrast, some countries do not have many of the CFC rules introduced in their legislation but are planning to change that. For example, Indonesia is going through a tax reform aiming to increase revenues and trying to implement BEPS, and this will likely cause the increase of tax compliance.[18]

With respect to new tax rules such as CFC legislation naturally comes the question concerning the impact of introducing new legislation in the state budget and for taxpayers. In this regard, there are different views if just looking at this issue from a financial point of view or also from administration costs and compliance perspectives that might be significant for taxpayers. Typical compliance costs would be costs for tax advisors, lawyers, finance staff, and tax planning.[19] CFC legislation increases these costs as taxpayers need to recalculate their income based on CFC rules and determine if they fulfill their scope so the process and administration is quite complex. The complexity of the tax system is also one of the key criteria of good tax systems. As this criteria is in conflict with the other criteria of a good tax system, a balanced combination needs to be found.

3. Complexity of CFC rules

CFC rules can be either entirely technical or provide more flexibility. The importance of the topic has also been discussed in the OECD BEPS Report 2015 on CFC rules, and it has been highlighted in the chapter "Work in relation to controlled foreign company rules" on page 2.[20] In the chapter on "share policy consideration", the need to set up a balance between administration costs and elimination of double taxation is highlighted.[21] This is further covered in the third policy consideration where the effectiveness of CFC rules is connected with a quite a "mechanical" application of CFC legislation. One of the countries that tends to adopt rules that are more mechanical is, for instance, the already mentioned case of In-

---

16 Michael Lang, Hans-Jorgen Aigner, and Ulrich Scheuerle, *CFC Legislation, Tax Treaties and EC Law* (Kluwer Law International B.V., 2004), 31.
17 'The Way Forward on Tax Measures Announced, but Not Enacted, by the Previous Government | Treasury Ministers', accessed 22 May 2020, https://ministers.treasury.gov.au/ministers/wayne-swan-2007/media-releases/way-forward-tax-measures-announced-not-enacted-previous.
18 Lang, Aigner, and Scheuerle, *CFC Legislation, Tax Treaties and EC Law*, 257–258.
19 Andrew Lymer and John Hasseldine, *The International Taxation System* (Springer Science & Business Media, 2012), 282.
20 'Oecd_discussion_draft_beps_action_3_strengthening_cfc_rules.Pdf', 2.
21 'Oecd_discussion_draft_beps_action_3_strengthening_cfc_rules.Pdf', 15.

donesia. Currently, the Indonesian tax administration focuses on taxpayers knowing their obligations, clear rules, and voluntary compliance as can be found in the chapter "Improving of Controlled Foreign Company current rules" of controlled foreign company legislation.[22] CFC rules apply in cases of 50 % of ownership or 50 % voting rights in a CFC, and it considers all income booked under retained earnings as the relevant tax base, not differentiating between passive or active income. The CFC income is included in the annual tax return for both individuals and companies.[23] Another country with a more mechanical approach is Poland. It provides its taxpayers with the list of factors that needs to be considered when determining the scope of CFC rules, and it also gives fixed tax rates for all types of income that lead to a decrease of profit shifting and also decreases administrative and compliance costs.[24]

However, this approach limits flexibility and, in fact, the tax administration rather prefers a more flexible application of the rules. Despite the fact that flexible rules can cause an increase in costs of compliance resulting from complexity, they are likely the choice as they are considered a more effective tool against base erosion and profit shifting. In that case, the administrative burden might increase, but the benefit of decreasing the profit shifting is considered higher and thus more relevant than the compliance costs of the taxpayer.[25] A good example is also the CFC legislation in the Czech Republic which is some sort of a new area in the taxation within the Czech Republic. It has both a flexible and mechanical part in the calculation. The flexible test is on the substantial economic activity while the mechanical test applies a 50 % threshold on control. The latter test is quite burdensome as it requires full proof by the taxpayer, and no assumptions are accepted. The Czech example leads to the question if the benefit of CFC rules will make up increased costs of both tax authorities and taxpayers.[26]

3.1. Disproportionate requirements in the burden of proof

The principle of proportionality is a general principle of EU law, and it states that the procedure must be appropriate for achieving a particular objective. This principle is defined in the glossary of the EU Regional Policy.[27] It ensures, among others, that tax authorities are not requesting unreasonable evidence from taxpayers. With regard to the proportionality of the measure, the ECJ emphasized that the CFC legislation must ensure that the CFC rules are not applied if the incorpora-

---

22 Lang et al., *Controlled Foreign Company Legislation*, 17:348.
23 Michael Lang et al., eds., *Controlled Foreign Company Legislation*, n.d., 338–346.
24 Lang et al., 17:416.
25 'Oecd_discussion_draft_beps_action_3_strengthening_cfc_rules.Pdf', 14–15.
26 Lang et al., *Controlled Foreign Company Legislation*, 17:166.
27 'Glossary', accessed 19 April 2021, https://ec.europa.eu/regional_policy/en/policy/what/glossary/p/proportionality.

tion of the subsidiary reflects economic reality. The principle of the proportionality has also been brought up in the *Cadbury Schweppes* case (C-196/04) in which the ECJ emphasizes that CFC rules should not apply if the foreign subsidiary carries out an economic activity, and the taxpayer should get a chance to proof that his subsidiary performs a genuine economic activity.[28]

To illustrate further, in Bulgaria, the principle of proportionality is reflected in the requirement for tax authorities to deliver the evidence of abusive practices before shifting the burden of proof to the taxpayer.[29] By contrast, it may be questioned whether the Italian CFC legislation is in line with the principle of proportionality as Italian shareholders bear the burden of providing the evidence in order not to be taxed on their foreign income in Italy.[30]

There are various theories on which the burden of proof should be imposed on a party. The general principle is that the burden should be divided between the taxpayers and the tax authorities. In some countries, preference is that the burden lies on the party that has easier access to the information; in others, the burden lies on the requestor of the information.[31] The persons that have to bear the burden of proof in the case of CFC rules are mostly taxpayers even though this has been changed in many countries. To give an example, based on information from tax news by Ulrika Lomas, in France, the burden of proof was on the tax authorities until the French tax reform. After the reform, the burden has been shifted to taxpayers.[32] The burden of proof is considered to be taxpayers' disadvantage as it increases his compliance costs and decreases his competitiveness compared to domestic companies.

In the communication from the commission to the council, it is considered that the burden of proof should not rest only with the taxpayer but other factors need to be taken in considerations such as *"general compliance capacity of the taxpayer and of the type of arrangement in question"*[33]. In this respect, it can be observed that the burden of proof is regulated quite differently among the various countries. For example, in Austria, an Austrian company with a foreign subsidiary has the obligation to accept the burden of proof despite the fact that the tax administration is usually the one that bears the costs of investigation. As in the

---

28 'CURIA – Documents', accessed 19 April 2021, https://curia.europa.eu/juris/document/document.jsf?text=&docid=56602&pageIndex=0&doclang=en&mode=lst&dir=&occ=first&part=1&cid=9674981.
29 Lang et al., *Controlled Foreign Company Legislation*, 141.
30 Lang et al., 17:272.
31 'Burden of Proof – Sample Chapter.Pdf', accessed 14 August 2020, https://www.ibfd.org/sites/ibfd.org/files/content/pdf/Burden%20of%20proof%20-%20Sample%20chapter.pdf.
32 'France Reforms CFC Legislation', accessed 14 August 2020, https://www.tax-news.com/news/France_Reforms_CFC_Legislation____57003.html.
33 'EUR-Lex – 52007DC0785 – EN', text/html; charset=UTF-8 (OPOCE), accessed 14 August 2020, https://eur-lex.europa.eu/legal-content/EN/TXT/HTML/?uri=CELEX:52007DC0785&from=GA.

case of CFCs, the tax authority might not be able to obtain all relevant documents, thus it can force *"reversal of the burden of proof"* on the taxpayer.[34] Additionally, in Spain, the burden of proof lies with the taxpayer who needs to provide documents that show the evidence proving that the foreign subsidiary was set up for economic reasons or having substance. In the case that this proof might be impossible from a compliance burden perspective, the burden can be shifted in exceptional circumstances to the tax authority.[35] By contrast, the Belgian approach is different, and the tax authority primarily bears the burden of the proof. This is even in the case that the authority concludes that some of the income should be attributed to the parent company. This is done through an "administrative tax procedure". Only in the case that the tax authorities attribute the entire income to the parent company does the burden shift to the taxpayer. There has also been a shift due to the new reporting obligation imposed on taxpayers.[36] In Luxembourg, for instance, the taxpayer is obligated to provide documentation related to a CFC per the tax authority request, and he is also obligated to prepare, on a yearly basis, the reports regarding the functions and risks of the CFC.[37]

The issues related to the burden of proof have already been brought up in ECJ case law. The one connected to a CFC was the *Cadbury Schweppes* case (C-196/04). In the opinion of the Advocate General on that case, the Member State should rely on the fact that subsidiaries are being established for genuine reasons and not for tax avoidance. The Advocate General also believes that the preparation of the proof that the UK parent company has to bear is not unreasonable as it would be done anyway as part of the tax checks that require companies to prepare to comply with national legislation.[38]

It is challenging to make the decision on who is the right person to bear the costs of the burden of proof. It is advisable that it should be the person who is the closest to the information, and that is usually the taxpayer as he usually prepares his other files that may be required, for instance, by transfer pricing reporting requirements.

---

34 Lang et al., *Controlled Foreign Company Legislation*, 85.
35 Lang et al., 17:527.
36 Lang et al., 17:69.
    The Ukrainian tax authority absorbs the burden of proof in connection with a CFC because there is presumption of 'taxpayer "good faith". The questionable transactions might then be challenged by tax authorities.
37 'Luxembourg Tax Authorities Issue Guidance on CFC Rules | Loyens & Loeff', accessed 14 August 2020, https://www.loyensloeff.com/en/en/news/news-articles/luxembourg-tax-authorities-issue-guidance-on-cfc-rules-n18595/.
38 'CURIA – Documents', accessed 19 April 2021, https://curia.europa.eu/juris/document/document.jsf?text=&docid=56602&pageIndex=0&doclang=en&mode=lst&dir=&occ=first&part=1&cid=9674981.

3.2. Causes of complexity of CFC rules
3.2.1. Classification of income

In relation to the complexity of tax systems, the definition of income, control, and addressees of the CFC rules play a significant role. Complexity related to the CFC income arises in many different aspects. Firstly, difficulties may arise in the definition of the CFC income and, secondly, in the determination and calculation of the CFC income. Most of the rules are therefore connected to the definition of income.[39]

To define the income, it is necessary to identify different categories of income. In this context, the OECD BEPS Action 3 Final Report on page 41 categorizes CFC income according to the following categories:

- Dividends
- Interest and other financing income
- Insurance income
- Sales and services income
- Royalties and other IP income[40]

For example, the Czech Republic follows this categorization and aims at covering only certain categories of income instead of focusing on the total income of the CFC. The categories include, for instance, interests, royalties, dividends, and income from the sale of shares. The income coming from these categories is attributed to the Czech controlling company.[41]

The OECD BEPS Action 3 Report, on pages 35–36, takes two approaches on how to determine CFC income. First, the *"form-based"* analysis looks at categories of income based on a formal classification. These categories would be determined according to the categories of CFC income previously mentioned. This approach has the disadvantage that even some active business activities might be covered by one of the above categories, or some types of income might be missing and would leave a certain risk of tax avoidance.[42]

Second, due to the possibility of tax evasion that might arise in the application of the form-based approach, the CFC rules apply an additional *"substance analysis"*. This approach analyses if there is income that derives from substantial activities undertaken by the CFC itself.[43] In this respect, OECD BEPs Action 3, on page 39, gives countries the option to choose one of three forms:

---

39 'Oecd_discussion_draft_beps_action_3_strengthening_cfc_rules.Pdf', 12.
40 'Oecd_discussion_draft_beps_action_3_strengthening_cfc_rules.Pdf', 35.
41 'Czech Republic – Corporate – Group Taxation', accessed 22 May 2020, https://taxsummaries.pwc.com/czech-republic/corporate/group-taxation.
42 'Oecd_discussion_draft_beps_action_3_strengthening_cfc_rules.Pdf', 35–36.
43 'Oecd_discussion_draft_beps_action_3_strengthening_cfc_rules.Pdf', 36.

- The *"substantial contribution analysis"* is the test that examines the contribution of CFC employees to the income. This method is not overly complex, but it does not provide a high protection against tax avoidance either. This analysis has been used, for instance, in *Denso* case no. 224 of 2016 when Japanese CFC rules were applied for the Denso Singaporean subsidiary as Singapore is a lower tax rate jurisdiction. The Supreme Court also examined the number of the employees to determine if the subsidiary has substance. As the Singaporean subsidiary performed the business, the CFC rules did not apply.[44]
- The *"viable independent entity analysis"* is the analysis of the function of the CFC and the ownership of the assets and risks. This method can be considered also suitable when aiming to decrease compliance costs, mostly as the analysis can use data from transfer pricing. However, a disadvantage is that it requires judgment that leads to administration and compliance costs.
- The *"employees and establishment analysis"* is the analysis of the CFC's activities and number of employees performing work for the CFC. This is the most mechanical approach from all three approaches. As it is quite mechanical, it reduces complexity and therefore the compliance and administration burdens. However, there is still a potential risk that this approach might increase some complexity.[45]

When comparing the approaches of the *"form base"* and *"substance analysis"*, the *"form base"* approach leads to less complexity due to its mechanical character and could be chosen in the case that the decrease of complexity would be the main objective of a country. However, as it gives room for tax avoidance, countries might rather choose the *"substance analysis"* instead. As this approach has three forms, it gives more opportunity to choose from which will better suit countries goals. Even though the *"substantial contribution analysis"* also has the advantage of lower compliance costs, it does not fully address the concern of missing control over tax avoidance. In terms of the substance analysis, the *"viable independent entity analysis"* could be the correct way to balance the compliance burden and protection against tax avoidance leveraging from work done in transfer pricing.

3.2.2. Attribution of income

The BEPS Action 3 Final Report from 2015 does not give an exact recommendation on income definition for CFC purposes only just possible approaches that comply with the OECD initiatives. Accordingly, the CFC income needs to be "attributable" to controlling parties and shareholders.

---

44 Courts of Japan, 'Japan vs Denso Singapore, November 2017, Supreme Court of Japan', *TPcases.Com* (blog), 27 November 2017, https://tpcases.com/japan-vs-denso-singapore-november-2017-supreme-court-of-japan/.
45 'Oecd_discussion_draft_beps_action_3_strengthening_cfc_rules.Pdf', 35–40.

There are two main approaches to attribute the CFC income to the controlling company, i.e. the *"full inclusion approach"* or the *"partial inclusion approach"*. Full inclusion considers the total income of the CFC as CFC income while the partial inclusion approach attributes only a certain category of income to the controlling company. The OECD Final Report does not give any recommendation as to which approach should be preferred.[46] According to the *"partial inclusion approach"*, for example, only the passive income is attributed to the controlling entity.[47] Passive income does not come from core business activities of the company such as dividends, interest, royalties. By contrast, active income is the income acquired from *"value-creating"* activities and is not considered as attributable income.[48] For instance, the partial inclusion approach has been applied in the Argentinian legislation according to which Argentinian taxpayers are taxed on the passive income earned by the CFC that is held by Argentinian taxpayers if more than 50% of CFC's income is passive and the tax rate is lower by 75% of the Argentine income tax rate.[49] By contrast, the Danish legislation is an example for which the legislator targets not just passive income but the total income of the subsidiary that qualifies as a CFC.[50] This was coming from the original attempt to prevent Danish companies from establishing subsidiaries in low tax countries and aiming not just at passive income but also on income from active business in the financial sector.[51]

Comparing both approaches, i.e. the *"full and partial inclusions"*, the *"full inclusion"* does not require calculating CFC income separately and, by contrast, *"partial inclusion"* requires the taxpayers to determine passive income. From a compliance perspective, *"full inclusion"* appears to be the better choice. However, it would lead to additional tax burden that is not connected with profit shifting which is the main focus of CFC legislation. This approach would also lead to lower attractivity of the country for multinational investors. There are other exceptions to ease the burden resulting from CFC legislation relating to the treat-

---

46   'Oecd_discussion_draft_beps_action_3_strengthening_cfc_rules.Pdf', 34.
47   Ina Kerschner and Maryte Somare, *Taxation in a Global Digital Economy: Schriftenreihe IStR Band 107* (Linde Verlag GmbH, 2017), 52.
      The differentiation between active and passive income was firstly considered for drafting US tax treaties with a source country having taxing rights on active income and a country of residence on passive income. This led to a desired outcome of balanced capital export neutrality for passive income and capital import neutrality for active income. This results from placing the taxpayer under CFC rules with value-creating activity in the same position as locally run businesses and eliminating competitors' advantages from which local taxpayers would otherwise benefit. 'Argentina – Corporate – Income Determination', accessed 22 May 2020, https://taxsummaries.pwc.com/argentina/corporate/income-determination.
48   'Oecd_discussion_draft_beps_action_3_strengthening_cfc_rules.Pdf', 35.
49   'Argentina – Corporate – Income Determination', accessed 22 May 2020, https://taxsummaries.pwc.com/argentina/corporate/income-determination.
50   'Denmark – Corporate – Group Taxation', accessed 22 May 2020, https://taxsummaries.pwc.com/denmark/corporate/group-taxation.
51   Lang, Aigner, and Scheuerle, *CFC Legislation, Tax Treaties and EC Law*, 168.

ment of passive income that will be covered in subchapter 4. For a more detailed analysis about the definition and the calculation of the CFC income, see Chapter on "The definition of CFC income".

3.2.3. Control

Control is another important factor that influences the complexity of CFC rules and thus the compliance and administration costs. Control is also covered by the BEPS Report on Action 3, page 27, which defines two standards in relation to CFC rules that need to be implemented by countries: the first one is the defining of which entities qualify as CFCs and the second is the threshold-requirement of 50% control.[52] According to the BEPS Report, pages 27–28, countries may opt for different types of control:

- Legal control – this type of control is looking at the percentage of voting rights. It is a mechanical test, so it is easier to apply for both taxpayers and administration.
- Economic control – this test *"recognizes that a resident can control an entity through an entitlement to the underlying value of the company even where they do not hold the majority of the shares"*.[53]
- De facto control – this test analyses tax residency and checks who is taking the main company decisions and who is influencing daily activities. This test requires complex analyses, and it leads to complexity and compliance burdens for taxpayers. However, it is a more flexible approach.[54] A more detailed analysis of this control follows in Chapter 3.3.
- Control based on consolidation – this test focuses on the analysis of companies' accounting principles. Moreover, it focuses on the persons who have impact on the companies' main decisions.[55] This approach is very complex and leads to higher compliance costs.

While the first two approaches are quite mechanical and should have a positive impact on compliance and administration costs, the last two are more targeted but, at the same time, more burdensome for taxpayers.[56]

In some countries, the taxpayers need to do a series of tests to determine the CFC profits. In the United Kingdom, for example, non-UK residents need to examine if the profits pass through the CFC "gateway". They are a series of tests that identify profits that are broadly, artificially diverted from the United Kingdome. For example, when profits are attributable to the United Kingdom due to significant

---

52   Sebastian Dueñas, 'CFC Rules Around the World | OECD CFC Rules | OECD Minimum Tax', *Tax Foundation* (blog), 17 June 2019, 11, https://taxfoundation.org/cfc-rules-around-the-world/.
53   'Oecd_discussion_draft_beps_action_3_strengthening_cfc_rules.Pdf', 27–28.
54   'Oecd_discussion_draft_beps_action_3_strengthening_cfc_rules.Pdf', 28.
55   'Oecd_discussion_draft_beps_action_3_strengthening_cfc_rules.Pdf', 28.
56   'Oecd_discussion_draft_beps_action_3_strengthening_cfc_rules.Pdf', 28.

people functions, those profits will be taxed in there unless one of four conditions is satisfied. The first is that obtaining a tax advantage is not the main purpose or one of the main purposes of the arrangement. A range of other tests may capture other CFC profits.[57]

The level of control can reduce the scope of CFC rules and therefore compliance and administration costs for minority shareholders as it allows focusing on shareholders who have a substantive influence in the decisions of the CFC.[58] The CFC rules provided by the BEPS Report give countries a wide scale of choice for the implementation in their domestic legislation. The different implementation might be quite complex for multinational enterprises as they need to keep track of the individual legislation and requirements that impact their compliance burden. For example, in the EU, despite the fact that there is minimum standard implemented, the states may act individually, however, they are not completely free in their choice of legislation. There is also no common definition of control in the EU.[59] The rates of control can go from 25% to 75%. To illustrate on the Czech example, a CFC is defined as a Czech non-resident company in which the Czech company participates by more than 50% in voting rights or profits.[60] By contrast, a Spanish parent company, for instance, must own over 50% of the non-resident subsidiary's equity and profits, and tax paid by the subsidiary must be under 75% of the tax that would be payable in Spain.[61] Portugal, for example, introduced control of "*25% of the share capital, voting rights, or rights on income or assets*"[62]. Different criteria for EU countries are causing complexity with regard to the compliance for taxpayers investing across the EU. Countries introducing CFC rules create certain complexity due to those compliance requirements. From a control perspective, legal and economical control are more in favour of a lower compliance burden and, in the case that compliance costs will be solely conditions for CFC rules, these two would be likely be introduced over de facto and consolidation control.

3.2.4. Scope of application

Another way to approach CFC legislation and its rules is the scope of application. According to the OECD BEPS Report, the countries may choose between two approaches. The first one is a "*transactional approach*". This approach differentiates

---

[57] 'United Kingdom – Other Taxes Impacting Corporate Entities', accessed 3 March 2020, http://taxsummaries.pwc.com/uk/taxsummaries/wwts.nsf/ID/United-Kingdom-Corporate-Other-taxes.
[58] 'Oecd_discussion_draft_beps_action_3_strengthening_cfc_rules.Pdf', 27.
[59] 'Document – European Union – The Role of the Concept of Control under CFC Legislation within the European Union Vis-à-Vis Third Countries – Tax Research Platform – IBFD', accessed 23 May 2020, https://research.ibfd.org/#/doc?url=/collections/et/html/et_2013_02_e2_4.html.
[60] 'Czech Republic – Corporate – Group Taxation'.
[61] 'Spain – Corporate – Group Taxation', accessed 24 May 2020, https://taxsummaries.pwc.com/spain/corporate/group-taxation.
[62] 'Portugal – Corporate – Group Taxation', accessed 24 May 2020, https://taxsummaries.pwc.com/portugal/corporate/group-taxation.

between active and passive income and focuses only on the latter, also called *"bad or tainted"* income[63]. The second one is the *"entity / jurisdictional approach"* that identifies countries with low tax rates. This approach is less burdensome because, in the case of a low tax rate in a respective jurisdiction, the total income of the CFC is attributed to the controlling entity. Hence, this approach has an *"all or nothing effect"*.[64]

Another classification of approaches that can be taken regarding CFC legislation are the global and the jurisdictional approaches. While the global approach *"applies CFC rules to all CFCs wherever they are resident and regardless of foreign tax rates"*,[65] the jurisdictional approach limits the scope to low tax jurisdictions and is more targeted. As the jurisdictional approach limits the scope of application of the CFC rules are considered less burdensome than the global approach.[66] Thus, the global approach is more complex and burdensome than the jurisdictional approach which is why some countries have changed their approach over the years. For example, in the Danish tax reform in 2017, the Danish rules were amended, and the requirement according to which the *"subsidiary should be subject to low taxation"* was repealed.[67]

As far as CFC rules are concerned, there are many other factors that cause complexity. Such a factor is, for example, the definition of the addressees of the CFC rules. The answer to the question of who is the addressee of the CFC rules also answers who has to absorb the burden of compliance. The OECD Report recommends applying CFC rules to corporate entities, trusts, partnerships, and permanent establishments (PE).[68] Another factor having impact on the complexity of CFC rules is the classification of a CFC in general, i.e. the criteria that need to be satisfied for a company to qualify as a CFC, which may also cause complexity.[69]

---

63 'Taxand-Asia-Senior-School-2018-DTA-Session-4-CFC.Pdf', 8, accessed 17 April 2020, https://www.taxand.com/wp-content/uploads/2018/07/Taxand-Asia-Senior-School-2018-DTA-Session-4-CFC.pdf. Even though there is still a difference on how scholars look at tainted income, it can either be characterized as profit of a CFC or passive income. The importance of this characteristic is due to its treatment in treaty provisions. Provision of business profit is covered by Article 7 OECD Model which gives taxing rights to a residence state if business is not carried out by a permanent establishment. If looking at it from the perspective of passive income, then different articles are consulted: Article 10 for dividends, Article 11 for interests, Article 12 for royalties, and Article 13 for capital gains. "Articles 10–12 refer to passive income which raise in one country and is paid to the resident of another country. They do not apply to passive income of the CFC that is raised in third country. CFC legislation does not treat CFC as transparent and it taxes dividend of CFC shareholders." Looking at this topic from a treaty perspective adds even more complexity to CFC rules.
64 'Taxand-Asia-Senior-School-2018-DTA-Session-4-CFC.Pdf', 8.
65 Kerschner and Somare, *Taxation in a Global Digital Economy*, 51.
66 Kerschner and Somare, 51.
67 Lang et al., *Controlled Foreign Company Legislation*, 236.
68 Kerschner and Somare, *Taxation in a Global Digital Economy*, 49.
69 For example, French companies are not classified as a CFC in case they can provide evidence that their foreign subsidiary carries out trading or manufacturing activities. Furthermore, CFC rules do not apply if subsidiaries are located in another EU country. For example, the United States applies a de minimus test where the total income of the CFC does not exceed a certain amount. See 'Taxand-Asia-Senior-School-2018-DTA-Session-4-CFC.Pdf'.

3.3. Increase of compliance burdens

To find the right balance between the compliance burden and the effectiveness of CFC legislation might be very challenging and, in many cases, countries rather opt for strengthening the CFC rules and accepting the related additional burden on the taxpayers and the tax administration. Typical methods and tools that increase compliance costs are substance analyses, inclusion of active and passive income, the de facto control, and the global approach.

Substance analyses can increase the compliance burden as they require complex and burdensome assessments depending on the form that the country legislators decide to opt for, if it is contribution of CFC employees to CFC income, independent entity analyses, or employee and premises resources needed by the CFC. All of these analyses require preparation work from the taxpayer and, at the end, build up his compliance costs. Another method that increases the compliance burden is inclusion of active and passive income in CFCs' income. It is the most burdensome in the case when a country chooses to apply the full inclusion method which considers CFC income as the whole income of CFCs. A further factor that increases the burden is the de facto control test. The control itself is the key part of CFC legislation. A "*de facto control*" is when a corporation is directly or indirectly controlled in any manner by another corporation, person, or group of persons.'[70] The de facto control test checks the residency of the taxpayer, for instance, based on where the top-level decisions are made or who significantly influences the company. On the one hand, de facto control requires lots of analyses and subjectivity so it implies a heavy compliance burden and uncertainty for taxpayers. Additionally, it is difficult for tax administration to challenge the taxpayer analyses due to the complexity of this control.[71] Many companies, for instance, hold their board meetings in the countries where they prefer to have their tax residency in order to comply with this control. According to Australian law, for example, an Australian company has de facto control over foreign company if it can influence the appointment of the directors in this company.[72] Moreover, complexity can be added in the case that the taxpayer is controlled by other parties. For example, in Ukraine, a resident becomes a controlling entity if he has 50% or more of interest in a foreign entity. The resident entity can also become a controlling person if it has at least 10% of interest and, at the same time, at least 50% of total interest in the foreign entity is owned by Ukrainian residents.[73] For the taxpayer, it might be difficult to maintain the information on other Ukrainian

---

[70] 'New Tax Rules Challenge Corporate Status', accessed 12 August 2020, https://www.mnp.ca/en/Posts-Site/Pages/new-tax-rules-challenge-corporate-status.aspx.
[71] 'Oecd_discussion_draft_beps_action_3_strengthening_cfc_rules.Pdf', 28.
[72] Australian Taxation Office, 'Foreign Income Return Form Guide 2020' (Australian Taxation Office), accessed 12 August 2020, https://www.ato.gov.au/Forms/Foreign-income-return-form-guide-2020/?page=3.
[73] Lang et al., *Controlled Foreign Company Legislation*, 782.

residents mainly because the situation might change during the time. Yet, some countries decided not to implement this control due to its complexity. For instance, the Spanish legislator has decided not to implement de facto control due to the difficulty to prove this control.[74] To decrease the burden, de facto control is often replaced with legal or economical control or a combination of them.[75] In this context, it is also questionable what will be the future of de facto control in the time during and after the pandemic. During the year of 2020, due to the Covid -19 pandemic, governments around the world took crisis measures to decrease the mobility of people and effectuate social distancing. This led to many employees being forced to work from home and, in some cases, the home office being in a different country than the employer. Additionally, meetings have been moved to the virtual world instead of with physical presence, so management and place of decisions might have shifted. As countries around the world try to support businesses and individuals during the pandemic, they likely do not strictly follow the de facto control. The OECD reacted fast to this situation, and it had already published the guidance on the Covid-19 impact related to tax treaties on 3 April 2020. Last, the global approach applies the CFC rules to all CFCs globally with no exceptions, for instance, for high tax jurisdictions. This seems to be the most burdensome method for the taxpayer. and it decreases the attractiveness of the country for foreign investors. As globalization had increasing trends over the last years, there are not many countries that would be willing to lose the advantage of competitiveness when it comes to foreign investments.

From the compliance burden perspective, the approaches that are having the most increasing effect on compliance are the global approach and full inclusion approach as they do not work with any rates, lists, or exceptions and require companies to include their whole income as the CFC's income. Therefore, it is recommended to opt for methods that are less burdensome but also do not give much room for tax avoidance.

4. Methods and tools to decrease the compliance burden

The main aim of CFC legislation is to prevent profit shifting between jurisdictions for the purpose of tax evasion. Yet, CFC legislation also brings additional burden to both sides, i.e. the taxpayer and the tax administration. To decrease this negative impact of CFC legislation, BEPS Action 3 guides towards rules that are more targeted and effective. The recommended way is to set up thresholds requirements that decrease the scope of CFC rules.[76] Thus, the most common

---

74 Lang, Aigner, and Scheuerle, *CFC Legislation, Tax Treaties and EC Law*, 508.
75 'Oecd_discussion_draft_beps_action_3_strengthening_cfc_rules.Pdf', 28.
76 'Oecd_discussion_draft_beps_action_3_strengthening_cfc_rules.Pdf', 19.

methods employed are the de minimis threshold, low tax thresholds, white list countries, and the excess profit approach.

The *"de minimis"* threshold is a targeted rule that excludes the CFC income from the parent company income if it falls under a certain threshold. Some countries provide thresholds by percentage and others by a fixed amount. The problematic aspect of this rule might be that the companies try to split the profit among more subsidiaries in order to fall under the threshold, and safeguards rule are implemented that again increase the compliance burden.[77] One of the countries that implemented a *"de minimis"* rule is, for instance, Germany. German law implemented both percentage and an amount ceiling. The German threshold for passive income is 10% of the total CFC income and the gross income of EUR 80,000.[78] Therefore, a CFC rule applies if this threshold is reached. Another example of a *"de minimis"* rule can be found in Luxembourg CFC legislation. When a company meets the control and ETR tests, it can still rely on the newly implemented rules and be excluded from the scope of the CFC rules. These rules consider a fixed amount of EUR 750,000 profit threshold and accounting profit to be below 10% of operating costs.[79] On the other hand, for instance, Belgium did not implement this rule due to the reason that the scope of CFC legislation in Belgium is narrow so there is no need for this rule. Some scholars consider Belgian's strict rules to be a competitive disadvantage of Belgian CFC legislation.[80]

The low-tax threshold also helps to decrease the compliance burden. It narrows the scope of CFC legislation with a focus on taxing only companies that are benefiting from lower tax rate jurisdictions and possible profit shifting. Even though this rule decreases the compliance burden, it might not fully protect from tax evasion as companies can try to shift their profit to medium tax jurisdictions.[81] Based on the OECD BEPS Report. the lower tax rate is either determined on a case-by-case basis or based on black and white lists. These lists simplify the whole process for both taxpayers and also the tax administration as checking the cases individually can be, on one hand, burdensome and, on the other, lacking certainty. Moreover, many countries consider an effective tax rate (ETR) rather than the statutory tax rate as the ETR can differ significantly from the statutory rate, and it is the rate that the taxpayer is interested in the most as it is an average tax rate at which a taxpayer pays its tax. Using the ETR requires more analyses as the taxpayer has to analyze the tax rules in the country in which the subsidiary is situated and to check its deductible and not deductible items. With the ETR, this approach

---

[77] 'Oecd_discussion_draft_beps_action_3_strengthening_cfc_rules.Pdf', 19–20.
[78] 'How Controlled Foreign Corporation Rules Look Around the World: Germany', *Tax Foundation* (blog), 18 February 2020, https://taxfoundation.org/germany-cfc-rules/.
[79] 'Luxembourg – Corporate – Group Taxation', accessed 10 August 2020, https://taxsummaries.pwc.com/luxembourg/corporate/group-taxation.
[80] Lang et al., *Controlled Foreign Company Legislation,104*.
[81] 'Oecd_discussion_draft_beps_action_3_strengthening_cfc_rules.Pdf', 21.

goes more toward the direction of a case-by-case scenario.[82] The ETR is used, for instance, by the Austrian legislation which considers a country to be a low tax jurisdiction if the ETR is 12.5% or less.[83] Another example comes from Chile where the minimum ETR needs to be at least 30% to avoid satisfying the CFC criteria.[84]

Another way to decrease the CFC burden are the so-called white list, black list, or grey list concepts. In BEPS Action 3, on page 22, it is included under the low tax threshold chapter, but it is a very effective tool. The white list is the list of countries that are out of scope of CFC legislation. Usually, the countries on the list are the ones that have signed tax treaties with the country in which the parent company is resident. The white list can also be used as a political tool on top of the tax one.[85] Sweden is one of the countries that is using it. If a company is resident in the country on the approved list, its income is exempted from the CFC rules. The countries are categorized into three groups: Firstly, fully included in the list, in case they have regular tax system; and, secondly partially included for countries with some beneficial tax regulations that exclude certain activities out of the list. The last category covers the countries that are not on the list and are subject to CFC rules.[86] Another list that countries are using is the black list. To illustrate, the Netherlands has the list of countries that must be viewed as low taxed for the purposes of the CFC legislation. Countries on this list are the ones that have a tax rate below 9% or are on the EU black list, for instance, Qatar, Jersey, and Bermuda.[87] Another type of list that countries opt to use is the grey list. New Zealand is currently using this list, however, in 2009, it was narrowed to Australia only. The main purpose of this list was to decrease compliance costs for the taxpayers who invested in countries with a tax rate similar to New Zealand.[88] These lists are strong tools for decreasing a potential compliance burden as they give certainty to taxpayers, and they do not require additional analyses and accounting requirements.

Another possible approach that countries can choose to decrease the compliance burden is the *"excess profits approach"*. It is targeting foreign companies in low tax jurisdictions with a focus on the profit that exceeds the normal returns coming from business activities, such as services and production. It targets profits made

---

82 'Oecd_discussion_draft_beps_action_3_strengthening_cfc_rules.Pdf', 21–24.
83 Lang et al., *Controlled Foreign Company Legislation*, 64.
84 Lang et al., 17:102.
85 Lang, Aigner, and Scheuerle, *CFC Legislation, Tax Treaties and EC Law*, 187.
86 '2018G_01616-181Gbl_Sweden Proposes Amendments to CFC Legislation.Pdf, accessed 11 August 2020, https://www.ey.com/Publication/vwLUAssets/Swedish_Ministry_of_Finance_proposes_amendments _to_CFC_legislation/$FILE/2018G_01616-181Gbl_Sweden%20proposes%20amendments%20to% 20CFC%20legislation.pdf.
87 'The Netherlands – Black List – CFC Tax Legislation', accessed 11 August 2020, https://www.tax-consultants-international.com/read/Netherlands_Black_List_CFC_tax_legislation?sub-list=5990&submenu=17169.
88 Lang et al., *Controlled Foreign Company Legislation*, 466–467.

from intangible property obtained from a related party. The company needs to calculate its normal return and then deduct it from its CFC income. The result is then income that is taxed under CFC rules. In this respect, the BEPS monitoring group also highlighted the advantage of this approach as leaving less room for abuse and being mostly easier for taxpayers to comply with and for a tax authority to check.[89] In this respect, it should be noted that the *"excess profits approach"* is more mechanical and easier than the categorical approach which will be described in next chapter. The formula used for the calculation of excess profit is composed of the *"rate of return"* which is the rate investors accept as return on their non-risk investments. It varies from country to country, but it is usually determined by a government bond rate. Another component of the formula is the *"eligible equity"* which is the equity used in the active business including the IP assets.[90]

There are many methods to decrease the compliance burden in the application of CFC rules. However, the countries that opt for decreasing the compliance burden need to be aware that this gives taxpayers more room for abusive tax behavior. It is necessary for lawmakers to decide what is their priority when creating and adjusting tax legislation. They might decide to decrease tax compliance at the costs of tax avoidance but having an advantage of luring international investors to their country. International investors usually bring more work, a decrease of the unemployment rate, and related employment benefits. Higher employment is strongly connected to higher personal income tax and VAT income revenue. Additionally, employment brings a higher standard of living for its residents. All of these benefits are not insignificant when lawmakers make their decisions, and they might decide for less burdensome CFC rules to allow them to access other benefits. Moreover, even though burdensome tax rules can also lead to lowering the competitiveness of countries, the rules and tools that aim at decreasing the compliance burden need to be chosen carefully. From the methods mentioned above, the one that gives the taxpayers the most certainty and also low compliance burden with a combination of high protection of abuse are black and white lists and the excess profit approach. Therefore, it would be advisable to opt for one of these methods.

5. CFC rules under the ATAD

The Anti-Tax Avoidance Directive can be also considered as a tool to decrease the compliance burden due to its main purpose of harmonization of some of the rules around the EU as stated by Council Directive (EU) 2016/1164 in paragraphs 2

---

89 'Ap3-Controlled-Foreign-Corporations.Pdf', accessed 14 August 2020, https://bepsmonitoring-group.files.wordpress.com/2015/05/ap3-controlled-foreign-corporations.pdf.
90 'Oecd_discussion_draft_beps_action_3_strengthening_cfc_rules.Pdf', 47–50.
   The formula used for calculation of excess profit would be: all income earned by CFC – normal return (rate of return) x (eligible equity) = excess profit.

and 3.[91] The main focus of the ATAD is on hybrid mismatches, interest deductions, and CFCs. Before the adoption of the ATAD, the EU states were inconsistent in their CFC legislation, and nearly half of them did not have any CFC rules.[92] Overly, the ATAD provides the minimum requirements that Member States should implement in their CFC legislations. The ATAD Article 7 CFC rules attribute income of foreign subsidiaries and PEs to the parent company if:

- the parent company holds at least 50 % of voting rights, capital, or profit share; and
- the tax paid by a foreign company is lower than the tax amount that would be paid by the parent company.[93]

As the determination of income is the main driver of CFC complexity, in its streamline approach, the ATAD offers two options of income definition in Article 7 of that ATAD which are described below under *"Model A"* and *"Model B"*.

5.1. Model A

The first option for a Member State, Model A, is to attribute predefined categories of foreign company passive income to the parent company income. The categories of income are listed in Article 7, paragraph 2 (a) of the ATAD and they include interests, royalties, dividends, income from financial leasing, banking, insurance, or invoicing artificial services.[94] This approach is also referred to as *"Model A"* or the *"tainted income approach"*. There is also a carve out that is applicable to EU/EEA countries if the foreign company performs substantive economic activity. In these cases, the CFC rules do not apply. However, this does not need to apply to non-EU/EEA countries.[95]

Countries that opted for Model A are, for instance, Austria, Croatia, Denmark, Hungary, the Netherlands, and Sweden.[96] This approach gives countries the possibility to include exemptions in order to decrease compliance burdens based on Article 7, paragraph 3. Hence, the Member States can decide not to treat foreign company as a CFC if:

- 1/3 or less of the income is in the category of passive income, or
- 1/3 or less of the passive income comes from intercompany transactions.[97]

---

91 'L_2016193EN.01000101.Xml', accessed 13 August 2020, https://eur-lex.europa.eu/legal-content/EN/TXT/HTML/?uri=CELEX:32016L1164&from=EN.
92 Lang et al., *Controlled Foreign Company Legislation*, 5.
93 'L_2016193EN.01000101.Xml', accessed 13 August 2020, https://eur-lex.europa.eu/legal-content/EN/TXT/HTML/?uri=CELEX:32016L1164&from=EN.
94 'L_2016193EN.01000101.Xml'.
95 'CFC Rules under ATAD', accessed 3 March 2020, https://tax.kpmg.us/articles/2019/beps-cfc-rules-under-atad.html.
96 'CFC Rules under ATAD'.
97 'L_2016193EN.01000101.Xml'.

Countries that did not choose to use any exceptions are Germany, Sweden, and the Czech Republic. One third of income exceptions is chosen by the majority of countries, for instance, Portugal, Poland, and Italy. Some countries such as Spain, Romania, and Austria decided to implement a combination of both exceptions. One interesting point to mention is that none of the countries that implemented this model decided to use the solitary exception on intercompany transactions.[98]

5.2. Model B

The second option for Member States is stated in Article 7, paragraph 2 (b). Income that falls into the scope of the CFC rules is coming from *"non-genuine arrangements"* the main purpose of which is to gain a tax advantage. Companies with *"non-genuine arrangements"* are considered to be the ones that do not bear the risks and do not have significant people functions.[99] This approach is also called *"Model B"* or the *"transactional approach"*. It also has built-in exceptions to decrease the CFC burden. In Article 7, paragraph 4 (a) and (b) state exceptions from the scope of the CFC rules for companies

- 'with accounting profits of no more than EUR 750 000, and non-trading income of no more than EUR 75 000; or
- of which the accounting profits amount to no more than 10 percent of its operating costs for the tax period.'[100]

The number of the countries that opted for this approach is lower than for the ones that decided to adopt *"Model A"*. For example, Slovakia, Luxembourg, Italy, Ireland, and Germany adopted *"Model B"*.[101] Regarding the exemptions, most of the countries opt for both exemptions. Only Estonia and Latvia adopted accounting profit threshold exemptions, and Slovakia and Belgium decided not to implement any exemptions.[102]

Most of the EU countries opted for *"Model A"* as it seems to be less complex and burdensome than *"Model B"*. As described in Chapters 3 and 4, less compliance burden is connected with choosing to build CFC rules on passive income instead of the inclusion of full income and also with possible exceptions connected with thresholds. *"Model A"* which also includes one of the exceptions seems to be the best way for countries to implement necessary CFC rules, on one hand and, decrease compliance on the other. EU countries can also adopt the black, white, and grey lists of third countries into their domestic legislation which, again, is the tool decreasing the compliance burden and giving certainty to taxpayers and tax administrations. As the ATAD provides the minimum requirements that countries need to implement, they are free to choose stricter rules,

---

98 'Dttl-Tax-Eu-Anti-Tax-Avoidance-Directive-Implementation-of-Controlled-Foreign-Company-Rules.Pdf', accessed 13 August 2020, https://www2.deloitte.com/content/dam/Deloitte/global/Documents/Tax/dttl-tax-eu-anti-tax-avoidance-directive-implementation-of-controlled-foreign-company-rules.pdf.
99 'L_2016193EN.01000101.Xml'.
100 'L_2016193EN.01000101.Xml'.
101 'CFC Rules under ATAD'.
102 'Dttl-Tax-Eu-Anti-Tax-Avoidance-Directive-Implementation-of-Controlled-Foreign-Company-Rules.Pdf'.

but that would also come with higher compliance and administration costs. What could be debatable on the ATAD is the fact that its main goal is harmonization, and it already offers two models, and each model has two possible exceptions. To reach the goal of harmonization, possibly one model with exceptions could have been presented.

5.3. The categorical approach

As the approach to classification of income is the main factor that influences the complexity of CFC legislation, it is important to consider it when implementing rules. In the previous sub-chapter dedicated to the ATAD rules, income and its categorization was the key element of *"Model A"* which was the preferred model between the Member States. Additionally, income is the main element of the transactional approach. Other approaches to income are also offered in the OECD BEPS Report. This subchapter focuses on the categorical approach. This approach brings individual rules to each type of income that falls under the scope of the CFC rules. There are two main categories of income, i.e. income that is considered active and passive income. This main categorization is important from a CFC perspective as many methods are focusing only on passive income. Based on the OECD BEPS Action 3, pages 45–46, three categories of income can be considered to be passive income with some exceptions. The first income category that is considered as passive income are dividends, however, with an exception if a foreign subsidiary has an active business. The second passive income category are interests and other types of financing income. The third category are sales, services, royalties, and IP income with exceptions if the income is earned by the foreign subsidiary itself. There is one active income category, which is insurance income, with the exception of the case when insurance comes from intercompany transactions and risk is shifted outside of a foreign subsidiary.[103]

The categorical approach should give companies more certainty as it is targeted at exact income categories, however, as every category also contains exceptions, this has an increasing impact on overall complexity. In the OECD BEPS Report, on page 46, the advantages and disadvantages of this approach are more analyzed. There might be preference from the countries to implement this approach as it gives flexibility to amend certain income categories if needed. Additionally, the categories are broader and combined so they are not broken into too many details. Another example for factors, however, that might increase the compliance burden may be generally-formulated anti-avoidance requirements. These requirements are targeting those specific transactions and structures that lead to tax avoidance. The compliance and administration burden depends a lot on if this requirement is set up as a regular one or it is an ad hoc requirement. An ad hoc requirement does not bring as much compliance burden as the one that needs to be

---

103 'Oecd_discussion_draft_beps_action_3_strengthening_cfc_rules.Pdf', 45–46.

done regularly. The main aspect of this requirement is that it should not be necessary in the case that CFC rules are set up correctly. So, in the case that a country determines its need, it would be considered as a factor that overly increases compliance costs.[104] For more information on anti-avoidance rules, you can refer to Chapter "Relationship between CFC rules and GAARs/PPT".

Despite the fact that the models mentioned above are implemented under the ATAD increase the compliance burden, they do accomplish their main purpose which is to ensure that taxpayers pay their fair share of taxes. The categorical approach is more mechanical than de facto control so even though it requires many analyses, it might be found to be less burdensome. It is interesting to note how de facto control has increased during the world pandemic as board meetings are held online and employees work from their homes abroad. This can lead, in the future, more towards shifting from de facto control to the categorical approach that has not been impacted by the world pandemic. The complexity of the methods brings little room for tax abuse and, therefore, it also brings fairness to the system.

6. Conclusion

The main difficulty that countries need to go through when adopting their CFC legislation, for instance, the rules, exceptions, and approaches, is to rightly balance their competitiveness for foreign investors with their state budget needs. Every country has its own program and financial needs to be able to perform its objectives in social areas. In most countries, the state budget is composed mostly from taxes, either individual, payroll, VAT or corporate. As CFC legislation influences both individual and corporate taxes, the pressure to design the CFC regimes is even more important. The importance of the topic is clearly expressed through the attention it also gets from the OECD and EU. Despite the fact that CFC legislation is domestic legislation, it particularly influences the behaviour of multinational companies. The attempt to set the minimum standards and to generally standardize the legislation is an important step towards ensuring a certain level of competitiveness and also decreasing the abuse attempts. However, both the OECD and the EU did not manage to find the answer to the question on how to decrease the compliance burdens without increasing opportunities for tax avoidance. CFC rules are depending on national policy makers, and it depends on their decision which direction they choose for their country to go, either for lower compliance burden and higher risk of profit shifting or for a higher compliance burden and less opportunities for tax avoidance. Countries attempt to overly create a fair tax environment for its taxpayers considering the potential compliance burdens and continuously trying to find the right balance.

---

104 'Oecd_discussion_draft_beps_action_3_strengthening_cfc_rules.Pdf', 21.

Another aim of this study was to identify the rules and approaches that have an increasing or decreasing impact on compliance and administration burdens. As administration and compliance burdens are directly linked, the administration burden has been included in this paper. To summarize, countries that decided to opt for rules with a decreasing effect on compliance and administration burdens can attract big multinational companies to come to their territory, and it may be economically beneficial for their country which can be very attractive for legislation makers.

The advantage of this approach is less complexity of the rules, easier checks, certainty, and potentially fewer cases for the court. However, there are disadvantages that might impact the decision of countries not to opt for these rules. A disadvantage of this approach is that this might also lead to a rise in tax avoidance and aggressive tax planning. This can also put domestic companies in a less favourable position as they do not have the same room for tax planning like the big multinational companies. That is why some countries would rather choose the rules that cause more compliance and administration burdens.

Yet, many countries rather decide to use more compliance demanding rules just to ensure lower tax avoidance. The risk of shifting the tax base to foreign countries with regimes that are more tax favourable can be mainly with regard to multinational companies. Advantages of implementing these rules is that there is less room for companies to shift their taxable profit to different countries, more taxes will remain in the countries' budget, and also the domestic companies can have the same conditions for businesses. Generally, there is no uniform way, and every approach to the CFC rules has its advantages and disadvantages, and it is very individual on each country which way it decides to go. As there is no harmonization on CFC legislation, it is also burdensome for multinationals to keep track on legislation requirements around the world.

This paper also identifies the difficulty for giving an exact answer on the compliance costs that each rule, exception, and approach may bring as not many detailed analyses are available and also because some of the factors are impossible to express in monetary terms. There cannot be a general answer to these problems and questions as every country needs to make its own decision that balances the compliance burden and tax avoidance depending on its objectives.

Series on International Tax Law

Band 2
Die unbeschränkte Steuerpflicht natürlicher Personen
Innerstaatliches Recht und Doppelbesteuerungsabkommen
Edgar Huemer
Wien 1996, 200 Seiten
ISBN 3-85122-538-4

Band 6
Die Auslegung von Doppelbesteuerungsabkommen in der Rechtsprechung der Höchstgerichte Deutschlands, der Schweiz und Österreichs
Lang/Mössner/Waldburger
Wien 1998, 136 Seiten
ISBN 3-85122-651-8

Band 7
Multilateral Tax Treaties
New Developments in International Tax Law
Lang/Loukota/Rädler/Schuch/Toifl/Urtz/Wassermeyer/Züger
Wien 1997, 264 Seiten
ISBN 3-85122-727-1

Band 14
Personengesellschaften im Internationalen Steuerrecht
Urtz/Züger
Wien 2001, 456 Seiten
ISBN 3-7073-0170-2

Band 16
Schiedsverfahren für Doppelbesteuerungsabkommen
Mario Züger
Wien 2001, 264 Seiten
ISBN 3-7073-0249-0

Band 20
Settlement of Disputes in Tax Treaty Law
Lang/Züger
Wien 2002, 596 Seiten
ISBN 3-7073-0265-2

Band 22
Personengesellschaften im Recht der Doppelbesteuerungsabkommen
Gerald Toifl
Wien 2003, 406 Seiten
ISBN 3-7073-0527-9

Band 24
Freistellungs- und Anrechnungsmethode in den Doppelbesteuerungsabkommen
Sutter/Wimpissinger
Wien 2002, 380 Seiten
ISBN 3-7073-0407-8

Band 25
Direct Taxation: Recent ECJ Developments
Michael Lang
Wien 2003, 208 Seiten
ISBN 3-7073-0436-1

Band 26
Avoidance of Double Non-Taxation
Michael Lang
Wien 2003, 504 Seiten
ISBN 3-7073-0489-2

Band 27
Unilaterale Maßnahmen zur Vermeidung der Doppelbesteuerung
Die Verordnung zu § 48 BAO
Bauer/Burgstaller/Haslinger/Herdin/Hofbauer/Lang/Loukota H./Loukota W./Schilcher/Schuch/Stefaner/Strasser/Sutter/Zieseritsch
Wien 2004, 288 Seiten
ISBN 3-7073-0536-8

Band 30
CFC Legislation
Lang/Aigner/Scheuerle/Stefaner
Wien 2004, 654 Seiten
ISBN 3-7073-0589-9

Band 33
Subject-to-tax-Klauseln in der
österreichischen Abkommenspraxis
Michael Schilcher
Wien 2004, 158 Seiten
ISBN 3-7073-0697-6

Band 35
WTO and Direct Taxation
Lang/Herdin/Hofbauer
Wien 2005, 772 Seiten
ISBN 3-7073-0710-7

Band 36
Das EG-Beihilfenverbot und sein
Durchführungsverbot in Steuersachen
Franz Philipp Sutter
Wien 2005, 414 Seiten
ISBN 3-7073-0762-X

Band 37
Die Auslegung von Quellenstaats-
regelungen in Doppelbesteuerungs-
abkommen
Christof Strasser
Wien 2005, 220 Seiten
ISBN 3-7073-0763-8

Band 38
Source versus Residence in
International Tax Law
Aigner/Loukota
Wien 2005, 630 Seiten
ISBN 3-7073-0764-6

Band 39
Tax Treaty Policy and Development
Stefaner/Züger
Wien 2005, 536 Seiten
ISBN 3-7073-0765-4

Band 40
Das Prinzip der Meistbegünstigung
im grenzüberschreitenden
Ertragsteuerrecht
Ines Hofbauer
Wien 2005, 244 Seiten
ISBN 3-7073-0880-4

Band 41
ECJ – Recent Developments in Direct
Taxation
Lang/Schuch/Staringer
Wien 2006, 358 Seiten
ISBN 3-7073-0878-2

Band 42
Mitarbeiter-Stock-Options im Recht der
Doppelbesteuerungsabkommen
Eva Burgstaller
Wien 2006, 296 Seiten
ISBN 3-7073-0947-9

Band 43
Double Taxation Conventions and
Social Security Conventions
Michael Lang
Wien 2006, 776 Seiten
ISBN 978-3-7073-0879-2

Band 44
EG-Grundfreiheiten und beschränkte
Steuerpflicht
Walter Loukota
Wien 2006, 344 Seiten
ISBN 978-3-7073-0948-5

Band 45
The Relevance of WTO Law for Tax
Matters
Herdin-Winter/Hofbauer
Wien 2006, 608 Seiten
ISBN 978-3-7073-1053-5

Band 46
Tax Treaty Law and EC Law
Lang/Schuch/Staringer
Wien 2007, 365 Seiten
ISBN 978-3-7073-0931-7

Band 47
Doppelbesteuerungsabkommen und
Europäisches Gemeinschaftsrecht
Georg Kofler
Wien 2007, 1200 Seiten
ISBN 978-3-7073-0849-5

Band 48
ECJ – Recent Developments in Direct
Taxation 2007
Lang/Schuch/Staringer
Wien 2007, 264 Seiten
ISBN 978-3-7073-1157-0

Series on International Tax Law

Band 49
The EU and Third Countries: Direct Taxation
Lang/Pistone
Wien 2007, 1072 Seiten
ISBN 978-3-7073-0932-4

Band 51
Taxation of Entertainers and Athletes
in International Tax Law
Loukota/Stefaner
Wien 2007, 502 Seiten
ISBN 978-3-7073-1205-8

Band 52
Conflicts of Qualification in
Tax Treaty Law
Burgstaller/Haslinger
Wien 2007, 406 Seiten
ISBN 978-3-7073-1204-1

Band 53
Common Consolidated Corporate
Tax Base
Lang/Pistone/Schuch/Staringer
Wien 2008, 1102 Seiten
ISBN 978-3-7073-1306-2

Band 54
Fundamental Issues and Practical
Problems in Tax Treaty Interpretation
Schilcher/Weninger
Wien 2008, 490 Seiten
ISBN 978-3-7073-1376-5

Band 55
EU Tax
Lang/Pistone/Schuch/Staringer
Wien 2008, 556 Seiten
ISBN 978-3-7073-1322-2

Band 56
Die japanischen Doppelbesteuerungs-
abkommen im Lichte des OECD- und
UN-Musterabkommens
Veronika Daurer
Wien 2008, 128 Seiten
ISBN 978-3-7073-1320-8

Band 57
ECJ – Recent Developments in Direct
Taxation 2008
Lang/Pistone/Schuch/Staringer
Wien 2008, 372 Seiten
ISBN 978-3-7073-1443-4

Band 58
Betriebsstättendiskriminierung
im Internationalen Steuerrecht
Werner Haslehner
Wien 2009, 408 Seiten
ISBN 879-3-7073-1574-5

Band 59
Recent Tax Treaty Development
around the Globe
Michael Lang
Wien 2009, 536 Seiten
ISBN 978-3-7073-1380-2

Band 60
Dual Residents in Tax Treaty Law and EC Law
Hofstätter/Plansky
Wien 2009, 528 Seiten
ISBN 978-3-7073-1461-2

Band 61
Taxation of Employment Income in
International Tax Law
Hohenwarter/Metzler
Wien 2009, 536 Seiten
ISBN 978-3-7073-1622-3

Band 62
Der Künstlerdurchgriff im nationalen und
internationalen Steuerrecht
Barbara Krüglstein
Wien 2009, 110 Seiten
ISBN 978-3-7073-1591-3

Band 63
Grenzen der Mitwirkungspflichten im
Lichte des Gemeinschaftsrechts
Michael Schilcher
Wien 2010, 304 Seiten
ISBN 978-3-7073-1623-3

Band 64
ECJ – Recent Developments in Direct
Taxation 2009
Lang/Pistone/Schuch/Staringer
Wien 2010, 272 Seiten
ISBN 978-3-7073-1697-1

Band 66
The EU's External Dimension in Direct
Tax Matters
Heidenbauer/Stürzlinger
Wien 2010, 488 Seiten
ISBN 978-3-7073-1774-9

Band 67
ECJ – Recent Developments in Direct
Taxation 2010
Lang/Pistone/Schuch/Staringer/Storck
Wien 2011, 240 Seiten
ISBN 978-3-7073-1847-0

Band 69
History of Tax Treaties
Ecker/Ressler
Wien 2011, 736 Seiten
ISBN 978-3-7073-2011-4

Band 70
Tax Treaty Case Law around the Globe – 2011
Lang/Pistone/Schuch/Staringer/Storck/de Broe/Essers/Kemmeren/Vanistendael
Wien 2011, 520 Seiten
ISBN 978-3-7073-1935-4

Band 71
Ausländische Stiftungen und vergleichbare Strukturen im österr. Steuerrecht
Uta Hammer
Wien 2012, 212 Seiten
ISBN 978-3-7073-2033-6

Band 73
ECJ – Recent Developments in Direct
Taxation 2011
Lang/Pistone/Schuch/Staringer/Storck
Wien 2012, 280 Seiten
ISBN 978-37073-2087-9

Band 74
International Group Financing and Taxes
Massoner/Storck/Stürzlinger
Wien 2012, 560 Seiten
ISBN 978-37073-2209-5

Band 75
Kurzfristige Arbeitnehmerüberlassung im Internationalen Steuerrecht
Kasper Dziurdź
Wien 2013, 256 Seiten
ISBN 978-3-7073-2190-6

Band 76
Doppelbesteuerungsabkommen Österreich-Kroatien
Lang/Simader
Wien 2013, 168 Seiten
ISBN 978-3-7073-2228-6

Band 77
ECJ – Recent Developments in Direct
Taxation 2012
Lang/Pistone/Schuch/Staringer/Storck
Wien 2013, 266 Seiten
ISBN 978-3-7073-2290-3

Band 78
Tax Treaty Case Law around the Globe 2012
Kemmeren/Smit/Essers/de Broe/Vanistendael/Lang/Pistone/Schuch/Staringer/Storck
Wien 2013, 400 Seiten
ISBN 978-3-7073-2291-0

Band 79
Limits to Tax Planning
Simader/Titz
Wien 2013, 624 Seiten
ISBN 978-3-7073-2408-2

Band 80
Exchange of Information for Tax Purposes
Günther/Tüchler
Wien 2013, 616 Seiten
ISBN 978-3-7073-2409-9

Band 81
Tax Treaty Case Law around the Globe 2013
Lang/Owens/Pistone/Schuch/Staringer/Storck/Essers/Kemmeren/Smit
Wien 2013, 392 Seiten
ISBN 978-3-7073-2655-0

Band 82
Kostenverteilungsverträge
Martin Lehner
Wien 2014, 616 Seiten
ISBN 978-3-7073-2656-7

Band 83
ECJ – Recent Developments in Direct
Taxation 2013
Lang/Pistone/Schuch/Staringer/Storck
Wien 2014, 240 Seiten
ISBN 978-3-7073-3055-7

Band 84
ECJ – Recent Developments in Value Added Tax
Lang/Pistone/Schuch/Staringer/Raponi
Wien 2014, 384 Seiten
ISBN 978-3-7073-2753-3

Series on International Tax Law

Band 85
Dependent Agents as Permanent Establishments
Lang/Pistone/Schuch/Staringer/Storck
Wien 2014, 312 Seiten
ISBN 978-3-7073-2460-0

Band 86
Tax Policy Challenges in the 21st Century
Petruzzi/Spies
Wien 2014, 752 Seiten
ISBN 978-3-7073-3129-5

Band 87
Doppelbesteuerungsabkommen Österreich–Slowenien
Lang/Daurer
Wien 2015, 144 Seiten
ISBN 978-3-7073-3160-8

Band 88
Die grundfreiheitliche Rechtsprechung des EuGH
Katharina Daxkobler
Wien 2015, 716 Seiten
ISBN 978-3-7073-3200-1

Band 89
Tax Treaty Case Law around the Globe 2014
Kemmeren/Smit/Essers/Lang/Owens/Pistone/Rust/Schuch/Staringer/Storck
Wien 2015, 432 Seiten
ISBN 978-3-7073-3084-7

Band 90
The OECD-Model-Convention and its Update 2014
Lang/Pistone/Rust/Schuch/Staringer/Storck
Wien 2015, 288 Seiten
ISBN 978-3-7073-3088-5

Band 91
ECJ – Recent Developments in Direct Taxation 2014
Lang/Pistone/Rust/Schuch/Staringer/Storck
Wien 2015, 260 Seiten
ISBN 978-3-7073-3316-9

Band 92
CJEU – Recent Developments in Value Added Tax 2014
Lang/Rust/Pistone/Schuch/Staringer/Raponi
Wien 2015, 264 Seiten
ISBN 978-3-7073-3340-4

Band 93
Global Trends in VAT/GST and Direct Taxes
Pfeiffer/Ursprung-Steindl
Wien 2015, 764 Seiten
ISBN 978-3-7073-3345-9

Band 94
Non-Discrimination in European and Tax Treaty Law
Dziurdź/Marchgraber
Wien 2015, 622 Seiten
ISBN 978-3-7073-3360-2

Band 95
Base Erosions and Profit Shifting (BEPS)
Lang/Pistone/Rust/Schuch/Staringer
Wien 2016, 368 Seiten
ISBN 978-3-7094-0734-9

Band 96
Transparenz – Eine neue Ära im Steuerrecht
Lang/Haunold
Wien 2016, 190 Seiten
ISBN 978-3-7073-3350-3

Band 97
Tax Treaty Case Law around the Globe 2015
Lang/Rust/Owers/Pistone/Schuch/Staringer/Storck/Essers/Kemmeren/Smit
Wien 2016, 384 Seiten
ISBN 978-3-7073-3381-7

Band 98
GAARS and Judicial Anti-Avoidance in Germany, the UK and the EU
Markus Seiler
Wien 2016, 374 Seiten
ISBN 978-3-7073-3515-6

Band 99
CJEU – Recent Developments in Value Added Tax 2015
Lang/Pistone/Rust/Schuch/Staringer/Raponi
Wien 2016, 376 Seiten
ISBN 978-3-7073-3532-3

Band 100
CJEU – Recent Developments in Direct Taxation 2015
Lang/Pistone/Rust/Schuch/Staringer/Storck
Wien 2016, 232 Seiten
ISBN 978-3-7073-3531-6

Band 101
Preventing Tax Treaty Abuse
Blum/Seiler
Wien 2016, 580 Seiten
ISBN 978-3-7073-3542-2

Series on International Tax Law

Band 102
Tax Treaty Case Law around the Globe 2016
Kemmeren/Smit/Essers/Lang/Owens/
Pistone/Rust/Schuch/Staringer/Storck
Wien 2017, 456 Seiten
ISBN 978-3-7073-3634-4

Band 103
CJEU – Recent Developments in Direct Taxation 2016
Lang/Pistone/Rust/Schuch/Staringer/Storck
Wien 2017, 248 Seiten
ISBN 978-3-7073-3697-9

Band 104
Limiting Base Erosion
Pinetz/Schaffer
Wien 2017, 568 Seiten
ISBN 978-3-7073-3758-7

Band 105
CJEU – Recent Developments in Value Added Tax
Lang/Pistone/Rust/Schuch/Staringer/Raponi
Wien 2017, 370 Seiten
ISBN 978-3-7073-3698-6

Band 106
Transparenz und Informationsaustausch
Lang/Haunold
Wien 2017, 144 Seiten
ISBN 978-3-7073-3768-6

Band 107
Taxation in a Global Digital Economy
Kerschner/Somare
Wien 2017, 488 Seiten
ISBN 978-3-7073-3778-5

Band 108
Tax Treaty Case Law around the Globe 2017
Lang/Rust/Owens/Pistone/Schuch/Staringer/
Storck/Essers/Smit/Kemmeren
Wien 2018, 440 Seiten
ISBN 978-3-7073-3788-4

Band 109
CJEU – Recent Developments in Value Added Tax 2017
Lang/Pistone/Rust/Schuch/Staringer/Pillet
Wien 2018, 408 Seiten
ISBN 978-3-7073-3901-7

Band 110
CJEU – Recent Developments in Direct Taxation 2017
Lang/Pistone/Rust/Schuch/Staringer/Storck
Wien 2018, 248 Seiten
ISBN 978-3-7073-3902-4

Band 111
OECD Arbitration in Tax Treaty Law
Majdanska/Turcan
Wien 2018, 768 Seiten
ISBN 978-3-7073-3903-1

Band 112
Tax Treaty Case Law around the Globe 2018
Kemmeren/Essers/Smit/Lang/Owens/Pistone/
Rust/Schuch/Staringer/Storck
Wien 2019, 478 Seiten
ISBN 978-3-7073-4022-8

Band 113
Transfer Pricing and Intangibles
Lang/Storck/Petruzzi/Risse
Wien 2019, 176 Seiten
ISBN 978-3-7073-4032-7

Band 114
CJEU – Recent Developments in Direct Taxation 2018
Lang/Rust/Schuch/Staringer/Storck/Pistone
Wien 2019
ISBN 978-3-7073-4121-8

Band 115
CJEU – Recent Developments in Value Added Tax 2018
Lang/Rust/Schuch/Staringer/Pistone/Pillet
Wien 2019
ISBN 978-3-7073-4122-5

Band 116
Transfer Pricing and Value Creation
Petruzzi/Tavares
Wien 2019
ISBN 978-3-7073-4123-2

Band 117
Special Features of the UN Model Convention
Binder/Wöhrer
Wien 2019
ISBN 978-3-7073-4124-9

Series on International Tax Law

Band 118
Attribution of Profits to Permanent Establishments
Lang/Storck/Petruzzi
Wien 2020
ISBN 978-3-7073-3313-8

Band 119
CJEU – Recent Developments in Direct Taxation 2019
Lang/Rust/Schuch/Staringer/Storck/Pistone
Wien 2020
ISBN 978-3-7073-4234-5

Band 120
Die Ergebnisabgrenzung bei verbundenen Unternehmen und Betreibsstätten post BEPS
Holzinger
Wien 2020
ISBN 978-3-7073-4184-3

Band 121
Tax Treaty Case Law around the Globe 2019
Lang/Rust/Owens/Pistone/Schuch/Staringer/Storck/Essers/Kemmeren/Öner/Smit
Wien 2020
ISBN 978-3-7073-4255-0

Band 122
Hybrid Entities in Tax Treaty Law
Govind/Van West
Wien 2020
ISBN 978-3-7073-4208-6

Band 123
CJEU – Recent Developments in Value Added Tax 2019
Kofler/Lang/Pistone/Rust/Schuch/Spies/Staringer/Pillet
Wien 2020
ISBN 978-3-7073-4290-1

Band 124
Concept and Implementation of CFC Legislation
Bravo/Miladinovic
Wien 2021
ISBN 978-3-7073-4405-9

Band 125
Access to Treaty Benefits
Auer/Dimitropoulou
Wien 2021
ISBN 978-3-7073-4406-6

Band 126
Tax Treaty Case Law around the Globe 2020
Lang/Rust/Owens/Pistone/Schuch/Staringer/Storck/Essers/Kemmeren/Öner/Smit/Kofler/Spies
Wien 2021
ISBN 978-3-7073-4442-4

Band 127
CJEU – Recent Developments in Direct Taxation 2020
Kofler/Lang/Rust/Schuch/Staringer/Storck/Pistone/Spies
Wien 2021
ISBN 978-3-7073-4450-9